MW00812863

Kawasaki
Vulcan 1500 & 1600
Service and Repair Manual

by Matthew Coombs

Models covered

(4913-320)

Vulcan VN1500. 1470cc. 1987 through 1999
Vulcan VN1500 Classic. 1470cc. 1996 through 2004
Vulcan VN1500 Classic Fl. 1470cc. 2000 through 2008
Vulcan VN1500 Nomad/Classic Tourer. 1470cc. 1998 through 2001
Vulcan VN1500 Nomad/Classic Tourer Fl. 1470cc. 2000 through 2004
Vulcan VN1500 Drifter. 1470cc. 1999 through 2004
Vulcan VN1500 Mean Streak. 1470cc. 2002 and 2003
Vulcan VN1600 Classic. 1552cc. 2003 through 2008
Vulcan VN1600 Mean Streak. 1552cc. 2004 through 2008
Vulcan VN1600 Nomad/Classic Tourer. 1552cc. 2005 through 2008

© Haynes Group Limited 2011

A book in the Haynes Service and Repair Manual Series

All rights reserved. No part of this book may be reproduced or transmitted in any form or by any means, electronic or mechanical, including photocopying, recording or by any information storage or retrieval system, without permission in writing from the copyright holder.

ISBN 978 1 78521 391 5

Library of Congress Control Number 2011922727

Haynes Group Limited
Haynes North America, Inc

www.haynes.com

Disclaimer

There are risks associated with automotive repairs. The ability to make repairs depends on the individual's skill, experience and proper tools. Individuals should act with due care and acknowledge and assume the risk of performing automotive repairs.

The purpose of this manual is to provide comprehensive, useful and accessible automotive repair information, to help you get the best value from your vehicle. However, this manual is not a substitute for a professional certified technician or mechanic.

This repair manual is produced by a third party and is not associated with an individual vehicle manufacturer. If there is any doubt or discrepancy between this manual and the owner's manual or the factory service manual, please refer to the factory service manual or seek assistance from a professional certified technician or mechanic.

Even though we have prepared this manual with extreme care and every attempt is made to ensure that the information in this manual is correct, neither the publisher nor the author can accept responsibility for loss, damage or injury caused by any errors in, or omissions from, the information given.

Contents

LIVING WITH YOUR KAWASAKI VULCAN

Introduction

Pre-ride checks

MAINTENANCE

Tune-up and routine maintenance

Contents

REPAIRS AND OVERHAUL

Engine, transmission and associated systems

Chassis components

Electrical system

Wiring diagrams

REFERENCE

Index

Kawasaki
The Green Meanies

by Julian Ryder

Kawasaki Heavy Industries

Kawasaki is a company of contradictions. It is the smallest of the big four Japanese manufacturers but the biggest company, it was the last of the four to make and market motorcycles yet it owns the oldest name in the Japanese industry, and it was the first to set up a factory in the USA. Kawasaki Heavy Industries, of which the motorcycle operation is but a small component, is a massive company with its heritage firmly in the old heavy industries like shipbuilding and railways; nowadays it is as much involved in aerospace as in motorcycles.

In fact it may be because of this that Kawasaki's motorcycles have always been quirky, you get the impression that they are designed by a small group of enthusiasts who are given an admirably free hand. More realistically, it may be that Kawasaki's designers have experience with techniques and materials from other engineering disciplines. Either way, Kawasaki have managed to be the factory who surprise us more than the rest. Quite often, they do this by totally ignoring a market segment the others are scrabbling over, but more often they hit us with pure, undiluted performance.

The origins of the company, and its name, go back to 1878 when Shozo Kawasaki set up a dockyard in Tokyo. By the late 1930s, the company was making its own steel in massive steelworks and manufacturing railway locos and rolling stock. In the run up to war, the Kawasaki Aircraft Company was set up in 1937 and it was this arm of the now giant operation that would look to motorcycle engine manufacture in post-war Japan.

They bought their high-technology experience to bear first on engines which were sold on to a number of manufacturers as original equipment. Both two- and four-stroke units were made, a 58 cc and 148 cc OHC unit. One of the customer companies was Meihatsu Heavy Industries, another company within the Kawasaki group, which in 1961 was shaken up and renamed Kawasaki Auto Sales. At the same time, the Akashi factory which was to be Kawasaki's main production facility until the Kobe earthquake of 1995, was opened.

Shortly afterwards, Kawasaki took over the ailing Meguro company, Japan's oldest motorcycle maker, thus instantly obtaining a range of bigger bikes which were marketed as Kawasaki-Meguros. The following year, the first bike to be made and sold as a Kawasaki was produced, a 125 cc single called the B8 and in 1963 a motocross version, the B8M appeared.

Model development

Kawasaki's first appearance on a road-race circuit came in 1965 with a batch of disc-valve 125 twins. They were no match for the opposition from Japan in the shape of Suzuki and Yamaha or for the fading force of the factory MZs from East Germany. Only after the other Japanese factories had

pulled out of the class did Kawasaki win, with British rider Dave Simmonds becoming World 125 GP Champion in 1969 on a bike that looked astonishingly similar to the original racer. That same year Kawasaki reorganised once again, this time merging three companies to form Kawasaki Heavy Industries. One of the new organisation's objectives was to take motorcycle production forward and exploit markets outside Japan.

KHI achieved that target immediately and set out their stall for the future with the astonishing and frightening H1. This three-cylinder air-cooled 500 cc two-stroke was arguably the first modern pure performance bike to hit the market. It hypnotised a whole generation of motorcyclists who'd never before encountered such a ferocious, wheelie inducing power band or such shattering straight-line speed allied to questionable handling. And as for the 750 cc version ...

The triples perfectly suited the late '60s, fitting in well with the student demonstrations of 1968 and the anti-establishment ethos of the Summer of Love. Unfortunately, the oil crisis would put an end to the thirsty strokers but Kawasaki had another high-performance ace up their corporate sleeve. Or rather they thought they did.

The 1968 Tokyo Show saw probably the single most significant new motorcycle ever made unveiled: the Honda CB750. At Kawasaki it caused a major shock, for they also had a 750 cc four, code-named New

The three cylinder two-stroke 750

The first Superbike, Kawasaki's 900 cc Z1

York Steak, almost ready to roll and it was a double, rather than single, overhead cam motor. Bravely, they took the decision to go ahead - but with the motor taken out to 900 cc. The result was the Z1, unveiled at the 1972 Cologne Show. It was a bike straight out of the same mould as the H1, scare stories spread about unmanageable power, dubious straight-line stability and frightening handling, none of which stopped the sales graph

rocketing upwards and led to the coining of the term 'superbike'. While rising fuel prices cut short development of the big two-strokes, the Z1 went on to found a dynasty, indeed its genes can still be detected in Kawasaki's latest products like the ZZ-R1100 (Ninja ZX-11).

This is another characteristic of the way Kawasaki operates. Models quite often have very long lives, or gradually evolve. There is

no major difference between that first Z1 and the air-cooled GPz range. Add water-cooling and you have the GPZ900, which in turn metamorphosed into the GPZ1000RX and then the ZX-10 and the ZZ-R1100. Indeed, the last three models share the same 58 mm stroke. The bikes are obviously very different but it's difficult to put your finger on exactly why.

Other models have remained effectively untouched for over a decade: the KH and KE single-cylinder air-cooled two-stroke learner bikes, the GT550 and 750 shaft-drive hacks favoured by big city despatch riders and the GPz305 being prime examples. It's only when they step outside the performance field that Kawasakis seems less sure. Their first factory customs were dire, you simply got the impression that the team that designed them didn't have their heart in the job. Only when the Classic range appeared in 1995 did they get it right.

Racing success

Kawasaki also have a more focused approach to racing than the other factories. The policy has always been to race the road bikes and with just a couple of exceptions that's what they've done. Even Simmonds' championship winner bore a strong resemblance to the twins they were selling in the late '60s and racing versions of the 500 and 750 cc triples were also sold as over-the-counter racers, the H1R and H2R. The 500 was in the forefront of the two-stroke assault on MV Agusta but wasn't a Grand Prix

One of the two-stroke engined KH and KE range - the KE100B

The GT750 - a favourite hack for despatch riders

The high-performance ZXR750

Through doing it their way Kawasaki developed a brand loyalty for their performance bikes that kept the Z1's derivatives in production until the mid-'80s and turned the bike into a classic in its model life. You could even argue that the Z1 lives on in the shape of the 1100 Zephyr's GPz1100-derived motor. And that's another Kawasaki invention, the retro bike. But when you look at what many commentators refer to as the retro boom, especially in Japan, you find that it is no such thing. It is the Zephyr boom. Just another example of Japan's most surprising motorcycle manufacturer getting it right again.

The Vulcans

If a motorcycle manufacturer is going to maintain a presence in the American market it has to have a big cruiser in its range, or preferably a family of them. Of the Japanese manufacturers, Kawasaki's image and other product lines made them least likely to succeed in this endeavour.

The company seemed only really enthusiastic about sports bikes, and pretty radical, cutting-edge designs at that. In the days of the UJM, the Universal Japanese Motorcycle, when all the Japanese makers' big bikes were air-cooled across the frame fours, they simply stuck a set of high bars on the standard model and added Ltd to the model name. There were also a couple of other half-hearted efforts with a twin; no-one was convinced.

It took until 1984 for Kawasaki to do what every maker who wanted to make an impact on the cruiser sector eventually had to do. Make a V-twin. The truth of this market sector is that if you want to compete with Harley-Davidson on their home turf then a bit of imitation is the sincerest form of flattery – and the route to sales success.

The first true Kawasaki cruiser was christened the Vulcan and the name has been

winner. It was the 750 that made the impact and carried the factory's image in F750 racing against the Suzuki triples and Yamaha fours.

The factory's decision to use green, usually regarded as an unlucky colour in sport, meant its bikes and personnel stood out and the phrase 'Green Meanies' fitted them perfectly. The Z1 motor soon became a full 1000 cc and powered Kawasaki's assault in F1 racing, notably in endurance which Kawasaki saw as being most closely related to its road bikes.

That didn't stop them dominating 250 and 350 cc GPs with a tandem twin two-stroke in the late '70s and early '80s, but their path-breaking monocoque 500 while a race winner never won a world title. When Superbike arrived, Kawasaki's road 750s weren't as track-friendly as the opposition's out-and-out race replicas. This makes Scott Russell's World title on the ZXR750 in 1993 even more praiseworthy, for the homologation bike, the ZXR750RR, was much heavier and much more of a road bike than the Italian and Japanese competition.

The company's Supersport 600 contenders have similarly been more sports-tourers than race-replicas, yet they too have been competitive on the track. Indeed, the flagship bike, the ZZ-R1100, is most definitely a sports tourer capable of carrying two people and their luggage at high speed in comfort all day and then doing it again the next day. Try that on one of the race replicas and you'll be in need of a course of treatment from a chiropractor.

VN1500 L Nomad/Classic Tourer

VN1500 N Classic

VN1600 A Classic

VN1600 B Mean Streak

used ever since for everything from 400 to 2000cc models, all of them cruisers. The first was a 750, although for its main market, the USA, it was a 700 because of government tariffs on imported motorcycles over that capacity. The first Vulcan stayed in Kawasaki's range for an astonishing 21 years during which time the company worked out the basic truths of the cruiser market. They are that technical innovation is not necessary but that a good, functional motorcycle can form the base of a surprisingly wide range of models.

From the inception of the range, Kawasaki used the Vulcan name as if it were that of the manufacturer and went for all the retro styling cues – wire wheels, instruments in a tank-mounted nacelle, lots of chrome. Maybe the name Kawasaki was just a bit too Japanese for the target market.

It wasn't long before Kawasaki followed another all-American dictum: 'You can't beat cubes.' In 1987 they launched the largest engine available in a motorcycle, a 102 x 90 mm, 1470cc V-twin with a single-pin crank and four valves per cylinder. Not surprisingly, it produced so much torque that it only needed a four-speed gearbox. In 2003, as Triumph took the largest capacity prize with the Rocket III, Kawasaki stroked the VN1500 by 5 mm to produce the 1552cc VN1600. Just as with the first, 750cc Vulcans, its big brother went basically unchanged for its model life. The twin carbs were reduced to one instrument in 1996 on Classic and Nomal/Classic Tourer models and fuel injection took over in 2000. For some reason, an extra speed was added to the box in '98. Other than that, the VN1500 was subtly and cleverly tweaked to produce significantly different models. The base model became the Classic while the addition of a screen and panniers produced the Classic Tourer. The Classic was resolutely retro in its styling while the Tourer's two-tone paint and panniers with chrome striping and handles were pure 1950s. The Drifter went even further back. Its valanced mudguards, finned exhausts, single seat and bullet lights harked back to the Indian V-twins of the inter-War years.

When Harley-Davidson invented the power cruiser with the V-Rod in 2001 the Japanese manufacturers responded, in Kawasaki's case with another Vulcan, the Mean Streak. Sports bike wheel sizes, upside-down forks, two bigger discs on the front and drag-strip styling gave a muscle bike feel very reminiscent of the Eliminator, a short-lived Kawasaki of the early 1980s. It may have taken twenty years for low-profile tyres on wide rims to become fashionable on a cruiser but the Vulcan Mean Streak is not likely to leave Kawasaki's range as quickly as the old Ninja-based Eliminator. Not if the longevity of the rest of the range is anything to go by.

Acknowledgements

Our thanks are due to Premier Bikes of Oxford who supplied the machine featured in the illustrations throughout this manual. We would also like to thank NGK Spark Plugs (UK) Ltd for supplying the colour spark plug condition photographs, the Avon Rubber Company for supplying information on tyre fitting and Draper Tools Ltd for some of the workshop tools shown.

Thanks are also due to Julian Ryder who wrote the introduction and to Kawasaki Motors Europe who supplied model photographs.

About this Manual

The aim of this manual is to help you get the best value from your motorcycle. It can do so in several ways. It can help you decide what work must be done, even if you choose to have it done by a dealer; it provides information and procedures for routine maintenance and servicing; and it offers diagnostic and repair procedures to follow when trouble occurs.

We hope you use the manual to tackle the work yourself. For many simpler jobs, doing it yourself may be quicker than arranging an appointment to get the motorcycle into a dealer and making the trips to leave it and pick it up. More importantly, a lot of money can be saved by avoiding the expense the shop must pass on to you to cover its labor and overhead costs. An added benefit is the sense of satisfaction and accomplishment that you feel after doing the job yourself.

References to the left or right side of the motorcycle assume you are sitting on the seat, facing forward.

We take great pride in the accuracy of information given in this manual, but motorcycle manufacturers make alterations and design changes during the production run of a particular motorcycle of which they do not inform us. No liability can be accepted by the authors or publishers for loss, damage or injury caused by any errors in, or omissions from, the information given.

The range was launched in the US in 1987 with the VN1500A and B models, with the A version lasting though to 1999 and having twin seats, alloy wheels and lower bars than the B version with its single seat and spoke wheels that was produced until 1992. The VN1500C was launched for the European market, and there was an L version of that in 1996 and 1997 that had lower bars for a more upright riding position, and spoke wheels.

The VN1500 Classic was launched in 1996 and was produced through to 2004, though in 2000 the Classic FI with fuel injection was launched to run alongside and was produced through to 2008. The VN1600 Classic was launched in 2003 and was produced alongside the 1500 until 2008. The Classic has spoke wheels and footboards.

The VN1500 Nomad/Classic Tourer was launched in 1998 and was produced through to 2001, though in 2000 the Nomad/Classic Tourer FI with fuel injection was launched to run briefly alongside and was produced through to 2004. The VN1600 Nomad/Classic Tourer was launched in 2005 and was produced until 2008. The Nomad/Classic Tourer has spoke wheels and footboards, as well as a windshield and saddlebags.

The VN1500 Drifter was launched in 1999 with a twin seat, then changed in 2001 to a single seat and was produced until 2004.

The VN1500 Mean Streak was launched in 2002 as the street version of the range, with uprated brakes and suspension and alloy wheels. In 2004 the Mean Streak was given the VN1600 engine and was produced until 2008.

The engine used across the range is a liquid-cooled V-twin with chain driven single overhead camshafts and hydraulic 'zero lash' valves operated via rockers. The transmission is four-speed on VN1500A, B and D models and five-speed on all other models, all constant mesh and driven via an hydraulic wet multi-plate clutch with back-torque limiter through to a front bevel gear, turning drive via a shaft to the final drive housing on the rear wheel.

VN1500A and B models have twin CV carburetors, and the Classic and Nomad/Classic Tourer have a single CV carburettor. All other models have a digital fuel injection system.

Identification numbers

Engine and frame numbers

The frame serial number is stamped into the right side of the steering head. The engine number is stamped into the left side of the crankcase and is visible from below the left side of the machine. Both of these numbers should be recorded and kept in a safe place so they can be given to law enforcement officials in the event of a theft.

The frame serial number and engine serial number should also be kept in a handy place (such as with your driver's license) so they are always available when purchasing or ordering parts for your machine.

The model code (e.g. VN1500-B1) can be determined from the frame serial numbers in the accompanying table.

Buying spare parts

Once you have found all the identification numbers, record them for reference when buying parts. Since the manufacturers change specifications, parts and vendors (companies that manufacture various components on the machine), providing the ID numbers is the only way to be reasonably sure that you are buying the correct parts.

Whenever possible, take the worn part to the dealer so direct comparison with the new component can be made. Along the trail from the manufacturer to the parts shelf, there are numerous places that the part can end up with the wrong number or be listed incorrectly.

The two places to purchase new parts for your motorcycle – the accessory store and the franchised dealer – differ in the type of parts they carry. While dealers can obtain virtually every part for your motorcycle, the accessory dealer is usually limited to normal high wear items such as shock absorbers, tune-up parts, various engine gaskets, cables, brake parts, etc. Rarely will an accessory outlet have major suspension components, cylinders, transmission gears, or cases.

Used parts can be obtained for considerably less than new ones, but you can't always be sure of what you're getting. Once again, take your worn part to the salvage yard for direct comparison.

Whether buying new, used or rebuilt parts, the best course is to deal directly with someone who specializes in parts for your particular make.

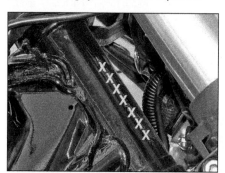

The frame number is stamped in the right-hand side of the steering head

The engine number is stamped in the bottom of the crankcase on the left-hand side of the engine

Model	Year	Initial frame number (according to market)
Vulcan 1500		
VN1500-A1	1987	JKBVNAA1*HA000021
VN1500-B1	1987	JKBVNAB1*HA000011 or JKBVNAB1*HA000001
VN1500-A2	1988	JKBVNAA1*JA001001 or VTN50A-001001
VN1500-B2	1988	JKBVNAB1*JA000301 or JKBVNAB1*JB500601 or VTN50A-003001
VN1500-A3	1989	JKBVNAA1*KA003001 or VTN50A-003001
VN1500-B3	1989	JKBVNAB1*KA002001 or VTN50B-002001
VN1500-A3	1990	JKBVNAA1*LA003001 or VTN50A-004001
VN1500-B3	1990	JKBVNAB1*LB501401 or VTN50B-003001
VN1500-A5	1991	JKBVNAA1*MA006001 or VTN50A-006001
VN1500-B5	1991	VTN50B-005001
VN1500-A5	1992	JKBVNAA1*NA009001 or VTN50A-009001
VN1500-B6	1992	VTN50B-009001
VN1500-A7	1993	JKBVNAA1*PA013001
VN1500-A8	1994	JKBVNAA1*RA020001
VN1500-A9	1995	JKBVNAA1*SA026001
VN1500-A10	1996	JKBVNAA1*TA040001
VN1500-A11	1997	JKBVNAA1*VA060001
VN1500-A12	1998	JKBVNAA1*WA075001
VN1500-A13	1999	JKBVNAA1*XA085001

Model	Year	Initial frame number (according to market)
Vulcan 1500 Classic		
VN1500-D1 (US, Canada, Australia)	1996	JKBVNAD1*TA000001
VN1500-D1 (Germany)	1996	VNT50D*000001
VN1500-D1 (General)	1996	VNT50A*040001
VN1500-D2 (US, Canada, Australia)	1997	JKBVNAD1*VA060001
VN1500-D2 (Germany)	1997	VNT50D*005001
VN1500-D2 (General)	1997	VNT50A*060001
VN1500-E1 (US, Canada)	1998	JKBVNAE1*WA000001
VN1500-E1 (Australia)	1998	JKBVNAE1*WA075001
VN1500-E1 (General)	1998	VNT50A*075001
VN1500-F1 (Germany)	1998	VNT50A*075001 or VNT50D*010001
VN1500-E2	1999	JKBVNAE1*XA085001 or JKBVNT50AEA085001
VN1500-F2	1999	JKBVNT50AFA085001
VN1500-E3	2000	JKBVNAE1*YA095001
VN1500-E4	2001	JKBVNAE1*1A101001
VN1500-E5	2002	JKBVNAE1*2A105001
VN1500-E6	2003	JKBVNAE1*3A110001
VN1500-E7	2004	JKBVNAE1*4A115001

Model	Year	Initial frame number (according to market)
Vulcan 1500 Classic FI		
VN1500-N1 (US, Canada, Australia)	2000	JKBVNAN1*YA000001
VN1500-N1 (General)	2000	JKBVNT50NNA000001
VN1500-N2 (US, Canada, Australia)	2001	JKBVNAN1*1A009001
VN1500-N2 (General)	2001	JKBVNT50NNA009001
VN1500-N3 (US, Canada, Australia)	2002	JKBVNAN1*2A015001
VN1500-N3 (General)	2002	JKBVNT50NNA015001
VN1500-N4	2005	JKBVNAN1*5A019001
VN1500N6F	2006	JKBVNAN1*6A025001
VN1500T6F	2006	JKBVNAT1*6A000001
VN1500N7F	2007	JKBVNAN1*7A028001
VN1500N8F	2008	JKBVNAN1*8A032001

Model	Year	Initial frame number (according to market)
Vulcan 1600 Classic		
VN1600-A1	2003	JKBVNKA1*3A000001 or JKBVNT60AAA000001
VN1600-A2	2004	JKBVNKA1*4A009001 or JKBVNT60AAA009001
VN1600-A3	2005	JKBVNKA1*5A013001 or JKBVNT60AAA013001
VN1600A6F	2006	JKBVNKA1*6A020001 or JKBVNT60AAA020001
VN1600E6F	2006	JKBVNKE1*6A000001
VN1600A7F	2007	JKBVNKA1*7A023001
VN1600A7FA	2007	JKBVNKA1*7A023001
VN1600A8F	2008	JKBVNKA1*8A026001
VN1600A8FA	2008	JKBVNKA1*8A026001

Model	Year	Initial frame number (according to market)
Vulcan 1500 Nomad/Classic Tourer		
VN1500-G1 (Australia)	1998	JKBVNAG1*WA000001
VN1500-G1 (General)	1998	JKAVNT50GGA000001
VN1500-H1 (Germany, Switzerland, Austria)	1998	JKAVNT50GHA000001
VN1500-G1/ G1A (US, Canada)	1999	JKBVNAG1*XA000001
VN1500-G2 (Australia)	2001	JKBVNAG1*XA010001
VN1500-G2 (General)	2001	JKAVNT50GGA010001
VN1500-H2 (Germany, Switzerland, Austria)	1998	JKAVNT50GHA010001
VN1500-G2A (US)	2000	JKBVNAG1*YA028001
VN1500-G3 (US)	2001	JKBVNAG1*1A033001

Model	Year	Initial frame number (according to market)
Vulcan 1500 Nomad/Classic Tourer FI		
VN1500-L1	2000	JKBVNAL1*YA000001 or JKBVNAL1*YA028001 or JKBVNT50GLA028001
VN1500-L2	2001	JKBVNAL1*1A007001 or JKBVNT50GLA033001
VN1500-L3	2002	JKBVNAL1*2A013001 or JKBVNT50GLA036001
VN1500-L4	2003	JKBVNAL1*3A020001 or JKBVNT50GLA040001
VN1500-L5	2004	JKBVNAL1*4A027001

Model	Year	Initial frame number (according to market)
Vulcan 1600 Nomad/Classic Tourer		
VN1600-D1	2005	JKBVNKD1*5A000001 or JKBVNT60ADA013001
VN1600D6F	2006	JKBVNKD1*6A006001 or JKBVNT60ADA020001
VN1600G6F	2006	JKBVNKG1*6A000001
VN1600D7F	2007	JKBVNKD1*7A011001
VN1600D7FA	2007	JKBVNKD1*7A011001
VN1600D8F	2008	JKBVNKD1*8A018001
VN1600D8FA	2008	JKBVNKD1*8A018001

Model	Year	Initial frame number (according to market)
Vulcan 1500 Drifter		
VN1500-J1	1999	JKBVNAJ1*XA000001 or JKBVNT50JJA000001 or VNT50J-000001
VN1500-J2	2001	JKBVNAJ1*YA010001 or JKBVNT50JJA010001
VN1500-R1	2001	JKBVNAR1*1A000001 or JKBVNT50JRA015001
VN1500-R2	2002	JKBVNAR1*2A005001 or JKBVNT50JRA005001
VN1500-R3	2003	JKBVNAR1*3A008001 or JKBVNT50JRA020001
VN1500-R4	2004	JKBVNAR1*4A010001

Model	Year	Initial frame number (according to market)
Vulcan 1500 Mean Streak		
VN1500-P1	2002	JKBVNAP1*2A000001 or JKBVNT50PPA000001
VN1500-P2	2003	JKBVNAP1*3A012001 or JKBVNT50PPA012001

Model	Year	Initial frame number (according to market)
Vulcan 1600 Mean Streak		
VN1600-B1	2004	JKBVNKB1*4A000001 or JKBVNT60BBA000001
VN1600-B2	2005	JKBVNKB1*5A005001 or JKBVNT60BBA005001
VN1600-B6F	2006	JKBVNKB1*6A010001 or JKBVNT60BBA010001
VN1600-F6F	2006	JKBVNKF1*6A000001
VN1600-B7F	2007	JKBVNKB1*7A013001 or JKBVNT60BBA013001
VN1600-B7FA	2007	JKBVNKB1*7A013001
VN1600-B8F	2008	JKBVNKB1*8A018001
VN1600-B8FA	2008	JKBVNKB1*8A018001

* denotes variable digit

Professional mechanics are trained in safe working procedures. However enthusiastic you may be about getting on with the job at hand, take the time to ensure that your safety is not put at risk. A moment's lack of attention can result in an accident, as can failure to observe simple precautions.

There will always be new ways of having accidents, and the following is not a comprehensive list of all dangers; it is intended rather to make you aware of the risks and to encourage a safe approach to all work you carry out on your bike.

Asbestos

● Certain friction, insulating, sealing and other products - such as brake pads, clutch linings, gaskets, etc. - contain asbestos. Extreme care must be taken to avoid inhalation of dust from such products since it is hazardous to health. If in doubt, assume that they do contain asbestos.

Fire

● Remember at all times that petrol is highly flammable. Never smoke or have any kind of naked flame around, when working on the vehicle. But the risk does not end there - a spark caused by an electrical short-circuit, by two metal surfaces contacting each other, by careless use of tools, or even by static electricity built up in your body under certain conditions, can ignite petrol vapour, which in a confined space is highly explosive. Never use petrol as a cleaning solvent. Use an approved safety solvent.

● Always disconnect the battery earth terminal before working on any part of the fuel or electrical system, and never risk spilling fuel on to a hot engine or exhaust.

● It is recommended that a fire extinguisher of a type suitable for fuel and electrical fires is kept handy in the garage or workplace at all times. Never try to extinguish a fuel or electrical fire with water.

Fumes

● Certain fumes are highly toxic and can quickly cause unconsciousness and even death if inhaled to any extent. Petrol vapour comes into this category, as do the vapours from certain solvents such as trichloro-ethylene. Any draining or pouring of such volatile fluids should be done in a well ventilated area.

● When using cleaning fluids and solvents, read the instructions carefully. Never use materials from unmarked containers - they may give off poisonous vapours.

● Never run the engine of a motor vehicle in an enclosed space such as a garage. Exhaust fumes contain carbon monoxide which is extremely poisonous; if you need to run the engine, always do so in the open air or at least have the rear of the vehicle outside the workplace.

The battery

● Never cause a spark, or allow a naked light near the vehicle's battery. It will normally be giving off a certain amount of hydrogen gas, which is highly explosive.

● Always disconnect the battery ground (earth) terminal before working on the fuel or electrical systems (except where noted).

Electricity

● When using an electric power tool, inspection light etc., always ensure that the appliance is correctly connected to its plug and that, where necessary, it is properly grounded (earthed). Do not use such appliances in damp conditions and, again, beware of creating a spark or applying excessive heat in the vicinity of fuel or fuel vapour. Also ensure that the appliances meet national safety standards.

● A severe electric shock can result from touching certain parts of the electrical system, such as the spark plug wires (HT leads), when the engine is running or being cranked, particularly if components are damp or the insulation is defective. Where an electronic ignition system is used, the secondary (HT) voltage is much higher and could prove fatal.

Remember...

✗ **Don't** start the engine without first ascertaining that the transmission is in neutral.

✗ **Don't** suddenly remove the pressure cap from a hot cooling system - cover it with a cloth and release the pressure gradually first, or you may get scalded by escaping coolant.

✗ **Don't** attempt to drain oil until you are sure it has cooled sufficiently to avoid scalding you.

✗ **Don't** grasp any part of the engine or exhaust system without first ascertaining that it is cool enough not to burn you.

✗ **Don't** allow brake fluid or antifreeze to contact the machine's paintwork or plastic components.

✗ **Don't** siphon toxic liquids such as fuel, hydraulic fluid or antifreeze by mouth, or allow them to remain on your skin.

✗ **Don't** inhale dust - it may be injurious to health (see Asbestos heading).

✗ **Don't** allow any spilled oil or grease to remain on the floor - wipe it up right away, before someone slips on it.

✗ **Don't** use ill-fitting spanners or other tools which may slip and cause injury.

✗ **Don't** lift a heavy component which may be beyond your capability - get assistance.

✗ **Don't** rush to finish a job or take unverified short cuts.

✗ **Don't** allow children or animals in or around an unattended vehicle.

✗ **Don't** inflate a tyre above the recommended pressure. Apart from overstressing the carcass, in extreme cases the tyre may blow off forcibly.

✔ **Do** ensure that the machine is supported securely at all times. This is especially important when the machine is blocked up to aid wheel or fork removal.

✔ **Do** take care when attempting to loosen a stubborn nut or bolt. It is generally better to pull on a spanner, rather than push, so that if you slip, you fall away from the machine rather than onto it.

✔ **Do** wear eye protection when using power tools such as drill, sander, bench grinder etc.

✔ **Do** use a barrier cream on your hands prior to undertaking dirty jobs - it will protect your skin from infection as well as making the dirt easier to remove afterwards; but make sure your hands aren't left slippery. Note that long-term contact with used engine oil can be a health hazard.

✔ **Do** keep loose clothing (cuffs, ties etc. and long hair) well out of the way of moving mechanical parts.

✔ **Do** remove rings, wristwatch etc., before working on the vehicle - especially the electrical system.

✔ **Do** keep your work area tidy - it is only too easy to fall over articles left lying around.

✔ **Do** exercise caution when compressing springs for removal or installation. Ensure that the tension is applied and released in a controlled manner, using suitable tools which preclude the possibility of the spring escaping violently.

✔ **Do** ensure that any lifting tackle used has a safe working load rating adequate for the job.

✔ **Do** get someone to check periodically that all is well, when working alone on the vehicle.

✔ **Do** carry out work in a logical sequence and check that everything is correctly assembled and tightened afterwards.

✔ **Do** remember that your vehicle's safety affects that of yourself and others. If in doubt on any point, get professional advice.

● If in spite of following these precautions, you are unfortunate enough to injure yourself, seek medical attention as soon as possible.

Note: *These checks are outlined in the owner's manual and covers those items which Kawasaki advise be inspected before you ride the motorcycle.*

Coolant level

> ⚠️ **Warning: DO NOT remove the filler neck pressure cap to add coolant. Topping up is done via the coolant reservoir tank filler. DO NOT leave open containers of coolant about, as it is poisonous.**

Before you start

✔ Make sure you have a supply of coolant available (a mixture of 50% distilled water and 50% corrosion inhibited ethylene glycol anti-freeze is needed).

✔ Always check the coolant level when the engine is cold.

Caution: Do not run the engine in an enclosed space such as a garage or workshop.

✔ Ensure the motorcycle is held vertical while checking the coolant level. Make sure the motorcycle is on level ground.

Bike care

● Use only the specified coolant mixture. It is important that anti-freeze is used in the system all year round, and not just in the winter. Do not top the system up using only water, as the system will become too diluted.

● Do not overfill the reservoir. If the coolant is significantly above the F (full) level line at any time, the surplus should be siphoned or drained off to prevent the possibility of it being expelled out of the overflow hose.

● If the coolant level falls steadily, check the system for leaks (see Chapter 1). If no leaks are found and the level continues to fall, fit a new pressure cap. If that does not solve the problem take the machine to a Kawasaki dealer for a pressure test.

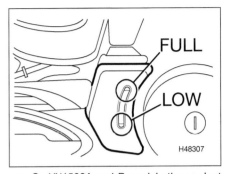

1 On VN1500A and B models the coolant reservoir is located on the lower right side of the bike. The coolant FULL and LOW level lines are visible on the side of the reservoir via the slot in the cover – the coolant level should be between the lines. If topping-up is required undo the screw and remove the cover.

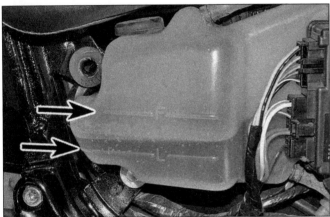

2 On all other models remove the right side cover (see Chapter 8). The coolant FULL and LOW level lines (arrowed) are visible on the side of the reservoir – the coolant level should be between the lines . . .

3 . . . if topping-up is required unscrew the reservoir bolts (arrowed) and displace the reservoir so the cap is clear of the seat.

4 Remove the reservoir cap.

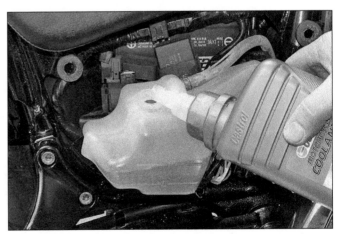

5 Add the specified coolant, using a clean funnel if required, to bring the level up to the FULL mark on the reservoir. Do not overfill. Refit the cap, then fit the reservoir and cover, according to model.

Brake and clutch fluid levels

> ⚠️ *Warning: Hydraulic fluid can harm your eyes and damage painted surfaces, so use extreme caution when handling and pouring it and cover surrounding surfaces with rag. Do not use fluid that has been standing open for some time, as it absorbs moisture from the air which can cause a dangerous loss of braking effectiveness.*

Before you start:
✔ Ensure the motorcycle and handlebars are positioned so the reservoir is horizontal while checking the levels.

✔ Make sure you have the correct hydraulic fluid. DOT 4 is recommended. Never mix different fluid types (i.e. do not mix DOT 4 with DOT 5), and never reuse old fluid.

✔ Wrap a rag around the reservoir being worked on to ensure that any spillage does not come into contact with painted surfaces.

Bike care:
● The fluid level in the reservoirs will change as the brake pads and clutch plates wear down.

● If any fluid reservoir requires repeated topping-up this is an indication of a hydraulic leak somewhere in the system, which should be investigated immediately.

● Check for signs of fluid leakage from the hydraulic hoses and components – if found, rectify immediately.

● Check the operation of both brakes and the clutch before taking the machine on the road; if there is evidence of air in the system (spongy feel to lever or pedal), it must be bled as described in Chapter 7 (brake) or Chapter 2 (clutch).

FRONT BRAKE AND CLUTCH

1 With the front brake fluid reservoir as level as possible, check that the fluid level is above the LOWER level line (arrowed) on the inspection window (early VN1500 models use a round reservoir, but the inspection window is the same).

2 If the level is below the LOWER level line, undo the cover screws and remove the cover, diaphragm plate (where fitted) and diaphragm.

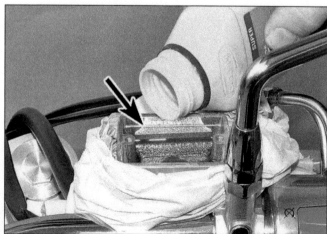

3 Top up with DOT 4 to the upper level line (arrowed) cast on the inside of the reservoir. Do not overfill, and take care to avoid spills (see **WARNING** above).

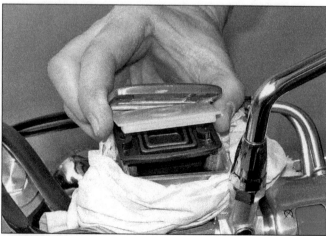

4 Wipe any moisture off the diaphragm with a clean absorbent shop towel. Compress the diaphragm, refit the diaphragm, plate and cover and tighten the screws.

REAR BRAKE

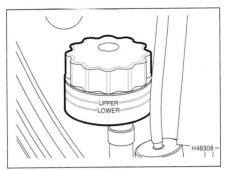

1 On VN1500A and B models remove the right side cover (see Chapter 8). The rear brake fluid level is visible through the reservoir body and must be between the UPPER and LOWER level lines.

2 On all other models the rear brake fluid level is visible through the reservoir body via the aperture in the reservoir cover and must be between the UPPER and LOWER level lines (arrowed) . . .

3 . . . if topping up is required remove the cover.

4 Unscrew the cap and remove the diaphragm plate and diaphragm.

5 Top up fluid to just below the UPPER line. Do not overfill, and take care to avoid spills (see **WARNING** on page 12).

6 Wipe any moisture off the diaphragm with a clean absorbent shop towel. Compress the diaphragm and fit the diaphragm plate and cap. Fit the cover.

Suspension, steering and final drive

Suspension and steering
● Check that the front and rear suspension operate smoothly without binding.
● Check that the suspension is adjusted as required.
● Check that the steering moves smoothly from lock-to-lock.

Final drive
● Inspect the final drive unit for oil leakage and check the oil level if leaks can be seen (see Chapter 1).

Legal and safety checks

Lighting and signalling:
● Take a minute to check that the headlight, tail light, brake light, instrument lights and turn signals all work correctly.
● Check that the horn sounds when the switch is operated.
● A working speedometer graduated in mph is a statutory requirement in the UK.

Safety:
● Check that the throttle grip rotates smoothly and snaps shut when released, in all steering positions. Also check for the correct amount of freeplay (see Chapter 1).
● Check that the engine shuts off when the kill switch is operated.
● Check that sidestand return springs hold the stand securely up when retracted.

Fuel:
● This may seem obvious, but check that you have enough fuel to complete your journey. If you notice signs of fuel leakage – rectify the cause immediately.
● Ensure you use the correct grade unleaded fuel – see Chapter 4A or 4B Specifications.

Engine oil level

Before you start

✔ Start the engine and allow it to reach normal operating temperature. *Caution: Do not run the engine in an enclosed space such as a garage or workshop.*
✔ Stop the engine and support the motorcycle on its sidestand. Allow it to stand undisturbed for a few minutes to allow the oil level to stabilize. Make sure the motorcycle is on level ground.
✔ The oil level is viewed through the window in the clutch cover on the right-hand side of the engine. Wipe the glass clean before inspection to make the check easier.

Bike care

● If you have to add oil frequently, you should check whether you have any oil leaks. If there is no sign of oil leakage from the joints and gaskets the engine could be burning oil (see *Troubleshooting*).

The correct oil

● Modern, high-revving engines place great demands on their oil. It is very important that the correct oil for your bike is used.
● Always top up with a good quality oil of the specified type and viscosity and do not overfill the engine.

Oil type	
All models	API grade SG, SH, SJ or SL with JASO MA motorcycle oil
Oil viscosity	
In normal climates	SAE 10W-40
In cold climates	SAE 10W-40 or 10W-50
In hot climates	SAE 20W-40 or 20W-50

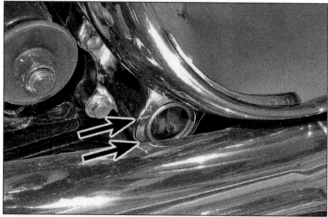

1 With the motorcycle held vertical, check the oil level in the inspection window at the bottom of the clutch cover. The level should lie between the upper and lower level marks (arrowed).

2 The oil filler cap is located either in the centre (VN1500A and B models) or at the top (all other models) of the right-hand crankcase cover. Unscrew the cap to add oil.

3 Add the specified oil, using a clean funnel if required, to bring the level up to the upper mark on the inspection window. Do not overfill.

4 Make sure the cap O-ring is in good condition and correctly seated before fitting cap.

Tires

The correct pressures
● The tires must be checked when **cold**, not immediately after riding. Note that low tire pressures may cause the tire to slip on the rim or come off. High tire pressures will cause abnormal tread wear and unsafe handling.
● Use an accurate pressure gauge.
● Proper air pressure will increase tire life and provide maximum stability and ride comfort.

Tire care
● Check the tires carefully for cuts, tears, embedded nails or other sharp objects and excessive wear. Operation of the motorcycle with excessively worn tires is extremely hazardous, as traction and handling are directly affected.
● Check the condition of the tire valve and ensure the dust cap is in place.
● Pick out any stones or nails which may have become embedded in the tire tread. If left, they will eventually penetrate through the casing and cause a puncture.
● If tire damage is apparent, or unexplained loss of pressure is experienced, seek the advice of a tire fitting specialist without delay.

Tire tread depth
● Make sure the amount of tread remaining is never below any legal limit specified in your country. Kawasaki recommends a minimum of 1 mm on the front tire. The minimum on the rear tire is 2 mm, or 3 mm if the motorcycle is ridden at speeds over 80 mph (130 kmh).
● Many tires now incorporate wear indicators in the tread. Identify the triangular pointer or 'TWI' mark on the tire sidewall to locate the indicator bar and replace the tire if the tread has worn down to the bar.

Tire pressures

VN1500	
Front	28 psi (1.93 Bar)
Rear	
Up to 97.5 kg (215 lbs) load	28 psi (1.93 Bar)
Over 97.5 kg (215 lbs) load	32 psi (2.2 Bar)
VN1500 Classic	
Front	28 psi (1.93 Bar)
Rear	36 psi (2.5 Bar)
VN1500 Classic FI	
Front	28 psi (1.93 Bar)
Rear	
Up to 97.5 kg (215 lbs) load	36 psi (2.5 Bar)
Over 97.5 kg (215 lbs) load	40 psi (2.8 Bar)
VN1600 Classic	
Front	28 psi (1.93 Bar)
Rear	36 psi (2.5 Bar)
Nomad/Classic Tourer	
Front	32 psi (2.2 Bar)
Rear	40 psi (2.8 Bar)
Drifter	
Front	28 psi (1.93 Bar)
Rear	
J1, J2, R1, R2 models	
Up to 97.5 kg (215 lbs) load	36 psi (2.5 Bar)
Over 97.5 kg (215 lbs) load	40 psi (2.8 Bar)
R3, R4 models	40 psi (2.8 Bar)
Mean Streak	
Front	36 psi (2.5 Bar)
Rear	36 psi (2.5 Bar)

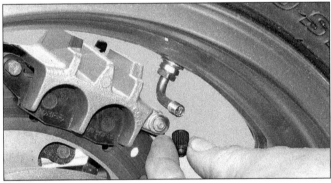

1 Remove the cap from the valve – do not forget to refit it afterwards.

2 Check the tire pressures when the tires are cold and keep them properly inflated.

3 Measure tread depth at the center of the tire using a tread depth gauge.

4 A tire tread wear indicator bar (arrowed) – their location markings (usually either an arrow, a triangle or the letters TWI) are marked on the sidewall.

Dimensions and weights

Note: *Specifications are for US market models – slight variances may occur in other countries. Add 0.5kg to dry weight for California models.*

VN1500A
Overall length . . . . 2390 mm
Overall width. . . . . 895 mm
Overall height . . . . 1190 mm
Wheelbase . . . . 1605 mm
Ground clearance. . . . . 150 mm
Seat height . . . . 720 mm
Weight (dry) . . . . 252 kg

VN1500B
Overall length . . . . 2370 mm
Overall width. . . . . 895 mm
Overall height . . . . 1210 mm
Wheelbase . . . . 1635 mm
Ground clearance. . . . . 165 mm
Seat height . . . . 710 mm
Weight (dry) . . . . 248 kg

VN1500 Classic
Overall length . . . . 2500 mm
Overall width. . . . . 965 mm
Overall height . . . . 1100 mm
Wheelbase . . . . 1660 mm
Ground clearance. . . . . 125 mm
Seat height . . . . 700 mm
Weight (dry) . . . . 292 kg

VN1500 Classic Fi
Overall length . . . . 2505 mm
Overall width. . . . . 995 mm
Overall height . . . . 1140 mm
Wheelbase . . . . 1665 mm
Ground clearance. . . . . 125 mm
Seat height . . . . 700 mm
Weight (dry) . . . . 299 kg

VN1600 Classic
Overall length . . . . 2505 mm
Overall width. . . . . 1040 mm
Overall height . . . . 1130 mm
Wheelbase . . . . 1680 mm
Ground clearance. . . . . 130 mm
Seat height . . . . 680 mm
Weight (dry) . . . . 306 kg

VN1500 Nomad/Classic Tourer
Overall length . . . . 2510 mm
Overall width. . . . . 960 mm
Overall height . . . . 1430 mm
Wheelbase . . . . 1665 mm
Ground clearance. . . . . 135 mm
Seat height . . . . 720 mm
Weight (dry) . . . . 331 kg

VN1500 Nomad/Classic Tourer Fi
Overall length . . . . 2510 mm
Overall width. . . . . 980 mm
Overall height . . . . 1430 mm
Wheelbase . . . . 1665 mm
Ground clearance. . . . . 135 mm
Seat height . . . . 720 mm
Weight (dry) . . . . 335 kg

VN1600 Nomad/Classic Tourer
Overall length . . . . 2515 mm
Overall width. . . . . 1040 mm
Overall height . . . . 1460 mm
Wheelbase . . . . 1690 mm
Ground clearance. . . . . 150 mm
Seat height . . . . 720 mm
Weight (dry) . . . . 350 kg

VN1500 Drifter
Overall length . . . . 2545 mm
Overall width. . . . . 980 mm
Overall height . . . . 1115 mm
Wheelbase . . . . 1655 mm
Ground clearance. . . . . 125 mm
Seat height . . . . 730 mm
Weight (dry) . . . . 303 kg

VN1500 Mean Streak
Overall length . . . . 2410 mm
Overall width. . . . . 850 mm
Overall height . . . . 1100 mm
Wheelbase . . . . 1705 mm
Ground clearance. . . . . 125 mm
Seat height . . . . 700 mm
Weight (dry) . . . . 289 kg

VN1600 Mean Streak
Overall length . . . . 2410 mm
Overall width. . . . . 850 mm
Overall height . . . . 1100 mm
Wheelbase . . . . 1705 mm
Ground clearance. . . . . 125 mm
Seat height . . . . 700 mm
Weight (dry) . . . . 290 kg

Engine

Type . . . . .Four-stroke 90° V-four
Capacity
   VN1500 models . . . . 1470 cc
   VN1600 models . . . . 1552 cc
Bore . . . . 102.0 mm
Stroke
   VN1500 models . . . . 90.0 mm
   VN1600 models . . . . 95.0 mm
Compression ratio 9:1
Cooling system. . . . . .Liquid cooled
Clutch. . . . . Wet multi-plate, hydraulic

Transmission

VN1500A, B and D models. . . . . .Four-speed constant mesh
All other models . . . . Five-speed constant mesh
Final drive. . . . . Shaft
Camshafts . . . . DOHC, chain-driven
Fuel system
   VN1500. . . . . .Twin Keihin CVK40 carburettors
   VN1500 Classic and Nomad/
      Classic Tourer . . . . .Single Keihin CVK40 carburettor
   All other models . . . . . . Digital fuel injection, 36mm throttle body
Starting system . . . . .Electric
Ignition system . . . . Battery and coil with electronic advance

Chassis

Frame type . . . . Steel cradle
Rake
   VN1500. . . . . 31°
   All other models . . . . 32°
Trail
   VN1500. . . . . 128 mm
   VN1500 Classic . . . . 123 mm
   VN1500 Classic Fi . . . . 165 mm
   VN1600 Classic . . . . 168 mm
   VN1500 Nomad/Classic Tourer . . . . 189 mm
   VN1600 Nomad/Classic Tourer . . . . 184 mm
   Drifter . . . . 165 mm
   Mean Streak . . . . 144 mm
Fuel tank capacity (including reserve)
   VN1500A. . . . . 16.0 litres
   VN1500B. . . . . 12.0 litres
   VN1500 Classic . . . . 16 litres
   VN1500 Classic Fi . . . . 19 litres
   VN1600 Classic . . . . 20 litres
   VN1500 Nomad/Classic Tourer . . . . 16 litres
   VN1500 Nomad/Classic Tourer Fi . . . . 16 litres
   VN1600 Nomad/Classic Tourer . . . . 20 litres
   Drifter J models . . . . 16 litres
   Drifter R models . . . . 19 litres
   Mean Streak . . . . 17 litres
Front suspension
   Type . . . . Oil-damped telescopic forks
   Travel . . . . 150 mm
   Adjustment . . . . none
Rear suspension
   Type . . . . Twin shock absorber and swingarm
   Travel (at axle)
      VN1500. . . . . 100 mm
      VN1500 Classic . . . . 87 mm
      VN1500 Classic Fi. . . . . 95 mm
      VN1600 Classic . . . . 95 mm
      VN1500 Nomad/Classic Tourer . . . . 100 mm
      VN1500 Nomad/Classic Tourer Fi. . . . . 100 mm
      VN1600 Nomad/Classic Tourer . . . . 99 mm
      Drifter . . . . 100 mm
      Mean Streak . . . . 87 mm
   Adjustment
      VN1500. . . . . Spring pre-load
      VN1500 Classic . . . . Spring pre-load
      VN1500 Classic Fi. . . . . Rebound damping, air pressure
      VN1600 Classic A1 and A2. Rebound damping, spring pre-load
      VN1600 Classic A3-on . . . . Rebound damping, air pressure
      Nomad/Classic Tourer . . . . Rebound damping, air pressure
      Drifter J1 . . . . Rebound damping, spring pre-load
      Drifter J2 and R. . . . . Rebound damping, air pressure
      Mean Streak . . . . Rebound damping, air pressure

Chassis (continued)

Wheels and tyres

VN1500A

Front	19 inch alloy, 100/90-19 57H tubeless tire
Rear	15 inch alloy, 150/90-15 74H tubeless tire

VN1500B

Front	19 inch steel spoke, 100/90-19 57H tube tire
Rear	15 inch steel spoke, 150/90-15 M/C 74H tube tire

VN1500 Classic

Front	16 inch steel spoke, 130/90-16 67H tube tire
Rear	16 inch steel spoke, 150/80-16 71H tube tire

VN1500 Classic Fi

Front	16 inch steel spoke, 130/90-16 M/C 67H tube tire
Rear	16 inch steel spoke, 150/80B-16 M/C 71H tube tire

VN1600 Classic

Front	16 inch steel spoke, 130/90-16 M/C 67H tube tire
Rear	16 inch steel spoke, 170/70B-16 M/C 75H tube tire

VN1500 Nomad/Classic Tourer

Front	16 inch alloy, 150/80-16 71H tubeless tire
Rear	16 inch alloy, 150/80-16 71H tubeless tire

VN1500 Nomad/Classic Tourer Fi

Front	16 inch alloy, 150/80-16 M/C 71H tubeless tire
Rear	16 inch alloy, 150/80B-16 M/C 71H tubeless tire

VN1600 Nomad/Classic Tourer

Front	16 inch alloy, 150/80-16 M/C 71H tubeless tire
Rear	16 inch alloy, 170/70B-16 M/C 75H tubeless tire

Drifter

Front	16 inch steel spoke, 130/90-16 M/C 67H tube tire
Rear	16 inch steel spoke, 150/80B-16 M/C 71H tube tire

Mean Streak

Front	17 inch alloy, 130/70R-17 M/C 62H tubeless tire
Rear	17 inch alloy, 170/70R-17 M/C 72H tubeless tire

Brakes

VN1500

Front	Single disc with single piston sliding caliper
Rear	Single disc with single piston sliding caliper

VN1500 Classic

Front	Single disc with twin piston sliding caliper
Rear	Single disc with single piston sliding caliper

VN1500 Classic Fi

Front	Single disc with twin piston sliding caliper
Rear	Single disc with twin piston sliding caliper

VN1600 Classic

Front	Twin discs with twin piston sliding calipers
Rear	Single disc with twin piston sliding caliper

VN1500 Nomad/Classic Tourer G1, G2, H1, H2

Front	Twin discs with twin piston sliding calipers
Rear	Single disc with single piston sliding caliper

VN1500 Nomad/Classic Tourer G3

Front	Twin discs with twin piston sliding calipers
Rear	Single disc with twin piston sliding caliper

VN1500 Nomad/Classic Tourer Fi

Front	Twin discs with twin piston sliding calipers
Rear	Single disc with twin piston sliding caliper

VN1600 Nomad/Classic Tourer

Front	Twin discs with twin piston sliding calipers
Rear	Single disc with twin piston sliding caliper

Drifter

Front	Single disc with twin piston sliding caliper
Rear	Single disc with twin piston sliding caliper

VN1500 Mean Streak P1, P2

Front	Twin disc with triple opposed-piston caliper
Rear	Single disc with twin piston sliding caliper

VN1600 Mean Streak B1

Front	Twin disc with triple opposed-piston caliper
Rear	Single disc with twin piston sliding caliper

VN1600 Mean Streak B2-on

Front	Twin disc with twin opposed-piston caliper
Rear	Single disc with twin piston sliding caliper

Chapter 1
Tune-up and routine maintenance

Contents

Degrees of difficulty

| **Easy,** suitable for novice with little experience | | **Fairly easy,** suitable for beginner with some experience | | **Fairly difficult,** suitable for competent DIY mechanic | | **Difficult,** suitable for experienced DIY mechanic | | **Very difficult,** suitable for expert DIY or professional | |

Engine

Spark plugs

Type

VN1500.	NGK DPR7EA-9 or ND X22EPR-U9
VN1500 Classic 1996 and 1997	NGK DPR7EA-9 or ND X22EPR-U9
VN1500 Classic 1998-on	NGK DPR5EA-9 or ND X16EPR-U9
VN1500 Nomad/Classic Tourer	NGK DPR5EA-9 or ND X16EPR-U9
VN1500 Nomad/Classic Tourer FI	NGK DPR6EA-9 or ND X20EPR-U9
VN1600 Nomad/Classic Tourer	NGK DPR6EA-9 or ND X20EPR-U9
Drifter and Mean Streak	NGK DPR6EA-9 or ND X20EPR-U9
Gap	0.8 to 0.9 mm (0.031 to 0.035 inch)

Engine idle speed

VN1500A	800+/-50 rpm
VN1500B	900+/-50 rpm
VN1500 Classic 1996 and 1997	
US	900+/-50 rpm
Austria, Germany, Switzerland	1000+/-50 rpm
VN1500 Classic 1998	
US (except California).	900+/-50 rpm
California, Austria, Germany, Switzerland	1000+/-50 rpm
VN1500 Classic 1999-on	800+/-50 rpm
VN1500 Nomad/Classic Tourer	800+/-50 rpm
VN1500 Nomad/Classic Tourer FI	950 rpm
VN1600 Nomad/Classic Tourer	950+/-50 rpm
Drifter and Mean Streak	950+/-50 rpm

Cylinder compression pressure

@ 300 rpm using starter motor.	340 to 590 kPa (50 to 85 psi)

Carburetor synchronization (VN1500 only)

Vacuum difference between cylinders	Less than 2 cm Hg (0.391 inch Hg)

Cylinder numbering

Front.	1
Rear	2

Chassis

Brake pad minimum thickness.	1.0 mm (0.040 inch)
Brake pedal position	
VN1500.	65 mm above top of footpeg
VN1500 Classic	125 mm above top of footboard
VN1500 Classic FI	95 mm above top of footboard
VN1600 Classic	110 mm above top of footboard
VN1500 Nomad/Classic Tourer	95 mm above top of footboard
VN1500 Nomad/Classic Tourer FI	95 mm above top of footboard
VN1600 Nomad/Classic Tourer	110 mm above top of footboard
Drifter J models	114 mm above top of footboard
Drifter R models	95 mm above top of footboard
Mean Streak	110 mm above top of footboard
Throttle grip freeplay	2 to 3 mm (0.08 to 0.12 inch)
Battery electrolyte specific gravity (VN1500A and B only).	1.280 at 68 degrees F (20 degrees C)
Tire pressures (cold).	See *Pre-ride checks*

Fluids and lubricants

Engine oil

Type	API grade SG, SH, SJ or SL with JASO MA motorcycle oil
Viscosity	
In normal climates	SAE 10W-40
In cold climates	SAE 10W-40 or 10W-50
In hot climates	SAE 20W-40 or 20W-50
Capacity	
VN1500, Classic up to 2001, and Nomad/Classic Tourer	
Oil change only.	2.5 liters (3.4 US qt, 4.4 Imp pt)
Oil and filter change	2.7 liters (4.2 US qt, 4.7 Imp pt)
Dry engine.	3.5 liters (3.4 US qt, 6.2 Imp pt)
All other models	
Oil change only.	2.9 liters (3.4 US qt, 5.1 Imp pt)
Oil and filter change	3.1 liters (4.2 US qt, 5.5 Imp pt)
Dry engine.	3.5 liters (3.4 US qt, 6.2 Imp pt)

Fluids and lubricants (continued)

Final drive oil
Type	API GL-5 Hypoid gear oil
Viscosity	
Above 41 degrees F (5 degrees C)...........................	SAE 90
Below 41 degrees F (5 degrees C)...........................	SAE 80
Capacity..	200 ml

Coolant
Type	Pre-mix coolant or 50% distilled water and 50% corrosion inhibited ethylene glycol anti-freeze
Capacity (all models, including reserve tank)....................	2.3 liters (2.4 US qt, 4.0 Imp pt)

Brake and clutch fluid
Type	DOT 4

Miscellaneous
Wheel bearings...	Medium weight, lithium-based multi-purpose grease
Swingarm pivot bearings	Medium weight, lithium-based multi-purpose grease
Cables and lever pivots	Aerosol cable lubricant
Sidestand pivot	Medium-weight, lithium-based multi-purpose grease
Brake pedal/shift lever pivots...............................	Cable lubricant or 10W30 motor oil
Throttle grip	Multi-purpose grease or dry film lubricant

Torque specifications
Cooling system air bleed valve (where fitted)....................	8 Nm (69 inch-lbs)
Final drive oil drain plug	8.8 Nm (78 inch-lbs)
Fork upper triple clamp bolts	
1500 models..	20 Nm (14.5 ft-lbs)
VN1600 Classic 2003 (A1) models and Drifter.................	20 Nm (14.5 ft-lbs)
VN1600 Classic 2004-on (A2-on and E) models	29 Nm (21 ft-lbs)
VN1600 Nomad/Classic Tourer and Mean Streak	29 Nm (21 ft-lbs)
Oil drain plug (in bottom of crankcase)	20 Nm (14.5 ft-lbs)
Oil screen cap (in left-hand side of crankcase)	20 Nm (14.5 ft-lbs)
Oil filter	18 Nm (159 inch-lbs)
Radiator drain bolt	
VN1500A and B	not available
All other VN1500 models	7.4 Nm (65 inch-lbs)
VN1600 models	2.2 Nm (19 inch-lbs)
Spark plugs	18 Nm (159 inch-lbs)
Steering stem nut or bolt	
VN1500A and B	39 Nm (29 ft-lbs)
VN1500 Classic	44 Nm (33 ft-lbs)
VN1500 Classic FI 2000 to 2002 (N1 to N3) models	54 Nm (40 ft-lbs)
VN1500 Classic FI 2003-on (N4-on) models	88 Nm (65 ft-lbs)
VN1600 Classic	88 Nm (65 ft-lbs)
Nomad/Classic Tourer	88 Nm (65 ft-lbs)
Drifter 1999 and 2000 (J1 and J2) models..................	88 Nm (65 ft-lbs)
Drifter 2001-on (R1-on) models	54 Nm (40 ft-lbs)
VN1500 Mean Streak	54 Nm (40 ft-lbs)
VN1600 Mean Streak	88 Nm (65 ft-lbs)
Water pump drain bolt	
VN1500A and B	not available
All other VN1500 models	10 Nm (65 inch-lbs)
VN1600 models	11 Nm (87 inch-lbs)

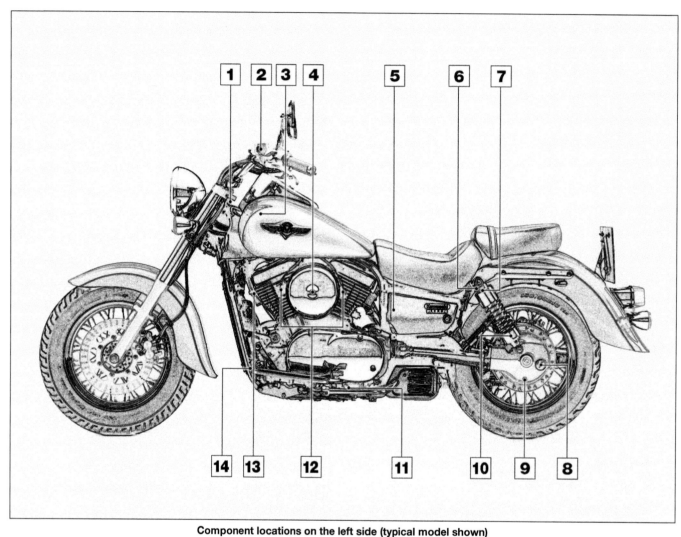

Component locations on the left side (typical model shown)

1 Steering head bearing adjuster
2 Clutch fluid reservoir
3 Cooling system pressure cap
4 Air filter
5 Battery

6 Rear shock air pressure valve
7 Rear shock damping adjuster
8 Final drive oil level/filler cap
9 Final drive oil drain bolt
10 Rear shock pre-load adjuster

11 Engine oil screen
12 Spark plugs
13 Air suction system valve
14 Coolant drain bolt in radiator

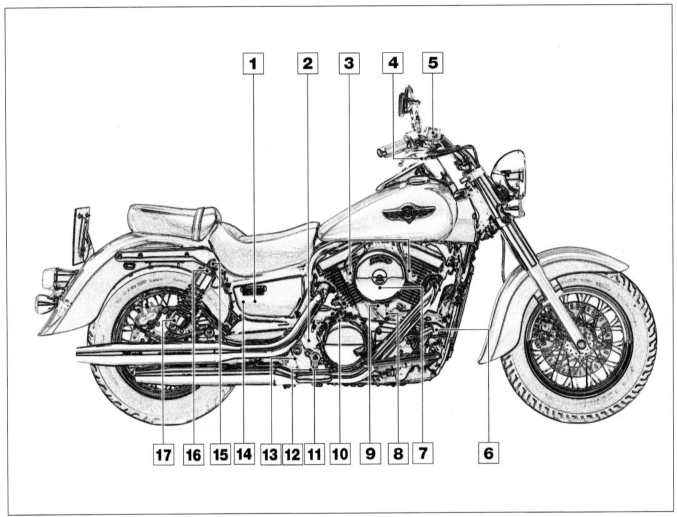

Component locations on the right side (typical model shown)

1 Coolant reservoir (except 1500A and B models)
2 Coolant reservoir (1500A and B models)
3 Spark plugs
4 Throttle cable upper adjusters
5 Front brake fluid reservoir

6 Rear brake fluid reservoir (except 1500A and B models)
7 Right-hand air filter (1500A and B models)
8 Coolant drain bolt on water pump
9 Idle speed adjuster
10 Engine oil filler cap
11 Engine oil level inspection window

12 Engine oil drain plug
13 Engine oil filter
14 Rear brake fluid reservoir (1500A and B models)
15 Rear shock air pressure valve
16 Rear shock damping adjuster
17 Rear shock pre-load adjuster

1 Maintenance schedule

Note: *The pre-ride inspection outlined in the owner's manual covers checks and maintenance that should be carried out on a daily basis. It's condensed and included here to remind you of its importance. Always perform the pre-ride inspection at every maintenance interval (in addition to the procedures listed). The intervals listed below are the shortest intervals recommended by the manufacturer for each particular operation during the model years covered in this manual. Your owner's manual may have different intervals for your model.*

Pre-ride

☐ Check the engine oil level
☐ Check the fuel level and inspect for leaks
☐ Check the engine coolant level and look for leaks
☐ Check the operation of both brakes – also check the fluid level and look for leakage
☐ Check the tires for damage, the presence of foreign objects and correct air pressure
☐ Check the throttle for smooth operation and correct freeplay
☐ Check the operation of the clutch – also check the fluid level and look for leakage
☐ Make sure the steering operates smoothly, without looseness and without binding
☐ Check for proper operation of the headlight, tail light, brake light, turn signals, indicator lights, speedometer and horn
☐ Make sure the sidestand returns to its fully up position and stays there under spring tension
☐ Make sure the engine STOP switch works properly

Every 4000 miles (6000 km) or 6 months

☐ Change the engine oil (Section 3)
☐ Check the battery (Section 4)

Every 4000 miles (6000 km)

☐ Clean and gap the spark plugs (Section 5)
☐ Check the brake pads for wear (Section 6)
☐ Check the brake system (Section 7)
☐ Check the clutch (Section 8)
☐ Check the tires and wheels (Section 9)
☐ Check the cooling system (Section 10)
☐ Check the steering (Section 11)
☐ Check the operation of the air suction valves (Section 12)
☐ Check the evaporative emission control system (California models) (Section 13)
☐ Check/adjust the throttle and choke operation and freeplay (Section 14)
☐ Check/adjust the idle speed – US and Canada VN1500A and B models (Section 15)
☐ Check/adjust the carburetor synchronization – US and Canada VN1500A and B models (Section 16)
☐ Check the fuel system and the condition of the fuel and vacuum hoses (Section 17)

Every 8000 miles (12,000 km)

All of the items under previous mileage and pre-ride headings plus:
☐ Change the engine oil and oil filter (Section 3)
☐ Check/adjust the idle speed – non US and Canada VN1500A and B models and all other models (Section 15)
☐ Check/adjust the carburetor synchronization – non US and Canada VN1500A and B models (Section 16)
☐ Lubricate all cables (Section 18)
☐ Lubricate the clutch and brake lever pivots (Section 18)
☐ Lubricate the shift/brake lever pivots and the sidestand pivot (Section 18)
☐ Replace the spark plugs (Section 5)
☐ Clean the air filter element (Section 19)
☐ Check the exhaust system for leaks and check the tightness of the fasteners (Section 20)
☐ Lubricate the swingarm bearings (Chapter 6)
☐ Lubricate the driveshaft joints (Chapter 6)*
☐ Check the tightness of all fasteners on the motorcycle (Section 21)
☐ Check the suspension (Section 22)
☐ Check the final drive differential oil level (Section 23)

The driveshaft joints should be lubricated after the first 8000 miles or 12,000 km, and thereafter every 24,000 miles or 36,000 km

Every 16,000 miles (24,000 km) or two years

☐ Change the coolant (Section 24)
☐ Change the fork oil (Chapter 6)
☐ Change the brake fluid (Chapter 7)
☐ Change the clutch fluid (Chapter 2)
☐ Lubricate the steering head bearings (Chapter 6)

Every 24,000 miles (36,000 km)

☐ Change the final drive differential oil (Section 23)
☐ Lubricate the driveshaft joints (Chapter 6)

Every two years

☐ Check and lubricate the wheel bearings (Chapter 7)
☐ Lubricate the speedometer gear (Chapter 9)

Every four years

☐ Replace the fuel hoses (Chapter 4A or 4B)
☐ Replace the brake hoses (Chapter 7)
☐ Replace the clutch hose(s) (Chapter 2)
☐ Overhaul the brake caliper(s) and master cylinder(s) (Chapter 7)
☐ Overhaul the clutch master and release cylinder(s) (Chapter 2)

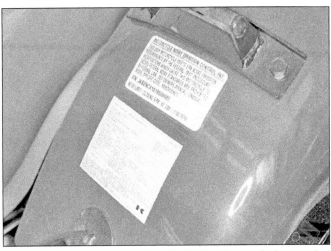

2.3 Decals in various locations include safety, emissions and maintenance information

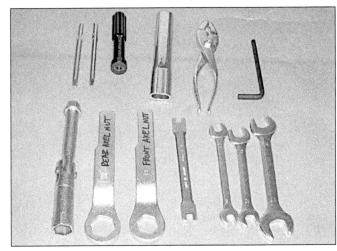

2.7 A typical toolkit provided with a motorcycle

2 Introduction to tune-up and routine maintenance

1 This Chapter covers the checks and procedures necessary for the tune-up and routine maintenance of your motorcycle. Section 1 covers the routine maintenance schedule, which is designed to keep the machine in proper running condition and prevent possible problems. The remaining Sections contain detailed procedures for carrying out the items listed on the maintenance schedule, as well as additional maintenance information designed to increase reliability.

2 Since routine maintenance plays such an important role in the safe and efficient operation of your motorcycle, it is presented here as a comprehensive check list. For the rider who does all of the bike's maintenance, these lists outline the procedures and checks that should be done on a routine basis.

3 Maintenance information is printed on decals in various locations on the motorcycle **(see illustration)**. If the information on the decals differs from that included here, use the information on the decal.

4 Deciding where to start or plug into the routine maintenance schedule depends on several factors. If you have a motorcycle whose warranty has recently expired, and if it has been maintained according to the warranty standards, you may want to pick up routine maintenance as it coincides with the next mileage or calendar interval. If you have owned the machine for some time but have never performed any maintenance on it, then you may want to start at the nearest interval and include some additional procedures to ensure that nothing important is overlooked. If you have just had a major engine overhaul, then you may want to start the maintenance

routine from the beginning. If you have a used machine and have no knowledge of its history or maintenance record, you may desire to combine all the checks into one large service initially and then settle into the maintenance schedule prescribed.

5 The Sections which outline the inspection and maintenance procedures are written as step-by-step comprehensive guides to the performance of the work. They explain in detail each of the routine inspections and maintenance procedures on the check list. References to additional information in applicable Chapters are also included and should not be overlooked.

6 Before beginning any maintenance or repair, the machine should be cleaned thoroughly, especially around the oil filter, spark plugs, cylinder head covers, side covers, carburetor(s), etc. Cleaning will help ensure that dirt does not contaminate the engine and will allow you to detect wear and damage that could otherwise easily go unnoticed.

7 The motorcycle comes from the factory with a tool kit that's useful for some of the maintenance procedures, as well as for emergency repairs **(see illustration)**. If the factory tool kit is missing or incomplete, you can put together your own or order the factory tool kit from a Kawasaki dealer.

3 Engine oil and filter – change

Special tool: *A filter removing tool is necessary for this job – there are several after-market options.*

⚠️ **Warning: Be careful when draining the oil, as the exhaust pipes, the engine, and the oil itself can cause severe burns. Wear protective gloves.**

1 Consistent routine oil and filter changes are the single most important maintenance procedure you can perform on a motorcycle. The oil not only lubricates the internal parts of the engine, transmission and clutch, but it also acts as a coolant, a cleaner, a sealant, and a protector. Because of these demands, the oil takes a terrific amount of abuse and should be replaced often with new oil of the recommended grade and type. Saving a little money on the difference in cost between a good oil and a cheap oil won't pay off if the engine is damaged. Make sure the oil has the JASO MA rating or anti-friction additives could cause the clutch to slip.

2 Before changing the oil and filter, warm up the engine so the oil will drain easily. Be careful when draining the oil, as the exhaust pipes, the engine, and the oil itself can cause severe burns.

3 Prop the motorcycle upright over a clean drain pan. Remove the oil filler cap to vent the crankcase and act as a reminder that there is no oil in the engine **(see illustration)**.

4 Remove the drain plug from the bottom of the crankcase and allow the oil to drain into

3.3 Unscrew the oil filler cap to act as a vent

3.4a Unscrew the oil drain plug . . .

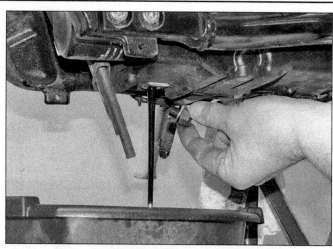

3.4b . . . and allow the oil to completely drain

3.5a Unscrew the cap . . .

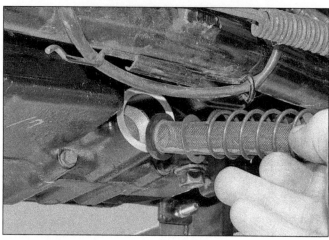

3.5b . . . and withdraw the spring and the screen

the pan **(see illustrations)**. Discard the sealing washer on the drain plug; it should be replaced with a new one whenever the plug is removed. If additional maintenance is planned for this time period, check or service another component while the oil is allowed to drain completely.

5 Unscrew the oil screen cap **(see illustration)**. Remove the cap and its O-ring, then pull the spring and oil screen out of the engine **(see illustration)**. Remove the spring and washer from the screen. Clean the screen in solvent and inspect it for damage. Fit the washer and

the spring back onto the screen, then reinstall it in the engine, rubber end first. Fit the cap, using a new O-ring if the old one is damaged **(see illustration)**. Tighten the cap to the torque listed in this Chapter's Specifications.

6 At every second oil change (i.e. at 8000 mile or 12,000 km intervals), as the oil is draining, remove the oil filter **(see illustration)**.

7 Wipe any remaining oil off the filter sealing area of the crankcase.

8 Coat the rubber gasket on a new filter with

HAYNES HiNT *As you unscrew the drain plug keep it pushed up against the crankcase, then when it is fully unscrewed pull it quickly away – this prevents oil running over your hand and the plug dropping in the drain tray.*

3.5c Replace the cap O-ring with a new one if necessary

3.6a Unscrew the filter using a filter removing socket or strap . . .

3.6b . . . and allow the oil to drain

clean engine oil **(see illustration)**. Install the filter and tighten it to the torque listed in this Chapter's Specifications **(see illustration)**.

9 Check the condition of the drain plug threads. If the plug has a magnetized tip clean off any debris stuck to it.

10 Fit a new sealing washer onto the drain plug, then fit the plug and tighten to the torque listed in this Chapter's Specifications. Avoid overtightening, as damage to the engine case will result.

11 Before refilling the engine, check the old oil carefully. If the oil was drained into a clean pan, small pieces of metal or other material can be easily detected. If the oil is very metallic colored, then the engine is experiencing wear from break-in (new engine) or from insufficient lubrication. If there are flakes or chips of metal in the oil, then something is drastically wrong internally and the engine will have to be disassembled for inspection and repair.

12 If there are pieces of fiber-like material in the oil, the clutch is experiencing excessive wear and should be checked.

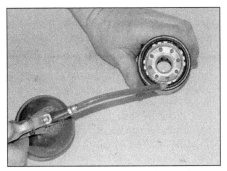

3.8a Smear clean oil onto the seal . . .

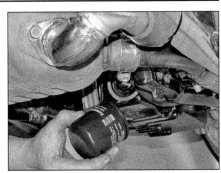

3.8b . . . then fit the filter and tighten it to the correct torque

13 If the inspection of the oil turns up nothing unusual, refill the crankcase to the proper level with the recommended oil **(see illustrations)**. Make sure the filler cap O-ring is in place then fit the cap **(see illustration)**. Start the engine and let it run for two or three minutes. Shut it off, wait a few minutes, then check the oil level. If necessary, add more oil to bring the level up to the Maximum mark. Check around the drain plug, screen cap and filter for leaks.

14 The old oil drained from the engine cannot be reused in its present state and should be disposed of. Check with your local refuse disposal company, disposal facility or environmental agency to see whether they will accept the oil for recycling. Don't pour used oil into drains or onto the ground. After the oil

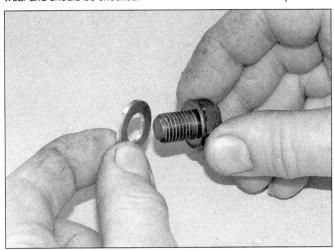

3.10 Fit a new sealing washer onto the drain plug

3.13a Add the specified type and amount of oil . . .

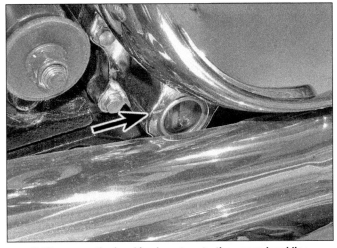

3.13b . . . so the level is almost up to the upper level line (arrowed)

3.13c Make sure the O-ring (arrowed) is in place and in good condition

has cooled, it can be drained into a suitable container (capped plastic jugs, topped bottles, milk cartons, etc.) for transport to one of these disposal sites.

Note: It is antisocial and illegal to dump oil down the drain. To find the location of your local oil recycling bank in the UK, call 08708 506 506 or visit www.oilbankline.org.uk

In the USA, note that any oil supplier must accept used oil for recycling.

4 Battery – check

⚠ *Warning: Be extremely careful when handling or working around the battery. The electrolyte is very*

caustic and an explosive gas (hydrogen) is given off when the battery is charging.
Note 1: *Checking of the electrolyte level and specific gravity applies only to standard (non-MF) fillable batteries, installed as original equipment on VN1500A and B models only. The maintenance-free (MF) batteries used on all other models do not require those periodic checks. Note that it is possible that the battery on some VN1500A and B models may have been replaced with an MF battery at some point over its life.*
Note 2: *On MF batteries do not attempt to remove the battery cell cap(s) to check the electrolyte level or battery specific gravity. Removal will damage the caps, resulting in electrolyte leakage and battery damage.*
1 Make sure the ignition is switched OFF. On VN1500A and B models remove the left side cover (see Chapter 8). On all other models remove the seat (the front seat on dual seat models) (see Chapter 8).

Standard battery – VN1500A and B
2 On VN1500A and B models the electrolyte level

is visible through the translucent battery case – it should be between the Upper and Lower level marks **(see illustration)**. If it is not easy to see remove the battery and clean the case.
3 If the level is low, remove the cell caps as required and fill each low cell to the upper level mark with distilled water **(see illustrations)**. Do not use tap water (except in an emergency), and do not overfill. The cell holes are quite small, so it may help to use a plastic squeeze bottle with a small spout to add the water. If the level is within the marks on the case, additional water is not necessary.
4 Next, check the specific gravity of the electrolyte in each cell with a small hydrometer made especially for motorcycle batteries. These are available from most dealer parts departments or motorcycle accessory stores.
5 Remove all the cell caps **(see illustration 4.3a)**. Draw some electrolyte from the first cell into the hydrometer and note the specific gravity **(see illustration)**. Compare the reading to the Specifications listed in this Chapter. Return the electrolyte to the

4.2 Make sure the level of the electrolyte is between the lines

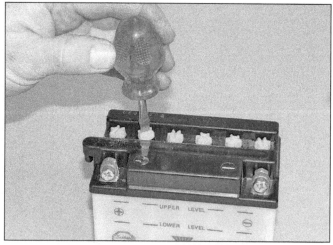

4.3a Remove the cap from relevant cell(s) . . .

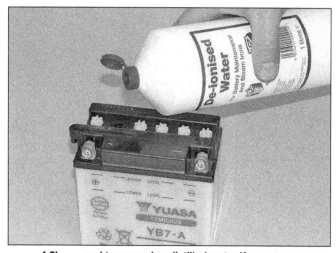

4.3b . . . and top up using distilled water if necessary

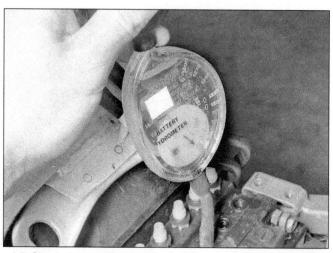

4.5 Check the specific gravity of each cell using an hydrometer

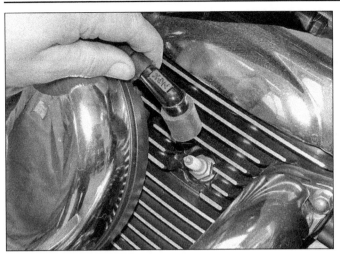

5.2a Pull the cap off the plug

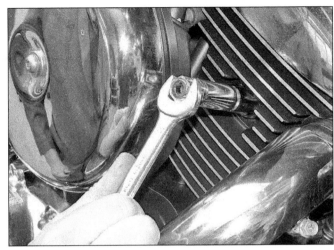

5.2b Unscrew the plug and lift it out with the tool - the rubber insert should grip around the plug top

appropriate cell and repeat the check for the remaining cells. When the check is complete, rinse the hydrometer thoroughly with clean water. Refit the cell caps.

6 If the specific gravity of the electrolyte in each cell is as specified, the battery is in good condition and is being charged by the machine's charging system.

7 If the specific gravity is low, the battery is not fully charged. This may be due to corroded battery terminals, a dirty battery case, a malfunctioning charging system, or loose or corroded wiring connections. On the other hand, it may be that the battery is worn out, especially if the machine is old, or that infrequent use of the motorcycle prevents normal charging from taking place.

8 Be sure to correct any problems and charge the battery if necessary.

All batteries

9 Check the battery terminals and leads are tight and free of corrosion. If corrosion is evident, disconnect the battery (see Chapter 9) and clean the terminals and lead ends with a wire brush or knife and emery paper. Apply a thin coat of petroleum jelly (Vaseline) or a dedicated battery terminal spray to the connections to slow further corrosion.

10 If the machine is not in regular use, disconnect

the battery and give it a refresher charge every month to six weeks (see Chapter 9). The state of charge of the battery can be assessed by measuring its open-circuit voltage.

11 Refer to Chapter 9 for additional battery maintenance and charging procedures.

5 Spark plugs – check and replacement

Check

1 This motorcycle is equipped with spark plugs that have an 18 mm wrench hex. Make sure your spark plug socket is the correct size before attempting to remove the plugs. Do not forget that each cylinder has two spark plugs. Work on one plug at a time.

2 Pull the spark plug cap off the spark plug **(see illustration)**. If available, use compressed air to blow any accumulated debris from around the spark plugs, and if not use a brush. Unscrew and remove the plug **(see illustration)**.

3 Inspect the electrodes for wear. Both the center and side electrodes should have square edges and the side electrode should be of

uniform thickness. Look for excessive deposits and evidence of a cracked or chipped insulator around the center electrode. Compare your spark plugs to the color spark plug reading chart on the inside rear cover. Check the threads, the washer and the ceramic insulator body for cracks and other damage.

4 If the electrodes are not excessively worn, and if the deposits can be easily re-moved with a wire brush, the plugs can be re-gapped and reused (if no cracks or chips are visible in the insulator). If in doubt concerning the condition of the plugs, replace them with new ones, as the expense is minimal.

5 Cleaning spark plugs by sandblasting is permitted, provided you clean the plugs with compressed air and a high flash-point solvent afterwards.

6 Check the gap between the electrodes – for best results, use a wire-type gauge rather than a flat gauge to check the gap **(see illustration)**. If the gap must be adjusted, bend the side electrode only and be very careful not to chip or crack the insulator nose **(see illustration)**.

7 Make sure the washer is in place before installing the plug. Fit the plug into the end of the tool, then use the tool to insert the plug **(see illustration)**. Alternatively there are dedicated plug insertion tools, or you can use

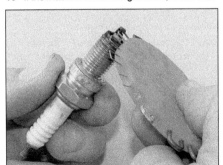

5.6a Using a wire gauge to measure the spark plug electrode gap

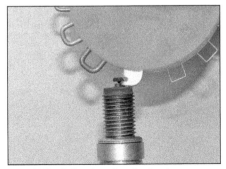

5.6b Adjusting the electrode gap

5.7 Insert the spark plug and tighten as described

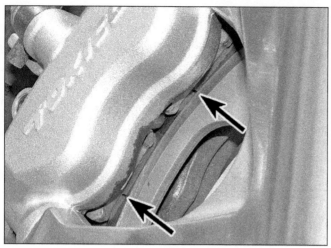

6.2 Front brake pad wear indicator cut-outs (arrowed) – Mean Streak B models

6.3 Rear brake pad friction material (arrowed) is easily visible

some hose (see **Haynes Hint**). Thread the plugs as far as possible into the head turning the tool or hose by hand, making sure they do not cross-thread.

HAYNES HINT *Slip a short length of hose over the end of the plug to use as a tool to thread it into place. The hose will grip the plug well enough to turn it, but will start to slip if the plug begins to cross-thread in the hole – this will prevent damaged threads.*

8 Once the plugs are finger tight, if a torque wrench is available, tighten the spark plugs to the torque listed in this Chapter's Specifications. If you do not have a torque wrench, tighten the plugs using a wrench until the washer seats on the cylinder head, then tighten them an additional 1/4 turn. Regardless of the method used, do not over-tighten them.
9 Reconnect the spark plug cap.

HAYNES HINT *Stripped plug threads in the cylinder head can be repaired with a thread insert – see 'Tools and Workshop Tips' in the Reference section.*

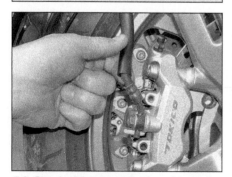

7.3 Check all hoses and unions for cracks and leaks

Replacement

10 At the prescribed interval, whatever the condition of the existing spark plugs, remove the plugs as described above and install new ones. Before installing new plugs, make sure they are the correct type and heat range.

6 Brake pads – wear check

1 Disc brake pads should be checked at the recommended intervals and replaced with new ones when worn beyond the limit listed in this Chapter's Specifications.
2 Each brake pad has wear indicators in the form of cut-outs or steps in the friction material. The wear indicators should be plainly visible by looking from below the front caliper(s), and from behind the rear caliper, but note that an accumulation of road dirt and brake dust could make them difficult to see **(see illustration)**. Where fitted remove the pad or caliper cover for an improved view.
3 If the indicators aren't visible, then the amount of friction material remaining should be, and it will be obvious when the pads need replacing **(see illustration)**. Kawasaki specify a minimum thickness of 1 mm. **Note:** *Some*

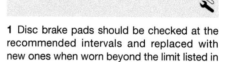

7.6 Turn the adjuster nut (arrowed) as required

after-market pads may use different indicators to those on the original equipment. Also check for uneven wear on all calipers with more than one piston, which is indicative of a sticking or seized piston. If found, the calipers must be overhauled (see Chapter 7).
4 If the pads are dirty or if you are in doubt as to the amount of friction material remaining, remove them for inspection (see Chapter 7). If the pads are excessively worn, also check the brake discs (see Chapter 7).
5 If the pads are worn to the limit, they must be replaced with new ones. Refer to Chapter 7 for details of pad removal and installation.

7 Brake system – general check

1 A routine general check of the brakes will ensure that any problems are discovered and remedied before the rider's safety is jeopardized.
2 Check the brake lever and pedal for loose connections, excessive play, bends, and other damage. Replace any damaged parts with new ones (see Chapter 7).
3 Make sure all brake fasteners are tight. Check the brake pads for wear (see Section 6) and make sure the fluid level in each reservoir is correct (see *Pre-ride checks* at the beginning of this manual). Look for leaks at the hose connections and check for cracks in the hoses **(see illustration)**. If the lever is spongy, bleed the brakes as described in Chapter 7.
4 Make sure the brake light operates when the front brake lever is pulled in. The front brake light switch is not adjustable. If it fails to operate properly, replace it with a new one (see Chapter 9).
5 Make sure the brake light is activated when the rear brake pedal is depressed approximately 15 mm (0.6 inch).
6 If it comes on late, after the brake is biting, or is permanently on, adjustment is necessary. Hold the switch and turn the adjusting nut on the switch body **(see illustration)** until the

7.7 Pull the lever away and turn the adjuster, aligning the required setting with the index mark

7.9 Slacken the locknut (arrowed) and turn the pushrod to adjust pedal position

brake light is activated when required – do not turn the switch itself. Turning the nut anti-clockwise (when looked at from the top) will cause the brake light to come on later, while turning it clockwise will cause it to come on sooner. If the switch doesn't operate the brake lights, check it as described in Chapter 9.

7 On many models the front brake lever has a span adjuster which alters the distance of the lever from the handlebar and can be set to suit rider preference. Each setting is identified by a number on the adjuster which aligns with the index mark on the lever. Push the lever away from the handlebar and turn the adjuster ring until the setting which best suits is obtained, then release the lever **(see illustration)**. Do not set the adjuster between the defined settings.

8 Rear brake pedal position is largely a matter of personal preference. Locate the pedal so that the rear brake can be engaged quickly and easily without excessive foot movement. The recommended factory setting is listed in this Chapter's Specifications.

9 Pedal position is adjusted by slackening the locknut on the master cylinder pushrod clevis and turning the pushrod using the hex at its top to change is effective length, thereby altering the position of the pedal **(see illustration)**.

8 Clutch

1 All models are fitted with an hydraulic clutch. Make sure the fluid level in the reservoir is correct (see *Pre-ride checks*).

2 Check the clutch lever pivot and pushrod for sloppy or rough action, excessive play, bends, and other damage. Replace any damaged parts with new ones (see Chapter 6). Clean and lubricate the lever pivot and pushrod components if its action is stiff or rough (see Section 18).

3 Check the operation of the clutch. If there

is evidence of air in the system (spongy feel to the lever, difficulty in engaging gear, drag when in gear), bleed the clutch (see Chapter 2). If the lever feels stiff or sticky, overhaul the release mechanism (see Chapter 2).

4 Look for leaks at the hose connections and check for cracks in the hoses, pipe and their joints – a hose runs from the master cylinder on the handlebar, along the top section of frame on the left-hand side, round the back of the engine to the release cylinder on the left side **(see illustration)**.

5 On many models the clutch lever has a span adjuster which alters the distance of the lever from the handlebar and can be set to suit rider preference. Each setting is identified by a number on the adjuster which aligns with the triangular index mark on the lever. Push the lever away from the handlebar and turn the adjuster ring until the setting which best suits is obtained, then release the lever **(see illustration)**. Do not set the adjuster between the defined settings.

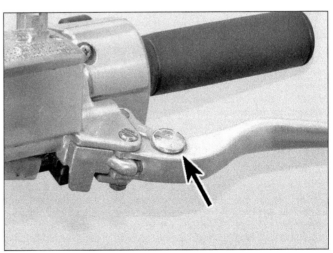

8.4 Clutch release cylinder and hydraulic hose (arrowed)

8.5 Clutch lever span adjuster (arrowed)

9.7 Check spoke tension and adjust if required using a spoke wrench – do not overtighten the spokes

9.10 Checking for play in the front wheel bearings

9 Tires/wheels and wheel bearings – general check

1 Routine tire and wheel checks should be made with the realization that your safety depends to a great extent on their condition.

Tires

2 Check the tires carefully for cuts, tears, embedded nails or other sharp objects and excessive wear. Operation of the motorcycle with excessively worn tires is extremely hazardous, as traction and handling are directly affected. Measure the tread depth at the center of the tire and replace worn tires with new ones when the tread depth is less than specified.
3 Repair or replace punctured tires as soon as damage is noted. Seek advice from a tire fitting specialist on the practicality and legality of tire repairs.
4 Check the tire pressures when the tires are cold and keep them properly inflated (see *Pre-ride checks*). Proper air pressure will increase tire life and provide maximum stability and ride comfort. Keep in mind that low tire pressures may cause the tire to slip on the rim or come off, while high tire pressures will cause abnormal tread wear and unsafe handling.
5 Check each valve stem locknut where present to make sure they are tight. Also, make sure the valve stem cap is in place and tight. If it is missing, fit a new one made of metal or hard plastic.

Cast wheels

6 The cast wheels used on some models are virtually maintenance-free, but they should be kept clean and checked periodically for cracks and other damage. Never attempt to repair damaged cast wheels; they must be replaced with new ones. Check that any wheel balance weights are fixed firmly to the wheel rim. If you suspect that a weight has fallen off, have

the wheel rebalanced by a motorcycle tire specialist.

Wire spoke wheels

7 Visually check the spokes for damage and corrosion. A broken or bent spoke must be replaced with a new one immediately because the load taken by it will be transferred to adjacent spokes which may in turn fail. Check the tension in each spoke by tapping each one lightly with a screwdriver and noting the sound produced – each should make the same sound of the correct pitch. Properly tensioned spokes will make a sharp pinging sound, loose ones will produce a lower pitch dull sound and tight ones will be higher pitched. If a spoke needs adjustment turn the adjuster at the rim using a spoke adjustment tool or an open-ended spanner **(see illustration)**.
8 Unevenly tensioned spokes will promote rim misalignment – refer to information on wheel runout in Chapter 7 and seek the advice of a Kawasaki dealer or wheel building specialist if the wheel needs realigning, which it may well do if many spokes are unevenly tensioned. Check front and rear wheel alignment as described in Chapter 7. Check that any wheel balance weights are fixed firmly to the wheel rim. If you suspect that a weight has fallen off, have the wheel rebalanced by a motorcycle tire specialist.

Wheel bearings

9 Wheel bearings will wear over a considerable mileage and should be checked periodically to avoid handling problems.
10 Support the motorcycle upright using an auxiliary stand so that the wheel being examined is off the ground. When checking the front wheel bearings turn the handlebars to full lock on one side so you have something to push against. Check for any play in the bearings by pushing and pulling the wheel against the hub **(see illustration)**. Also rotate the wheel and check that it turns smoothly and without any grating noises.

11 If any play is detected in the hub, or if the wheel does not rotate smoothly (and this is not due to brake or transmission drag), remove the wheel and inspect the bearings for wear or damage (see Chapter 7).

10 Cooling system – check

> ⚠ *Warning: The engine must be cool before beginning this procedure.*

Note: *Refer to 'Pre-ride checks' at the beginning of this manual and check the coolant level before performing this check.*
1 The entire cooling system should be checked carefully at the recommended intervals. Look for evidence of leaks, check the condition of the coolant, check the radiator for clogged fins and damage, and make sure the fan operates when required.
2 Examine each of the rubber coolant hoses along its entire length. Look for cracks, abrasions and other damage. Squeeze each hose at various points **(see illustration)**. They should feel firm, yet pliable, and return to their original shape when released. If they are dried out or hard, replace them with new ones.

10.2 Check all the coolant hoses as described

10.4 Check the pump drain hole or hose (arrowed) for signs of leakage

10.6 Check the radiator – bent fins can be straightened with a small screwdriver

3 Check for evidence of leaks at each cooling system joint. Tighten the hose clamps carefully to prevent future leaks.

4 Check the drain hole on the underside of the pump or the bottom of the drain hose connected to the pump (according to model) for signs of leakage **(see illustration)**. If the pump mechanical seal fails, the drain allows the coolant to escape. If the oil seal fails, the drain allows the oil to escape. If on inspection the drain shows signs of coolant leakage, replace the mechanical seal with a new one. If there are signs of oil leakage replace the oil seal with a new one (see Chapter 3). A whitish emulsion of oil and coolant mean both seals have failed.

5 Check the radiator for evidence of leaks and other damage. Leaks in the radiator leave telltale scale deposits or coolant stains on the outside of the core below the leak. If leaks are noted, remove the radiator (refer to Chapter 3) and have it repaired at a radiator shop or replace it with a new one. **Caution:** *Do not use a liquid leak stopping compound to try to repair leaks.*

6 Check the radiator fins for mud, dirt and insects, which may impede the flow of air through the radiator. If the fins are dirty, force water or low pressure compressed air through the fins from the rear of the radiator. If the fins

10.7 Remove the pressure cap as described

are bent or distorted, straighten them carefully with a screwdriver **(see illustration)**.

7 For access to the cooling system pressure cap remove the fuel tank (see Chapter 4A for carburetor models and Chapter 4B for fuel injection models) – note that on some models you may be able to access the cap after removing or displacing the instrument cluster from the tank, leaving the tank in place – it will depend mostly on the size and strength of your hands. Remove the pressure cap by turning it counterclockwise until it reaches a stop. If you hear a hissing sound (indicating there is still pressure in the system), wait until it stops. Now, press down on the cap and continue turning the cap counterclockwise until it can be removed **(see illustration)**.

> **⚠ Warning: Do not remove the pressure cap when the engine is hot. It is good practice to cover the cap with a heavy cloth and turn the cap slowly anti-clockwise. If you hear a hissing sound (indicating that there is still pressure in the system), wait until it stops, then continue turning the cap until it can be removed.**

8 Check the condition of the coolant in the system. If it is rust colored or if accumulations of scale are visible, drain, flush and refill the system with new coolant. Check the antifreeze content of the coolant with an antifreeze hydrometer. Sometimes coolant may look like it's in good condition, but might be too weak to offer adequate protection. If the hydrometer indicates a weak mixture, drain, flush and refill the cooling system (see Section 24).

9 Check the cap gaskets for cracks and other damage. If you have been experiencing an unexplainable loss of coolant have the cap pressure tested by a dealer service department, or just replace it with a new one – they are not expensive. Fit the cap by turning it clockwise until it reaches the first stop, then push down on the

cap and continue turning until it can turn no further.

10 Start the engine and let it reach normal operating temperature, then check for leaks again. As the coolant temperature increases, the fan should come on automatically and the temperature should begin to drop. If it does not, refer to Chapter 3 and check the fan and fan circuit carefully.

11 If the coolant level is consistently low, and no evidence of leaks can be found, and the cap has been tested or a new one has been fitted, have the entire system pressure checked by a Kawasaki dealer service department, motorcycle repair shop or service station.

11 Steering head bearings – check and adjustment

1 Steering head bearings can become dented, rough or loose during normal use of the machine. In extreme cases, worn or loose steering head bearings can cause steering wobble which is potentially dangerous.

Check

2 To check the bearings, prop the bike securely upright and block it so the front wheel is raised off the ground.

3 Point the wheel straight ahead and slowly move the handlebars from side-to-side. Dents or roughness in the bearing races will be felt and the bars will not move smoothly. Again point the wheel straight-ahead, and tap the front of the wheel to one side. The wheel should 'fall' under its own weight to the limit of its lock, indicating that the bearings are not too tight (take into account the restriction that cables and wiring may have). Check for similar movement to the other side.

4 Next, grasp the fork legs and try to move

11.4 Checking for play in the steering head bearings

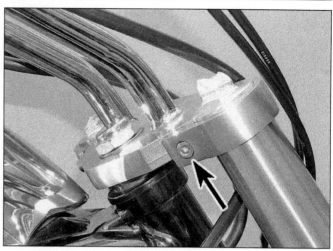

11.6 Slacken the fork clamp bolt (arrowed) on each side – Mean Streak shown

11.7a Unscrew the steering stem nut . . .

11.7b . . . and remove the washer . . .

the wheel forward and backward **(see illustration)**. Any looseness in the steering head bearings will be felt. If play is felt in the bearings, adjust the steering head as follows:

> **HAYNES HiNT** *Make sure you are not mistaking any movement between the bike and stand, or between the stand and the ground, for freeplay in the bearings. Do not pull and push the forks too hard – a gentle movement is all that is needed. Freeplay between the fork tubes due to worn bushes can also be misinterpreted as steering head bearing play – do not confuse the two.*

Adjustment

5 Remove the fuel tank (see Chapter 4A or 4B). If necessary, for access to the steering stem nut/bolt displace the handlebar assembly and rest it on some rag (see Chapter 6).

6 Loosen the fork pinch bolts in the upper triple clamp **(see illustration)**.

7 Unscrew the steering stem nut or bolt (according to model) and remove the washer, and where fitted the O-ring **(see illustrations)**. Ease the triple clamp up off the forks **(see illustration)**. Where fitted remove the tabbed washer from the bearing adjuster nut **(see illustration)**.

11.7c . . . and where fitted the O-ring . . .

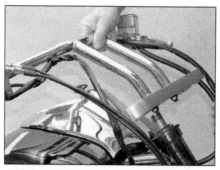

11.7d . . . then gently ease the handlebar/ triple clamp assembly up off the forks

8 Use a spanner wrench (C-spanner) or a suitable drift located in the notches in the adjuster nut to adjust the bearings – on VN1500A and B and Classic models with two nuts together turn them as a pair, turning the lower nut when loosening and turning the upper nut when tightening **(see illustration)**.

9 If the steering is loose, tighten it by turning the adjuster clockwise, and if the steering

11.7e Remove the tabbed washer where fitted

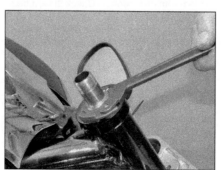

11.8 Adjust the bearings as described using a C-spanner

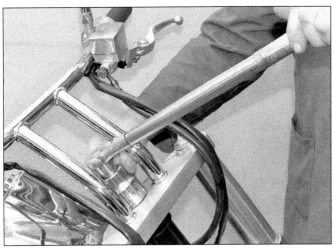

11.10 Tighten the steering stem nut or bolt to the correct torque

12.2 Front cylinder reed valve housing (arrowed)

is tight, loosen it by turning the adjuster counterclockwise. Turn the nut only a small amount at a time, and after each movement repeat the checks outlined above (Steps 2 to 4) until the bearings are correctly set. The object is to set the adjuster nut so that the bearings are under a very light loading, just enough to remove any freeplay.
Caution: Take great care not to apply excessive pressure because this will cause premature failure of the bearings.
10 Fit the tabbed washer where removed, locating the tabs in the adjuster notches **(see illustration 11.7e)**. Fit the upper triple clamp **(see illustration 11.7d)**. Grease and fit the O-ring where removed, using a new one if necessary **(see illustration 11.7c)**. Fit the washer and the nut or bolt **(see illustrations 11.7b and a)**, then tighten the nut or bolt to the torque value listed at the beginning of the Chapter for your model **(see illustration)**. Next tighten the fork pinch bolts, again to

the torque value listed for your model **(see illustration 11.6)**.
11 Recheck the steering head bearings as described above. If necessary, repeat the adjustment procedure. Reinstall all parts previously removed.

Bearing lubrication and replacement

12 Refer to Chapter 6 for steering head bearing lubrication and replacement procedures.

12 Air suction system reed valves – check

1 The air suction reed valves are one-way check valves that allow fresh air to flow into the exhaust ports. The system uses the suction developed by the exhaust pulses to

pull air from the air filter, through a hose to the air switching valve, through a pair of hoses and a pair of reed valves, and finally into the exhaust ports. The introduction of fresh air helps ignite any fuel that may not have been burned by the normal combustion process.
2 First make sure all the hoses are in good condition are securely connected at each end **(see illustration)**. Replace any cracked or hardened hoses with new ones.
3 Depending on the model you are working on, for access to remove the valve from the front cylinder you may have to remove the horn (see Chapter 9) and/or displace the radiator (see Chapter 3). For access to remove the valve from the rear cylinder you may have to remove the exhaust (see Chapter 4A or 4B).
4 Disconnect the hose from the valve **(see illustration)**. Remove the bolts, lift off the cover and remove the gasket and reed valve **(see illustration)**.

12.4a Release the clamp (arrowed) and detach the hose

12.4b Remove the cover, gasket and valve

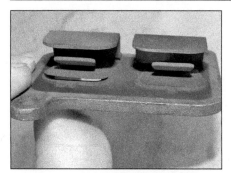

12.5 Check each reed valve as described

5 Check the valve for cracks, warping, burning or other damage, and make sure the reed lifts and seats correctly **(see illustration)**. Check the area where the reeds contact the valve holder for scratches, separation and grooves. If any of these conditions are found, replace the valve.

6 Wash the valve with solvent if carbon has accumulated between the reed and the valve holder.

7 Installation of the valves is the reverse of removal. Be sure to use a new gasket. See Chapter 4A or 4B for the air switching valve.

13 Evaporative emission control system (California models only) – check

1 This system, installed on California models to conform to stringent emission control standards, routes fuel vapors from the fuel system into the engine to be burned, instead of letting them evaporate into the atmosphere. When the engine

isn't running, vapors are stored in a carbon canister.

Hoses

2 To begin the inspection of the system, remove the seat, fuel tank and side covers (see Chapters 4A or 4B and 8). Inspect the hoses from the fuel tank, carburetor(s) or throttle body and liquid/vapor separator to the canister for cracking, kinks or other signs of deterioration. Replace them with new ones if necessary.

Component inspection

3 Label and disconnect the hoses, then remove the separator and canister from the machine (see Chapter 4).

4 Check the separator closely for cracks or other signs of damage. If these are found, replace it.

5 Inspect the canister for cracks or other signs of damage. Tip the canister so the nozzles point down. If fuel runs out of the canister, the liquid/vapor separator is probably bad. The fuel inside the canister has probably caused damage, so it would be a good idea to replace it also.

14 Throttle and choke operation/grip freeplay – check and adjustment

Throttle check

1 With the engine stopped, make sure the throttle grip rotates easily from fully closed to fully open with the front wheel turned at various angles. The grip should return automatically from fully open to fully closed when released. If the throttle sticks, check

the throttle cables for cracks or kinks in the housings. Also, make sure the inner cables are clean and well-lubricated.

2 Check for a small amount of freeplay in the cable before the throttle opens by lightly turning the grip and compare the freeplay to the value listed in this Chapter's Specifications **(see illustration)**.

Throttle cable adjustment

Note: *These motorcycles use two throttle cables – a throttle opening or accelerator cable and a throttle closing or decelerator cable.*

3 Freeplay adjustments are initially made at the throttle twistgrip end of the cable.

4 Loosen the locknut on the adjuster on each cable and turn the adjusters fully in **(see illustration)**.

5 Turn the adjuster on the throttle closing cable until it just becomes tight, but not so it starts to pull the throttle open. Tighten the locknut.

6 Turn the adjuster on the throttle opening cable until the specified freeplay is obtained at the throttle grip, then tighten the locknut.

7 Check that the throttle twistgrip operates smoothly and snaps shut quickly when released.

8 On VN1500A and B models, if you cannot adjust the cables as specified, reset the adjusters so freeplay is at a maximum as in Step 4. Loosen the locknuts securing the cables in the bracket on the carburetors, and adjust each cable as described in Steps 5 and 6 by turning the adjusters above the locknuts, then tighten the locknuts. Finally make any minor and subsequent adjustments using the adjusters at the twistgrip.

9 On VN1500 Classic and Nomad/Classic Tourer models, if you cannot adjust the cables as specified, reset the adjusters so freeplay is at a maximum as in Step 4. Remove the fuel

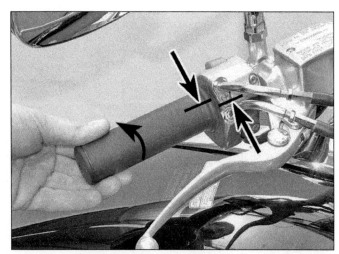

14.2 Throttle cable freeplay is measured in terms of the amount of twistgrip rotation before the throttle opens

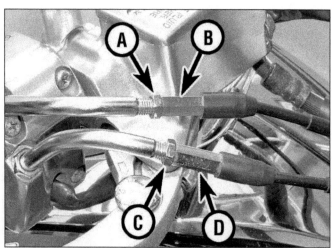

14.4 Throttle opening cable locknut (A) and adjuster (B), throttle closing cable locknut (C) and adjuster (D)

tank (see Chapter 4A). Loosen the locknuts on the adjusters roughly half way along the cables, and adjust each cable as described in Steps 5 and 6 by turning the adjusters, then tighten the locknuts. Finally make any minor and subsequent adjustments using the adjusters at the twistgrip.

10 On VN1500 Classic FI, Nomad/Classic Tourer FI and all Drifter models, if you cannot set the correct freeplay in the opening cable as specified, reset the adjuster so freeplay is at a maximum as in Step 4. Remove the fuel tank (see Chapter 4B). Loosen the locknut on the adjusters roughly half way along the opening cable, and adjust the cable as described in Step 6 by turning the adjuster, then tighten the locknut. Finally make any minor and subsequent adjustments using the adjusters at the twistgrip.

11 Mean Streak models and VN1600 Classic and Nomad/Classic Tourer models do not have any adjusters other than those at the twistgrip.

12 If the cable cannot be adjusted as specified, replace the cables with new ones (see Chapter 4A or 4B).

 Warning: Turn the handlebars all the way through their travel with the engine idling. Idle speed should not change. If it does, the cables may be routed or adjusted incorrectly. Correct this condition before riding the bike.

Choke check

Note: *On fuel injection models the choke knob should only be used if the bike cannot be started normally, for example in extreme cold or high altitude. The fuel injection system has its own automatic fast idle system that uses information from the sensors to adjust for cold starting as required.*

13 Inspect the choke knob, and its cable where fitted. The choke should pull out smoothly and easily and stay out by itself. If it doesn't, lubricate the cable or linkage mechanism as required (see Section 18).

15 Idle speed – check and adjustment

1 The idle speed should be checked and adjusted at the specified maintenance intervals and when it is obviously too high or too low. On VN1500A and B models, the carburetors should be synchronized as described in Section 16 as part of the procedure. Before adjusting the idle speed, make sure the spark plugs are in good condition and the gaps are correct (see Section 5). Also, with the engine running turn the handlebars back-and-forth and see if the idle speed changes as this is done. If it does, the throttle cable may not be adjusted correctly, or it may be incorrectly routed or worn out. Be sure to correct this problem before proceeding.

2 The engine must be at normal operating temperature, which is usually reached after 10 to 15 minutes of stop and go riding. Make sure the choke knob is pushed fully in.

3 With the engine idling turn the adjusting knob as required, until the idle speed listed in this Chapter's Specifications is obtained **(see illustration)**.

4 Snap the throttle open and shut a few times, then recheck the idle speed. If necessary, repeat the adjustment procedure.

5 If a smooth, steady idle can't be achieved refer to Chapter 4A on carburetor models and Chapter 4B on fuel injection models for additional information.

16 Carburetor synchronization (VN1500A and B models) – check and adjustment

 Warning: Gasoline is extremely flammable, so take extra precautions when you work on any part of the fuel system. Don't smoke or allow open flames or bare light bulbs near the work area, and don't work in a garage where a natural gas-type appliance (such as a water heater or clothes dryer) is present. If you spill any fuel on your skin, rinse it off immediately with soap and water. When you perform any kind of work on the fuel system, wear safety glasses and have a fire extinguisher suitable for a class B type fire (flammable liquids) on hand.

1 Carburetor synchronization is simply the process of adjusting the carburetors so they pass the same amount of fuel/air mixture to each cylinder. This is done by measuring the vacuum produced in each cylinder. Carburetors that are out of synchronization will result in increased fuel consumption, increased engine temperature, less than ideal throttle response and higher vibration levels.

2 To synchronize the carburetors, you will need a manometer, such as the Morgan Carbtune Pro4, or a set of vacuum gauges, suitable for a twin cylinder engine, with the necessary adapters and hoses to fit the take-off points **(see illustration)**. When using such equipment always read the instructions supplied with it. The hoses usually have some form of restrictor in them for damping the movement of the manometer rod or gauge needle – make sure these are fitted correctly if not already in place otherwise it

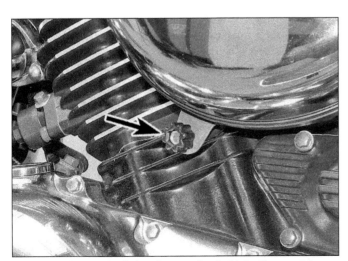

15.3 Idle speed adjuster (arrowed) – fuel injection models

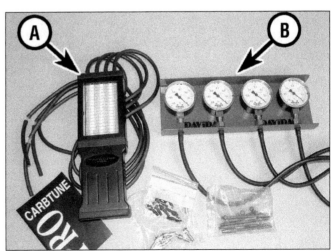

16.2 The Carbtune manometer (A) and a set of vacuum gauges (B), and the various adapters that come with them – each set is available in twin format

will be difficult to get an accurate reading, and that in the case of the Carbtune the hoses are connected with the restrictors closest to the take-off points on the throttle bodies.

3 A manometer can be purchased from a motorcycle dealer or accessory shop and should have the necessary rubber hoses supplied with it for hooking into the vacuum hose fittings on the carburetors.

4 A ready-made vacuum gauge setup can also be purchased from a dealer, or one can be fabricated from commonly available hardware and automotive vacuum gauges, but note that gauges on a home-made set-up must be calibrated first.

5 The manometer is the more reliable and accurate instrument, and for that reason is preferred over the vacuum gauge setup; however, if the mercury type is used, since mercury is a liquid, and extremely toxic, extra precautions must be taken during use and storage of the instrument.

6 Because of the nature of the synchronization procedure and the need for special instruments, most owners leave the task to a dealer service department or a reputable motorcycle repair shop.

7 Start the engine and let it run until it reaches normal operating temperature, then shut it off.

8 Detach the bike's vacuum hoses from the fittings on the carburetors.

9 Connect the vacuum gauge or manometer hoses to the fittings according to the manufacturer's instructions. Make sure there are no leaks in the setup, as false readings will result.

10 Start the engine and make sure the idle speed is correct.

11 The vacuum readings for both of the cylinders should be the same, or at least within the tolerance listed in this Chapter's Specifications. If the vacuum readings vary, adjust as necessary.

12 To perform the adjustment, synchronize the carburetors by turning the butterfly valve hex-headed screw as needed, until the vacuum is identical or nearly identical for both cylinders. Turn the screw inward to increase vacuum at the rear carburetor; turn it outward to decrease vacuum at the rear carburetor.

13 When the adjustment is complete, recheck the vacuum readings and idle speed, then stop the engine. Remove the vacuum gauge or manometer and attach the bike's vacuum hoses to the fittings on the carburetors.

17 Fuel system – check

⚠ **Warning: Gasoline is extremely flammable, so take extra precautions when you work on any part of the fuel system. Don't smoke or allow open flames or bare light bulbs**

near the work area, and don't work in a garage where a natural gas-type appliance (such as a water heater or clothes dryer) is present. If you spill any fuel on your skin, rinse it off immediately with soap and water. When you perform any kind of work on the fuel system, wear safety glasses and have a fire extinguisher suitable for a class B type fire (flammable liquids) on hand.

1 On carburetor models check the fuel tank, the fuel tap, the fuel pump, the fuel filter, the fuel hoses and the carburetor(s) for leaks and evidence of damage. When checking the tank check the underside, particularly around the level sensor plate and tap or hose unions, according to model.

2 On fuel injection models check the fuel tank, the fuel hoses, the fuel filter on 2000 (L1) model Nomad/Classic Tourer and 1999 and 2000 (J1 and J2) model Drifters (particularly around the fuel injector) for leaks and evidence of damage. When checking the tank check the underside, particularly around the fuel pump and level sensor (where fitted) plate(s).

3 If carburetor gaskets are leaking, the carburetor(s) should be disassembled and rebuilt by referring to Chapter 4A. If the fuel tap or a hose union is leaking, tightening the fasteners may help. If leakage persists, the tap should be removed and repaired or replaced with a new one.

4 If there is leakage from around a mounting plate on the underside of the tank check the fasteners are tight according to the torque listed in Chapter 4A or 4B according to the component and model, and check the relevant Section within the Chapter for any tightening sequence. If leakage persists remove the component and replace the seal or gasket with a new one.

5 If the fuel hoses or vacuum hoses are cracked or otherwise deteriorated, replace them with new ones.

6 On carburetor models, the fuel filter, which is connected in-line between the tap and the pump, may become clogged and should be replaced with a new one periodically – remove the tank to access the filter (see Chapter 4A), then release the hose clamps and detach the filter. Fit the new filter with the arrow pointing in the direction of fuel flow (i.e. from the tank to the pump). Make sure the hoses are pushed fully onto the unions and secure them with the clamps. Also there are two strainers fitted inside the tank, part of the hose unions on VN1500A and B models and part of the tap on Classic and Nomad/Classic Tourer models – every so often remove and drain the tank (see Chapter 4A). Remove the unions or tap. Clean the strainers in solvent, then blow them through with compressed air, and check them for splits or holes. Replace any worn or damaged components with new ones. Use new O-rings on A and B models, and a new tap seal and nylon washers on Classic and Nomad/Classic Tourer models (do not use metal washers).

7 On 2000 (L1) model Nomad/Classic Tourer and 1999 and 2000 (J1 and J2) model Drifters the fuel filter is in-line between the tank and the throttle body – remove the tank (see Chapter 4B). The filter should last the life of the bike under normal circumstances. To remove it remove the rubber cover where fitted, then release and detach the fuel hose from the top of the filter – note how everything is fitted for correct installation. Displace or remove the vacuum sensor and atmospheric sensor. Remove the filter and its holder, noting how they fit. On installation make sure everything is correctly aligned and routed. Make sure the stoppers on the filter do not touch the filter holder, and make sure the clamp screw is horizontal and the hose damper sleeve or rubber cover is correctly positioned so the hose and clamp do not contact the underside of the tank. There is a fuel strainer on the intake side of the pump which can be cleaned if necessary after removing the pump (see Chapter 4B).

8 On all other fuel injection models the filter is inside the tank and is part of the pump assembly. The filter should last the life of the bike under normal circumstances. It is not possible to clean it and it is not available separately from the complete pump assembly. There is a fuel strainer on the intake side of the pump which can be cleaned if necessary after removing the pump (see Chapter 4B).

9 After any servicing work on the fuel system check carefully for leaks, both before and after starting the engine, and before taking the bike out on the road.

18 Lubrication – general

1 Since the controls, cables and various other components of a motorcycle are exposed to the elements, they should be lubricated periodically to ensure safe and trouble-free operation.

2 The footpegs, clutch and brake lever, brake pedal, shift lever and sidestand pivots should be lubricated frequently. In order for the lubricant to be applied where it will do the most good, the component should be disassembled. However, if chain and cable lubricant is being used, it can be applied to the pivot joint gaps and will usually work its way into the areas where friction occurs. If motor oil or light grease is being used, apply it sparingly as it may attract dirt (which could cause the controls to bind or wear at an accelerated rate). **Note:** *One of the best lubricants for the control lever pivots is a dry-film lubricant (available from many sources by different names).*

3 The throttle cables and choke cable where fitted should be lubricated with aerosol cable lubricant which is specially formulated for

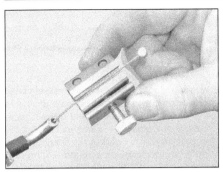

18.3a Fit the cable into the adapter . . .

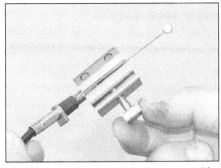

18.3b . . . and tighten the screw to seal it in . . .

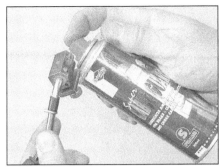

18.3c . . . then apply the lubricant using the nozzle provided inserted in the hole in the adapter

use on motorcycle control cables. Small adapters for pressure lubricating the cables with spray can lubricants are available and ensure that the cable is lubricated along its entire length **(see illustrations)**. See Chapter 4A or 4B for the cable removal procedure. **Note:** *While you're lubricating, check the end of each cable for fraying. Replace frayed cables.*

4 Where fitted the speedometer cable should be detached from the speedometer

19.8a Undo the screw . . .

and lubricated in the same way (see Chapter 9).

5 Refer to Chapter 6 for the swingarm bearing lubrication procedure.

19 Air filter element – servicing

VN1500A and B

1 Remove the fuel tank (see Chapter 4A). Remove the frame covers and the radiator cover. There is an air filter on each side of the bike **(see illustration 12.2 in Chapter 4A)**.

2 Undo the air filter cover bolts and remove the cover.

3 Remove the filter mounting bolts and take out the filter. Separate the foam element from the core.

4 Wipe out the housing and cover with a clean rag.

5 Check the element for tears or other

damage. Replace the element with a new one if it's damaged.

6 Clean the element with solvent. If compressed air is available, use it to clean the element by blowing from the inside out (from the mesh side toward the foam side). If the foam is extremely dirty or torn, replace the element with a new one. Squeeze the element dry.

7 Soak the element in clean SAE 30 engine oil. Squeeze as much oil as possible out of the element, then squeeze the element inside a clean rag to remove more oil.

All other models

8 The air filter is in the housing on the left-hand side. Undo the centre screw and remove the washer and the cover, then remove the air filter element **(see illustrations)**.

9 Wipe out the housing and cover with a clean rag, then place a clean rag in the duct to keep out dirt.

10 Tap the element on a hard surface to remove the dirt. Finish cleaning by blowing compressed air from the inside of the element

19.8b . . . and remove the cover . . .

19.8c . . . and the filter element

19.10 Blow compressed air through from the inside

to the outside **(see illustration)**. Check the element for damage and replace it with a new one if necessary.

All models

11 Reinstall the filter by reversing the removal procedure. Make sure the element is seated properly in the filter housing before installing the cover. Make sure the cover seal is in good condition and correctly in place.

20 Exhaust system – check
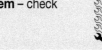

1 Periodically check all of the exhaust system joints for leaks and loose fasteners. If tightening the clamp bolts fails to stop any leaks, replace the gaskets with new ones (a procedure which requires disassembly of the system – see Chapter 4A or 4B).
2 The exhaust pipe flange nuts at the cylinder heads are especially prone to loosening, which could cause damage to the head. Check them frequently and keep them tight.

21 Fasteners – check

1 Since vibration of the machine tends to loosen fasteners, all nuts, bolts, screws, etc. should be periodically checked for proper tightness.
2 Pay particular attention to the following:
  Spark plugs
  Engine oil drain plug
  Oil filter
  Oil screen cap
  Coolant drain plug
  Levers and pedal
  Footpegs and sidestand
  Engine mount bolts
  Front fork clamp bolts, rear shock absorber nuts and swingarm pivot bolt
  Brake system
  Front and rear wheel axles
3 If a torque wrench is available, use it along with the torque specifications at the beginning of this, or other, Chapters.

22 Suspension – check

1 The suspension components must be maintained in top operating condition to ensure rider safety. Loose, worn or damaged suspension parts decrease the vehicle's stability and control.
2 While standing alongside the motorcycle, hold the front brake on and push on the handlebars to compress the forks several times. See if they move up-and-down smoothly without binding. If binding is felt, the forks should be disassembled and inspected as described in Chapter 6.

3 Carefully inspect the area around the fork seals for any signs of fork oil leakage **(see illustration)**. If leakage is evident, the seals must be replaced as described in Chapter 6. Also check the inner tube surface for evidence of pitting and corrosion in the area of the tube that slides past the seal and that could cause the seals to blow in the future – you can clean up any rust and carefully take off the sharp edges of any pits using a fine abrasive paper and then treat with oil, but the only real cure is to have the tube re-chromed. On models with shrouded forks, inspection of the fork inner tube and seal area is only possible if the shrouds are removed. Due to the protection offered by the shrouds however, it is unlikely the inner tubes will have sustained damage and it is suggested that the inspection can be limited to a check of fork action as described in Step 2 and to check that there is no sign of oil leakage.
4 Check the tightness of all suspension nuts and bolts to be sure none have worked loose.
5 Inspect the rear shock absorber(s) for fluid leakage and tightness of the mounting nuts. If leakage is found, the shock(s) should be replaced. Replace both shocks as a pair.
6 Prop the bike securely upright on an auxiliary stand so the rear wheel is off the ground. Grab the swingarm on each side, just ahead of the axle **(see illustration)**. Rock the swingarm from side to side – there should be no discernible movement at the rear. If there's a little movement or a slight clicking can be heard, make sure the pivot bolt is tightened to the correct torque for the model (see Chapter 6). If the bolt is tight but movement is still noticeable, the swingarm will have to be removed and the bearings replaced as described in Chapter 6.
7 Next, grasp the top of the rear wheel and pull it upwards – there should be no discernible freeplay before the shock absorbers compress

22.3 Check the fork inner tube surface (arrowed) for oil leakage, corrosion and pitting

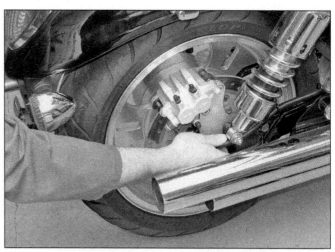

22.6 Checking for play in the swingarm pivot

(see illustration). Any freeplay felt in indicates worn bushes or bearings in the shock absorber or swingarm. The worn components must be identified and replaced with new ones (see Chapter 6).

22.7 Checking for play in the rear shock mountings

23 Final drive oil – level check and oil change

Oil level check

1 Final drive oil level should be checked at the specified maintenance interval. Before every ride, take a quick look for signs of leakage around the final drive housing.

2 Support the bike securely upright on level ground. If the machine has been ridden recently, make sure the final drive unit is cool to the touch before checking the level.

3 Remove the filler plug from the final drive housing (see illustration).

4 Look inside the hole and check the oil level

– it should be even with the bottom of the hole (see illustration).

5 If it's low, add oil of the type listed in this Chapter's Specifications with a funnel or hose until it is at the correct level (see illustration).

6 Clean any debris off the magnetic centre in the plug (see illustration) – an excess or any large bits of metal are a cause for concern. Check the condition of the filler plug O-ring and fit a new one if necessary. Make sure the O-ring is correctly seated then fit the filler plug.

Oil change

7 Ride the bike to warm the oil so it will drain completely, then prop it securely upright on level ground.

8 Remove the filler plug from the final drive housing (see illustration 23.3).

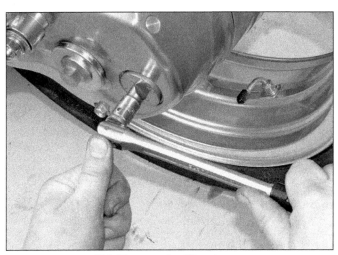

23.3 Unscrew the filler plug . . .

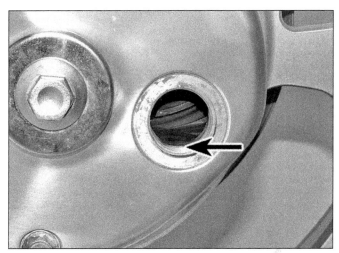

23.4 . . . and check the oil is level with the bottom edge of the hole (arrowed)

23.5 Top the oil level up if necessary

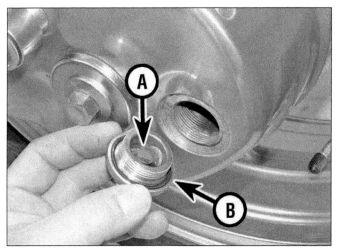

23.6 Clean any debris off the magnet (A). Make sure the O-ring (B) is in place and in good condition

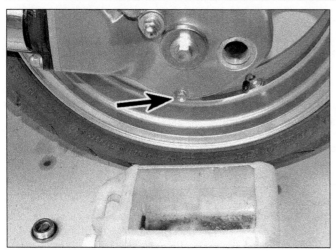

23.9 Unscrew the drain plug (arrowed) and allow the oil to drain completely

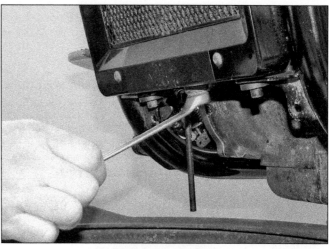

24.3a Unscrew the bolt . . .

9 Place a drain tray below the housing. Remove the drain plug and let the oil drain for 10 to 15 minutes **(see illustration)**. Discard the drain plug sealing washer – a new one must be used.

10 Clean the drain plug, reinstall it using a new sealing washer and tighten it to the torque listed in this Chapter's Specifications.

11 Fill the final drive unit to the correct level with the type of oil listed in this Chapter's Specifications **(see illustration 23.5)** – the oil should be level with the bottom of the filler hole **(see illustration 23.4)**.

12 Clean any debris off the magnetic centre in the plug **(see illustration 23.6)** – an excess or any large bits of metal are a cause for concern. Check the condition of the filler plug O-ring and fit a new one if necessary. Make sure the O-ring is correctly seated then fit the filler plug.

---

24 Cooling system – draining, flushing and refilling

⚠ *Warning: Allow the engine to cool completely before performing this maintenance operation. Also, don't allow antifreeze to come into contact with your skin or painted surfaces of the motorcycle. Rinse off spills immediately with plenty of water. Antifreeze is highly toxic if ingested. Never leave antifreeze lying around in an open container or in puddles on the floor; children and pets are attracted by its sweet smell and may drink it. Check with local authorities about disposing of used antifreeze. Many communities have collection centers which will see that antifreeze is disposed of safely. Antifreeze is also combustible, so don't store or use it near open flames.*

Draining

1 For access to the cooling system pressure cap remove the fuel tank (see Chapter 4A for carburetor models and Chapter 4B for fuel injection models) – note that on some models you may be able to access the cap after removing or displacing the instrument cluster from the tank, leaving the tank in place – it will depend mostly on the size and strength of your hands. Remove the pressure cap by turning it counterclockwise until it reaches a stop. If you hear a hissing sound (indicating there is still pressure in the system), wait until it stops. Now, press down on the cap and continue turning the cap counterclockwise until it can be removed **(see illustration 10.7)**.

2 On VN1500A and B models remove the radiator cover.

3 Place a large, clean drain pan under the radiator. Remove the drain bolt from the bottom of the radiator and allow the coolant to drain into the pan **(see illustrations)**. A new sealing washer (where fitted) is needed, but keep the old one for use during flushing if required.

4 Either place some absorbent rag under the water pump drain, or place the drain pan

under the engine on the right-hand side and prepare a chute (you could cut one out of a plastic drinks bottle) to go from the pump to the tray to avoid getting coolant on the engine – note that the amount of residual coolant in the pump will be minimal and so some rag should suffice. Remove the drain bolt from the pump and allow the remaining coolant to drain **(see illustration)**. A new sealing washer is needed, but keep the old one for use during flushing if required.

5 Refer to Chapter 3 and remove and drain the coolant reservoir. Wash the reservoir out with water, then refit it.

Flushing

6 Flush the system with clean tap water by inserting a garden hose in the radiator filler neck. Allow the water to run through the system until it is clear when it exits the drain bolt holes. If the radiator is extremely corroded, remove it (see Chapter 3, and have it cleaned at a radiator shop.

7 Clean the drain holes, then fit and tighten the drain bolts using the old sealing washers.

8 Fill the cooling system with clean water mixed with a flushing compound. Make sure the flushing compound is compatible

24.3b . . . and allow the system to drain

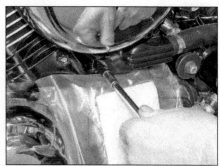

24.4 Unscrew the bolt and drain any coolant from the pump

with aluminum components, and follow the manufacturer's instructions carefully.

9 Start the engine and allow it to reach normal operating temperature. Let it run for about ten minutes.

10 Stop the engine. Let the machine cool for a while, then cover the pressure cap with a heavy rag and turn it counterclockwise to the first stop, releasing any pressure that may be present in the system. Once the hissing stops, push down on the cap and remove it completely.

11 Drain the system once again.

12 Fill the system with clean water, then repeat Steps 8, 9 and 10.

Refilling

13 Fit the radiator drain bolt using a new sealing washer where fitted and tighten the bolt to the torque listed in this Chapter's Specifications for your model where given **(see illustration 24.3a)**. Repeat for the pump drain bolt.

14 Slowly fill the system with the proper coolant mixture (see this Chapter's Specifications) **(see illustration)**. **Note:** *Pour the coolant in slowly to minimise the amount of air entering the system, and when full carefully waggle the bike from side to side and squeeze the hoses to dislodge any trapped air.*

15 When the system is full (all the way up to the top of the radiator cap seat in the filler neck), slacken the top rear bolt on the water pump and turn it out a few times (but do not remove it) until coolant seeps out around the threads **(see illustration)** – this bleeds any air out of the top of the pump. Now, on all models except VN1600 Classic and Nomad/Classic Drifter models, unscrew the air bleed valve in front of the filler neck and check that coolant is visible to the top of the hole **(see illustration)**. If not add more coolant until it is. Fit the bleed valve and tighten to the listed torque.

16 Fit the pressure cap. Also top up the coolant reservoir to the FULL line.

17 Install the fuel tank if removed, and the instrument cluster, as required. On VN1500A and B models install the radiator cover. Start the engine and allow it to run until the cooling fan kicks in, then turn the engine off. Check the system for leaks.

24.14 Slowly fill the system and bleed it as described

18 Allow the engine to cool, then check the coolant level in the reservoir (see *Pre-ride checks*) at the beginning of this manual. If the coolant level is low, add the specified mixture until it reaches the FULL mark in the reservoir.

19 Do not dispose of the old coolant by pouring it down a drain. Instead, pour it into a heavy plastic container, cap it tightly and take it to an authorized disposal site.

24.15a Slacken the top rear bolt to bleed any air from the pump . . .

24.15b . . . then remove the bleed valve where fitted and check the level

Chapter 2
Engine, clutch and transmission

Contents

Degrees of difficulty

Easy, suitable for novice with little experience 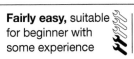	**Fairly easy,** suitable for beginner with some experience	**Fairly difficult,** suitable for competent DIY mechanic	**Difficult,** suitable for experienced DIY mechanic	**Very difficult,** suitable for expert DIY or professional

Specifications

General

Type	Four-stroke 90° V-four
Capacity	
VN1500 models	1470 cc
VN1600 models	1552 cc
Bore	102.0 mm
Stroke	
VN1500 models	90.0 mm
VN1600 models	95.0 mm
Compression ratio	9:1
Cylinder numbering	
Front	1
Rear	2

Camshaft chain

20-link length	
Standard	127.0 to 127.4 mm (5.0 to 5.015 inches)
Limit	128.9 mm (5.074 inches)

Camshafts – VN1500A and B models

Lobe height (intake)
  Standard . . . . 33.812 to 33.912 mm (1.332 to 1.336 inch)
  Minimum . . . . 33.710 mm (1.328 inch)
Lobe height (exhaust)
  Standard . . . . 33.494 to 33.594 mm (1.320 to 1.324 inch)
  Minimum . . . . 33.39 mm (1.315 inch)
Bearing inside diameter
  Standard . . . . 25.000 to 25.021 mm (0.9843 to 0.9851 inch)
  Maximum . . . . 25.08 mm (0.9874 inch)
Journal diameter
  Standard . . . . 24.959 to 24.980 mm (0.9826 to 0.9835 inch)
  Minimum . . . . 24.93 mm (0.9815 inch)
Bearing clearance
  Standard . . . . 0.020 to 0.062 mm (0.0008 to 0.0024 inch)
  Limit . . . . 0.15 mm (0.006 inch)

Camshafts and rockers –
Classic, Classic FI, Nomad/Classic Tourer, Nomad/Classic Tourer FI, Drifter and Mean Streak

Lobe height (intake)
  VN1500 Classic and Nomad/Classic Tourer models (except Switzerland)
    Standard . . . . 33.480 to 33.600 mm (1.3184 to 1.3229 inch)
    Minimum . . . . 33.380 mm (1.314 inch)
  VN1600 Classic and all Mean Streak models
    Standard . . . . 33.928 to 34.044 mm (1.3357 to 1.3403 inch)
    Minimum . . . . 33.830 mm (1.3319 inch)
  All other models
    Standard . . . . 33.800 to 33.920 mm (1.3309 to 1.3354 inch)
    Minimum . . . . 33.700 mm (1.327 inch)
Lobe height (exhaust)
  VN1500 Classic and Nomad/Classic Tourer models (except Switzerland)
    Standard . . . . 33.360 to 33.460 mm (1.3144 to 1.3183 inch)
    Minimum . . . . 33.260 mm (1.310 inch)
  VN1600 Classic and all Mean Streak models
    Standard . . . . 33.741 to 33.857 mm (1.3284 to 1.3329 inch)
    Minimum . . . . 33.640 mm (1.324 inch)
  All other models
    Standard . . . . 33.480 to 33.600 mm (1.3184 to 1.3229 inch)
    Minimum . . . . 33.380 mm (1.314 inch)
Bearing inside diameter
  Large journals
    Standard . . . . 25.000 to 25.021 mm (0.9843 to 0.9851 inch)
    Maximum . . . . 25.08 mm (0.9874 inch)
  Small journal
    Standard . . . . 17.000 to 17.021 mm (0.6693 to 0.6701 inch)
    Maximum . . . . 17.08 mm (0.6724 inch)
Journal diameter
  Large journals
    Standard . . . . 24.959 to 24.980 mm (0.9826 to 0.9835 inch)
    Minimum . . . . 24.93 mm (0.9815 inch)
  Small journal
    Standard . . . . 16.966 to 16.984 mm (0.6680 to 0.6687 inch)
    Minimum . . . . 16.93 mm (0.6665 inch)
Bearing clearance
  Large journals
    Standard . . . . 0.020 to 0.062 mm (0.0008 to 0.0024 inch)
    Limit . . . . 0.15 mm (0.006 inch)
  Small journal
    Standard . . . . 0.016 to 0.055 mm (0.0006 to 0.0022 inch)
    Limit . . . . 0.14 mm (0.0055 inch)
Camshaft runout (total indicator reading)
  Standard . . . . 0.02 mm (0.0008 inch) max
  Limit . . . . 0.1 mm (0.004 inch)
Rocker arm inside diameter
  Standard . . . . 16.0 to 16.018 mm (0.630 to 0.631 inch)
  Maximum . . . . 16.05 mm (0.632 inch)
Rocker shaft diameter
  Standard . . . . 15.966 to 15.984 mm (0.628 to 0.629 inch)
  Minimum . . . . 15.94 mm (0.627 inch)

Cylinder head, valves and valve springs

Compression pressure	340 to 590 kPa (50 to 85 psi) @ 300 rpm using starter motor
Cylinder head warpage limit.	0.05 mm (0.002 inch)
Valve stem bend (total indicator reading)	
Standard	
VN1500A and B	0.02 mm (0.0008 inch) max
All other models	0.01 mm (0.0004 inch) max
Limit	0.05 mm (0.002 inch)
Valve stem diameter	
Standard	
Intake	6.965 to 6.980 mm (0.2742 to 0.2748 inch)
Exhaust.	6.955 to 6.970 mm (0.2738 to 0.2744 inch)
Minimum	
Intake	6.95 mm (0.2736 inch)
Exhaust.	6.94 mm (0.2732 inch)
Valve guide inside diameter (intake and exhaust)	
Standard.	7.000 to 7.015 mm (0.2756 to 0.2762 inch)
Maximum	7.08 mm (0.2787 inch)
Valve stem-to-guide clearance (wobble method – see text)	
Standard	
Intake	0.05 to 0.13 mm (0.0020 to 0.0051 inch)
Exhaust.	0.08 to 0.16 mm (0.0031 to 0.0063 inch)
Minimum	
Intake	0.27 mm (0.0106 inch)
Exhaust.	0.30 mm (0.0118 inch)
Valve head thickness	
Standard (intake and exhaust)	0.9 to 1.1 mm (0.0354 to 0.0433 inch)
Minimum	
Intake	
VN1500A and B and VN1500 Classic.	0.5 mm (0.020 inch)
All other models	0.7 mm (0.028 inch)
Exhaust.	0.5 mm (0.020 inch)
Valve seat width	
Intake	
Mean Streak	0.8 to 1.2 mm (0.031 to 0.047 inch)
All other models	0.5 to 1.0 mm (0.020 to 0.040 inch)
Exhaust.	0.5 to 1.0 mm (0.020 to 0.040 inch)
Valve spring free length	
VN1500A and B	
Standard	
Inner	37.8 mm (1.489 inch)
Outer.	42.3 mm (1.666 inch)
Minimum	
Inner	36.2 mm (1.426 inch)
Outer.	40.7 mm (1.604 inch)
VN1500 Classic 1996 and 1997 (D1 and D2) models	
Front cylinder intake valves	
Standard – inner	39.82 mm (1.567 inch) (orange)
Standard – outer.	44.76 mm (1.762 inch) (orange)
Minimum – inner	38.3 mm (1.509 inch)
Minimum – outer	43.2 mm (1.700 inch)
All other valves – D1 models	
Standard – inner	37.8 mm (1.489 inch) (yellow)
Standard – outer.	42.3 mm (1.666 inch) (yellow)
Minimum – inner	36.4 mm (1.434 inch)
Minimum – outer	40.7 mm (1.604 inch)
All other valves – D2 models	
Standard.	42.3 mm (1.666 inch) (purple)
Minimum.	40.7 mm (1.604 inch)
All other models	
Standard	
Inner	39.82 mm (1.567 inch) (orange)
Outer.	44.76 mm (1.762 inch) (orange)
Minimum	
Inner	38.3 mm (1.509 inch)
Outer.	43.2 mm (1.700 inch)

Cylinders

Bore diameter

  Standard... 102.000 to 102.012 mm (4.0157 to 4.0162 inches)

  Limit .... 102.1 mm (4.020 inches)

Taper limit.. 0.05 mm (0.002 inch)

Out-of-round limit... 0.05 mm (0.002 inch)

Pistons and rings

Piston diameter

  Standard... 101.942 to 101.957 mm (4.0135 to 4.0140 inches)

  Limit .... 101.79 mm (4.007 inches)

Piston-to-cylinder clearance .... 0.043 to 0.070 mm (0.0017 to 0.0028 inch)

Oversize pistons and rings.................................. +0.5 mm (0.020 inch)

Ring side clearance

  1500 models

    Standard

      Top – A and B models............................. 0.03 to 0.07 mm (0.0012 to 0.0028 inch)

      Top – all other models............................ 0.035 to 0.07 mm (0.0014 to 0.0028 inch)

      Second .... 0.02 to 0.06 mm (0.0007 to 0.0023 inch)

    Maximum

      Top .... 0.17 mm (0.0067 inch)

      Second .... 0.16 mm (0.0062 inch)

  1600 models

    Standard

      Top .... 0.05 to 0.09 mm (0.0020 to 0.0035 inch)

      Second .... 0.03 to 0.07 mm (0.0012 to 0.0028 inch)

    Maximum

      Top .... 0.19 mm (0.0075 inch)

      Second .... 0.17 mm (0.0067 inch)

Ring groove width

  1500 models

    Standard

      Top – A and B models............................. 1.02 to 1.04 mm (0.0402 to 0.0410 inch)

      Top – all other models............................ 1.025 to 1.04 mm (0.0404 to 0.0410 inch)

      Second .... 1.21 to 1.23 mm (0.0476 to 0.0484 inch)

      Oil .... Not specified

    Maximum

      Top .... 1.12 mm (0.044 inch)

      Second .... 1.31 mm (0.052 inch)

  1600 models

    Standard

      Top .... 1.24 to 1.26 mm (0.0488 to 0.0496 inch)

      Second .... 1.22 to 1.24 mm (0.0483 to 0.0488 inch)

      Oil .... Not specified

    Maximum

      Top .... 1.34 mm (0.053 inch)

      Second .... 1.32 mm (0.052 inch)

Ring thickness

  Standard

    Top

      1500 models... 0.97 to 0.99 mm (0.0382 to 0.0390 inch)

      1600 models... 1.17 to 1.19 mm (0.0461 to 0.0468 inch)

    Second .... 1.17 to 1.19 mm (0.0461 to 0.0468 inch)

    Oil .... Not specified

  Minimum

    Top

      1500 models... 0.90 mm (0.035 inch)

      1600 models... 1.10 mm (0.043 inch)

    Second .... 1.10 mm (0.043 inch)

    Oil .... Not specified

Ring end gap

  Standard

    Top

      1500 models... 0.30 to 0.40 mm (0.0118 to 0.0157 inch)

      1600 models... 0.25 to 0.35 mm (0.0098 to 0.0138 inch)

    Second .... 0.40 to 0.55 mm (0.0157 to 0.0217 inch)

    Oil .... 0.30 to 0.90 mm (0.0118 to 0.0350 inch)

  Limit

    Top .... 0.7 mm (0.028 inch)

    Second .... 0.8 mm (0.031 inch)

    Oil .... 1.2 mm (0.047 inch)

Clutch

Clutch fluid	DOT 4
Diaphragm spring free height	
VN1500A and B models	
Standard	4.7 mm (0.185 inch)
Limit	4.4 mm (0.174 inch)
VN1500 Mean Streak	
Standard	6.0 mm (0.235 inch)
Limit	5.6 mm (0.220 inch)
All other models thru' 2006	
Standard	4.3 mm (0.169 inch)
Limit	4.0 mm (0.158 inch)
All models from 2007-on	
Standard	4.4 mm (0.174 inch)
Limit	4.1 mm (0.161 inch)
Friction plate thickness	
Standard	3.3 to 3.5 mm (0.130 to 0.138 inch)
Minimum	3.1 mm (0.122 inch)
Friction and steel plate warpage	
Standard	0.2 mm (0.008 inch) or less
Limit	0.3 mm (0.012 inch)

Oil pump

Oil pressure	345 to 440 kPa (50 to 64 psi) @ 2000 rpm, oil temp 90 to 100°C (194 to 212°F)

Crankshaft and bearings

Main bearing journal diameter	
VN1500A and B	
Standard	54.981 to 55.000 mm (2.1646 to 2.1670 inch)
Limit	54.96 mm (2.164 inch)
All other models	
Standard	54.986 to 55.000 mm (2.1664 to 2.1670 inch)
Limit	54.96 mm (2.164 inch)
Main bearing diameter	
VN1500A and B	
Standard	55.030 to 55.049 mm (2.1682 to 2.1689 inch)
Limit	55.08 mm (2.170 inch)
All other models	
Standard	55.025 to 55.038 mm (2.1663 to 2.1668 inch)
Limit	55.07 mm (2.168 inch)
Main bearing/journal clearance	
VN1500A and B	
Standard	0.030 to 0.068 mm (0.0012 to 0.0027 inch)
Limit	0.10 mm (0.004 inch)
All other models	
Standard	0.025 to 0.052 mm (0.0010 to 0.0020 inch)
Limit	0.10 mm (0.004 inch)
Crankshaft runout limit	0.05 mm (0.002 inch)
Crankshaft side clearance	
Standard	0.05 to 0.55 mm (0.002 to 0.021 inch)
Limit	0.75 mm (0.029 inch)
Crankshaft web length	
Standard	96.85 to 96.95 mm (3.813 to 3.817 inch)
Limit	96.6 mm (3.803 inch)

Connecting rods and bearings

Connecting rod side clearance	
Standard	0.16 to 0.46 mm (0.007 to 0.018 inch)
Maximum	0.7 mm (0.027 inch)
Connecting rod bearing oil clearance	
Standard	0.026 to 0.057 mm (0.001 to 0.002 inch)
Maximum	0.10 mm (0.004 inch)
Connecting rod big-end bore diameter	
No circle around rod weight mark	58.000 to 58.010 mm (2.2835 to 2.2839 inch)
Circle around rod weight mark	58.011 to 58.020 mm (2.2839 to 2.2842 inch)
Connecting rod journal (crank pin) diameter	
No circle on crank throw	54.981 to 54.991 mm (2.1646 to 2.1650 inch)
Circle on crank throw	54.992 to 55.000 mm (2.1650 to 2.1654 inch)
Connecting rod bend and twist limit	0.2 mm (0.008 inch) per 100 mm (3.94 inches)

Shift mechanism

Shift linkage rod standard length (including locknuts)
  VN1500A and B and Classic . . . .   88.5 mm (3.48 inches)
  All other models . . . .   111 to 113 mm (4.37 to 4.44 inches)
Shift fork groove width
  Standard. . . . .   6.05 to 6.15 mm (0.2382 to 0.2421 inch)
  Maximum . . . .   6.3 mm (0.2480 inch)
Shift fork ear thickness
  Standard. . . . .   5.9 to 6.0 mm (0.2323 to 0.2362 inch)
  Minimum. . . . .   5.8 mm (0.2283 inch)
Shift fork guide pin diameter
  Standard. . . . .   7.9 to 8.0 mm (0.3110 to 0.3150 inch)
  Minimum. . . . .   7.8 mm (0.3071 inch)
Shift drum groove width
  Standard. . . . .   8.05 to 8.20 mm (0.3169 to 0.3228 inch)
  Maximum . . . .   8.3 mm (0.3268 inch)

Torque specifications

Engine mountings

VN1500A and B
  Through-bolt nuts. . . . .   44 Nm (33 ft-lbs)
  Right frame member bolts/nuts . . . .   44 Nm (33 ft-lbs)
  Front bracket to frame bolts. . . . .   24 Nm (17.5 ft-lbs)
VN1500 Classic, Nomad/Classic Tourer, and Drifter 1999 and 2000 (J) models
  Through-bolt nuts. . . . .   44 Nm (33 ft-lbs)
  Right frame member bolts/nuts . . . .   44 Nm (33 ft-lbs)
  Front bracket to frame bolts. . . . .   23 Nm (17 ft-lbs)
  Rear bracket to frame bolts . . . .   23 Nm (17 ft-lbs)
All other models
  Through-bolt nuts. . . . .   44 Nm (33 ft-lbs)
  Right frame member bolts/nuts . . . .   44 Nm (33 ft-lbs)
  Front bracket to frame bolts. . . . .   25 Nm (18 ft-lbs)
  Rear bracket to frame bolts . . . .   25 Nm (18 ft-lbs)

Engine components

Balancer driven gear/left balancer weight bolt
  VN1500A and B . . . .   93 Nm (69 ft-lbs)
  All other models . . . .   85 Nm (63 ft-lbs)
Camshaft chain tensioner
  VN1500A and B . . . .   Not available
  All other models
    Tensioner mounting bolts
      1500 models except Mean Streak . . . .   10 Nm (88 inch-lbs)
      1600 models and all Mean Streaks. . . . .   11 Nm (96 inch-lbs)
    Tensioner cap . . . .   20 Nm (14.5 ft-lbs)
    Tensioner locking bolt. . . . .   5 Nm (44 inch-lbs)
Camshaft sprocket bolts . . . .   15 Nm (11 ft-lbs)
Clutch cover bolts . . . .   11 Nm (96 inch-lbs)
Clutch hose banjo bolts . . . .   25 Nm (18 ft-lbs)
Clutch master cylinder clamp bolts
  VN1500A and B models. . . . .   9 Nm (80 inch-lbs)
  All other models . . . .   10 Nm (88 inch-lbs)
Clutch nut. . . . .   147 Nm (108 ft-lbs)
Connecting rod nuts. . . . .   59 Nm (44 ft-lbs)
Crankcase bolts
  6 mm bolts
    VN1500A and B . . . .   9 Nm (80 inch-lbs)
    All other VN1500 models . . . .   10 Nm (88 inch-lbs)
    VN1600 models . . . .   11 Nm (96 inch-lbs)
  8 mm bolts . . . .   21 Nm (15 ft-lbs)
  10 mm bolts . . . .   39 Nm (29 ft-lbs)
Cylinder head nuts . . . .   25 Nm (18 ft-lbs)
Cylinder nuts . . . .   25 Nm (18 ft-lbs)
External oil pipe or hose
  Oil pipe banjo bolts – VN1500A and B models . . . .   12 Nm (104 inch-lbs)
  Oil hose union bolts and banjo bolt – all other models . . . .   10 Nm (88 inch-lbs)
Internal oil pipe bolts . . . .   10 Nm (88 inch-lbs)
Oil pressure relief valve . . . .   15 Nm (11 ft-lbs)

Torque specifications (continued)

Engine components (continued)

Oil pump bolts
1500 engines	10 Nm (88 inch-lbs)
1600 engines	11 Nm (96 inch-lbs)
Primary drive gear bolt	147 Nm (108 ft-lbs)
Rocker case cover bolts	9 Nm (80 inch-lbs)

Rocker case nuts/bolts
12 mm nuts	78 Nm (58 ft-lbs)
8 mm nuts	25 Nm (18 ft-lbs)
6 mm bolts	9 Nm (80 inch-lbs)
Rocker shafts	25 Nm (18 ft-lbs)
Spark plug retainer	12 Nm (104 inch-lbs)
Starter clutch housing bolts	15 Nm (11 ft-lbs)

Starter clutch/right balancer weight bolt
VN1500A and B	93 Nm (69 ft-lbs)
All other models	85 Nm (63 ft-lbs)
Transmission output shaft bearing retainer bolts	11 Nm (96 inch-lbs)

Transmission output shaft damper cam nut
1500 engines except Classic FI models	225 Nm (165 ft-lbs)
VN1500 Classic FI models and all 1600 engines	195 Nm (144 ft-lbs)
Water pump idle shaft holder bolts	8 Nm (70 inch-lbs)

1 General information

The engine/transmission unit on all models is a water-cooled V-twin. The valves are operated by single overhead camshafts which are chain driven off the crankshaft. Twin balancer weights on each end of a shaft at the front of the engine keep things smooth. The engine/transmission assembly is constructed from aluminum alloy. The crankcase is divided horizontally.

The crankcase incorporates a wet sump, pressure-fed lubrication system which uses a gear-driven oil pump, oil filter, mesh oil screen, a relief valve and an oil pressure switch.

Power from the crankshaft is routed to the transmission via the clutch, which is of the wet, multi-plate type and is gear-driven off the crankshaft. The transmission is a four speed (VN1500A and B models and VN1500 Classic D models) or five-speed (all other models), constant-mesh unit. Drive is turned through 90° in a front bevel gear housing then to the rear wheel via a shaft and final drive housing.

2 Cylinder compression – check

Note: *Each cylinder has a decompression mechanism on the camshaft to assist starting, which is why the compression values listed in the Specifications are lower than you would expect for a healthy engine. Bear in mind when assessing measured values that do not correspond to that specified that there could be a fault with the decompression mechanism.*

1 Among other things, poor engine performance may be caused by leaking valves, a leaking head gasket, or worn pistons, rings and/or cylinder walls. A cylinder compression check will help pinpoint these conditions and can also indicate the presence of excessive carbon deposits in the cylinder heads.

2 The only tools required are a compression gauge and a spark plug wrench. Depending on the outcome of the initial test, a squirt-type oil can may also be needed.

3 Run the engine until it reaches normal operating temperature.

4 Remove one spark plug from the cylinder being tested, and detach the lead from the other plug on that cylinder (see Chapter 1). Remove both spark plugs from the cylinder not being tested. Work carefully – don't strip the spark plug hole threads and don't burn your hands.

5 Install the compression gauge in the spark plug hole of the cylinder being tested **(see illustrations)**. Hold or block the throttle wide open.

6 Crank the engine over until the gauge reading stops increasing, observing the initial movement of the compression gauge needle as well as the final total gauge reading. Repeat the procedure for the other cylinder, removing and installing the plugs as specified in Step 4. Compare the results to the compression value listed in this Chapter's Specifications.

7 If the compression in both cylinders built up quickly and evenly to the specified amount, you can assume the engine upper end is in good mechanical condition. Worn or sticking piston rings and worn cylinders will produce very little initial movement of the gauge needle, but compression will tend to build up gradually as the engine spins over. Valve and valve seat leakage, or head gasket leakage, is indicated by low initial compression which does not tend to build up.

8 To further confirm your findings, add a small amount of engine oil to each cylinder by inserting the nozzle of a squirt-type oil can through the spark plug holes. The oil will tend to seal the piston rings if they are leaking. Repeat the test for the other cylinder.

9 If the compression increases significantly after the addition of the oil, the piston rings and/or cylinders are definitely worn. If the compression does not increase, the pressure is leaking past the valves or the head gasket. Leakage past the valves may be due to burned, warped or cracked valves or valve

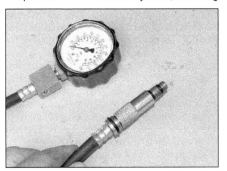

2.5a Fit an adapter onto the gauge hose if necessary . . .

2.5b . . . then thread the gauge into the spark plug hole

seats, valves that are hanging up in the guides or a damaged hydraulic valve lifter.

10 If compression readings are considerably higher than specified, the combustion chambers are probably coated with excessive carbon deposits. It is possible (but not very likely) for carbon deposits to raise the compression enough to compensate for the effects of leakage past rings or valves. Remove the cylinder heads and carefully decarbonize the combustion chambers.

3 Engine oil pressure – check

1 An oil pressure check can provide useful information about the condition of the engine and its lubrication system.

2 The oil pressure warning light should come on when the ignition switch is turned ON and extinguish a few seconds after the engine is started. If the oil pressure light comes on whilst the engine is running, low oil pressure is indicated – stop the engine immediately and carry out an oil level check (see *Pre-ride checks*). If the oil level is good next check the switch and its circuit (see Chapter 9). If that is good check the oil pressure as follows.

3 To check the oil pressure, a suitable gauge and adapter to thread in the place of the oil pressure switch are needed. Kawasaki can provide a gauge and adapter (part Nos. 57001-125 and 57001-1033), or the gauge and adapter can be obtained from a tool supplier, but make sure you get the correct adapter.

4 Remove the oil pressure switch (see Chapter 9) and screw the gauge adapter in its place – be prepared for some oil spillage, and if preferred drain the oil first (see Chapter 1). Connect the oil pressure gauge to the adapter. Replenish the engine oil and/or check the oil level (see *Pre-ride checks*).

5 Warm the engine up to normal operating temperature.

6 Briefly increase the engine speed to 2000 rpm whilst watching the gauge reading. The oil pressure should be similar to that given in the Specifications.

7 If the pressure is too low, either the pressure relief valve is stuck open, the oil pump or its drive mechanism is faulty, the oil screen is blocked, or there is other engine damage resulting in an internal leak. Also make sure the correct grade oil is being used. Begin diagnosis by checking the oil strainer and relief valve, then the oil pump (see Section 30). If those items check out okay, chances are the bearing oil clearances are excessive and the engine needs to be overhauled.

8 If the pressure is too high, either the filter or an oil passage is clogged, the relief valve is stuck closed or the wrong grade of oil is being used.

9 Stop the engine. Drain the engine oil if required. Remove the gauge and adapter. Fit the oil pressure switch (see Chapter 9) then replenish the engine oil (see Chapter 1).

⚠ *Warning: Be careful when removing the pressure gauge adapter as the exhaust pipes, the engine and the oil itself can cause severe burns.*

4 Operations possible with the engine in the frame

The components and assemblies listed below can be removed without having to remove the engine from the frame. If, however, a number of areas require attention at the same time, removal of the engine is recommended. For the alternator see Chapter 9.

> *Cam chain tensioners*
> *Gearshift mechanism external components*
> *Water pump*
> *Starter motor*
> *Starter clutch and right balancer weight*
> *Balancer weights*
> *Clutch assembly and primary drive*

5 Operations requiring engine removal

On all models, it is necessary to remove the engine/transmission assembly from the frame and separate the crankcase halves to gain access to the following components:

> *Rocker arms, shafts and cases*
> *Cylinder heads*
> *Cylinders and pistons*
> *Camshaft chains*
> *Oil pump*
> *Crankshaft, connecting rods and bearings*
> *Transmission shafts*
> *Shift drum and forks*
> *Balancer shaft*

6 Major engine repair – general note

1 It is not always easy to determine when or if an engine should be completely overhauled, as a number of factors must be considered.

2 High mileage is not necessarily an indication that an overhaul is needed, while low mileage, on the other hand, does not preclude the need for an overhaul. Frequency of servicing is probably the single most important consideration. An engine that has regular and frequent oil and filter changes, as well as other required maintenance, will most likely give many miles of reliable service. Conversely, a neglected engine, or one which has not been broken in properly, may require an overhaul very early in its life.

3 Exhaust smoke and excessive oil consumption are both indications that piston rings and/or valve guides are in need of attention. Make sure oil leaks are not responsible before deciding that the rings and guides are bad. Refer to Section 2 and perform a cylinder compression check to determine for certain the nature and extent of the work required.

4 If the engine is making obvious knocking or rumbling noises, the connecting rod and/or main bearings are probably at fault.

5 Loss of power, rough running, excessive valve train noise and high fuel consumption rates may also point to the need for an overhaul, especially if they are all present at the same time. If a complete tune-up does not remedy the situation, major mechanical work is the only solution.

6 An engine overhaul generally involves restoring the internal parts to the specifications of a new engine. During an overhaul the piston rings are replaced and the cylinder walls are bored and/or honed. If a rebore is done, then an oversize set of pistons and rings are also required. The main and connecting rod bearings and transmission shaft bearings are generally replaced with new ones and, if necessary, the crankshaft is also replaced. Generally the valves are serviced as well, since they are usually in less than perfect condition at this point. While the engine is being overhauled, other components such as the carburetors (where fitted) and the starter motor can be rebuilt also. The end result should be a like-new engine that will give as many trouble free miles as the original.

7 Before beginning the engine overhaul, read through all of the related procedures to familiarize yourself with the scope and requirements of the job. Overhauling an engine is not all that difficult, but it is time consuming. Plan on the motorcycle being tied up for a minimum of two weeks. Check on the availability of parts and make sure that any necessary special tools, equipment and supplies are obtained in advance.

8 Most work can be done with typical shop hand tools, although a number of precision measuring tools are required for inspecting parts to determine if they must be replaced. Often a dealer service department or motorcycle repair shop will handle the inspection of parts and offer advice concerning reconditioning and replacement. As a general rule, time is the primary cost of an overhaul so it doesn't pay to install worn or substandard parts.

9 As a final note, to ensure maximum life and minimum trouble from a rebuilt engine, everything must be assembled with care in a spotlessly clean environment.

7 Engine – removal and installation

⚠ *Warning: The engine is very heavy. Engine removal and installation should be done with the aid of at least two assistants to avoid damage or injury that could occur if the engine is*

7.1a Bike supported using wood blocks and a metal bar as shown . . .

7.1b . . . with the bar secured to the frame

dropped. *An hydraulic floor jack should be used to support and lower the engine if possible (they can be rented at low cost).*

Removal

1 Prop the bike securely upright using an auxiliary stand or stands **(see illustrations)** – the arrangement shown imitates the Kawasaki purpose-made stand, but you need to remove some of the assemblies detailed below (i.e. the exhaust etc) before fitting it. Tie the front brake lever to the handlebar so the brake is on. Work can be made easier by raising the machine to a suitable working height on an hydraulic ramp or a suitable platform. Make sure the motorcycle is secure and will not topple over (also see *Tools and Workshop Tips* in the Reference section).

VN1500A and B

2 Remove the seat and the side covers (see Chapter 8). Disconnect the battery (see Chapter 9).
3 Remove the fuel tank (see Chapter 4A). Remove the frame covers (see Chapter 8).
4 Drain the engine oil and the coolant (see Chapter 1).
5 Remove the air filter housings (see Chapter 4A). Remove the horn (see Chapter 9).
6 Remove the radiator and coolant reservoir (see Chapter 3).
7 Remove the left-hand footpeg (see Chapter 8). Remove the left-hand engine cover. Displace the clutch release cylinder (see Section 19) – there is no need to disconnect the hose, but fit cable-ties around the cylinder and piston to prevent the piston creeping out.
8 Remove the shift pedal (see Section 21).
9 Remove the exhaust downpipes (see Chapter 4).
10 Detach the air suction valve hose from the front cylinder. Detach the coolant hoses from the cylinder heads. Remove the air surge tank ducts. Remove the thermostat housing and its hoses. Remove the surge tank.
11 Remove the ignition switch (see Chapter 9). Remove the coolant reservoir bracket. Detach the air suction valve hose from the rear

cylinder. Remove the ignition coil assembly (see Chapter 5).
12 Remove the carburetors if required, or if not just disconnect the throttle cables and hoses (see Chapter 4A). Plug the intake openings with clean rags if you remove the carburetors.
13 Mark and disconnect the wires from the oil pressure switch, and neutral switch. Unplug the brake light switch, alternator, sidestand and pick-up coil electrical connectors (see Chapters 5 and 9).
14 Disconnect the starter motor lead **(see illustration 7.42a)**. Disconnect the engine ground cable **(see illustration 7.42b)**.

VN1500 Classic and Nomad/Classic Tourer

15 Remove the seat and the side covers (see Chapter 8). Disconnect the battery (see Chapter 9). Remove the engine protection bar where fitted.
16 Remove the fuel tank (see Chapter 4A).
17 Drain the engine oil and the coolant (see Chapter 1).
18 Remove the air filter housings, the fuel pump, and the surge tank (see Chapter 4A).
19 Detach the spark plug caps. Detach the air suction valve hoses.
20 Release the wiring ties on the right-hand side of the frame. Disconnect the cooling fan and rear brake light switch wiring connectors. Remove the radiator (see Chapter 3).
21 Remove the shift pedals (see Section 21). Remove the left-hand engine cover **(see illustration 7.37)**.
22 Mark and disconnect the oil pressure switch, neutral switch, sidestand switch, alternator, pick-up coil, and regulator/rectifier wiring connectors **(see illustration 7.38)**. Detach the starter motor lead.
23 Displace the clutch release cylinder (see Section 19) – there is no need to disconnect the hose, but fit cable-ties around the cylinder and piston to prevent the piston creeping out.
24 Remove the horn (see Chapter 9).
25 Detach the coolant hoses from the cylinder heads.

26 Remove the carburetor (see Chapter 4A). Plug the intake openings with clean rags.
27 Remove the exhaust downpipes (see Chapter 4A).
28 Disconnect the starter motor lead **(see illustration 7.42a)**. Disconnect the engine ground cable **(see illustration 7.42b)**.

VN1500 Classic FI and Nomad/Classic Tourer FI, all Mean Streak models, all Drifter models

29 Remove the seat and the side covers (see Chapter 8). Disconnect the battery (see Chapter 9). Remove the engine protection bar where fitted.
30 Remove the fuel tank (see Chapter 4B).
31 Drain the engine oil and the coolant (see Chapter 1).
32 Remove the air filter housings (see Chapter 4B). Remove the air suction valve and hoses (see Chapter 4B).
33 Disconnect the throttle cables (see Chapter 4B). Disconnect the fuel injector and throttle sensor wiring connectors (see Chapter 4B). Disconnect the fuel and vacuum hoses as required so the throttle body is free to be removed with the engine. Where fitted disconnect the oil reserve tank hose.
34 Detach the spark plug caps. Release the rear cylinder right side lead from the throttle body and position the leads clear **(see illustration)**.

7.34 Release the HT lead from its tie to the throttle body (arrowed)

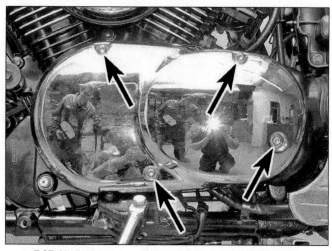

7.37 Undo the screws (arrowed) and remove the cover

7.38 Disconnect the various wiring connectors

35 Remove the horn (see Chapter 9).

36 Release the wiring clips on the right-hand side of the frame. Disconnect the cooling fan and rear brake light switch wiring connectors (see Chapters 3 and 9). Remove the radiator (see Chapter 3).

37 Remove the shift pedal(s) (see Section 21). Remove the left side engine cover (not fitted on Drifter 1999 and 2000 (J1 and J2) models) **(see illustration)**. On Drifter 1999 and 2000 (J1 and J2) models remove the connector cover from the top of the alternator cover, noting the collars and dampers and how they locate.

38 Mark and disconnect the oil pressure switch, neutral switch, sidestand switch, alternator, pick-up coil, and regulator/rectifier wiring connectors, and on all except Nomad/Classic Tourer 2000 (L1) models and Drifter 1999 and 2000 (J1 and J2) models the speed sensor connector **(see illustration)**.

39 Displace the clutch release cylinder (see Section 19) – there is no need to disconnect the hose, but fit cable-ties around the cylinder and piston to prevent the piston creeping out.

40 Detach the coolant hoses from the cylinder heads.

41 Remove the exhaust downpipes (see Chapter 4B).

42 Disconnect the starter motor lead **(see**

illustration). Disconnect the engine ground cable **(see illustration)**.

VN1600 Classic and Nomad/Classic Tourer

43 Remove the seat and the side covers (see Chapter 8). Disconnect the battery (see Chapter 9). Remove the engine protection bars where fitted.

44 Remove the fuel tank (see Chapter 4B).

45 Drain the engine oil and the coolant (see Chapter 1).

46 Remove the air filter housings (see Chapter 4B). Remove the air suction valve and hoses (see Chapter 4B).

47 Remove the exhaust downpipes (see Chapter 4).

48 Remove the radiator and thermostat housing (see Chapter 3).

49 Remove the ignition coils (see Chapter 5).

50 Remove the shift pedals (see Section 21). Remove the left-hand engine cover **(see illustration 7.37)**.

51 Disconnect the throttle cables (see Chapter 4B). Disconnect the fuel injector and throttle sensor wiring connectors (see Chapter 4B). Disconnect the fuel and vacuum hoses as required so the throttle body is free to be removed with the engine.

52 Detach the spark plug caps. Release the rear cylinder right side lead from the throttle

body and position the leads clear **(see illustration 7.34)**.

53 Remove the horn (see Chapter 9). Release the choke knob and cable.

54 Mark and disconnect the oil pressure switch, neutral switch, sidestand switch, alternator, pick-up coil, and speed sensor wiring connectors **(see illustration 7.38)**. Remove the regulator/rectifier assembly (see Chapter 9).

55 Remove the clutch hose bracket and displace the release cylinder (see Section 19) – there is no need to disconnect the hose from the cylinder, but fit cable-ties around the cylinder and piston to prevent the piston creeping out.

56 Remove the rear brake fluid reservoir cover and displace the reservoir. On Classic models remove the cover from the left-hand side of the swingarm.

57 Disconnect the starter motor lead **(see illustration 7.42a)**. Disconnect the engine ground cable **(see illustration 7.42b)**.

All models

58 Remove the final drive housing (see Chapter 6). Pull the rubber boot off the front of the swingarm **(see illustration)**. Rotate the driveshaft to put the shaft locking pin hole in an accessible position. Depress the locking pin using a suitable tool and push the shaft back off the engine to disengage

7.42a Pull back the boot, unscrew the nut and detach the lead

7.42b Unscrew the bolt (arrowed) and detach the cable

7.58a Pull the boot off the swingarm

the driveshaft **(see illustration)**. Retrieve the driveshaft locking pin for safekeeping using a magnet **(see illustration)**.

59 Position an hydraulic or mechanical jack under the engine with a block of wood between the jack head and sump **(see illustration 7.63)**. Make sure the jack is centrally positioned so the engine will not topple in any direction when the last mounting bolt is removed. Raise the jack to take the weight of the engine, but make sure it is not lifting the bike and taking the weight of that as well. The idea is to support the engine so that there is no pressure on any of the mounting bolts once they have been slackened, so they can be easily withdrawn. Note that it may be necessary to alter the position of the jack as some of the bolts are removed to relieve the stress transferred to the other bolts. Make a note of which side the two through bolts go in from as it varies from model to model.

60 On VN1500A and B models unscrew the front mounting bracket bolts – refer to the illustrations relating to Step 61 as a guide. Unscrew the nut on the end of each through-bolt. Withdraw the rear through-bolt. Unscrew the nuts and bolts securing the frame member on the right side and displace it and lay it on some rag on the ground, making sure no strain is placed on the rear brake hose. Withdraw the front through-bolt and remove the bracket from the front of the frame.

61 On all other models remove the blanking caps from any frame bolts **(see illustration)**. Unscrew the front mounting bracket bolts on the right side **(see illustration)**. Unscrew the nuts and bolts securing the frame member

7.58b Depress the pin and push the shaft back . . .

on the right side and displace it and lay it on some rag on the ground, making sure no strain is placed on the rear brake hose **(see illustrations)**. Unscrew the nut on the end of the front through-bolt and remove the cap **(see illustration)**. Unscrew the front

7.61a Remove the blanking caps from the bolts where fitted

7.61c Unscrew the nuts and remove the front bolts . . .

7.61d . . . then unscrew the rear bolts . . .

7.61f Unscrew the nut and remove the bush cap

7.61g Unscrew the left side bracket bolts . . .

7.58c . . . then remove the pin and keep it safe

mounting bracket bolts on the left side **(see illustration)**. Withdraw the front through-bolt and remove the bracket from the front of the frame **(see illustration)**. Unscrew the nut on the end of the rear through-bolt, then unscrew the rear bracket bolts on the right side and

7.61b Unscrew the front bracket bolts on the right side

7.61e . . . and displace the right section of frame along with the footpeg/board and rear brake assembly

7.61h . . . then withdraw the front through-bolt and remove the bracket

7.61i Unscrew the through-bolt nut and the bracket bolts . . .

7.61j . . . and remove the bracket, noting the cap

7.61k Unscrew the bracket bolts . . .

remove the bracket, noting the bush cap **(see illustrations)**. Unscrew the rear bracket bolts on the left side **(see illustration)**. Withdraw the rear through-bolt and remove the bracket **(see illustration)**.

62 Make sure there are no wires or hoses

7.61l . . . then withdraw the through-bolt and remove the bracket

still attached to the engine and connected to something on the frame. Make sure everything that needs to be has been removed or displaced.
63 With the help of at least two assistants, slowly and carefully guide the engine out the right side, away from the bike **(see illustration)**.

7.63 Carefully manoeuvre the engine out to the right

64 Remove the driveshaft locking pin spring if required **(see illustration)**. Check the condition of all rubber mounting bushes **(see illustration)** – remove them from their mounts if required and replace them with new ones if necessary.

Installation

65 Installation is the reverse of removal. Note the following points:

a) *Make sure all rubber mounting bushes are correctly in place. If they have been removed make sure they are clean if being reused, or fit new ones if necessary. Lubricate the bushes with soapy water or a rubber lubricant before fitting.*

b) *Make sure the clutch release cylinder and its hose are correctly positioned. Make sure the driveshaft spring (if removed) is fitted, and the pin and access hole are aligned in an accessible position **(see illustration)**. Smear some high temperature grease over the drive shaft splines.*

c) *Make sure the driveshaft rubber boot is fitted **(see illustration)**. Make sure the boot does not get caught inside the front of the swingarm.*

d) *Do not forget to fit the bush caps with the through bolts and their nuts. Don't tighten any of the engine mounting bolts until they all have been installed. Tighten the engine mounting bolts and nuts to the torque value listed in the Specifications.*

e) *Fit the shaft locking pin **(see illustration 7.64a)**. Align the hole in the universal joint rim with the shaft locking pin, then depress the pin and slide the shaft on so the pin engages **(see illustration)**. Try*

7.64a Remove the spring as shown if required

7.64b Check the condition of all mounting bushes and hardware

7.65b Make sure the spring is inside the splined coupling

7.65c Make sure the rubber boot is fitted if removed

7.65e Align the pin and the hole then depress the pin and push the shaft over it

to move the shaft back again – it should be locked in place. Position the rubber boot over the front of the swingarm *(see illustration 7.58a)*.

f) Use new gaskets at all exhaust pipe connections.

g) Refill the engine with oil and coolant (see Chapter 1).

h) Adjust the throttle cables, choke (see Chapter 1).

i) Start the engine and check that there are no oil or coolant leaks. Adjust the idle speed (see Chapter 1).

8 Engine disassembly and reassembly – general information

1 Before disassembling the engine, clean the exterior with a degreaser and rinse it with water. A clean engine will make the job easier and prevent the possibility of getting dirt into the internal areas of the engine.

2 In addition to the precision measuring tools mentioned earlier, you will need a torque wrench and a valve spring compressor, various other special tools that are mentioned in the relevant Section, and a good selection of general workshop tools, including sockets, spanners, hex bits, screwdrivers and pliers, suitable for motorcycle work. Some new, clean engine oil of the correct grade and type, some engine assembly lube (or moly-based grease), a tube of Kawasaki Bond liquid gasket (part no. 92104-1064) or equivalent, a tube of Kawasaki Bond liquid gasket RTV (silicone) sealant (part no. 56019-120) or equivalent, and some non-permanent thread locking compound, will also be required. Although it may not be considered a tool, if you are checking bearing oil clearances some Plastigage (type HPG-1) should also be obtained.

3 Some blocks of wood are often very useful to act as supports for the engine. If you have an automotive-type engine stand, an adapter plate can be made from a piece of plate, some angle iron and some nuts and bolts.

4 When disassembling the engine, keep "mated" parts together (including gears, cylinders, pistons, etc. that have been in contact with each other during engine operation). These "mated" parts must be reused or replaced as an assembly.

5 A complete engine/transmission disassembly should be done in the following general order with reference to the appropriate Sections.

Remove the rocker cases
Remove the cylinder heads
Remove the cylinders
Remove the pistons
Remove the clutch and the primary drive gear
Remove the starter clutch
Remove the external shift mechanism
Remove the left-hand balancer weight
Separate the crankcase halves
Remove the crankshaft and connecting rods
Remove the balancer shaft
Remove the transmission and shift drum/ forks assembly

6 Reassembly is accomplished by reversing the general disassembly sequence.

9 Camshaft chain tensioners – removal and installation

Caution: Once you start to remove the tensioner bolts, you must remove the tensioner all the way and reset it before tightening the bolts. The tensioner extends and locks in place, so if you loosen the bolts part way and then retighten them, the tensioner or cam chain will be damaged. Do not turn the engine over with a tensioner removed.

VN1500A and B

Removal

1 Unscrew the tensioner cap bolt and remove the spring. Discard the sealing washer as a new one must be used.

2 Unscrew the tensioner mounting bolts and withdraw the tensioner from the engine.

3 Remove the gasket and discard it – a new

one must be used on installation. Remove all traces of old gasket from the tensioner and cylinder block mating surfaces.

Inspection

4 Lift the ratchet on the plunger and check that the plunger moves smoothly and freely in and out of the body **(see illustration 9.13)**. With the plunger extended and the ratchet locked, make sure you cannot push the plunger into the body. Replace the tensioner with a new one if there are any faults.

Installation

5 Ensure the tensioner and cylinder block mating surfaces are clean and dry. Clean the mounting bolt threads.

6 Lift the ratchet on the plunger and push the plunger fully into the body **(see illustration 9.13)**.

7 Fit a new gasket onto the tensioner body. Fit the tensioner with the arrow pointing up. Apply a suitable non-permanent thread locking compound to the bolt threads and tighten the bolts.

8 Fit a new sealing washer and the spring onto the tensioner cap bolt, then insert the spring and tighten the bolt – as the spring is compressed you should hear the plunger push out over the ratchet mechanism to tension the chain.

All other models

Removal

9 To remove the front cylinder tensioner, remove the lower air cleaner duct and the left-hand air cleaner base holder (see Chapter 4A or 4B). To remove the rear cylinder tensioner remove the rear exhaust downpipe (see Chapter 4A or 4B) – on VN1600 models you can remove the tensioner with the exhaust in place, but access is improved with the cover removed.

10 Slacken the tensioner locking bolt **(see illustration)**. Unscrew the tensioner cap and remove the inner spring, the bearing retainer, bearing and outer spring. Remove the O-ring and discard it – a new one must be fitted

11 Unscrew the tensioner mounting bolts and withdraw the tensioner from the engine **(see illustration)**.

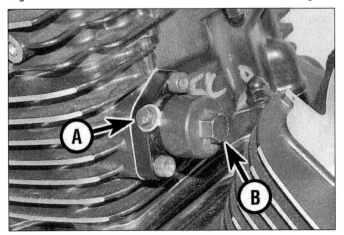

9.10 Slacken the locking bolt (A) then unscrew the cap (B)

9.11 Unscrew the bolts (arrowed) and remove the tensioner

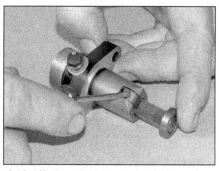

9.13 Lift the ratchet and check the action of the plunger

9.16a Fit the outer spring . . .

9.16b . . . then the bearing . . .

9.16c . . . and hold the bearing down while tightening the locking bolt

9.16d Fit the retainer onto the bearing

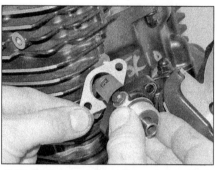

9.17 Fit the tensioner using a new gasket

12 Remove the gasket and discard it – a new one must be used on installation. Remove all traces of old gasket from the tensioner and cylinder block mating surfaces.

Inspection

13 Lift the ratchet on the plunger and check that the plunger moves smoothly and freely in and out of the body **(see illustration)**. With the plunger extended and the ratchet locked make sure you cannot push the plunger into the body. Replace the tensioner with a new one if there are any faults.

Installation

14 Ensure the tensioner and cylinder block mating surfaces are clean and dry.
15 Lift the ratchet on the plunger and push the plunger fully into the body **(see illustration 9.13)**.

16 Fit the outer spring into the tensioner **(see illustration)**. Fit the bearing against the spring and push it in until it seats, holding it there with a screwdriver while you tighten the locking bolt finger-tight **(see illustrations)**. Fit the retainer **(see illustration)**.
17 Fit a new gasket onto the tensioner body **(see illustration)**. Fit the tensioner with the locking bolt facing up and out and tighten the bolts to the torque listed in this Chapter's Specifications.
18 Fit a new O-ring onto the tensioner **(see illustration)**. Fit the inner spring into the tensioner. Fit the cap, locating the outer end of the inner spring into the recess, and tighten it to the torque listed in this Chapter's Specifications **(see illustration)**.
19 Unscrew the locking bolt – you should

hear the outer spring click **(see illustration)**. Now tighten the locking bolt to the torque listed in this Chapter's Specifications.
20 Install the air cleaner base and air duct and/or the exhaust pipe as required (see Chapter 4A or 4B).

10 Rocker case covers –
removal and installation

Removal

1 Remove the engine from the frame (see Section 7).
2 On VN1500A and B models unscrew the bolts and remove the side covers, then unscrew the bolts and remove the top cover.

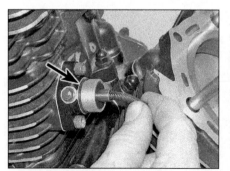

9.18a Fit a new O-ring (arrowed), then fit the inner spring . . .

9.18b . . . and the cap

9.19 Unscrew the locking bolt to release the outer spring, then tighten it

10.3 Unscrew the bolts and remove the cover

10.5a Remove the springs . . .

10.5b . . . then pick the filters out

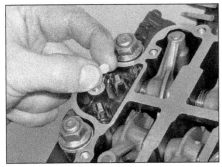

10.7a Fit new filters, then fit the springs

10.7b Fill the recess with oil

10.8 Seat the new gasket over the dowels (arrowed) where fitted

3 On all other models unscrew the bolts and remove the cover **(see illustration)**.

4 Remove the gasket. Remove the locating dowels if loose (not fitted on VN1500A and B models).

5 Remove the hydraulic lifter oil filter springs and filters from the rocker case **(see illustrations)** – discard the filters, new ones must be used.

Installation

6 Clean the mating surfaces of the cylinder head and the valve cover, making sure you remove all traces of old gasket.

7 Fit new hydraulic lifter filters **(see illustration)**. Fit the springs onto the filters **(see illustration 10.5a)**. Fill the recess with

new engine oil of the specified type **(see illustration)** (see Chapter 1).

8 Fit the locating dowels if removed (not fitted on VN1500A and B models). Fit the new gasket **(see illustration)**.

9 On VN1500A and B models make sure the rubber damper is correctly fitted in the top cover, then fit the cover and tighten the bolts to the torque listed in this Chapter's Specifications. Fit the side covers.

10 On all other models make sure the rubber dampers are correctly fitted then fit the cover and tighten the bolts in the sequence shown to the torque listed in this Chapter's Specifications **(see illustrations)**. Make sure the oil hoses route correctly under the left side of the rear cover **(see illustration)**.

11 Install the engine (see Section 7).

11 Rocker cases – removal and installation

Removal

1 Remove the engine from the frame (see Section 7).

2 On VN1600 models remove the throttle body assembly (see Chapter 4B).

3 Remove the rocker case cover(s) (see Section 10). On VN1500A and B remove the alternator outer cover (see Chapter 9).

4 Remove the spark plugs (see Chapter 1).

5 On all except VN1500A and B models unscrew the timing inspection cap and the crankshaft end cap from the alternator cover on the left-hand

10.10a Make sure the dampers are in place (front cover shown) . . .

10.10b . . . then fit the cover and tighten the bolts in the order shown . . .

10.10c . . . when fitting the rear cover make sure the oil hoses route correctly

11.5 Remove the crankshaft end cap (A) and the timing inspection cap (B)

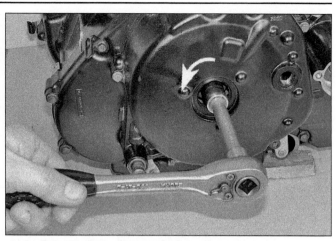

11.6a Turn the engine anti-clockwise using a socket on the rotor bolt

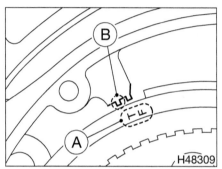

11.6b Front cylinder timing mark (A) and static timing mark (B) – VN1500A and B models

side of the engine (see illustration). Check the condition of the cap O-rings and replace them with new ones if necessary.

6 The engine must be turned so the piston in the cylinder being worked on is at top dead centre (TDC) on its compression stroke so that the valves are closed – turn the engine anti-clockwise using a suitable socket on the alternator rotor bolt. To set the front cylinder at TDC turn the engine until the index line marked **F** on the rotor aligns with the static

11.6c Front cylinder timing mark (A) and static timing mark (B) – all other models

timing mark on the alternator inner cover on VN1500A and B models and the notch in the inspection hole on all other models, and the upright F on the camshaft sprocket is at the top (see illustrations) – do not confuse the upright F with an F on its side next to a line (this mark is used when installing the camshaft). To set the rear cylinder at TDC turn the engine until the index line marked **R** on the rotor aligns with the static timing mark on the alternator inner cover on VN1500A and B

models and the notch in the inspection hole on all other models, and the upright R on the camshaft sprocket is at the top – do not confuse the upright R with an R on its side next to a line (this mark is used when installing the camshaft). If the F or R on the sprocket is not visible (you need to look carefully as they are not that easy to see), rotate the engine anti-clockwise one full turn (360°) until the mark on the rotor again aligns with the static timing mark – the mark on the sprocket will now be at the top. When turning the engine with one rocker case removed hold the non-chain end of the camshaft down, and when turning the engine with one camshaft removed hold the chain up to prevent it binding.

7 On VN1500A and B models unscrew the oil pipe banjo bolt. Discard the sealing washers – new ones must be used. If the cylinder head(s) is/are being removed as well then unscrew all three banjo bolts (one on each rocker case and one on the crankcase) and the pipe bracket bolt and remove the pipe from the engine.

8 On all other models unscrew the oil hose union bolt and detach the hose (see illustration). Discard the O-ring – a new one must be used.

11.6d The timing mark (arrowed) on the sprocket is difficult to see – do not confuse with the same letter on its side

11.8 Unscrew the bolt and detach the oil hose

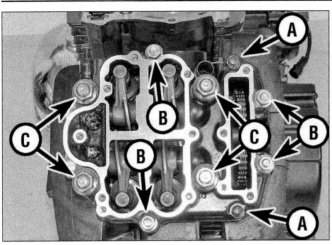

11.10 Rocker case bolts (A), small nuts (B) and large nuts (C)

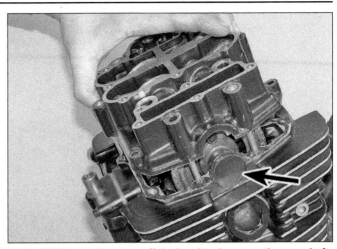

11.11 Lift the rocker case off the head and remove the camshaft cap (arrowed)

9 Remove the cam chain tensioner (see Section 9).

10 The rocker case is secured by two bolts, four small nuts and four large nuts **(see illustration)** – unscrew the bolts first, then the small nuts, then the large nuts, slackening them evenly and a little at a time in a criss-cross pattern.

11 Lift the rocker case off the cylinder head, using a screwdriver or similar in the leverage points to initially release it if necessary **(see illustration)**. Remove the camshaft end cap. Remove the dowels if loose. Mark the case with an F or R according to its cylinder (i.e. Front or Rear).

12 If required remove the rocker shafts and arms (see Section 12).

13 Clean all traces of old sealant off the rocker case and cylinder head mating surfaces and the camshaft end cap and its cut-outs.

Installation

14 If removed install the rocker shafts and arms (see Section 12). Lubricate the camshaft journals and lobes with molybdenum disulphide oil (engine oil and molybdenum grease mixed in the ratio 10:1).

15 Refer to Section 13, Step 20 and make sure the timing marks for the cylinder being worked on are correct.

11.16a Fit the end cap – you may have to shift the camshaft slightly to get it correctly seated

16 Clean the mating surfaces of the cylinder head and the rocker case and the end cap cut-outs and the end caps themselves with solvent, removing all traces of old sealant. Apply fresh silicone sealant all round the end cap and fit it onto the cylinder head **(see illustration)**. Apply the sealant to the mating surface of the rocker case **(see illustration)**. Fit the dowels if removed. Fit the case onto the cylinder head **(see illustration 11.11)** – make sure you fit the case you marked F onto the front

11.16b Apply sealant to the mating surface

cylinder head, and the case marked R onto the rear.

17 Lubricate the 12 mm nut threads and seating surface and each side of the nut washers with molybdenum disulphide oil (engine oil and molybdenum grease mixed in the ratio 10:1) **(see illustration)**. Fit the nuts with the washers and tighten them finger-tight. Fit the 8 mm nuts and the 6 mm bolts and tighten them finger-tight. Now tighten the 12 mm nuts evenly and a bit at a time in the sequence shown (1 to 4) to the torque listed in this Chapter's Specifications **(see illustration)**. Next tighten the 8 mm nuts

11.17a Lubricate the large nuts and washers before fitting them

11.17b Rocker case nut and bolt tightening sequence

11.18a Tighten the nuts (arrowed) at the front . . .

11.18b . . . and at the back of each cylinder

11.22 Fit a new O-ring smeared with oil into the groove in the union

11.23 Fit the caps using new O-rings if necessary

Section 10). On VN1500A and B install the alternator outer cover (see Chapter 9).

26 On VN1600 models install the throttle body assembly (see Chapter 4B).

27 Install the engine in the frame (see Section 7).

12 Rocker shafts, rocker arms and hydraulic lifters – removal, inspection and installation

Removal

Note: *Keep all mated parts together and in order so they can be reinstalled in their original locations – a compartmentalized container with code numbers and letters written on each compartment is a convenient way to keep parts together.*

1 Remove the rocker case (see Section 11). Note the relative positions of the arms and springs according to the side of the case they fit on (i.e. intake or exhaust).

2 Unscrew the intake rocker shaft and remove the rocker arms and springs, noting how they fit **(see illustrations)**. Slide the arms back onto the shaft in the correct order so mated parts remain together. Repeat for the exhaust rocker shaft. Note that of the four arms fitted to each head, three are identical, with the arm on the cam chain side of the exhaust shaft being the different one.

3 Remove the O-rings from each shaft and discard them **(see illustration 12.12)** – new ones must be be used.

4 If necessary pull the hydraulic lifters out of their bores **(see illustration)** – if it is not necessary it is best to leave them in to avoid the procedures in Steps 9 to 11 that will have to be carried out if they are disturbed.

Caution: Do not hit or drop the hydraulic lifters as the plunger may not operate correctly.

Inspection

5 Clean the rockers and shaft with solvent and dry them off. Blow through the oil passages in the rocker arms with compressed air, if available. Inspect the rocker arm faces for

(5 to 8) in the same way to the torque listed in this Chapter's Specifications, then finally tighten the 6 mm bolts to the torque listed in this Chapter's Specifications. Go round all the nuts and bolts again in the same sequence (1 to 10) with the torque wrench set to the correct torque for each nut or bolt.

18 Tighten the cylinder head and cylinder nuts to the torque listed in this Chapter's Specifications **(see illustrations)** – if the head hasn't been removed they may not tighten much or at all, but if they have become loose having removed the rocker case it is essential they are tightened.

19 Install the cam chain tensioner (see Section 9).

20 When both rocker cases and tensioners have been installed, but before fitting the rocker case covers, turn the engine anti-

clockwise through two full turns and check again that the timing marks on both cylinders align correctly (see Step 6).

21 On VN1500A and B models fit the oil pipe using a new sealing washer on each side of each union as required according to what has been removed and tighten the banjo bolts to the torque listed in this Chapter's Specifications. If necessary also tighten the pipe bracket bolt.

22 On all other models fit the oil hose using a new O-ring smeared with oil and tighten the union bolt to the torque listed in this Chapter's Specifications **(see illustration)**.

23 On all except VN1500A and B models fit the timing inspection cap and crankshaft end cap using new O-rings if necessary and tighten them **(see illustration)**.

24 Install the spark plugs (see Chapter 1).

25 Install the rocker case cover(s) (see

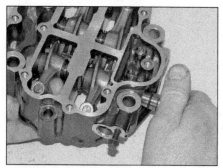

12.2a Unscrew the shaft and remove the rocker arms . . .

12.2b . . . and springs as you withdraw it

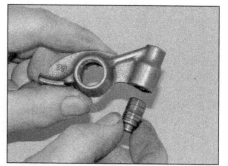

12.4 Remove the lifters from the arms only if necessary

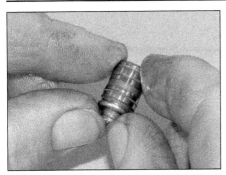

12.8 Check the performance of the lifter as described

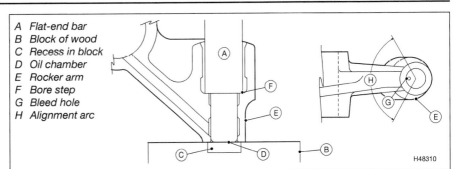

A Flat-end bar
B Block of wood
C Recess in block
D Oil chamber
E Rocker arm
F Bore step
G Bleed hole
H Alignment arc

12.9 Recess the chamber as shown

pits, spalling, score marks and rough spots. Check the rocker arm-to-shaft contact areas, as well. Look for cracks in each rocker arm. If the faces of the rocker arms are damaged, check the corresponding camshaft lobes (see Section 13) and replace all worn or damaged components with new ones, preferably as a whole set.

6 Inspect the surfaces of the rocker arm shafts, in the area where the rocker arms ride, and the corresponding bores of the arms. If either the shaft or the rocker arms are visibly worn or damaged, replace them as a set. On all except VN1500A and B models, for which no specifications are given, you can measure the diameter of riding points on the shaft and the internal diameter of each rocker arm bore to determine the extent of wear.

7 Make sure the oil holes in the hydraulic lifters are clear. Check the lifters and their bores for wear, scuff marks, scratches and other damage. Check the contact tip of the lifter and the top of the valve stem it contacts for wear. Kawasaki doesn't provide specifications or wear tolerances for the lifters or their bores. If wear or damage is found, replace the worn parts.

8 Lifter performance can be tested as follows: bleed the air from the lifter as described in Step 10. Remove the lifter from the oil and remove the pin. Push the plunger into the lifter – it should not push in **(see illustration)**. If it does, repeat the air bleeding procedure and try again – if the plunger still moves in the lifter is faulty.

Rocker arm assembly and hydraulic lifter bleeding

Note: *Work on one rocker arm and its lifter at a time, keeping mated parts together.*

9 If new rocker arms are being installed and the oil chambers that come with them are not already fitted into them, the chambers must be aligned and recessed in the arms as follows: prepare a block of wood with a recess cut into it and a flat-ended piece of bar to fit into the lifter bore in the arm as shown in the diagram **(see illustration)**. Set the oil chamber bleed hole within the 120° arc as shown and push the bar down until the rim of the oil chamber is level with the step in the bore.

10 Before fitting the lifters into the arms the lifters must be bled of air as follows: get a thumbtack (drawing pin) and cut off the tip of the pin, leaving 2.1 to 2.3 mm (0.0827 to 0.0906 in) of shaft protruding from the cap – there must be no more than 2.3 mm or the lifter could be damaged **(see illustration)**. Grind the end of the shaft so it is smooth. Prepare a container with enough clean engine oil in it to cover the lifter. Fit the pin into the hole in the top of the lifter and hold it in place – this keeps the oil check valve open. Submerge the lifter in the oil bath. Now push the plunger in and out to bleed the air from it, replacing it with oil **(see illustration)**.

11 Put the rocker arm in the container of engine oil so it is covered. Push the lifter into the arm, making sure the plunger end faces out **(see illustration)**. From here on take care not to let either the lifter or the oil within it and the rocker arm to come out.

Installation

Note: *Make sure all components are returned to their original positions in the rocker case. Remember that of the four arms fitted to each head, three are identical, with the arm on the cam chain side of the exhaust shaft being the different one.*

12 Fit new O-rings onto each rocker shaft and smear them with clean oil **(see illustration)**.

13 Work with the rocker case upside down. Slide each shaft in turn into the rocker case and position each spring and arm as the shaft is inserted – on the intake shaft the spring fits first, then the arm, and on the exhaust side the

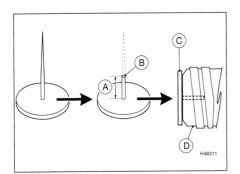

12.10a Lifter bleeding set-up

A Thumbtack needle length
B Thumbtack needle ground end
C Thumbtack inserted
D Hydraulic lifter

12.10b Bleeding air from the lifter with the thumbtack in place

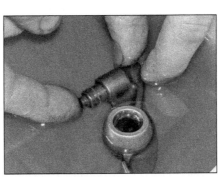

12.11 Keep the rocker submerged when fitting the lifter

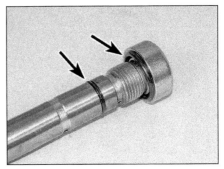

12.12 Fit new O-rings (arrowed) onto the shaft

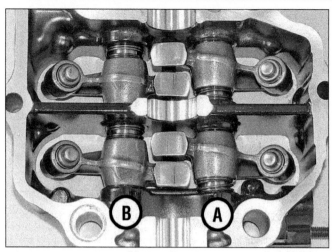

12.13 The springs and arms must be laid out as shown – A, intake side; B, exhaust side

13.2 Disengage the chain and lift the camshaft out

arm fits first, then the spring **(see illustration)**. Make sure the lifters and oil do not come out of the arms.

14 Tighten the rocker shafts to the torque listed in this Chapter's Specifications.

15 Install the rocker case (see Section 11).

13 Camshafts – removal, inspection and installation

Removal

1 Remove the rocker cases (see Section 11).

2 Pull up on the camshaft chain and carefully guide the camshaft out, bringing the decompression mechanism with it **(see illustration)**. **Note:** *Don't remove the sprockets from the camshafts unless absolutely necessary.* Drop the chain into the tunnel so it rests on the spark plug retainer. Cover the top of the cylinder head with a rag to prevent foreign objects from falling into the engine. Note that each camshaft is different – the rear cylinder camshaft has a groove cut in the section just behind the sprocket flange for identification.

3 The decompression mechanism for each camshaft is slightly different – if you want to remove them from the camshafts mark each one F or R according to the camshaft it fits on. Remove them from the end of each camshaft, noting how they locate **(see illustration)**.

Camshaft inspection

4 Clean the camshaft and blow the oil passages through with compressed air.

5 Inspect the bearing surfaces of the rocker case and cylinder head and the corresponding journals on the camshafts **(see illustration)**. Look for score marks, deep scratches and evidence of spalling (a pitted appearance). Check the oil passages for clogging.

6 Check the camshaft lobes for heat discoloration (blue appearance), score marks, chipped areas, flat spots and spalling. Measure the height of each lobe with a micrometer **(see illustration)** and compare the results to the minimum height listed in this Chapter's Specifications. If damage is noted or wear is excessive, the camshaft must be replaced with a new one.

7 Next, check the camshaft journal oil clearances – this is done using a product

called Plastigauge, available direct from the manufacturer or from good automotive suppliers. Follow the manufacturer's instructions. Work on one head at a time and make sure the correct camshaft and rocker case are fitted to ensure all mated parts are kept together. Remove the rocker shafts and arms from the rocker case (see Section 12). Clean the camshaft and the bearing surfaces in the cylinder head and rocker case with a clean lint-free cloth, then lay the camshaft in the cylinder head.

8 Cut some strips of Plastigauge and lay one piece on each journal, parallel with the camshaft centreline. Make sure the rocker case dowels are fitted. Fit the rocker case onto the head. Lubricate the 12 mm nut threads and seating surface and each side of the nut washers with molybdenum disulphide oil (engine oil and molybdenum grease mixed in the ratio 10:1). Fit the nuts with the washers and tighten them evenly and a little at a time in a criss-cross sequence to the torque setting specified at the beginning of the Chapter. While doing this, don't let the camshafts rotate, or the Plastigauge will be disturbed and you will have to start again.

9 Now unscrew the rocker case nuts evenly

13.3 Remove the decompression mechanism from the end of the shaft if required

13.5 Check all corresponding bearing surfaces for wear and damage

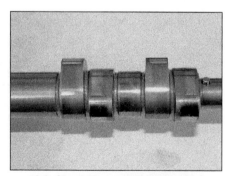

13.6 Check the camshaft lobes and measure their height

13.11 Camshaft sprocket bolts (arrowed)

and a little at a time in a criss-cross sequence, and lift off the case.

10 To determine the oil clearance, compare the crushed Plastigauge (at its widest point) on each journal to the scale printed on or contained in the Plastigauge container. Compare the results to this Chapter's Specifications. If the oil clearance is greater than specified, replace the camshaft with a new one and recheck the clearance. If the clearance is still too great, also replace the cylinder head and rocker case with new ones.

11 Except in cases of oil starvation, the cam chain should wear very little – refer to Section 24 to remove and check it if required. Check the sprocket for wear, cracks and other damage, and replace it with a new one if necessary. If the sprocket teeth are worn, the cam chain is also worn, and so probably is the sprocket on the crankshaft. If severe wear is apparent, the entire engine should be disassembled for inspection. The camshaft sprockets can be replaced separately from the camshafts **(see illustration)**. The sprocket for the front cylinder camshaft is marked F, and that for the rear is marked R. Clean the threads of the bolts and apply non-permanent thread locking agent, and tighten them to the torque listed in this Chapter's Specifications.

Decompression mechanism inspection

12 If the decompression mechanism fails, either compression will not be released when starting the engine, or decompression remains when the engine has started and is running. Check the action of the mechanism **(see illustration)**. Replace the mechanism with a new one if necessary.

Installation

13 If you removed the sprocket from the camshaft, refer to Step 11 and install it.

14 If removed, fit the decompression mechanism onto the camshaft, aligning the pin with the cut-out **(see illustration 13.3)** – make sure you fit the correct mechanism to the correct shaft according to the marks made on removal as they are different – on early models the mechanism for the rear camshaft has a yellow spring, while on all other models they are identifiable by the look of them from the inner face **(see illustration)**.

15 When turning the engine in any of the following three steps, make sure that the loose cam chain(s) is/are held taut to prevent it/them dropping and jamming.

16 If the camshafts from both cylinder heads have been removed, turn the engine anti-clockwise **(see illustration 11.6a)** until the index line marked **F** on the alternator rotor aligns with the static timing mark on the alternator inner cover on VN1500A and B models **(see illustration 11.6b)**, and the notch in the inspection hole on all other models **(see illustration 11.6c)**, so that the front piston is at TDC, and install the front cylinder camshaft as described in steps 19-on. Then turn the engine anti-clockwise 310° until the index line marked **R** on the rotor aligns with the static timing mark on VN1500A and B models and the notch in the inspection hole on all other models so the rear cylinder piston is at TDC,

and install the rear cylinder camshaft in the same way.

17 If only the camshaft from the front cylinder head has been removed, and the engine has been turned since removing it (or if you are any doubt as to the position of the engine), remove the rear cylinder rocker case cover(s) (see Section 10), then turn the engine until it is positioned as though you were going to remove the rear rocker case as described in Section 11, Step 6, then from there turn the engine anti-clockwise 410° so that the line marked **F** on the alternator rotor aligns with the static timing mark on VN1500A and B models and the notch in the inspection hole on all other models, so that the front piston is at TDC, and install the front cylinder camshaft as described in steps 19-on.

18 If only the camshaft from the rear cylinder head has been removed, and the engine has been turned since removing it (or if you are any doubt as to the position of the engine), remove the front cylinder rocker case cover(s) (see Section 10), then turn the engine until it is positioned as though you were going to remove the front rocker case as described in Section 11, Step 6, then from there turn the engine anti-clockwise 310° so that the line marked **R** on the alternator rotor aligns with the static timing mark on VN1500A and B models and the notch in the inspection hole on all other models, so that the rear piston is at TDC, and install the rear cylinder camshaft as described in steps 19-on.

19 Make sure the bearing surfaces in the cylinder head and the camshaft bearing journals are clean, then lubricate them with molybdenum disulphide oil (engine oil and molybdenum grease mixed in the ratio 10:1).

20 Make sure you have the correct camshaft for the cylinder being worked on – the rear cylinder camshaft has a groove cut in the section just behind the sprocket flange for

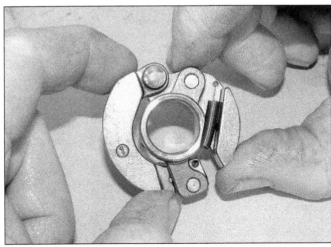

13.12 Check the movement of the weight and that it returns under spring pressure

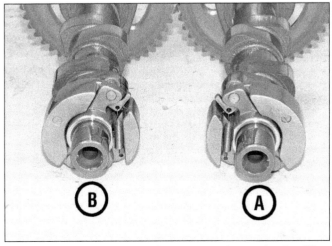

13.14 Front cylinder camshaft decompression mechanism (A), rear cylinder mechanism (B)

13.20a Rear cylinder camshaft has a groove (arrowed) in the rib

13.20b Front cylinder camshaft sprocket timing mark positions

13.20c Rear cylinder camshaft sprocket timing mark positions

13.20d Pull up on the front run of the chain to remove all slack

identification **(see illustration)**. Lay the camshaft onto the head with the lines on the sprocket parallel with the cylinder head top surface and the F or R line the correct way up and at the front **(see illustration)**. Fit the cam chain around the sprocket as you install the camshaft, pulling up on the front run of the chain to remove all slack in the front run between the crankshaft and the camshaft **(see illustration)**. With the camshaft seated on the head push the tensioner blade in with your finger or a suitable tool inserted in the tensioner hole to take up the slack in the chain and make sure the marks on the rotor and sprocket are in exact alignment as described. If not disengage the chain from the sprocket and turn the camshaft as required, then refit the chain and check the marks again.

21 Install the rocker case (see Section 11) – if both camshafts have been removed, after fitting one camshaft install the rocker case for that shaft before fitting the other shaft (see Section 11).

22 When both camshafts and rocker cases

and tensioners have been installed, but before fitting the rocker case covers, turn the engine anti-clockwise through two full turns and check again that the timing marks on both cylinders align correctly (see Step 6 in Section 11).

14 Cylinder heads –
removal and installation

Removal

1 Remove the engine from the frame (see Section 7).
2 Remove the carburetor(s) or throttle body if not already done (see Chapter 4A or 4B).
3 Unscrew the spark plug retainer from each head – to do this you need a 27 mm hex bit, available from Kawasaki (part no. 57001-1210) or from a good motorcycle accessory dealer or tool supplier. If you don't have the special tool, you can use a large bolt head to fit and either

thread nuts onto it, tighten them together, then fit a spanner onto the inner nut, or cut the bolt head off and weld it to a 3/8-inch drive socket adapter **(see illustration)**. Hook the cam chain onto some wire to keep it held up, then withdraw the retainer. Discard the O-rings on the retainer – new ones must be used.
4 Detach or release any other hoses or pipes and/or remove the air suction valves as

14.3 Fabricated tool made out of nuts and a bolt to remove the retainer (arrowed)

14.8 Carefully lift the head up off the cylinder

14.15 Fit the dowels (arrowed) then lay the new gasket on the cylinder

14.16 Each head is identified by a letter cast into it

required according to models and what has been removed/detached for engine removal.

5 Remove the rocker case and camshaft for the cylinder being worked on (see Sections 11 and 13).

6 On VN1500A and B models, if not already done when removing the rocker case(s), unscrew the oil pipe banjo bolts and bracket bolt and remove the pipe. Discard the sealing washers – new ones must be used.

7 Unscrew the two nuts from the underside of the cylinder head, one at the front and one at the back **(see illustrations 11.18a and b)**.

8 Have some rag to hand to catch any residual coolant. Lift the cylinder head off the cylinder **(see illustration)**. If the head is stuck, use two wooden dowels inserted into the intake or exhaust ports to lever the head off. Don't attempt to pry the head off by inserting a screwdriver between the head and the cylinder block – you'll damage the sealing surfaces. Note that the head for the front cylinder is marked F, and that for the rear is marked R – if you can't see the marks make your own.

9 Lift the head gasket off the cylinder **(see illustration 14.15)**. A new one must be used on installation.

10 Locate the two dowel pins, either in the underside of the head or the top of the cylinder, to make sure they haven't fallen into the engine. Remove them for safekeeping if loose.

11 Stuff a clean rag into the cam chain tunnel to prevent the entry of debris.

12 Check the cylinder head gasket and

the mating surfaces on the cylinder head and block for signs of leakage, which could indicate warpage. Refer to Section 15 and check the flatness of the cylinder head.

13 Clean all traces of old gasket material from the cylinder head and block. If a scraper is used, take care not to scratch or gouge the soft aluminium. Be careful not to let any of the gasket material fall into the crankcase, the cylinder bore or the water passages.

Installation

14 Wipe over the mating surfaces of the cylinder and cylinder head with solvent. Lubricate the cylinder bores with engine oil.

15 Make sure the dowels are in place, then lay the new gasket in place on the cylinder **(see illustration)**. Never reuse the old gasket and don't use any type of gasket sealant.

16 Make sure you have the cylinder head marked F for the front cylinder and that marked R for the rear **(see illustration)**, then carefully lower the head over the studs and onto the dowels and gasket **(see illustration 14.8)**. It is helpful to have an assistant support the camshaft chain with a piece of wire so it doesn't fall and become kinked or detached from the crankshaft. When the head is resting against the cylinder, wire the cam chain to another component to keep tension on it.

17 Fit the two nuts onto the underside of the cylinder head, one at the front and one at the back, and tighten them lightly at this stage **(see illustration)** – they will be fully tightened after installing the rocker case.

18 Fit new O-rings smeared with grease onto

the spark plug retainer **(see illustration)**. Lift the cam chain and insert the retainer, making sure it fits through the loop of the chain, then tighten the retainer to the torque listed in this Chapter's Specifications **(see illustration)**.

19 Install the other cylinder head if removed in the same way.

20 Install the camshafts and rocker cases (see Sections 11 and 13) – on VN1500A and B models, after fitting the cases fit the oil pipe (Section 11, step 21).

21 Connect any other hoses or pipes and/ or install the air suction valves as required according to models and what has been removed/detached.

22 Install the remaining components according to Section 11, then install the engine.

15 Cylinder heads and valves – disassembly, inspection and reassembly

1 Because of the complex nature of this job and the special tools and equipment required, most owners leave servicing of the valves, valve seats and valve guides to a professional. However, you can make an initial assessment of whether the valves are seating correctly, and therefore sealing, by tilting the head and pouring a small amount of solvent into each of the valve intake and exhaust ports in turn. If the solvent leaks past either valve into the combustion chamber area the valve is not seating correctly and sealing.

2 With the correct tools (a valve spring

14.17 Fit the nuts, but don't fully tighten them yet

14.18a Fit new O-rings (arrowed) . . .

14.18b . . . then lift the chain and fit the retainer through it

15.7a Fit the valve spring compressor as shown . . .

15.7b . . . making sure it locates correctly both on the top of the spring retainer . . .

compressor is essential – make sure it is suitable for motorcycle work), you can also remove the valves and associated components from the cylinder head, clean them and check them for wear to assess the extent of the work needed, and, unless seat cutting or guide replacement is required, grind in the valves and reassemble them in the head.

3 A dealer service department or specialist can replace the guides and re-cut the valve seats.

4 After the valve service has been performed, be sure to clean the head very thoroughly before installation to remove any metal particles or abrasive grit that may still be present from the valve service operations. Use compressed air, if available, to blow out all the holes and passages.

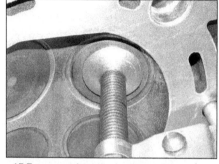

15.7c . . . and on the bottom of the valve

15.7d Remove the keepers . . .

Disassembly

5 Remove the cylinder head from the engine (see Section 14). Before the valves are removed, scrape away any traces of gasket material from the head gasket sealing surface. Work slowly and do not nick or gouge the soft aluminum of the head. Gasket removing solvents, which work very well, are available at most motorcycle shops and auto parts stores. Carefully scrape all carbon deposits out of the combustion chamber area. A hand held wire brush or a piece of fine emery cloth can be used once the majority of deposits have been scraped away. Do not use a

wire brush mounted in a drill motor, or one with extremely stiff bristles, as the head material is soft and may be eroded away or scratched by the wire brush.

6 Before proceeding, arrange to label and store the valves along with their related components so they can be kept separate and reinstalled in the same valve guides they are removed from (again, plastic bags work well for this).

7 Compress the valve spring on the first valve with a spring compressor, making sure it is correctly located onto each end of the valve assembly **(see illustration)** – on the top of the valve the adaptor needs to be about the same size as the spring retainer –

if it is too small it will be difficult to remove and install the keepers **(see illustration)**. On the underside of the head make sure the plate on the compressor only contacts the valve and not the soft aluminium of the head **(see illustration)** – if the plate is too big for the valve, use a spacer between them. Do not compress the springs any more than is absolutely necessary. Remove the keepers. Carefully release the valve spring compressor and remove the retainer, springs and the valve from the head **(see illustrations)**. If the valve binds in the guide (won't pull through), push it back into the head and deburr the area around the keeper groove with a very fine file or whetstone **(see illustration)**.

15.7e . . . the spring retainer and spring . . .

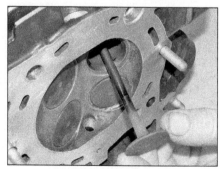

15.7f . . . and the valve

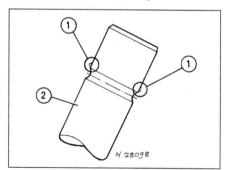

15.7g If the valve stem (2) won't pull through the guide, deburr the area (1) above the collet groove

15.9a Pull the seal off the valve stem . . .

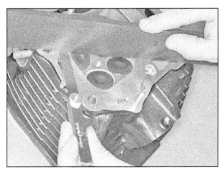

15.9b . . . then remove the spring seats

15.14a Check for warpage using a straight-edge and feeler gauge set to the maximum warpage . . .

8 Repeat the procedure for the remaining valves. Remember to keep the parts for each valve together so they can be reinstalled in the same location.

9 Once the valves have been removed and labeled, pull off the valve stem seals with pliers or a dedicated tool if available and discard them (the old seals should never be reused), then remove the spring seats **(see illustrations)**.

10 Next, clean the cylinder head with solvent and dry it thoroughly. Compressed air will speed the drying process and ensure that all holes and recessed areas are clean.

11 Clean all of the parts with solvent and dry them thoroughly. Do the parts from one valve at a time so that no mixing between valves occurs.

12 Scrape off any deposits that may have formed on the valve, then use a motorized wire brush to remove deposits from the valve heads and stems. Again, make sure the valves do not get mixed up.

Inspection

13 Inspect the head very carefully for cracks and other damage. If cracks are found, a new head will be required. Check the cam bearing surfaces for wear and evidence of seizure. Check the rocker arms and camshafts for wear as well (see Sections 12 and 13).

14 Using a precision straightedge and a feeler gauge, check the head gasket mating surface for warpage. Lay the straightedge lengthwise, across the head and diagonally (corner-to-corner), intersecting the head bolt holes. Try to slip a feeler gauge of the same thickness

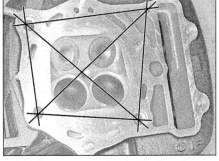

15.14b . . . measuring in the directions shown

as the warpage limit listed in this Chapter's Specifications under it, on either side of the combustion chamber **(see illustrations)**. If the feeler gauge can be inserted between the head and the straightedge, the head is warped and must either be machined or, if warpage is excessive, replaced with a new one.

15 Examine the valve seats. If they are pitted, cracked or burned, the head will require valve service that is beyond the scope of the home mechanic. Measure the valve seat width and compare it to this Chapter's Specifications **(see illustration)**. If it is not within the specified range, or if it varies around its circumference, valve service work is required.

16 Clean the valve guides to remove any carbon buildup, then flush them with solvent and dry them.

17 Next check the valve stem-to-guide

15.15 Measure the valve seat width

clearance using the wobble method as follows: fit each valve in its guide in turn so that its face is above the seat. Mount a dial gauge at right angles against the side of the valve stem as close to the cylinder head as possible and measure the amount of side clearance (wobble) between the valve stem and its guide in two directions **(see illustration)**. If the side clearance exceeds the limit specified, remove the valve and measure the valve stem diameter **(see illustration)**. Also measure the inside diameter of the guide with a small hole gauge and micrometer **(see illustration)**. Measure the guides at each end and at the centre to determine if they are worn unevenly. Replace any component that is worn beyond its specifications with a new one. If the valve guide is within specifications, but is worn unevenly, it should be replaced.

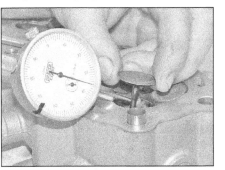

15.17a Measure the amount of valve wobble using a dial gauge as shown

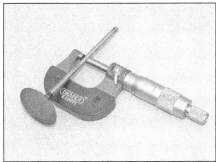

15.17b Measure the valve stem diameter with a micrometer

15.17c Measure the valve guide with a small bore gauge then measure the bore gauge with a micrometer

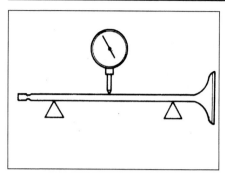

15.18 Check for runout in the valve stem using V-blocks and a dial gauge

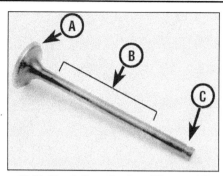

15.19 Check the valve face (A), stem (B) and keeper groove (C) for wear and damage

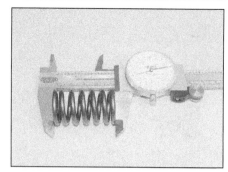

15.20a Measure the free length of the valve springs . . .

18 Check the valve stem for bending. Set the valve in a V-block with a dial indicator touching the middle of the stem **(see illustration)**. Rotate the valve and note the reading on the gauge. If the stem runout exceeds the value listed in this Chapter's Specifications, replace the valve.

19 Carefully inspect each valve face for cracks, pits and burned spots. Check the valve stem and the keeper groove area for cracks **(see illustration)**. Rotate the valve and check for any obvious indication that it is bent. Check the end of the stem for pitting and excessive wear. The presence of any of the above conditions indicates the need for valve servicing.

20 Check the end of each valve spring for wear and pitting. Measure the free length and compare it to this Chapter's Specifications **(see illustration)**. Any springs that are shorter than specified have sagged and should not be

reused. Stand the spring on a flat surface and check it stands square **(see illustration)**.

21 Check the spring retainers and keepers for obvious wear and cracks. Any questionable parts should not be reused, as extensive damage will occur in the event of failure during engine operation.

22 If the inspection indicates that no service work is required, the valve components can be reinstalled in the head.

Reassembly

23 Before installing the valves in the head, they should be lapped to ensure a positive seal between the valves and seats. This procedure requires fine valve lapping compound (available at auto parts stores) and a valve lapping tool (either hand-held or drill driven – note that some drill-driven tools specify using only a fine grinding compound). If a lapping tool is not available, a piece of rubber or plastic hose can be slipped over the

valve stem (after the valve has been installed in the guide) and used to turn the valve.

24 Apply a small amount of fine lapping compound to the valve face **(see illustration)**, then slip the valve into the guide. **Note:** *Make sure the valve is installed in the correct guide and be careful not to get any lapping compound on the valve stem.*

25 Attach the lapping tool to the valve and rotate the tool between the palms of your hands. Use a back-and-forth motion (as though rubbing your hands together) rather than a circular motion (i.e. so that the valve rotates alternately clockwise and anti-clockwise rather than in one direction only) **(see illustration)**. If a motorised tool is being used, take note of the correct drive speed for it – if your drill runs too fast and is not variable, use a hand tool instead. Lift the valve off the seat and turn it at regular intervals to distribute the grinding compound properly. Continue the grinding procedure until the valve face and seat contact area is of uniform width, and unbroken around the entire circumference.

26 Carefully remove the valve from the guide and wipe off all traces of lapping compound. Use solvent to clean the valve and wipe the seat area thoroughly with a solvent soaked cloth. Repeat the procedure for the remaining valves.

27 Working on one valve at a time, lay the spring seats in place in the cylinder head **(see illustration 15.9b)**.

28 Fit a new valve stem seal squarely onto the guide and push it on using a stem seal fitting tool or an appropriate size deep socket until it is felt to clip into place **(see illustrations)**. If

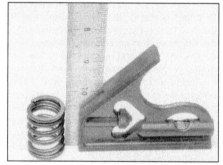
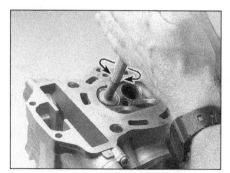

15.20b . . . and check them for bend

15.25 Using a valve lapping tool

15.24 Apply small dabs of the paste around the circumference of the valve

15.28a Fit a new valve stem seal . . .

15.28b . . . and press it squarely into place using a deep socket of the appropriate size

15.30a Fit the springs . . .

15.30b . . . then fit the retainer shouldered side down

15.33 Tap the top of each valve stem to seat the keepers

the seal gets cocked and distorts when fitting it use a new one.

29 Coat the valve stem with molybdenum disulphide grease then install it into its guide **(see illustration 15.7f)**. Check that the valve moves up-and-down freely in the guide.

30 Next fit the inner and outer springs, with their closer-wound coils facing down **(see illustration)**. Fit the spring retainer, with its shouldered side facing down so that it fits into the top of the springs **(see illustration)**.

31 Apply a small amount of grease to the keepers to help hold them in place. Compress the valve springs with a spring compressor, making sure it is correctly located onto each end of the valve assembly (see Step 7) **(see illustrations 15.7a, b and c)**. Do not compress the springs any more than is necessary to slip the keepers into place. Locate each keeper in turn into the groove in the valve stem using a screwdriver with a dab of grease on it **(see illustration 15.7d)**. Carefully release the compressor, making sure the keepers seat and lock in the retaining groove.

32 Repeat the procedure for the remaining valves. Remember to keep the parts for each valve together and separate from the other valves so they can be reinstalled in the same location.

33 Support the cylinder head on blocks so the valves can't contact the work surface, then

tap the end of each valve stem lightly to seat the keepers in their grooves **(see illustration)**.

 HAYNES HiNT *Check for proper sealing of the valves by pouring a small amount of solvent into each of the valve ports.* **If the solvent leaks past any valve into the combustion chamber the valve grinding operation on that valve should be repeated.**

16 Cylinders – removal, inspection and installation

Removal

1 Remove the engine from the frame (see Section 7).

2 Following the procedure given in Section 14, remove the cylinder head. Make sure the crankshaft is positioned at Top Dead Center (TDC) for the cylinder you're working on.

3 Remove the cam chain guide, noting how it locates **(see illustration 24.4)**. Note that the guide for the front cylinder is marked F, and that for the rear is marked R – if you can't see the marks make your own.

4 Get some absorbent rag or tissue to absorb the coolant in the cylinder jacket, or make a chute out of some flexible plastic that can channel the coolant into a container. Unscrew the drain bolt and drain the coolant from the cylinder **(see illustration)**. Discard the drain bolt sealing washer – a new one must be used.

5 Unscrew the two nuts securing the cylinder, one at the front and one at the back **(see illustration 16.4)**.

6 When removing the cylinder try not to let the chain drop – pass the chain down the tunnel and wire it to another component.

7 Lift the cylinder straight up to remove it **(see illustration)**. If it's stuck, tap gently around its perimeter with a soft-faced hammer. Don't attempt to pry between the block and the crankcase, as you will ruin the sealing surfaces. As you lift, keep a finger on the piston to prevent the connecting rod falling against the crankcase, and be careful not to let these drop into the engine. Note that the front cylinder is marked F, and the rear is marked R – if you can't see the marks make your own.

8 Stuff clean shop towels around the piston and into the cam chain tunnel. Remove the gasket and discard it – a new one must be used **(see illustration 16.17)**. Remove the dowels for safekeeping if loose.

9 Clean all traces of old gasket material

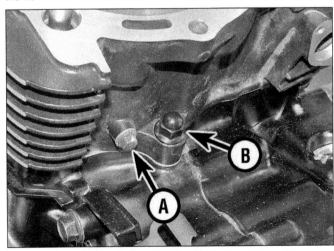

16.4 Cylinder drain bolt (A), retaining nut (B) – rear

16.7 Carefully lift the cylinder up off the crankcase

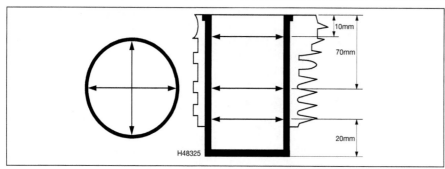

16.11a Measure the cylinder bore in the directions shown . . .

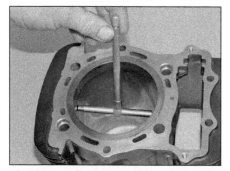

16.11b . . . using a telescoping gauge, then measure the gauge with a micrometer

from the mating surfaces of the cylinder and crankcase.

Inspection

Caution: *Don't attempt to separate the liners from the cylinder block.*

10 Check the cylinder walls carefully for scratches and score marks.

11 Using the appropriate precision measuring tools, check each cylinder's diameter 10 mm down from the top, 70 mm down from the top, and 20 mm up from the bottom of the cylinder bore, parallel to the crankshaft axis **(see illustrations)**. Next, measure each cylinder's diameter at the same three locations across the crankshaft axis. Compare the results to this Chapter's Specifications. If the cylinder walls are tapered, out-of-round, worn beyond the specified limits, or badly scuffed or scored, have them rebored and honed by a dealer service department or a motorcycle repair shop. If a rebore is done, oversize pistons and

16.21a Carefully lower the cylinder onto the piston . . .

16.17 Lay the new gasket over the dowels (arrowed) and onto the crankcase

rings will be required as well. **Note:** *Pistons are available in one oversize only – +0.5 mm (+0.020 in)*. Make sure the person doing the rebore maintains the specified piston-to-bore clearance with the new piston.

12 If the precision measuring tools are not available, a dealer service department or motorcycle repair shop will make the measurements and offer advice concerning servicing of the cylinders.

13 If they are in reasonably good condition and not worn to the outside of the limits, and if the piston-to-cylinder clearances can be maintained properly (see Section 17), then the cylinders do not have to be rebored; honing is all that is necessary.

14 To perform the honing operation you will need the proper size flexible hone with fine stones, or a "bottle brush" type hone, plenty of light oil or honing oil, some shop towels and an electric drill motor. Hold the cylinder block in a vise (cushioned with soft jaws or wood blocks)

16.21b . . . and carefully feed each ring into the bore as you lower the cylinder

when performing the honing operation. Mount the hone in the drill motor, compress the stones and slip the hone into the cylinder. Lubricate the cylinder thoroughly, turn on the drill and move the hone up and down in the cylinder at a pace which will produce a fine crosshatch pattern on the cylinder wall with the crosshatch lines intersecting at approximately a 60-degree angle. Be sure to use plenty of lubricant and do not take off any more material than is absolutely necessary to produce the desired effect. Do not withdraw the hone from the cylinder while it is running. Instead, shut off the drill and continue moving the hone up and down in the cylinder until it comes to a complete stop, then compress the stones and withdraw the hone. Wipe the oil out of the cylinder and repeat the procedure on the remaining cylinder. Remember, do not remove too much material from the cylinder wall. If you do not have the tools, or do not desire to perform the honing operation, a dealer service department or motorcycle repair shop will generally do it for a reasonable fee.

15 Next, the cylinders must be thoroughly washed with warm soapy water to remove all traces of the abrasive grit produced during the honing operation. Be sure to run a brush through the bolt holes and flush them with running water. After rinsing, dry the cylinders thoroughly and apply a coat of light, rust-preventative oil to all machined surfaces.

Installation

16 Check that the mating surfaces of the cylinder block and crankcase are free from oil or pieces of old gasket.

17 If removed, fit the dowels into the crankcase and push them firmly home. Remove the rags from around the piston and the cam chain tunnel, taking care not to let the connecting rod fall against the crankcase. Lay the new base gasket in place, locating it over the dowels and making sure all the holes align **(see illustration)**. Never re-use the old gasket.

18 Lubricate the cylinder bore, piston and rings with plenty of clean engine oil.

19 Slowly rotate the crankshaft until the piston is at top dead center.

20 Attach a piston ring compressor to the piston and compress the piston rings. A large hose clamp can be used instead – just make sure it doesn't scratch the piston, and don't tighten it too much. If the tools are not available you will have to compress and feed each ring into the bore by hand.

21 Make sure you fit the cylinder marked F at the front and that marked R at the rear. Install the cylinder over the piston and carefully lower it down until the piston crown fits into the cylinder liner **(see illustration)**. While doing this, pull the camshaft chain up, using a hooked tool or a piece of coat hanger. Push down on the cylinder, making sure the piston doesn't get cocked sideways and the rings enter the bore – if a compressor tool is used remove it as soon as the lower ring is in, and if a tool is not being used carefully compress and feed each ring into the bore by hand as it is lowered **(see illustration)**. A wood or plastic hammer handle can be used to gently tap the cylinder down, but don't use too much force or the piston will be damaged or a ring or rings could break.

22 When the cylinder seats on the crankcase fit the nuts and tighten them lightly at this stage **(see illustration 16.4)** – they will be fully tightened after installing the rocker case.

23 Fit the cam chain guides, making sure they seat correctly **(see illustration 24.4 and 24.10)** -- make sure you fit the guide marked F into the front cylinder and that marked R into the rear.

24 Hold the cam chains up and turn the crankshaft to check that everything moves as it should.

25 Fit the cylinder drain bolt using a new sealing washer **(see illustration 16.4)**.

26 Install the cylinder heads and all other removed components and assemblies.

17 Pistons – removal, inspection and installation

1 The pistons are attached to the connecting rods with piston pins that are a slip fit in the pistons and rods.

2 Before removing the pistons from the rods, if not already in place stuff a clean shop towel into each crankcase hole, around the connecting rod. This will prevent the circlips from falling into the crankcase if they are inadvertently dropped.

Removal

3 Using a sharp scribe, scratch F or R denoting the position of each piston (front or rear cylinder) into its crown. Each piston should have either an arrow pointing toward the front of the engine or a circle in the forward side of the piston, according to model. If it is not visible, scribe an arrow into the front side of the piston crown before removal.

4 Support the piston and remove the circlip on one side with needle-nose pliers or a pointed tool **(see illustration)**. Push the piston pin out from the other side with fingers **(see illustration)**. If the pin won't come out, heat the piston using a hot air gun to expand it.

Inspection

5 Before the inspection process can be carried out, the pistons must be cleaned and the old piston rings removed.

6 Using a piston ring installation tool if required, or your fingers, carefully remove the rings from the pistons (see Section 18). Do not nick or gouge the pistons in the process. Carefully note which way up each ring fits and in which groove as they must be installed in their original positions if being reused.

7 Scrape all traces of carbon from the tops of the pistons. A hand-held wire brush or a piece of fine emery cloth can be used once most of the deposits have been scraped away. Do not, under any circumstances, use a wire brush

17.4a Prise out the circlip using a suitable tool in the notch . . .

mounted in a drill motor to remove deposits from the pistons; the piston material is soft and will be eroded away by the wire brush.

8 Use a piston ring groove cleaning tool to remove any carbon deposits from the ring grooves. If a tool is not available, a piece broken off the old ring will do the job. Be very careful to remove only the carbon deposits. Do not remove any metal and do not nick or gouge the sides of the ring grooves.

9 Once the deposits have been removed, clean the pistons with solvent and dry them thoroughly. Make sure the oil return holes below the oil ring grooves are clear.

10 If the pistons are not damaged or worn excessively and if the cylinders are not rebored, new pistons will not be necessary. Normal piston wear appears as even, vertical wear on the thrust surfaces of the piston and slight looseness of the top ring in its groove. New piston rings, on the other hand, should always be used when an engine is rebuilt.

11 Carefully inspect each piston for cracks around the skirt, at the pin bosses and at the ring lands.

12 Look for scoring and scuffing on the thrust faces of the skirt, holes in the piston crown and burned areas at the edge of the crown. If the skirt is scored or scuffed, the engine may have been suffering from overheating and/or abnormal combustion, which caused excessively high operating temperatures. The oil pump and cooling system should be checked thoroughly. A hole in the piston crown, an extreme to be sure, is an indication that abnormal combustion (pre-ignition)

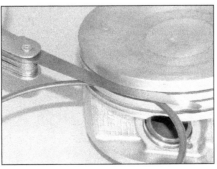

17.13 Measure the piston ring-to-groove clearance with a feeler gauge

17.4b . . . then push out the pin and separate the piston from the rod

was occurring. Burned areas at the edge of the piston crown are usually evidence of spark knock (detonation). If any of the above problems exist, the causes must be corrected or the damage will occur again.

13 Measure the piston ring-to-groove clearance by laying each piston ring in its groove and slipping a feeler gauge in beside it **(see illustration)**. Make sure you have the correct ring for the groove (see Section 18, Step 11). Check the clearance at three or four locations around the groove. If the clearance is greater than specified, measure the thickness of each ring and the width of each groove and replace the components worn beyond their limits with new ones, though if wear like this is evident it is advisable to replace all pistons and rings as a complete new set.

14 Check the piston-to-bore clearance by measuring the bore (see Section 16) and the piston diameter. Make sure that the pistons and cylinders are correctly matched. Measure the piston across the skirt on the thrust faces at a 90-degree angle to the piston pin, about 5 mm up from the bottom of the skirt **(see illustration)**. Subtract the piston diameter from the bore diameter to obtain the clearance. If it is greater than specified, the cylinders will have to be rebored and new oversized pistons and rings installed. If the appropriate precision measuring tools are not available, have the cylinders and pistons checked by a dealer service department or a motorcycle repair shop.

15 Apply clean engine oil to the pin, insert it into the piston and check for freeplay

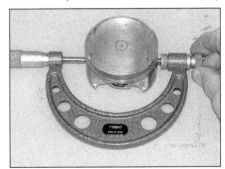

17.14 Measure the piston diameter with a micrometer at the specified distance from the bottom of the skirt

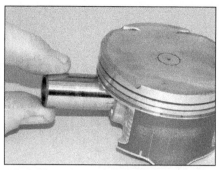

17.15 Fit the pin into the piston and check for any freeplay

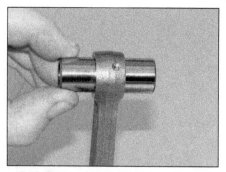

17.16 Fit the pin into the connecting rod and check for any freeplay

17.21a Seat the piston on the connecting rod . . .

by rocking the pin back-and-forth **(see illustration)**. If the pin is loose, new pistons and pins must be installed.

16 Repeat Step 15, this time inserting the pin into the connecting rod **(see illustration)**. Replace the piston and pin if the pin is worn; replace the connecting rod if the pin bore is worn.

17 Refer to Section 18 and install the rings on the pistons.

Installation

18 Make sure there is plenty of rag stuffed around each connecting rod to prevent anything falling into the engine.

19 Lubricate the piston pin, the piston pin bore and the connecting rod small-end bore with molybdenum disulphide oil (engine oil and molybdenum grease mixed in the ratio 10:1).

20 When fitting the pistons onto the connecting rods make sure the arrow points to the front of the engine or the circle on the piston crown faces the front of the engine.

21 Fit a **new** circlip into one side of the piston (do not reuse old circlips). Line up the piston on its correct connecting rod, and insert the piston pin from the other side **(see illustrations)**. Secure the pin with the other **new** circlip **(see illustration)**. When fitting the circlips, compress them only just enough to fit them in the piston, and make sure they are properly seated in their grooves with the open end away from the removal notch.

22 Install the cylinder (see Section 16).

17.21b . . . then push the pin through . . .

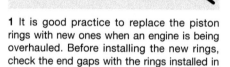

18 Piston rings – installation

1 It is good practice to replace the piston rings with new ones when an engine is being overhauled. Before installing the new rings, check the end gaps with the rings installed in the bore, as follows.

2 Lay out the pistons and the new ring sets so the rings will be matched with the same piston and cylinder during the end gap measurement procedure and engine assembly.

3 Insert the top (No. 1) ring into the bottom of the cylinder and square it up with the cylinder walls by pushing it in with the top of the piston **(see illustrations)**. The ring should be about one inch above the bottom edge of the cylinder. To measure the end gap, slip a feeler gauge between the ends of the

17.21c . . . and fit a new circlip into the groove

ring and compare the measurement to the Specifications **(see illustration)**.

4 If the gap is larger or smaller than specified, double check to make sure that you have the correct rings before proceeding.

5 If the gap is too small, the ring ends may come in contact with each other during engine operation, which can cause serious damage.

6 Excess end gap is not critical unless it is greater than the specified limit for the ring being checked. Again, double check to make sure you have the correct rings for your engine.

7 Repeat the procedure for each ring that will be installed in the first cylinder and for each ring in the remaining cylinder. Remember to keep the rings, pistons and cylinders matched up.

8 Once the ring end gaps have been checked/corrected, the rings can be installed on the pistons.

18.3a Fit the ring in the bore . . .

18.3b . . . and set it square using the piston . . .

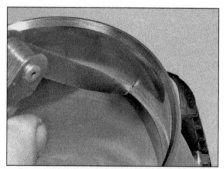

18.3c . . . then measure the end gap using a feeler gauge

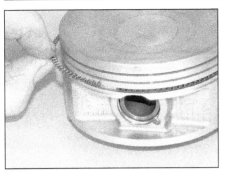

18.9a Fit the oil ring expander in its groove . . .

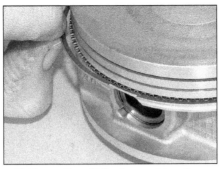

18.9b . . . then fit the lower side rail . . .

18.9c . . . and the upper side rail on each side of it

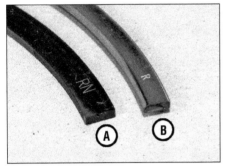

18.11a Note the letters on the rings which must face up – middle ring (A), top ring (B)

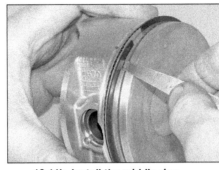

18.11b Install the middle ring . . .

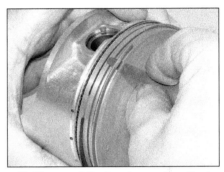

18.13 . . . and the top ring as described

9 The oil control ring (lowest on the piston) is installed first. It is composed of three separate components. Slip the expander into the groove, making sure the ends butt against each other and do not overlap **(see illustration)**. Next install the lower side rail **(see illustration)**. Do not use a piston ring installation tool on the oil ring side rails as they may be damaged. Instead, place one end of the side rail into the groove between the spacer expander and the ring land. Hold it firmly in place and slide a finger around the piston while pushing the rail into the groove. Next, install the upper side rail in the same manner **(see illustration)**.

10 After the three oil ring components have been installed, check to make sure that both the upper and lower side rails can be turned smoothly in the ring groove.

11 Install the second compression ring (middle ring) next. It can be readily distinguished from the top compression ring by the letters RN and its cross-section shape **(see illustration)**. Fit the ring with the RN mark on one end facing up. Do not mix the top and middle rings **(see illustration)**.

12 To avoid breaking the ring, use a piston ring installation tool and make sure that the identification mark is facing up. Fit the ring into the middle groove on the piston. Do not expand the ring any more than is necessary to slide it into place.

13 Finally, install the top compression ring into the top groove in the same manner. Make sure the identifying mark R is facing up **(see illustration)**.

14 Repeat the procedure for the remaining piston and rings. Be very careful not to confuse the middle and top rings.

15 Once the rings have been properly installed, check they move freely without snagging and stagger the end gaps as shown, including those of the oil ring side rails **(see illustration)**.

19 Clutch release mechanism – removal, overhaul and installation

⚠ *Warning: If the master or release cylinder is in need of an overhaul all old fluid should be flushed from the system (see Step 58). Overhaul must be done in a spotlessly clean work area to avoid contamination and possible failure of the hydraulic system components. Do not, under any circumstances, use petroleum-based solvents to clean the parts – use DOT 4 fluid or denatured alcohol. To prevent damage from spilled fluid, always cover paintwork when working on the system.*

Master cylinder

Note: *If the master cylinder is being overhauled (usually due to sticking or poor action, or fluid leaks) read through the entire procedure first and make sure that you have obtained all the new parts required, including some new DOT 4 brake/clutch fluid – a rebuild kit is*

available that includes the piston, seal, cup and spring – do not reassemble the master cylinder without the rebuild kit – a new seal and cup must be used. The pushrod, rubber boot and circlip are available separately if required.

Removal

1 Disconnect the wiring connector from the

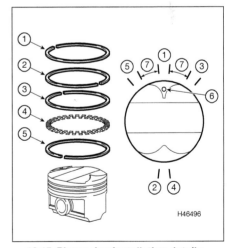

18.15 Piston ring installation details – stagger the ring end gaps as shown

1 Top ring	6 Mark on piston
2 Second ring	crown faces front
3 Upper side rail	of engine
4 Oil ring expander	7 30 ° to 40°
5 Lower side rail	

19.1 Disconnect the wiring connector

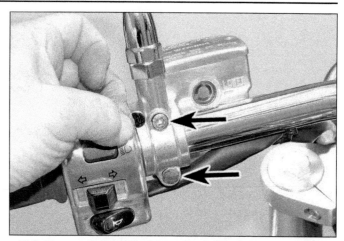

19.2 Remove the blanking caps where fitted, then unscrew the clamp bolts (arrowed)

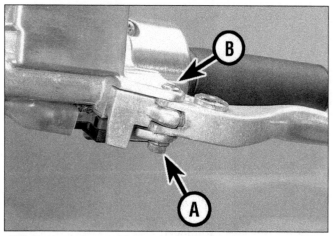

19.3 Unscrew the nut (A) then the screw (B) and remove the lever

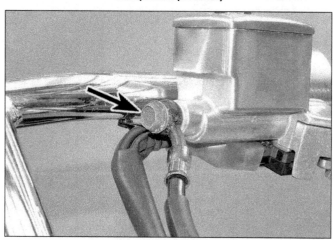

19.5 Clutch hose banjo bolt (arrowed)

clutch switch **(see illustration)**. Remove the mirror (see Chapter 8).
2 If the master cylinder is just being displaced, unscrew the master cylinder clamp bolts and remove the clamp, then position the master cylinder assembly clear of the handlebar **(see illustration)**. Ensure no strain is placed on the

hydraulic hose. Keep the reservoir upright to prevent air entering the system.
3 If the master cylinder is being overhauled remove the locknut from the underside of the lever pivot bolt, then unscrew the bolt **(see illustration)**.
4 Slacken the reservoir cover screws.

5 Unscrew the clutch hose banjo bolt and detach the banjo union, noting its alignment with the master cylinder, and catching any residual fluid in a rag **(see illustration)**. Use plastic foodwrap to seal the banjo union and secure the hose in an upright position to minimise fluid loss if the system hasn't been drained. Discard the sealing washers as new ones must be fitted on reassembly.
6 Unscrew the master cylinder clamp bolts and remove the clamp, then lift the master cylinder and reservoir away from the handlebar **(see illustration 19.2)**.
7 Remove the reservoir cover, diaphragm plate and diaphragm. Drain the brake fluid from the master cylinder and reservoir into a suitable container. Wipe any remaining fluid out of the reservoir with a clean rag.
8 If required, undo the screw securing the clutch switch and remove the switch.

Overhaul

9 Carefully remove the pushrod and rubber boot from the master cylinder **(see illustration)**.
10 Depress the piston and use circlip pliers to remove the circlip, then slide out the

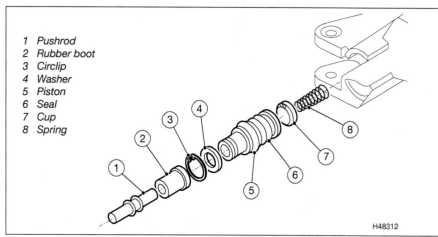

1 Pushrod
2 Rubber boot
3 Circlip
4 Washer
5 Piston
6 Seal
7 Cup
8 Spring

H48312

19.9 Clutch master cylinder components

washer, piston assembly and spring, noting how they fit. If they are difficult to remove, apply low pressure compressed air to the fluid outlet. Lay the parts out in the proper order to prevent confusion during reassembly.

11 Clean the master cylinder and reservoir with clean brake/clutch fluid. If compressed air is available, blow it through the fluid galleries to ensure they are clear (make sure the air is filtered and unlubricated).

Caution: Do not, under any circumstances, use a petroleum-based solvent to clean master cylinder parts.

12 Check the master cylinder bore for corrosion, scratches, nicks and score marks. If damage or wear is evident, the master cylinder must be replaced with a new one. If the master cylinder is in poor condition, then the release cylinder should be checked as well.

13 The piston, seal, cup and spring are all included in the master cylinder rebuild kit. Use all of the new parts, regardless of the apparent condition of the old ones. Lubricate the master cylinder bore with new brake fluid.

14 Smear the cup with silicone grease or new brake fluid. Fit the open side of the cup onto the narrow end of the spring, locating the peg in the hole where present. Fit the spring wide end first into the master cylinder, and push the cup in, making sure its lip does not turn inside out.

15 If not already in place smear the seal with silicone grease or new brake fluid and fit it into its groove in the piston so the flared side will fit into the master cylinder first.

16 Lubricate the piston and seal with silicone grease or clean brake fluid. Slide the piston into the master cylinder and up against the cup and spring. Make sure the lips on the seal do not turn inside out. Push the piston in to compress the spring, then fit the washer and the new circlip, making sure it locates in the groove.

17 Smear the pushrod and rubber boot with silicone grease. Lubricate the pushrod tips and inside the rubber boot with silicone grease. Fit the pushrod into the boot so the rounded end will fit into the master cylinder and locate the outer lip of the boot in the groove. Press the wide rim of the boot into place in the end of the cylinder.

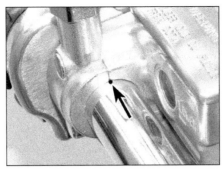

19.19 Align the clamp joint with the punch mark (arrowed)

Installation

18 If removed, fit the clutch switch onto the master cylinder.

19 Attach the master cylinder to the handlebar, aligning the clamp joint with the punch mark on the top of the handlebar, then fit the back of the clamp with the mirror mount facing up **(see illustration)**. Tighten the upper bolt to the torque listed in this Chapter's Specifications, then tighten the lower bolt.

20 Connect the clutch hose to the master cylinder, using new sealing washers on each side of the banjo fitting. Align the hose as noted on removal **(see illustration 19.5)**. Tighten the banjo bolt to the torque listed in this Chapter's Specifications.

21 Install the clutch lever – tighten the pivot bolt lightly, then tighten the locknut **(see illustration 19.3)**. Check the action of the lever.

22 Connect the clutch switch wiring **(see illustration 19.1)**.

23 Fill the fluid reservoir with new DOT 4 fluid (see *Pre-ride checks*). Refer to Step 44 and bleed the air from the system.

24 Check the operation of the clutch before riding the motorcycle.

Release cylinder

Note: *If the release cylinder is being overhauled (usually due to sticking or poor action, or fluid leaks) read through the entire procedure first and make sure that you have obtained all the new parts required, including some new DOT 4 brake/clutch fluid – do not reassemble*

19.26 Clutch hose banjo bolt (arrowed)

the release cylinder using the old seal – a new one must be used.

Removal

25 On all models except VN1500A and B and Drifter 1999 and 2000 (J1 and J2) models remove the shift pedal(s) (see Section 21), then remove the left side engine cover **(see illustration 7.37)**. On Drifter 1999 and 2000 (J1 and J2) models remove the connector cover from the top of the alternator cover, noting the collars and dampers and how they locate.

26 If required unscrew the clutch hose banjo bolt and detach the banjo union, noting its alignment with the master cylinder, and catching any residual fluid in a rag **(see illustration)**. Use plastic foodwrap to seal the banjo union and secure the hose in an upright position to minimise fluid loss if the system hasn't been drained. Discard the sealing washers as new ones must be fitted on reassembly.

27 Unscrew the release cylinder bolts, noting the wiring guide and how it locates where fitted, and remove the cylinder, taking care to catch residual fluid in a rag **(see illustration)**. Remove the spacer/gasket and discard it as a new one must be used. If the cylinder is not being overhauled fit cable-ties around the cylinder and piston to prevent the piston creeping out **(see illustration)**.

28 If required (for example if you are going to remove the front bevel gear housing) withdraw the pushrod, noting which way round it fits **(see illustration)**. Check the condition of the

19.27a Unscrew the bolts (arrowed), noting the wiring guide

19.27b Use cable-ties to prevent piston creep

19.28a Withdraw the pushrod (arrowed) if required

19.28b Lever the seal out

pushrod seal. If it has been leaking, hook or lever it out **(see illustration)**.

Overhaul

29 Clean the exterior of the cylinder with denatured alcohol or brake system cleaner.

30 Withdraw the piston from the cylinder **(see illustration)**. If the piston cannot be withdrawn by hand, it can be pushed out by applying compressed air to the clutch hose union hole. Only low pressure should be required, such as is generated by a foot pump. Wrap the release cylinder in a wad of rag to prevent the piston being forcibly expelled.

31 Remove the spring.

32 Carefully remove the fluid seal from the piston, noting which way round it fits. Discard the seals as a new one must be used.

33 Clean the piston and cylinder with clean brake fluid or denatured alcohol. If compressed air is available, use it to dry the parts thoroughly (make sure it's filtered and unlubricated).

Caution: Do not, under any circumstances, use a petroleum-based solvent to clean release cylinder parts.

34 Inspect the cylinder bore and piston for signs of corrosion, nicks and burrs and loss of plating. If surface defects are present, the cylinder assembly must be replaced with a new one. If it is in bad shape the master cylinder should also be checked.

35 Lubricate the fluid seal with new brake/clutch fluid. Fit the fluid seal onto the piston so its flared side will face into the cylinder.

36 Fit the narrow end of the spring over the boss on the inner end of the piston.

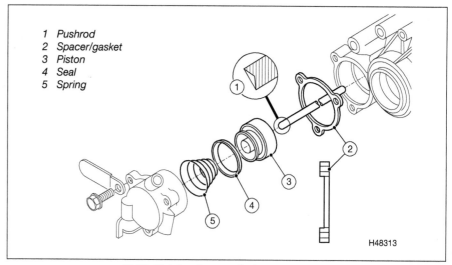

1 Pushrod
2 Spacer/gasket
3 Piston
4 Seal
5 Spring

H48313

19.30 Clutch release cylinder components

37 Lubricate the cylinder with clean brake fluid and fit the spring and piston into the bore. Make sure the spring remains correctly positioned and make sure the fluid seal does not dislodge or turn inside out as you push it in. Using your thumbs, push the piston all the way in, making sure it enters the bore squarely.

Installation

38 Clean the release cylinder and crankcase mating surfaces. Clean the threads of the bolts. Remove the cable-ties from around the cylinder and piston if fitted.

39 If removed fit a new pushrod seal **(see illustration)**. Make sure the pushrod is straight and clean, then smear the shaft with oil and the flat end with molybdenum disulphide grease, then slide it into place flat end first so the cupped end will face the release cylinder **(see illustration)**.

40 Smear molybdenum disulphide grease into the centre of the piston where the pushrod seats. Fit a new gasket/spacer with the stepped side facing out, then fit the release cylinder and tighten the bolts, not forgetting the wiring guide where fitted **(see illustration)**.

41 If detached connect the clutch hose to the release cylinder, using new sealing washers on

each side of the banjo fitting. Align the hose as noted on removal **(see illustration 19.26)**. Tighten the banjo bolt to the torque listed in this Chapter's Specifications.

42 Fill the master cylinder to the correct level with new DOT4 hydraulic fluid (see *Pre-ride checks*) and bleed the hydraulic system (see Step 44). Check for leaks and thoroughly test the operation of the clutch before riding the motorcycle.

43 Install the engine cover or connector cover as required according to model.

Clutch release mechanism bleeding

44 Bleeding the clutch is simply the process of removing air from the clutch fluid reservoir, the hose and the release cylinder. Bleeding is necessary whenever an hydraulic connection is loosened, after a component or hose is replaced with a new one, or when the master cylinder or release cylinder is overhauled. Leaks in the system may also allow air to enter, but leaking clutch fluid will reveal their presence and warn you of the need for repair.

45 To bleed the clutch, you will need some new DOT 4 brake/clutch fluid, a length of clear flexible hose, a small container partially filled with clutch fluid, some rags, a ring spanner to fit the release cylinder bleed valve,

19.39a Fit a new pushrod seal

19.39b Fit the pushrod flat-end first so the cupped end faces out

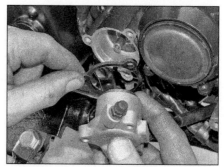

19.40 Fit the release cylinder using a new spacer/gasket

19.48 Pull the cap off the bleed valve (arrowed)

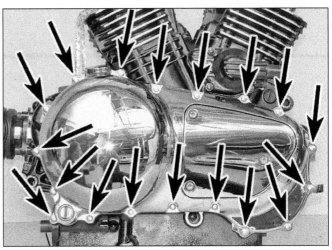

20.4 Right crankcase cover bolts (arrowed)

and to make the task simpler an assistant. Bleeding kits that include the hose, a one-way valve and a container are available relatively cheaply from a good auto store, and simplify the task as you don't need an assistant. Alternatively you can use a commercially available vacuum-type bleeding tool – follow the manufacturer's instructions.

46 On all models except VN1500A and B and Drifter 1999 and 2000 (J1 and J2) models remove the shift pedal(s) (see Section 21), then remove the left side engine cover **(see illustration 7.37)**. On Drifter 1999 and 2000 (J1 and J2) models remove the connector cover from the top of the alternator cover, noting the collars and dampers and how they locate.

47 Remove the reservoir cap, diaphragm plate (where fitted) and diaphragm. Slowly pump the clutch lever a few times, until no air bubbles can be seen floating up from the holes in the bottom of the reservoir. This bleeds the air from the master cylinder end of the line. Temporarily refit the reservoir cap.

48 Pull the dust cap off the end of the bleed valve **(see illustration)**. Fit a ring spanner onto the valve, positioning it so it can turn a ¼ turn anti-clockwise without snagging. Attach one end of the clear vinyl or plastic hose to the bleed valve and submerge the other end in the clean clutch fluid in the container.

49 Check the fluid level in the reservoir. Do not allow the fluid level to drop below the lower mark during the procedure.

50 Carefully pump the clutch lever three or four times, then hold it in and open the bleed valve. When the valve is opened, clutch fluid will flow out of the bleed pipe and into the clear tubing, and the lever will move toward the handlebar. If there is air in the system there will be air bubbles in the fluid coming out of the pipe.

51 Tighten the bleed valve, then release the clutch lever gradually. Repeat the process until

no air bubbles are visible in the fluid leaving the pipe, topping-up the reservoir as required. On completion, disconnect the hose, then tighten the bleed valve and fit the dust cap.

52 Check the fluid level in the reservoir, then fit the diaphragm, diaphragm plate and cover (see *Pre-ride checks*). Wipe up any spilled clutch fluid. Check the entire system for fluid leaks.

Fluid change

53 Changing the clutch fluid is a similar process to bleeding the clutch and requires the same tools (see Step 45) plus a syringe for siphoning the fluid out of the reservoir (though if one isn't available it is no problem to displace the reservoir and tip the fluid out, or to soak up with some kitchen towel or similar). Make sure that the container is large enough to take all the old fluid when it is flushed out of the system.

54 Follow Steps 46 and 48, then remove the reservoir cap, diaphragm plate (where fitted) and diaphragm and siphon the old fluid out of the reservoir. Fill the reservoir with new clutch fluid, then carefully pump the clutch lever three or four times and hold it in while opening the bleed valve. When the valve is opened, clutch fluid will flow out of the release cylinder into the clear tubing.

55 Tighten the bleed valve, then release the clutch lever gradually. Repeat the process until new fluid can be seen emerging from the release cylinder bleed valve – keep the reservoir topped-up with new fluid to above the LOWER level at all times or air may enter the system and greatly increase the length of the task.

> **HAYNES HiNT** *Old clutch fluid is invariably darker in colour than new fluid, making it easy to see when all old fluid has been expelled from the system.*

56 Disconnect the hose, then tighten the bleed valve and fit the dust cap.

57 Top-up the reservoir, then fit the diaphragm, diaphragm plate and cap (see *Pre-ride checks*). Wipe up any spilled clutch fluid. Check the entire system for fluid leaks.

Draining the system for overhaul

58 Draining the brake fluid is again a similar process to bleeding the brakes. Follow the procedure described above for changing the fluid, but quite simply do not put any new fluid into the reservoir – the system fills itself with air instead. An alternative is to use a commercially available vacuum-type brake bleeding tool – follow the manufacturer's instructions.

20 Clutch – removal, inspection and installation

Clutch removal

Note: *An air impact wrench is required to slacken the clutch nut to avoid over-loading the back-torque limiter mechanism.*

1 Drain the engine oil (see Chapter 1).

2 Remove the front cylinder exhaust (see Chapter 4A or 4B).

3 Refer to Section 7 and displace the frame member from the right side of the frame and lay it on some rag on the ground, making sure no strain is placed on the rear brake hose.

4 Unscrew the right crankcase cover bolts and remove the cover **(see illustration)** – there are a couple of leverage points to help release the cover if necessary. **Note:** *As each bolt is removed, store it in its relative position in a cardboard template of the crankcase halves (see illustration 25.11c). This will ensure all bolts are installed in the correct location on reassembly.* Remove the gasket and discard it – a new one must be used.

5 Release the retaining ring and remove the

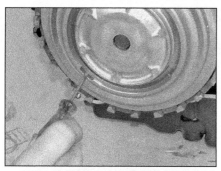

20.5a Release the retaining ring and remove the spring plate

20.5b Draw the pushrod end-piece out, noting the washer and bearing

20.6 Use an air wrench to unscrew the nut

spring plate **(see illustration)**. Remove the pushrod end piece along with its washer and needle bearing **(see illustration)**.

6 Unscrew the clutch nut using an air wrench **(see illustration)**.

20.7 Remove the springs and holder as an assembly

7 Remove the spring holder assembly, keeping all components together and in order **(see illustration)**.

8 Draw the clutch assembly off the shaft **(see illustration)**. Slide the needle bearing, sleeve

20.8 Draw the rest of the clutch off the shaft as an assembly

and inner thrust washer off the shaft **(see illustrations 20.20c, b and a)**.

9 To disassemble the clutch assembly remove the pressure plate and the clutch plates – keep the plates in order if they are being re-used **(see illustration)**.

10 Remove the clutch centre and back-torque limiter from the housing, noting the washer and drive sleeve **(see illustrations 20.23b and a)**.

Inspection

11 Examine the splines on both the inside and the outside of the drive sleeve and in the back-torque assembly **(see illustration)**. If any wear is evident, replace the components with new ones.

12 Measure the free height of the clutch diaphragm spring and compare the results to this Chapter's Specifications **(see illustration)**. If the spring has sagged, or if cracks are noted, replace it with a new one.

13 If the lining material of the friction plates smells burnt or if it is glazed, new parts are required. If the metal clutch plates are scored or discolored, they must be replaced with new ones. Measure the thickness of each friction plate **(see illustration)** and compare the results to this Chapter's Specifications. Replace the friction plates as a set if they are near the wear limit.

14 Lay all metal and friction plates, one at a time, on a perfectly flat surface (such as a piece of plate glass) and check for warpage by trying to slip a 0.012-inch (0.3 mm) feeler gauge between the flat surface and the plate **(see illustration)**. Do this at several places around

20.9 Remove the pressure plate and clutch plates

20.11 Check the splines for wear and damage

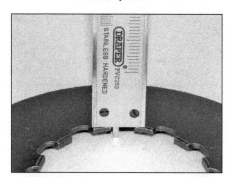

20.12 Measuring spring free height

20.13 Measuring clutch friction plate thickness

20.14 Check the plain plates for warpage

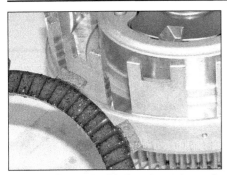

20.15a Check the friction plate tabs and housing slots . . .

20.15b . . . and the metal plate teeth and centre slots as described

20.17 Check the pushrod end-piece and its bearing

the plate's circumference. If the feeler gauge can be slipped under the plate, it is warped and should be replaced with a new one.

15 Inspect the friction plate tabs and the clutch housing slots for burrs and indentations on the edges **(see illustration)**. Similarly check for wear between the inner teeth of the metal plates and the slots in the clutch centre **(see illustration)**. Wear of this nature will cause clutch drag and slow disengagement during gear changes as the plates will snag when the pressure plate is lifted. With care a small amount of wear can be corrected by dressing with a fine file, but if this is excessive the worn components should be replaced with new ones.

16 Check the clutch pressure plate for wear and damage. If problems such as excessive engine braking and rear wheel hop have occurred the pressure plate gap could be too small. If clutch slip and a spongy feel to the lever (which bleeding the system does

not cure) occur the gap could be too big. Thinner and thicker metal plates are available to address this problem – if the gap is too small a thinner plate can be fitted to repair the problem, and if the gap is too big a thicker plate can be fitted. Before doing this make sure all other possible causes have been checked. Confirmation of an incorrect gap can be got through a complicated measurement procedure best carried out by a Kawasaki dealer – take the clutch assembly along and ask them to check.

17 Check the pushrod end-piece, washer and bearing for wear or damage and replace them with new ones if necessary **(see illustration)**.

18 Check the dogs and slots between the back-torque limiter and clutch centre for wear and damage **(see illustration)**. The back-torque limiter components can be removed and checked, but a press is needed. With the assembly face down and a suitable

interface between the press shaft and the spring holder, press the holder just enough to remove the retaining ring, then slowly release it and remove the outer spring seat, the springs and the inner spring seat, and the spacer and damper cam **(see illustration)**. Check all components for wear and damage, replacing parts with new ones as required. Reassembly the components in the hub in reverse order. Make sure the retaining ring is correctly located before releasing the press.

Installation

19 Clean all traces of old gasket material from the clutch cover and crankcase.

20 Lubricate the inner thrust washer, sleeve and needle roller bearing with clean engine oil and slide them in that order onto the transmission shaft **(see illustrations)**.

21 Fit the clutch housing over the needle bearing **(see illustration)**.

20.18a Check the dogs in the clutch centre and their slots in the limiter

20.18b Compress the springs as described and remove the retaining ring (arrowed)

20.20a Slide the thrust washer . . .

20.20b . . . sleeve . . .

20.20c . . . and needle bearing on . . .

20.21 . . . then fit the housing onto the bearing

20.22a Fit the thrust washer . . .

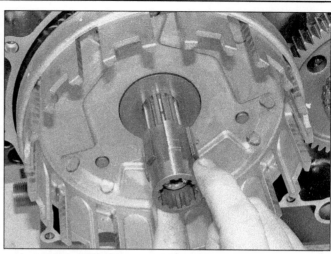

20.22b . . . and the drive sleeve

20.23a Fit the back-torque limiter onto the sleeve, engaging the splines . . .

20.23b . . . then fit the clutch centre onto the back-torque limiter, engaging the dogs in the slots

22 Fit the outer thrust washer followed by the drive sleeve, with its plain end outermost **(see illustrations)**.

23 Slide the back-torque limiter assembly onto the shaft, then fit the clutch centre onto the limiter **(see illustrations)**.

24 Coat the clutch friction and metal plates with engine oil. Install the clutch plates, starting with a friction plate, then fitting a metal plate, and alternating them until all are fitted **(see illustrations)**. On all but the last friction plate, position the friction plate tabs in the clutch housing main grooves. The tabs of the last friction plate go in the shallow grooves **(see illustration)**. Fit the pressure plate **(see illustration)**.

25 Where fitted fit the spring seat onto the spring holder **(see illustration)**. On all models fit the main diaphragm spring onto the holder, concave side facing up **(see illustration)**. Smear the back torque limiter springs with grease and fit them onto the spring holder, first one concave side up, second one concave side down, third one concave side up, as shown **(see illustrations)**.

26 Fit the spring holder assembly into the clutch **(see illustration 20.7)**.

27 Lubricate the clutch nut threads and seating surface with molybdenum disulphide oil (engine oil and molybdenum grease mixed in the ratio 10:1). Fit the nut and tighten it

20.24a Fit a friction plate . . .

20.24b . . . then a metal plate, and so on . . .

20.24c . . . locating the tabs of the final friction plate in the shallow slots . . .

20.24d . . . then fit the pressure plate

20.25a Fit the spring holder

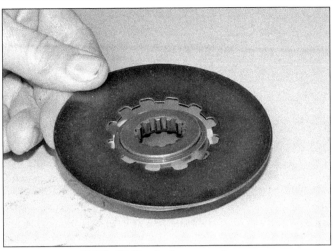

20.25b Fit the diaphragm spring . . .

20.25c . . . and the back-torque springs as described . . .

finger-tight **(see illustration 20.6)**. Lock the teeth of the primary drive and driven gear teeth together where they mesh on the top using a piece of aluminium (DO NOT use steel), an aluminium or copper washer or penny, or some stout rag **(see illustration)**. With the gears locked tighten the clutch nut to the torque listed in this Chapter's Specifications **(see illustration)**. Remove the locking tool.

28 Fit the pushrod end piece along with the needle bearing and washer **(see illustration 20.5b)**.

29 Fit the spring plate and secure it with the retaining ring, making sure it seats correctly in its groove **(see illustrations)** – if the plate does not seat correctly the release cylinder piston has probably crept out – push on the plate until it seats.

30 Make sure the right crankcase cover dowels are in place **(see illustration)**. Fit a new gasket. Position the cover on the engine, and tighten the bolts in a criss-cross pattern to the torque listed in this Chapter's Specifications **(see illustration)**.

31 Refer to Section 7 and install the frame member.

32 Install the front cylinder exhaust (see Chapter 4A or 4B).

33 Fill the crankcase with the recommended type and amount of engine oil (see Chapter 1).

20.25d . . . so the profile is as shown

20.27a Lock the primary drive and driven gear teeth as described . . .

20.27b . . . and tighten the clutch nut to the specified torque

20.29a Fit the spring plate . . .

20.29b . . . and secure it with the retaining ring

20.30a Locate the new gasket over the dowels (arrowed) . . .

20.30b . . . then fit the cover

21.2a Note the alignment of the punch mark . . .

21.2b . . . then unscrew the bolt and draw the pedal off the shaft

21.6a Note the alignment of the punch mark then unscrew the bolt and draw the arm off the shaft . . .

21 External shift mechanism – removal, inspection and installation

Shift pedal(s) and linkage

Removal

1 Remove the footpeg or board according to model (see Chapter 8). Before removing the shift pedal(s), note any existing manufacturer's alignment punch marks or other marks previously made where present, or make your own as described in the relevant Step if none are visible or they are unclear.

2 On VN1500A and B and Mean Streak models mark the alignment of the pedal clamp slit with the linkage shaft then unscrew the pedal pinch bolt and slide the pedal off the shaft (see illustrations).

3 On VN1500 Classic 1996 to 2004 (D, E and F models) models mark the alignment of the rear pedal shaft with the slit in the front pedal clamp, then unscrew the pedal pinch bolt and slide the pedal off the shaft. Now mark the alignment of the front pedal clamp slit with the linkage shaft then unscrew the pedal pinch bolt and slide the pedal off the shaft.

4 On all other models mark the alignment of the rear pedal clamp slit with the linkage shaft then unscrew the pedal pinch bolt and slide the pedal off the shaft. Now mark the

alignment of the front pedal clamp slit with the linkage shaft then unscrew the pedal pinch bolt and slide the pedal off the shaft.

5 Remove the left side engine cover **(see illustration 7.37)** (not fitted on Drifter J models). On all except VN1500A and B models remove the alternator outer cover (see Chapter 9, Section 34, Step 2) – there is no need to remove the engine from the frame.

6 To remove the linkage assembly mark the alignment of the linkage arm clamp slit with the shift mechanism shaft, then unscrew the pinch bolt and slide the arm off the shaft and remove the shaft stub from the inner cover **(see illustrations)**.

Installation

7 Clean and grease the pivot sections of the linkage shaft, and the splines on each shaft and in each pedal, as required according to model.

8 Fit the stub end of the linkage shaft into its bore in the alternator inner cover **(see illustration 21.6b)**. Fit the linkage arm onto the shift shaft, aligning the marks, and tighten the pinch bolt **(see illustration 21.6a)**.

9 On all except VN1500A and B models install the alternator outer cover (see Chapter 9).

10 The remainder of installation is the reverse of removal – align the pedal(s) as noted on removal.

Adjustment

11 Adjustment of the pedal position(s) can

be made to suit if required by moving the linkage arm around the shaft by one or more splines, following the procedure for your model above **(see illustration)**. Alternatively finer adjustment can be made by changing the linkage rod length – loosen the locknuts on the rod and rotate the rod to shorten or lengthen it, then tighten the locknuts. **Note:** *The linkage rod has left-hand threads on the rear end, meaning the locknut on that end will have to be turned clockwise to loosen it. The left-hand threads mean the rod will thread simultaneously into or out of the arm at each end depending on which way it is turned, thereby changing its effective length. There is a length specified for each model at the beginning of the Chapter which along with the standard alignment of the pedals on the shafts gives the recommended position of the pedal(s).*

Shift mechanism

Removal

12 Remove the front bevel gear housing (see Chapter 6).

13 Note how the shift shaft is installed, then push the pawl plate off the end of the shift drum and pull the shaft/arm assembly out of the crankcase together with the return spring **(see illustration)**. Note the washer on the shaft and take care not to lose it.

14 Note how the gear positioning lever and

21.6b . . . and the stub out of the cover

21.11 Adjustment can be made either by shifting the arm around the shaft, or slackening the locknuts (arrowed) and turning the rod

21.13 Push the pawl plate away and pull the shaft out

21.14 Unscrew the bolt and remove the lever and its spring

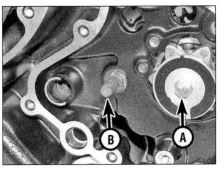

21.15 Neutral plate/shift drum cam screw (A), return spring pin (B)

21.17 Check the lever, roller and cam plate detents

the spring ends locate, then unscrew the bolt and remove the lever and spring **(see illustration)**.

15 If the neutral switch contact plate or shift drum cam needs to be removed, unscrew the bolt, then pull off the plate and cam, taking care not to lose the small locating pins between the plate and cam and between cam and drum **(see illustration)**.

Inspection

16 Check the shift shaft for bends and damage to the splines. If either condition is found it will have to be replaced with a new one.

17 Check the condition of the gear positioning lever and shift drum cam **(see illustration)**. Replace them if they are cracked or distorted.

18 Check the pawl plate arms for cracks, distortion and wear, paying special attention to the tips of the pawls where they engage the

shift drum cam **(see illustration)**. Make sure the pawl plate slides smoothly and freely on its backing plate and returns under pressure of its spring **(see illustration)**. Replace any worn or damaged components with new ones – all components are available individually.

19 Check the return spring pawl plate spring and lever spring for cracks and distortion **(see illustration)**. Make sure the return spring pin is tight **(see illustration 21.15)**. If it is loose, unscrew it, clean the threads and apply a non-permanent locking compound, then reinstall the pin and tighten it securely.

20 Replacement of the shaft seal in the front bevel gear housing is covered in Chapter 6.

Installation

21 If you removed the shift drum cam and neutral switch contact plate, install them, fitting the locating pins and aligning the cam and plate with them. Clean the threads of

the screw and apply non-permanent thread locking agent. Tighten the screw securely.

22 Clean the threads of the positioning lever bolt and apply non-permanent thread locking agent. Align the shift drum so it is in neutral and so that the roller will locate in the neutral detent. Install the positioning lever **(see illustration)**. Ensure that the legs of the return spring locate correctly against the crankcase and lever so it is tensioned. Tighten the bolt securely.

23 Slide the shift shaft into place, pushing the pawl plate against the spring to clear the shift drum cam **(see illustration 21.13)**. Once the shaft is in place, release the pawl and let it engage with the shift drum cam. Make sure the washer is on the shaft **(see illustration)**.

24 Check everything is correctly positioned **(see illustration)**.

25 Install the front bevel gear housing (see Chapter 6).

21.18a Check the selector arm pawls and cam plate pins

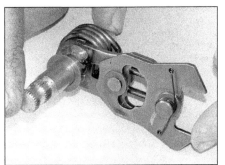

21.18b Check the pawl plate slides smoothly and easily

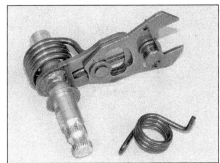

21.19 Check the springs

21.22 Fit the lever, locating the spring ends and roller while threading the bolt in

21.23 Make sure the washer is on the shaft

21.24 The installed assembly should be as shown

22.4 Remove the gear/weight assembly, then remove the sleeve from it

22.6 Note and mark the alignment of the gear with the weight, then lift the gear off

22.9 Alternate holed and solid segments as shown

22 Balancer weights, starter clutch and torque limiter – removal, inspection and installation

Left balancer weight

Removal

1 Remove the alternator inner cover (see Chapter 9, Section 34 or 35, according to model, following the relevant steps only – do not remove the alternator rotor yet if you need to hold it to unscrew the balancer weight bolt as in Step 2).

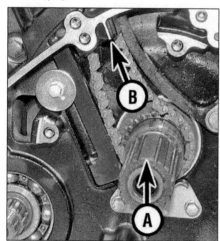

22.10 Turn the crankshaft to align the wide spline (A) with the static mark (B)

22.12a Slide the gear/weight assembly onto the shaft

2 Referring to the illustrations in Section 34 of Chapter 9, counter-hold the alternator rotor using a rotor strap or the left balancer weight using a holding tool and loosen the balancer bolt. Note that if you are also removing the right balancer weight/starter clutch assembly slacken the bolt now (see Step 21). Remove the alternator rotor, and where fitted the inner stator (see Chapter 9) – on models without an inner stator note the alignment of the rotor and balancer gear marks. On models with an inner stator remove a spark plug from each cylinder (see Chapter 1), then turn the engine using a socket on the rotor bolt and align the marks on the left balancer weight and the drive gear – these marks must be aligned when installing the rotor later. Slide the drive gear off.

3 Unscrew the balancer bolt and remove the washer (see illustration 22.14).

4 Draw the balancer driven gear/weight as an assembly off the shaft, noting the sleeve (see illustration).

5 On models with an inner alternator stator slide the balancer drive gear off the shaft.

6 If required lift the driven gear off the weight, noting its alignment (make a mark between them to be sure), and remove the rubber dampers, noting how they fit (see illustration).

Inspection

7 Check the balancer drive and driven gears for wear or damage and replace if problems are found.

8 Check the rubber dampers for wear or deterioration and replace them if their condition is in doubt.

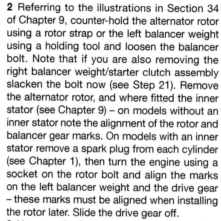

22.12b Fit the sleeve into the gear

Installation

9 If removed fit the damper segments onto the weight – on all except VN1500A and B models alternate solid segments with holed segments as shown (see illustration). Fit the gear onto the weight with the holes aligned as shown, or aligning the marks made on removal (see illustration 22.6).

10 Turn the crankshaft to align the wide spline with the timing mark on the crankcase (see illustration).

11 On models with an inner alternator stator slide the balancer drive gear onto the shaft, aligning the wide splines.

12 Slide the balancer driven gear/weight assembly onto the shaft, aligning the wide splines (see illustration) – on models with an inner alternator stator align the mark on the driven gear with that on the drive gear, turning the balancer shaft as required to achieve this. Fit the sleeve (see illustration).

13 Install the inner stator where fitted, and on all models the alternator rotor – when fitting the rotor make sure the marks are aligned correctly (see Chapter 9).

14 Lubricate the threads and seating surface of the balancer bolt with molybdenum disulphide oil (engine oil and molybdenum grease mixed in the ratio 10:1). Fit the bolt with its washer and tighten to the torque listed in this Chapter's Specifications, counter-holding the alternator rotor as before (see illustration).

15 Install the alternator inner cover (see Chapter 9).

22.14 Fit the bolt with its washer and tighten to the specified torque

22.19 Remove the washer

22.20 Remove the starter driven gear, turning it clockwise as you do

22.24 Draw the starter clutch/balancer assembly off the shaft

Right balancer weight, starter clutch and torque limiter

Starter clutch check

16 Remove the starter motor (see Chapter 9).
17 Try to turn the torque limiter gear in both directions. It should turn freely clockwise and lock anti-clockwise. If it turns both ways or neither way, or if wear or damage can be seen, remove the components for investigation.

Removal

18 Remove the right crankcase cover (see Section 20).
19 Remove the washer from the starter torque limiter **(see illustration)**.
20 Draw the starter driven gear out of the clutch hub, turning it clockwise as you do **(see illustration)**.
21 Counter-hold the primary drive gear bolt **(see illustration 23.2b)** and unscrew the starter clutch/balancer bolt, removing it with its washer **(see illustration 22.33)**. If the primary drive gear has been removed hold the alternator rotor using a rotor strap or the left balancer weight using a holding tool instead.
22 Remove the needle roller bearing, the washer and the sleeve **(see illustration 22.32c, b and a)**.
23 Remove the starter torque limiter **(see illustration 22.31)**.
24 Take the starter clutch/balancer weight assembly off **(see illustration)**.

22.26a Check the rollers and the corresponding surface on the hub

22.26b Check the bearing, sleeve and inner surface of the gear hub

Inspection and disassembly

25 Check the gears for wear or damage. Replace them if problems are found.
26 Check the rollers inside the starter clutch for scoring or wear, and check the outer surface of the driven gear hub **(see illustration)**. Check their retainer for damage and make sure all the rollers are securely retained. Also check the inner surface of the hub and the bearing and sleeve **(see illustration)**.
27 Fit the driven gear into the starter clutch and try to turn it in both directions **(see illustration)**. It should turn freely clockwise and lock anti-clockwise. If it turns both ways or neither way, or if wear or damage can be seen, replace it.

28 To remove the starter clutch from the balancer weight hold the weight using a rotor strap around its rim or in a vise and unscrew the bolts securing the starter clutch housing **(see illustration)**. Lift the housing off and remove the roller assembly, noting which way round everything fits. Install a new roller assembly on the balancer with its flanged side innermost, then fit the housing over it with its grooved side outermost. Clean the threads of the bolts and apply non-permanent thread locking agent, and tighten them to the torque listed in this Chapter's Specifications.
29 Check the torque limiter for wear on the gear teeth, damage or discoloration (indicating overheating) **(see illustration)**. Replace it if problems are found. Check the bearings, one in the crankcase **(see illustration 22.31)** and

22.27 Make sure the gear turns freely clockwise and locks anti-clockwise

22.28 Unscrew the bolts and separate the weight from the clutch

22.29a Draw the gear shaft out of the limiter and check all teeth for wear and damage

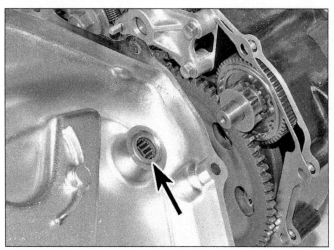

22.29b **Check the bearing in the cover (arrowed) and the one in the crankcase**

22.31 **Fit the torque limiter into its bearing (arrowed)**

one in the crankcase cover **(see illustration)**, and replace them with new ones if necessary – refer to *Tools and Workshop Tips* for more information.

Installation

30 Slide the balancer weight/starter clutch assembly onto the shaft, aligning the wide splines **(see illustration 22.24)**.

31 Lubricate the starter torque limiter shaft with molybdenum disulphide oil (engine oil and molybdenum grease mixed in the ratio 10:1) and fit it into its bearing with the large pinion innermost, engaging it with the starter motor shaft if installed **(see illustration)**.

32 Lubricate the sleeve, washer and needle bearing with oil and fit them in that order **(see illustrations)** – make sure the washer stays seated on the sleeve and does not slip down behind it to rest on the shaft.

33 Lubricate the threads and seating surface of the starter clutch/balancer bolt with molybdenum disulphide oil (engine oil and molybdenum grease mixed in the ratio 10:1). Fit the bolt with its washer and tighten to the torque listed in this Chapter's Specifications, counter-holding the primary drive gear bolt as before **(see illustration)**.

34 Lubricate the outside of the driven gear hub. Fit the gear into the clutch, turning it

clockwise as you push it in **(see illustration 22.20)**.

35 Fit the washer onto the starter torque limiter **(see illustration 22.19)**.

36 Install the right crankcase cover (see Section 20).

---

23 Primary drive gear – removal, inspection and installation

Removal

1 Remove the right crankcase cover (see Section 20, Steps 1 to 4).

2 Lock the teeth of the primary drive and driven gear teeth together where they mesh on the top using a piece of aluminium (DO NOT use steel), an aluminium or copper washer or penny, or some stout rag.**(see illustration 20.27a)**. Slacken the primary gear bolt **(see illustration)**.

3 Remove the clutch (see Section 20).

4 Remove the washer from the starter torque limiter **(see illustration 22.19)**. Draw the starter driven gear out of the clutch hub, turning it clockwise as you do **(see illustration 22.20)**.

22.32a **Fit the sleeve . . .**

22.32b **. . . then washer . . .**

22.32c **. . . and the bearing**

22.33 **Fit the bolt with its washer and tighten to the specified torque**

23.2 **Lock the gear teeth together and unscrew the bolt**

23.5 Unhook the spring, then unscrew the bolts (arrowed) and remove the tensioner/shaft holder

23.6a Unscrew and remove the bolt and washer

5 Unhook the water pump chain tensioner spring **(see illustration)**. Unscrew the idle shaft holder bolts and remove the tenisoner/shaft holder assembly. Note the dowels **(see illustration 23.14a)**.

6 Unscrew and remove the primary drive gear bolt and washer **(see illustration)**. Remove the washer from the water pump idle shaft **(see illustration)**. Draw the water pump drive and outer idle sprockets and chain off **(see illustration)** – note how the outer idle sprocket locates over the drive pin and withdraw the pin form the shaft for safekeeping **(see illustration)**.

7 Slide the primary drive gear off the shaft **(see illustration 23.11)**.

Inspection

8 Check the primary drive gear for worn or damaged teeth and replace it with a new one if necessary. If the gear is worn or damaged, also check the clutch housing gear – you may need to replace the clutch housing as well. Check the splines on the shaft and in the gear.

9 Remove the tensioner assembly from the shaft holder **(see illustration)**. Check the chain tensioner blade and spring and

the water pump idle shaft bearing for wear and damage and replace components with new ones as required – refer to *Tools and Workshop Tips* in the Reference Section for bearing checks and removal and installation methods.

10 Check the sprocket teeth for wear and damage. Check the splines on the shaft and in the pump drive sprocket.

Installation

11 Slide the primary drive gear onto the shaft

with its raised boss innermost and aligning the wide splines **(see illustration)**.

12 Turn the water pump idle shaft so the hole for the drive pin is horizontal, then fit the pin **(see illustration 23.6d)**. Fit the chain and sprockets, aligning the wide spline on the drive sprocket with that on the shaft **(see illustration 23.6c)**. Fit the washer onto the idle shaft **(see illustration 23.6b)**.

13 Lubricate the threads and seating surface of the primary drive gear bolt with molybdenum disulphide oil (engine oil and molybdenum grease mixed in the ratio 10:1). Fit the bolt

23.6b Remove the idle shaft washer . . .

23.6c . . . then draw the chain and sprockets off . . .

23.6d . . . and remove the drive pin

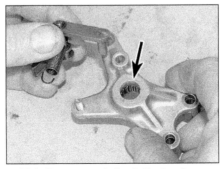

23.9 Remove and check the tensioner assembly and the shaft bearing (arrowed)

23.11 Slide the gear onto the shaft

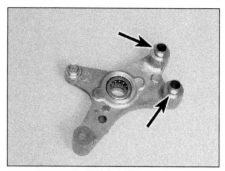

23.14a Lubricate the bearing and make sure the dowels (arrowed) are fitted

23.14b Fit the tensioner/shaft holder assembly . . .

23.14c . . . making sure the blade and spring are all correctly located

with its washer and tighten it finger-tight **(see illustration 23.6a)**.

14 Lubricate the needle bearing in the idle shaft holder with oil and make sure the dowels are in place **(see illustration)**. Fit the holder and tighten the bolts to the to the torque listed in this Chapter's Specifications **(see illustration)**. Check the tensioner is seated correctly on the chain then hook up the spring **(see illustration)**.

15 Fit the starter driven gear into the clutch hub, turning it clockwise as you do **(see illustration 22.20)**. Fit the starter torque limiter washer **(see illustration 22.19)**.

16 Install the clutch (see Section 20).

17 Lock the teeth of the primary drive and driven gear teeth together where they mesh on the underside and tighten the primary

gear bolt to the torque listed in this Chapter's Specifications **(see illustrations)**.

18 Install the right crankcase cover (see Section 20).

24 Camshaft chains and guides – removal, inspection and installation

Removal

1 Remove the cylinder head(s) (see Section 14).

2 For the front cylinder, remove the alternator rotor and where fitted the inner alternator stator (see Chapter 9). On models with an

inner stator slide the balancer drive gear off the shaft.

3 For the rear cylinder, remove the primary drive gear (see Section 23).

4 Before removing the guides note that the guide for the front cylinder is marked F, and that for the rear is marked R – if you can't see the marks make your own. Note the retaining washer for the front cylinder guide and the tab for the rear guide, each secured to the crankcase by a bolt. Lift the cam chain guide blade out, noting how it locates **(see illustration)**.

5 Unscrew the tensioner blade bolts and remove the blade **(see illustration)** – lift it out the top on the front cylinder, and draw it out the bottom on the rear cylinder **(see illustrations)**.

23.17a Lock the primary drive and driven gear teeth as described . . .

23.17b . . . and tighten the bolt to the specified torque

24.4 Lift the guide blade out of the tunnel

24.5a Unscrew the tensioner blade bolts (arrowed) – front cylinder blade shown

24.5b Lift the front cylinder blade out from the top . . .

24.5c . . . and draw the rear cylinder blade out from the bottom

24.6a Unscrew the bolts (arrowed) and remove the chain guide . . .

24.6b . . . then remove the chain

6 Unscrew the chain guide bolts and remove the guide **(see illustration)**. Mark the outer face of the chain so it can be installed the same way round if being reused. Disengage and remove the chain **(see illustration)**.

Inspection

7 Pull the chain tight to eliminate all slack and measure the length of twenty links, pin-to-pin **(see illustration)**. Compare your findings to this Chapter's Specifications and replace the chain with a new one if it has stretched beyond the limit.

8 Also check the chains for binding and obvious damage.

9 Check the chain guides for deep grooves, cracking and other obvious damage, replacing them if necessary.

Installation

10 Installation is the reverse of removal. Clean the threads of the chain guide and tensioner blade bolts and apply fresh threadlock. Make sure the retaining washer for the front cylinder chain guide and the tab for the rear guide are fitted and the bolts are tight. Make sure guide blades are fitted in the correct place according to their mark (Step 4) – locate the

lugs in the cut-outs in the top of the block **(see illustration)**. On models with an inner alternator stator slide the balancer drive gear onto the shaft, aligning the wide splines – also make sure you align the mark on the drive gear with that on the driven gear, turning the gears as required to achieve this.

25 Crankcase – disassembly and reassembly

1 To access the crankshaft, connecting rods, bearings, transmission components, oil pump, balancer shaft and water pump seals, the crankcase must be split into two parts.

2 Remove the engine (see Section 7). Remove the oil filter (see Chapter 1).

Disassembly

3 Remove the rocker cases, camshafts, cylinder heads, cylinders and pistons (see Sections 11, 13, 14, 16 and 17).

4 On all except VN1500A and B models (on which the external oil pipe should already have been removed when removing the rocker cases or cylinder heads) unscrew the oil hose banjo bolt and remove the hoses **(see illustration)**. Discard the sealing washers – new ones must be used.

5 Remove the alternator rotor and left balancer, and the starter clutch and right balancer (see Section 22).

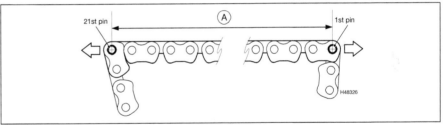

24.7 Stretch the chain and measure the length of 20 links (A)

24.10 Seat the lugs in the cut-outs

25.4 Unscrew the bolt (arrowed) and detach the hoses

25.7a Withdraw the shaft . . .

25.7b . . . and remove the sprocket

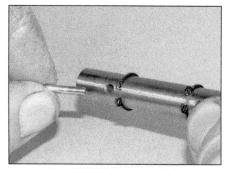

25.7c Remove the drive pin for safekeeping

25.7d Lift the chain off the driven sprocket

25.10a Remove the retaining ring . . .

6 If required remove the water pump impeller (see Chapter 3) – this can be done later if you have a holding tool for the driven sprocket as shown in Chapter 3, or not at all if there is no need to strip the pump.

7 Remove the clutch and primary drive gear (see Sections 20 and 23). Withdraw the water pump idle shaft and remove the inner idle sprocket (see illustrations) – note the drive pin in the shaft and how it locates in the sprocket, and remove it for safekeeping (see illustration). Remove the chain from the driven sprocket (see illustration).

8 Remove the cam chains and guides (see Section 24).

9 Remove the shift mechanism (see Section 21).

10 If the transmission assembly is to be removed from the crankcase, remove the retaining ring from the end of the output shaft and slide the needle bearing off (see illustrations). Unscrew the bearing retainer bolts and remove the retainers (see illustration). Counter-hold the damper cam using either the Kawasaki tool (part no. 57001-1025) or a suitable C-spanner, locating the hook end in the hole in the cam and the handle against the engine mounting bolt lug (see illustration). With the damper cam securely held unscrew the nut, then slide cam off the shaft (see illustration). On all

25.10b . . . and slide the bearing off

25.10c Unscrew the bolts (arrowed) and remove the retainers

25.10d Lock the shaft using the tool or a C-spanner as shown and unscrew the nut . . .

25.10e . . . then slide the damper cam off

25.11a Right side 8 mm crankcase bolts (arrowed)

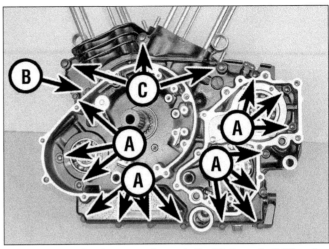

25.11b Left side 6 mm crankcase bolts (A), 8 mm bolt (B) and 10 mm bolts (C)

1600 engine models discard the nut – a new one must be used.

11 Remove the 8 mm crankcase bolts from the right side of the crankcase **(see illustration)**. Remove the 6 mm bolts, then the 8 mm bolt and then the 10 mm bolts in the left side of the crankcase **(see illustration)**. **Note:** *As each bolt is removed, store it in its relative position in a cardboard template of the crankcase halves* **(see illustration)**. *This will ensure all bolts are installed in the correct location on reassembly.*

12 Carefully lay the crankcase on wooden blocks on its left side so the shafts are supported clear of the bench and the crankcase is level. Carefully prise the crankcase apart using a suitable screwdriver in the two prise points – do not prise in any other place as you can easily damage the mating surface which could cause an oil leak after assembly **(see illustrations)**.

13 Carefully lift the right crankcase half up off the left half **(see illustration)** – the crankshaft, balancer shaft and transmission components will stay in the left half. Remove the oil passage O-ring and discard it – a new one must be used **(see illustration 25.20b)**. Remove the two dowels if loose **(see illustration 25.20a)**.

14 Refer to Sections 26 through 33 for procedures on the internal components of the crankcase.

Reassembly

15 Remove all traces of sealant from the crankcase mating surfaces. Be careful not to let any fall into the case as this is done.

16 Make sure the following components are in place inside the crankcase:

a) *Oil return pipes, crankcase breather baffle and strainer*
b) *Transmission shafts, shift drum and forks*
c) *Balancer shaft*
d) *Crankshaft and connecting rods*
e) *Oil pump*
f) *Internal oil pipes*
g) *Oil pressure relief valve*
h) *Water pump shaft and drive chain guide*

17 Check the position of the shift drum, shift forks and transmission shafts – make sure they're in the neutral position.

18 Pour some engine oil over the transmission gears, the crankshaft main bearings and the shift drum. Don't get any oil on the crankcase mating surface.

19 Wipe over the mating surface of each half with a clean rag and some solvent. Apply a thin, even bead of silicone sealant to the mating surface of the right half as shown **(see illustration)**.

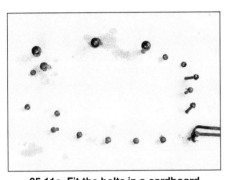

25.11c Fit the bolts in a cardboard template as shown

25.12a There is a pry point at the front . . .

25.12b . . . and one at the back

25.13 Carefully separate the crankcase halves

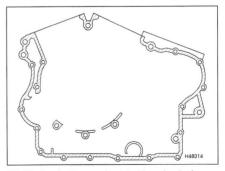

25.19 Apply the sealant to the shaded area as shown

25.20a Fit the dowels (arrowed) . . .

25.20b . . . and a new O-ring

25.23a Crankcase 8 and 10 mm bolt tightening sequence in the right . . .

25.23b . . . and left side positions

Caution: Apply the sealant only to the shaded areas. Don't apply an excessive amount of sealant, as it will ooze out when the case halves are assembled. Don't apply sealant to the oil passage at the back of the crankcase or the section for the oil strainer bore.

20 Fit the two dowels if removed **(see illustration)**. Fit a new O-ring onto the oil passage **(see illustration)**.

21 Carefully fit the right crankcase half down onto the left crankcase half, making sure the dowels locate correctly **(see illustration 25.13)**. Check that the lower crankcase half is correctly seated.

Caution: The crankcase halves should fit together without being forced. If the casings are not correctly seated, remove the right crankcase half and investigate the problem. Do not attempt to pull them together using the crankcase bolts as the casing will crack and be ruined.

22 Install the right crankcase bolts and tighten them so they are just snug, then sit the crankcase upright and install the left bolts, again tightening them so they are just snug **(see illustrations 25.11a and b)**.

23 Tighten the 8 mm bolts and 10 mm bolts in each half in the sequence shown to the torque listed in this Chapter's Specifications for each size bolt **(see illustrations)**.

24 Now tighten the 6 mm bolts to the torque listed in this Chapter's Specifications. Now go round all bolts again, checking they are at the correct torque for each size bolt.

25 Turn the crankshaft (supporting the connecting rods as you do so they don't contact the crankcase walls), balancer shaft, input shaft and output shaft to make sure they turn freely. Make sure you can select first gear by turning the shift drum. **Note:** *Because the positive neutral finder locks out second through fifth gears when the output shaft isn't spinning, you can't check second through fifth gears.*

26 If the transmission assembly was removed, slide the damper cam onto the output shaft **(see illustration 25.10e)**. Lubricate the threads and seating surface of the nut (using a new nut on 1600 engines) with molybdenum disulphide oil (engine oil and molybdenum grease mixed in the ratio 10:1), then thread it on **(see illustration)**. Hold the cam using the same tool as before but locating it on the opposite side as shown

25.26a Fit the nut . . .

and tighten the nut to the torque listed in this Chapter's Specifications **(see illustration)**. Clean the threads of the transmission output shaft bearing retainer bolts. Apply fresh threadlock, fit the retainers and tighten the bolts to the listed torque **(see illustration 25.10c)**. Lubricate the needle bearing and slide it onto the shaft then fit a new retaining ring, seating it in the groove **(see illustrations 25.10b and a)**.

27 The remainder of installation is the reverse of removal, with the following additions:

a) *Make sure the water pump drive chain and sprockets are fitted before the primary drive gear **(see illustrations 25.7d, c, b and a)**.*

b) *On all except VN1500A and B models fit the oil hoses using new sealing washers, making sure the thick one is between the two hose unions, the shorter hose to the rear cylinder rocker case is on the top, and the hoses are aligned as shown **(see illustration 25.4)**. Tighten the banjo bolt to the torque listed in this Chapter's Specifications.*

c) *Be sure to refill the engine oil and coolant.*

26 Crankcase components – inspection and servicing

1 After the crankcases have been separated and the crankshaft, balancer shaft, transmission shafts and shift drum and forks, and oil pump and internal oil pipes have been removed, clean the crankcases thoroughly with new solvent and dry with compressed air.

2 Blow through all oil passages and pipes with compressed air.

3 Remove all traces of old gasket sealant from the crankcase mating surfaces. Minor damage to the surfaces can be cleaned up with a fine sharpening stone. **Caution:** *Be very careful not to nick or gouge the crankcase mating surfaces or leaks will result. Check both crankcase sections very carefully for cracks and other damage.*

4 If any damage is found that can't be repaired, replace the crankcase halves as a set.

25.26b . . . then lock the shaft and tighten the nut to the specified torque

Bearing replacement

5 Check all the bearings in each crankcase half for wear or damage **(see illustration)**. Inspection of the crankshaft main bearings, which are replaced as a unit with the case halves, is described in Section 28. Rotate the other bearings with your fingers and check for roughness, looseness or noise. Replace bearings that are in doubtful condition with new ones (Steps 6 to 8). For water pump shaft seal and bearing replacement, see Chapter 3. Refer to *Tools and Workshop Tips* in the Reference Section for bearing checks and removal and installation methods.

6 Unbolt the bearing retainer from bearings so equipped **(see illustration)**. Before removing the balancer shaft bearing from the right crankcase remove the oil return pipe assembly **(see illustration)**, and before removing the transmission input shaft bearing remove the internal oil pipe (see Section 30). Note which way the marked side of the bearing faces and install the new bearing the same way round. The bearings are a tight fit and Kawasaki recommend the use of an hydraulic press or puller to remove them. If such equipment is not available, place the case half in an oven heated to about 200-degrees F (100-degrees C) and allow it to heat up, then drive the bearings out with a socket or bearing driver that seats on the inner race **(see illustration)**.

7 Before installing the bearings, allow them to sit in the freezer overnight, and about fifteen minutes before installation, place the case half in an oven heated to about 200-degrees F

26.5 Apart from the large ball bearings, there are various small needle bearings (arrowed)

(100-degrees C) and allow it to heat up. The bearings are an interference fit and this will ease installation.

> ⚠️ *Warning: Before heating the case, wash it thoroughly with soap and water so that no explosive fumes are present. Also, don't use a flame to heat the case.*

8 Install ball bearings using a press if available, or with a socket or bearing driver that bears against the bearing outer race (do not use the inner race), and press or drive them in until they contact the seat. Needle bearings should be pressed or drawn into place, not driven.

27 Connecting rod bearings – general note

1 Even though connecting rod bearings are generally replaced with new ones during the engine overhaul, the old bearings should be retained for close examination as they may reveal valuable information about the condition of the engine.

2 Bearing failure occurs mainly because of lack of lubrication, the presence of dirt or other foreign particles, overloading the engine and/or corrosion. Regardless of the cause of bearing failure, it must be corrected before the engine is reassembled to prevent it from happening again.

3 When examining the bearings, remove them from the connecting rods and caps and lay them out on a clean surface in the

26.6a Transmission input shaft bearing retainer bolts (arrowed)

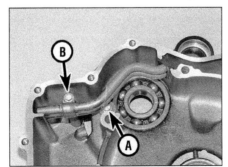

26.6b Balancer shaft bearing retainer bolt (A) – unscrew the bolt (B) and remove the oil pipes first

26.6c A socket can be used to drive bearings out

same general position as their location on the crankshaft journals. This will enable you to match any noted bearing problems with the corresponding side of the crankshaft journal.

4 Dirt and other foreign particles get into the engine in a variety of ways. It may be left in the engine during assembly or it may pass through filters or breathers. It may get into the oil and from there into the bearings. Metal chips from machining operations and normal engine wear are often present. Abrasives are sometimes left in engine components after reconditioning operations such as cylinder honing, especially when parts are not thoroughly cleaned using the proper cleaning methods. Whatever the source, these foreign objects often end up imbedded in the soft bearing material and are not easily recognized. Large particles will not imbed in the bearing and will score or gouge the bearing and journal. The best prevention for this cause of bearing failure is to clean all parts thoroughly and keep everything spotlessly clean during engine reassembly. Frequent and regular oil and filter changes are also recommended.

5 Lack of lubrication or lubrication breakdown has a number of interrelated causes. Excessive heat (which thins the oil), overloading (which squeezes the oil from the bearing face) and oil leakage or throw off (from excessive bearing clearances, worn oil pump or high engine speeds) all contribute to lubrication breakdown. Blocked oil passages will also starve a bearing and destroy it. When lack of lubrication is the cause of bearing failure, the bearing material is wiped or extruded from the steel backing of the bearing. Temperatures may increase to the point where the steel backing and the journal turn blue from overheating.

6 Riding habits can have a definite effect on bearing life. Full throttle low speed operation, or lugging the engine, puts very high loads on bearings, which tend to squeeze out the oil film. These loads cause the bearings to flex, which produces fine cracks in the bearing face (fatigue failure). Eventually the bearing material will loosen in pieces and tear away from the steel backing. Short trip riding leads to corrosion of bearings, as insufficient engine heat is produced to drive off the condensed water and corrosive gases produced. These products collect in the engine oil, forming acid and sludge. As the oil is carried to the engine bearings, the acid attacks and corrodes the bearing material.

7 Incorrect bearing installation during engine assembly will lead to bearing failure as well. Tight fitting bearings which leave insufficient bearing oil clearances result in oil starvation. Dirt or foreign particles trapped behind a bearing insert result in high spots on the bearing which lead to failure.

8 To avoid bearing problems, clean all parts thoroughly before reassembly, double check all bearing clearance measurements and lubricate the new bearings with engine assembly lube or moly-based grease during installation.

28.2 Lift the balancer shaft out . . .

28.3 . . . then lift the crankshaft out

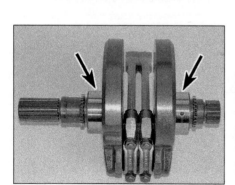

28.7 Check and measure the main bearing journals (arrowed) . . .

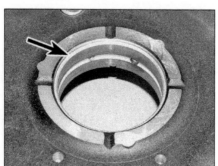

28.10 . . . and the main bearings themselves (arrowed)

28 Crankshaft, balancer shaft and main bearings – removal, inspection and installation

Removal

1 Remove the engine and separate the crankcase halves (see Sections 7 and 25).

2 Lift the balancer shaft out of its bearing **(see illustration)** – you may have to turn the crankshaft slightly if the web interferes with the balancer shaft flange.

3 Carefully lift the crankshaft out (it is heavier than you may think!) and set it on a clean surface **(see illustration)**.

Crankshaft inspection

4 If required and not already done, mark and remove the connecting rods from the crankshaft (see Section 29).

5 Clean the crankshaft with solvent, using a rifle-cleaning brush to scrub out the oil passages. If available, blow the crank dry with compressed air.

6 Check the camshaft chain sprockets on the crankshaft for chipped teeth and other wear, and if not already done also check the sprockets on the camshafts. If any undesirable conditions are found, replace the crankshaft with a new one. Check the chains as described in Section 24. Check the rest of the crankshaft for cracks and other damage.

7 Set the crankshaft on V-blocks and check the runout with a dial indicator touching each of the main journals **(see illustration)**. Compare your findings with this Chapter's Specifications. If the runout exceeds the limit, replace the crank.

8 Check the main journals for uneven wear, scoring and pits. Measure the diameter of the crankshaft journals with a micrometer and compare your findings with this Chapter's Specifications. Also, by measuring the diameter at a number of points around each journal's circumference, you'll be able to determine whether or not the journal is out-of-round. Take the measurement at each end of the journal to determine if the journal is tapered.

9 If any crank journal has worn down past the service limit, replace the crankshaft with a new one.

10 Using a telescoping gauge and a micrometer, measure the diameters of the main bearings, then compare the measurements with those listed in this Chapter's Specifications **(see illustration)**. If the measurements are beyond the specified limit, the crankcase halves must be replaced as a set – the bearings are not available separately.

Installation

11 Lubricate the bearings with molybdenum disulphide oil (engine oil and molybdenum grease mixed in the ratio 10:1).

12 If removed fit the connecting rods onto the crankshaft (see Section 29).

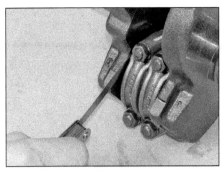

29.1 Measuring the connecting rod side clearance

29.2 Connecting rod weight grade letters are across the front

29.3 Connecting rod cap nuts (arrowed)

13 Carefully lower the crankshaft into place, making sure the left-hand rod is aligned with the rear cylinder cut-out and the right-hand rod is aligned with the front (see illustration 28.3).

14 Fit the flanged end of the balancer shaft into its bearing (see illustration 28.2) – you may have to turn the crankshaft slightly if the web interferes with the flange.

15 Assemble the case halves (see Section 25).

29 Connecting rods and bearings – removal, inspection, bearing selection and installation

Removal

1 Remove the crankshaft (see Section 28). Before removing the connecting rods from the crankshaft, measure the side clearance between the rods and the crank web with a feeler gauge (see illustration). If the clearance is greater than that listed in this Chapter's Specifications, the rods will have to be replaced with new ones.

2 Label the rods with cylinder letters, FF for front and RR for rear, marking across the rod and the cap on the rear face. The letter across the rod and cap on the front face indicates the weight grade, and because this could (as shown) be an F making a double FF on the rear face means you can't get muddled up (see illustration).

3 Unscrew the bearing cap nuts, separate the cap from the rod, then detach the rod from

the crankshaft (see illustration). If the cap is stuck, tap on the ends of the rod bolts with a soft face hammer to free them.

4 If required separate the bearing inserts from the rods and caps, but make sure you keep them in order so they can be reinstalled in their original locations if being reused (see illustration). Wash the parts in solvent and dry them with compressed air, if available.

Inspection

5 Check the connecting rods for cracks and other obvious damage.

6 Refer to Section 27 and examine the connecting rod bearing inserts. If they are scored, badly scuffed or appear to have been seized, new bearings must be installed. Always replace the bearings in the connecting rods as a set. If they are badly damaged, check the corresponding crankshaft journal. Evidence of extreme heat, such as discoloration, indicates that lubrication failure has occurred. Be sure to thoroughly check the oil pump and pressure relief valve as well as all oil holes and passages before reassembling the engine.

7 Have the rods checked for twist and bending at a dealer service department or other motorcycle repair shop.

Bearing selection

8 If the bearings and journals appear to be in good condition, check the oil clearances as follows, working on one rod at a time:

9 Start with the rod for the number one cylinder (front). Wipe the bearing inserts and the connecting rod and cap clean, using a lint-free cloth.

10 Fit the bearing inserts into the connecting rod and cap. Make sure the tab on the bearing engages with the notch in the rod or cap.

11 Wipe off the connecting rod journal with a lint-free cloth. Lay a strip of Plastigage across the top of the journal, parallel with the journal axis (see illustration). Assemble the connecting rod to its proper journal, making sure the previously applied marks correspond to each other and the weight grade letter faces the front of the crankshaft.

12 Lubricate the threads and seating surface of the nuts with molybdenum disulphide oil (engine oil and molybdenum grease mixed in the ratio 10:1). Fit the nuts and tighten to the torque listed in this Chapter's Specifications, but don't allow the connecting rod to rotate at all.

13 Unscrew the nuts and remove the connecting rod and cap from the journal, being very careful not to disturb the Plastigage. Compare the width of the crushed Plastigage to the required scale (metric or imperial) printed in the Plastigage envelope to determine the bearing oil clearance (see illustration).

14 If the clearance is within the range listed in this Chapter's Specifications and the bearings are in perfect condition, they can be reused. If the clearance is beyond the standard range, but within the service limit, replace the bearing inserts with inserts that have blue paint marks, then check the oil clearance once again (these are the thickest bearing inserts, and may be thick enough to bring bearing clearance with the specified range). Always replace all of the inserts at the same time.

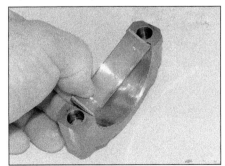

29.4 Remove the bearing inserts if required

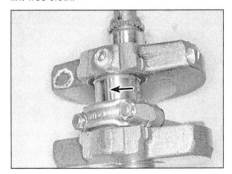

29.11 Lay a strip of Plastigage (arrowed) across the journal parallel to the centreline

29.13 Measure the width of the crushed Plastigage using the correct scale

29.16 Measure the diameter of the journal

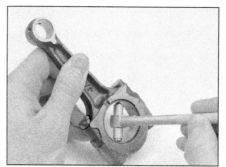

29.20a Assemble the connecting rod and measure the bore diameter

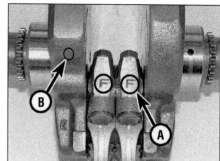

29.20b Connecting rod bore diameter is denoted by a circle or no circle around the weight grade letter (A); crankpin diameter by a circle or no circle on the web (B)

15 The clearance might be slightly greater than the standard clearance, but that doesn't matter, as long as it isn't greater than the maximum clearance or less than the minimum clearance.

16 If the clearance is greater than the service limit listed in this Chapter's Specifications, measure the diameter of the connecting rod journal with a micrometer and compare your findings with this Chapter's Specifications **(see illustration)**. Also, by measuring the diameter at a number of points around the journal's circumference, you'll be able to determine whether or not the journal is out-of-round. Take the measurement at each end of the journal to determine if the journal is tapered.

17 If any journal has worn down past the service limit, replace the crankshaft with a new one.

18 If the diameter of the journal isn't less than the service limit but differs from the original according to any markings on the crankshaft web as described in the Specifications, apply new marks with a hammer and punch **(see illustration 29.20b)**.

• If the journal measures within the "no mark" range listed in this Chapter's Specifications, don't make any marks on the crank (there shouldn't be one there anyway).

• If the journal measures within the "O" mark range listed in this Chapter's Specifications, make a "O" mark on the crank in the area indicated (if not already there).

19 Remove the bearing inserts from the connecting rod and cap, then assemble the

cap to the rod. Tighten the nuts to the torque listed in this Chapter's Specifications.

20 Using a telescoping gauge and a micrometer, measure the inside diameter of the connecting rod **(see illustration)**. The mark around the weight grade letter (if any) on the connecting rod should coincide with the measurement, but if it doesn't, make a new mark **(see illustration)**.

• If the inside diameter measures within the "no mark" range listed in this Chapter's Specifications, don't make any mark on the rod (there shouldn't be one there anyway).

• If the inside diameter measures within the "O" mark range, make a "O" mark on the rod (it should already be there).

21 By referring to the accompanying table, select the correct connecting rod bearing inserts – the colour code should be marked on the edge of the insert.

Big-end marking	Connecting rod marking	Bearing insert colour	Part Number
None	O	Brown	92028-1476
None	None	Black	92028-1475
O	O	Black	92028-1475
O	None	Blue	92028-1474

22 Repeat the bearing selection procedure for the remaining connecting rod.

Installation

23 Wipe off the bearing inserts, connecting rods and caps. Fit the inserts into the rods and

caps, using your hands only, making sure the tabs on the inserts engage with the notches in the rods and caps **(see illustration)**. When all the inserts are installed, lubricate their bearing surface with molybdenum disulphide oil (engine oil and molybdenum grease mixed in the ratio 10:1). Do not lubricate the surfaces of the rod and cap or the non-bearing surfaces of the inserts.

24 Assemble each connecting rod to its proper journal, making sure the previously applied marks correspond to each other and the weight grade letter faces the front of the crankshaft **(see illustration)**. If new rods are being installed, they should both have the same weight grade to minimize vibration **(see illustration 29.2)**.

25 When you're sure the rods are positioned correctly, lubricate the threads and seating surface of the nuts with molybdenum disulphide oil (engine oil and molybdenum grease mixed in the ratio 10:1). Fit the nuts and tighten to the torque listed in this Chapter's Specifications **(see illustration)**.

26 Turn the rods on the crankshaft. If either of them feels tight, tap on the bottom of the connecting rod caps with a hammer – this should relieve stress and free them up. If it doesn't, recheck the bearing clearance.

27 As a final step, recheck the connecting rod side clearance (see Step 1). If the clearances aren't correct, find out why before proceeding with engine assembly.

29.23 Locate the tab on the insert in the notch (arrowed)

29.24 Assemble the rods and caps . . .

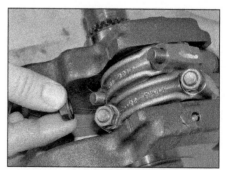

29.25 . . . and tighten the nuts to the specified torque

30.3 Oil pressure relief valve (arrowed)

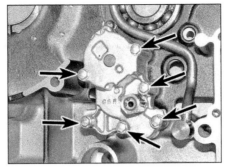

30.4a Unscrew the bolts (arrowed) . . .

30.4b . . . and remove the pump

30 Oil pump, pressure relief valve and internal oil pipes – removal, inspection and installation

Oil pump and pressure relief valve

1 If not already done, and the engine is still in the frame and can be run, refer to Section 3 and perform an oil pressure check. **Note:** *Kawasaki doesn't provide wear tolerances for the oil pump and no individual components are available. If you are rebuilding the engine, it's a good idea to install a new oil pump.*

Removal

2 Remove the engine and separate the crankcase halves (see Sections 7 and 25).
3 If required unscrew the oil pressure relief valve **(see illustration)**.
4 Unscrew the bolts securing the pump and lift it out of the crankcase **(see illustrations)**. Remove the oil passage O-rings **(see illustration)** – new ones must be used. Remove the dowels if loose **(see illustration)**.
5 Release the circlip that secures the oil pump shaft and remove the washer **(see illustrations)**. Draw the gear and shaft out, noting the washer **(see illustration)**. A new circlip should be used on installation.

Inspection

6 Check the driven gear for worn or damaged teeth. Also check the drive gear on the back of the clutch housing.

30.4c Remove the O-rings (arrowed) . . .

7 Check the shaft bearing in the crankcase for wear or damage and replace it with a new one if any problems are found **(see illustration 30.5c)**. Refer to tools and Workshop Tips in the Reference Section for bearing checks and removal and installation methods.
8 To check the relief valve first remove it from the pump if not already done. Using a wood or plastic tool, push the steel ball or plunger (according to model) into the valve body and check that it moves smoothly and freely against spring pressure and returns to its original position when released. If not, clean the valve in solvent, then blow it with compressed air. Recheck the action of the valve – if it is still not good replace it with a new one. Individual components are not available and Kawasaki specify it should not be disassembled or its performance could be affected.

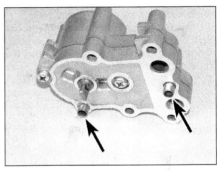

30.4d . . . and the dowels if loose

Installation

9 Installation is the reverse of removal, with the following additions:
a) Lubricate the shaft bearing with oil. Make sure the outer washer is on the shaft before fitting it, and fit the inner washer before securing the shaft with a new circlip **(see illustrations 30.5c, b and a)**.
b) Fit new O-rings onto the oil passages **(see illustration 30.4c)**.
c) Before installing the pump body, prime it by pouring oil into the passages while turning the shaft by hand – this will ensure that it begins to pump oil quickly.
d) Make sure the dowels are fitted **(see illustration 30.4d)**. Align the tab on the pump with the slot in the drive shaft **(see illustration 30.4b)**. Tighten the pump mounting bolts to the torque listed in this

30.5a Release the circlip . . .

30.5b . . . remove the washer . . .

30.5c . . . and draw the gear out, noting the washer (arrowed)

Chapter's Specifications (see illustration 30.4a).

e) *Clean the threads of the pressure relief valve and apply non-permanent thread locking agent, then tighten it to the torque listed in this Chapter's Specifications.*

Internal oil pipes

10 Remove the engine and separate the crankcase halves (see Sections 7 and 25).

11 Remove the crankshaft (see Section 28).

12 There is a pipe in each crankcase half **(see illustrations)**. Unscrew the oil pipe retainer and support bolts and remove the retainer. Carefully ease the pipe unions out of the oil passage bores **(see illustration)**. Discard the O-rings – new ones must be used.

13 Installation is the reverse of removal. Use new O-rings smeared with grease and push the unions fully into the bores until they seat **(see illustration)**. Clean the threads of the bolts and apply non-permanent threadlock, and tighten the bolts to the torque listed in this Chapter's Specifications.

---

31 Shift drum and forks –
removal, inspection and installation

Removal

1 See Section 32.

Inspection

2 Inspect the selector forks for any signs of wear or damage, especially around the fork

31.2 Check the fit of each fork in its pinion

31.5 Check the guide pins and their grooves in the drum

30.12a Internal oil pipe (arrowed) – right side

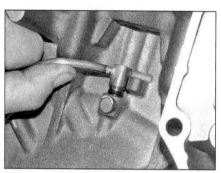

30.12c Carefully ease the pipe unions out of their bores

ends where they engage with the groove in the pinion. Check that each fork fits correctly in its pinion groove **(see illustration)**. Measure the thickness of the fork ends and the width of their groove and compare the readings to the

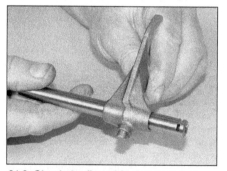

31.3 Check the fit and feel of each fork on the shaft

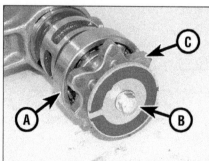

31.6 Check the bearing (A) – to replace it remove the neutral plate (B) and cam (C)

30.12b Internal oil pipe (arrowed) – left side

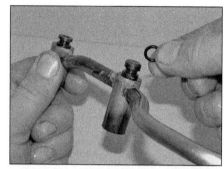

30.13 Fit a new O-ring onto each union

specifications. Check closely to see if the forks are bent. If the forks are in any way damaged or are worn beyond their specifications they must be replaced with new ones.

3 Check that the forks fit correctly on the shaft and drum **(see illustration)**. They should move freely with a light fit but no appreciable freeplay. Replace the forks and/or shaft and drum with new ones if they are worn. Check that the shaft holes in the crankcase are neither worn nor damaged.

4 Check the selector fork shaft is straight by rolling it along a flat surface. A bent shaft will cause difficulty in selecting gears and make the gearchange action heavy. Replace the shaft with a new one if it is bent.

5 Inspect the selector drum grooves and selector fork guide pins for signs of wear or damage **(see illustration)**. Measure the diameter of each pin and the width of its groove and compare the readings to the specifications. If either component shows signs of wear or damage the fork(s) and drum must be replaced with new ones.

6 Check that the selector drum bearing rotates freely and has no sign of freeplay between it and the drum **(see illustration)**. To fit a new bearing, remove the neutral switch contact plate and shift drum cam (see Section 21, Step 15). Remove the old bearing and fit a new one, then fit the cam and plate (Section 21, Step 21).

Installation

7 See Section 32.

32.3 Unscrew the bolts (arrowed) and remove the plate

32.5a Withdraw the shaft . . .

32.5b . . . and remove the right fork

32 Transmission shafts –
removal and installation

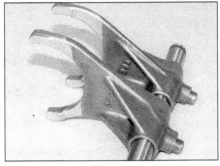

32.5c The forks have identification numbers to ensure correct fitment

32.5d Lift the transmission shafts and selector drum out together

Removal

1 Remove the engine and separate the crankcase halves (see Sections 7 and 25).
2 Remove the internal oil pipe from the left-hand crankcase half (see Section 30).
3 Unscrew the shift drum bearing retainer plate bolts and remove the plate (see illustration). Turn the drum to align the cam peaks with the cut-outs in the case.
4 On VN1500A, B and Classic D models mark the top of the right selector fork R and the left one L. Withdraw the fork shaft and pivot the forks away from the shift drum. Remove the drum. Remove the forks – fit the forks back onto the shaft in the correct order and way round. Lift the input shaft and output shaft out of the case together.
5 On all other models withdraw the selector fork shaft and remove the right fork (see illustrations). Note that the two forks that fit on the shaft are marked with numbers – the right-hand fork is marked 269 or 293 (according to model), and the left-hand fork is marked 270, and the marks face the left side of the engine (see illustration). Lift the input shaft, output shaft and shift drum and forks out of the case as a complete assembly and lay them on the bench (see illustration). Remove the left fork (see illustration 32.9d). Fit the forks back onto the shaft in the correct

order and way round. Lift the shift drum off the transmission shafts (see illustration 32.9c). To remove the fork from the drum remove the split pin and withdraw the guide pin, then slide the fork off, noting that the number 292 marked on one side faces the right end of the drum (see illustration 32.9a).
6 Refer to Section 33 for transmission shaft disassembly and Section 31 for shift drum and fork inspection.

Installation

7 Lubricate the fork ends, bores, guide pins and shaft with molybdenum disulphide oil (engine oil and molybdenum grease mixed in the ratio 10:1) before installing them.
8 On VN1500A, B and Classic D models position both transmission shafts together so their related pinions engage. Grasp the shafts and locate them in the case, making sure they seat correctly. Fit the fork you marked L into

its groove in the input shaft pinion and the fork you marked R into its groove in the output shaft pinion. Fit the shift drum, aligning it so the cam peaks fit through the cut-outs in the case, and pivot the forks around so the guide pins seat in the grooves. Fit the fork shaft. Rotate the shift drum as required into the neutral position.
9 On all other models, if removed fit the centre fork onto the shift drum with the number 292 facing the right end of the drum (see illustration). Centre the guide pin bore above the middle groove in the drum and fit the guide pin. Secure it using a new split pin inserted from the right-hand end of the drum and bend its ends round. Position both transmission shafts together so their related pinions engage (see illustration). Fit the shift drum fork into the groove in its pinion and lay the drum on the transmission shafts (see illustration). Fit the fork marked 270, number facing the left

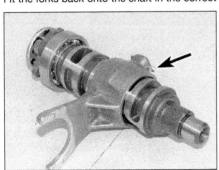

32.9a Make sure the centre fork and its guide pin split pin (arrowed) are fitted as shown

32.9b Lay the shafts together . . .

32.9c . . . then position the selector drum . . .

32.9d . . . and the left fork

32.9e Turn the drum so the neutral detent (arrowed) is positioned as shown

When disassembling the transmission shafts, place the parts on a long rod or thread a wire through them to keep them in order and facing the proper direction.

end, into its groove in the output shaft pinion **(see illustration)**. Grasp the shafts, drum and forks and locate them in the case, making sure they seat correctly, and aligning the drum so the cam peaks fit through the cut-outs in the case **(see illustration 32.5d)**. Rotate the shift drum as required into the neutral position **(see illustration)**. Fit the fork marked 269 or 293, number facing the left, into its groove in the output shaft pinion and locate its guide pin in the groove in the drum **(see illustration 32.5b)**. Fit the fork shaft **(see illustration 32.5a)**.

10 Check that the shafts turn freely – in neutral you should be able to hold the output shaft still and turn the input shaft.

11 Clean the threads of the shift drum bearing retainer plate bolts. Apply some non-permanent threadlock, then fit the plate and tighten the bolts **(see illustration 32.3)**.

12 Fit the internal oil pipe into the left-hand crankcase half (see Section 30).

---

33 Transmission shafts –
disassembly, inspection and reassembly

1 Remove the transmission shafts from the crankcase (see Section 32). Always disassemble the transmission shafts separately to avoid mixing up the components.

VN1500A and B and Classic D models – 4 speed transmission

Input shaft disassembly

2 Remove the snap-ring from the left end of the shaft and slide the needle bearing off **(see illustration)**.

3 Slide the thrust washer and the 4th and 2nd gear pinions off the shaft.

4 Remove the circlip securing the 3rd gear pinion, then slide the washer and the pinion off the shaft.

5 The 1st gear pinion is integral with the shaft.

Inspection

6 Wash all of the components in clean solvent and dry them off. Blow through the oil holes with compressed air if available.

7 Check the needle bearing, referring to *Tools and Workshop Tips* in the Reference Section. If required replace it with a new one.

8 Check the gear teeth for cracking, chipping, pitting and other obvious wear or damage. Any pinion that is damaged as such must be replaced with a new one.

9 Inspect the dogs and the dog holes in the gears for cracks, chips, and excessive wear especially in the form of rounded edges **(see illustration)**. Make sure mating gears engage properly. Replace the paired gears as a set if necessary.

10 Check for signs of scoring or bluing on the pinions, bushes where fitted, and shaft. This could be caused by overheating due to inadequate lubrication. Make sure the oil retention dimples on fitted bushes are visible **(see illustration)** – if not the bush is worn.

Check that all the oil holes and passages are clear. Replace any damaged or worn pinions or bushes.

11 Check that each pinion moves freely on the shaft or its bush where fitted but without undue freeplay. Check that each bush moves freely on the shaft but without undue freeplay.

12 The shaft is unlikely to sustain damage unless the engine has seized, placing an unusually high loading on the transmission, or the machine has covered a very high mileage. Check the surface of the shaft, especially

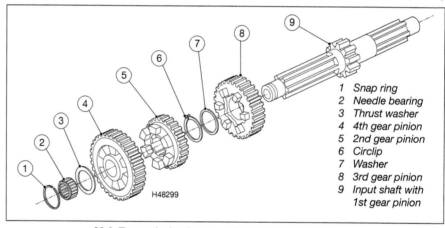

1 Snap ring
2 Needle bearing
3 Thrust washer
4 4th gear pinion
5 2nd gear pinion
6 Circlip
7 Washer
8 3rd gear pinion
9 Input shaft with 1st gear pinion

H48299

33.2 Transmission input shaft components – 4-speed

33.9 Check the dogs and dog holes for rounding and wear

33.10 Check the oil retention dimples in the bushes

where a pinion turns on it, and replace the shaft if it has scored or picked up, or if there are any cracks. Damage of any kind can only be cured by replacement.

13 Check the washers and replace any that are bent or worn. Use new ones if in any doubt. Replace all circlips with new ones.

Input shaft reassembly

14 During reassembly, apply molybdenum disulphide oil (engine oil and molybdenum grease mixed in the ratio 10:1) to the mating surfaces of the shaft, pinions and bushes.

15 When installing the circlips, do not expand their ends any further than is necessary and position them with each end aligned with a spline **(see illustration 33.43d)**. Make sure the round edged side of the circlip faces the pinion it secures so the sharp edged side takes the thrust of the pinion.

16 Slide the 3rd gear pinion onto the shaft with the dogs facing away from the 1st pinion, then slide the washer on **(see illustration 33.2)**. Fit the circlip, making sure it is locates correctly in its groove.

17 Slide the 2nd gear pinion onto the shaft with the selector fork groove away from the 3rd pinion, and aligning the oil holes.

18 Slide the 4th gear pinion onto the shaft with the raised centre facing out, then fit the thrust washer.

19 Slide the needle bearing on, then fit the snap-ring into its groove.

20 Check that all components have been correctly installed **(see illustration 33.2)**.

Output shaft disassembly

21 Remove the snap-ring from the right-hand end of the shaft and slide the needle bearing off **(see illustration)**.

22 Slide the thrust washer off the shaft, followed by the 1st gear pinion, and the thrust washer.

23 The 3rd gear pinion has three steel balls in it for the positive neutral finder mechanism. These lock the pinion to the shaft unless it is spun rapidly enough to fling the balls outward. To remove the pinion, place the shaft vertical with the pinion uppermost, then hold the 2nd gear pinion below it and spin the 3rd gear pinion and shaft while pulling the pinion up **(see illustration 33.50)**; it may take several attempts to disengage the pinion from the shaft, but it will slide off easily once it is disengaged – make sure it doesn't fly off the top of the shaft as you remove it as the steel balls will drop out. After it is removed, collect the three steel balls from the slots inside it **(see illustration 33.60a)**.

Caution: Don't pull the gear up too hard or fast – the balls will fly out of the gear.

24 Remove the circlip securing the 2nd gear pinion, then slide the splined washer, the pinion and its bush off the shaft.

25 Mark the outer face of the 4th gear pinion then slide it off the shaft. The circlip behind it can stay in place, or remove it if required, noting that if so it must be replaced with a new one.

1 Snap ring
2 Needle bearing
3 Thrust washer
4 1st gear pinion
5 Thrust washer
6 3rd gear pinion
7 Circlip
8 Washer
9 2nd gear pinion
10 2nd gear pinion bush
11 4th gear pinion
12 Circlip
13 Steel balls (3 off)

H48300

33.21 Transmission output shaft components – 4-speed

Inspection

26 Refer to Steps 6 to 13 above.

Output shaft reassembly

27 During reassembly, apply molybdenum disulphide oil (engine oil and molybdenum grease mixed in the ratio 10:1) to the mating surfaces of the shaft, pinions and bushes.

28 When installing the circlips, do not expand their ends any further than is necessary and position them with each end aligned with a spline **(see illustration 33.43d)**. Make sure the round edged side of the circlip faces the pinion it secures so the sharp edged side takes the thrust of the pinion.

29 If removed, fit a new circlip for the 4th gear pinion, making sure it locates correctly in the groove **(see illustration 33.21)**. Slide the 4th gear pinion onto the shaft with the side you marked facing out.

30 Slide the 2nd gear pinion bush onto the shaft with its shouldered end facing the 4th gear pinion and aligning the oil holes. Slide the 2nd gear pinion onto the bush with its recessed side facing out. Slide the splined washer on. Fit the circlip, making sure it is locates correctly in its groove in the shaft.

31 Lubricate the positive neutral finder mechanism balls with engine oil – don't use grease as it will impair the action of the mechanism. Fit the balls into the holes with the narrow outer ends in the 3rd gear pinion **(see illustrations 33.60a and b)**. Place the pinion onto the bench with its selector fork groove facing up. Place the end of the output

shaft down into the gear and hold the shaft vertical – the holes in the pinion that contain the balls must align with the slots in the shaft spline grooves **(see illustration 33.60c)**. Lift the gear up the shaft until it is in place, then tilt the shaft horizontal and turn it slowly, then check that the pinion cannot slide off.

32 Slide the thrust washer onto the shaft, then slide the 1st gear pinion on with its more recessed side facing the 3rd gear pinion. Fit the thrust washer.

33 Slide the needle bearing on, then fit the snap-ring into its groove.

34 Check that all components have been correctly installed **(see illustration 33.21)**.

All other models – 5 speed transmission

Input shaft disassembly

35 Remove the snap-ring from the end of the shaft and slide the bearing and the thrust washer off **(see illustrations 33.46c, b and a)**.

36 Remove the circlip securing the 2nd gear pinion and slide it off, followed by the 5th gear pinion, its bush and the splined washer **(see illustration and 33.45e, d, c, b and a)**.

37 Remove the circlip securing the 3rd gear pinion, then slide the pinion off the shaft **(see illustrations 33.44b and a)**.

38 Remove the circlip securing the 4th gear pinion, then slide the splined washer and the pinion off the shaft **(see illustrations 33.43c, b and a)**.

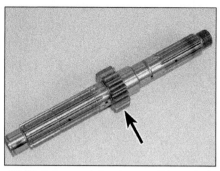

33.39 1st gear pinion (arrowed) is part of the shaft

33.43a Slide the 4th gear pinion . . .

33.43b . . . and the splined washer onto the shaft . . .

33.43c . . . and secure them with the circlip . . .

33.43d . . . making sure it locates properly in its groove

33.44a Slide the 3rd gear pinion onto the shaft . . .

39 The 1st gear pinion is integral with the shaft **(see illustration)**.

Inspection

40 Refer to Steps 6 to 13 above.

Input shaft reassembly

41 During reassembly, apply molybdenum disulphide oil (a 50/50 mixture of molybdenum disulphide grease and clean engine oil) to the mating surfaces of the shaft, pinions and bushes.

42 When installing the circlips, do not expand their ends any further than is necessary and position them with each end aligned with a spline **(see illustration 33.43d)**. Make sure the round edged side of the circlip faces the direction thrust so the sharp edged side takes the thrust of the pinion it seats against.

43 Slide the 4th gear pinion onto the shaft with its recessed side facing the 1st gear pinion **(see illustration)**. Slide the splined

washer onto the shaft, then fit the circlip, making sure that it locates correctly in the groove in the shaft **(see illustrations)**.

44 Slide the 3rd gear pinion onto the shaft with the selector fork groove facing out, and aligning the oil holes **(see illustration)**. Fit the circlip, making sure it is locates correctly in its groove in the shaft **(see illustrations)**.

45 Slide the splined washer onto the shaft, followed by the 5th gear pinion splined bush,

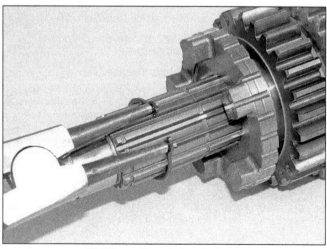

33.44b . . . then fit the circlip . . .

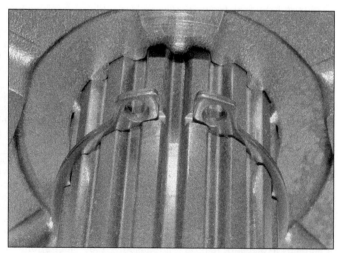

33.44c . . . making sure it locates properly in its groove

33.45a Slide the splined washer onto the shaft . . .

33.45b . . . followed by the 5th gear pinion bush . . .

33.45c . . . then fit the 5th gear pinion onto the bush

33.45d Slide the 2nd gear pinion onto the shaft . . .

33.45e . . . then fit the circlip . . .

33.45f . . . making sure it locates properly in its groove

aligning the oil holes **(see illustrations)**. Slide the 5th gear pinion onto the bush with its recessed side facing the 3rd gear pinion **(see illustration)**. Slide the 2nd gear pinion onto the shaft with its recessed side facing out, then fit the circlip, making sure it locates correctly in the groove **(see illustrations)**.

46 Fit the thrust washer, then slide the needle bearing on and fit the snap-ring into its groove **(see illustrations)**.

47 Check that all components have been correctly installed **(see illustration)**.

Output shaft disassembly

48 Remove the snap-ring from the end of the shaft and slide the bearing off **(see illustrations 33.62b and a)**.

49 Slide the thrust washer off the shaft, followed by the 1st gear pinion and the thrust washer **(see illustrations 33.61c, b and a)**.

50 The 4th gear pinion has three steel balls in it for the positive neutral finder mechanism. These lock the pinion to the shaft unless it is spun rapidly enough to fling the balls outward. To remove the pinion, place the shaft vertical

33.46a Fit the thrust washer . . .

with the pinion uppermost, then hold the 3rd gear pinion below it and spin the 4th gear pinion and shaft while pulling the pinion up up **(see illustration)**; it may take several attempts to disengage the pinion from the shaft, but

33.46b . . . and the needle bearing . . .

33.46c . . . then fit the snap ring into its groove

33.47 The complete assembly should be as shown

33.50 Hold the 3rd gear pinion, then spin and lift off the 4th gear pinion

33.57a Slide the 2nd gear pinion onto the shaft . . .

33.57b . . . followed by the splined washer . . .

33.57c . . . and secure them with the circlip . . .

33.57d . . . making sure it locates in the groove

it will slide off easily once it is disengaged – make sure it doesn't fly off the top of the shaft as you remove it as the steel balls will drop out. After it is removed, collect the three steel balls from the slots inside it **(see illustration 33.60a)**.
Caution: Don't pull the gear up too hard or fast – the balls will fly out of the gear.
51 Remove the circlip securing the 3rd gear pinion, then slide the splined washer, the pinion and its bush, and the splined washer off the shaft **(see illustrations 33.59e, d, c, b and a)**.

52 Remove the circlip securing the 5th gear pinion, then slide the pinion off the shaft **(see illustrations 33.58b and a)**.
53 Remove the circlip securing the 2nd gear pinion, then slide the splined washer and the pinion off the shaft **(see illustrations 33.57c, b and a)**.

Inspection

54 Refer to Steps 6 to 13 above.

Output shaft reassembly

55 During reassembly, apply molybdenum disulphide oil (a 50/50 mixture of molybdenum disulphide grease and clean engine oil) to the mating surfaces of the shaft, pinions and bushes.
56 When installing the circlips, do not expand their ends any further than is necessary and position them with each end aligned with a spline **(see illustration 33.43d)**. Make sure the round edged side of the circlip faces the direction thrust so the sharp edged side takes the thrust of the pinion it seats against.
57 Slide the 2nd gear pinion onto the shaft with its recessed side facing away from the flange, followed by the splined washer **(see illustrations)**. Fit the circlip, making sure it is locates correctly in its groove in the shaft **(see illustrations)**.
58 Slide the 5th gear pinion onto the shaft with its selector fork groove facing away from the 2nd gear pinion and aligning the oil holes, then fit the circlip, making sure it is locates correctly in its groove in the shaft **(see illustrations)**.
59 Slide the splined washer and the 3rd gear pinion bush onto the shaft, aligning the oil holes, then slide the 3rd gear pinion onto its bush with its recessed side facing away from the 5th gear pinion **(see**

37.58a Slide the 5th gear pinion onto the shaft . . .

33.58b . . . and secure it with the circlip . . .

33.58c . . . making sure it locates in the groove

33.59a Slide the splined washer onto the shaft . . .

33.59b . . . followed by the 3rd gear pinion bush . . .

33.59c . . . then fit the pinion onto the bush

33.59d Slide the splined washer onto the shaft . . .

33.59e . . . then fit the circlip . . .

33.59f . . . making sure it locates in the groove

illustrations). Slide the splined washer on, then fit the circlip, making sure it is locates correctly in its groove in the shaft **(see illustrations)**.

60 Lubricate the positive neutral finder mechanism balls with engine oil – don't use grease as it will impair the action of the mechanism. Fit the balls into the holes with the narrow outer ends in the 4th gear pinion **(see illustrations)**. Hold the shaft upright on the bench. Carefully slide the 4th gear

pinion onto the shaft with its selector fork groove facing down, and aligning the holes that contain the balls with the slots in the shaft, keeping it horizontal so the balls do not slide out **(see illustration)**. When the pinion is in place, tilt the shaft horizontal and turn it slowly, then check that the pinion cannot slide off.

61 Slide the thrust washer onto the shaft, then slide the 1st gear pinion on with its recessed side facing the 4th gear pinion

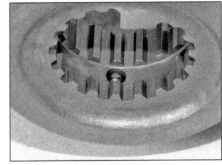

33.60a Fit the balls into the holes . . .

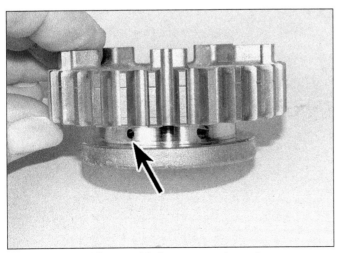

33.60b . . . with the narrow outer ends

33.60c Slide the 4th gear pinion down onto the shaft, aligning the narrow ball holes with the slots (arrowed)

33.61a Slide the thrust washer onto the shaft . . .

33.61b . . . followed by the 1st gear pinion . . .

33.61c . . . and the thrust washer

(see illustration). Fit the thrust washer (see illustration).
62 Slide the needle bearing on, then fit the snap-ring into its groove (see illustrations).
63 Check that all components have been correctly installed (see illustration).

34 Initial start-up and break-in procedure

1 Make sure the engine oil and coolant levels are correct (see *Pre-ride checks*). Make sure there is fuel in the tank.
2 Turn the engine kill switch to the ON position and shift the gearbox into neutral. Turn the ignition ON.
3 Start the engine and allow it to run at a moderately fast idle until it reaches operating temperature.

⚠ *Warning: If the oil pressure warning light doesn't go off, or it comes on while the engine is running, stop the engine immediately.*

4 If a lubrication failure is suspected, stop the engine immediately and try to find the cause. If an engine is run without oil, even for a short period of time, severe damage will occur.
5 Check carefully for oil and coolant leaks and make sure the transmission and controls, especially the brakes, function properly before road testing the machine.
6 Any rebuilt engine needs time to break-in, even if parts have been installed in their original locations. For this reason, treat the machine gently for the first few miles to make sure oil has circulated throughout the engine and any new parts installed have started to seat.

7 Even greater care is necessary if the engine has been rebored or a new crankshaft has been installed. In the case of a rebore, the engine will have to be broken in as if the machine were new. This means greater use of the transmission and a restraining hand on the throttle until at least 500 miles (800 km) have been covered. There's no point in keeping to any set speed limit – the main idea is to keep from lugging the engine and to gradually increase performance until the 500 mile (800 km) mark is reached. These recommendations can be lessened to an extent when only a new crankshaft is installed. Experience is the best guide, since it's easy to tell when an engine is running freely.
8 Make sure an initial oil and filter change is done after running the rebuilt engine for about 600 miles (1000 km).

33.62a Fit the needle bearing . . .

33.62b . . . then fit the snap ring into its groove

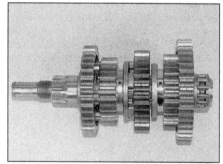

33.63 The complete assembly should be as shown

Chapter 3
Cooling system

Contents

Degrees of difficulty

Easy, suitable for novice with little experience	Fairly easy, suitable for beginner with some experience	Fairly difficult, suitable for competent DIY mechanic	Difficult, suitable for experienced DIY mechanic	Very difficult, suitable for expert DIY or professional

Specifications

General

Coolant type and mixture ratio.	See Chapter 1
Coolant capacity	See Chapter 1
Filler cap pressure rating	1.0 to 1.2 Bar (14 to 18 psi)

Cooling fan thermostatic switch

VN1500A and B

Switch closes (fan ON).	94 to 100°C (201 to 212°F)
Switch opens (fan OFF)	around 90°C (194°F)
Resistance	
Switch closed (on)	Less than 0.5 ohms
Switch open (off).	More than 1 M-ohm

All other models

Switch closes (fan ON).	100 to 110°C (212 to 230°F)
Switch opens (fan OFF)	around 98 °C (203 °F)
Resistance	
Switch closed (on)	Less than 0.5 ohms
Switch open (off).	More than 1 M-ohm

Temperature light sender

Switch closes (light ON)	110 to 120°C (230 to 248°F)
Switch opens (light OFF)	108°C (226°F)

Thermostat

Thermostat rating	
Opening temperature	
VN1500A and B models	80 to 84° C (176 to 183° F)
All other models	58 to 62° C (136 to 144° F)
Valve travel (when fully open)	Not less than 8 mm (5/16-inch) at 95° C (203° F)

Torque specifications

Coolant pipe bolts to cylinder head	10 Nm (88 inch-lbs)
Coolant temperature sender unit	7.8 Nm (69 inch-lbs)
Thermostatic fan switch	
VN1500A and B	7.8 Nm (69 inch-lbs)
All other models	18 Nm (13 ft-lbs)
Water pump impeller bolt	10 Nm (88 inch-lbs)
Water pump cover bolts.	10 Nm (88 inch-lbs)

1 General information

The models covered by this manual are equipped with a liquid cooling system that uses a water/antifreeze mixture to carry away excess heat produced during the combustion process. The cylinders are surrounded by water jackets through which the coolant is circulated by the water pump. The pump is mounted to the right side of the crankcase and is driven by chain and sprockets running off the right-hand end of the crankshaft. The coolant passes internally up around the cylinders, through the water passages in the cylinder heads, out through a pair of tubes and hoses and into the thermostat housing. The hot coolant then flows down into the radiator (which is mounted on the front of the frame to take advantage of maximum air flow), where it is cooled by the passing air, through another hose and back to the water pump, where the cycle is repeated.

An electric fan, mounted behind the radiator and automatically controlled by a thermostatic switch in the radiator, draws cooling air through the radiator when the motorcycle is not moving. Under certain conditions, the fan may come on even after the engine is stopped, and the ignition switch is off, and may run for several minutes.

The coolant temperature sender unit (not fitted on VN1500A and B models), threaded into the radiator, senses the temperature of the coolant and controls the coolant temperature warning light on the instrument cluster.

On models with fuel injection an engine coolant temperature (ECT) sensor is threaded into the thermostat housing and provides the ICU with information on engine temperature.

The entire system is sealed and pressurized. The pressure is controlled by a valve which is part of the radiator cap. By pressurizing the coolant, the boiling point is raised, which prevents premature boiling of the coolant. An overflow hose, connected between the radiator and reservoir tank, directs coolant to the tank when the radiator cap valve is opened by excessive pressure. The coolant is automatically siphoned back to the radiator as the engine cools.

Many cooling system inspection and service procedures are part of routine maintenance and are included in Chapter 1.

⚠ **Warning: Do not allow antifreeze to come in contact with your skin or painted surfaces of the motorcycle. Rinse off spills immediately with plenty of water. Antifreeze is highly toxic if ingested. Never leave antifreeze lying around in an open container or in puddles on the floor; children and pets are attracted by its sweet smell and may drink it. Check with local authorities about disposing of used antifreeze. Many communities have collection centers which will see that antifreeze is disposed of safely.**

⚠ **Warning: Do not remove the pressure cap when the engine and radiator are hot. Scalding hot coolant and steam may be blown out under pressure, which could cause serious injury. To open the pressure cap, wait until the engine has cooled. When the engine has cooled, place a thick rag, like a towel, over the radiator cap; slowly rotate the cap counterclockwise to the first stop. This procedure allows any residual pressure to escape. When the steam has stopped escaping, press down on the cap while turning counterclockwise and remove it.**

Caution: At all times use the specified type of anti-freeze, and always mix it with distilled water in the correct proportion or purchase pre-mix coolant. The anti-freeze contains corrosion inhibitors which are essential to avoid damage to the cooling system. A lack of these inhibitors could lead to a build-up of corrosion which would block the coolant passages, resulting in overheating and severe engine damage. Distilled water must be used as opposed to tap water to avoid a build-up of scale which would also block the passages.

2 Radiator cap – check

If problems such as overheating and loss of coolant occur, check the entire system as described in Chapter 1. If no problems can be found have the radiator cap opening pressure checked by a dealer service department or service station equipped with the special tester required to do the job. If the cap is defective, replace it with a new one.

3 Coolant reservoir – removal and installation

VN1500A and B models

1 Undo the screw on the top of the reservoir cover, then remove the cover.
2 Detach the overflow hose from the top of the reservoir inner wall.
3 The reservoir has two pegs, one on the inner wall and one on the bottom, that fit into grommets. Release the pegs, then open the cap and pour the coolant into a suitable container. Disconnect the bottom hose and remove the reservoir.
4 Installation is the reverse of removal. Fill the reservoir with the specified coolant (see Chapter 1).

All other models

5 Remove the right side cover (see Chapter 8).
6 Displace the junction box from its rubber holder, and if required release the holder from the reservoir (see illustration).
7 Detach the overflow hose from the top of the reservoir.
8 Unscrew the reservoir bolts, then remove the cap, detach the bottom hose and drain the coolant into a suitable container, either via the hose union or the filler orifice (see illustration).
9 Installation is the reverse of the removal steps. Fill the reservoir with the specified coolant (see Chapter 1).

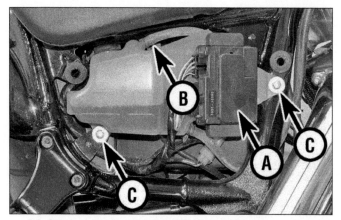

3.6 Displace the junction box (A), then detach the overflow hose (B). Reservoir mounting bolts (C)

3.8 Detach the bottom hose and drain the reservoir

4.1a Disconnect the fan assembly connector (arrowed) . . .

4.1b . . . and the fan switch connector (arrowed)

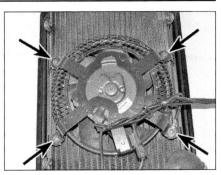

4.10 Fan assembly bolts (arrowed)

4 Cooling fan and thermostatic switch – check and replacement

Note: *If overheating occurs during normal use of the motorcycle fully check the cooling system as described in Chapter 1.*

Check

1 If the engine is overheating and the cooling fan isn't coming on, first check the fuses (see Chapter 9). If a fuse is blown, check the circuit for a short to ground (see the *Wiring diagrams* at the end of this book). If the fuses are all good, on VN1500A and B models disconnect the fan electrical connector, and on all other models disconnect the fan and fan switch connectors **(see illustrations)** – remove the fuel tank for access where necessary (see Chapter 4A or 4B). Using two jumper wires, apply battery voltage (+ to blue wire) to the terminals in the fan motor side of the electrical connector on VN1500A and B models, and the positive (+) to the blue wire terminal in the switch connector and the negative (–) to the black/yellow wire in the main connector on all other models. If the fan doesn't work, replace the motor.

2 If the fan does come on, the problem lies in the thermostatic fan switch, the junction box (containing the cooling fan relay) on VN1500A and B models except A9-on or the separate cooling fan relay on A9-on models, or the wiring that connects the components. Remove the jumper wires and reconnect the electrical connector to the fan.

3 If you're working on a VN1500A or B model (with a single-wire fan switch connector), disconnect the connector from the switch, attach a jumper wire to the harness side of the connector and ground the other end of the jumper wire. If the fan comes on, the circuit to the motor is good, and the thermostatic fan switch is faulty.

4 If you're working on any other model (with a double-wire fan switch connector), disconnect the connector **(see illustration 4.1b)**. Connect the terminals in the harness side of the connector together with a jumper wire. If the fan comes on, the circuit to the motor is good and the switch is faulty. If the fan still doesn't

work, check the wiring back to the junction box fuse.

5 If the fan is on the whole time, disconnect the wiring – the fan should stop. If it does the switch is faulty; if it doesn't there is a fault in the wiring.

6 If you're working on a VN1500A or B model except A9-on, and the fan still doesn't work, check the fan relay, located in the junction box – remove the seat to access it (see Chapter 8). Repeatedly touch the jumper wire to ground as detailed in Step 3 – if you feel and hear a clicking inside the relay, the relay is good and the fault must lie in the wiring from the relay to the fan motor. If no clicking is heard in the relay, the fault could lie in the wiring from the thermostatic fan switch to the relay, or in the relay itself. If all wiring checks out OK, remove the junction box and test the relay as follows. Set a multimeter to test for continuity and connect its probes to terminals 2 and 5 **(see illustration 6.2a in Chapter 9)**. There should be no continuity (infinite resistance). Using a fully-charged 12 volt battery and two insulated jumper wires, connect the positive (+) terminal of the battery to terminal 2 on the relay box, and the negative (–) terminal to terminal 4. At this point the multimeter should read 0 ohms (continuity). If this is the case the relay is proven good. If the relay still indicates no continuity (infinite resistance) across its terminals, it is faulty and the junction box must be replaced with a new one – individual relays are not available.

7 If you're working on a VN1500A9-on model, and the fan still doesn't work, locate the fan relay. Repeatedly touch the jumper wire to ground as detailed in Step 3 – if you feel and hear a clicking inside the relay, the relay is good and the fault must lie in the wiring from the relay to the fan motor. If no clicking is heard in the relay, the fault could lie in the wiring from the thermostatic fan switch to the relay, or in the relay itself. If all wiring checks out OK, replace the relay with a new one.

8 The switch reacts to temperature, closing (turning on) and opening (turning off) in the temperature ranges given in the Specifications at the beginning of the chapter. While in theory it is possible to bench test the behavior of the switch at those temperatures, in practice the test is difficult to set up and perform. You can however test the switch in the bike, though less accurately. Disconnect the switch wiring connector. Connect the probes of a multimeter

set to read resistance to the switch terminal (+) and body (-) on VN1500A and B models, and to the terminals on all other models. When the engine is cold the ohmmeter reading should be very high (approx 1 M-ohm) indicating that the switch is open (OFF). Run the engine until it is hot – when it is very hot the meter reading should drop to less than 0.5 ohms, indicating that the switch has closed (ON). On all except VN1500A and B models if the fan has not come on by the time the temperature warning light in the instrument cluster comes on, then the switch is faulty. Now turn the engine off. As the temperature falls, and after the warning light (where fitted) goes out, the meter reading should again show very high resistance, indicating that the switch has opened (OFF). If the meter readings obtained are different, or they are obtained at different temperatures, then the switch is faulty and must be replaced with a new one.

Replacement

Fan motor

 Warning: The engine must be completely cool before beginning this procedure.

9 Disconnect the cable from the negative terminal of the battery and remove the radiator (see Section 7).

10 Release and disconnect the wiring as required. Unscrew the bolts securing the fan bracket to the radiator **(see illustration)**. Note which bolt secures the fan motor ground wire. Separate the fan from the radiator.

11 Installation is the reverse of the removal steps.

Thermostatic fan switch

 Warning: The engine must be completely cool before beginning this procedure.

12 Disconnect the cable from the negative terminal of the battery and remove the radiator (see Section 7).

13 Disconnect the switch wiring where not already done **(see illustration 4.1b)**, then unscrew the switch from the radiator.

14 Install the switch and tighten it to the torque listed in this Chapter's Specifications for your model.

15 Connect the wiring and install the radiator.

5.1 Temperature sender unit (arrowed)

5 Coolant temperature light and sender unit – check and replacement

Note: *If overheating occurs during normal use of the motorcycle fully check the cooling system as described in Chapter 1.*

Check

1 All except VN1500A and B models are equipped with a coolant temperature warning light in the instrument cluster, actuated by the temperature sender unit in the bottom of the radiator **(see illustration)**. When the ignition is switched on the temperature warning light should come on temporarily, then go out – this serves as an indication that the circuit and bulb or LED are functioning correctly (if not, refer to Chapter 9).

2 If the engine has been overheating but the warning light hasn't been coming on, turn the ignition on, then disconnect the electrical connector from the sender unit.

3 Connect one end of a jumper wire to the sender unit wire and connect the other end of the jumper wire to ground. The warning light should come on. If it does the sender unit is faulty.

4 If the light is on the whole time, disconnect the wiring – the light should go out. If it does the sender is faulty; if it doesn't there is a fault in the wiring.

5 The sender reacts to temperature, closing (turning on) and opening (turning off) at the temperature ranges given in the Specifications at the beginning of the chapter. While in theory it is possible to bench test the behavior of the switch at those temperatures, in practice the test is difficult to set up and perform. You can test the resistance of the switch in the bike with the engine cold. Disconnect the switch wiring connector. Connect the probes of a multimeter set to read resistance to the switch terminal (+) and body (-). When the engine is cold the ohmmeter reading should be very high (approx 1 M-ohm) indicating that the switch is open (OFF). If the reading is around zero ohms, indicating that the switch is closed (ON), the switch is faulty. Note that you should not attempt to test the closing temperature of the switch in the bike.

Replacement

Sender unit

> ⚠ **Warning:** *The engine must be completely cool before beginning this procedure.*

6 Disconnect the cable from the negative terminal of the battery and remove the radiator (see Section 7).

7 Disconnect the sender wiring where not already done **(see illustration 5.1)**. Unscrew the sender unit from the radiator. If it is to be reused clean all old sealant off the threads.

8 Apply some silicone sealant to the threads and quickly install the unit, tightening to the torque listed in this Chapter's Specifications.

9 Connect the wiring and install the radiator.

Coolant temperature bulb or LED

10 Refer to Chapter 9.

6 Thermostat and housing – removal, check and installation

> ⚠ **Warning:** *The engine must be completely cool before beginning this procedure.*

1 The thermostat is automatic in operation and should give many years service without requiring attention. In the event of a failure, the valve will probably jam open, in which case the engine will take much longer than normal to warm up. Conversely, if the valve jams shut, the coolant will be unable to circulate and the engine will overheat. Neither condition is acceptable, and the fault must be investigated promptly.

Removal

Note: *On fuel injection models the thermostat can be removed without having to first remove the housing from the bike if required – ignore Step 4.*

2 Refer to Chapter 1 and partially drain the cooling system – there is no need to fully drain it unless required, approximately 200 ml (6.7 US fl oz) is sufficient, so the level is below that of the thermostat housing.

3 Remove the fuel tank (see Chapter 4A or 4B). On VN1500A and B models remove the fuel filter (see Chapter 4A). On VN1500 Classic and Nomad/Classic Tourer models remove the surge tank (see Chapter 4A).

4 To remove the thermostat housing, release and detach the hoses **(see illustration)**. On fuel injection models disconnect the ECT sensor wiring connector **(see illustration)**. Unbolt the thermostat housing and remove it.

5 To remove the thermostat on carburetor models undo the cover screws, detach the cover and draw the thermostat out. Remove the O-ring and discard it – a new one must be used.

6 To remove the thermostat on fuel injection

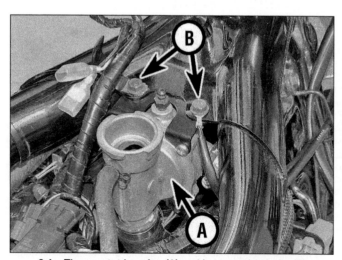

6.4a Thermostat housing (A) and its mounting bolts (B)

6.4b Disconnect the ECT sensor wiring connector (arrowed)

6.6a Disconnect the AP sensor wiring connector (arrowed)

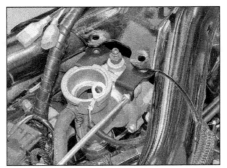

6.6b Undo the screws, detach the cover . . .

6.6c . . . and remove the thermostat . . .

models, if the housing has not been removed unscrew the housing mounting bolts **(see illustration 6.4a)** and disconnect the AP sensor wiring connector **(see illustration)**. Undo the cover screws, detach the cover and draw the thermostat out **(see illustrations)**. Remove the O-ring and discard it **(see illustration)** – a new one must be used.

Check

7 Remove any coolant deposits, then visually check the thermostat for corrosion, cracks and other damage. If it was open when it was removed, the thermostat is defective.
8 To check the thermostat operation, submerge it in a container of the specified coolant (50/50 antifreeze and water) along with a thermometer **(see illustration)**. The thermostat should be suspended so it does not touch the sides of the container.

 Warning: Antifreeze is poisonous. Do not use a cooking pan to test the thermostat.

9 Gradually heat the water in the container with a hot plate or stove and check the temperature when the thermostat first starts to open. Compare the opening temperature to the values listed in this Chapter's Specifications.
10 Continue heating the water until the valve is fully open. Using adequate protection against the hot thermostat measure how far the thermostat valve has opened and

6.6d . . . and the O-ring

compare to the value listed in this Chapter's Specifications.
11 If these specifications are not met, or if the thermostat doesn't open while the water is heated, or if you are in any doubt about the performance of the thermostat, replace it with a new one – they are not expensive.

Installation

12 Installation is the reverse of the removal steps, with the following additions:
 a) If the thermostat housing was removed on fuel injection models, do not forget to connect the ECT sensor wiring **(see illustration 6.4b)**.
 b) Fit the thermostat into the housing with the hole at the top **(see illustration 6.4c)**.

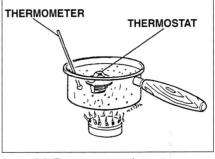

6.8 Thermostat testing set-up

 c) Fit a new O-ring in the groove in the thermostat cover **(see illustration 6.4d)**.
 d) Fill the cooling system with the recommended coolant (see Chapter 1).

7 Radiator – removal and installation

 Warning: The engine must be completely cool before beginning this procedure.

1 Drain the cooling system (see Chapter 1). On VN1500A and B models remove the frame covers (see Chapter 8). On Mean Streak models remove the horn (see Chapter 9).
2 Disconnect the fan motor/fan switch/ temperature sender wiring connector(s), according to model **(see illustrations 4.1a and 5.1)**. Free the wiring from any clips or ties and feed it back to the fan, noting its routing.
3 Loosen the clamps securing the hoses to the pump on the right and the radiator on the left **(see illustrations)**. Work the hoses free, taking care not to damage the unions in the process.
4 On VN1500A and B models unscrew the radiator mounting bolts, one at the top and two at the bottom, noting the earth wire secured by the bottom left one. Take the radiator out.
5 On all other models , unscrew the mounting bolt at the top of the radiator, then lift the

7.3a Detach the hoses (arrowed) from the pump . . .

7.3b . . . and from the left-hand side of the radiator

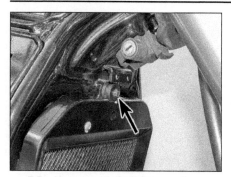

7.5a Unscrew the bolt (arrowed) . . .

7.5b . . . then lift the radiator posts out of the bushes . . .

7.5c . . . and remove the radiator

radiator bottom posts out of the mounting bushings **(see illustrations)**.

6 Inspect the mounting bushings. Replace them if they're cracked or deteriorated.

7 Installation is the reverse of the removal steps, with the following additions:
a) Don't forget to connect the wiring.
b) On VN1500A and B don't forget to connect the earth lead with the bottom left bolt.
c) Fill the cooling system with the recommended coolant (see Chapter 1).

8 Water pump – check, removal and installation

⚠ **Warning: The engine must be completely cool before beginning this procedure.**

Check

1 Visually check the area around the water pump for coolant leaks. Try to determine if the leak is simply the result of a loose hose clamp or deteriorated hose, or defective cover gasket.

2 Check the drain hole on the underside of the pump or the bottom of the drain hose connected to the pump and routed round the front of the engine for signs of leakage **(see illustration)**. If the pump mechanical seal fails, the drain allows the coolant to escape. If the oil seal fails, the drain allows the oil to escape. If on inspection the drain shows signs of coolant leakage, replace the mechanical seal with a new one. If there are signs of oil leakage replace the oil seal with a new one (see Chapter 2). A whitish emulsion of oil and coolant mean both seals have failed.

3 To check inside the pump, drain the coolant following the procedure in Chapter 1.

4 Remove the pump cover (see Step 8).

5 Try to wiggle the pump impeller back-and-forth and in-and-out. If you can feel movement, the water pump seals and bearings must be replaced.

6 Check the impeller blades for corrosion. If they are heavily corroded, replace the impeller and flush the system thoroughly (it would also be a good idea to check the internal condition of the radiator).

Removal

7 Drain the coolant (see Chapter 1).

8 To remove the cover, on VN1500A and B models unscrew the inlet pipe bolts, and on all other models, release the clamp and detach the hose from the cover **(see illustration 7.3a)**. Unscrew the cover bolts, noting how the two rear ones secure the idle speed adjuster bracket on some models, and remove the cover, pulling it off the pipe on VN1500A and B models **(see illustration)**. Remove the cover gasket and discard it – a new one must be used. Remove the dowels if loose. Note that new sealing washers must be fitted with the rear cover bolts on installation, and that on models with the idle speed adjuster bracket there are four washers, one on each side of each bracket hole. Discard the pipe O-ring on VN1500A and B models – a new one must be used.

9 To remove the impeller with the engine in the frame shift the transmission into first gear and, with the rear tire in contact with the floor, press the brake pedal. If the engine has been removed how you hold the impeller depends on what has and has not been removed – you can hold the driven sprocket using a holding tool as shown if the front cylinder and pump drive chain have been removed **(see**

8.2 Check the pump drain hole or hose (arrowed) for leakage

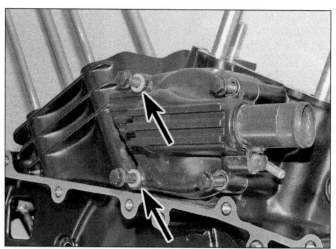

8.8 Unscrew the bolts, noting the sealing washers (arrowed), and remove the cover

8.9a You can hold the sprocket using a holding tool . . .

8.9b . . . or jam the gears as described

8.9c Unscrew the bolt . . .

8.9d . . . and remove the impeller

8.9e Remove the O-ring

8.9f Check the impeller seating seal surface (arrowed)

illustration), and if not you can lock the primary drive and driven gears together using a piece of aluminium (do not use steel) or stout rag where the teeth mesh on the underside if the right crankcase cover has been removed (see illustration). Note that you cannot hold the impeller itself as it is not keyed to its shaft and will turn on it. With the shaft locked unscrew the impeller nut, turning it clockwise as it has left-hand threads, and take the impeller off the shaft (see illustrations). Remove the O-ring from the shaft (see illustration) – a new one must be used. Check the condition of the seating seal on the inner face of the impeller for wear and damage and if any is evident replace the impeller with a new one (see illustration).

10 If only the mechanical seal needs to be replaced you can remove it and fit a new one now, but if other components are being removed and replaced do not remove the seal yet. To replace it now, pry its flange loose from the bore with a sharp screwdriver and pull the seal out with pliers (see illustration). Tap the new one squarely in using a 28 mm socket or other suitable tool that bears only on the seating rim of the seal, and tap it in until it seats (see illustration). Note: The new seal is coated with adhesive on the outside. Don't apply sealant to the seal or its bore.

11 To remove the oil seal and bearings separate the crankcase halves (see Chapter 2). Withdraw the shaft (see illustration).

12 Remove the unsealed bearing from inside the crankcase using a knife-edged puller with slide-hammer attachment (see illustration).

8.10a Lever up the seal flange (arrowed) using a suitable tool (shown with shaft removed)

8.10b Drive the new seal in using a suitable socket

8.11 Withdraw the pump shaft

8.12a Remove the unsealed bearing . . .

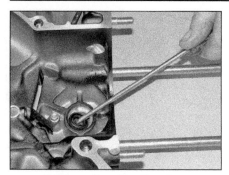

8.12b . . . then the oil seal . . .

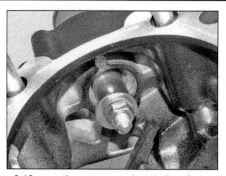

8.12c . . . then set up a drawbolt using a small socket on the bearing inner race on the inside . . .

8.12d . . . and a large socket around (not touching) the seal on the outside . . .

8.12e . . . and tighten the inner nut . . .

8.12f . . . to push the sealed bearing and mechanical seal out into the large socket

Remove the oil seal using seal hook or screwdriver **(see illustration)**. Push the sealed bearing and mechanical seal out together using two sockets and a drawbolt arrangement as shown **(see illustrations)**.

13 Push the new sealed bearing in using a similar drawbolt and socket arrangement, but working in the opposite direction **(see illustration)**.

14 Smear the outer rim of the new oil seal with oil and fit it with its open end facing as shown into the inside of the crankcase, using a washer and socket to drive it in and setting it level with the rim of its bore so it does not contact the sealed bearing **(see illustrations)**. When fitted coat the lips with high temperature grease.

8.13a Fit the new sealed bearing . . .

8.13b . . . using a similar set-up but using a socket that contacts the outer race . . .

8.13c . . . the opposite way round

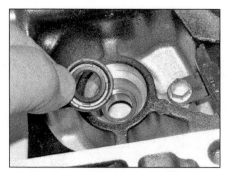

8.14a Fit the new oil seal as shown . . .

8.14b . . . then lay a washer over it as protection . . .

8.14c . . . and drive it in using a socket

8.15 Drive the unsealed bearing in using a socket on the outer race

8.16a Fit the mechanical seal using a G-clamp to draw it in via a socket on the outside on the seal rim . . .

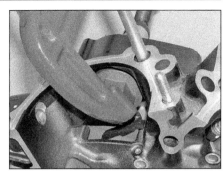

8.16b . . . and a suitable interface against the crankcase on the inside

15 Drive the new unsealed bearing **(see illustration 8.12a)** in until it seats using socket or bearing drive located on the outer race **(see illustration)**.

16 Fit the new mechanical seal **(see illustration 8.10b)** and press it in using a 28 mm socket or other suitable tool that bears only on the seating rim of the seal and using a G-clamp as shown, so the seal is drawn squarely in until it seats by turning the clamp bolt **(see illustrations)**. Make sure the rim is correctly seated all the way round **(see illustration 8.10a)**. Do not use a drawbolt arrangement as the threads of the stud could damage the seal lips.

Installation

17 Carefully insert the shaft through the bearings and seals **(see illustration 8.11)**. Fit a new O-ring smeared with oil into the groove in the outer end of the shaft **(see illustration 8.9e)**. Coat the seating seal on the inner face of the impeller with coolant **(see illustration 8.9f)**. Fit the impeller and tighten the bolt, turning it anti-clockwise **(see illustrations 8.9d and c)** – tighten it to the torque listed in the Specifications now if you have a suitable method of locking the shaft (do not hold the impeller), otherwise lock it later using one of the methods described in Step 9 at the appropriate stage (if locking the primary drive and driven gears fit the locking tool where the gear teeth mesh at the top). The important thing is DO NOT forget to tighten it at some point.

18 Reassemble the crankcase halves (see Chapter 2).

19 Clean all traces of old gasket from the cover and housing mating surfaces. On VN1500A and B models fit a new O-ring onto the coolant pipe. Fit a new gasket, locating it over the dowels **(see illustration)**. Fit the cover, seating the pipe as you do on VN1500A and B models **(see illustration)**. Fit the bolts using new sealing washers and not forgetting the idle speed adjuster bracket where fitted, and tighten the bolts to the torque listed in the Specifications **(see illustration 8.8)**. On VN1500A and B models tighten the pipe bolts.

20 Fill the system with the specified coolant (see Chapter 1).

9 Coolant hoses and pipes – removal and installation

Removal

1 Before removing a hose, drain the coolant (see Chapter 1).

2 Use a screwdriver to release or slacken the larger-bore hose clamps, then slide them back along the hose and clear of the union spigot **(see illustrations 7.3a and b)**. The smaller-bore hoses are secured by spring clamps which can be expanded by squeezing their ears together with pliers.

Caution: The radiator unions are fragile. Do not use excessive force when attempting to remove the hoses.

3 If a hose proves stubborn, release it by rotating it on its union before working it off. If all else fails, cut the hose with a sharp knife. Whilst this means replacing the hose with a new one – it is preferable to buying a new radiator.

4 The outlet pipe on each cylinder head can be removed by unscrewing the bolt **(see illustration)**. If the pipe is removed, the O-ring must be replaced with a new one.

Installation

5 Slide the clamps onto the hose and then work the hose on to its union as far as the spigot where present.

> **HAYNES HiNT** *If the hose is difficult to push on its union, soften it by soaking it in very hot water, or alternatively a little soapy water on the union can be used as a lubricant.*

6 Rotate the hose on its unions to settle it in position before sliding the clamps into place and tightening them.

7 If the outlet pipe on the cylinder head has been removed, fit a new O-ring smeared with grease into the groove. Fit the pipe and tighten the bolt to the torque setting specified at the beginning of the Chapter.

8 Refill the cooling system with fresh coolant (see Chapter 1) and check the coolant level (see *Pre-ride checks*).

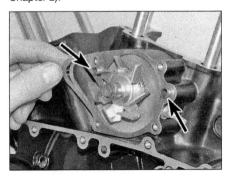

8.19a Fit a new gasket onto the dowels (arrowed) . . .

8.19b . . . then fit the cover

9.4 Coolant outlet pipe bolt (arrowed)

Notes

Chapter 4A
Fuel and exhaust systems – carburetor models

Contents

Degrees of difficulty

Easy, suitable for novice with little experience	Fairly easy, suitable for beginner with some experience	Fairly difficult, suitable for competent DIY mechanic	Difficult, suitable for experienced DIY mechanic	Very difficult, suitable for expert DIY or professional

Specifications

General

Fuel grade .... Unleaded, minimum octane rating 91 RON
Carburetor type
  VN1500A and B models.................................... Keihin CVK36 x 2
  VN1500 Classic and Nomad/Classic Tourer models .... Keihin CVK40 x 1
Idle speed... See Chapter 1

Jet sizes

VN1500A

Main jet
  Standard
    Front cylinder carburetor
      California   118
      All others   112
    Rear cylinder carburetor
      California   118
      US 49-state and Canada   115
      All others   112
  High altitude (above 4000 ft)
    Front cylinder carburetor
      California   115
      All others   110
    Rear cylinder carburetor
      California   115
      All others   112
Jet needle
  Front carburetor
    California N53U
    Switzerland N67F
    All others N53S
  Rear carburetor
    California N53V
    US 49-state and Canada N53T
    Switzerland N67G
    All others N67A
Pilot screw (turns out – see text)
  US and Switzerland 2¼
  All others 1½

VN1500B

Main jet
  Standard
    Front cylinder carburetor   130
    Rear cylinder carburetor   132
  US model high altitude (above 4000 ft)
    Front cylinder carburetor   128
    Rear cylinder carburetor   130
Jet needle
  Front carburetor
    California N36R
    Switzerland N77D
    All others N36P
  Rear carburetor
    California N36S
    Switzerland N77D
    All others N36Q
Pilot screw (turns out – see text)
  US and Switzerland 2¼
  All others 1½

VN1500 Classic – D models

Main jet
  Switzerland   140
  All others   132
  US high altitude (above 4000 ft)   130
Main air jet   100
Needle jet   6
Jet needle
  Switzerland N2PS
  All others N3RB
Pilot jet
  Standard   45
  US high altitude (above 4000 ft)   42

Jet sizes (continued)

VN1500 Classic – D models (continued)
Pilot air jet
    Switzerland.. 70
    All others.. 50
Pilot screw (turns out – see text)
    Switzerland.. 1¼ ± ¼
    All others.. 2 ± ¼
Starter (choke) jet... 60

VN1500 Classic – E and F models
Main jet
    Standard.. 138
    US high altitude (above 4000 ft)........................... 135
Main air jet... 100
Needle jet.. 6
Jet needle.. N2PY
Pilot jet
    Standard.. 45
    US high altitude (above 4000 ft)........................... 42
Pilot air jet... 50
Pilot screw (turns out – see text)............................ 2 ± ¼
Starter (choke) jet... 65

VN1500 Nomad/Classic Tourer
Main jet
    Standard.. 142
    US high altitude (above 4000 ft)........................... 140
Main air jet... 100
Needle jet.. 6
Jet needle.. N2PY
Pilot jet
    Standard.. 45
    US high altitude (above 4000 ft)........................... 42
Pilot air jet... 95
Pilot screw (turns out – see text)
    Switzerland (except H2 models)............................ 1¼ ± ¼
    All others.. 1¾ ± ¼
Starter (choke) jet... 65

Fuel level
VN1500A and B models
    Front carburetor... 2.2 ± 1 mm
    Rear carburetor.. 4.2 ± 1 mm
VN1500 Classic and Nomad/Classic Tourer models .... 0 to 2 mm below float chamber mating surface

Float height
VN1500A and B models..................................... Not available
VN1500 Classic and Nomad/Classic Tourer models .... 19 ± 2 mm

Air switching valve test vacuum
VN1500A and B models..................................... 35 to 43 kPa (260 to 320 mm-Hg)
VN1500 Classic and Nomad/Classic Tourer
    US and Canada Classic D models......................... 57 to 65 kPa (430 to 490 mm-Hg)
    All other models... 49 to 57 kPa (370 to 430 mm-Hg)

Fuel level sensor
Resistance
    Full position .... 4 to 10 ohms
    Empty position .... 90 to 100 ohms

Throttle sensor
Output voltage
    Throttle closed .... 0.9 to 1.1 volts
    Throttle fully open.. 4.06 to 4.26 volts

1 General information

The fuel supply system consists of the fuel tank, fuel tap, fuel filter, fuel pump, carburetor(s) and the connecting lines, hoses and control cables.

The carburetors used on VN1500A and B models are two constant vacuum Keihins with butterfly-type throttle valves. Classic and Nomad/Classic Tourer models use a single constant vacuum Keihin. For cold starting, an enrichment circuit is actuated by a choke lever mounted on the left side of the carburetor on VN1500A and B models, mounted on the left-hand side behind the rear cylinder and linked to the carburetor by cable on Classic models, and mounted on the left-hand side of the frame at the front and linked to the carburetor by cable on Classic and Nomad/Classic Tourer models. Classic models from 1998-on (E and F models) and all Nomad/Classic Tourer models have a throttle sensor fitted on the carburetor that relays information on throttle angle to the ICU.

A fuel level sensor in the form of a float on an arm inside the tank actuates the fuel gauge in the instrument cluster.

2 Fuel tank – removal and installation

⚠️ **Warning: Gasoline is extremely flammable, so take extra precautions when you work on any part of the fuel system. Don't smoke or allow open flames or bare light bulbs near the work area, and don't work in a garage where a natural gas-type appliance (such as a water heater or clothes dryer) is present. Since gasoline is carcinogenic, wear fuel-resistant gloves when there's a possibility of being exposed to fuel, and, if you spill any fuel on your skin, rinse it off immediately with soap and water. Mop up any spills immediately and do not store fuel-soaked rags where they could ignite. When you perform any kind of work on the fuel system, wear safety glasses and have a fire extinguisher suitable for a Class B type fire (flammable liquids) on hand.**

Removal

1 Remove the seat (see Chapter 8).
2 Disconnect the cable from the negative terminal of the battery (see Chapter 9).
3 On all except VN1500B models remove the instrument housing from the top of the tank (see Chapter 9).
4 Turn the fuel tap off. Disconnect the fuel hose from the carburetor side of the fuel tap, being prepared with a rag to catch the residual fuel.

5 Unscrew the tank mounting bolts **(see illustrations)**. Note the collars in the rubber grommets and remove them for safekeeping if required.
6 Lift and support the rear of the tank and disconnect the fuel level sensor wiring connector. Mark and disconnect the breather hose and, on California models, the evaporative emission control system hoses from the tank. Note any color code markings on the hoses; if they're obscured, make your own so the hoses can be reconnected properly.
7 Slide the tank to the rear to disengage the rubber dampers from the cups, then carefully lift the tank away from the machine.
8 To drain the tank connect a suitable hose to the tap outlet union and place the other end in a container suitable for storing fuel. Open the tap on its reserve setting and allow the tank to drain – note that however hard you try there will probably always be a small amount of fuel left in the far recesses of the tank.

Installation

9 Before installing the tank, check the condition of the rubber mounting dampers and grommets and the hoses on the underside of the tank – if they're hardened, cracked, or show any other signs of deterioration, replace them with new ones.
10 When installing the tank, reverse the above procedure. Make sure the tank seats properly and does not pinch any control cables or wires. If difficulty is encountered when trying to slide the tank dampers into the cups, a small amount of light oil should be used to lubricate them.

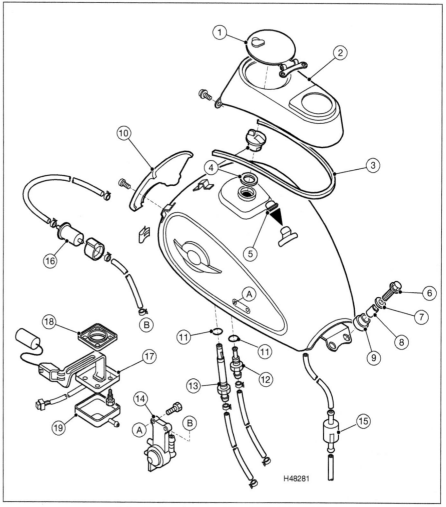

H48281

2.5a Fuel tank assembly – VN1500A and B

1 Filler cap cover (A models)	6 Bolt	13 Hose union
2 Instrument housing (A models)	7 Washer	14 Fuel tap
3 Seal (A models)	8 Collar	15 Drain
4 Filler cap and seal (A models)	9 Grommet	16 Filter
5 Rubber (A models)	10 Trim	17 Level sensor
	11 O-ring	18 Seal
	12 Hose union	19 Cover

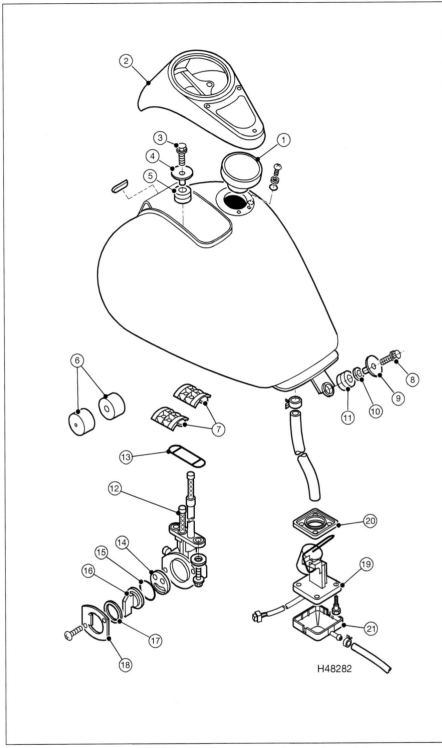

H48282

2.5b Fuel tank assembly – VN1500 Classic and Nomad/Classic Tourer

1 Filler cap
2 Instrument housing
3 Bolt
4 Collar
5 Grommet
6 Rubber support
7 Rubber support
8 Bolt

9 Collar
10 Spacer (Nomad/Classic Tourer)
11 Grommet
12 Strainer
13 Seal
14 Flow plate

15 O-ring
16 Tap lever
17 Seal
18 Tap plate
19 Level sensor
20 Seal
21 Cover

3 Fuel tap –
removal and installation

⚠️ **Warning: Gasoline is extremely flammable, so take extra precautions when you work on any part of the fuel system. Don't smoke or allow open flames or bare light bulbs near the work area, and don't work in a garage where a natural gas-type appliance (such as a water heater or clothes dryer) is present. Since gasoline is carcinogenic, wear fuel-resistant gloves when there's a possibility of being exposed to fuel, and, if you spill any fuel on your skin, rinse it off immediately with soap and water. Mop up any spills immediately and do not store fuel-soaked rags where they could ignite. When you perform any kind of work on the fuel system, wear safety glasses and have a fire extinguisher suitable for a Class B type fire (flammable liquids) on hand.**

Removal

1 Remove and drain the tank (see Section 2) **(see illustration 2.5a or b)**.

2 Place the tank upside down on a cushion of clean rag – make sure the tank is adequately cushioned around the sides so it is stable.

3 On VN1500A and B models disconnect the hoses from the tap, then unscrew the bolts and remove the tap. If required unscrew the hose unions from the tank to access the strainers for cleaning. Discard the sealing washers or O-rings – new ones must be used

4 On Classic and Nomad/Classic Tourer models unscrew the tap bolts, noting the nylon washers, and draw it out of the tank. Discard the sealing ring – a new one must be used.

5 Clean the strainers with solvent, and carefully blow them through with low pressure compressed air if available, then check for holes and splits in the gauze. Replace the strainers with new ones if available separately, or fit new unions or a new tap according to model.

6 If the tap has been leaking and tightening the assembly screws does not cure the problem check with a dealer as to the availability of internal components. If they are available disassemble the tap and replace worn or damaged parts and seals with new ones. If parts are not available replace the tap with a new one.

Installation

7 Installation is the reverse of removal. Use new O-rings, sealing washers and sealing rings according to model – on Classic and Nomad/Classic Tourer models do not replace the nylon washers with any of another material. Make sure the tank seats properly and does not pinch any control cables or wires. If difficulty is encountered when trying to slide the tank dampers into the cups, a small amount of light oil should be used to lubricate them.

4 Fuel tank – cleaning and repair

All repairs to the fuel tank should be carried out by a professional who has experience in this critical and potentially dangerous work. Even after cleaning and flushing of the fuel system, explosive fumes can remain and ignite during repair of the tank.

5 Idle fuel/air mixture adjustment – general information

1 Due to the increased emphasis on controlling motorcycle exhaust emissions, certain governmental regulations have been formulated which directly affect the carburetion of this machine. In order to comply with the regulations, the carburetors on some models have a metal sealing plug pressed into the hole over the pilot screw (which controls the idle fuel/air mixture) on each carburetor, so they can't be tampered with. These should only be removed in the event of a complete carburetor overhaul (described in Section 9), and even then the screws should be returned to their original settings. The pilot screws on other models are accessible, but the use of an exhaust gas analyzer is the only accurate way to adjust the idle fuel/air mixture and be sure the machine doesn't exceed the emissions regulations.
2 If the engine runs extremely rough at idle or continually stalls, and if a carburetor overhaul does not cure the problem, take the motorcycle to a Kawasaki dealer service department or other repair shop equipped with an exhaust gas analyzer. They will be able to properly adjust the idle fuel/air mixture to achieve a smooth idle and restore low speed performance.
3 Pilot screw settings (expressed as the number of turns out from the fully screwed in position) are given in the Specifications. These are standard settings if installing a new screw.

6 Carburetor overhaul – general information

1 Poor engine performance, hesitation, hard starting, stalling, flooding and backfiring are all signs that major carburetor maintenance may be required.
2 Keep in mind that many problems are incorrectly diagnosed as carburetor problems, and are really mechanical problems within the engine or malfunctions within the ignition system. Try to establish for certain that the carburetors are in need of a major overhaul before beginning.

3 Check the fuel tap strainers, the fuel filter, the fuel lines, the tank cap vent, the intake duct or manifold clamps and bolts, the vacuum hoses, the air filter element, the cylinder compression, the spark plugs, the air suction system and on VN1500A and B models the carburetor synchronization before assuming that a carburetor overhaul is required.
4 Most carburetor problems are caused by dirt particles, varnish and other deposits which build up in and block the fuel and air passages. Also, in time, gaskets and O-rings shrink or deteriorate and cause fuel and air leaks which lead to poor performance.
5 When the carburetor is overhauled, it is generally disassembled completely and the parts are cleaned thoroughly with a carburetor cleaning solvent and dried with filtered, unlubricated compressed air. The fuel and air passages are also blown through with compressed air to force out any dirt that may have been loosened but not removed by the solvent. Once the cleaning process is complete, the carburetor is reassembled using new gaskets, O-rings and, generally, a new inlet needle valve and seat.
6 Before disassembling the carburetor(s), make sure you have a carburetor rebuild kit (which will include all necessary O-rings and other parts), or all of the individual components required if a kit is not available, some carburetor cleaner, a supply of rags, some means of blowing out the carburetor passages and a clean place to work. On VN1500A and B models It is recommended that only one carburetor be overhauled at a time to avoid mixing up parts.

7 Carburetor(s) – removal and installation

⚠️ **Warning: Gasoline is extremely flammable, so take extra precautions when you work on any part of the fuel system (see the Warning in Section 2).**
Note: *If you are removing the carburetor(s) for disassembly and inspection refer to Section 10 and check the fuel level first – the level cannot be checked after removal, and can only be adjusted with the carburetor(s) disassembled.*

VN1500A and B models

Removal

1 Remove the fuel tank (see Section 2).
2 On the right side unscrew the carburetor cover, then remove its bracket **(see illustration 8.1)**. Detach the vacuum hose.
3 On the left side undo the throttle cable bracket screw, detach the bracket, and free the cable ends from the throttle cam. Detach the vacuum hose.
4 Slacken the clamp screws securing the carburetors in the air ducts and intake ducts on each side.

5 Remove the fuel pump, detaching the hose from the carburetors (see Section 16).
6 Disconnect the air suction hose from the rear of the surge tank (see Section 12). Remove the air duct for the front carburetor from the surge tank. Push the surge tank forwards.
7 Detach the carburetors, then twist them clockwise and lift them out.
8 After the carburetors have been removed, stuff clean rags into the intake ducts to prevent the entry of dirt or other objects.
9 If required loosen the intake duct clamps and remove them from the engine, noting their orientation – look for any cylinder marks (F and R for front and rear), or make your own marks if they aren't visible.

Installation

10 Installation is the reverse of removal, noting the following:
   a) Lubricate the air and intake ducts with light oil to ease their fitment onto the carburetors. Align any notches in the ducts with the tabs.
   b) Make sure the intake manifolds and their clamping band screws are positioned correctly
   c) Make sure all hoses are in good condition, correctly routed and securely connected.
   d) Lightly lubricate the ends of the throttle cables with multi-purpose grease before connecting them to the cam. Make sure the hole on the bracket locates over the peg. Adjust the throttle grip freeplay (see Chapter 1).
   e) Check for fuel leaks.
   f) Check and, if necessary, adjust the idle speed and carburetor synchronization (see Chapter 1).
Caution: Tape over or stuff clean rag into each cylinder head intake after removing the throttle body assembly to prevent anything from falling in.

Classic and Nomad/Classic Tourer models

Removal

11 Remove the fuel tank (see Section 2).
12 Release the choke knob from its holder.
13 Remove the right side air filter housing (see Section 12). Unbolt the housing bracket from the engine.
14 Disconnect the fuel and air hoses from the carburetor.
15 On all except D models remove the air surge tank (see Section 12). Drain the cooling system (see Chapter 1). Detach the coolant hoses from the carburetor – the top-side hose should be easily accessible, but if required detach the hose on the right side after displacing the carburetor. Disconnect the throttle sensor wiring connector.
16 Slacken the clamp screw securing the carburetor to the intake manifold. Pull the carburetor out of the manifold and out to the right. Undo the throttle cable bracket screw, detach the bracket, and free the cable ends

from the throttle cam. Take the carburetor out.
17 If necessary, remove the intake manifold bolts and take the manifold off the engine.

Installation

18 Installation is the reverse of removal, noting the following:
a) If removed fit the intake manifold using new sealing rings.
b) Lightly lubricate the ends of the throttle cables with multi-purpose grease before connecting them to the cam. Make sure the cut-out in the bracket locates over the peg.
c) Make sure all hoses are in good condition, correctly routed and securely connected.
d) On all except D models fill the cooling system (see Chapter 1).
e) Adjust the throttle grip freeplay (see Chapter 1).
f) Check for fuel leaks, and on all except D models for coolant leaks.
g) Check and, if necessary, adjust the idle speed (see Chapter 1).

8 Carburetor separation (VN1500A and B models)

1 The carburetor diaphragms and jets can be removed for cleaning and inspection without separating the carburetors from each other **(see illustration)**. The float chambers are contained within the center section of the carburetor assembly, so individual carburetor bodies must be removed from the center section to inspect the floats and adjust the fuel level.
2 Remove the carburetors (see Section 7).
3 Undo the choke rod bracket screws and detach the bracket and rod from the front carburetor.
4 Undo the choke rod pivot screw on the rear carburetor and detach the rod.
5 Remove the cotter pin and plastic washer, then detach the throttle link from the carburetor.
6 Undo the float chamber screws and separate the carburetor bodies from the center section.
7 Reassemble the carburetors in a reverse order.

9 Carburetor(s) – disassembly, cleaning and inspection

Warning: Gasoline is extremely flammable, so take extra precautions when you work on any part of the fuel system (see the Warning in Section 2).

Disassembly

1 Remove the carburetor(s) from the machine as described in Section 7. Set the assembly

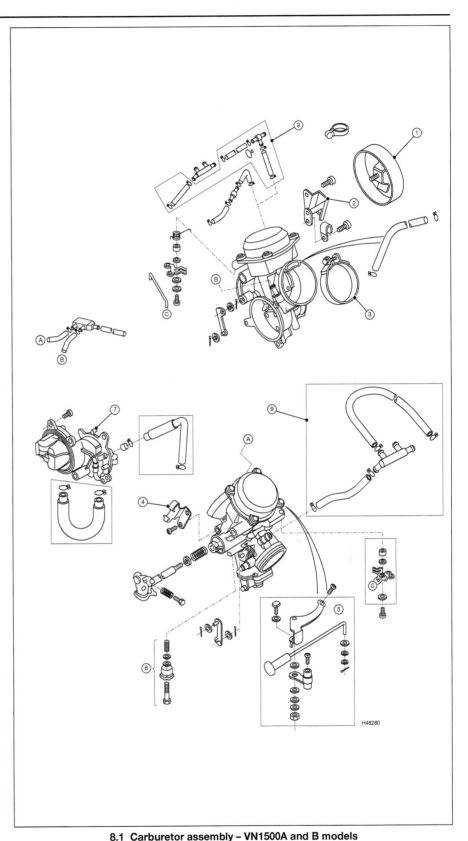

8.1 Carburetor assembly – VN1500A and B models

1 Cover
2 Bracket
3 Clamp
4 Throttle cable bracket
5 Choke rod assembly
6 Idle speed adjuster
7 Float chamber

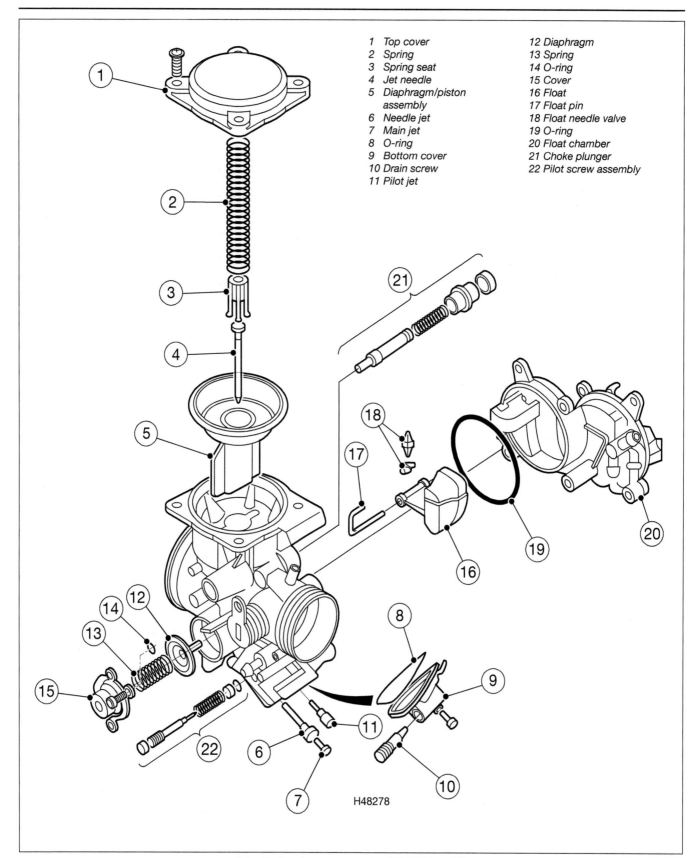

1 Top cover
2 Spring
3 Spring seat
4 Jet needle
5 Diaphragm/piston
    assembly
6 Needle jet
7 Main jet
8 O-ring
9 Bottom cover
10 Drain screw
11 Pilot jet
12 Diaphragm
13 Spring
14 O-ring
15 Cover
16 Float
17 Float pin
18 Float needle valve
19 O-ring
20 Float chamber
21 Choke plunger
22 Pilot screw assembly

H48278

9.2a Carburetor components – VN1500A and B

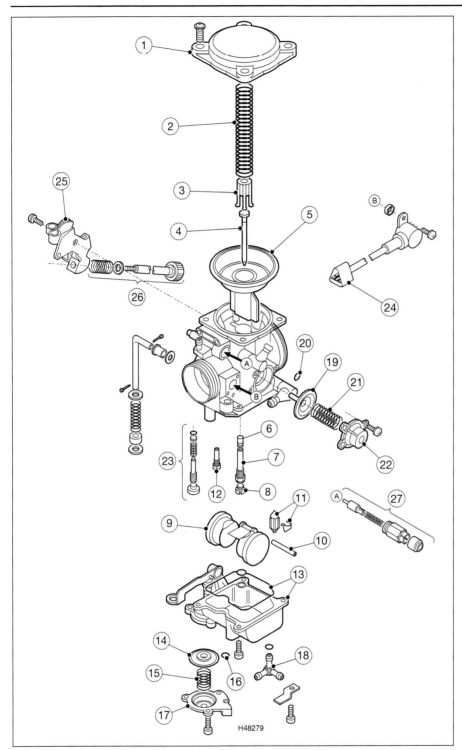

9.2b Carburetor components – Classic and Nomad/Classic Tourer

1 Top cover	10 Float pin	19 Diaphragm
2 Spring	11 Float needle valve	20 O-ring
3 Spring seat	12 Pilot jet	21 Spring
4 Jet needle	13 Float chamber and O-ring	22 Cover
5 Diaphragm/piston assembly	14 Diaphragm	23 Pilot screw assembly
6 Needle jet	15 Spring	24 Throttle sensor
7 Needle jet holder	16 O-ring	25 Throttle cable bracket
8 Main jet	17 Cover	26 Idle speed adjuster
9 Float	18 Hose union	27 Choke plunger

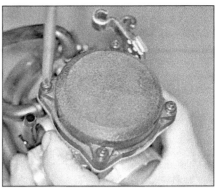

9.2c Undo the cover screws . . .

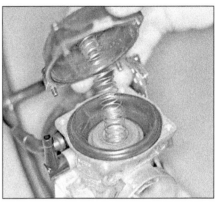

9.2d . . . lift the cover off and remove the spring

on a clean working surface. If you're planning to work on the floats of a VN1500A or B model, or if the float chamber O-rings have been leaking, separate the carburetors (see Section 8).

2 Remove the four screws securing the top cover to the carburetor body **(see illustrations)**. Lift the cover off and remove the piston spring.

3 Peel the diaphragm away from its groove in the carburetor body, being careful not to tear it. Lift out the diaphragm/piston assembly **(see illustration)**.

4 Remove the piston spring seat and

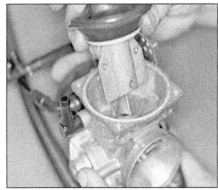

9.3 Lift the diaphragm/piston assembly out

separate the needle from the piston **(see illustrations)**.

VN1500A and B models

5 Refer to the exploded view **(see illustration 9.2a)** and note the following:

6 Make sure your screwdrivers are the correct size for the screws being undone.

7 Remove the bottom cover and O-ring for access to the jets **(see illustration)**.

8 Pull out the float pin with needle-nosed pliers to remove the floats **(see illustration)**.

9 When removing the diaphragm covers, do not lose the small O-ring in the passage next to the diaphragm **(see illustration)**.

10 The pilot (idle mixture) screw is located in a passage in the carburetor body. On US models, this screw is hidden behind a plug which will have to be removed if the screw is to be taken out. The usual way to do this is to drill a hole in the plug, then pry it out. Be careful not to drill into the screw. Record the pilot screw's position (see **Haynes Hint**). Now remove the pilot screw along with its spring, washer and O-ring **(see illustration)**.

11 The choke plunger can be removed from each carburetor by unscrewing the nut that retains it to the carburetor body **(see illustration)**.

 HAYNES HiNT *To record the pilot screw's current setting, turn the screw in until it seats lightly, counting the exact number of turns. Now unscrew and remove the pilot screw.*

9.4a Remove the spring seat . . .

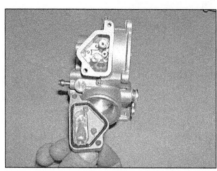

9.7 Remove the bottom cover with its O-ring for access to the jets

9.4b . . . then push the jet needle up from the bottom

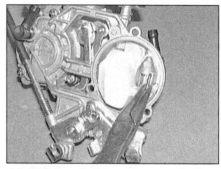

9.8 Withdraw the pin and remove the float

Classic and Nomad/Classic Tourer models

12 Refer to the exploded view **(see illustration 9.2b)** and note the following:

13 Make sure your screwdrivers are the correct size for the screws being undone.

14 Remove the float chamber cover and O-ring for access to the jets and floats **(see illustration)**. Hold the needle jet holder with a wrench while you unscrew the main jet **(see illustration)**. Note which way the needle jet goes in the bore **(see illustration)**.

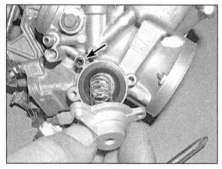

9.9 Note the O-ring (arrowed) around the air passage

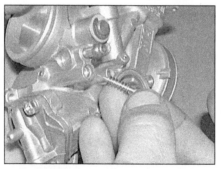

9.10 Remove the pilot screw and its spring, washer and O-ring as described

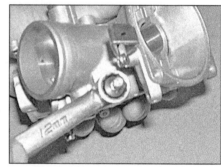

9.11 Unscrew the choke plunger

9.14a Remove the float chamber with its O-ring for access to the jets and float

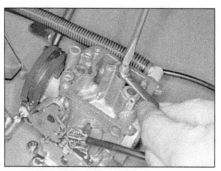

9.14b Hold the needle jet holder and unscrew the main jet from it

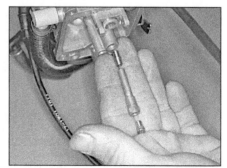

9.14c Main jet, needle jet holder and needle jet

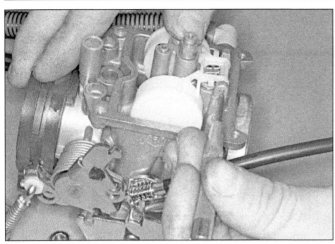

9.15a Push the pivot pin out . . .

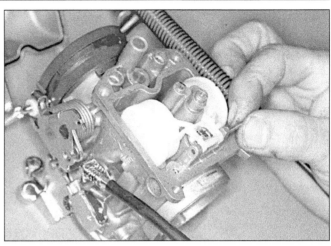

9.15b . . . then withdraw it and remove the float

15 Push out the float pin to remove the float **(see illustrations)**.

16 When removing the diaphragm covers, do not lose the small O-ring in the passage next to the diaphragm **(see illustration)**.

17 The pilot (idle mixture) screw is located in a passage in the carburetor body. On US models, this screw is hidden behind a plug which will have to be removed if the screw is to be taken out. The usual way to do this is to drill a hole in the plug, then pry it out. Be careful not to drill into the screw. Record the pilot screw's setting (see **Haynes Hint**). Now remove the pilot screw along with its spring, washer and O-ring.

18 The choke plunger is part of the choke cable. To remove it, unscrew it from the carburetor, then compress the spring and slip the cable end out of the plunger **(see illustrations)**.

Cleaning

Caution: Use only a carburetor cleaning solution that is safe for use with plastic parts (be sure to read the label on the container).

19 Submerge the metal components in the carburetor cleaner for approximately thirty minutes (or longer, if the directions recommend it).

20 After the carburetor has soaked long enough for the cleaner to loosen and dissolve most of the varnish and other deposits, use a brush to remove the stubborn deposits. Rinse it again, then dry it with compressed air. Blow out all of the fuel and air passages in the main and upper body.

Caution: Never clean the jets or passages with a piece of wire or a drill bit, as they will be enlarged, causing the fuel and air metering rates to be upset.

Inspection

21 Check the operation of the choke plunger. If it doesn't move smoothly, replace it, along with the return spring. Check the tapered end of plunger for wear and replace if it's worn.

22 Check the tapered portion of the pilot screw for wear or damage. Replace the pilot screw if necessary.

23 Check the carburetor body, float bowl and top cover for cracks, distorted sealing surfaces and other damage. If any defects are found, replace the faulty component, although replacement of the entire carburetor will probably be necessary (check with your parts supplier for the availability of separate components).

24 Check the diaphragms for splits, holes and general deterioration. Holding it up to a light will help to reveal problems of this nature.

25 Insert the vacuum piston in the carburetor body and see that it moves up-and-down smoothly. Check the surface of the piston for wear. If it's worn excessively or doesn't move smoothly in the bore, replace the carburetor.

26 Check the jet needle for straightness by rolling it on a flat surface (such as a piece of glass). Replace it if it's bent or if the tip is worn.

27 Check the tip of the fuel inlet valve needle. If it has grooves or scratches in it, it must be replaced. Push in on the rod in the other end of the needle, then release it – if it doesn't spring back, replace the valve needle.

28 Check the O-rings. Replace them if they're damaged.

29 Operate the throttle shaft to make sure the throttle butterfly valve opens and closes smoothly. If it doesn't, replace the carburetor.

30 Check the floats for damage. This will usually be apparent by the presence of fuel inside one of the floats. If the floats are damaged, they must be replaced.

---

10 Carburetor(s) – reassembly and fuel level adjustment

Caution: When installing the jets, be careful not to over-tighten them – they're made of soft material and can strip or shear easily.

Note: *When reassembling the carburetors, be sure to use the new O-rings, gaskets and other parts supplied in the rebuild kit. Refer to illustrations 9.2a and 9.2b.*

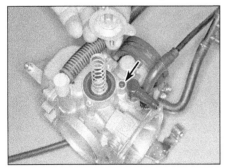

9.16 Note the O-ring (arrowed) around the air passage

9.18a Compress the spring . . .

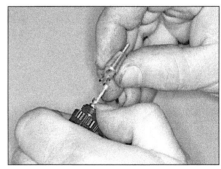

9.18b . . . and slip the cable out of the plunger

Reassembly

1 If the choke plunger was removed, install it in its bore, followed by its spring and nut. Tighten the nut securely and install the cap.

2 Install the pilot screw (if removed) along with its spring, washer and O-ring, turning it in until it seats lightly. Now, turn the screw out the number of turns that was previously recorded. If you're working on a US model, install a new metal plug in the hole over the screw after the carburettor(s) is fitted and the exhaust gas CO content has been checked on an exhaust gas analyser. Apply a little bonding agent around the circumference of the plug after it has been seated.

3 Install the pilot jet, needle jet, needle jet holder and main jet. If you're working on a VN1500A or B model, install the O-ring and bottom cover.

4 Drop the jet needle down into its hole in the vacuum piston and fit the spring seat over the needle. Make sure the spring seat doesn't cover the hole at the bottom of the vacuum piston – reposition it if necessary.

5 Install the diaphragm/vacuum piston assembly into the carburetor body. Lower the spring into the piston. Seat the bead of the diaphragm into the groove in the top of the carburetor body, making sure the diaphragm isn't distorted or kinked. This isn't always an easy task. If the diaphragm seems too large in diameter and doesn't want to seat in the groove, place the top cover over the carburetor diaphragm, insert your finger into the throat of the carburetor and push up on the vacuum piston. Push down gently on the top cover – it should drop into place, indicating the diaphragm has seated in its groove.

6 Install the top cover, tightening the screws securely.

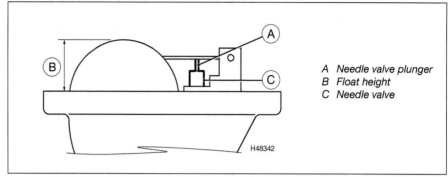

A *Needle valve plunger*
B *Float height*
C *Needle valve*

10.9 Let the float hang down so its tang touches the needle valve but doesn't compress it

VN1500A and B models

7 Place the floats in their installed position and push the float pin into place. Tap the pin over the carburetor body until it's fully installed.

8 No specification is given for measuring the float height. If the fuel level as measured before was incorrect, bend the float tang in small increments to adjust the float position as required. Repeat the procedure for the other float.

Classic and Nomad/Classic Tourer models

9 Invert the carburetor. Attach the fuel inlet valve needle to the float. Set the float into position in the carburetor, making sure the valve needle seats correctly. Install the float pivot pin. To check the float height, hold the carburetor so the float hangs down, then tilt it back until the valve needle is just seated (the rod in the end of the valve shouldn't be compressed). Measure the distance from the carburetor body to the top of the float **(see illustration)** and compare your measurement to the float height listed in this Chapter's Specifications. If it isn't as specified, carefully bend the tang that contacts the valve needle up or down until the float height is correct.

10 Install the O-ring into the groove in the float bowl. Place the float bowl on the carburetor and install the screws, tightening them securely.

Fuel level adjustment

VN1500A and B models

⚠️ *Warning: Gasoline is extremely flammable, so take extra precautions when you work on any part of the fuel system (see the Warning in Section 2).*

11 The carburetors must be installed on the engine for this procedure.

12 Place the motorcycle in a perfectly upright position. Set the fuel tap to the RES position so fuel will flow into the carburetors. **Note:** *This can also be done if the engine has been removed from the motorcycle – place the engine in an upright position and temporarily connect the fuel tank to the carburetors.*

13 Attach Kawasaki service tool no. 57001-1017 to the drain fitting on the bottom of the carburetor assembly (both will be checked) **(see illustration)**. This is a clear plastic tube graduated in millimeters. An alternative is to use a length of clear plastic tubing and an accurate ruler. Hold the graduated tube (or the free end of the clear plastic tube) against the carburetor body, as shown in the accompanying illustration. If the Kawasaki tool is being used, raise the zero mark to a point several millimeters above the upper edge of the coasting enricher cover lower screw (the zero point). If a piece of clear plastic tubing is being used, make a mark on the tubing at this point.

14 Unscrew the drain screw at the bottom of the float bowl a couple of turns, then let fuel flow into the tube. Wait for the fuel level to stabilize, then slowly lower the tube until the zero mark is level with the upper edge of the coasting enricher diaphragm screw (the zero point). **Note:** *Don't lower the zero mark below the zero point, then bring it back up –*

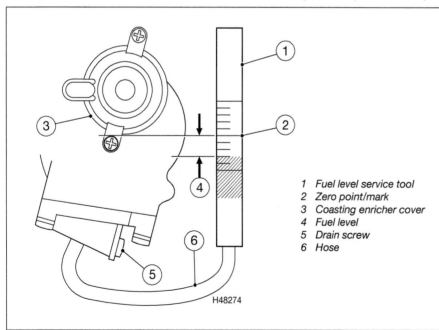

1 *Fuel level service tool*
2 *Zero point/mark*
3 *Coasting enricher cover*
4 *Fuel level*
5 *Drain screw*
6 *Hose*

10.13 Fuel level check set-up – VN1500A and B

the reading won't be accurate. If this happens accidentally, dump the fuel out of the hose and start again.

15 Measure the distance between the mark and the top of the fuel in the tube or gauge. This distance is the fuel level – write it down on a piece of paper, screw in the drain screw, close off the fuel supply, then move on to the next carburetor and check it the same way.

16 Compare your fuel level readings to the value listed in this Chapter's Specifications. If the fuel level in either carburetor is not correct, separate the carburetors for access to the float bowl and bend the tang (see Step 8), as necessary, then recheck the fuel level.

Classic and Nomad/Classic Tourer models

⚠ *Warning: Gasoline is extremely flammable, so take extra precautions when you work on any part of the fuel system (see the Warning in Section 2).*

17 Place the motorcycle in a perfectly upright position. Set the fuel tap to the RES position so fuel will flow into the carburetor. **Note:** *This can also be done if the engine has been removed from the motorcycle – place the engine in an upright position and temporarily connect the fuel tank to the carburetor.*

18 Attach Kawasaki service tool no. 57001-1017 to the drain fitting on the bottom of the carburetor assembly **(see illustration)**. This is a clear plastic tube graduated in millimeters. An alternative is to use a length of clear plastic tubing and an accurate ruler. Hold the graduated tube (or the free end of the clear plastic tube) against the carburetor body, as shown in the accompanying illustration. If the Kawasaki tool is being used, raise the zero mark to a point several millimeters above the float chamber /carburetor body mating surface (the zero point). If a piece of clear plastic tubing is being used, make a mark on the tubing at this point.

19 Unscrew the drain screw at the bottom of the float bowl a couple of turns, then let fuel flow into the tube. Wait for the fuel level to stabilize, then slowly lower the tube until the zero mark is level with the chamber/body mating surface (the zero point). **Note:** *Don't lower the zero mark below the zero point, then bring it back up – the reading won't be accurate. If this happens accidentally, dump the fuel out of the hose and start again.*

20 Measure the distance between the mark and the top of the fuel in the tube or gauge. This distance is the fuel level – write it down on a piece of paper, screw in the drain screw, close off the fuel supply, then move on to the next carburetor and check it the same way.

21 Compare your fuel level readings to the value listed in this Chapter's Specifications. If the fuel level is not correct, remove the float bowl and bend the tang up or down (see Step 9), as necessary, then recheck the fuel level.

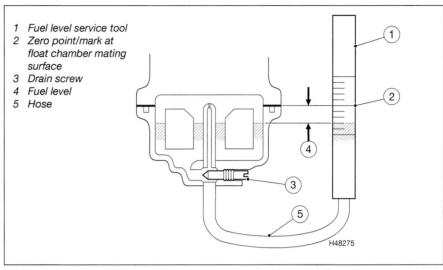

1 Fuel level service tool
2 Zero point/mark at float chamber mating surface
3 Drain screw
4 Fuel level
5 Hose

H48275

10.18 Fuel level check set-up – Classic and Nomad/Classic Tourer

 HAYNES HiNT *Bending the tang up increases the float height and lowers the fuel level – bending it down decreases the float height and raises the fuel level.*

11 Throttle cables – removal and installation

Removal

1 Remove the fuel tank (see Section 2).

2 Undo the screw securing the accelerator cable retainer and slacken the locknut on the decelerator cable at the handlebar. Slacken the cable adjuster locknuts and screw the adjusters in to create as much slack as possible (see Chapter 1).

3 Undo the throttle housing screws and separate the halves.

4 Detach the cable ends from the pulley and draw the cables out of the housing.

VN1500A and B models

5 Loosen the locknuts and free the cables from their brackets at the carburetor.

6 Detach the cable ends from the throttle cam.

7 Remove the cables, noting how they are routed.

Classic and Nomad/Classic Tourer models

8 Remove the carburetor from the engine (see Section 7), but do not detach the cable bracket.

9 Instead release the clip from the bracket. Draw the cable housings up out of the bracket and slip them out.

10 Detach the cable ends from the throttle cam.

11 Remove the cables, noting how they are routed.

Installation

12 Route the cables into place. Make sure they don't interfere with any other components and aren't kinked or bent sharply.

13 Lubricate the end of the accelerator cable with multi-purpose grease and connect it to the throttle pulley at the carburetor. Pass the inner cable through the slot in the bracket, then seat the cable housing in the bracket.

14 Repeat the previous step to connect the decelerator cable.

15 If you're working on a Classic or Nomad/Classic Tourer, reinstall the carburetor (see Section 7).

16 Fit the cables into the switch housing and connect the cables to the throttle grip pulley. Do not yet tighten the retainer plate screw or locknut.

17 Install the cable/switch housing, locating the pin in the hole in the handlebar, and tighten the screws. Align the cable elbows and tighten the retainer screw and locknut.

18 Adjust throttle cable freeplay (see Chapter 1).

19 Turn the handlebars back and forth to make sure the cables don't cause the steering to bind.

20 Operate the throttle and check the cable action. The cables should move freely and the throttle pulley at the carburetor should move back and forth in response to both acceleration and deceleration. If the cables don't operate properly, find and fix the problem before you put the fuel tank back on.

21 Install the fuel tank (see Section 2).

22 Start the engine. With the engine idling, turn the handlebars all the way to left and right while listening for changes in idle speed. If idle speed increases as the handlebars turn, the cables are improperly routed. This is dangerous. Find the problem and fix it before riding the bike.

12 Air filter housings, ducts and surge tank – removal and installation

VN1500A and B models

Filter housings and ducts

1 Remove the air filter elements (see Chapter 1).
2 Unbolt the air filter housing from the engine **(see illustration)**. Remove the duct, noting which way round it fits.

3 Installation is the reverse of the removal steps. Fit the duct with its UPPER mark at the top. Apply a light oil to the surge tank/air duct and housing joints to ease fitment. Make sure all duct joint seals are in good condition and replace them with new ones if necessary. The left and right air filter housings are identical, but are marked R and L for identification as the mounting brackets differ – if the brackets don't seem to align with their mounting points, the housings may be on the wrong side of the bike.

Surge tank

4 Remove the fuel tank (see Section 2). Remove the thermostat housing (see Chapter 3).
5 Remove the filter housings and ducts.
6 Disconnect the surge tank hoses and the air ducts and remove the tank from the frame.
7 Installation is the reverse of the removal steps. Make sure all duct joint seals are in good condition and replace them with new ones if necessary.

Classic and Nomad/Classic Tourer models

Right filter housing

8 Remove the cover **(see illustration)**.
9 Undo the screws and bolt and displace the housing base from its mounting bracket. Disconnect the crankcase breather hose. Release the air duct clamp on the carburetor and remove the base. Note that there are captive nuts in slots in the end of the lower air duct for the base screws – remove them for safekeeping.
10 Installation is the reverse of removal. Make sure all duct joint seals are in good condition or replace them with new ones. Make sure the air duct nuts are in place. Note that the gap between the carburetor air duct clamp tabs should be 7.5 to 8.5 mm.

Left filter housing

11 Remove the fuel tank (see Section 2).
12 Remove the surge tank.
13 Remove the air filter element (see Chapter 1).
14 Undo the screws and bolt and remove the housing base, detaching the EVAP hose on California models. Note that there are captive nuts in slots in the end of the lower air duct for the base screws – remove them for safekeeping.
15 Installation is the reverse of removal. Make sure all duct joint seals are in good condition and replace them with new ones if necessary. Make sure the air duct nuts are in place.

Surge tank

16 Remove the fuel tank (see Section 2).
17 Undo the screw at the rear of the tank **(see illustration 12.8)**. Push the tank down and to the right to clear the holder, then remove it.
18 Installation is the reverse of removal. Make sure all duct joint seals are in good condition and replace them with new ones if necessary.

Lower air duct

19 Remove the carburetor and inlet manifold (see Section 7).
20 Remove the right and left filter housings. Remove the housing mounting brackets.
21 Unbolt the air filter housing from its mounting bracket. Disconnect the hoses from the back and top of the housing and remove it.
22 Detach the air suction system hose, then draw the lower air duct out.
23 Installation is the reverse of removal. Make sure all duct joint seals are in good condition and replace them with new ones if necessary.

12.2 Air filter housings, ducts and surge tank – VN1500A and B

1	Cover	5	Housing	9	Duct
2	Filter element	6	Duct	10	Duct
3	Filter core	7	Air switching valve	11	Duct
4	Seal	8	Surge tank	12	Drain

H48283

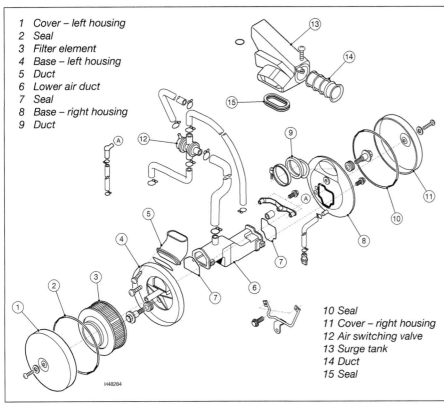

1 Cover – left housing
2 Seal
3 Filter element
4 Base – left housing
5 Duct
6 Lower air duct
7 Seal
8 Base – right housing
9 Duct

10 Seal
11 Cover – right housing
12 Air switching valve
13 Surge tank
14 Duct
15 Seal

H48284

12.8 Air filter housings, ducts and surge tank – Classic and Nomad/Classic Tourer

13 Exhaust system –
removal and installation

VN1500A models

1 Undo the cover screws on the lower muffler and remove the cover **(see illustration)**.
2 Loosen the muffler clamps. Unscrew the muffler assembly bracket bolt and detach the mufflers from the power chamber.
3 Slacken the front exhaust pipe clamp bolt. Unscrew the pipe holder nuts and remove the holders. Detach the pipe from the cylinder head and the power chamber.
4 Slacken the rear exhaust pipe clamp bolt. Unscrew the pipe holder nuts and remove the holders. Undo the power chamber mounting bolts and remove the power chamber and rear pipe together. Detach the pipe from the chamber.
5 Remove the gasket from each pipe port in the cylinder head – new ones must be used. Check the condition of the sealing rings between the pipes/mufflers and power chamber and replace them with new ones if necessary.
6 Installation is the reverse of the removal steps, with the following additions:
  a) Use new gaskets in the exhaust ports, and new sealing rings where necessary.
  b) Make sure all rubber mounting grommets are in good condition and correctly fitted.

13.1 Exhaust system – VN1500A

1 Pipe holder nuts
2 Pipe holders
3 Gasket
4 Exhaust pipe – left
5 Exhaust pipe – right
6 Sealing ring
7 Power chamber
8 Muffler – lower
9 Muffler – upper

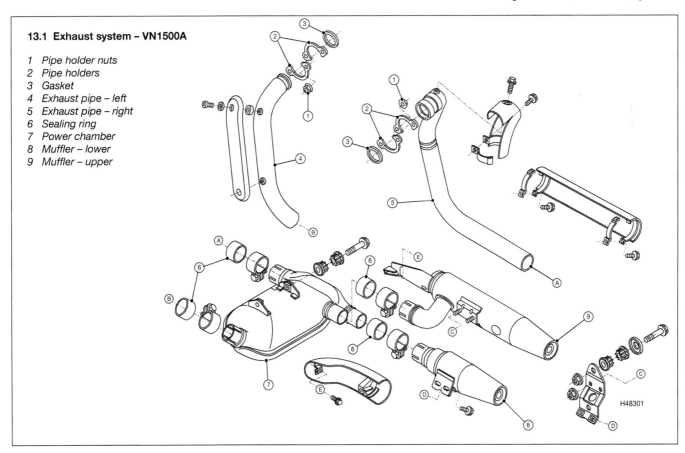

H48301

c) *Do not fully tighten any of the nuts/bolts until all components of the system are in place.*

d) *Tighten the exhaust pipe holder nuts at the cylinder heads evenly.*

e) *Tighten the remaining nuts and bolts.*

f) *Warm up the engine to normal operating temperature, let it cool, then retighten all of the nuts and bolts.*

VN1500B models

7 Loosen the joint pipe clamp bolt **(see illustration)**.

8 Unscrew the left pipe holder nuts and remove the holders. Unscrew the left muffler bolt and remove the left pipe.

9 Unscrew the right pipe holder nuts and remove the holders. Unscrew the right muffler bolt and the joint pipe bolt and remove the right pipe.

10 Installation is the reverse of removal, with the following additions:

a) *Use new gaskets in the exhaust ports, and new sealing rings where necessary.*

b) *Make sure all rubber mounting grommets are in good condition and correctly fitted.*

c) *Do not fully tighten any of the nuts/bolts until all components of the system are in place.*

d) *Tighten the exhaust pipe holder nuts at the cylinder heads evenly.*

e) *Tighten the remaining nuts and bolts.*

f) *Warm up the engine to normal operating temperature, let it cool, then retighten all of the nuts and bolts.*

Classic and Nomad/Classic Tourer models

11 Release the clamps securing the pipe

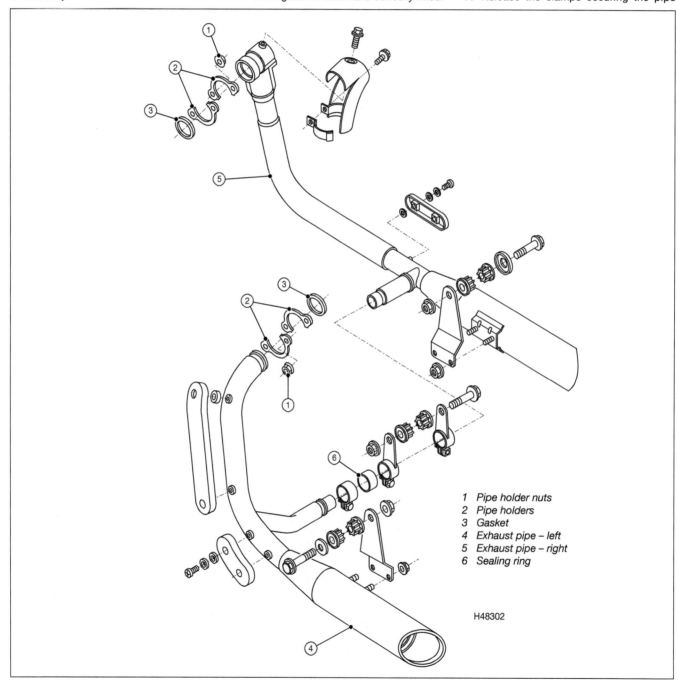

1 Pipe holder nuts
2 Pipe holders
3 Gasket
4 Exhaust pipe – left
5 Exhaust pipe – right
6 Sealing ring

H48302

13.7 Exhaust system – VN1500B

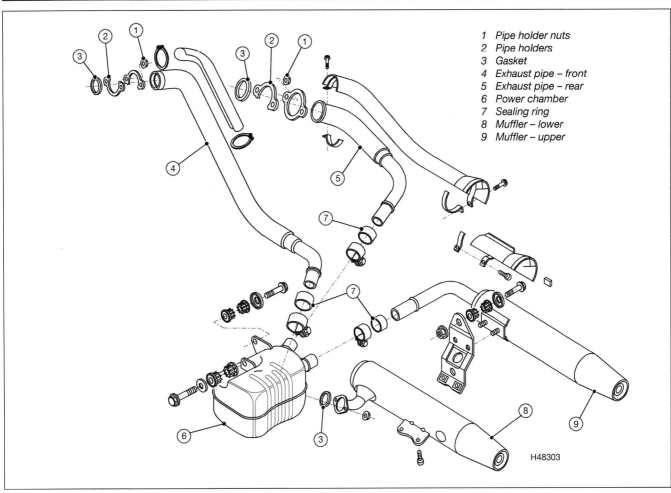

1   Pipe holder nuts
2   Pipe holders
3   Gasket
4   Exhaust pipe – front
5   Exhaust pipe – rear
6   Power chamber
7   Sealing ring
8   Muffler – lower
9   Muffler – upper

13.11 Exhaust system – Classic and Nomad/Classic Tourer

covers, then slide the clamps off the hooks and remove the covers **(see illustration)**.

12 Slacken the clamp bolts securing the pipes in the power chamber.

13 Unscrew the power chamber mounting bolt on the right side and slacken the bolt on the left side.

14 Unscrew the pipe holder nuts and remove the holders. Detach the pipes from the cylinder head and the power chamber.

15 Unscrew the bolt securing the cover to the right side muffler, then draw the cover forward to release the hook.

16 On Classic models unscrew the lower muffler flange nuts and mounting bolts and remove the lower muffler. Slacken the upper muffler clamp bolt, then unscrew the mounting bolt and remove the upper muffler.

17 On Nomad/Classic Tourer models remove the saddlebags. Slacken the muffler clamp bolt, then unscrew the muffler mounting bolts and remove the muffler.

18 Installation is the reverse of the removal steps, with the following additions:

a) *Use new gaskets in the exhaust ports, and new sealing rings where necessary.*

b) *Make sure all rubber mounting grommets*

are in good condition and correctly fitted.

c) *Do not fully tighten any of the nuts/bolts until all components of the system are in place.*

d) *Tighten the exhaust pipe holder nuts at the cylinder heads evenly.*

e) *Tighten the remaining nuts and bolts.*

f) *Warm up the engine to normal operating temperature, let it cool, then retighten all of the nuts and bolts.*

14 Air suction system switching valve – operational test

1 The air switching valve(s) is/are part of the air suction system. VN1500A and B models have two valves, one feeding the suction valve for each cylinder, while Classic and Nomad/Classic Tourer models have the one valve feeding both suction valves **(see illustration 12.2 or 12.8)**. Routine checking procedures are described in Chapter 1. If you suspect the valve has failed (for example, if the bike runs poorly at low speed or backfires during deceleration), test it as follows:

2 Remove the fuel tank (see Section 2), and on Classic and Nomad/Classic Tourer models the surge tank (see Section 12). Remove the valve and its hoses from the motorcycle.

3 Connect a vacuum pump to the thin vacuum hose on top of the valve.

4 Try to blow air into the large air inlet hose on the bottom of the valve. It should flow easily through the valve when there's no vacuum applied to the vacuum line.

5 Operate the vacuum pump and raise vacuum to the value listed in this Chapter's Specifications. The valve should close, making it impossible to blow air into the hose.

6 If the valve doesn't perform as described, replace it with a new one.

15 Evaporative emission control system (California models) – removal and installation

1 The evaporative emission control system used on California models prevents fuel vapor from escaping into the atmosphere. When the engine isn't running, the vapor is stored in a canister, then routed into the combustion

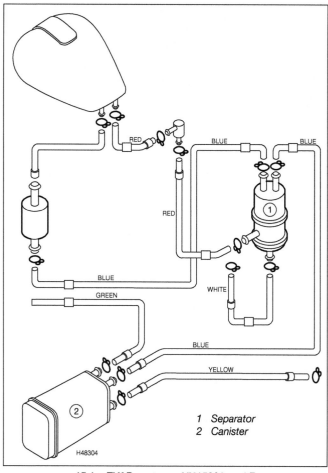

15.1a EVAP system – VN1500A and B

1 Separator
2 Canister

15.1b EVAP system – Classic and Nomad/Classic Tourer

1 Canister
2 Separator
3 To air switching valve
4 To carburetor
5 To air filter housing

chambers for burning when the engine starts **(see illustrations)**.

2 The hoses should be checked periodically for loose connections, damage and deterioration. Tighten or replace the hoses as needed.

3 To remove the canister, disconnect the hoses and lift the canister out of its holder.

4 To remove the liquid/vapor separator, disconnect its hoses and remove it from the mounting strap. Keep the separator in an upright position while it's out of the bike.

5 Installation is the reverse of the removal steps.

16 Fuel pump – check, removal and installation

Check

1 The fuel pump is located under the fuel tank. It runs when the starter button is pressed, and as required when the engine is running to maintain the correct level of fuel in the carburettor float chamber(s). When the float needle vale shuts off the flow into the chamber(s) back pressure in the line stops the pump.

2 Remove the pump. Using a fully charged 12V battery, connect the positive (+) terminal to the black/yellow (VN1500A and B) or yellow (Classic and Nomad/Classic Tourer) wire terminal in the pump side of the connector using an auxiliary lead, and connect the negative (-) terminal to the green (VN1500A and B) or black/yellow (Classic and Nomad/ Classic Tourer) wire terminal – the pump should operate. If it doesn't measure the resistance between the blue and black/yellow wire terminals on VN1500A and B or black and yellow terminals on Classic and Nomad/ Classic Tourer – the reading should be about 20 K-ohms. If not replace the pump with a new one.

3 If the pump runs you can have it pressure checked by a dealer.

4 If the pump is fine check the wiring, connectors and terminals, and then the other components, in the pump circuit for physical damage or loose or corroded connections and rectify as necessary (see Electrical system fault finding and the *Wiring Diagrams* in Chapter 9).

Removal

5 Remove the fuel tank (see Section 2).

6 On VN1500A and B models unscrew the pump bracket bolts and displace the pump, then disconnect the wiring connector and detach the hoses, marking which fits where.

7 On Classic and Nomad/Classic Tourer models disconnect the pump wiring connector and hoses, noting which fits where – be prepared with some rag to catch any residual fuel. Displace the fuel filter from its mount and remove it. Unscrew the pump bracket bolts and remove the pump

Installation

8 Installation is the reverse of removal, noting the following:

a) *On VN1500A and B models, with the pump positioned with the wiring at the bottom and the hose unions at the top, the hose from the filter fits onto the left-hand union on the pump.*

b) *On Classic and Nomad/Classic Tourer models fit the hose from the filter onto the union marked IN on the pump, and make sure the filter is fitted with its flow arrow pointing in the direction of flow from the tank to the pump.*

c) *Make sure the hoses are fully pushed onto their unions and are securely held by the clamps – use new clamps if necessary. Check for leaks when running the engine.*

17 Fuel gauge and level sensor – check, removal and installation

 Warning: Refer to the precautions given in Section 1 before starting work.

Check

Note: Refer to *Electrical System Fault Finding and to the wiring diagram for your model in Chapter 9.*

1 The circuit consists of the sensor mounted in the tank and the gauge in the instrument cluster **(see illustration 2.5a or b).**

2 Remove the fuel tank (see Section 2). On models with a tank mounted gauge reconnect the instrument wiring connector.

3 To check the gauge prepare an auxiliary piece of wire with bared ends to jump between the terminals in the loom side of the level sensor wiring connector. Turn the ignition ON. The gauge needle should be on E. Now use the auxiliary wire to briefly bridge the terminals in the connector – the gauge should read F. Do not leave the wire connected for longer than is necessary to assess the movement of the needle. If the gauge functions as described the level sensor is faulty. If not check the wiring between the connector and the gauge for physical damage or loose or corroded connections and rectify as necessary (see *Electrical System Fault Finding* and the *Wiring Diagrams* in Chapter 9). Also make sure there is battery voltage at the brown or brown/red wire terminal in the loom side of the instrument wiring connector with the ignition ON. If the circuit is good the gauge is faulty.

4 To check the level sensor remove it from the tank. Make sure the float arm moves up and down smoothly and freely – if not replace the sensor with a new one. Connect an ohmmeter between the terminals in the sensor wiring connector and check the resistance is 4 to 10 ohms with the float arm in the full position and 90 to 100 ohms in the empty position. If not, the sensor is faulty.

Removal

Fuel gauge

5 Refer to Chapter 9.

Fuel level sensor

6 Remove and drain the fuel tank (see Section 2). Place it upside down on a cushion of rag so it is adequately protected and supported.

7 Unscrew the sensor mounting plate bolts. Lift the mounting plate and carefully draw the sensor float arm out of the tank. Remove the seal and discard it – a new one must be used.

Installation

8 Installation is the reverse of removal, noting the following:
   a) *Fit the sensor using a new seal.*
   b) *Tighten the bolts evenly and a little at a time in a criss-cross sequence.*
   c) *Check for leaks when running the engine.*

18 Throttle sensor – check, adjustment and replacement

Note: *The throttle sensor is fitted on Classic E and F models and Nomad/Classic Tourer G and H models only.*

Check and adjustment

1 Make sure the idle speed is correctly adjusted (see Chapter 1).

2 Remove the fuel tank (see Section 2).

3 Using a voltmeter, insert the positive probe into the back of the sensor wiring connector yellow/white wire terminal, and the negative probe into the black/blue wire terminal **(see illustration 9.2b).** If the probes cannot be inserted into the connector, disconnect it and prepare some auxiliary wires to run between the terminals of each connector half, with a small portion of the insulation cut away so that the meter probes can be connected to them using crocodile clips. Alternatively, and preferably, prepare two insulated terminals midway along each wire to accept the meter probes. There is a harness adapter available from Kawasaki (part no. 57001-1400) if preferred.

Caution: Do not allow the bare sections of wire to contact each other or any other part of the motorcycle. Make sure the wires connect between the correct terminals – do not get them crossed.

4 Turn the ignition on. Check the voltage output of the sensor with the throttle closed and compare it to the output specified at the beginning of the Chapter. If the recorded output differs from that specified, slacken the sensor mounting screws and rotate the sensor until the output is within the specified range, then tighten the screws evenly. If it cannot be adjusted to within the range, see Step 6.

5 Now check the voltage output of the sensor with the throttle fully open and compare it to the output specified at the beginning of the Chapter. If the recorded output differs from that specified, slacken the sensor mounting screws and rotate the sensor until the output is within the specified range, then tighten the screws evenly. Check the voltage again with the throttle closed. If the sensor cannot be adjusted to within the range for both positions see Step 7.

6 If no reading is obtained, disconnect the relevant ignition control unit wiring connector (see Chapter 5) and check the connectors for loose or corroded terminals. Test the wiring between the terminals of the sensor wiring connector and the corresponding terminals on the ignition control unit (ICU) connector for continuity. If not, this is probably due to a damaged or broken wire between the connectors; pinched or broken wires can usually be repaired. Also check the sensor for cracks and other damage. If the wiring and connectors are good, see Step 7.

7 If the sensor is suspected of being faulty, you can take it to a Kawasaki dealer for testing. If it is confirmed to be faulty, it must be replaced with a new one; the sensor is a sealed unit and cannot therefore be repaired. If the sensor is good, have the ICU checked by the dealer.

Replacement

8 Remove the carburetor (see Section 7).

9 Undo the sensor mounting screws and remove the sensor, noting how it fits.

10 Install the sensor and lightly tighten the screws, then install the carburetor and adjust the sensor as described above until the correct output voltage is obtained. On completion, tighten the screws evenly.

Notes

Chapter 4B
Fuel and exhaust systems – fuel injection models

Contents

Degrees of difficulty

Easy, suitable for novice with little experience	**Fairly easy,** suitable for beginner with some experience	**Fairly difficult,** suitable for competent DIY mechanic	**Difficult,** suitable for experienced DIY mechanic	**Very difficult,** suitable for expert DIY or professional

Specifications

Fuel
Grade . . . . Unleaded. Minimum 91 RON (Research Octane Number)

Fuel injection system
Throttle body type . . . . Mitsubishi twin barrel 36 mm
Idle speed. . . . . See Chapter 1
Idle speed control (ISC) valves
   Resistance . . . . 13.6 to 20.4 ohms
Fuel pump
   Fuel pressure
      All VN1500 models and VN1600 Mean Streak
         Ignition ON, fuel pump running. . . . . 46 psi (3.2 Bar)
         Ignition ON, fuel pump off, system pressurised . . . . 41 psi (2.9 Bar)
         Engine idling . . . . 38 psi (2.7 Bar)
      VN1600 Classic and Nomad/Classic Tourer
         Ignition ON, fuel pump running. . . . . 44 psi (3.1 Bar)
         Ignition ON, fuel pump off, system pressurised . . . . 41 psi (2.9 Bar)
         Engine idling . . . . 44 psi (3.1 Bar)
   Minimum fuel flow rate
      All VN1500 models and VN1600 Mean Streak. . . . . 75 ml or more every 3 seconds
      VN1600 Classic and Nomad/Classic Tourer. . . . . 67 ml or more every 3 seconds

Engine management system sensors

Atmospheric pressure (AP) sensor

Input voltage	4.75 to 5.25 volts
Output voltage	3.74 to 4.26 volts at standard atmospheric pressure

Engine coolant temperature (ECT) sensor

Resistance @ 20°C (68°F)	2.162 to 3.112 K-ohms
Resistance @ 50°C (122°F)	0.785 to 1.049 K-ohms
Resistance @ 100°C (212°F)	207 to 253 ohms

Fuel injector resistance

All VN1500 models and VN1600 Mean Streak	14.2 to 14.8 ohms at 20°C (68°F)
VN1600 Classic and Nomad/Classic Tourer	11.7 to 12.3 ohms at 20°C (68°F)

Intake air pressure (IAP) sensor

Input voltage	4.75 to 5.25 volts
Output voltage	3.74 to 4.26 volts at standard atmospheric pressure

Intake air temperature (IAT) sensor resistance

At 0°C (32°F)	5.4 to 6.6 K-ohms
At 20°C (68°F)	2.26 to 2.86 K-ohms
At 80°C (176°F)	0.29 to 0.39 K-ohms

Throttle position (TP) sensor

Input voltage	4.75 to 5.25 volts
Output voltage	
Throttle closed	approx. 0.584 to 0.604 volts as throttle is opened
Throttle fully open	approx. 4.29 to 4.59 volts as throttle is opened
Resistance	4 to 6 K-ohms

Tip-over (TO) sensor

Input voltage	Battery voltage
Output voltage	
Sensor upright	0.4 to 1.4 volts
Sensor tilted	3.7 to 4.4 volts

Air switching valve

Test vacuum

Drifter J models	45 to 53 kPa (340 to 400 mm-Hg)
VN1500 Mean Streak models	43 to 50 kPa (320 to 380 mm-Hg)
VN1500 Classic, Nomad/Classic Tourer and Drifter R models	49 to 57 kPa (370 to 430 mm-Hg)
VN1600 Classic and Nomad/Classic Tourer	49 to 65 kPa (370 to 490 mm-Hg)
Resistance – VN1600 Mean Streak only	18 to 22 ohms

Torque settings

Engine coolant temperature (ECT) sensor	18 Nm (13 ft-lbs)
Fuel pump bolts	
Oval pump plate	7 Nm (61 inch-lbs)
Round pump plate	10 Nm (88 inch-lbs)
Intake manifold flange bolts	12 Nm (106 inch-lbs)
Throttle body bracket bolts	12 Nm (106 inch-lbs)

1 General information and precautions

General information

The fuel supply system consists of the fuel tank, fuel pump, pressure regulator, filter, a level sensor, the fuel hose(s), fuel injectors, throttle body, and control cables. Power to the fuel pump, injectors and ICU is switched on and off by the fuel injection system power relay. The injection system supplies fuel and air to the engine via a single 36 mm throttle body and a twin bore manifold. The injectors are operated by the Ignition Control Unit (ICU) using the information obtained from the various sensors it monitors. Refer to Section 8 for more information on the operation of the fuel injection system.

All models have a fuel gauge and/or warning light in the instrument cluster, actuated by a level sensor inside the fuel tank.

Precautions

⚠️ **Warning: Petrol (gasoline) is extremely flammable, so take extra precautions when you work on any part of the fuel system. Always remove the battery (see Chapter 9). Don't smoke or allow open flames or bare light bulbs near the work area, and don't work in a garage where a natural gas-type appliance is present. If you spill any fuel on your skin, rinse it off immediately with soap and water. When you perform any kind of work on the fuel system, wear safety glasses and have a fire extinguisher suitable for a class B type fire (flammable liquids) on hand.**

Residual pressure will remain in the system after the motorcycle has been used. Before disconnecting any fuel hose, ensure the ignition is switched OFF and make sure you have some absorbent rag to catch any fuel. It is vital that no dirt or debris is allowed to enter any part of the system. Any foreign matter in the fuel system components could result in injector damage or malfunction. Ensure the ignition is switched OFF before disconnecting or reconnecting any fuel injection system wiring connector. If a connector is disconnected or reconnected with the ignition switched ON, the ignition control unit (ICU) may be damaged.

Always perform service procedures in a

well-ventilated area to prevent a build-up of fumes.

Never work in a building containing a gas appliance with a pilot light, or any other form of naked flame. Ensure that there are no naked light bulbs or any sources of flame or sparks nearby.

Do not smoke (or allow anyone else to smoke) while in the vicinity of petrol (gasoline) or of components containing it. Remember the possible presence of vapour from these sources and move well clear before smoking.

Check all electrical equipment belonging to the house, garage or workshop where work is being undertaken (see the *Safety first!* section of this manual). Remember that certain electrical appliances such as drills, cutters etc, create sparks in the normal course of operation and must not be used near petrol (gasoline) or any component containing it. Again, remember the possible presence of fumes before using electrical equipment.

Always mop up any spilt fuel and safely dispose of the rag used.

Any stored fuel that is drained off during servicing work must be kept in sealed containers that are suitable for holding petrol (gasoline), and clearly marked as such; the containers themselves should be kept in a safe place. Note that this last point applies equally to the fuel tank if it is removed from the machine; also remember to keep its filler cap closed at all times.

Read the *Safety first!* section of this manual carefully before starting work.

2 Fuel tank – removal and installation

⚠️ **Warning: Refer to the precautions given in Section 1 before starting work.**

Note: *Removing the tank involves a certain amount of unavoidable fuel spillage, which is obviously dangerous. Refer to the precautions given in Section 1 before starting work, and have plenty of rag to hand. Once the tank has been removed, rest it on some soft rag to prevent damaging the paintwork or hose unions. Try to time the removal procedure with a near empty tank, which makes it much easier to lift.*

Removal

1 Make sure the fuel cap is secure. Remove the seat(s) (see Chapter 8). Disconnect the battery negative (–) lead (see Chapter 9).
2 Remove the instrument/warning light housing (according to model) from the tank (see Chapter 9). On VN1600 models and all Mean Streak models disconnect the ignition switch wiring connector **(see illustration)**. If required remove the switch (see Chapter 9).
3 Disconnect the fuel pump and fuel level sensor wiring connector(s) and release the wiring from the guide where fitted **(see illustration)**.
4 If required pump the fuel from the tank using a commercially available fuel pump suitable for petrol and store it in a suitable container.

5 Unscrew the tank mounting bolt(s)/nut, according to model, noting any washers(s) and collar(s) **(see illustration)**. Lift the rear of the tank and disconnect the breather/overflow/EVAP hoses as required according to model, marking each hose according to its location.
6 Place a rag under the fuel pump. On all except 1600 Classic and Nomad/Classic Tourer models detach the fuel return hose, catching any residual fuel in the rag **(see illustration)**.
7 Press in the tabs on the supply hose joint and pull it off the union, again catching any fuel **(see illustration)**.
8 Clamp all hoses and fit blanking caps onto all hose unions.
9 Carefully lift the tank off the frame and remove it **(see illustration)**.
10 Check all the tank rubbers for signs of damage or deterioration and replace them with new ones if necessary.

Installation

11 Installation is the reverse of removal, noting the following:
  a) *Depending on how the tank has been stood and how full it is there is the possibility of fuel having made its way into the breather pipe which could spurt out of the union on the base when it is moved – be prepared with some rag for this. Once the tank is upright the pipe will fill itself with air.*
  b) *Make sure all mounting rubbers and collars are in place.*

2.2 Disconnect the ignition switch wiring connector

2.3 Disconnect the pump/level sensor wiring connector(s) and release any guide

2.5 Unscrew the bolt and detach the hose where fitted . . .

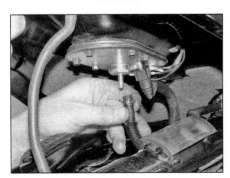

2.6 . . . the fuel return hose where fitted . . .

2.7 . . . and disconnect the fuel supply hose

2.9 Carefully lift the tank off and remove it

2.11 The front of the tank on this model has a grommet that locates over a peg

4.2a Disconnect the fuel hose as described for your model – Mean Streak shown

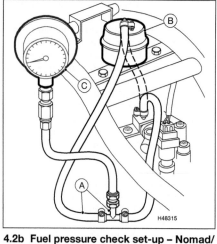

4.2b Fuel pressure check set-up – Nomad/ Classic Tourer L1 and Drifter J models

A Fuel gauge   B Fuel filter
   adapter and hose C Fuel gauge

c) *Make sure the tank locates correctly (see illustration).*
d) *Press the fuel supply hose joint onto its union until it clicks into place (see illustration 2.7). Make sure the fuel hose is secure by pulling and pushing the joint on the union – the hose should not come off, but there should be about 5 mm movement. If the joint does not slide, remove and refit it.*
e) *Make sure the fuel return hose (where fitted) is pushed fully onto its union and is secured with the clamp (see illustration 2.6).*
f) *Make sure the breather/overflow/EVAP hoses are correctly routed.*
g) *Make sure all wiring connectors are securely clicked together.*
h) *Start the engine and check that there is no sign of fuel leakage.*

3 Fuel tank –
cleaning and repair

All repairs to the fuel tank should be carried out by a professional who has experience in this critical and potentially dangerous work. Even after cleaning and flushing of the fuel system, explosive fumes can remain and ignite during repair of the tank.

4 Fuel pressure – check

1 To check the fuel pressure, a suitable gauge, gauge adapter and hoses are needed.

Kawasaki provides service tools (Pt. Nos. 57001-1417 and 57001-125 or 57001-1593, 57001-1607 and 57001-125, according to model – ask your dealer) for this purpose.
2 Remove the fuel tank (see Section 2). Disconnect the fuel hose from the top of the fuel filter on Drifter J models and Nomad/ Classic Tourer L1 models, from the fuel rail on 1600 Classic and Nomad/Classic Tourer models (disconnect the wiring connector from the rear injector to improve access, then reconnect it), and from the delivery pipe to the fuel rail on all other models **(see illustration)**. Use the hoses and adapter to connect the gauge between the fuel tank and the fuel rail as shown for your model **(see illustrations)**. Position the tank back on the frame, connecting all hoses and wiring.

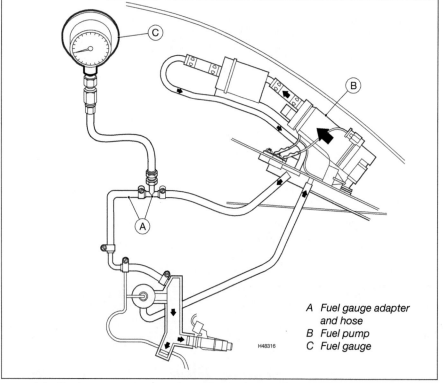

A *Fuel gauge adapter and hose*
B *Fuel pump*
C *Fuel gauge*

4.2c Fuel pressure check set-up – Classic, Nomad/Classic Tourer L2-on and Mean Streak models

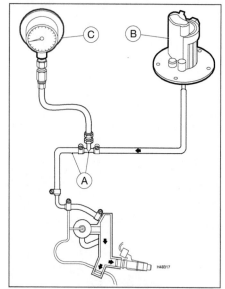

4.2d Fuel pressure check set-up – 1600 Classic and Nomad/Classic Tourer models

A *Fuel gauge   B Fuel pump
   adapter and hose C Fuel gauge*

3 Turn the ignition switch ON and check the pressure reading on the gauge as the pump runs for 3 seconds and pressurizes the system, then with the system pressurised when the pump has stopped. Start the engine and check the pressure with the engine idling. In each case the pressure should be as specified at the beginning of this Chapter. Note that the gauge needle will fluctuate, so take the reading at the mid-point of its extremes.

4 Turn the ignition OFF and disconnect the gauge and adapters. Use a rag to catch any residual fuel as before. Connect the fuel hose (see Section 2).

5 If the pressure is too low, check for a leak in the fuel supply system, including the fuel rail and injectors. If there is no leakage the pick-up or filter could be blocked, or the pump could be faulty. See Chapter 1 for the filter and Section 5 for the pump.

6 If the pressure is too high, either the pressure regulator on the fuel rail or the check valve in the fuel pump is faulty or the fuel hose or injector(s) is/are clogged.

5 Fuel pump – check, removal and installation

Warning: Refer to the precautions given in Section 1 before starting work.

Check

1 The fuel pump is located inside the fuel tank. When the ignition is switched ON, it should be possible to hear the pump run for a few seconds until the system is up to pressure. If you can't hear anything, open the filler cap and check again. Next check the fuel injection system fuse (see Chapter 9), then the relay (see Section 6). If all is good, check the wiring, connectors and terminals for physical damage or loose or corroded connections and rectify as necessary (see Chapter 9, Section 2 and the *Wiring Diagrams*). If the pump still will not run, proceed as follows.

2 Remove the seat(s) (see Chapter 8).

3 Ensure the ignition is switched OFF. Locate the fuel pump wiring connector **(see illustration 2.3)**.

4 With the connector still connected, and using needle probes inserted into the pump side of the connector, connect the positive (+) lead of a voltmeter to the yellow/red wire terminal on 1600 Classic and Nomad/Classic Tourer models or the white/red wire terminal on all other models, and the negative (–) lead to the black/white wire terminal. Switch the ignition ON whilst noting the reading obtained on the meter.

5 If battery voltage is present for a few seconds, the fuel pump circuit is operating correctly and the fuel pump itself is faulty and must be replaced with a new one.

6 If no reading is obtained, check the yellow/red or white/red wire and connectors between the fuel tank and the pump relay for continuity using the wiring diagrams at the end of Chapter 9, and check for continuity to

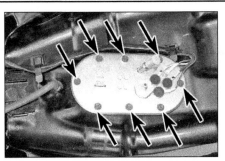

5.9a Unscrew the bolts (arrowed – Mean Streak shown) . . .

the ICU in the black/white wire. If continuity (zero resistance) is not present, locate the break in the wire or faulty connector and repair or replace as required. Make sure all the connectors are free from corrosion and are securely connected. Repair/replace the wiring as necessary and clean the connectors using electrical contact cleaner. If this fails to reveal the fault, check the following components.

a) *Engine stop switch, ignition switch, ignition fuse (see Chapter 9).*
b) *Tip over sensor (see Section 10).*
c) *Ignition control unit (ICU) (see Chapter 5).*

Removal

7 Remove the fuel tank (see Section 2).

8 If not already done pump the fuel from the tank using a commercially available fuel pump suitable for petrol (gasoline) and store it in a suitable container. Place the tank upside down on some clean rag. Release the wiring from any retaining tabs.

9 Make a note of which way round the pump mounting plate is positioned on your model, i.e.

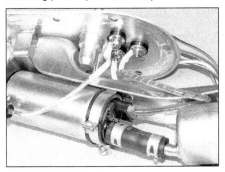

5.10a Check all the wiring terminals . . .

5.11a Fit the new seal . . .

whether the wiring is to the back or the front of the tank. Unscrew the fuel pump mounting plate bolts **(see illustration)**. Carefully withdraw the pump assembly from the tank **(see illustration)**. On models with an oval pump plate make a note of where the tab on the pump seal is positioned on your model **(see illustration 5.11b)**. Remove the seal and discard it – a new one must be used on installation **(see illustration 5.11a)**. The pump comes as a complete assembly and no individual components are available.

Installation

10 Make sure the wiring terminal screws and nuts are tight **(see illustration)**. Make sure the strainer is clean **(see illustration)** – if necessary clean it using solvent and blow it dry with compressed air.

11 Clean the threads of the pump bolts. Ensure the mounting plate and tank surfaces are clean and dry, then fit the new seal – on models with an oval pump plate fit the tab on the seal in the same position as noted on removal **(see illustrations)**.

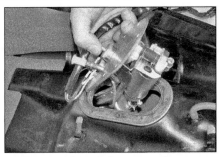

5.9b . . . and carefully remove the pump

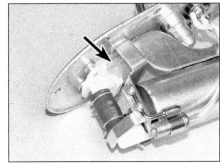

5.10b . . . and the strainer (arrowed)

5.11b . . . with the tab (arrowed) positioned as shown where relevant

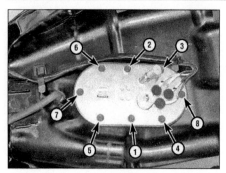

5.13a Fuel pump bolt tightening sequence – oval plate

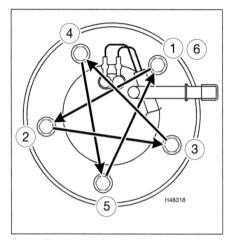

5.13b Fuel pump bolt tightening sequence – round plate

6.2a Fuel injection system power relay (arrowed)

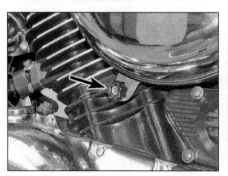

7.3a Release the adjuster (arrowed) from its holder

12 Carefully manoeuvre the pump assembly into the tank, making sure the wiring is positioned as noted on removal on models with an oval pump plate, and the fuel hose union points to the back on models with a round plate (see illustration 5.9b).

13 Apply a suitable non-permanent thread locking compound to the bolts and tighten them finger-tight. Now tighten them evenly and a little at a time in the sequence shown for your model and to the torque setting specified at the beginning of the Chapter for your model (see illustrations).

14 Secure the wiring in any retaining tabs previously released.

15 Install the fuel tank (see Section 2).

6 Fuel injection system power relay – check

1 Remove the coolant reservoir (see Chapter 3).

2 Pull the relay off its mounting and disconnect the wiring connector (see illustration). Using a multimeter or test light, check for continuity between terminals 3 and 4 on the relay (see illustration). There should be no continuity. Now use jumper wires to connect the positive (+) terminal of a fully charged 12 volt battery to terminal 1 on the relay and the negative (–) battery terminal to relay terminal 2. There

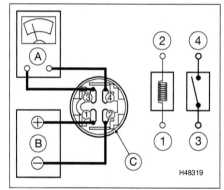

6.2b Fuel injection system power relay test set-up

A Multimeter   B Battery   C Relay

7.3b Undo the screw and remove the cover

should now be continuity shown across terminals 3 and 4. If the relay fails either of the checks, replace it with a new one.

3 If the relay is good, check for battery voltage at the brown/red and yellow/red wire terminals on the loom side of the wiring connector with the ignition and kill switch ON. If there is no voltage at the brown/red wire, check the ignition fuse and circuit, and if there is no voltage at the yellow/red wire check the fuel injection fuse and circuit and its components, referring to the relevant wiring diagram at the end of Chapter 9. If voltage is present, check the wiring between the relay and the pump wiring connector and the ICU for continuity. If all is good the ICU could be faulty (see Chapter 5).

7 Air filter housings and lower air duct – removal and installation

Right filter housing

1 Remove the fuel tank (see Section 2).

2 Disconnect the ISC valve/IAT sensor sub-loom wiring connector (see illustration). Feed the wiring down to the housing, noting its routing.

3 Release the idle speed adjuster (see illustration). Remove the housing cover (see illustration).

4 Detach the ISC valve hoses from the pipes (see illustration).

5 Undo the screws and bolt and displace the

7.2 Disconnect the wiring connector

7.4 Detach the hoses (arrowed) from the pipes

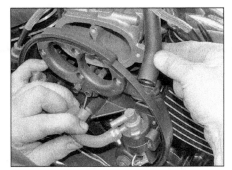

7.5a Undo the screws and bolt (arrowed) and displace the housing . . .

7.5b . . . then disconnect the air suction hose . . .

7.5c . . . the crankcase breather hose and the drain hose (arrowed)

7.5d Retrieve the captive nuts . . .

7.5e . . . and note the O-rings (arrowed)

7.8a Undo the screws and bolts (arrowed) and remove the housing

housing base from its mounting bracket (see illustrations). Detach the air suction system hose, crankcase breather hose, and drain hose (see illustrations). Note that there are captive nuts in slots in the end of the lower air duct for the base screws – remove them for safekeeping (see illustration). Also note the O-rings on the ISC air pipes (see illustration).
6 Installation is the reverse of removal. Make sure all duct joint seals are in good condition or replace them with new ones. Make sure the ISC O-rings and air duct nuts are in place (see illustrations 7.5e and d). Clean the threads of the screws for the air duct and apply non-permanent thread locking compound.

Left filter housing

7 Remove the air filter element (see Chapter 1).
8 Undo the screws and bolts and remove the housing base, detaching the EVAP hose on

California models (see illustration). Note that there are captive nuts in slots in the end of the lower air duct for the base screws – remove them for safekeeping (see illustration).
9 If required unscrew the bolts and remove the bracket (see illustration).
10 Installation is the reverse of removal. Make sure all duct joint seals are in good condition or replace them with new ones. Make sure the air duct nuts are in place (see illustration 7.8b). Clean the threads of the screws for the air duct and apply non-permanent thread locking compound.

Lower air duct

11 Remove the throttle body and inlet manifold (see Section 11).
12 Draw the lower air duct out (see illustration). If required remove the drain hose.
13 Installation is the reverse of removal. Make

sure you fit the drain hose under the duct, with the plugged end facing the left. Make sure all duct joint seals are in good condition or replace them with new ones.

8 Fuel injection system – description

1 The fuel injection system consists of the fuel circuit and the electronic control circuit.
2 The fuel circuit consists of the tank, pump, filter, pressure regulator, throttle body, inlet manifold and injectors. Fuel is pumped under pressure from the tank to the fuel rail, from which the individual injectors are fed. Operating pressure is maintained by the pressure regulator. The injectors spray pressurised fuel into the inlet manifold where it mixes with air and vaporises, before

7.8b Retrieve the captive nuts

7.9 Unscrew the bolts (arrowed) and remove the bracket

7.12 Draw the duct out from between the cylinders

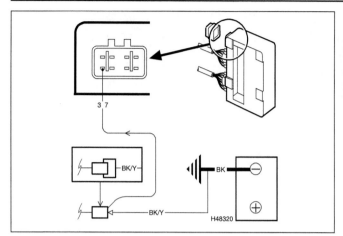

9.1 Fault diagnosis set-up

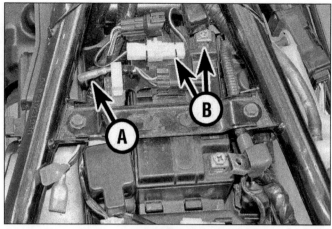

9.2 Connect the female bullet connector with the yellow wire (A) to the negative connector or battery negative terminal (B) as required

entering the cylinder where it is compressed and ignited. Cold starting is enabled using idle speed control (ISC) valves actuated by the ICU as required according to information on engine coolant temperature received from the ECT sensor.

3 The electronic control circuit consists of the ignition control unit (ICU), which operates and co-ordinates both the fuel injection and ignition systems, and the various sensors which provide the ICU with information on engine operating conditions. Power to the system is controlled by a relay.

4 The ignition control unit (ICU) monitors signals from the following sensors.
● Atmospheric pressure (AP) sensor
● Intake air pressure (IAP) sensor
● Intake air temperature (IAT) sensor
● Engine coolant temperature (ECT) sensor
● Throttle position (TP) sensor
● Tip-over (TO) sensor
● Pick-up coils

5 Based on the information it receives, the ICU calculates the appropriate ignition and fuel requirements of the engine. By varying the length of the electronic pulse it sends to each injector, the ICU controls the length of time the injectors are held open and thereby the amount of fuel that is supplied to the engine.

6 The FI warning light should come on briefly when the ignition is switched ON, then go out – this serves as a check that the circuit is working correctly. If the light comes on and stays on a fault has occurred. If the light does not come on at all check the instrument cluster (see Chapter 9). If there is a problem with the system as a whole check the fuses (see Chapter 9) and the power relay (see Section 6).

7 In the event of an abnormality in any of the sensor signals, the ICU will determine whether the engine can still be run safely. If it can, a back-up mode substitutes the sensor signal with a fixed signal, restricting performance but allowing the bike to be ridden home or to a dealer. In some cases the engine will continue to run after a fault has been registered, but once stopped the engine will not be able to

be restarted. If the fault is serious, the fuel injection system will be shut down and the engine will not run.

8 After the engine has been stopped, the appropriate self-diagnostic fault code can be accessed. See Section 9 for fault diagnosis.

9 Fuel injection system – fault diagnosis

1 On 1500 Classic and Nomad/Classic Tourer FI models and all Drifter models, if the FI warning light comes on, enter fault diagnosis mode as follows to read the fault code: remove the seat(s) (see Chapter 8). Lift the ICU out, leaving it connected. Remove the blanking cap from the small socket on the ICU. Prepare an auxiliary lead to connect between the diagnosis (no. 37) terminal on the ICU and the connector on the end of the black/yellow wire from the battery negative (-) terminal, or alternatively connect directly to the negative terminal itself **(see illustration)**. Make sure the ignition is OFF. Connect the wire as described. Turn the ignition ON. The FI light should start to flash the fault code (see Step 4). Keep the lead connected until you have finished reading the fault code. Disconnect the lead to exit diagnosis mode, then turn the ignition OFF.

2 On all Mean Streak models, if the FI warning light comes on, enter fault diagnosis mode as follows to read the fault code: remove the seat (see Chapter 8). Identify the self diagnosis single female bullet connector on the end of the yellow wire coming from the ICU **(see illustration)**. Prepare an auxiliary lead to connect between the diagnosis connector and the connector on the end of the black/yellow wire from the battery negative (-) terminal, or alternatively connect directly to the negative terminal itself. Make sure the ignition is OFF. Connect the wire as described. Turn the ignition ON. The FI light should start to flash the fault code (see Step 4). Keep the lead connected until you have finished reading

the fault code. Disconnect the lead to exit diagnosis mode, then turn the ignition OFF.

3 On 1600 Classic and Nomad/Classic Tourer models, if the FI warning light comes on, enter fault diagnosis mode as follows to read the fault code: remove the seats (see Chapter 8). Identify the self diagnosis single female bullet connector on the end of the yellow wire coming from the ICU **(see illustration 9.2)**. Prepare an auxiliary lead to connect between the diagnosis connector and the battery negative (-) terminal. Make sure the ignition is OFF. Connect the wire as described. Turn the ignition ON. Push the mode button on the bottom left of the instrument cluster to display the tripmeter. Now push the select button down for more than 2 seconds – the letters FI are shown on the LCD display. The FI light should start to flash the fault code (see Step 4). To exit diagnosis mode, either push the reset button for more than 2 seconds, or push the mode button to display the trip meter, or turn the ignition OFF.

4 The FI warning light emits short (0.3 second) flashes to give out the fault code. All codes are two digit. The first digit is indicated by the first set of flashes, then there is a gap of 1 second, then the second digit is indicated by a second set of flashes. For example, one flash followed by a 1 second gap followed by three flashes indicates the fault code number 13; four flashes followed by a 1 second gap followed by two flashes indicates the fault code number 42. If there is only one code it is continuously repeated until diagnosis mode is exited. If there is more than one fault code, the codes are repeated three times each in ascending order, with a 3 second gap between each code (for example two codes of 13 and 42 are actually displayed 13, 13, 13, 42, 42, 42). Once all codes have been revealed, the ICU will continuously run through the code(s) stored in its memory, revealing each one in turn with a 3 second gap between them. The fault codes are shown in the table.

5 The fault codes remain stored in the ICU's memory log.

Fault code	Faulty component – ICU response	Possible causes
11	Throttle position sensor – engine will continue to run but with reduced performance	Faulty wiring or wiring connector Faulty, damaged or improperly installed sensor Faulty ICU
12	Intake air pressure sensor – engine will run	Faulty wiring or wiring connector Faulty, damaged or improperly installed sensor Detached, pinched or blocked hose Faulty ICU
13	Intake air temperature sensor – engine will run, intake temperature signal fixed at 45°C	Faulty wiring or wiring connector Faulty, damaged or improperly installed sensor Faulty ICU
14	Coolant temperature sensor – engine will run, coolant temperature signal fixed at 86°C	Faulty wiring or wiring connector Faulty, damaged or improperly installed sensor Faulty ICU
15	Atmospheric pressure sensor – engine will run, air pressure signal fixed at 760 mmHg	Faulty wiring or wiring connector Faulty sensor Faulty ICU
21	No. 1 (front) cylinder pick-up coil – engine will continue to run using signal from No. 2 coil – if both coils faulty engine will stop	Faulty wiring or wiring connector Faulty, damaged or improperly installed sensor or timing rotor Faulty ICU
22	No. 2 (rear) cylinder pick-up coil – engine will continue to run using signal from No. 1 coil – if both sensors faulty engine will stop	Faulty wiring or wiring connector Faulty, damaged or improperly installed sensor or timing rotor Faulty ICU
31	Tip-over sensor – engine will not run, fuel and ignition systems turned OFF	Machine overturned Faulty wiring or wiring connector Faulty damaged or improperly installed speed sensor Faulty ICU
41	No. 1 front) cylinder injector – engine will run on other cylinder, fuel supply to No. 1 cylinder cut	Faulty wiring or wiring connector Faulty or damaged injector Faulty ICU
42	No. 2 (rear) cylinder injector – engine will run on other cylinder, fuel supply to No. 2 cylinder cut	Faulty wiring or wiring connector Faulty or damaged injector Faulty ICU
45	Fuel pump – engine will stop	Faulty wiring or wiring connector Faulty pump Faulty ICU
51	No. 1 (front) cylinder ignition coil – engine will run on other cylinder, fuel supply to No. 1 cylinder cut	Faulty wiring or wiring connector Faulty or damaged ignition coil Faulty ICU
52	No. 2 cylinder ignition coil – engine will run on other cylinder, fuel supply to No. 2 cylinder cut	Faulty wiring or wiring connector Faulty or damaged ignition coil Faulty ICU

6 Once the code(s) has/have been revealed, identify the fault using the table above, then refer to Step 10 for checking procedures.

7 The sensors can be checked using home equipment. If a fault appears, use the fault code table above to identify which component is faulty. First ensure that the relevant system wiring connectors are securely connected and free of corrosion – poor connections are the cause of the majority of problems. Also check the wiring itself for any obvious faults or breaks, and use a continuity tester to check the wiring between the component, its connectors and the ICU, referring to electrical system fault finding and the wiring diagrams in Chapter 9. Next remove the sensor(s) in question (see Section 10) and check that the sensing head is clean and not obstructed by anything. On the IAP sensor, make sure the vacuum hose is securely connected at both ends and has no cracks or splits. Any checks that can realistically be made on the sensor with home equipment are given in Section 10.

If this fails to locate and/or solve the problem, the motorcycle should be taken to a Kawasaki dealer for testing.

10 Fuel injection system – sensor check, removal and installation

Caution: Ensure the ignition is switched OFF before disconnecting/reconnecting any fuel injection system wiring connector. If a connector is disconnected/reconnected with the ignition switched ON the ignition control unit (ICU) could be damaged.

Throttle position (TP) sensor

Check

1 Remove the fuel tank (see Section 2).
2 Check the sensor resistance as follows: disconnect the sensor wiring connector **(see illustration)**. Connect the positive (+) probe of an ohmmeter to the blue/white wire terminal

on the sensor, then connect the negative (–) lead to the brown/black wire terminal. The resistance should be 4 to 6 K-ohms. If not, the sensor is faulty.

Removal and installation

3 The throttle sensor is an integral part of the throttle body and is not available separately.

10.2 Throttle position sensor wiring connector (arrowed)

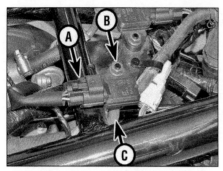

10.5 IAP sensor wiring connector (A), nut or bolt (B) and vacuum hose (C)

If the sensor is faulty, a complete new throttle body will have to be installed, though it is worth checking with a Kawasaki dealer to see if anything can be done to avoid this.

Intake air pressure (IAP) sensor

4 Remove the fuel tank (see Section 2).
5 Disconnect the wiring connector **(see illustration)**.
6 Unscrew the nut or bolt (according to model) and displace the sensor from its bracket, then detach the vacuum hose from the underside and remove the sensor.
7 Installation is the reverse of removal.

Intake air temperature (IAT) sensor

Check

8 Remove the sensor (see below).
9 Check the sensor resistance as follows: connect the positive probes of an ohmmeter to the terminals on the sensor. The resistance should be 2.26 to 2.86 K-ohms at 20°C (68°F) and 5.4 to 6.6 K-ohms at 0°C (32°F) – to simplify the test use your judgement to assess the resistance at room temperature where you are, then place the sensor in the fridge or freezer and again make a judgement as to the reading you should obtain. The main thing is that the resistance is roughly correct and that it changes when temperature changes. If not, the sensor is faulty.

Removal and installation

10 Remove the right side air filter housing (see Section 7).
11 Disconnect the sensor wiring connector **(see illustration)**.

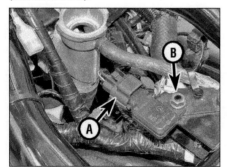

10.20 Disconnect the wiring connector (A) then unscrew the nut (B)

12 Unscrew the nut and remove the sensor **(see illustration)**.
13 Installation is the reverse of removal.

Engine coolant temperature (ECT) sensor

Check

14 The resistance of the sensor changes with temperature – see the Specifications at the beginning of the chapter. While in theory it is possible to bench test the sensor at those temperatures, in practice the test is difficult to set up and perform. You can however test the resistance of the sensor at room temperature as described for the IAT sensor in Step 9, again using your judgement as to what results should be achieved in relation to the specifications listed.

Removal and installation

15 Remove the thermostat housing (see Chapter 3).
16 Unscrew and remove the sensor from the housing.
17 If you are refitting the same sensor clean any old sealant off the threads. Apply some silicone sealant to the threads and tighten the sensor to the torque listed in the Specifications.
18 Install the thermostat housing (see Chapter 3).

Atmospheric pressure (AP) sensor

19 Remove the fuel tank (see Section 2).
20 Disconnect the wiring connector **(see illustration)**.
21 Unscrew the nut and remove the sensor.

10.11 Disconnect the wiring connector (arrowed) . . .

10.24 Tip-over sensor (arrowed) – Mean Streak

22 Installation is the reverse of removal.

Tip-over (TO) sensor

Removal

23 On 1500 Classic, Nomad/Classic Tourer and Drifter models remove the seat (see Chapter 8). Undo the screw and remove the battery holder. With the exception of Drifter J1 models undo the sensor bracket screw. Disconnect the wiring connector and remove the sensor. Separate the sensor from its bracket if required, noting which way round and up it fits.
24 On Mean Streak models remove the seat (see Chapter 8). Unscrew the sensor mounting bolt or lift the sensor off its mount, according to model, then disconnect the wiring connector and remove the sensor **(see illustration)**. Where fitted separate the sensor from its bracket if required, noting which way round and up it fits.
25 On 1600 Classic and Nomad/Classic Tourer models remove the fuel tank (see Section 2). Remove the frame cover on each side. On Nomad/Classic Tourer models displace the IAP sensor from the bracket. Unscrew the bracket nuts and remove the sensor. Separate the sensor from its bracket if required, noting which way round and up it fits.

Installation

26 Installation is the reverse of removal. Make sure the sensor is fitted with its UP arrow pointing upwards and facing the rear on Drifter J1 models and the front on all other models **(see illustration)**. On 1500 Classic

10.12 . . . then unscrew the nut and remove the sensor

10.26 Fit the sensor with the UP mark facing up and mounted as described for your model

11.3a Release and disconnect the plug leads, then unscrew the bolts (arrowed) . . .

11.3b . . . and remove the bar and bracket

11.4a Undo the screw (arrowed) . . .

11.4b . . . and detach the cable end

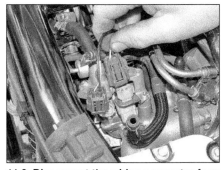

11.6 Disconnect the wiring connector from each injector

11.7a Detach the vacuum hose (arrowed) . . .

and Nomad/Classic Tourer, Drifter and Mean Streak models make sure the peg on the bracket locates in the hole in the frame.

11 Throttle body – removal and installation

⚠ Warning: Refer to the precautions given in Section 1 before starting work.

Removal
1 Remove the fuel tank (see Section 2).
2 On 1600 Classic and Nomad/Classic Tourer models remove the thermostat housing (see Chapter 3).

3 Remove the air filter housing on each side (see Section 7). Release the spark plug leads on the right side from their clips and pull the caps off the plugs, then secure the leads clear of the throttle body **(see illustration)**. Unscrew the spark plug lead holder bar bolts and remove the bar, then unscrew the throttle body bracket bolts and remove the bracket **(see illustration)**.
4 Undo the choke cable retainer screw and remove the retainer, then detach the cable end from the throttle body **(see illustrations)**.
5 Detach the throttle cables (see Section 14).
6 Disconnect the throttle sensor wiring connector **(see illustration 10.2)**. Disconnect the fuel injector wiring connectors **(see illustration)**.

7 Detach the vacuum hose at the T-joint **(see illustration)**. Detach the ISC valve hoses from the top of the throttle body **(see illustration)** – this gives a bit more clearance and eases removal.
8 Disconnect the fuel hose from the top of the fuel filter on Drifter J models and Nomad/Classic Tourer L1 models, from the fuel rail on 1600 Classic and Nomad/Classic Tourer models, and from the delivery pipe to the fuel rail on all other models **(see illustration 4.2a)** – mark the end of the hose so you don't get it the wrong way round on installation.
9 Where fitted unscrew the oil hose holder bolts and remove the holders **(see illustration)**.
10 Stick masking tape over the rocker cover

11.7b . . . and the ISC hoses (arrowed)

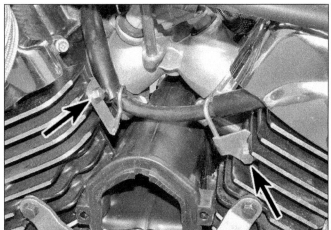

11.9 Unscrew the bolts (arrowed) and remove the holders

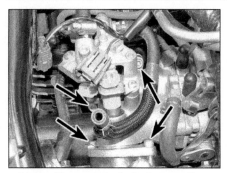

11.10a Unscrew the bolts (arrowed) . . .

11.10b . . . and manoeuvre the throttle body assembly to the right

11.10c Remove the seal (arrowed) from each flange and fit new ones on installation

cases on the right side. Unscrew the intake manifold flange bolts and take the manifold/throttle body assembly off the engine and manoeuvre it carefully out the right side **(see illustrations)**. Remove the sealing ring from each manifold flange **(see illustration)** – new ones must be used.

11 If required remove the fuel injectors (see Section 12).

12 If required detach the ISC pipes from the manifold, then unscrew the manifold bolts and detach it from the throttle body **(see illustrations)**. Remove the seal – a new one must be used. Remove the dowels if loose.

Caution: Do not snap the throttle cam from fully open to fully closed once the cables have been disconnected because this can lead to engine idle speed problems.

Caution: Tape over or stuff clean rag into each cylinder head intake after removing the throttle body assembly to prevent anything from falling in.

Caution: Do not immerse the throttle body in cleaning agent as the throttle sensor will be damaged.

Caution: The throttle body assembly must be treated as a complete unit. Do not loosen any nuts/bolts/screws other than as directed here or in the next Section as they are pre-set at the factory to ensure correct operation. The only components on the assembly which are serviceable are the manifold, the fuel injectors (see Section 12), the various hoses and pipes and the wiring.

Installation

13 Installation is the reverse of removal, noting the following:

a) *If removed wipe over the manifold/throttle body mating surfaces with solvent. Fit the manifold onto the throttle body using a new seal, make sure the dowels are fitted, and tighten the bolts evenly, making sure the seal remains in its groove and does not get pinched.*

b) *If the flanges have been removed from the manifold fit them with their ribbed side facing up. Fit the new sealing rings onto the intake manifold flanges with their narrow side facing into the flange and make sure they are centred (see illustration 11.10c).*

c) *Wipe over the flange mating surface on the cylinder head with solvent.*

d) *Carefully manoeuvre the throttle body assembly in the from the right and tighten the flange bolts finger-tight only at first. After fitting the throttle body bracket (see Step 3) tighten the bracket bolts first, then the flange bolts, to the torque listed in the Specifications.*

e) *Lightly lubricate the ends of the throttle and choke cables with multi-purpose grease before connecting them.*

f) *Make sure all hoses are in good condition, correctly routed and securely connected.*

g) *Make sure all wiring connectors are securely connected.*

h) *Adjust the throttle grip freeplay (see Chapter 1).*

i) *Check that there are no fuel leaks.*

j) *Check, and if necessary adjust, the idle speed (see Chapter 1).*

12 Fuel injectors – check, removal and installation

 Warning: Refer to the precautions given in Section 1 before starting work.

Check

1 If the engine runs, check the operation of each injector in the throttle bodies using a sounding rod. Remove the left side air filter housing (see Section 7). Start the engine and allow it to idle. Check each injector emits a 'clicking' noise. If either injector is silent, either the injector or its wiring harness is faulty.

2 If the engine does not run, remove the fuel tank (Section 2). Disconnect the wiring connector from each injector **(see illustration 11.6)**. Connect an ohmmeter between the terminals of each injector in turn and measure the resistance **(see illustration)**. Compare the reading for each injector to that given in the Specifications. If the resistance of any injector differs greatly from that specified a new injector should be installed.

3 If the injectors are good check for battery voltage at the white/red wire terminal in each wiring connector, with the connector connected (insert needle probes into the back of the connector) and the fuel pump wiring connected. Turn the ignition switch ON – there

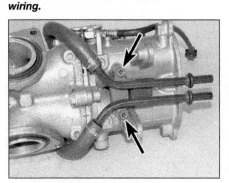

11.12a Unscrew the bolts (arrowed) and detach the pipes . . .

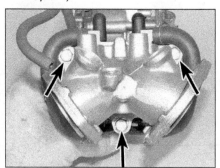

11.12b . . . then unscrew the bolts (arrowed) and detach the manifold

12.2 Checking injector resistance

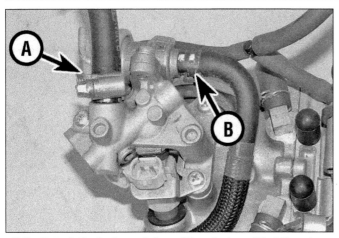

12.5a Detach the fuel supply hose (A) and where fitted the return hose (B) . . .

12.5b . . . and the vacuum hose (arrowed)

should be voltage for three seconds. If there is no voltage, check the white/red wire to the power relay for continuity, then check the relay itself (Section 6). Also check for continuity in the wiring from each injector to the ICU. If all is good check the ICU (Chapter 5).

Removal

4 Remove the fuel tank (see Section 2). If required remove the throttle body (see Section 11).

5 If the throttle body has not been removed release the clamp and detach the fuel supply hose, being prepared with a rag to catch any residual fuel **(see illustration)**. On all except 1600 Classic and Nomad/Classic Tourer models also detach the return hose and the vacuum hose from the pressure regulator **(see illustration)**.

6 If the throttle body has not been removed disconnect the wiring connector from each injector **(see illustration 11.6)**.

7 Undo the fuel rail screws and remove the injector retainer(s), where fitted **(see illustrations)**. Carefully lift off the fuel rail and injectors as an assembly **(see illustration)**. Remove the seals from the injectors, or from the injector seats in the throttle bodies. Discard them as new ones must be used. Note the dowels and collar where fitted and remove them if loose.

8 If required remove the injectors from the fuel rail **(see illustration)**. Remove and discard the O-rings – they must be replaced with new ones **(see illustration)**.

Installation

9 Installation is the reverse of removal, noting the following:
  a) *If the injectors have been removed from their rail fit a new O-ring smeared with clean engine oil onto each one, locating it in the groove* **(see illustration 12.8b)**.
  b) *Fit a new seal smeared with oil onto each injector seat with the conical side facing the nozzle* **(see illustration 12.7c)**.

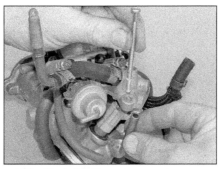

12.7a Undo the long screw and remove the spacer . . .

  c) *Make sure the dowels are in place* **(see illustration 12.7c)**. *Fit the fuel rail assembly onto the throttle bodies, making sure each injector locates correctly and the seals stay in place. Fit the fuel rail screws with the retainer(s) and collar as fitted according to model and tighten them* **(see illustrations 12.7b and a)**.
  d) *Make sure the fuel supply and return hoses are pushed fully onto their unions and are secured by the clamps* **(see illustration 12.5a)**. *Do not forget to fit the vacuum hose onto the pressure regulator* **(see illustration 12.5b)**.

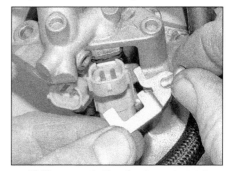

12.7b . . . undo the short screws and remove the retainer(s) where fitted . . .

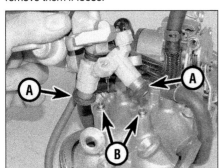

12.7c . . . then lift the fuel rail/injector assembly off and remove the seals (A) and the dowels (B) if loose

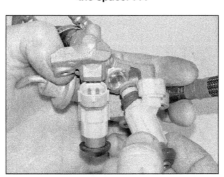

12.8a Pull the injector out of the rail . . .

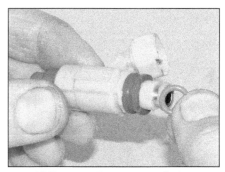

12.8b . . . and remove the O-ring

13.3 Fuel pressure regulator screws (arrowed)

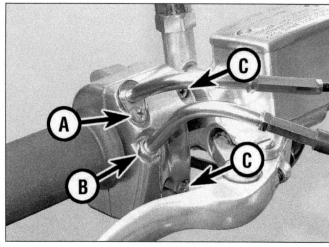

14.2 Undo the screw (A) and slacken the nut (B). Switch housing screws (C)

e) Make sure the wiring connectors are secure **(see illustration 11.6)**.

f) Run the engine and check that the fuel system is working correctly before taking the machine out on the road.

13 Fuel pressure regulator – removal and installation

 Warning: Refer to the precautions given in Section 1 before starting work.

Removal

1 On 1600 Classic and Nomad/Classic Tourer models the regulator is incorporated in the fuel pump and is not available separately.

2 On all other models remove the fuel rail (see Section 12).

3 Undo the regulator screws and detach the regulator from the rail **(see illustration)**. Remove the strainer. Remove the O-ring – a new one must be used.

4 Clean the strainer in solvent and check it for splits and holes – replace it with a new one if necessary.

Installation

5 Installation is the reverse of removal, noting the following:

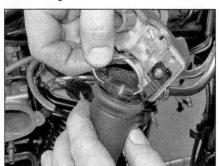

14.4a Detach the cable ends . . .

a) Fit the regulator using a new O-ring, locating it in the groove.

b) Do not forget to fit the strainer.

14 Throttle cables – removal and installation

 Warning: Refer to the precautions given in Section 1 before proceeding.

Removal

1 Remove the fuel tank (see Section 2).

14.3a Detach the housing from the handlebar . . .

14.4b . . . and remove the cables

2 Undo the screw securing the accelerator cable retainer and slacken the locknut on the decelerator cable at the handlebar **(see illustration)**. Slacken the cable adjuster locknuts and screw the adjusters in to create as much slack as possible (see Chapter 1).

3 Undo the throttle housing screws and separate the halves and slide the twistgrip off the bar **(see illustrations)**.

4 Detach the cable ends from the pulley and remove the cables from the housing **(see illustrations)**.

5 Release the retaining clip from the cable bracket on the throttle body **(see illustration)**.

14.3b . . . and slide the twistgrip off

14.5a Release the clip . . .

14.5b . . . then draw the cables up . . .

14.6 . . . and detach the ends from the cam

14.9a Fit the cable end into the cam . . .

14.9b . . . and seat the cable in the bracket

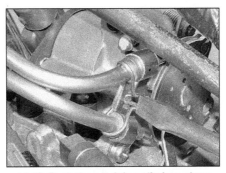

14.10 Push the retaining clip into place

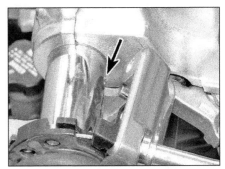

14.12 Locate the pin in the hole

Draw the cable housings up out of the bracket and slip them out **(see illustration)**.

6 Detach the cable ends from the throttle cam **(see illustration)**.

7 Remove the cables, noting how they are routed.

Installation

8 Route the cables into place. Make sure they don't interfere with any other components and aren't kinked or bent sharply.

9 Lubricate the end of the lower cable with multi-purpose grease and connect it to the throttle cam on the throttle body **(see illustration)**. Slip the inner cable through the slot in the bracket, then seat the cable elbow in the bracket **(see illustration)**.

10 Repeat the previous step to connect the upper cable **(see illustrations 14.6 and 14.5b)**. Push the clip into place **(see illustration)**.

11 Fit the cables into the switch housing and connect the cables to the throttle grip pulley **(see illustrations 14.4b and a)**. Do not yet tighten the retainer plate screw or locknut. Slide the twistgrip onto the handlebar **(see illustration 14.3b)**.

12 Install the cable/switch housing, locating the pin in the hole in the handlebar, and tighten the screws **(see illustration)**. Align the cable elbows and tighten the retainer screw and locknut **(see illustration 14.2)**.

13 Adjust throttle cable freeplay (see Chapter 1).

14 Turn the handlebars back and forth to make sure the cables don't cause the steering to bind.

15 Operate the throttle and check the cable

action. The cables should move freely and the throttle cam should move back and forth in response to both acceleration and deceleration. If the cables don't operate properly, find and fix the problem before you put the fuel tank back on.

16 Install the fuel tank (see Section 2).

17 Start the engine. With the engine idling, turn the handlebars all the way to left and right while listening for changes in idle speed. If idle speed increases as the handlebars turn, the cables are improperly routed. This is dangerous. Find the problem and fix it before riding the bike.

15 Fuel gauge and/or warning light and level sensor(s) – check, removal and installation

Warning: Refer to the precautions given in Section 1 before starting work.

Check

Note: *Refer to Electrical System Fault Finding and to the Wiring Diagram for your model in Chapter 9.*

1 The circuit consists of the sensor(s) mounted in the tank and the gauge and/or warning light in the instrument cluster. VN1500 Classic, Nomad/Classic Tourer and Drifter models have a variable level sensor connected to the gauge and an on/off sensor that is part of the fuel pump and connected to the fuel warning light. VN1600 Classic and Nomad/Classic Tourer models have a variable sensor

connected to the gauge and an on/off sensor connected to the fuel warning light combined in one unit. Mean Streak models have an on/off sensor that is part of the fuel pump and connected to the fuel warning light.

2 Prepare an auxiliary piece of wire with bared ends to jump between the terminals in the loom side of the sensor wiring connector.

3 Remove the seat(s) (see Chapter 8), and if necessary the fuel tank (see Section 2), to access the level sensor wiring connector(s).

4 To test the warning light disconnect the relevant wiring connector according to model – refer to the wiring diagrams. Turn the ignition ON and briefly connect across the warning light terminals in the loom side of the connector using the jumper wire – the warning light should come on. If it does the circuit is good and the sensor is faulty. If it doesn't check the wiring to the instrument cluster for continuity.

5 To check the gauge disconnect the relevant wiring connector according to model – refer to the wiring diagrams. Turn the ignition ON. The gauge should be on E. Now use the auxiliary wire to briefly bridge the terminals in the connector – the gauge should read F. Do not leave the wire connected for longer than is necessary to assess the movement of the needle. If the gauge functions as described the level sensor is faulty. If not check the wiring between the connector and the gauge for physical damage or loose or corroded connections and rectify as necessary (see *Electrical System Fault Finding* and the *Wiring Diagrams* in Chapter 9). If the circuit is good the gauge is faulty.

16.1a Front pipe cover clamps (arrowed)

16.1b Rear pipe cover clamps (arrowed)

16.1c Muffler cover clamp (arrowed)

16.2 Slacken the pipe clamp bolts (arrowed)

6 To check the variable level sensor remove it from the tank. Make sure the float arm moves up and down smoothly and freely – if not replace the sensor with a new one. Connect an ohmmeter between the terminals in the sensor wiring connector and check the resistance varies as you move the arm up and down. If not, the sensor is faulty.

Removal
Fuel gauge or warning light
7 Refer to Chapter 9.

Fuel level sensor
8 On VN1500 Classic, Nomad/Classic Tourer, Drifter and Mean Streak models the on/off

sensor is part of the fuel pump assembly and is not available separately.
9 To remove the variable sensor, and the combined sensors on VN1600 Classic and Nomad/Classic Tourer models, remove and drain the fuel tank (see Section 2). Place it upside down on a cushion of rag so it is adequately protected and supported.
10 Unscrew the sensor mounting plate bolts. Lift the mounting plate and carefully draw the sensor float arm out of the tank. Remove the seal and discard it – a new one must be used.

Installation
11 Installation is the reverse of removal, noting the following:

a) Fit the variable sensor using a new seal.
b) Tighten the bolts evenly and a little at a time in a criss-cross sequence.
c) Check for leaks when running the engine.

16 Exhaust system – removal and installation

⚠ **Warning: If the engine has been running the exhaust system will be very hot. Allow the system to cool before carrying out any work.**

HAYNES HiNT *Exhaust system clamp bolts tend to become corroded and seized. It is advisable to spray them with WD40 or a similar product before attempting to slacken them.*

Removal
1 Release the clamps securing the pipe and muffler covers, then slide the clamps off the hooks and remove the covers **(see illustrations)**.
2 Slacken the clamp bolts securing the pipes in the power chamber **(see illustration)**.
3 Unscrew the power chamber mounting bolt on the right side and slacken the bolt on the left side **(see illustrations)**.

16.3a Unscrew the right side bolt (arrowed) . . .

16.3b . . . and slacken the left side bolt

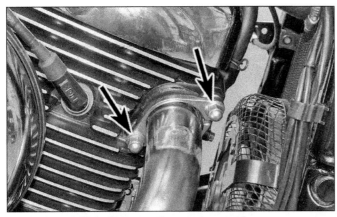

16.4a Unscrew the nuts (arrowed) . . .

16.4b . . . and remove the holders

16.4c Remove the front pipe . . .

16.4d . . . and remove the rear pipe

4 Unscrew the pipe holder nuts and remove the holders **(see illustrations)**. Detach the pipes from the cylinder head and the power chamber **(see illustrations)**.

5 Where fitted remove the saddlebags.

6 On Classic and Mean Streak models unscrew the muffler assembly bracket nut **(see illustration)**. Support the muffler/power chamber assembly and then unscrew the chamber bolt on the left **(see illustration 16.3b)**, withdraw the muffler bolt and remove the assembly. If required unscrew the lower muffler flange nuts and the upper muffler clamp bolt and separate the muffler assembly from the power chamber, then if required

unscrew the muffler nuts and separate them from the bracket **(see illustrations)**.

7 On Nomad/Classic Tourer and Drifter models slacken the muffler clamp bolt, then unscrew the muffler mounting bolts and remove the muffler. After removing both mufflers unscrew the power chamber bolt on the left side and remove the chamber.

Installation

8 Installation is the reverse of the removal steps, with the following additions:
  a) *Use new gaskets in the exhaust ports*
  (see illustration).

16.6a Unscrew the nut (arrowed)

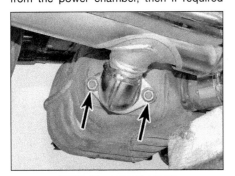

16.6b Unscrew the nuts
(arrowed) . . .

16.6c . . . and slacken the clamp bolt and detach the muffler assembly from the power chamber

16.8a Use new gaskets . . .

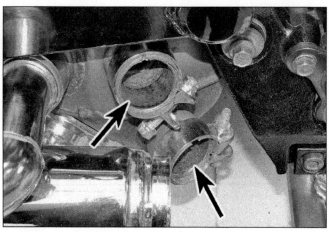

16.8b ... and new sealing rings (arrowed) where necessary

16.8c Make sure the rubber bushes are in good condition

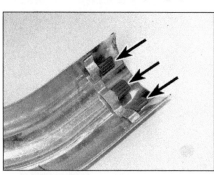

16.8g Make sure the cover rubbers (arrowed) are in good condition

b) Use new sealing rings where necessary (see illustration).

c) Make sure all rubber mounting bushes are in good condition and correctly fitted (see illustration).

d) Do not fully tighten any of the nuts/bolts until all components of the system are in place.

e) Tighten the exhaust pipe holder nuts at the cylinder heads evenly.

f) Tighten the remaining nuts and bolts.

g) Warm up the engine to normal operating temperature, let it cool, then retighten all of the nuts and bolts.

h) Make sure cover rubbers are in place and in good condition (see illustration).

17 Idle speed control (ISC) valves – operational test

1 The ISC valves control a flow of air into each inlet manifold for cold starting. They are opened and closed as required by the ICU, acting on information from the engine coolant temperature sensor. There is a valve for each duct of the inlet manifold.

2 To access the valves remove the right side air filter housing cover (see Section 7). Detach the outlet hose from the valve, then disconnect the wiring connectors, marking which fits where (see illustration). Remove the valve.

3 Try to blow air into the air inlet at the top of the valve. The valve should be closed. Now connect a battery to the terminals using suitable leads, connecting the positive (+) terminal to the white/red wire terminal. The valve should now be open, allowing the passage of air through it. If not replace the valve with a new one.

4 If required check the resistance of the valve windings using an ohmmeter connected to the terminals – it should be as specified at the beginning of the chapter.

5 If the valve is good, check for battery voltage at the white/red wire with the ignition on. If there is no voltage check the wire for continuity to the power relay, then check the relay (see Section 6). If all is good check for continuity in the green/yellow wire or green/black wire (according to valve) to the ICU.

6 If no problems can be found but there is a problem with cold starting or idle speed, check the ECT sensor. If that is good the ICU could be faulty

18 Air suction system switching valve – operational test

1 The air switching valve is part of the air suction system. Routine checking procedures are described in Chapter 1. If you suspect the valve has failed (for example, if the bike runs poorly at low speed or backfires during deceleration), test it as follows according to model:

2 Remove the fuel tank (see Section 2). Remove the valve and its hoses from the motorcycle (see illustrations).

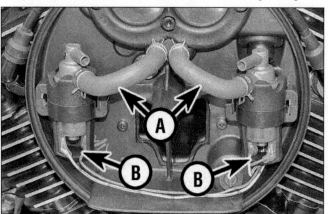

17.2 ISC valve outlet hoses (A) and wiring connectors (B)

18.2a Disconnect the wiring connector (arrowed) or detach the vacuum hose, according to model

18.2b Release the clamp and detach the front hose (arrowed) . . .

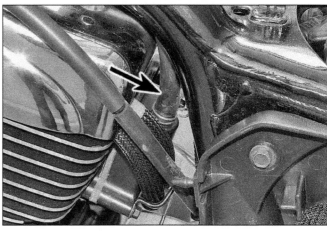

18.2c . . . and the rear hose (arrowed) and remove the valve

3 On 1600 Mean Streak models try to blow air into the air inlet hose **(see illustration)**. The valve should be open and air should flow through it. Now connect a battery to the terminals using suitable leads, connecting the terminals as shown **(see illustration)**. The valve should now be closed, allowing no air through it. If not replace the valve with a new one. If required check the resistance of the valve windings using an ohmmeter connected to the terminals – it should be as specified at the beginning of the chapter.

4 On all other models connect a vacuum pump to the thin vacuum hose on top of the valve. Try to blow air into the large air inlet hose on the bottom of the valve. It should flow easily through the valve when there's no vacuum applied to the vacuum line. Operate the vacuum pump and raise vacuum to the value listed in this Chapter's Specifications. The valve should close, making it impossible to blow air into the hose.

5 If the valve doesn't perform as described, replace it with a new one.

19 Evaporative emission control system (California models) – general information

1 The evaporative emission control system used on California models prevents fuel vapor from escaping into the atmosphere. When the engine isn't running, the vapor is stored in a canister, then routed into the combustion chambers for burning when the engine starts.

2 The hoses should be checked periodically for loose connections, damage and deterioration. Tighten or replace the hoses as needed.

3 To remove the canister, disconnect the hoses and lift the canister out of its holder.

4 To remove the liquid/vapor separator,

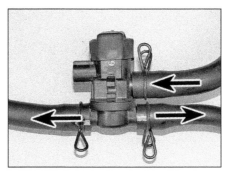

18.3a Air should flow through the valve as shown

disconnect its hoses and remove it from the mounting strap. Keep the separator in an upright position while it's out of the bike.

5 Installation is the reverse of the removal steps.

20 Catalytic converter – general information

General information

1 A catalytic converter is incorporated in the exhaust system power chamber to minimise the level of exhaust pollutants released into the atmosphere. It is an open-loop, system with no feedback to the ICU.

2 The catalytic converter consists of a canister containing a fine mesh impregnated with a catalyst material, over which the hot exhaust gases pass. The catalyst speeds up the oxidation of harmful carbon monoxide, unburned hydrocarbons and soot, effectively reducing the quantity of harmful products released into the atmosphere via the exhaust gases.

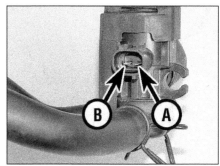

18.3b Connect the positive terminal to the terminal (A), negative to (B)

Precautions

3 The catalytic converter is a reliable and simple device which needs no maintenance in itself, but there are some facts of which an owner should be aware if the converter is to function properly for its full service life.

● DO NOT use leaded or lead replacement petrol (gasoline) – the additives will coat the precious metals, reducing their converting efficiency and will eventually destroy the catalytic converter.

● Always keep the ignition and fuel systems well-maintained in accordance with the manufacturer's schedule – if the fuel/air mixture is suspected of being incorrect have it checked on an exhaust gas analyser.

● If the engine develops a misfire, do not ride the bike at all (or at least as little as possible) until the fault is cured.

● DO NOT use fuel or engine oil additives – these may contain substances harmful to the catalytic converter.

● DO NOT continue to use the bike if the engine burns oil to the extent of leaving a visible trail of blue smoke.

● Avoid bump-starting the bike unless absolutely necessary.

Chapter 5
Ignition system

Contents

Degrees of difficulty

Easy, suitable for novice with little experience	Fairly easy, suitable for beginner with some experience	Fairly difficult, suitable for competent DIY mechanic	Difficult, suitable for experienced DIY mechanic	Very difficult, suitable for expert DIY or professional

Specifications

Ignition coil

VN1500A and B models
  Primary resistance .... 1.7 to 2.5 ohms
  Secondary resistance.................................. 18 to 26 K-ohms
All other models
  Primary resistance .... 1.9 to 2.9 ohms
  Secondary resistance.................................. 18 to 28 K-ohms
Arcing distance....................................... min. 6 mm (1/4 inch)

Pickup coil resistance

VN1500A and B models.................................. 440 to 490 ohms
All other models .... 380 to 560 ohms

---

1 General information

These motorcycles are equipped with a battery operated, fully transistorized, breakerless ignition system. The system consists of the following components:

  Pickup coils
  Ignition control unit (ICU)
  Battery and fuses
  Ignition coils
  Spark plugs
  Stop and ignition switches
  Primary and secondary circuit wiring

All models are fitted with a fully transistorised electronic ignition system that, due to its lack of mechanical parts, is totally maintenance-free. The system comprises a pair of pick-up coils, one for each cylinder, with triggers on the alternator rotor, an ignition control unit (ICU), and a pair of ignition coils, again one for each cylinder, with each coil firing two spark plugs per cylinder - refer to

Wiring Diagrams at the end of Chapter 9 for details.

The triggers magnetically operate the pick-up coils as the crankshaft rotates. The pick-up coils send signals to the ignition control unit, which then supplies the ignition HT coils with the power necessary to produce a spark at the plugs.

The ICU incorporates an electronic advance system.

The system incorporates a safety interlock circuit which will cut the ignition if the sidestand is extended whilst the engine is running and in gear. It also prevents the engine from being started if the sidestand is down and the engine is in gear. The engine can be started with the sidestand up when it is in gear as long as the clutch lever is pulled in.

Some models are fitted with an immobiliser system which will not allow the engine to be started unless the correct key is used.

Because of their nature, the individual ignition system components can be checked but not repaired. If ignition system troubles

occur, and the faulty component can be isolated, the only cure for the problem is to replace the part with a new one. Keep in mind that most electrical parts, once purchased, can't be returned. To avoid unnecessary expense, make very sure the faulty component has been positively identified before buying a replacement part.

2 Ignition system – check

 Warning: Because of the very high voltage generated by the ignition system, extreme care should be taken to avoid electrical shock when these checks are performed.

1 If the ignition system is the suspected cause of poor engine performance or failure to start, a number of checks can be made to isolate the problem.

2 Make sure the ignition stop switch is in the Run or On position.

2.3 Pull the cap off the spark plug

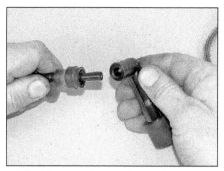

2.5a Unscrew the cap from the lead . . .

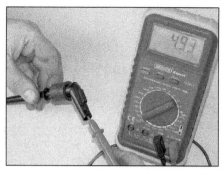

2.5b . . . and check the resistance of the cap

Engine will not start

3 Pull one of the spark plug caps off its plug **(see illustration)**. Connect the cap to a spare spark plug and lay the plug on the engine with the threads contacting the engine. If it's necessary to hold the spark plug, use an insulated tool. Crank the engine over and make sure a well-defined, blue spark occurs between the spark plug electrodes.

⚠ *Warning: DO NOT remove one of the spark plugs from the engine to perform this check – atomized fuel being pumped out of the open spark plug hole could ignite, causing severe injury!*

4 If no spark occurs, the following checks should be made:

5 Unscrew a spark plug cap from a plug lead and check the cap resistance with an ohmmeter **(see illustrations)**. If the resistance is infinite, replace it with a new one. Repeat this check on the other plug caps.

6 Make sure all relevant electrical connectors are clean and tight. Refer to the wiring diagrams at the end of this book and check all wires for shorts, opens and correct installation.

7 Check the battery voltage with a voltmeter and the specific gravity with a hydrometer (see Chapter 1). If the voltage is less than 12-volts or if the specific gravity is low, recharge the battery.

8 Check the ignition fuse and the fuse connections, and on fuel injection models check the injection system fuse. If the fuse is blown, replace it with a new one; if the connections are loose or corroded, clean or repair them.

9 Refer to Section 3 and check the ignition coil primary and secondary resistance.

10 Refer to Section 4 and check the pickup coil resistance.

11 Refer to Chapter 9 and check the clutch, neutral and sidestand switches and the starter interlock circuit diodes.

12 On carburetor models, if the preceding checks produce positive results but there is still no spark at the plug, have the ICU checked by a Kawasaki dealer service department or other repair shop equipped with the special tester required.

13 On fuel injection models, if the preceding checks produce positive results but there is still no spark at the plug, check the injection system power relay and tip-over sensor. If they are good have the ICU checked by a Kawasaki dealer service department or other repair shop equipped with the special tester required.

Engine starts but misfires

14 If the engine starts but misfires, make the following checks before deciding that the ignition system is at fault.

15 The ignition system must be able to produce a spark across a six millimeter (1/4-inch) gap (minimum). Test tools are commercially available **(see illustration)**. Make sure the tool electrodes are positioned six millimeters apart.

16 Connect one of the spark plug wires to the test tool electrode, then connect or touch the other end to a good engine ground (earth).

17 Crank the engine over (it may start and run on the remaining cylinder) and see if well-defined, blue sparks occur between the

test fixture electrodes. If the minimum spark gap test is positive, the ignition coil for that cylinder is functioning properly. Repeat the check on a spark plug wire that is connected to the other coil. If the spark will not jump the gap during either test, or if it is weak (orange colored), refer to Section 3 and perform the HT coil checks described.

3 Ignition coils – check, removal and installation

Check

1 The coils can be checked visually (for cracks and other damage) and the primary and secondary coil resistances can be measured with an ohmmeter. If the coils are undamaged, and if the resistances are as specified, they are probably capable of proper operation.

2 Remove the coil(s).

3 To check the coil primary resistance, place the ohmmeter selector switch in the Rx1 position, then connect one ohmmeter lead to one of the primary terminals and the other ohmmeter lead to the other primary terminal **(see illustration)**. Compare the measured resistance to the value listed in this Chapter's Specifications. If it's not as specified, the coil is probably defective.

4 To check the coil secondary resistance unscrew the caps from the leads **(see illustration 2.5a)**. Place the ohmmeter selector switch in the Rx1000 (K-ohm) position, then connect the meter lead probes into the bare ends of the HT leads **(see illustration)**.

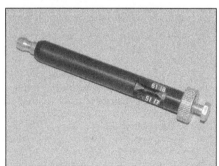

2.15 Typical ignition system spark gap testing tool

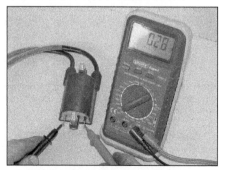

3.3 To test the coil primary resistance, connect the multimeter leads to the primary wiring terminals

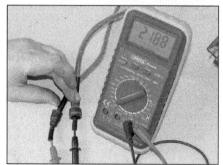

3.4 To test the coil secondary resistance, connect the multimeter probes to the HT lead ends

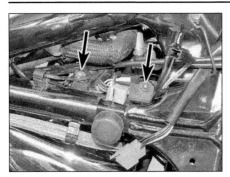

3.17a Disconnect the wiring connectors to access the nuts (arrowed) . . .

3.17b . . . on each side as required according to model

3.17c Displace the coil, draw it out, then disconnect the primary wiring

Compare the measured resistance to the values listed in this Chapter's Specifications.

5 If the secondary resistances are not as specified, unscrew the spark plug lead retainers from the coil, detach the leads and check the resistance again. If it is now within specifications, one or both of the leads are bad. If it's still not as specified, the coil is probably defective.

6 In order to determine conclusively that the ignition coils are defective, they should be tested by an authorized Kawasaki dealer service department which is equipped with the special electrical tester required for this check.

Removal and installation

VN1500A and B models

7 Remove the seat (see Chapter 8). Remove the coolant reservoir (see Chapter 3), then remove the reservoir bracket.

8 Displace the ignition switch from the frame.

9 Detach the hose from the rear cylinder air suction system reed valve housing.

10 Release the HT leads from their ties then pull the caps off the plugs. Feed the leads back to the coils, noting their routing. Also disconnect the primary circuit wiring connector and feed that down to the coils.

11 Remove the blanking plug from each

side of the coil assembly cover. Unscrew the bolt on each side and carefully draw the coil assembly out to the right.

12 Unscrew the bolts and remove the cover.

13 Mark the locations of the primary circuit wiring connectors, then disconnect them. Undo the coil mounting bolts, then detach the coil from the bracket.

14 Installation is the reverse of removal. If a new coil is being installed, the lead should come with it but you will need the old plug caps, or new ones as preferred. Make sure any bracket or earth wire previously released is secured with the coil. Make sure the primary circuit electrical connectors are attached to the proper terminals.

All other models

15 Remove the fuel tank (see Chapter 4A or 4B).

16 Release the HT leads from their clips then pull the caps off the plugs **(see illustration 2.3)**.

17 Move aside any hoses and/or disconnect any wiring connectors that are in the way of the coil mounting nuts, as required according to model **(see illustrations)**. Support the coil with one hand and unscrew the nuts **(see illustration)**, then displace the coil and draw it out and disconnect the primary circuit connectors, noting which goes where – also

note any bracket or earth lead secured with them, according to model.

18 Installation is the reverse of removal. If a new coil is being installed, the lead should come with it but you will need the old plug caps, or new ones as preferred. Make sure any bracket or earth wire previously released is secured with the coil. Make sure the primary circuit electrical connectors are attached to the proper terminals.

4 Pickup coils – check, removal and installation

Check

1 On VN1500A and B models remove the ignition coil assembly (see Section 3).

2 On Drifter J models remove the connector cover on the left side of the engine. On all other models remove the shift pedals (see Chapter 2), then remove the left side engine cover **(see illustration)**.

3 Follow the pickup coil wiring from the point where it leaves the alternator cover and disconnect it at the connector, referring to the Wiring Diagrams in Chapter 9 for wire colors **(see illustration)**.

4 Connect the probes of an ohmmeter to the

4.2 Unscrew the bolts (arrowed) and remove the cover

4.3 Except on VN1500A and B models the wiring connector is under the cover

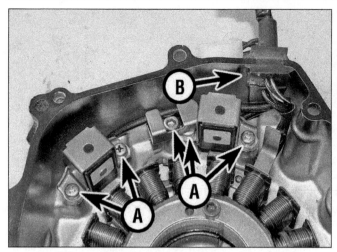

4.9 Wiring guide and pick-up coil screws (A) and wiring grommets (B) – VN1600 shown

5.4 Ignition control unit (arrowed) – UK model VN1600 Mean Streak

black and black/yellow wire terminals in the coil side of the connector to test the pick-up coil for the front cylinder, and to the black/red and black/white wire terminals for the rear cylinder coil, and measure the resistance. Compare the resistance readings with the value listed in this Chapter's Specifications.

5 Set the ohmmeter on the highest resistance range. Measure the resistance between a good ground and each terminal in the electrical connector. The meter should read infinity.

6 If a pickup coil fails either of the above tests, both coils must be replaced with a new set.

Removal

7 On VN1500A and B models remove the ignition coil assembly (see Section 3). Follow the pickup coil wiring from the point where it leaves the alternator cover and disconnect it at the connector.

8 Remove the alternator outer cover (see Chapter 9, Section 34). Note the layout of the coils and the routing of the wiring before removing them.

9 Undo the wiring guide screw where fitted and the pickup coil mounting screws **(see illustration)**. Remove the wiring guide where fitted, slip the grommet(s) out of the slot and remove the pickup coil(s) together with the wiring harness, and on Mean Streak models the brackets with their dampers.

Installation

10 Position the pickup coils and wiring guide where fitted in the alternator cover, on Mean Streak models fitting the dampers and brackets, and fit the screws, tightening them securely. Apply a small amount of silicone sealant to the grommet on the wiring harness and seat the grommet securely in the notch **(see illustration 4.9)**.

11 Install the alternator outer cover and connect the wiring (see Chapter 9). On VN1500A and B models install the ignition coil assembly (see Section 3).

5 Ignition control unit (ICU) – removal, check and installation

Check

1 On carburetor models a special tester is required to accurately measure the resistance values across the various terminals of the ICU. Take the unit to a Kawasaki dealer service department or other repair shop equipped with this tester.

2 On fuel injection models it is not possible to test the ICU. If it is suspected of being faulty, first check the ignition and injection system fuses (see Chapter 9), then check the injection

system power relay (see Chapter 4B). If all appears good, refer to the wiring diagrams at the end of Chapter 9 and check that the power circuit wiring between the fuses, relay and the ICU, and the earth circuit wiring from the ICU to ground, shows continuity, and the connectors are secure and clean. If all is good, the ICU could well be faulty – substitution with one known to be good is the only way to determine this conclusively.

Removal and installation

3 On carburetor models remove the right side cover (see Chapter 8). On Classic and Nomad/Classic Tourer models remove the coolant reservoir (see Chapter 3). Disconnect the wiring connectors then unscrew the bolts and remove the ICU.

4 On fuel injection models remove the seat(s) (see Chapter 8). Unscrew the battery holder bolt and remove the holder. Move aside any wiring and electrical components as required. On the Mean Streak model photographed removal of the battery gave better access, but whether you need to depends on your model and the type of ICU fitted. Lift the ICU out and disconnect the connector(s) **(see illustration)** – on models with a single connector slide the locking device across to release the connector.

5 Installation is the reverse of removal.

Chapter 6
Steering, suspension and final drive

Contents

Degrees of difficulty

| Easy, suitable for novice with little experience | 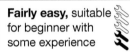 | Fairly easy, suitable for beginner with some experience | | Fairly difficult, suitable for competent DIY mechanic | | Difficult, suitable for experienced DIY mechanic | | Very difficult, suitable for expert DIY or professional | |

Specifications

Front fork oil

VN1500A
Type . . . . SAE 10W20 fork oil
Amount
    Dry fill . . . . 436 ± 2.5 ml
    At oil change. . . . . 370 ml
Oil level (spring removed and fork fully compressed). . . . . 124 ± 7 mm

VN1500B
Type . . . . SAE 10W20 fork oil
Amount
    Dry fill . . . . 474 ± 2.5 ml
    At oil change. . . . . 405 ml
Oil level (spring removed and fork fully compressed). . . . . 140 ± 7 mm

VN1500 Classic
Type . . . . SAE 10W20 fork oil
Amount
    Dry fill . . . . 464 ± 2.5 ml
    At oil change. . . . . 395 ml
Oil level (spring removed and fork fully compressed). . . . . 137 ± 2 mm

VN1500 Classic FI
Type . . . . Showa SS-8 or SAE 10W20 fork oil
Amount
    Dry fill . . . . 467 ± 2.5 ml
    At oil change. . . . . 395 ml
Oil level (spring removed and fork fully compressed). . . . . 137 ± 2 mm

VN1600 Classic
Type . . . . KHL34-G10 (Kayaba) fork oil
Amount
    Dry fill . . . . 521 ± 2 ml
    At oil change. . . . . 445 ml
Oil level (spring removed and fork fully compressed). . . . . 120 mm

Front fork oil (continued)

VN1500 Nomad/Classic Tourer
  Type . . . . SAE 10W20 fork oil
  Amount
    Dry fill . . . . 431 ± 2.5 ml
    At oil change . . . . 365 ml
  Oil level (spring removed and fork fully compressed) . . . . 176 ± 2 mm
VN1500 Nomad/Classic Tourer FI
  Type . . . . SAE 10W20 fork oil
  Amount
    Dry fill . . . . 397 ± 2.5 ml
    At oil change . . . . 338 ml
  Oil level (spring removed and fork fully compressed) . . . . 165 ± 2 mm
VN1600 Nomad/Classic Tourer
  Type . . . . KHL34-G10 (Kayaba) fork oil
  Amount
    Dry fill . . . . 513 ± 4 ml
    At oil change . . . . 440 ml
  Oil level (spring removed and fork fully compressed) . . . . 135 ± 2 mm
Drifter
  Type . . . . SAE 10W20 fork oil
  Amount
    Dry fill . . . . 419 ± 2.5 ml
    At oil change . . . . 356 ml
  Oil level (spring removed and fork fully compressed)
    J models . . . . 176 ± 2 mm
    R models . . . . 169 ± 2 mm
Mean Streak
  Type
    2002 and 2003 (1500P) models . . . . SAE 10W20 fork oil
    2004-on (1600B and F) models . . . . Showa SS-8 or SAE 10W20 fork oil
  Amount
    Right-hand fork
      Dry fill . . . . 507 ± 2.5 ml
      At oil change . . . . 430 ml
    Left-hand fork
      Dry fill . . . . 601 ± 2.5 ml
      At oil change . . . . 510 ml
  Oil level (spring removed and fork fully compressed)
    Right-hand fork . . . . 142 mm
    Left-hand fork . . . . 136 mm

Rear shock absorber settings

Shock absorber settings
  VN1500A and B, VN1500 Classic, VN1600 Classic A1/A2
    Standard pre-load position 2
    Pre-load range . . . . 1 to 5
  All other models
    Standard rebound damper position 2
    Rebound range . . . . 1 to 4
    Air pressure . . . . 0 to 43 psi (2.97 Bar)

Torque specifications

Fork damper rod bolt
  VN1500 models . . . . 20 Nm (174 inch-lbs)
  VN1600 Classic, Nomad/Classic Tourer and Drifter . . . . 30 Nm (22 ft-lbs)
  Mean Streak . . . . 20 Nm (174 inch-lbs)
Fork inner bolt (Mean Streak only, left-hand fork) . . . . 98 Nm (72 ft-lbs)
Fork pinch bolts – lower triple clamp
  VN1500A and B . . . . 52 Nm (38 ft-lbs)
  VN1500 Classic and Nomad/Classic Tourer . . . . 34 Nm (25 ft-lbs)
  VN1500 Classic FI and Nomad/Classic Tourer FI . . . . 20 Nm (174 inch-lbs)
  VN1600 Classic and Nomad/Classic Tourer . . . . 29 Nm (21 ft-lbs)
  Drifter . . . . 34 Nm (25 ft-lbs)
  Mean Streak 1500P models . . . . 20 Nm (174 inch-lbs)
  Mean Streak 1600B models . . . . 29 Nm (21 ft-lbs)

Torque specifications (continued)

Fork pinch bolts – upper triple clamp
VN1600 Classic A2-on, VN1600 Nomad/Classic Tourer	29 Nm (21 ft-lbs)
Mean Streak	29 Nm (21 ft-lbs)
All other models	20 Nm (174 inch-lbs)

Fork top bolts
VN1600 Classic and Nomad/Classic Tourer.	22 Nm (16 ft-lbs)
Mean Streak	34 Nm (25 ft-lbs)

Front bevel gear housing bolts
M8 bolts
VN1500A and B	25 Nm (18 ft-lbs)
VN1500 Classic D models	25 Nm (18 ft-lbs)
VN1500 Nomad/Classic Tourer G and H models	25 Nm (18 ft-lbs)
All other models	29 Nm (21 ft-lbs)
M6 bolts marked 9	12 Nm (104 inch-lbs)
M6 bolts unmarked.	9 Nm (78 inch-lbs)

Final drive housing nuts
VN1500A and B and Classic D models	29 Nm (22 ft-lbs)
All other models	34 Nm (25 ft-lbs)
Handlebar clamp pinch bolts – VN1500A and B	59 Nm (43 ft-lbs)
Handlebar stud nuts – Mean Streak.	34 Nm (25 ft-lbs)
Handlebar bracket bolts and stud nuts – all other models	34 Nm (25 ft-lbs)

Steering stem nut or bolt
VN1500A and B	39 Nm (29 ft-lbs)
VN1500 Classic	44 Nm (33 ft-lbs)
VN1500 Classic FI 2000 to 2002 (N1 to N3) models	54 Nm (40 ft-lbs)
VN1500 Classic FI 2005-on (N4-on) models	88 Nm (65 ft-lbs)
VN1600 Classic	88 Nm (65 ft-lbs)
Nomad/Classic Tourer	88 Nm (65 ft-lbs)
Drifter 1999 and 2000 (J1 and J2) models	88 Nm (65 ft-lbs)
Drifter 2001-on (R1-on) models	54 Nm (40 ft-lbs)
VN1500 Mean Streak	54 Nm (40 ft-lbs)
VN1600 Mean Streak	88 Nm (65 ft-lbs)

Rear shock absorber mounting nuts
VN1500A and B	30 Nm (22 ft-lbs)
All other models	34 Nm (25 ft-lbs)

Swingarm pivot bolt
VN1500A and B	98 Nm (72 ft-lbs)
VN1500 Classic and Nomad/Classic Tourer.	125 Nm (94 ft-lbs)
VN1500 Classic FI and VN1600 Classic.	108 Nm (80 ft-lbs)
VN1500 Nomad/Classic Tourer FI	125 Nm (94 ft-lbs)
Drifter J models	125 Nm (94 ft-lbs)
Drifter R models and Mean Streak P models.	110 Nm (79.6 ft-lbs)
Mean Streak B and F models.	108 Nm (80 ft-lbs)

1 General information

The front forks on these models are of the coil spring, hydraulically-damped telescopic type, conventionally mounted on all except Mean Streak models, that have upside-down forks.

The rear suspension consists of two coil spring shock absorbers and a swingarm, which contains a passage for the driveshaft.

The final drive uses a front bevel gear at the engine, a driveshaft and a final bevel drive housing at the rear wheel. A rubber damper mechanism is fitted between the rear wheel coupling and the wheel hub.

2 Handlebar – removal and installation

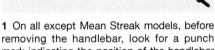

1 On all except Mean Streak models, before removing the handlebar, look for a punch mark indicating the position of the handlebar in the brackets. Make your own mark if you can't see one.
2 On all except Mean Streak models, carefully pry the trim plugs out of the handlebar bolts.
3 If the handlebar is being displaced from the top yoke for access to other components, such as the forks or the steering head, simply undo the nuts on the underside of the top yoke on VN1500A and B and Mean Streak models, or the bracket bolts on all other models, and lift the handlebar off. It's not necessary to disconnect the cables, wires or hoses, but support the assembly on plenty of rag and tie it in place as required to avoid contact with other components and unnecessary strain on the cables, wires and hoses.
4 If the handlebar is being completely removed for replacement or other purposes, disconnect the throttle cables (see Chapter 4A or 4B), displace the handlebar switch housings (see Chapter 9), and displace the clutch and front brake master cylinders (see Chapters 2 and 7 respectively).
5 Check the handlebar for cracks and distortion and replace it if any undesirable conditions are found.

6 Installation is the reverse of the removal steps, with the following additions:

a) *On VN1500A and B and Mean Streak models, tighten the stud nuts to the torque listed in this Chapter's Specifications.*

b) *On all other models, align the punch mark on the back of the handlebar with the top surface of the bottom section of the bracket, then tighten the forward bolt on each bracket to the torque listed in this Chapter's Specifications, then tighten the rear bolt. This will leave a gap at the rear of the bracket. Don't try to close the gap by tightening the bolts further or the brackets will break.*

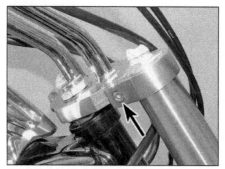

3.7 Slacken the bolt (arrowed) in the upper triple clamp

3.8 Loosen the top bolt now if required

3 Forks – removal and installation

Removal

1 Note the routing of the cables, hose and wiring around the forks. Mark each fork according to the side it fits on. Note the setting of the top of the fork in respect to the upper surface of the top triple clamp.

2 On VN1600 Nomad/Classic Tourer models remove the windshield (see Chapter 8). On VN1600 Classic and Nomad/Classic Tourer models remove the headlight and its shell (see Chapter 9). Unscrew the fork cover bolts and remove the windshield brackets where fitted and the front cover.

3 On VN1500 Classic and all Mean Streak models slacken the front turn signal clamp bolt or nut.

4 Remove the front wheel (see Chapter 7).

5 Remove the front fender (see Chapter 8).

6 Release any wiring or hose clamps or straps from the fork tubes.

7 Loosen the fork pinch bolt in the upper triple clamp **(see illustration)**.

8 On VN1500 Nomad/Classic Tourer FI models remove the fork cap. On VN1500 Nomad/Classic Tourer FI models, VN1600 Classic and Nomad/Classic Tourer models, and all Mean Streak models, if the fork oil is being changed or the fork is being disassembled slacken

the top bolt now, then lightly retighten it **(see illustration)**.

9 Loosen the fork pinch bolt(s) in the lower triple clamp **(see illustration)**. Twist the fork tube and slide the fork downward and out of the triple clamps **(see illustration)**. On VN1600 Classic and Nomad/Classic Tourer models note the rubber damper that fits inside the bottom of the fork shroud which has probably come away with the fork.

Installation

10 Remove all traces of corrosion from the fork tube and the triple clamps. Make sure you install each fork on its correct side as marked on removal. On VN1600 Classic and Nomad/Classic Tourer models fit the rubber damper that fits inside the bottom of the fork shroud onto the inner tube just above the dust seal, making sure it is the correct way up.

11 Slide the fork up through the lower triple clamp and into the upper one, making sure all cables, hoses and wiring are routed on the correct side of the fork **(see illustration 3.9b)**. Set the top of the fork tube (the top of the tube itself, not the cap or top bolt) flush with the upper surface of the upper clamp **(see illustration)**. Tighten the lower triple clamp pinch bolt(s) to the torque setting specified at the beginning of the Chapter – on models with two bolts tighten the bolts evenly and a bit at a time to ensure even seating of the clamp, and after the second bolt has reached its torque check the first bolt again **(see illustration 3.9a)**.

12 On VN1500 Nomad/Classic Tourer FI models, VN1600 Classic and Nomad/Classic Tourer models and all Mean Streak models, if the fork has been dismantled or if the fork oil was changed, tighten the fork top bolt to the specified torque setting **(see illustration 3.8)**. On VN1500 Nomad/Classic Tourer FI models fit the fork cap.

13 Tighten the upper triple clamp pinch bolt to its specified torque setting **(see illustration 3.7)**. On VN1600 Classic and Nomad/Classic Tourer models fit the rubber damper up into the bottom of the fork shroud.

14 Install the remaining components in a reverse of the removal procedure according to model, referring to the relevant Chapters. Check the operation of the front forks and brake before taking the machine out on the road.

4 Fork oil – change

1 After a high mileage the fork oil will deteriorate and its damping and lubrication qualities will be impaired. Always change the oil in both fork legs.

VN1500A and B models

2 Support the bike upright using an auxiliary stand, making sure it is secure. Position a jack with a block of wood on the jack head under

3.9a Slacken the bolt(s) (arrowed) in the lower triple clamp

3.9b Draw the fork down and out of the triple clamps

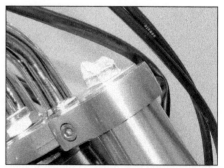

3.11 Set the top of the tube flush with the upper triple clamp so the cap or bolt is proud

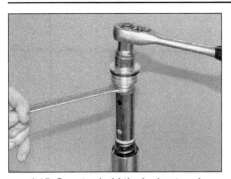

4.15 Counter-hold the locknut and unscrew and remove the top bolt

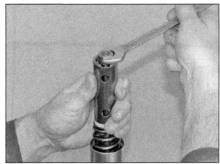

4.16a Thread the locknut up, but not off, the rod

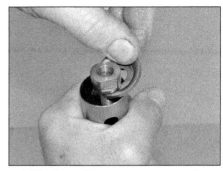

4.16b Grasp the spacer, compress the spring and slip the slotted washer out

the engine to support the motorcycle when the fork caps are removed.

3 Displace the handlebar from the upper triple clamp (see Section 2).

4 Remove the fork cap **(see illustration 4.38)**.

5 Push the top plug downward against spring pressure with a suitable tool, then hold it down while removing the retaining ring, and then carefully release the spring pressure and remove the plug.

6 Remove the spacer and the washer. Withdraw the spring.

7 Place a drain pan under the fork leg and undo the drain screw. Allow the fork oil to drain for several minutes.

 Warning: Do not allow the fork oil to contact the brake disc, pads or tire. If it does, clean the disc with brake system cleaner, wipe off the tire, and replace the pads with new ones before riding the motorcycle.

8 Check the drain screw sealing washer for damage and replace it if with a new one if necessary. Clean the threads of the drain screw, then apply some fresh non-permanent threadlock, fit the sealing washer and tighten the screw.

9 Pour the type and amount of fork oil, listed in this Chapter's Specifications, into the top of the fork tube. Slowly pump the forks a few times to purge the air.

10 Fully compress the front forks (you may need an assistant to do this). Insert a stiff tape measure or a marked rod into the centre of the fork tube and measure the distance from

the oil to the top of the fork tube. Compare your measurement to the value listed in this Chapter's Specifications. Drain or add oil, as necessary, until the level is correct.

11 Check the condition of the O-ring on the top plug and replace it with a new one if necessary, then coat it with a thin layer of multi-purpose grease. Fit the fork spring with its narrow end facing down, then fit the washer and the spacer. Seat the top plug on the spacer then push it down against the spring pressure and fit the retaining ring into its groove. Fit the cap.

12 Repeat the procedure on the other fork. Note that it is essential that the oil quantity and level is identical in each fork.

Mean Streak models

Right-hand fork

13 Remove the fork (see Section 3) – make sure the top bolt is loosened while the leg is still held in the bottom triple clamp.

14 Unscrew the fork top bolt from the top of the inner tube **(see illustration 4.24)**. The bolt will remain on the damper rod, held by the locknut.

15 Slide the outer tube down gently until it seats on the bottom. Counter-hold the locknut and unscrew the top bolt **(see illustration)**.

16 Thread the locknut up to the top of the rod, so that half of its threads are exposed. Grasp the spacer and push it against the spring then slip the slotted washer out from under the nut

and slowly release the pressure on the spring. Remove the spacer, then lift the spring out of the tube **(see illustrations)**.

17 Invert the fork leg over a suitable container and pump the fork tubes and damper rod several times to expel as much oil as possible **(see illustration 4.29)**. Support the fork upside down in the container for a while to allow as much oil as possible to drain, then pump the fork and rod again. If the oil contains metal particles inspect the fork bushes for wear (see Section 5). Wipe any excess oil off the spring and spacer.

18 Stand the fork upright. Slowly pour in the specified quantity of the specified grade of fork oil **(see illustration 4.30a)**. Now pump the fork and damper rod slowly at least ten times each to distribute the oil evenly and expel all air from the damper. Slide the outer tube and damper rod down gently until they seat. Measure the oil level from the top of the tube **(see illustration 4.30b)**. Add or subtract oil until it is at the level specified at the beginning of this Chapter.

19 Thread an M12 x 1.25 bolt into the exposed locknut threads **(see illustration)**. Pull the damper rod out as far as possible using the bolt head as a handle. Fit the spring with the tapered end at the top. Keeping the damper rod extended, fit the spacer, locating the nylon collar in the top of the spring **(see illustration)**.

20 Keeping the damper rod extended push down on the spacer to compress the spring and slip the washer under the locknut

4.16c Remove the spacer and the spring

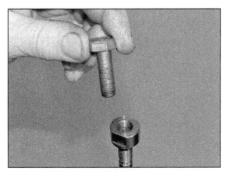

4.19a Thread a bolt into the exposed locknut threads to use as a handle to keep the rod extended

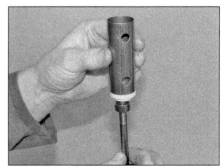

4.19b Fit the spring, then fit the spacer

4.20a Fit the slotted washer under the locknut

4.20b Thread the top bolt onto the rod

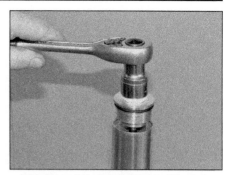

4.24 Thread the top bolt out of the tube

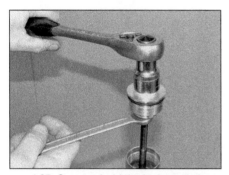

4.25 Counter-hold the locknut and unscrew and remove the top bolt

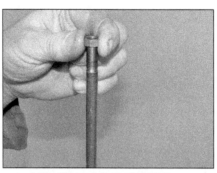

4.26a Thread the locknut off . . .

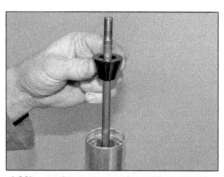

4.26b . . . then remove the rubber stopper

(see illustration). Remove the bolt (see illustration 4.19a). Thread the locknut all the way down the rod (see illustration 4.16a). Thread the top bolt onto the damper rod

4.27a Clamp the bottom of the fork as shown

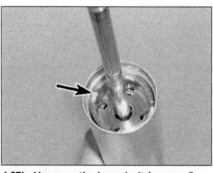

4.27b Unscrew the inner bolt (arrowed) . . .

4.27c . . . using a tool as described . . .

4.27d . . . and remove the damper rod assembly

(see illustration). Counter-hold the locknut using a spanner as before and tighten the top bolt securely against it (see illustration 4.15).

21 Check the condition of the O-ring on the top bolt and replace it with a new one if necessary. Smear some fork oil onto the O-ring. Extend the inner tube and thread the top bolt into it, making sure it does not cross-thread, and tighten it as much as possible holding the inner tube by hand (see illustration 4.35). Note: Tighten the top bolt to the specified torque setting when the fork has been installed in the bike and is held in the bottom triple clamp, but before the top triple clamp bolt is tightened.

22 Install the fork (see Section 3).

Left-hand fork

23 Remove the fork (see Section 3) – make sure that the top bolt is loosened while the leg is still held in the bottom triple clamp.

24 Unscrew the fork top bolt from the top of the inner tube (see illustration). The bolt will remain on the damper rod, held by the locknut on its top.

25 Slide the outer tube down gently until it seats on the bottom. Counter-hold the locknut and unscrew the top bolt (see illustration).

26 Thread the locknut off the rod, then remove the rubber stopper (see illustrations).

27 Clamp the bottom of the fork in a vice, using some thick card against the jaws as protection (see illustration). Using either the Kawasaki tool (part no. 57001-1502) or a suitable equivalent peg spanner (see Tool Tip), unscrew the inner bolt and lift out the damper rod assembly (see illustrations).

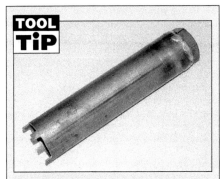

TOOL TiP

You can fabricate a tool out of a piece of steel tube the same diameter as the inner bolt with castellations 7 mm wide and 4.5 mm deep cut into one end so they fit into the slots, and a nut welded onto the other as shown.

28 Remove the spacer, then hook the washer and spring out of the tube **(see illustrations)**.
29 Invert the fork over a suitable container and pump the fork tubes to expel as much fork oil as possible **(see illustration)**. Support the fork upside down in the container for a while to allow as much oil as possible to drain, then pump the fork again. If the fork oil contains metal particles inspect the fork bushes for wear (see Section 5). Wipe any excess oil off the spring and spacer.
30 Stand the fork upright. Slowly pour in the specified quantity of the specified grade of fork oil **(see illustration)**. Slide the outer tube down gently until it seats on the bottom. Measure the oil level from the top of the tube **(see**

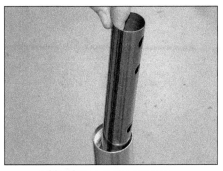

4.28a Remove the spacer . . .

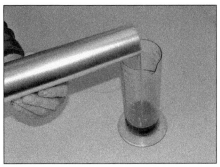

4.29 Drain the oil as described

illustration). Add or subtract oil until it is at the level specified at the beginning of this Chapter.
31 Fit the spring with the tapered end at the top **(see illustration)**. Fit the washer and the spacer **(see illustrations)**.

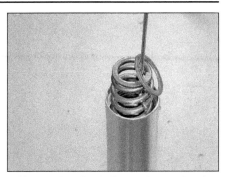

4.28b . . . then hook the washer and spring out

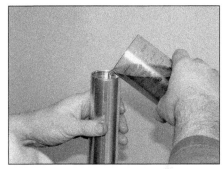

4.30a Pour the oil into the top of the tube and distribute and bleed it as described . . .

32 Fit the damper assembly into the fork **(see illustration)**. Fit the inner bolt and tighten it to the torque listed in the Specifications using the same tool as on removal **(see illustration and 4.27c)**.

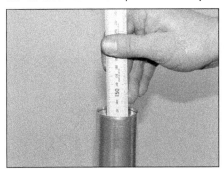

4.30b . . . then measure the level as described using a ruler

4.31a Fit the spring . . .

4.31b . . . the washer . . .

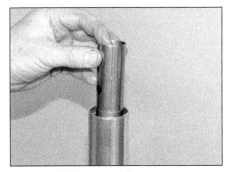

4.31c . . . and the spacer

4.32a Fit the damper assembly . . .

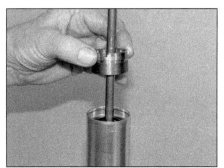

4.32b . . . then fit the bolt and tighten it using the tool

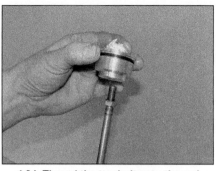

4.34 Thread the top bolt onto the rod

4.35 Check and lubricate its O-ring, then thread the top bolt into the tube

33 Fit the rubber stopper onto the inner bolt, then thread the locknut onto the damper rod until it seats **(see illustrations 4.26b and a)**.
34 Thread the top bolt onto the rod **(see illustration)**. Counter-hold the locknut using a spanner as before and tighten the top bolt securely against it **(see illustration 4.25)**.
35 Check the condition of the O-ring on the top bolt and replace it with a new one if necessary. Smear some fork oil onto the O-ring. Extend the inner tube and thread the top bolt into it, making sure it does not cross-thread, and tighten it as much as possible holding the inner tube by hand **(see illustration)**. **Note:** *Tighten the top bolt to the*

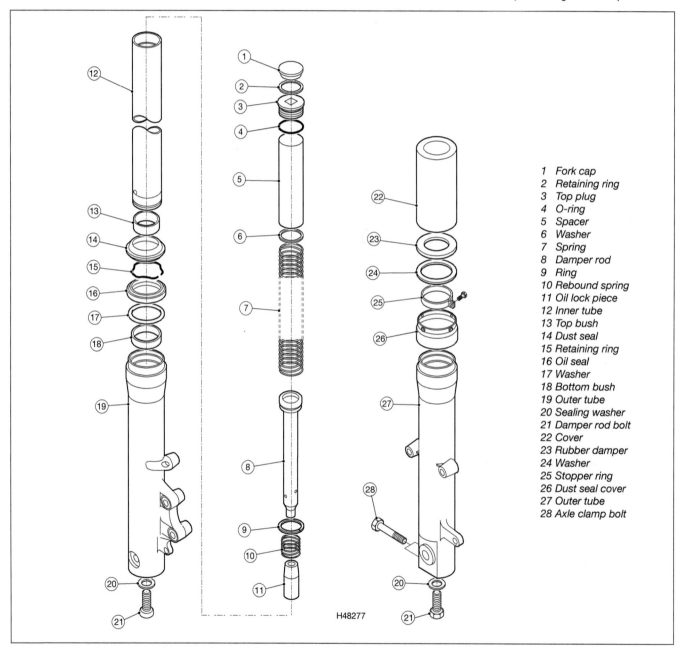

1 Fork cap
2 Retaining ring
3 Top plug
4 O-ring
5 Spacer
6 Washer
7 Spring
8 Damper rod
9 Ring
10 Rebound spring
11 Oil lock piece
12 Inner tube
13 Top bush
14 Dust seal
15 Retaining ring
16 Oil seal
17 Washer
18 Bottom bush
19 Outer tube
20 Sealing washer
21 Damper rod bolt
22 Cover
23 Rubber damper
24 Washer
25 Stopper ring
26 Dust seal cover
27 Outer tube
28 Axle clamp bolt

H48277

4.38 Front fork components - all VN1500 models except Nomad/Classic Tourer FI and Mean Streak

specified torque setting when the fork has been installed in the bike and is held in the bottom triple clamp, but before the top triple clamp bolt is tightened.

36 Install the fork (see Section 3).

All other models

37 Remove the forks (see Section 3) – on VN1500 Nomad/Classic Tourer FI and VN1600 models make sure that the top bolts are loosened while the forks are still held in the bottom triple clamp. Support the fork leg in an upright position.

38 On all VN1500 models except Nomad/ Classic Tourer FI, remove the fork cap **(see illustration)**. Push the top plug downward against spring pressure with a suitable tool, then hold it down while removing the retaining ring, and then carefully release the spring pressure and remove the plug.

39 On VN1500 Nomad/Classic Tourer FI models, remove the fork cap **(see illustration)**. Unscrew the fork top bolt from the top of the inner tube – the bolt will remain on the damper rod, held by the locknut on its top. Slide the outer tube down gently until it seats on the bottom. Hold the top bolt and push the spring down to expose the locknut, and fit a spanner onto it. Counter-hold the locknut and unscrew the top bolt. Hold the spring and remove the spanner, then slowly release the spring.

40 On VN1600 models unscrew the fork top bolt from the top of the inner tube **(see illustration)** – the bolt is under pressure from the fork spring; use a ratchet tool so it does not need to be removed from the bolt as you unscrew it, and maintain some downward pressure on it, particularly as you come to the end of the threads, or alternatively hold the tool still and twist the fork tube to unthread it from the bolt.

41 On VN1600 models and all Drifter models remove the spacer and the washer.

42 Withdraw the spring, noting which way up it fits.

43 Invert the fork over a suitable container and pump the fork tubes to expel as much fork oil as possible **(see illustration 4.29)**. Support the fork upside down in the container for a while to allow as much oil as possible to drain, then pump the fork again. If the fork oil contains metal particles inspect the fork bushes for wear (see Section 5). Wipe any excess oil off the spring and spacer.

44 Stand the fork upright. Slowly pour in the specified quantity of the specified grade of fork oil **(see illustration 4.30a)**. Slide the inner tube down gently until it seats on the bottom. Measure the oil level from the top of the tube **(see illustration 4.30b)**. Add or subtract oil until it is at the level specified at the beginning of this Chapter.

45 Fit the spring, on VN1500 models with the tapered end at the bottom.

46 On VN1600 models and all Drifter models fit the washer and the spacer.

47 On all VN1500 models except Nomad/ Classic Tourer FI, check the condition of the

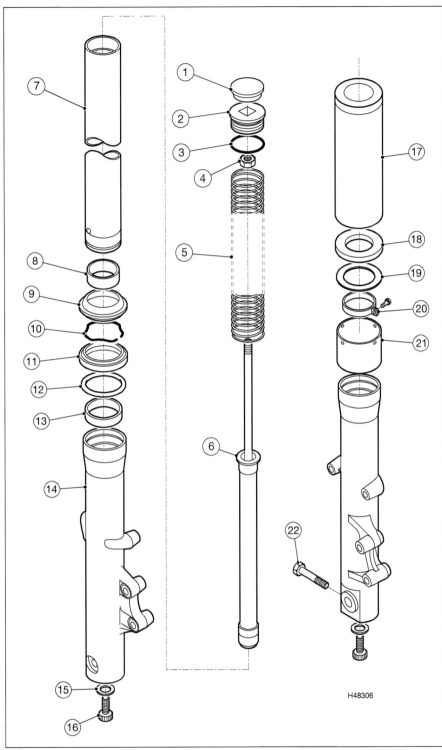

H48306

4.39 Front fork components - VN1500 Nomad/Classic Tourer FI

1 Fork cap	9 Dust seal	16 Damper cartridge bolt
2 Top bolt	10 Retaining ring	17 Cover
3 O-ring	11 Oil seal	18 Rubber damper
4 Locknut	12 Washer	19 Washer
5 Spring	13 Bottom bush	20 Stopper ring
6 Damper cartridge	14 Outer tube	21 Dust seal cover
7 Inner tube	15 Sealing washer	22 Axle clamp bolt
8 Top bush		

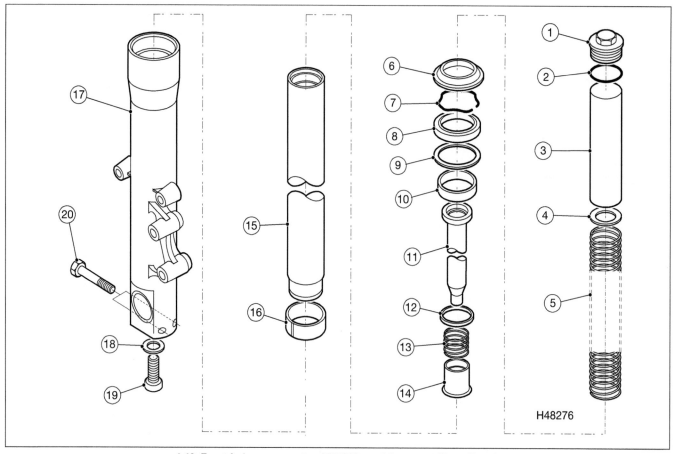

4.40 Front fork components - VN1600 models except Mean Streak

1 Top bolt	6 Dust seal	11 Damper rod	16 Bottom bush
2 O-ring	7 Retaining ring	12 Ring	17 Outer tube
3 Spacer	8 Oil seal	13 Rebound spring	18 Sealing washer
4 Washer	9 Washer	14 Oil lock piece	19 Damper rod bolt
5 Spring	10 Top bush	15 Inner tube	20 Axle clamp bolt

O-ring on the top plug and replace it with a new one if necessary. Smear some fork oil onto the O-ring. Extend the inner tube and have an assistant hold it. Seat the top plug on the spacer then push it down against the spring pressure and fit the retaining ring into its groove. Fit the cap.

48 On VN1500 Nomad/Classic Tourer FI models, check the condition of the O-ring on the top bolt and replace it with a new one if necessary. Smear some fork oil onto the O-ring. Keeping the damper rod extended push down on the spring and thread the top bolt onto the damper rod. Compress the spring and fit the spanner onto the locknut. Counter-hold the locknut and tighten the top bolt securely against it. Extend the inner tube and thread the top bolt into it, making sure it does not cross-thread, and tighten it as much as possible holding the inner tube by hand. **Note:** *Tighten the top bolt to the specified torque setting when the fork has been installed in the bike and is held in the bottom triple clamp, but before the top triple clamp bolt is tightened.*

49 On VN1600 models check the condition of the O-ring on the top bolt and replace it with a new one if necessary. Smear some fork oil onto the O-ring. Extend the inner tube and thread the top bolt into it, making sure it does not cross-thread, and tighten it as much as possible holding the inner tube by hand **(see illustration 4.35)**. **Note:** *Tighten the top bolt to the specified torque setting when the fork*

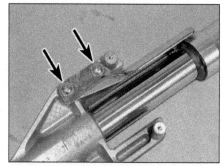

5.1 Undo the screws (arrowed) and remove the protector

has been installed in the bike and is held in the bottom triple clamp, but before the top triple clamp bolt is tightened.

50 Repeat the procedure on the other fork. Note that it is essential that the oil quantity and level is identical in each fork.

51 Install the forks (see Section 3).

5 Forks – disassembly, inspection and reassembly

Mean Streak models

Disassembly

1 Remove the forks – make sure the top bolts are loosened while the forks are still held in the bottom triple clamp (see Section 3). Always dismantle the fork legs separately to avoid interchanging parts and thus causing an accelerated rate of wear. Store all components in separate, clearly marked containers. Remove the fork protector **(see illustration)**.

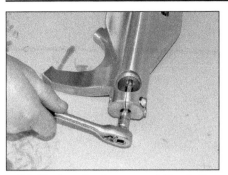

5.2 Slacken the damper cartridge bolt

5.5 Prise out the dust seal using a flat-bladed screwdriver

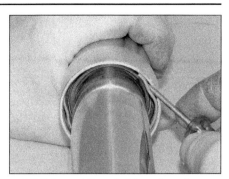

5.6 Prise out the retaining clip using a flat-bladed screwdriver

2 When working on the right fork, lay the fork flat on the bench with the caliper mounting lugs to the left, then hold the fork down and slacken the damper cartridge bolt in the base of the fork **(see illustration)**. If the damper cartridge rotates inside the fork whilst attempting to unscrew the bolt, compress the fork so that the spring exerts pressure on the cartridge body whilst the bolt is unscrewed. Alternatively, if available use an air wrench.

3 Refer to Section 4, Steps 14 to 17 for the right-hand fork and 24 to 29 for the left fork, and drain the oil form the fork.

4 On the right fork remove the damper cartridge bolt and its sealing washer from the bottom **(see illustration 5.2)**. Discard the sealing washer as a new one must be used on reassembly. Withdraw the damper cartridge from inside the fork. Remove the oil lock piece from the bottom of the damper.

5 Carefully prise out the dust seal from the bottom of the outer tube **(see illustration)**.

6 Carefully prise out the oil seal retaining clip, taking care not to scratch the surface of the inner tube **(see illustration)**.

7 To separate the inner and outer tubes it is necessary to displace the bottom bush and oil seal from the bottom of the outer tube. The top bush on the inner tube will not pass through the bottom bush, and this can be used to good effect. Grasp the inner tube in one hand and the outer tube in the other and compress them slightly, then pull them apart so that the top bush strikes the bottom bush **(see illustration)**. Repeat this operation until the bottom bush and seal are tapped out **(see illustration)**.

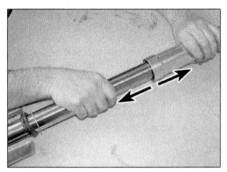

5.7a Repeatedly draw the tubes apart . . .

8 Remove the top bush from the inner tube by carefully levering its ends apart using a screwdriver **(see illustration)**. Slide the bottom bush, the oil seal washer, the oil seal, the retaining clip and the dust seal off the inner tube, noting which way up they fit. Discard the oil seal as a new one must be used. Kawasaki recommend that new bushes and a new retaining ring should also be used. Check the condition of the dust seal and use a new one if necessary.

Inspection

9 Clean all parts in solvent and blow them dry with compressed air, if available.

10 Check the fork inner tube for score marks, dents, pitting, scratches, flaking of its surface and excessive or abnormal wear. Fit a new tube if any are found. Check the inner tube for runout using V-blocks and a dial gauge and replace it with a new one if necessary.

5.7b . . . until the seal and bush are displaced

> ⚠ **Warning: If the inner tube is bent, it should not be straightened; replace it with a new one.**

11 Check the fork outer tube for cracks. Check the fork seal seat and housing for nicks, gouges and scratches. If damage is evident, leaks will occur. Also check the oil seal washer for damage or distortion and fit a new one if necessary.

12 Check the spring for cracks and other damage. Measure the spring free length and compare the measurement to the specifications at the beginning of the Chapter **(see illustration)**. If it is defective or sagged below the service limit, replace the springs in both forks with new ones. Never renew only one spring.

13 Examine the working surfaces of the two bushes (i.e. the inner surface of the bottom bush and the outer surface of the top bush) **(see illustration)**; if the grey Teflon outer

5.8 Remove the top bush as described, then slide all other components off

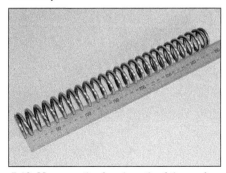

5.12 Measure the free length of the spring

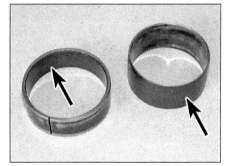

5.13 Check the working surface (arrowed) of each bush for wear

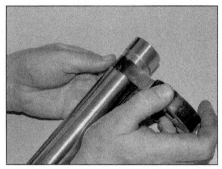

5.16a Wrap some tape over the ridges

5.16b Slide all components on as described . . .

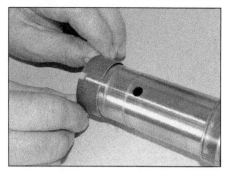

5.16c . . . then remove the tape and fit the top bush

surface has been worn away to reveal the copper inner surface over more than 75% of the surface area, or if the bushes are scored or badly scuffed, they must be replaced with new ones. Kawasaki recommend that new bushes should be used whenever the forks are disassembled.

14 On the right fork check the damper cartridge and rod for damage and wear. Hold the body of the cartridge and pump the rod in and out. If any wear or damage is found, or if the rod does not move smoothly in the damper, a new damper must be installed.

15 On the left fork check the damper, spring and rod for damage and wear **(see illustration 4.27d)**. Check the rubber stopper for cracks and hardening. If any wear or damage is found, new parts must be installed.

Reassembly

16 Wrap some insulating tape over the ridges

on the end of the inner tube to protect the lips of the new oil seal as it is installed **(see illustration)**. Apply a smear of the specified clean fork oil to the lips of the dust seal and the inner surface of the bottom bush, and smear molybdenum disulphide grease to the lips of the oil seal. Slide the dust seal, the retaining clip, the oil seal, and the oil seal washer onto the inner tube, making sure the dust seal is the correct way round and that the marked side of the oil seal faces the dust seal **(see illustration)**. Next slide the bottom bush on. Remove the insulating tape then fit the top bush into its recess **(see illustration)**.

17 Apply a smear of the specified clean fork oil to the outer surface of each bush, then carefully insert the inner tube fully into the outer tube **(see illustration)**.

18 Support the fork upside down. Align the slit in the bottom bush with one side of the

fork – it should not face the front or back. Press the bottom bush squarely into its recess in the outer tube as far as possible. Slide the oil seal washer on top of the bush, and keep the oil seal, the retaining clip and the dust seal out of the way by sliding them up the tube. If necessary, tape them to the caliper bracket to prevent them from falling down and interfering as the bush is drifted into place.

19 Using either the special service tool (Pt. No. 57001-1530) or a suitable drift, carefully drive the bottom bush fully into its recess – the oil seal washer prevents damaging the edges of the bush **(see illustration)**. If using a drift, wrap tape around it and the fork inner tube to prevent scratching the chrome. Make sure the bush enters the recess squarely. It is best to make sure that the inner tube is withdrawn as much as possible from the outer tube so that any accidental scratching is confined to the area that does not affect the oil seal.

20 Lift the washer to check the bush is seated fully and squarely in its recess in the outer tube, then wipe the recess clean and re-seat the washer.

21 Drive the oil seal into place as described in Step 19 until the retaining clip groove is visible.

22 Once the oil seal is correctly seated, fit the retaining clip, making sure it is correctly located in its groove, then press the dust seal into position **(see illustrations)**.

23 On the right fork clean the threads of the damper rod bolt. Lay the fork flat on the bench with the caliper mounting lugs to the right. Fit the oil lock piece onto the bottom of the damper cartridge. Slide the cartridge fully into the fork. Fit a new sealing washer onto the cartridge bolt and apply a few drops of a suitable non-permanent thread locking compound. Fit the bolt into the bottom of the fork and thread it into the cartridge, tightening it to the torque setting specified at the beginning of the Chapter **(see illustration 5.2)**. If the damper cartridge rotates inside the tube as you tighten the bolt, wait until the fork is fully reassembled and tighten it then (the pressure of the spring on the cartridge will prevent it from turning).

24 Refer to Section 4, Steps 18 to 21 for the right-hand fork and 30 to 35 for the left fork and fill the fork with oil and finish reassembly.

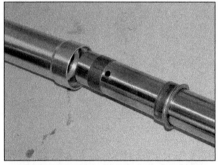

5.17 Fit the inner tube into the outer tube

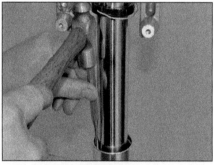

5.19 Drive the bottom bush and oil seal in as described

5.22a Fit the retaining clip into its groove . . .

5.22b . . . then press the dust seal into place

25 If the damper rod bolt in the right fork requires tightening (see Step 23), place the fork upside down on the floor, using a rag to protect it, then have an assistant compress the fork so that maximum spring pressure is placed on the damper cartridge head while tightening the bolt to the specified torque setting.

26 Install the forks (see Section 3).

All other models

Disassembly

27 Remove the forks – on VN1600 models make sure the top bolts are loosened while the forks are still held in the bottom triple clamp (see Section 3). Always dismantle the fork legs separately to avoid interchanging parts and thus causing an accelerated rate of wear. Store all components in separate, clearly marked containers **(see illustration 4.38, 4.39 and 4.40, according to model)**.

28 On VN1500 Classic FI, Nomad/Classic Tourer and Nomad/Classic Tourer FI, and Drifter models, slide the cover up off the fork and remove the rubber damper and washer. Unscrew the stopper ring bolt and remove the ring. Carefully prise the dust seal cover up and slide it off.

29 Lay the fork flat on the bench, hold it down and slacken the damper rod bolt in the base of the outer tube. If the bolt does not slacken but instead the rod turns with the bolt inside the fork, try compressing the fork so that more pressure is exerted on the damper rod head, or if available use an air-ratchet.

30 Refer to Section 4, Steps 38 to 43, and drain the oil form the fork.

31 Remove the damper cartridge bolt and its copper sealing washer from the bottom of the outer tube. Discard the sealing washer as a new one must be used on reassembly. On VN1500 Nomad/Classic Tourer FI models remove the damper cartridge. On all other models tip the damper rod out.

32 Carefully prise out the dust seal from the top of the outer tube **(see illustration 5.5)**.

33 Carefully prise out the oil seal retaining clip, taking care not to scratch the surface of the inner tube **(see illustration 5.6)**.

34 To separate the inner and outer tubes it is necessary to displace the top bush and oil seal from the top of the outer tube. The bottom bush on the inner tube will not pass through the top bush, and this can be used to good effect. Grasp the inner tube in one hand and the outer tube in the other and compress them slightly, then pull them apart so that the bottom bush strikes the top bush **(see illustration 5.7a)**. Repeat this operation until the top bush and seal are tapped out **(see illustration 5.7b)**.

35 Slide the oil seal, the oil seal washer and top bush off the inner tube, noting which way up they fit. Discard the oil seal as a new one must be used. Kawasaki recommend that new bushes and a new retaining ring should also be used. Check the condition of the dust seal and use a new one if necessary. Do not

remove the bottom bush from the inner tube unless it is being replaced with a new one.

36 Tip the oil lock piece out of the outer tube.

Inspection

37 Clean all parts in solvent and blow them dry with compressed air, if available. Check the inner fork tube for score marks, scratches, flaking of the chrome finish and excessive or abnormal wear. Look for dents in the outer tube and replace the tubes in both forks if any are found. Check the fork seal seat for nicks, gouges and scratches. If damage is evident, leaks will occur.

38 Check the inner tube for runout using V-blocks and a dial gauge and replace it with a new one if necessary.

 Warning: If the inner tube is bent, it should not be straightened; replace it with a new one.

39 Check the working surface of each bush for wear **(see illustration 5.13)** – the surface should be Teflon grey all over. If the Teflon has worn to expose the material below replace the bushes with new ones. Kawasaki recommend that new bushes should be used whenever the forks are disassembled. To remove the bottom bush from the inner tube carefully lever its ends apart using a screwdriver and slide it out of its recess **(see illustration 5.8)**.

40 Check the springs (both the main spring and the rebound spring on the damper rod) for cracks and other damage. Measure the main spring free length and compare the measurement to the specifications at the beginning of the Chapter **(see illustration 5.12)**. If it is defective or sagged below the service limit, replace the main springs in both forks with new ones. Never replace only one spring.

41 On all except VN1500 Nomad/Classic Tourer FI models check the damper rod, and in particular the ring in its head, for damage and wear, and replace it with a new one if necessary. Check the oil lock piece for damage. Check the rebound spring.

42 On VN1500 Nomad/Classic Tourer FI models check the damper cartridge and rod for damage and wear. Hold the body of the cartridge and pump the rod in and out. If any wear or damage is found, or if the rod does not move smoothly in the damper, a new damper must be installed.

Reassembly

43 If removed fit the bottom bush into its recess in the bottom of the inner tube. Apply a smear of the specified clean fork oil to the bush.

44 On all except VN1500 Nomad/Classic Tourer FI models, if removed, fit the rebound spring onto the damper rod, and fit the ring into its groove in the head. Slide the damper rod into the top of the inner tube and all the way down so it protrudes from the bottom. Fit the oil lock piece onto the bottom of the rod, then push the rod back into the tube so the oil lock piece fits into the bottom.

45 On VN1500 Nomad/Classic Tourer FI models slide the damper cartridge into the top of the inner tube and all the way down so

it protrudes from the bottom. Fit the oil lock piece onto the bottom of the cartridge, then push the rod back into the tube so the oil lock piece fits into the bottom.

46 Lay the fork flat on the bench. Slide the inner tube fully into the outer tube.

47 Clean the threads of the damper rod bolt. Fit a new copper sealing washer onto the damper bolt and apply a few drops of a suitable non-permanent thread locking compound. Fit the bolt into the bottom of the outer tube and tighten it to the specified torque setting. If the damper rod or cartridge rotates inside the tube as you tighten the bolt, wait until the fork is fully reassembled and tighten it then (the pressure of the spring on the cartridge should prevent it from turning, especially if you compress the fork).

48 Apply a smear of the specified clean fork oil to the inner surface of the top bush. Slide the bush down the inner tube and seat it in the top of the outer tube. Align the slit in the bush with one side of the fork – it should not face the front or back. Slide the oil seal washer onto the bush.

49 Support the fork upright. Using a suitable drift with tape wrapped around it to prevent scratching the chrome, carefully drive the bush fully and squarely into its recess, moving it round to exert even pressure – the oil seal washer prevents damaging the rim of the bush **(see illustration 5.19)**. Make sure the bush enters the recess squarely. It is best to make sure that the fork inner tube is withdrawn as much as possible from the outer tube so that any accidental scratching is confined to the area that does not affect the oil seal.

50 Lift the washer to check the bush is seated fully and squarely in its recess in the outer tube, then wipe the recess clean and re-seat the washer.

51 Apply a smear of grease to the oil seal lips. Slide the seal onto the inner tube with its marked side facing up. Drive the seal into place as described in Step 49 until the retaining clip groove is visible.

52 Fit the retaining clip, making sure it is correctly located in its groove **(see illustration 5.22a)**.

53 Lubricate the lips of the new dust seal then slide it down the fork tube and press it into position **(see illustration 5.22b)**.

54 Refer to Section 4, Steps 44 to 50 and fill the fork with oil and finish reassembly.

55 If the damper rod bolt requires tightening (see Step 47), place the fork upside down on the floor, using a rag to protect it, then have an assistant compress the fork so that maximum spring pressure is placed on the damper rod head/dampercartridge while tightening the bolt to the specified torque setting.

56 On VN1500 Classic FI, Nomad/Classic Tourer and Nomad/Classic Tourer FI, and Drifter models, fit the dust seal cover, aligning it so the notch faces the back, and tapping it into place until it seats. Fit the stopper ring, washer, rubber damper and cover.

57 Install the fork (see Section 3).

6.4a Support the bike securely . . .

6.4b . . . and prevent movement by locking the rear brake on

6 Steering head bearings – replacement

1 If the steering head bearing check/adjustment (see Chapter 1) does not remedy excessive play or roughness in the steering head bearings, the entire front end must be disassembled and the bearings and races replaced with new ones.

Disassembly

2 Remove the fuel tank (see Chapter 4A or 4B).

3 Remove the headlight, front turn signals and bracket, covers, brackets and guides as required according to model so that there is nothing left fixed to either the upper or lower triple clamp – refer to the relevant chapters as required, and note the routing of all wiring, cables and hoses. Also look for the L and R marks on some components denoting the side they fit on.

4 Refer to Section 3 and remove the front forks. Make sure the bike is adequately supported – on the motorcycle photographed, axle stands were used as shown and the rear brake held on with a piece of wood (see illustrations).

5 Refer to Section 2 and displace the handlebars if required by unscrewing the nuts below the triple clamp and lifting the complete assembly off the triple clamp – although they can be left in place.

6 Unscrew the steering stem nut or bolt (according to model) and remove the washer, and where fitted the O-ring (see illustrations). Ease the triple clamp up off the steering stem (see illustrations).

7 On VN1500A and B and Classic models, while supporting the lower triple clamp, unscrew the two nuts using a spanner wrench (C-spanner) or a suitable drift located in the notches, then remove the bearing cap and lower the steering stem out.

8 On all other models remove the tabbed washer from the bearing adjuster nut (see

6.6a Unscrew the nut or bolt . . .

6.6b . . . and remove the washer . . .

6.6c . . . and where fitted the O-ring

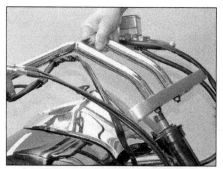

6.6d Lift the upper triple clamp (and handlebar assembly if not displaced) off the steering stem

6.6e One method of supporting the assembly

6.8a Remove the tabbed washer . . .

6.8b . . . then unscrew the nut . . .

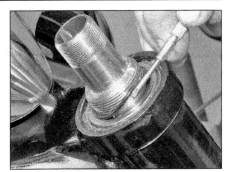

6.8c . . . remove the O-ring . . .

6.8d . . . and remove the triple clamp/
steering stem

6.9 Remove the upper bearing

6.11 Check the outer races for wear and
damage

illustration). While supporting the lower triple clamp, unscrew the nut using a spanner wrench (C-spanner) or a suitable drift located in the notches, then remove the bearing cap if it didn't come away with the nut, and the O-ring, and lower the triple clamp/steering stem out (see illustrations). Check the condition of both O-rings and replace them with new ones if necessary.

Inspection

9 Remove the upper bearing from the steering head (see illustration).
10 Clean all the parts with solvent and dry them thoroughly, using compressed air, if available. If you do use compressed air, don't let the bearings spin as they're dried – it could ruin them. Wipe the old grease out of the frame steering head and bearing races.
11 Examine the outer races in the steering

head for cracks, dents, and pits (see illustration). If even the slightest amount of wear or damage is evident, the races should be replaced with new ones.
12 To remove the outer races, drive them out of the steering head with Kawasaki tool no. 57001-1107 or equivalent drift – using a standard drift will not work as there is no protruding lip for purchase. A slide-hammer with the proper internal-jaw puller will also work (see illustrations). When installing the races, use Kawasaki press shaft no. 57001-1075 and drivers no. 57001-1106 and 57001-1076 on VN1500A and B and Classic models, and 57001-1077 on all other models, or tap them gently into place with a hammer and bearing driver or a large socket, or use a drawbolt arrangement (see illustration). Do not strike the bearing surface or the race will be damaged.

HAYNES HINT *Since the races are an interference fit in the frame, installation will be easier if the new races are left overnight in a refrigerator. This will cause them to contract and slip into place in the frame with very little effort.*

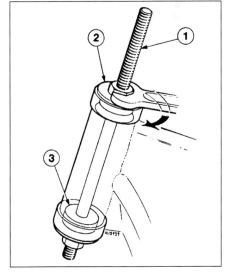

6.12c Drawbolt arrangement for fitting
steering stem bearing races

1 *Long bolt or threaded bar*
2 *Thick washer*
3 *Guide for lower race*

6.12a Fit the puller attachment and
expand it behind the race . . .

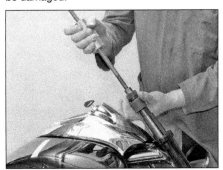

6.12b . . . then fit the slide-hammer and jar
the race out

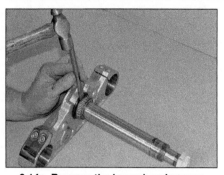

6.14a Remove the lower bearing race using a cold chisel . . .

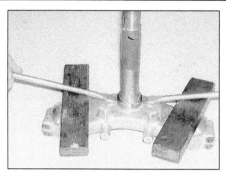

6.14b . . . and screwdrivers . . .

13 Check the bearings for wear. Look for cracks, dents, and pits in the inner races, flat spots on the bearings, and distortion to the cage. If a new bearing is required, replace both of them as a set.

14 The lower bearing is an interference fit on the stem – only remove it if a new one is being fitted, or if a new grease seal (fitted under the bearing) is needed. To remove the lower bearing, on all except VN1500A and B and Classic models thread the nut onto the stem to protect the threads and cover the nut

in masking tape to protect its surface, then on all models place the stem on its side and use a cold chisel to drive the bearing inner race up **(see illustrations)**. Once displaced it can be worked free using levers on either side.

15 Check the grease seal under the lower bearing and replace it with a new one if necessary.

16 Inspect the steering stem/lower triple clamp for cracks and other damage. Do not attempt to repair any steering components. Replace them with new parts if defects are found.

17 Check the bearing cap seal – if it's worn or deteriorated, replace it with a new one. On all except VN1500A and B and Classic models remove the nut from the cap first if they are together.

18 Pack the bearings with a high-quality bearing grease. Coat the outer races with grease also.

19 Fit the grease seal onto the steering stem. Fit the lower bearing and drive it onto the steering stem using Kawasaki stem bearing driver no. 57001-137 and adapter no. 57001-1074 on VN1500A and B and Classic models, and 57001-1344 and 57001-1345 on all other models. If you don't have access to these tools, a section of pipe with a diameter the same as the inner race of the bearing can be used **(see illustration)**. Drive the bearing on until it is fully seated.

Reassembly

VN1500A and B and Classic models

20 Insert the steering stem/lower triple clamp into the frame head. Fit the upper bearing and the bearing cap. Fit the adjusting nut with its shoulder down (against the bearing). Using a C-spanner, tighten the nut while moving the lower triple clamp back and forth. Continue to tighten the nut to approximately 39 Nm/29 ft-lbs until the steering head becomes tight – you can calculate the torque by applying a measured amount of force to the wrench handle at a measured distance from the center of the nut **(see illustration)**. Check that there is no play and the stem turns smoothly. Now back the nut off until there is some play in the bearings, then retighten it until the play is taken up – make sure there is no more play, but don't overtighten, though, or the steering will be too tight and the bearings may be damaged. Make sure the steering head turns smoothly. Fit the locknut.

21 Install all removed components and assemblies except the fuel tank, tightening the steering stem bolt to the specified torque for your model. Now make a final check and adjustment of the bearings as described in Chapter 1, then install the fuel tank.

All other models

22 If new bearings are being fitted follow Step 23, if the old bearings are being reused follow Step 24.

23 Insert the steering stem/lower triple clamp into the frame head **(see illustration 6.8d)**. Fit the upper bearing **(see illustration 6.9)**. Do not fit the O-ring at this stage. Fit the bearing cap and adjusting nut **(see illustration)**. Using a C-spanner, tighten the nut while moving the lower triple clamp back and forth. Continue to tighten the nut to approximately 78 Nm/58 ft-lbs until the steering head becomes tight – you can calculate the torque by applying a measured amount of force (440N, 45kgf or 99lb) to the wrench handle at a measured distance 180 mm or 7 inches) from the center of the nut **(see illustration 6.20)**. Check that there is no play and the stem turns smoothly.

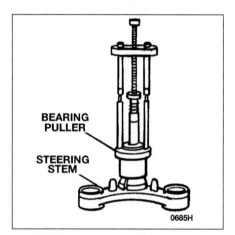

6.14c . . . or a puller if necessary

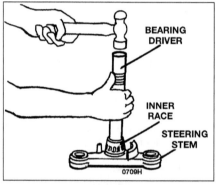

6.19 Drive the new bearing on using a suitable bearing driver or a length of pipe that bears only against the inner race and not against the rollers or cage

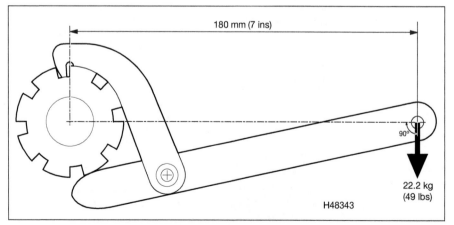

6.20 To get the correct torque apply the illustrated pulling force the distance shown from the nut centre

Now remove the nut and bearing cap and fit the O-ring, smearing it with grease (see illustration). Fit the cap/nut again and tighten it to 20 Nm/14 ft-lbs on VN1500 Nomad/Classic Tourer, Nomad/Classic Tourer FI and Drifter J models, and 5 Nm/43 inch-lbs on all other models, until the play is taken up – make sure there is no more play, but don't overtighten, though, or the steering will be too tight and the bearings may be damaged. Make sure the steering head turns smoothly. Fit the tabbed washer (see illustration 6.8a). Install all removed components and assemblies except the fuel tank – smear O-ring under the stem nut washer with grease and tighten the nut to the specified torque for your model. Now make a final check and adjustment of the bearings as described in Chapter 1.

24 Insert the steering stem/lower triple clamp into the frame head (see illustration 6.8d). Fit the upper bearing (see illustration 6.9). Fit the O-ring, smearing it with grease (see illustration 6.22b). Fit the bearing cap and adjusting nut (see illustration 6.22a). Using a C-spanner, tighten the nut while moving the lower triple clamp back and forth to 20 Nm/14 ft-lbs on VN1500 Nomad/Classic Tourer, Nomad/Classic Tourer FI and Drifter J models, and 5 Nm/43 inch-lbs on all other models, until the play is taken up – make sure there is no more play, but don't overtighten, though, or the steering will be too tight and the bearings may be damaged. Make sure the steering head turns smoothly. Fit the tabbed washer (see illustration 6.8a). Install all removed components and assemblies except the fuel tank – smear O-ring under the stem nut washer with grease and tighten the nut to the specified torque for your model. Now make a final check and adjustment of the bearings as described in Chapter 1.

25 Install the fuel tank and any other components not already installed.

---

7 Rear shock absorbers –
removal, inspection and
installation

Removal

1 Support the bike upright using an auxiliary stand – the rear wheel must be off the ground so all weight is off the rear suspension. If both shock absorbers are being removed place a piece of wood under the rear wheel to fill the gap so the wheel does not drop when the second shock is removed. Tie the front brake lever to the handlebar.

2 Where fitted remove the saddlebags.

3 Unscrew the shock absorber upper and lower nuts and remove the washers (see illustration). Draw the shock evenly off the motorcycle (see illustration).

Inspection

4 Check the bush in the bottom of the shock absorber, and in the top on all models except

6.23a Fit the bearing cap and nut

VN1600 and all Mean Streaks, for wear or damage (see illustration). Replace the bush(es) with new ones if necessary (and if available for your model – check with your dealer). A drawbolt arrangement is the best way to remove and install the bushes – one can be made up as described in *Tools and Workshop Tips* in the Reference section.

5 On VN1600 and all Mean Streak models withdraw the collar from the top mount (see illustration). Clean off old grease and dirt. Check the condition of the grease seals and bearing. If required lever out the grease seals. Fit the collar back in and check for play between it and the bearing. Refer to *Tools and Workshop Tips* (Section 5) in the Reference section for more information on bearings. If the bearing is worn drive it out of the bore using a suitable driver or socket or draw it out using a drawbolt (one can be made up as described in *Tools and Workshop Tips* in the

7.3a Unscrew the nuts and remove the washers . . .

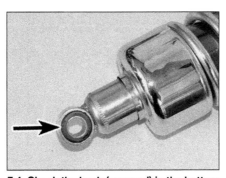

7.4 Check the bush (arrowed) in the bottom mount and where fitted in the top mount

6.23b Fit the greased O-ring

Reference section) – do not re-use the bearing after removing it. The new bearing should be pressed or drawn in, not driven in. When fitting the new bearing make sure it is central in the bore.

6 Lubricate the bearing, collar and new seals with a multi-purpose grease. Press the new seals squarely into place. Fit the collar with its shouldered end facing the inner side of the shock absorber (identifiable by the fact the air valve faces the front (see illustration 7.5).

7 Check the shock absorber for obvious physical damage and oil leakage, and the spring for looseness, cracks or signs of fatigue. Parts are not available for the shock absorber itself. If it is worn or damaged, it must be replaced with a new one.

Installation

8 Installation is the reverse of the removal procedure. Where fitted install the shock with

7.3b . . . and draw the shock off its mounts

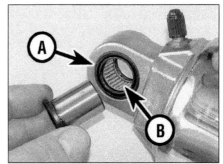

7.5 Withdraw the collar and check the seals (A) and bearing (B)

**9.7a Swingarm cover screws (arrowed) –
VN1600 Mean Streak shown**

**9.7b Pull the boot forward off the
swingarm**

9.8 Remove the pivot cap

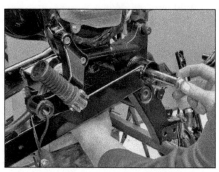

**9.9 Unscrew and withdraw the pivot bolt
and remove the swingarm**

the air valves at the top and facing outward and/or forward (according to model) **(see illustration 7.3b)**. Fit the plain washer first, then the spring washer **(see illustration 7.3a)**. Tighten the shock absorber nuts to the torque values listed in this Chapter's Specifications.

8 Swingarm bearings – check

1 Refer to Chapter 7 and remove the rear wheel, then refer to Section 7 and remove the rear shock absorbers.
2 Grasp the rear of the swingarm with one hand and place your other hand at the junction of the swingarm and the frame. Try to move the rear of the swingarm from side-to-side. Any wear (play) in the bearings should be felt as movement between the swingarm and the frame at the

front. The swingarm will actually be felt to move forward and backward at the front (not from side-to-side). If any play is noted, first make sure the swingarm pivot bolt is correctly tightened (see Section 9) – if it is, the bearings should be replaced with new ones (see Section 10).
3 Next, move the swingarm up and down through its full travel. It should move freely, without any binding or rough spots. If it does not move freely, refer to Section 10 for servicing procedures.

9 Swingarm – removal and installation

Removal

1 Support the bike upright using an auxiliary stand – the rear wheel must be off the ground

so all weight is off the rear suspension. Place a piece of wood under the rear wheel to fill the gap so the wheel does not drop when the shock absorbers are removed. Tie the front brake lever to the handlebar.
2 Remove the mufflers (see Chapter 4A or 4B).
3 On all except VN1500A and B models the rear brake hose passes through one or two closed guides on the swingarm – either detach the brake hose from the caliper and draw it through the guide(s), or displace the rear master cylinder and remove the rear brake system along with the swingarm, as preferred or required. Refer to Chapter 7 for all details on the brake system, including bleeding it afterwards if the hose is detached. If you detach the hose from the caliper also free it from its other guides.
4 Remove the rear wheel (see Chapter 7). On VN1500A and B models free the rear brake hose from its guides.
5 Remove the shock absorbers (see Section 7).
6 Remove the final drive housing (see Section 11).
7 Remove the swingarm cover(s) **(see illustrations)**.
8 On all except VN1500A and B models remove the swingarm pivot cap **(see illustration)**.
9 Support the swingarm. Unscrew and withdraw the swingarm pivot bolt, then manoeuvre the swingarm out to the rear, drawing it off the driveshaft **(see illustration)**.
10 Check the pivot bearings (see Section 10).

Installation

11 Lubricate all pivot components with fresh grease, referring to Section 10 if not already done.
12 Position and support the swingarm so its pivot holes are aligned with the holes in the frame, then slide the pivot bolt in and tighten to the torque listed in this Chapter's Specifications for your model **(see illustration 9.9)**.
13 Raise and lower the swingarm to make sure it moves freely without binding or interference. Check swingarm bearing play as described in Section 8.
14 The remainder of installation is the reverse of the removal steps.

10 Swingarm bearings – replacement

1 Bearing replacement isn't complicated, but it requires a blind hole (expanding) puller and a slide-hammer.
2 Remove the swingarm (see Section 9).
3 Pry out the swingarm seals then remove the bearing sleeves and the central spacer **(see illustrations)**.

**10.3a Remove the seal and the sleeve on
each side . . .**

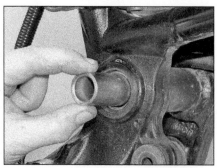

10.3b . . . and withdraw the spacer

4 Remove the bearings with a blind hole puller **(see illustration)**.

5 Drive the new bearing in, with its marked side facing out, using a suitable bearing driver that locates fully on the cage face, and preferably one with a shouldered centre that just fits inside the bearing.

6 Pack the bearing with bearing grease. Coat the central spacer and sleeves with the same grease before fitting them **(see illustrations 10.3b and a)**. Press the new seals in and smear the lips with the grease.

7 Install the swingarm (see Section 9).

11 Final drive housing – removal, inspection and installation

Removal

1 If required drain the final drive oil (see Chapter 1) – note that oil will not leak out under normal circumstances, only if a seal has failed or if the housing is not supported upright, in which case it could come out of the breather.

2 Remove the left shock absorber (see Section 7).

3 Remove the rear wheel (see Chapter 7).

4 Where fitted remove the cover from the left side of the swingarm **(see illustration 9.7a)**.

5 Unscrew the final drive housing nuts and take the housing off the swingarm **(see illustrations)**. Note the spring fitted on the shoulder of the nut and remove it for safekeeping **(see illustration)**. On VN1600 Classic and Nomad/Classic Tourer and all Mean Streak models remove the gasket from the housing mating surface **(see illustration)** – Kawasaki specify to use a new one.

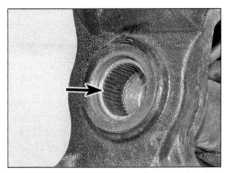

10.4 Remove the bearings (arrowed) using a puller

Inspection

6 Rotate the driveshaft joint in the front of the final drive housing – check it rotates smoothly and freely and that the power is transmitted correctly through the bevel gear assembly to the output boss. If there are any signs of roughness or notchiness or any evidence of wear or excessive backlash, the unit must be disassembled and examined further. Remove the filler plug and look into the hole, using a flashlight if necessary, for obvious signs of damage such as broken gear teeth.

7 Check the housing for any evidence of oil leakage from the seals.

8 Check the splines for wear and damage. If any is evident on the front splines check the driveshaft (see Section 12), and if any is evident on the output boss check the rear wheel coupling (Chapter 7).

9 If attention to the final drive housing is required, the complete unit should be taken to a Kawasaki dealer or service agent who will

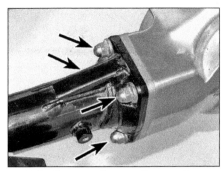

11.5a Unscrew the nuts (arrowed) . . .

have the necessary special tools and expertise to carry out the rather complicated inspection and overhaul procedure.

Installation

10 Installation is the reverse of the removal steps, with the following additions:

a) Clean all the old grease off the splines and smear some fresh high temperature grease on.

b) On VN1600 Classic and Nomad/Classic Tourer and all Mean Streak models fit the gasket onto the housing mating surface **(see illustration 11.5d)**.

c) Fit the narrow end of the spring onto the shouldered section of the nut **(see illustration 11.5c)**.

d) Push the housing against the swingarm to compress the spring and seat the flange, and tighten the nuts to the torque listed in this Chapter's Specifications **(see illustration)**.

e) If drained fill the final drive unit with oil (see Chapter 1).

12 Front bevel gear housing and driveshaft – removal, inspection and installation

Front bevel gear housing

Removal

1 Remove the engine (see Chapter 2).

2 Mark the alignment of the shift linkage arm clamp slit with the shift mechanism shaft, then unscrew the pinch bolt and slide the arm off the shaft **(see illustration)**.

11.5b . . . and remove the housing

11.5c Remove the spring . . .

11.5d . . . and the gasket where fitted

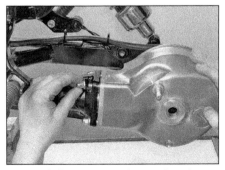

11.10 Push the housing against the swingarm when fitting the nuts

12.2 Note the alignment, then unscrew the bolt and slide the arm off

12.4 Remove the boot

12.5a Front bevel gear housing bolts (arrowed) . . .

12.5b . . . store the bolts and associated washers/guides in a template as shown

12.6 Remove the damper cam and spring from the housing

12.7a Lever out the shift shaft seal . . .

3 If required remove the neutral switch and speed sensor (see Chapter 9).

4 Remove the rubber boot **(see illustration)**.

5 Slacken the bevel gear housing bolts evenly in a criss-cross pattern, then remove them, noting the positions of the bolts with the washers **(see illustration)**. **Note:** *As each bolt is removed, store it in its relative position in a cardboard template of the crankcase halves along with the washers, wiring clamp where fitted and clutch hose holder* **(see illustration)**. *This will ensure all bolts are installed in the correct location on reassembly.* Draw the housing off the engine **(see illustration 12.13a)**. Remove the gasket and discard it **(see illustration 12.12)** – a new one must be

used. Remove the dowels if loose. Note there is a washer on the shift shaft – make sure it is not stuck to the cover.

6 If required remove the damper cam and spring **(see illustration)**.

7 Lever out the shift shaft and clutch pushrod oil seals **(see illustrations)** – new ones must be fitted.

Inspection

8 Rotate the pinion coupling on the bevel gear housing with fingers and check for rough or noisy movement. Check for signs of oil leakage around the pinion and drive coupling. Visual inspection of the internal components isn't possible without disassembling the unit.

9 Bevel gear housing overhaul is a complicated procedure that requires several special tools, for which there are no readily available substitutes. If there's visible wear or damage, or if differential rotation is rough or noisy, take it to a Kawasaki dealer for disassembly and further inspection.

Installation

10 Fit new shift shaft and clutch pushrod oil seals – either push them in with your fingers or use a socket to drive them in if necessary **(see illustrations)**. Smear the seal lips with grease.

11 Lubricate the shaft splines with grease. Fit the spring and damper cam onto the shaft in the housing **(see illustration 12.6)**.

12.7b . . . and the pushrod seal

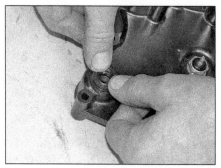

12.10a Fit the new shift shaft seal . . .

12.10b . . . and the pushrod seal

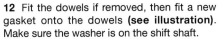

12.12 Fit the new gasket onto the dowels (arrowed)

12.13a Fit the housing . . .

12.13b . . . then fit the bolts and tighten as described

12 Fit the dowels if removed, then fit a new gasket onto the dowels **(see illustration)**. Make sure the washer is on the shift shaft.

13 Locate the housing and fit the bolts along with their washers, wiring clamp where fitted and clutch hose holder, and tighten them all finger-tight **(see illustrations)**. Now tighten the bolts numbered 1 and 2 a bit at a time alternately until the housing is seated **(see illustration)**. Now tighten all the bolts evenly and a little at a time in the sequence shown to the torque settings listed in the Specifications – make sure you distinguish firstly between the M8 and M6 bolts, and secondly between the unmarked M6 bolts and those marked with a 9, when determining the torque to apply.

14 Fit the shift linkage arm onto the shift mechanism shaft, aligning the mark, and tighten the pinch bolt **(see illustration 12.2)**.

15 If removed install the neutral switch and speed sensor (see Chapter 9).

16 Fit the rubber boot **(see illustration)**.

17 Install the engine (see Chapter 2).

Driveshaft

Removal

18 If the front bevel gear housing is in place remove the swingarm (see Section 9). Rotate the driveshaft to put the shaft locking pin hole in an accessible position. Depress the locking pin using a suitable tool and pull the shaft off **(see illustration)**. Retrieve the driveshaft locking pin for safekeeping, and remove the spring if required **(see illustrations)**.

19 If the engine has been removed pull the driveshaft forward out of the swingarm.

Inspection

20 Check the driveshaft for bending or other visible damage such as step wear of the splines. If the shaft is bent, or the splines at either end are worn, replace the shaft with a new one.

21 Hold the driveshaft firmly in one hand and try to twist the universal joint **(see illustration)**. If there's play between the couplings in the joint, replace the shaft with a new one.

Installation

22 Installation is the reverse of removal, with the following additions:

  a) Lubricate the splines at the each end with high-temperature grease.

  b) Make sure the driveshaft rubber boot, spring (if removed) and locking pin are fitted, and the pin is in an accessible position. Smear some high temperature grease over the drive shaft splines.

12.13c Front bevel gear housing bolt numbering

12.16 Fit the boot, aligning the tabs as shown

12.18a Depress the pin and push the shaft back . . .

12.18b . . . then remove the pin and keep it safe

12.18c Remove the spring if required, noting how it fits

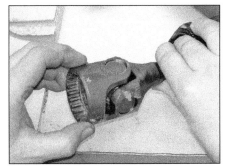

12.21 Check for any play between the universal joint couplings

12.22 Align the hole with the pin, then depress the pin and slide the shaft over

13.3 Release the snap ring from its groove

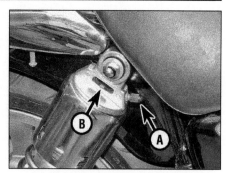

14.2 Air pressure valve (A), rebound damping adjuster dial (B)

c) *Align the hole in the universal joint rim with the shaft locking pin, then depress the pin and slide the shaft on so the pin engages* **(see illustration)**. *Try to move the shaft back again – it should be locked in place. Position the rubber boot over the front of the swingarm.*

13 Rear wheel coupling/ rubber damper – check and replacement

1 Remove the rear wheel (see Chapter 7).
2 Check for play between the coupling and the damper segments – if any is evident replace the damper with a new one.
3 Remove the large snap-ring that secures the coupling to the wheel **(see illustration)**. Lift the rear wheel coupling from the wheel – if it is tight use a puller.
4 Lift the rubber damper from the wheel.
5 Installation is the reverse of the removal

procedure. Check the condition of the hub O-ring and replace it with a new one if necessary. Smear the O-ring with grease. Use a new snap-ring if the old one has deformed – on later models Kawasaki specify to use a new one whatever the apparent condition of the old.

14 Rear shock absorbers – adjustment

Warning: Ensure that the suspension settings are equal in both shocks or unstable handling may occur.

Spring preload

1 The rear spring preload is adjusted by turning the adjusting sleeve with the hook wrench included in the bike's tool kit. Compare preload with the values listed in this Chapter's Specifications and adjust as needed.

Air pressure

2 Remove the cap from the air pressure valve **(see illustration)**. The recommended air pressure range is listed in this Chapter's Specifications and can be adjusted between the values as required. Press the valve core in to release pressure. Apply only low pressure air using a manual pump – do not use an air compressor.
Caution: Don't exceed the maximum pressure listed in this Chapter's Specifications or the shock seals may be damaged.

Rebound damping

3 The damping is adjusted by turning the dial on the top of the shock, aligning the setting required with the index mark **(see illustration 14.2)**. Compare damping with the values listed in this Chapter's Specifications and adjust as needed.

Chapter 7
Brakes, wheels and tires

Contents

Degrees of difficulty

Easy, suitable for novice with little experience	**Fairly easy,** suitable for beginner with some experience	**Fairly difficult,** suitable for competent DIY mechanic	**Difficult,** suitable for experienced DIY mechanic	**Very difficult,** suitable for expert DIY or professional

Specifications

Brakes

Brake fluid type	DOT 4
Brake pad minimum thickness.	See Chapter 1

Front disc thickness
    VN1500A, VN1600 Classic, VN1600 Nomad/Classic Tourer, all Mean Streak models

Standard.	4.8 to 5.1 mm (0.189 to 0.200 inch)
Minimum.	4.5 mm (0.177 inch)

    All other VN1500 models and Drifter models

Standard.	5.8 to 6.2 mm (0.228 to 0.244 inch)
Minimum.	5.5 mm (0.217 inch)

Rear disc thickness – all models

Standard.	6.8 to 7.2 mm (0.268 to 0.283 inch)
Minimum.	6.0 mm (0.236 inch)
Disc runout (maximum)	0.3 mm (0.012 inch)
Brake pedal position	See Chapter 1

Wheels and tires

Cast alloy wheels – VN1500 models

Wheel runout limit
    Axial (side-to-side) . . . .   0.5 mm (0.020 inch)
    Radial (out-of-round) . . . .   0.8 mm (0.031 inch)
Axle runout limit (front and rear) . . . .   0.2 mm (0.008 inch) per 100 mm (3.94 inches) of axle length
Tire pressures and sizes . . . .   See *Pre-ride checks*

Cast alloy wheels – VN1600 models

Wheel runout limit
    Axial (side-to-side) . . . .   1.0 mm (0.039 inch)
    Radial (out-of-round) . . . .   1.0 mm (0.039 inch)
Axle runout limit (front and rear) . . . .   0.2 mm (0.008 inch) per 100 mm (3.94 inches) of axle length
Tire pressures and sizes . . . .   See *Pre-ride checks*

Wire spoke wheels

Wheel runout limit
    Axial (side-to-side) . . . .   2.0 mm (0.078 inch)
    Radial (out-of-round)
        VN1500B and Classic . . . .   2.0 mm (0.078 inch)
        VN1500 Classic FI and Drifter . . . .   1.5 mm (0.059 inch)
Axle runout limit (front and rear) . . . .   0.2 mm (0.008 inch) per 100 mm (3.94 inches) of axle length
Tire pressures and sizes . . . .   See *Pre-ride checks*

Torque specifications

Brake caliper bleed valves . . . .   8 Nm (69 inch-lbs)
Brake disc bolts
    VN1500 Classic D models . . . .   23 Nm (16.5 ft-lbs)
    All other models . . . .   27 Nm (20 ft-lbs)
Brake hose banjo bolts . . . .   25 Nm (18 ft-lbs)
Brake pad pin bolts – Mean Streak 1600B2-on . . . .   15 Nm (11 ft-lbs)
Caliper body joining bolts – Mean Streak
    1500P and 1600B1 models . . . .   21 Nm (15 ft-lbs)
    1600B2-on . . . .   22 Nm (16 ft-lbs)
Caliper mounting bolts
    Single piston sliding calipers . . . .   32 Nm (24 ft-lbs)
    Twin piston sliding and opposed piston calipers . . . .   34 Nm (25 ft-lbs)
Front wheel axle or axle nut
    VN1500A and B . . . .   88 Nm (65 ft-lbs)
    All other models . . . .   108 Nm (80 ft-lbs)
Front wheel axle pinch bolt(s)
    VN1500A and B . . . .   29 Nm (22 ft-lbs)
    VN1500 Classic and Classic FI . . . .   34 Nm (25 ft-lbs)
    VN1500 Nomad/Classic Tourer and Nomad/Classic Tourer FI . . . . . .   34 Nm (25 ft-lbs)
    VN1600 Classic A1 models . . . .   20 Nm (15 ft-lbs)
    VN1600 Classic A2-on models . . . .   29 Nm (21 ft-lbs)
    VN1600 Nomad/Classic Tourer . . . .   29 Nm (21 ft-lbs)
    Drifter . . . .   34 Nm (25 ft-lbs)
    VN1500 Mean Streak . . . .   25 Nm (18 ft-lbs)
    VN1600 Mean Streak . . . .   29 Nm (21 ft-lbs)
Rear wheel axle nut . . . .   108 Nm (80 ft-lbs)
Rear brake caliper bracket stopper bolt
    VN1500A and B . . . .   32 Nm (24 ft-lbs)
    All other models . . . .   64 Nm (47 ft-lbs)

1 General information

The motorcycles covered by this manual are equipped with hydraulic disc brakes on both wheels. VN1500A and B models have a single-piston sliding caliper at the front and the rear. VN1500 Classic models have a twin piston sliding caliper at the front, and a single piston sliding caliper at the rear up to and including E3 (2000) models, and thereafter a twin piston sliding caliper. VN1500 Nomad/ Classic Tourer (except G3 models) models have twin piston sliding calipers at the front and a single piston sliding caliper at the rear. VN1500 Nomad/Classic Tourer G3 models, Nomad/Classic Tourer FI models and VN1600 Nomad/Classic Tourer models have twin piston sliding calipers, two at the front and one at the rear. VN1500 Classic FI models, VN1600 Classic models and Drifter models have a twin piston sliding caliper at the front and rear. Mean Streak P and B1 models have opposed six piston calipers at the front and a twin piston sliding caliper at the rear. Mean Streak B2-on models have opposed four piston calipers at the front and a twin piston sliding caliper at the rear.

VN1500B models, VN1500 Classic and Classic FI models and Drifter models have wire spoke wheels with tubed tires. VN1500A models,

VN1600 Classic models, all Nomad/Classic Tourer models and all Mean Streak models have cast alloy wheels with tubeless tires.

Caution: Disc brake components rarely require disassembly. Do not disassemble components unless absolutely necessary. If any hydraulic brake line connection in the system is loosened, the entire system should be disassembled, drained, cleaned and then properly filled and bled upon reassembly. Do not use solvents on internal brake components. Solvents will cause seals to swell and distort. Use only clean brake fluid or alcohol for cleaning. Use care when working with brake fluid as it can injure your eyes and it will damage painted surfaces and plastic parts.

2 Brake pads – replacement

Warning: The dust created by the brake system may contain asbestos, which is harmful to your health. Never blow it out with compressed air and don't inhale any of it. An approved filtering mask should be worn when working on the brakes.

Note: *Do not operate the brake lever while the pads are out of the caliper.*

Single-piston sliding calipers

Note: *Pad replacement procedures are the same for front and rear single-piston calipers.*

1 Unscrew the caliper mounting bolts **(see illustration)**. Slide the caliper off the disc.
2 Support the caliper so it doesn't hang by the brake hose.
3 Push the caliper bracket in (toward the piston) until the pad pins clear the holes in the pad **(see illustration)**.
4 Remove the pads from the caliper **(see illustration)**.
5 Inspect the surface of each pad for contamination and check that the friction material has not worn beyond its service limit (see Chapter 1). If any pad is worn down to, or beyond, the service limit wear indicator (i.e. the wear indicator is no longer visible), is fouled with oil or grease, or heavily scored or damaged, fit a new set of pads. **Note:** *It is not possible to degrease the friction material; if the pads are contaminated in any way they must be replaced with new ones.*
6 If the pads are in good condition clean them carefully, using a fine wire brush which is completely free of oil and grease to remove all traces of road dirt and corrosion. Using a pointed instrument, dig out any embedded particles of foreign matter. If required, spray with a dedicated brake cleaner to remove any dust.
7 Slide the caliper off the bracket. Note the pad spring in the top of caliper and the pad guides on the caliper bracket and remove them if required for cleaning or replacement, noting

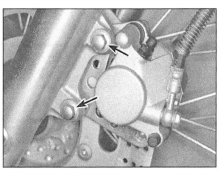

2.1 Unscrew the bolts (arrowed) and slide the caliper off the disc

how they fit. Clean off all traces of corrosion and hardened grease from the slider pins and from their rubber boots. Check the slider pin boots for cracks and splits and replace them with new ones if necessary, making sure they locate correctly.
8 Check the condition of the brake disc (see Section 4).
9 Clean around the exposed section of the piston to remove any dirt or debris that could cause the seals to be damaged. Push the piston into the caliper, as far as possible if new pads are being fitted, or just a little if the old pads are still serviceable. Keep an eye on the fluid level in the master cylinder reservoir – it may be necessary to remove the cap, plate and diaphragm and siphon out some fluid (see *Pre-ride checks*). If you can't depress the piston with thumb pressure, try using a G-clamp (with rag or card to protect the caliper body), or a piece of wood as leverage, or place the old pads back in the caliper and use a metal bar or a screwdriver inserted between them (but take care not to damage the friction surface if the pads are being reused) **(see illustration 2.24a)**. If available you can use a proper piston-pushing tool **(see illustration 2.24b)**.
10 If the piston is difficult to push back, remove the bleed valve cap, then attach a length of clear hose to the bleed valve and place the open end in a suitable container, then open the valve and try again (see Section 7). Take great care not to draw any air into the system. If in doubt, bleed the brake afterwards. If the piston has seized, apply the brake lever

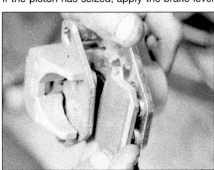

2.4 . . . then lift the pads out

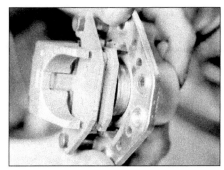

2.3 Slide the bracket in until the pad is clear of the pins . . .

(front) or pedal (rear) and check whether the piston moves at all. If it moves out but can't be pushed back in, it is likely there is some hidden corrosion stopping it. If it doesn't move at all, or to fully clean and inspect the piston, overhaul the caliper (see Section 3).
11 Make sure the pad spring and guides are correctly in place. Apply some silicone grease to the slider pins and inside the boots. Slide the caliper back onto the bracket, making sure the boots locate correctly around the base of the pins to provide a seal.
12 When fitting the pads into the caliper make sure the friction material on each pad faces the other.
13 Install both pads in the caliper and pull the caliper bracket out, so the pins locate in the holes in the inner pad.
14 Slide the caliper onto the disc and tighten the mounting bolts to the torque listed in this Chapter's Specifications.
15 Operate the brake lever (front) or pedal (rear) until the pads contact the disc. Check the level of fluid in the hydraulic reservoir and top-up if necessary (see *Pre-ride checks*).
16 Check the operation of the brake before riding the motorcycle.

Twin-piston sliding calipers

Note: *Pad replacement procedures are the same for front and rear dual-piston calipers.*
17 Unscrew the caliper mounting bolts **(see illustration)**. Slide the caliper and pads off the disc.
18 Support the caliper so it doesn't hang by the brake hose.

2.17 Unscrew the bolts (arrowed) and slide the caliper off the disc

2.19a Remove the clip . . .

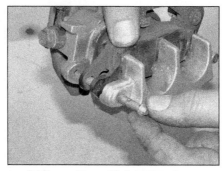

2.19b . . . then withdraw the pin . . .

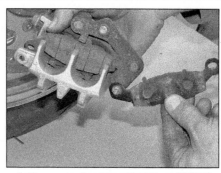

2.19c . . . and remove the inner pad . . .

19 Remove the retaining clip from the pad pin **(see illustration)**. Withdraw the pad pin **(see illustration)**. Pivot the inner pad up and slide it off its post, then remove the outer pad, noting how it locates **(see illustrations)**.

20 Inspect the surface of each pad for contamination and check that the friction material has not worn beyond its service limit (see Chapter 1). If any pad is worn down to, or beyond, the service limit wear indicator (i.e. the wear indicator is no longer visible), is fouled with oil or grease, or heavily scored or damaged, fit a new set of pads. **Note:** *It is not possible to degrease the friction material; if the pads are contaminated in any way they must be replaced with new ones.*

21 If the pads are in good condition clean them carefully, using a fine wire brush which is completely free of oil and grease to remove

all traces of road dirt and corrosion. Using a pointed instrument, dig out any embedded particles of foreign matter. If required, spray with a dedicated brake cleaner to remove any dust.

22 Slide the caliper off the bracket **(see illustration)**. Clean off all traces of corrosion and hardened grease from the slider pins and from their rubber boots. Check the slider pin boots for cracks and splits and replace them with new ones if necessary, making sure they locate correctly. Note the pad spring in the top of caliper and the pad guide on the caliper bracket and remove them if required for cleaning or replacement, noting how they fit **(see illustrations)**.

23 Check the condition of the brake disc (see Section 4).

24 Clean around the exposed section of

each piston to remove any dirt or debris that could cause the seals to be damaged. Push the pistons into the caliper, as far as possible if new pads are being fitted, or just a little if the old pads are still serviceable. Keep an eye on the fluid level in the master cylinder reservoir – it may be necessary to remove the cap, plate and diaphragm and siphon out some fluid (see *Pre-ride checks*). If you can't depress the pistons with thumb pressure, try using a G-clamp (with rag or card to protect the caliper body), or a piece of wood as leverage, or place the old pads back in the caliper and use a metal bar or a screwdriver inserted between them (but take care not to damage the friction surface if the pads are being reused), **(see illustration)**. If available you can use a proper piston-pushing tool **(see illustration)**.

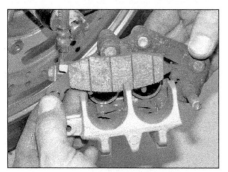

2.19d . . . and the outer pad

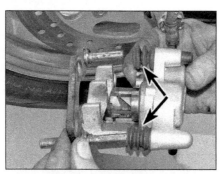

2.22a Slide the caliper off the bracket, and clean and check the pins and boots (arrowed) . . .

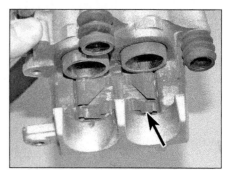

2.22b . . . the spring (arrowed) . . .

2.22c . . . and the guide

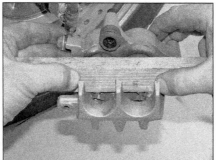

2.24a Push the piston in using one of the methods described . . .

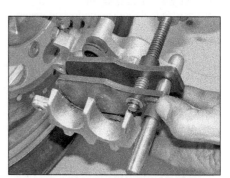

2.24b . . . or using a purpose built commercial tool

2.29 Slide the caliper onto the disc and fit the bolts

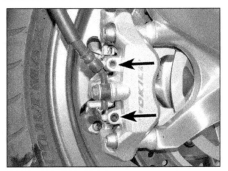

2.33a Slacken the pad pins (arrowed) . . .

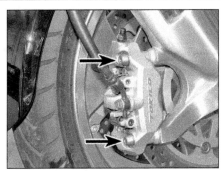

2.33b . . . then unscrew the mounting bolts (arrowed) and slide the caliper off the disc

25 If the pistons are difficult to push back, remove the bleed valve cap, then attach a length of clear hose to the bleed valve and place the open end in a suitable container, then open the valve and try again (see Section 7). Take great care not to draw any air into the system. If in doubt, bleed the brake afterwards. If a piston appears seized, first block or hold the other piston using wood or cable-ties, then apply the brake lever (front) or pedal (rear) and check whether the piston moves at all. If it moves out but can't be pushed back in, it is likely there is some hidden corrosion stopping it. If it doesn't move at all, or to fully clean and inspect the pistons, overhaul the caliper (see Section 3).

26 Make sure the pad spring and guides are correctly in place **(see illustrations 2.22b and c)**. Apply some silicone grease to the slider pins and inside the boots. Slide the caliper back onto the bracket, making sure the boots locate correctly around the base of the pins to provide a seal **(see illustration 2.22a)**.

27 When fitting the pads into the caliper make sure the friction material on each pad faces the other.

28 Fit the outer pad, making sure it locates correctly **(see illustration 2.19d)**. Slide the inner pad onto its post then pivot it down into the caliper **(see illustration 2.19c)**. Press both pads against the spring to align the holes, then insert the pad pin and secure it with the retaining clip **(see illustrations 2.19b and a)**.

29 Slide the caliper onto the disc and tighten the mounting bolts to the torque listed in this Chapter's Specifications **(see illustration)**.

30 Operate the brake lever (front) or pedal (rear) until the pads contact the disc. Check the level of fluid in the hydraulic reservoir and top-up if necessary (see *Pre-ride checks*).

31 Check the operation of the brake before riding the motorcycle.

Opposed-piston calipers (Mean Streak models)

32 On six piston calipers unscrew the pad spring bolts and remove the spring. Unscrew the caliper mounting bolts and slide the caliper off the disc. Remove the retaining clip from the pad pin. Withdraw the pad pin and remove the pads.

33 On four piston calipers slacken the pad pins **(see illustration)**. Unscrew the caliper mounting bolts and slide the caliper off the disc **(see illustration)**. Work on one pair of pads at a time. Unscrew and remove the pad pin, then remove the pad spring and withdraw the pads from the caliper **(see illustrations)**.

34 Inspect the surface of each pad for contamination and check that the friction material has not worn beyond its service limit (see Chapter 1). If any pad is worn down to, or beyond, the service limit wear indicator (i.e. the wear indicator is no longer visible), is fouled with oil or grease, or heavily scored or damaged, fit a complete set of new pads.

Note: *It is not possible to degrease the friction material; if the pads are contaminated in any way they must be replaced with new ones.*

35 If the pads are in good condition clean them carefully, using a fine wire brush which is completely free of oil and grease to remove

all traces of road dirt and corrosion. Using a pointed instrument, dig out any embedded particles of foreign matter. If required, spray with a dedicated brake cleaner to remove any dust.

36 Check the condition of the brake disc (see Section 4).

37 Remove all traces of corrosion from the pad pin(s) and check it/them for wear and damage.

38 Clean around the exposed section of each piston to remove any dirt or debris that could cause the seals to be damaged. On four piston calipers block the gap between the fitted pair of pads with a suitable tool. If new pads are being fitted, now push the pistons all the way back into the caliper to create room for them; if the old pads are still serviceable push the pistons in a little way. To push the pistons back use finger pressure or a piece of wood as leverage, or place the old pads back in the caliper and use a metal bar or a screwdriver inserted between them (but take care not to damage the friction surface if the pads are being reused), or use grips and a piece of wood, with rag or card to protect the caliper body **(see illustration)**. On six piston calipers you can use a proper piston-pushing tool **(see illustration 2.24b)**. Depending on the fluid level in the reservoir it may be necessary to remove the cap, plate and diaphragm and siphon out some fluid (see *Pre-ride checks*). If the pistons are difficult to push back, remove the bleed valve cap, then attach a length of clear hose to the bleed valve and place the open end in a suitable container, then open

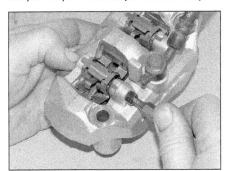

2.33c Unscrew the pin and remove the spring (arrowed) . . .

2.33d . . . and the pads

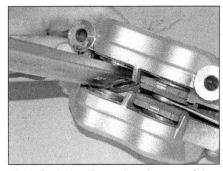

2.38 Push the pistons in using one of the methods described

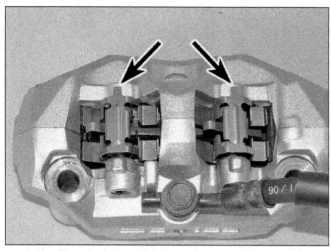
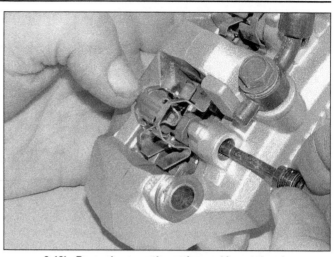

2.42a The tabs (arrowed) face the inner side of the caliper

2.42b Press down on the spring and insert the pin

the valve and try again (see Section 8). Take great care not to draw any air into the system. If in doubt, bleed the brake afterwards.

39 If a piston appears seized, first block or hold the other piston(s) using wood or cable-ties, then apply the brake lever and check whether the piston in question moves at all. If it moves out but can't be pushed back in, it is likely there is some hidden corrosion stopping it. If it doesn't move at all, or to fully clean and inspect the pistons, overhaul the caliper (see Section 3).

40 When fitting the pads into the caliper make sure the friction material on each pad faces the other.

41 On six piston calipers fit the pads into the caliper, making sure they locate correctly. Align the holes, then insert the pad pin and fit the retaining clip. Slide the caliper onto the disc making and tighten the mounting bolts to the torque setting specified at the beginning of the Chapter. Fit the pad spring and tighten the bolts.

42 On four piston calipers fit the pads up into the caliper **(see illustration 2.33d)**. Fit the pad spring with the side tab facing the inner side of the caliper **(see illustration)**. Insert the pad pin, then press down on the spring leaf and slide the pin all the way through and tighten it finger-tight **(see illustration)**. Repeat the

procedure for the other pair of pads. Slide the caliper onto the disc and tighten the mounting bolts to the torque setting specified at the beginning of the Chapter **(see illustration)**. Tighten the pad pins to the specified torque setting **(see illustration 2.33a)**.

43 Operate the brake lever until the pads contact the disc. Check the level of fluid in the hydraulic reservoir and top-up if necessary (see *Pre-ride checks*).

44 Check the operation of the front brake before riding the motorcycle.

3 Brake calipers – removal, overhaul and installation

⚠ *Warning: If a caliper is being completely removed, or is in need of an overhaul, it is best to drain all old brake fluid from the system, then fill with new fluid after the overhaul (see Section 7). Overhaul of the brake calipers must be done in a spotlessly clean work area to avoid contamination and possible failure of the brake hydraulic system components. Do not, under any circumstances, use petroleum-based solvents to clean brake parts. Use clean DOT 4 brake fluid, dedicated brake cleaner*

or denatured alcohol only, as described. To prevent damage from spilled brake fluid, always cover paintwork when working on the braking system.

Note: *If you are only displacing the caliper and are not overhauling or completely removing it, don't disconnect the brake hose from it.*

Removal

1 If you're just displacing the caliper(s) for wheel removal, unscrew the mounting bolts and slide the caliper off the disc **(see illustration 2.1 or 2.17 or 2.33b)**. Tie the caliper back so no strain is placed on the hose.

2 If the caliper is being completely removed or overhauled, unscrew the brake hose banjo bolt and detach the hose, noting how it aligns with the caliper **(see illustrations)**. Seal the end of the banjo union with plastic foodwrap and secure the hose in an upright position to minimise fluid loss, and wrap some rag or tissue around the caliper to catch the fluid inside. Discard the sealing washers, as new ones must be fitted on reassembly. Refer to Section 2 to remove the caliper and the brake pads.

Overhaul

3 Clean the exterior of the caliper with denatured alcohol or brake system cleaner. Have some clean rag ready to catch any spilled brake fluid.

2.42c Slide the caliper onto the disc and fit the bolts

3.2a Brake hose banjo bolt (arrowed) – twin piston sliding caliper

3.2b Brake hose banjo bolt (arrowed) – four opposed-piston caliper

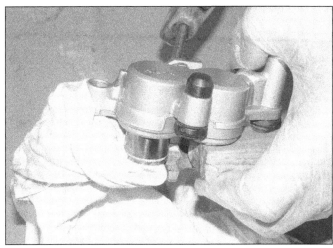

3.4a Apply compressed air to the fluid passage . . .

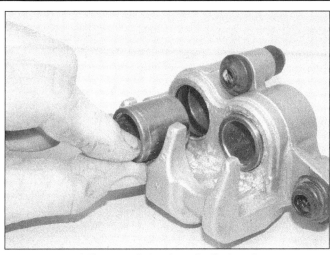

3.4b . . . until the piston is displaced

4 On sliding calipers, if not already done slide the caliper off its bracket, then remove the pad spring from the caliper **(see illustrations 2.22a and b)**. Stuff some stout rag or place a piece of wood between the piston(s) and the caliper body – it should be just thick enough to stop the piston(s) leaving the bores entirely. Apply compressed air gradually and progressively, starting with a fairly low pressure, to the fluid inlet on the caliper and allow the piston(s) to ease out of the bore(s) **(see illustrations)**. On twin piston calipers make sure the pistons are displaced evenly, using a small piece of wood to block one while the other moves if necessary.

5 On opposed piston calipers, unscrew the caliper body joining bolts and separate the body halves, catching any residual fluid with the rag **(see illustrations)**. Remove the caliper body O-ring(s) and obtain new ones for reassembly **(see illustration)**. Place one of the caliper halves piston-up on the bench. When working on the outer caliper half, make sure the bleed valve is tight, and find a suitable bolt to block the fluid inlet banjo bolt bore and thread it in. Get a wad of rag and place the caliper piston side down onto the rag. Apply compressed air gradually and progressively, starting with a fairly low pressure, to the fluid passage on the caliper joint and allow the pistons to ease out of their bores, controlling

them with hand pressure on the caliper **(see illustration)**. Make sure the pistons are displaced evenly, using pressure to block one while the other moves if necessary. Repeat the procedure for the other caliper half.

6 If a piston is stuck in its bore due to corrosion, the caliper should be replaced with a new one. Do not try to remove a piston by levering it out or by using pliers or other grips.

7 With the exception of single piston calipers mark each piston and the caliper body to ensure that the pistons can be matched to their original bores on reassembly.

8 Remove the dust seal(s) and the piston seal(s) from the piston bore(s) using a soft

wooden or plastic tool to avoid scratching the bore(s) **(see illustration)**. Discard the seals as new ones must be fitted on reassembly.

9 Clean the piston(s) and bore(s) with clean DOT 4 brake fluid. If compressed air is available, blow it through the fluid galleries in the caliper to ensure they are clear (make sure it is filtered and unlubricated).

Caution: Do not, under any circumstances, use a petroleum-based solvent to clean brake parts.

10 Inspect the caliper bore(s) and piston(s) for signs of corrosion, nicks and burrs and loss of plating. If surface defects are present, the piston(s) and/or the caliper assembly must

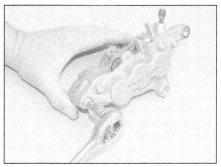

3.5a Unscrew the bolts (on the back on four-piston calipers) . . .

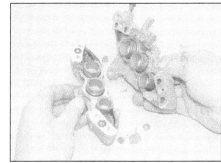

3.5b . . . and separate the halves

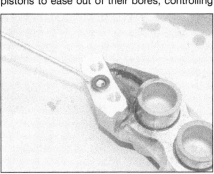

3.5c Remove the O-ring(s) and discard it/ them

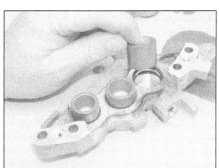

3.5d Apply compressed air to the fluid passage until the pistons are displaced

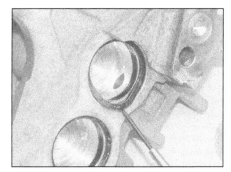

3.8 Remove the seals and discard them

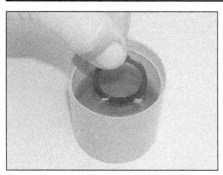

3.11a Lubricate the new piston seal with brake fluid . . .

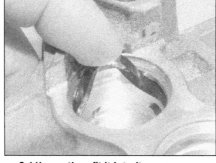

3.11b . . . then fit it into its groove . . .

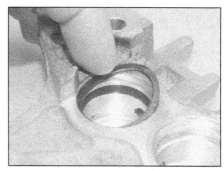

3.12 . . . followed by the new dust seal

be replaced with new ones. If one caliper is in poor condition, the other caliper(s) and the master cylinder should also be checked.

11 Lubricate the new piston seal(s) with clean brake fluid and fit it/them into the inner groove(s) in the caliper bore(s) **(see illustrations)**. On six piston calipers note that there are two sizes of bore in each caliper and care must therefore be taken to ensure that the correct size seals are fitted to the correct bores – the same applies when fitting the new dust seals and pistons.

12 Lubricate the new dust seal(s) with clean brake fluid and fit it/them into the outer groove(s) in the caliper bore(s) **(see illustration)**.

13 Lubricate the piston(s) with clean brake fluid and fit it/them, closed-end first, into the caliper bores, taking care not to displace the seals **(see illustration)**. Using your thumbs, push the piston(s) all the way in, making sure they enter the bore squarely.

14 On sliding calipers, clean off all traces of corrosion and hardened grease from the slider pins and the rubber boots. Check the boots for cracks and splits and replace them with new ones if necessary, making sure they locate correctly **(see illustration 2.22a)**. Fit the pad spring into the caliper, and make sure they guide(s) is/are on the bracket **(see illustrations 2.22b and c)**. Slide the caliper onto the bracket, making sure the boots locate correctly around the base of the pins to provide a seal.

15 On opposed piston calipers, lubricate the new caliper body O-ring(s) with clean DOT 4 brake fluid and fit it/them into the caliper body **(see illustration)**. Join the two halves of the caliper body together, ensuring that the O-ring(s) stay(s) in place **(see illustration)**. Tighten the caliper body joining bolts evenly to the torque setting specified at the beginning of the Chapter **(see illustration)**.

Installation

16 If removed, install the brake pads (see Section 2).

17 Slide the caliper onto the disc, making sure the pads fit on each side of the disc **(see illustration 2.29 or 2.42c)**.

18 Fit the caliper mounting bolts and tighten them to the torque setting specified at the beginning of the Chapter.

19 If removed, connect the brake hose to the caliper using new sealing washers **(see illustration)**. Align the hose correctly **(see illustration 3.2a or b)**. Tighten the banjo bolt to the specified torque setting for your model.

20 Top up the hydraulic reservoir with DOT 4 brake fluid (see *Pre-ride checks*) and bleed the system as described in Section 7. Check that there are no fluid leaks and test the operation of the brake before riding the motorcycle.

4 Brake discs – inspection, removal and installation

Inspection

1 Visually inspect the surface of the disc for score marks and other damage. Light scratches are normal after use and won't affect brake operation, but deep grooves and heavy score marks will reduce braking efficiency and accelerate pad wear. If the disc is badly grooved it must be replaced with a new one.

2 The disc must not be machined or allowed to wear down to a thickness less than the service limit as listed in this Chapter's Specifications.

3.13 Fit the piston and push it all the way in

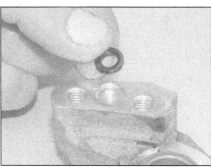

3.15a Fit the new O-ring(s) . . .

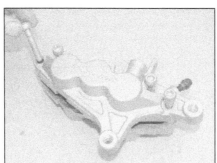

3.15b . . . then join the caliper halves . . .

3.15c . . . install the bolts and tighten them to the specified torque

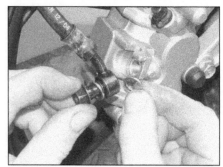

3.19 Always use new sealing washers and align the hose correctly

4.2 Measure the thickness of the disc

4.3 Checking disc runout with a dial gauge

4.5 Brake disc bolts (arrowed) – rear disc on VN1600 Mean Streak shown

The minimum thickness may also be stamped on the disc. Check the thickness of the disc in the middle of the pad contact area using a micrometer **(see illustration)** – do not measure across the rim of the disc with a ruler. Replace the disc with a new one if necessary.

3 To check disc runout, support the bike securely upright using an auxiliary stand so the wheel being checked is off the ground. Mount a dial indicator to a fork leg (front disc) or swingarm (rear disc) with the plunger on the indicator touching the surface of the disc about 1/2-inch from the outer edge **(see illustration)**. **Note:** *You may have to remove the saddlebag and/or muffler to check the rear disc according to model (see Chapter 4).* Slowly turn the wheel and watch the indicator needle, comparing your reading with the limit listed in this Chapter's Specifications. If the runout is greater than allowed, check the hub bearings for play (see Chapter 1). If the bearings are worn, replace them and repeat this check. If the disc runout is still excessive, remove it as described below and check for any corrosion between the disc and the hub. If the seat is clean you can also try moving the disc around the wheel one bolt hole at a time and after each movement rechecking for runout. Otherwise replace the disc with a new one.

Removal

4 Remove the wheel (see Section 10 or 11). **Caution: Don't lay the wheel down and allow it to rest on the disc – the disc could become warped. Set the wheel on wood blocks so the wheel rim supports the weight of the wheel.**

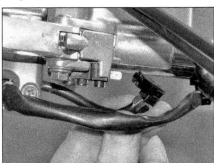

5.3 Disconnect the brake light switch wires

5 If you are not replacing the disc with a new one, mark the relationship of the disc to the wheel, so it can be installed in the same position. Unscrew the disc bolts, loosening them evenly and a little at a time in a criss-cross pattern to avoid distorting the disc, then remove the disc **(see illustration)**. On the front discs on VN1500 Nomad/Classic Tourer and Nomad/Classic Tourer FI models and Mean Streak models with four piston calipers, remove the gasket between the disc and the hub – a new one must be used.

Installation

6 Before installing the disc, make sure there is no dirt or corrosion where it seats on the hub. If the disc does not sit flat when it is bolted down, it will appear to be warped when checked or when the front brake is used.

7 On the front discs on VN1500 Nomad/ Classic Tourer and Nomad/Classic Tourer FI models and Mean Streak models with four piston calipers fit new gaskets.

8 Fit the disc onto the wheel with its marked side facing out, aligning the previously applied matchmarks (if you're reinstalling the original disc), and making sure the arrow points in the direction of normal rotation.

9 Clean the threads of the disc mounting bolts, then apply a suitable non-permanent thread locking compound. Fit the bolts and tighten them evenly and a little at a time in a criss-cross pattern to the torque setting specified at the beginning of this Chapter. Clean the disc using acetone or brake system cleaner. If a new disc has been fitted, remove any protective coating from its working surfaces and fit new brake pads.

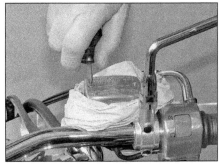

5.4 Slacken the cover screws

10 Install the wheel (see Section 10 or 11).

11 Check the operation of the brake before riding the motorcycle.

5 Master cylinders – removal, overhaul and installation

⚠️ **Warning: If the brake master cylinder is in need of an overhaul it is best to drain all old brake fluid from the system, then fill with new fluid after the overhaul (see Section 7). Overhaul must be done in a spotlessly clean work area to avoid contamination and possible failure of the brake hydraulic system components. Do not, under any circumstances, use petroleum-based solvents to clean brake parts. Use clean DOT 4 brake fluid, dedicated brake cleaner or denatured alcohol only, as described. To prevent damage from spilled brake fluid, always cover paintwork when working on the braking system.**

1 If the master cylinder is leaking fluid, or if the lever does not produce a firm feel when the brake is applied, and bleeding the brakes does not help, master cylinder overhaul is recommended. Before disassembling the master cylinder, read through the entire procedure and make sure that you have the correct rebuild kit, and any other parts you may require not included in the kit – ask your dealer. Also, you will need some new DOT 4 brake fluid, some clean rags and internal snap-ring pliers.

2 Disassembly, overhaul and reassembly of the brake master cylinder must be done in a spotlessly clean work area to avoid contamination and possible failure of the brake hydraulic system components.

Removal

Note: *If you are only displacing the master cylinder and are not overhauling or completely removing it, don't disconnect the brake hose from it.*

Front master cylinder

3 Disconnect the brake light switch wiring connectors **(see illustration)**.

4 If required loosen, but do not remove, the screws holding the reservoir cap in place **(see illustration)**.

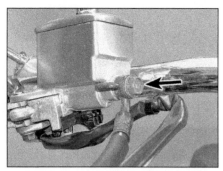

5.5 Brake hose banjo bolt (arrowed)

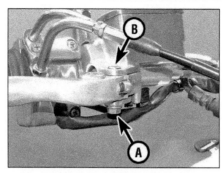

5.6 Unscrew the nut (A), then undo the bolt (B) and remove the lever

5.7a Remove the blanking caps where fitted . . .

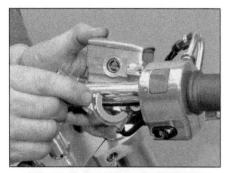

5.7b . . . then unscrew the bolts and detach the master cylinder

5.8a Remove the reservoir cover

5 If required unscrew the brake hose banjo bolt and detach the hose from the master cylinder, noting how it aligns **(see illustration)**. Seal the end of the banjo union with plastic foodwrap and secure the hose in an upright position to minimise fluid loss, and wrap some rag or tissue around the master cylinder to catch the fluid inside.

6 If required unscrew the locknut from the underside of the lever pivot bolt, then unscrew the bolt **(see illustration)**.

7 Where fitted remove the blanking caps from the master cylinder clamp bolts **(see illustration)**. Unscrew the bolts and detach

the master cylinder from the handlebar **(see illustration)**.

Caution: Do not tip the master cylinder upside down or brake fluid will run out.

Rear master cylinder

8 On VN1500A and B models remove the right side cover (see Chapter 8). On all other models remove the protective cover from the brake fluid reservoir **(see illustration)**. On all models unbolt the reservoir **(see illustration)**.

Note: *Keep the reservoir upright so brake fluid doesn't spill out.*

9 If required unscrew the brake hose banjo bolt and detach the hose from the master

cylinder, noting how it aligns. Seal the end of the banjo union with plastic foodwrap and secure the hose in an upright position to minimise fluid loss, and wrap some rag or tissue around the master cylinder to catch the fluid inside.

10 On VN1500A and B models remove the cotter pin, washer and clevis pin joining the pushrod to the brake pedal linkage. Unscrew the master cylinder mounting bolts and take the master cylinder off, together with the fluid reservoir.

11 On all other models slacken the master cylinder mounting bolts **(see illustration 5.8b)**. Unbolt the right footpeg/floorboard bracket from the motorcycle and support it with cable-ties, string or a bungee cord **(see illustration)**. Remove the cotter pin, washer and clevis pin joining the pushrod to the brake pedal lever. Unscrew the master cylinder mounting bolts and take the master cylinder off, together with the fluid reservoir.

Overhaul

12 Unscrew the reservoir cap and remove the diaphragm plate and rubber diaphragm, then tip the brake fluid into a suitable container. Wipe any remaining fluid out of the reservoir with a clean rag.

13 Carefully remove the rubber dust boot

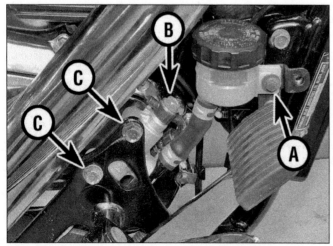

5.8b Reservoir bolt (A), brake hose banjo bolt (B), master cylinder bolts (C)

5.11 Floorboard bracket bolts (arrowed)

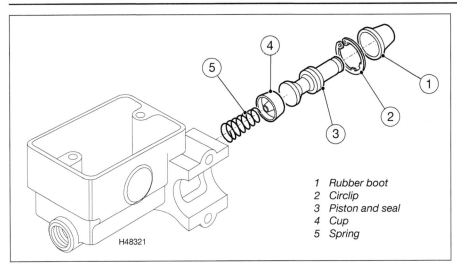

5.13a Front brake master cylinder components

1 Rubber boot
2 Circlip
3 Piston and seal
4 Cup
5 Spring

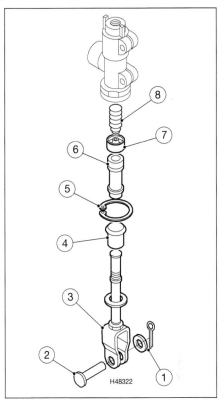

5.13b Rear brake master cylinder components

1 Cotter pin and washer	4 Rubber boot
2 Clevis pin	5 Circlip
3 Clevis and pushrod assembly	6 Piston and seal
	7 Cup
	8 Spring

from the end of the master cylinder **(see illustrations)**. Remove the snap-ring and slide out the pushrod (rear master cylinder), piston assembly and the spring. Lay the parts out in the proper order to prevent confusion during reassembly.

14 Clean all of the non-replacement parts with brake system cleaner (available at auto parts stores), denatured alcohol or clean brake fluid.

Caution: Do not, under any circumstances, use a petroleum-based solvent to clean brake parts. If compressed air is available, use it to dry the parts thoroughly (make sure it's filtered and unlubricated). Check the master cylinder bore for corrosion, scratches, nicks and score marks. If damage is evident, the master cylinder must be replaced with a new one. If the master cylinder is in poor condition, then the caliper should be checked as well. Make sure the ports in the bottom of the master cylinder are clear. If the small relief port is clogged, the brakes will drag.

15 Remove the old cup and seal from the piston and/or spring and fit the new ones. If a new piston is included in the rebuild kit, use it regardless of the condition of the old one. If a new rubber boot is being fitted, on the rear master cylinder remove the old one from the pushrod and fit the new one.

16 Before reassembling the master cylinder, soak the piston and the cup and seal in clean brake fluid for ten to fifteen minutes. Lubricate the master cylinder bore with clean brake fluid, then carefully insert the spring and piston assembly and related parts in the reverse order of disassembly. Make sure the lips on the cup and seal do not turn inside out when they are slipped into the bore.

17 Depress the piston, using the pushrod on the rear master cylinder, then fit the snap-ring with the sharp side facing out, making sure it locates in the groove. Seat the rubber dust boot in the master cylinder, and around the

piston tip (front) or pushrod (rear) if not already done.

Installation

18 Installation is the reverse of removal, noting the following:

a) *On the front master cylinder fit the master cylinder clamp with the mirror mount at the top and/or UP mark facing up, and align the clamp/master cylinder mating surfaces with the punch mark on the handlebar (see illustration). Tighten the upper bolt first, then the lower bolt – there will be a gap at the bottom. Do not forget to connect the brake light switch wiring.*

b) *On the rear master cylinder use a new cotter pin and bend its ends round the clevis pin.*

c) *Connect the brake hose to the master cylinder using new sealing washers and tighten the banjo bolt to the torque listed in this Chapter's Specifications.*

d) *Fill the fluid reservoir with new DOT 4 brake fluid (see Pre-ride) checks). Refer to Section 7 and bleed the air from the system.*

e) *Check the operation of the brakes and brake light before taking the bike out on the road.*

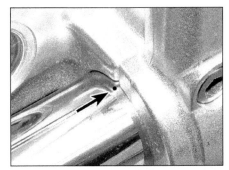

5.18 Align the clamp mating surfaces with the punch mark (arrowed)

6 Brake hoses – inspection and replacement

Inspection

1 Twist and flex the rubber hose while looking for cracks, bulges and seeping fluid **(see illustration)**. Check extra carefully around the areas where the hose connects to the banjo fittings, as these are common areas for hose failure.

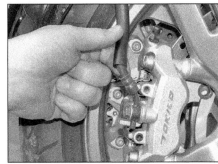

6.1 Flex the hose to check for cracks

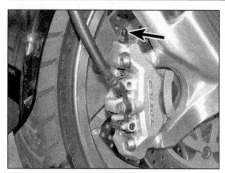

7.5a Caliper bleed valve (arrowed) – four piston caliper

7.5b Caliper bleed valves (arrowed) – twin piston sliding caliper, rear

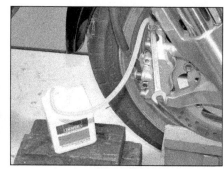

7.5c One of several commercially available one-man bleeding kits

Replacement

2 Drain all old brake fluid from the system (see Section 7).

3 The brake hoses have banjo fittings on each end. Cover the surrounding area with plenty of rags and unscrew the banjo bolt at each end of the hose, noting the alignment of the fitting with the master cylinder or brake caliper **(see illustrations 3.2a and b, 5.5 and 5.8b)**. Free the hose from any clips or guides and remove it, noting its routing. Discard the sealing washers. **Note:** *Do not operate the brake lever or pedal while a brake hose is disconnected.*

4 Position the new hose, making sure it isn't twisted or otherwise strained, and ensure that it is correctly routed through any clips or guides and is clear of all moving components. Make sure the elbow locates correctly.

5 Check that the fittings align correctly, then install the banjo bolts, using new sealing washers on both sides of the fittings **(see illustration 3.19)**. Tighten the banjo bolts to the torque setting specified at the beginning of this Chapter.

6 Refill the system with new DOT 4 brake fluid and bleed the air from it (see Section 7).

7 Check the operation of the brakes before riding the motorcycle.

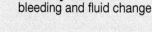

7 Brake system –
bleeding and fluid change

Bleeding

1 Bleeding the brakes is simply the process of removing any air from the brake fluid reservoir, master cylinder, hose(s) and the brake caliper(s). Bleeding is necessary whenever a brake system hydraulic connection is loosened, after a component or hose is replaced with a new one, or when the master cylinder or caliper is overhauled. Leaks in the system may also allow air to enter, but leaking brake fluid will reveal their presence and warn you of the need for repair.

2 To bleed the brakes, you will need some new DOT 4 brake fluid, a length of clear flexible hose, a small container partially filled with clean brake fluid, some rags, a spanner (preferably a ring spanner) to fit the brake caliper bleed valve, and possibly help from an assistant. Bleeding kits that include the hose, a one-way valve and a container are available relatively cheaply from a good auto store, and simplify the task as you don't need an assistant.

3 Cover painted components to prevent damage in the event that brake fluid is spilled.

4 Refer to 'Pre-ride checks' and remove the reservoir cover or cap, diaphragm plate (where fitted) and diaphragm and slowly pump the brake lever (front brake) or pedal (rear brake) a few times, until no air bubbles can be seen floating up from the holes in the bottom of the reservoir. This bleeds the air from the master cylinder end of the line. Temporarily refit the reservoir cover or cap.

5 Pull the dust cap off the bleed valve **(see illustrations)**. If using a ring spanner fit it onto the valve **(see Haynes Hint)**. Attach one end of the hose to the bleed valve and, if not using a kit, submerge the other end in the clean brake fluid in the container **(see illustration)**.

6 Check the fluid level in the reservoir. Do not allow the fluid level to drop below the lower mark during the procedure.

7 Carefully pump the brake lever or pedal three or four times and hold it in (front) or down (rear) while opening the bleed valve **(see illustration)**. When the valve is opened, brake fluid will flow out of the caliper into the clear tubing, and the lever will move toward the handlebar, or the pedal will move down. If there is air in the system there will be air bubbles in the brake fluid coming out of the caliper.

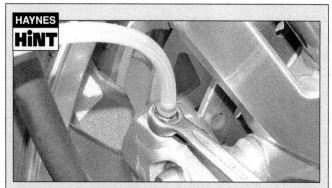

HAYNES HINT

To avoid damaging the bleed valve during the procedure, loosen it and then tighten it temporarily with a ring spanner before attaching the hose. With the hose attached, the valve can then be opened and closed either with an open-ended spanner, or by leaving the ring spanner located on the valve and fitting the hose above it.

7.7 Pump the lever then open the valve

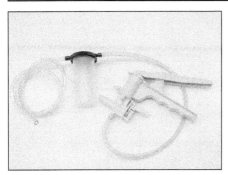

7.17 This tool creates a vacuum to suck the fluid out

8.2 Slacken the pinch bolt (arrowed)

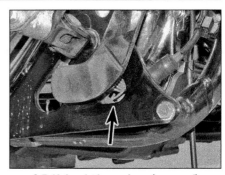

8.5 Unhook the springs (arrowed)

8 Tighten the bleed valve, then release the brake lever or pedal gradually. Repeat the process until no air bubbles are visible in the brake fluid leaving the caliper, and the lever or pedal is firm when applied, topping the reservoir up when necessary. On completion, disconnect the hose, then tighten the bleed valve to the torque setting specified at the beginning of this Chapter and fit the dust cap. On twin front disc models carry out the process on both front calipers. Where the rear caliper has two bleed valves, carry out the process using the other valve.

> **HAYNES HiNT** *If it is not possible to produce a firm feel to the lever or pedal, the fluid may be aerated. Let the brake fluid in the system stabilise for a few hours and then repeat the procedure when the tiny bubbles in the system have settled out, or you could try a commercially available vacuum-type brake bleeding tool (see illustration 7.17).*

9 Top-up the reservoir, then install the diaphragm, diaphragm plate (where fitted), and cover or cap (see *Pre-ride checks*). Wipe up any spilled brake fluid. Check the entire system for fluid leaks.
10 Check the operation of the brakes before riding the motorcycle.

Fluid change

11 Changing the brake fluid is a similar process to bleeding the brakes and requires the same materials plus a suitable tool (such as a syringe) for siphoning the fluid out of the reservoir. Also ensure that the container is large enough to take all the old fluid when it is flushed out of the system.
12 Follow Steps 3 and 5, then remove the reservoir cover or cap, diaphragm plate (where fitted) and diaphragm and siphon the old fluid out of the reservoir. Wipe the reservoir clean. Fill the reservoir with new brake fluid, then carefully pump the brake lever or pedal three or four times and hold it in (front) or down (rear) while opening the caliper bleed valve. When the valve is opened, brake fluid will flow out of the caliper into the clear tubing, and the lever will move toward the handlebar, or the pedal will move down.

13 Tighten the bleed valve, then release the brake lever or pedal gradually. Keep the reservoir topped-up with new fluid to above the LOWER level at all times or air may enter the system and greatly increase the length of the task. Repeat the process until new fluid can be seen emerging from the caliper bleed valve.

> **HAYNES HiNT** *Old brake fluid is invariably much darker in colour than new fluid, making it easy to see when all old fluid has been expelled from the system.*

14 Disconnect the hose, then tighten the bleed valve to the specified torque setting and fit the dust cap. On twin front disc models carry out the process on both front calipers. Repeat the process on the rear caliper's other bleed valve, where applicable.
15 Top-up the reservoir, then install the diaphragm, diaphragm plate (where fitted), and cover or cap (see *Pre-ride checks*). Wipe up any spilled brake fluid. Check the entire system for fluid leaks.
16 Check the operation of the brakes before riding the motorcycle.

Draining the system for overhaul

17 Draining the brake fluid is again a similar process to bleeding the brakes. Follow the procedure described above for changing the fluid, but quite simply do not put any new fluid into the reservoir – the system fills itself with air instead. An alternative is to use a commercially available vacuum-type brake bleeding tool **(see illustration)** – follow the manufacturer's instructions.

8 Brake pedal – removal and installation

Removal

1 On VN1500A and B models remove the cotter pin, washer and clevis pin joining the pushrod to the brake pedal lever.
2 Slacken the brake pedal lever pinch bolt **(see illustration)**. On all except VN1500A and B models slacken the master cylinder bolts **(see illustration 5.8b)**.

3 Unbolt the right footpeg or floorboard bracket from the frame **(see illustration 5.11)**.
4 Turn the bracket around. Remove the cotter pin, washer and clevis pin and disconnect the pedal lever from the linkage on VN1500A and B models and from the master cylinder pushrod on all other models **(see illustration 5.13b)**.
5 Unhook the brake pedal spring and brake light switch spring **(see illustration)**.
6 On all except VN1500A and B models unscrew the master cylinder bolts and displace the cylinder from the bracket.
7 Look for alignment marks on the pedal shaft and lever or make your own if you can't see them. Remove the pedal pinch bolt and pull the lever off the pedal shaft.
8 On models with a floorboard remove the floorboard E-clips and pivot pins and detach the floorboard from the bracket. On all models pull the brake pedal out of the bracket.

Installation

9 Installation is the reverse of the removal steps, with the following additions:
a) Lubricate the pedal shaft with multi-purpose grease.
b) Make sure the pedal shaft is correctly aligned in the lever according to the punch marks present or made.
c) Tighten the pedal pinch bolt and footpeg/ floorboard bracket bolts securely.
d) Check brake pedal height (position) and adjust as necessary (see Chapter 1).
e) Check the operation of the brakes before riding the motorcycle.

9 Wheels – inspection, repair and alignment check

Inspection and repair

1 Clean the wheels thoroughly to remove mud and dirt that may interfere with the inspection procedure or mask defects. Make a general check of the wheels and tires as described in Chapter 1.
2 Jack the bike up and support it so the wheel you're inspecting is off the ground. With the wheel in the air, attach a dial indicator to the fork tube or the swingarm and position the pointer against the side of the rim **(see**

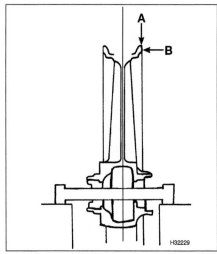

9.2 Check the wheel for radial (out-of-round) runout (A) and axial (side-to-side) runout (B)

illustration). Spin the wheel slowly and check the side-to-side (axial) runout of the rim, then compare your readings with the value listed in this Chapter's Specifications. In order to accurately check radial runout with the dial indicator, the wheel would have to be removed

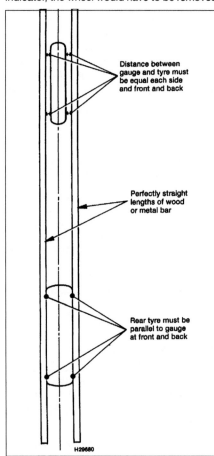

9.12 Wheel alignment check using a straight-edge

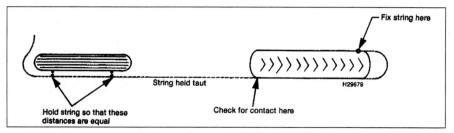

9.9 Wheel alignment check using string

from the machine and the tire removed from the wheel. With the axle clamped in a vise, the wheel can be rotated to check the runout.

3 An easier, though slightly less accurate, method is to attach a stiff wire pointer to the fork tube or the swingarm and position the end a fraction of an inch from the wheel (where the wheel and tire join). If the wheel is true, the distance from the pointer to the rim will be constant as the wheel is rotated. Repeat the procedure to check the runout of the rear wheel. **Note:** *If wheel runout is excessive, refer to the appropriate Section in this Chapter and check the wheel bearings very carefully before replacing the wheel.*

4 Cast alloy wheels should also be visually inspected for cracks, flat spots on the rim and other damage. Since tubeless tires are involved, look very closely for dents in the area where the tire bead contacts the rim. Dents in this area may prevent complete sealing of the tire against the rim, which leads to deflation of the tire over a period of time.

5 If damage is evident on a cast alloy wheel, or if runout in either direction is excessive, the wheel will have to be replaced with a new one. Never attempt to repair a damaged cast alloy wheel. Rim runout on a wire spoked wheel can be corrected by spoke tension adjustment or rim replacement, but this is a task for a wheel building expert.

Alignment check

6 Misalignment of the wheels, which may be due to a cocked rear wheel or a bent frame or triple clamps, can cause strange and possibly serious handling problems. If the frame or triple clamps are at fault, repair by a frame specialist or replacement with new parts are the only alternatives.

7 To check the alignment you will need an assistant, a length of string or a perfectly straight piece of wood and a ruler. A plumb bob or other suitable weight will also be required.

8 Support the bike upright on an auxiliary stand. Measure the width of both tires at their widest points. Subtract the smaller measurement from the larger measurement, then divide the difference by two. The result is the amount of offset that should exist between the front and rear tires on both sides.

9 If a string is used, have your assistant hold one end of it about half way between the floor and the rear axle, touching the rear sidewall of the tire **(see illustration)**.

10 Run the other end of the string forward

and pull it tight so that it is roughly parallel to the floor. Slowly bring the string into contact with the front sidewall of the rear tire, then turn the front wheel until it is parallel with the string. Measure the distance from the front tire sidewall to the string.

11 Repeat the procedure on the other side of the motorcycle. The distance from the front tire sidewall to the string should be equal on both sides.

12 As was previously pointed out, a perfectly straight length of wood may be substituted for the string **(see illustration)**. The procedure is the same.

13 If the distance between the string and tire is greater on one side, or if the rear wheel appears to be cocked, refer to Chapter 6 and make sure the swingarm pivot is tight.

14 If the front-to-back alignment is correct, the wheels still may be out of alignment vertically.

15 Using the plumb bob, or other suitable weight, and a length of string, check the rear wheel to make sure it is vertical. To do this, hold the string against the tire upper sidewall and allow the weight to settle just off the floor. When the string touches both the upper and lower tire sidewalls and is perfectly straight, the wheel is vertical. If it is not, adjust the stand until it is.

16 Once the rear wheel is vertical, check the front wheel in the same manner. If both wheels are not perfectly vertical, the frame and/or major suspension components are bent.

10 Front wheel – removal, inspection and installation

Removal

1 Position the motorcycle on an auxiliary stand so that the front wheel is off the ground. Always make sure the motorcycle is properly supported.

2 Displace the front brake caliper(s) (see Section 3). Support the caliper(s) with a cable-tie or a bungee cord so that no strain is placed on the hydraulic hose(s). There is no need to disconnect the hose(s). **Note:** *Do not operate the front brake lever with the caliper(s) removed.*

VN1500 models except Mean Streak

3 Where fitted detach the speedometer cable from the drive unit.

4 Unscrew the axle nut.

5 Loosen the axle clamp bolt in the bottom of the right fork **(see illustration 10.9)**.

6 Insert a punch or similar tool into the hole in the right side of the axle. Support the wheel, then pull the axle out and carefully lower the wheel to the ground.

7 Draw the wheel forwards and to one side if required to clear the mudguard – if your jack isn't high enough you will have to remove the mudguard (see Chapter 8). Remove the speedometer drive unit, and its driveplate on VN1500A and B models) from the right side where fitted, or the spacer. Remove the spacer from the left side – on models with a spacer on each side the shorter one fits on the left side.

Caution: Don't lay the wheel down and allow it to rest on a disc – the disc could become warped. Set the wheel on wood blocks so the disc doesn't support the weight of the wheel. If the axle is corroded, remove the corrosion with wire wool.

VN1500 Mean Streak and all VN1600 models

8 Where fitted remove the cap from the left end of the axle.

9 Loosen the axle clamp bolts in the bottom of the right fork **(see illustration)**.

10 Unscrew the axle using a 22 mm hex key, then support the wheel, withdraw the axle and carefully lower the wheel to the ground **(see illustrations)**.

11 Draw the wheel forwards and to one side if required to clear the mudguard – if your jack isn't high enough you will have to remove the mudguard (see Chapter 8). Remove the spacer from each side **(see illustration)** – they are the same. **Note:** *Do not operate the front brake lever with the wheel*

removed. *To prevent accidental operation of the brake, slip a piece of wood between the brake pads.*

Inspection

12 Check the axle (Section 11, Step 9).
13 Check the condition of the wheel bearings (see Section 12).

Installation

VN1500 models except Mean Streak

14 Clean all old grease off the axle, spacer(s), speedometer drive unit where fitted, and grease seals. Apply fresh grease to all components as you fit them.

15 On VN1500A and B models fit the speedometer drive unit driveplate, locating the tabs in the cut-outs. On all models with a speedometer cable, fit the drive unit in place in the right side of the hub locating the tabs in the cut-outs. Fit the spacer into the left-side. Slide the wheel into place.

16 On models without a speedometer cable, fit the spacers into the hub, shorter one on the left side.

17 Manoeuvre the wheel into position between the forks. Lift the wheel, making sure everything stays in place, and on models with a speedometer drive unit locate the stop between the lugs on the fork, and slide the axle through from the right side.

18 Fit the axle nut and tighten to the torque listed in this Chapter's Specifications. Tighten the axle clamp bolt to the torque listed in this Chapter's Specifications.

19 Install the brake caliper(s).

20 Connect the speedometer cable where fitted.

21 Apply the front brake, pump the forks up and down several times and check for binding and proper brake operation.

VN1500 Mean Streak and all VN1600 models

22 Clean all old grease off the axle, spacers, and grease seals. Apply fresh grease to the spacers and axle as you fit them.

23 Fit a spacer into the seal in each side of the wheel **(see illustration 10.11)**.

24 Manoeuvre the wheel into position between the forks. Lift the wheel, making sure the spacers stay in place, and slide the axle through from the right side **(see illustration 10.10b)**. Tighten the axle to the torque listed in this Chapter's Specifications.

25 Install the brake calipers.

26 Lower the bike so the wheel is on the ground, then pump the forks up and down without applying the brake – a block in front of the wheel makes this easier, or move the bike so the wheel is against a wall or similar solid object. Now tighten the axle clamp bolts on the bottom of the right fork to the listed torque **(see illustration 10.9)** – tighten the bolts alternately and evenly, and when the toque has been reached on the second bolt recheck the first bolt.

27 Apply the front brake, pump the forks up and down several times and check for binding and proper brake operation.

11 Rear wheel – removal, inspection and installation

Removal

1 Position the motorcycle on an auxiliary stand so that the rear wheel is off the ground. Always make sure the motorcycle is properly supported. Tie the front brake lever to the handlebar.

2 Where fitted remove the saddlebags and saddlebag bracket.

3 Remove the rear fender (see Chapter 8).

4 Remove the mufflers (see Chapter 4A or 4B).

5 Displace the rear brake caliper (see Section 3). Unscrew the caliper bracket stopper bolt **(see illustration)**.

10.9 Loosen the axle clamp bolts (arrowed)

10.10a Unscrew the axle using a 22 mm hex bit . . .

10.10b . . . then support the wheel and withdraw the axle

10.11 Remove the spacer from each side

11.5 Unscrew the bracket stopper bolt (arrowed)

11.6 Bend the pin ends straight, remove the pin and unscrew the nut (arrowed)

11.7a Withdraw the axle with its washer

11.7b Remove the wheel spacer

11.7c Draw the wheel off the final drive housing and lower to the ground

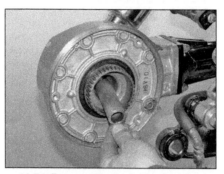

11.7d Remove the final drive housing spacer

6 Remove the cotter pin from the axle nut **(see illustration)**. Unscrew the axle nut and remove the washer **(see illustration 11.15)**.
7 Support the wheel and slide the axle out **(see illustration)**. Remove the caliper bracket **(see illustration 11.13)**. Remove the spacer from the right side of the hub **(see illustration)**. Pull the wheel to the right to clear the final drive housing, lower the wheel and remove it from the swingarm **(see illustration)**. Remove the spacer from the final drive housing **(see illustration)**.
8 Clean all old grease off the axle, spacers and final drive coupling splines.

Inspection

9 Clean all old grease off the axle, then remove any corrosion with wire wool. Check the axle is straight by rolling its shaft along a true surface. If the equipment is available set the axle on V-blocks and check it for runout

using a dial indicator. If the axle exceeds the maximum allowable runout limit listed in this Chapter's Specifications, it must be replaced with a new one.
10 Check the condition of the wheel bearings (see Section 12).

Installation

11 Clean all old grease off the axle, spacers, grease seal and final drive coupling splines. Apply fresh molybdenum disulphide grease. Fit the spacer into the final drive housing **(see illustration 11.7d)**.
12 Manoeuvre the wheel into place, then lift it onto the final drive housing, engaging the coupling splines **(see illustration 11.7c)**.
13 Fit the spacer into the seal on the right side of the wheel hub **(see illustration 11.7b)**. Fit the brake caliper bracket between the spacer and swingarm on the right side and tighten the stopper bolt finger-tight **(see illustration)**.

14 Slide the axle with its washer in from the left side and through the caliper bracket **(see illustration 11.7a)**.
15 Fit the axle nut with its washer **(see illustration)**.
16 Tighten the axle nut to the torque listed in this Chapter's Specifications. Install a new cotter pin, tightening the axle nut an additional amount, if necessary, to align the hole in the axle with the castellations on the nut **(see illustration)**. Bend the ends of the pin around the nut **(see illustration 11.6)**.
17 Tighten the caliper bracket stopper bolt to the torque listed in this Chapter's Specifications.
18 The remainder of installation is the reverse of the removal steps.
19 Check the operation of the brake carefully before riding the motorcycle.

12 Wheel bearings – inspection and maintenance

Front wheel bearings

1 Remove the wheel (see Section 10). If required remove the brake disc(s) (see Section 4) to prevent damage or distortion during bearing removal – if left in place, take care to support the wheel on wood blocks so that the wheel rim supports the weight of the wheel.
2 On all models with a speedometer cable except VN1500A and B models remove the circlip securing the driveplate then remove the plate. A new circlip should be used.
3 Lever out the bearing seal from the left side

11.13 Fit the caliper bracket and tighten the stopper bolt finger-tight

11.15 Fit the washer and axle nut

11.16 Fit a new pin between the castellations and through the axle

12.3 Lever out the bearing seal

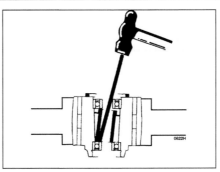

12.5a Locate the drift as shown . . .

12.5b . . . and drive the bearing out

using a flat-bladed screwdriver or a seal hook **(see illustration)**. Where fitted also remove the seal from the right side. Take care not to damage the hub. Discard the seal(s) as new ones must be fitted on reassembly.

4 Inspect the bearings – check that the inner race turns smoothly and that the outer race is a tight fit in the hub (see Tools and Workshop Tips (Section 5) in the Reference Section). **Note:** *Do not remove the bearings unless they are going to be replaced with new ones because removal will destroy them.*

5 If the bearings are worn, remove the circlip from the right side on Mean Streak models and the left side on all others **(see illustration 12.19)**. Remove the bearings using a metal rod (preferably a brass punch) inserted through the centre of the opposite bearing and locating it on the inner race, pushing the bearing spacer aside to expose it **(see illustration)**. Curve the end of the drift to obtain better purchase if necessary. Strike the drift with a hammer, working evenly around the bearing, to drive it from the hub **(see illustration)**. Remove the spacer which fits between the bearings, noting which way round it fits if shaped at one end. Turn the wheel over and remove the other bearing.

6 If the bearings are difficult to remove as described remove them using an internal expanding puller with slide-hammer attachment, which can be obtained commercially – select the correct attachment and locate it behind the inner race of the bearing, then tighten the inner bolt to expand and lock the puller. Attach the slide-hammer, hold the wheel firmly down and jar the bearing out. Having removed the first bearing remove the spacer which fits between the bearings. Turn the wheel over and remove the other bearing using the same procedure.

7 Thoroughly clean the hub area of the wheel with a suitable solvent and inspect the bearing seats for scoring and wear. If the seats are damaged, consult a Kawasaki dealer before reassembling the wheel.

8 Drive the new bearings into the hub with the marked side facing outwards using a bearing driver or suitable socket that bears on the outer race **(see illustration)** – do not drive the bearings in by the inner race. Make sure the bearing fits squarely and all the way into its seat.

9 Turn the wheel over then fit the bearing spacer and the other new bearing.

12.8 Using a socket to drive the bearing in

10 Fit the new circlip into its groove in the right side on Mean Streak models and the left side on all others **(see illustration 12.19)**.

11 Apply a smear of grease to the new seal(s), then press it/them into the hub with your fingers or drive it/them in using a piece of wood or a socket and level it with the rim **(see illustration)** – all models have a seal in the left side, all models without a speedometer cable and VN1500A and B models also have one in the right.

12 On all models with a speedometer cable except VN1500A and B models fit the speedometer driveplate, locating the tabs in the cut-outs, then fit a new circlip into the groove.

13 Install the brake disc(s) if removed (see Section 4). Clean the disc(s) using brake system cleaner.

14 Install the wheel (see Section 10).

Rear wheel bearings

15 Remove the wheel (see Section 11). If required remove the brake disc (see Sec-

12.16 Lever out the bearing seal

12.11 Press the new seal into place – using a piece of wood across the seal sets it flush with the rim of the housing

tion 4) to prevent it being damaged or distorted during bearing removal – if you do leave it in place, take care to support the wheel on wood blocks so that the wheel rim supports the weight of the wheel.

16 Lever out the bearing seal from the right-hand side of the hub using a flat-bladed screwdriver or a seal hook **(see illustration)**. Take care not to damage the hub. Discard the seal as a new one should be fitted on reassembly.

17 Inspect the bearings in both sides of the hub – check that the inner race turns smoothly, quietly and freely and that the outer race is a tight fit in the hub. **Note:** *Do not remove the bearings unless they are going to be replaced with new ones.*

18 If the bearings are worn, remove the circlip from the right side **(see illustration)** – a new one should be used. Remove the bearings using a metal rod (preferably a brass punch) inserted through the centre of the opposite

12.18 Remove the circlip (arrowed)

12.23 Press the new seal into place – using a piece of wood across the seal sets it flush with the rim of the housing

bearing and locating it on the inner race, pushing the bearing spacer aside to expose it **(see illustration 12.5a)**. Curve the end of the drift to obtain better purchase if necessary. Strike the drift with a hammer, working evenly around the bearing, to drive it from the hub **(see illustration 12.5b)**. Remove the spacer which fits between the bearings, noting which way round it fits if shaped at one end. Turn the wheel over and remove the remaining bearing using the same procedure.

19 If the bearings are difficult to remove as described, remove them using an internal expanding puller with slide-hammer attachment, which can be obtained commercially – select the correct attachment and locate it behind the inner race of the bearing, then tighten the inner bolt to expand and lock the puller. Attach the slide-hammer, hold the wheel firmly down and jar the bearing out. Having removed the first bearing remove the spacer which fits between the bearings. Turn the wheel over and remove the remaining bearing using the same procedure.

20 Thoroughly clean the hub area of the wheel with a suitable solvent and inspect the bearing seats for scoring and wear. If the seats are damaged, consult a Kawasaki dealer before reassembling the wheel.

21 Drive the new bearings into the hub with the marked side facing outwards using a bearing driver or suitable socket that bears on the outer race **(see illustration 12.8)** – do not drive the bearings in by the inner race. Make sure the bearing fits squarely and all the way into its seat.

22 Turn the wheel over then install the bearing spacer and the other new bearing.

23 Fit the new circlip into its groove in the right side **(see illustration 12.18)**. Apply a smear of grease to the new seal, then press it into the hub with your fingers or drive it in using a piece of wood or a socket and level it with the rim **(see illustration)**.

24 Check the rear wheel coupling/rubber dampers (see Chapter 6).

25 Install the brake disc if removed (see Section 4). Clean the disc using brake system cleaner.

26 Install the wheel (see Section 11).

13 Tube tires (wire spoke wheels) – removal and installation

1 Tires with inner tubes are used as standard equipment on VN1500B models, VN1500 Classic and Classic FI models and Drifter models. Refer to the *Pre-ride checks* listed at the beginning of this manual for tire maintenance, and to Chapter 1 for wheel maintenance.

2 When selecting new tires, refer to the tire information in the Owner's Handbook. Ensure that front and rear tire types are compatible, the correct size and correct speed rating; if necessary seek advice from a Kawasaki dealer or tire fitting specialist **(see illustration 15.5)**.

3 To properly remove and install tires, you will need at least two motorcycle tire irons, some water and a tire pressure gauge.

Removal

4 Begin by removing the wheel from the motorcycle. If the tire is going to be re-used, mark it next to the valve stem, wheel balance weight or rim lock.

5 Deflate the tire by removing the valve stem core. When it is fully deflated, push the bead of the tire away from the rim on both sides. In some extreme cases, this can only be accomplished with a bead breaking tool, but most often it can be carried out with tire irons. Riding on a deflated tire to break the bead is not recommended, as damage to the rim and tire will occur.

6 Dismounting a tire is easier when the tire is warm, so an indoor tire change is recommended in cold climates. The rubber gets very stiff and is difficult to manipulate when cold.

7 Place the wheel on a thick pad or old blanket. This will help keep the wheel and tire from slipping around.

8 Once the bead is completely free of the rim, lubricate the inside edge of the rim and the tire bead with soap and water or rubber lubricant (do not use any type of petroleum-based lubricant, as it will cause the tire to deteriorate). Remove the locknut and push the tire valve through the rim.

9 Insert one of the tire irons under the bead of the tire at the valve stem and lift the bead up over the rim. This should be fairly easy. Take care not to pinch the tube as this is done. If it is difficult to pry the bead up, make sure that the rest of the bead opposite the valve stem is in the dropped center section of the rim.

10 Hold the tire iron down with the bead over the rim, then move about 1 or 2 inches to either side and insert the second tire iron. Be careful not to cut or slice the bead or the tire may split when inflated. Also, take care not to catch or pinch the inner tube as the second tire iron is levered over. For this reason, tire irons are recommended over screwdrivers or other implements.

11 With a small section of the bead up over the rim, one of the levers can be removed and reinserted 1 or 2 inches farther around the rim

until about 1/4 of the tire bead is above the rim edge. Make sure that the rest of the bead is in the dropped center of the rim. At this point, the bead can usually be pulled up over the rim by hand.

12 Once all of the first bead is over the rim, the inner tube can be withdrawn from the tire and rim. Push in on the valve stem, lift up on the tire next to the stem, reach inside the tire and carefully pull out the tube. It is usually not necessary to completely remove the tire from the rim to repair the inner tube. It is sometimes recommended though, because checking for foreign objects in the tire is difficult while it is still mounted on the rim.

13 To remove the tire completely, make sure the bead is broken all the way around on the remaining edge, then stand the tire and wheel up on the tread and grab the wheel with one hand. Push the tire down over the same edge of the rim while pulling the rim away from the tire. If the bead is correctly positioned in the dropped center of the rim, the tire should roll off and separate from the rim very easily. If tire irons are used to work this last bead over the rim, the outer edge of the rim may be marred. If a tire iron is necessary, be sure to pad the rim as described earlier.

14 Refer to Section 14 for inner tube repair procedures.

Installation

15 Mounting a tire is basically the reverse of removal. Some tires have a balance mark and/or directional arrows molded into the tire sidewall. Look for these marks so that the tire can be installed properly. The dot should be aligned with the valve stem.

16 If the tire was not removed completely to repair or replace the inner tube, the tube should be inflated just enough to make it round. Sprinkle it with talcum powder, which acts as a dry lubricant, then carefully lift up the tire edge and install the tube with the valve stem next to the hole in the rim. Once the tube is in place, push the valve stem through the rim and start the locknut on the stem.

17 Lubricate the tire bead, then push it over the rim edge and into the dropped center section opposite the inner tube valve stem. Work around each side of the rim, carefully pushing the bead over the rim. The last section may have to be levered on with tire irons. If so, take care not to pinch the inner tube as this is done.

18 Once the bead is over the rim edge, check to see that the inner tube valve stem is pointing to the center of the hub. If it's angled slightly in either direction, rotate the tire on the rim to straighten it out. Run the locknut the rest of the way onto the stem but don't tighten it completely.

19 Inflate the tube to approximately 1-1/2 times the pressure listed in the Chapter 1 Specifications and check to make sure the guidelines on the tire sidewalls are the same distance from the rim around the circumference of the tire.

 Warning: Do not overinflate the tube or the tire may burst, causing serious injury.

TIRE CHANGING SEQUENCE - TUBED TIRES

1 Deflate tire. After pushing tire beads away from rim flanges push tire bead into well of rim at point opposite valve. Insert tire lever adjacent to valve and work bead over edge of rim.

2 Use two levers to work bead over edge of rim. Note use of rim protectors.

3 Remove inner tube from tire.

4 When first bead is clear, remove tire as shown.

5 When fitting, partially inflate inner tube and insert in tire.

6 Work first bead over rim and feed valve through hole in rim. Partially screw on retaining nut to hold valve in place.

7 Check that inner tube is positioned correctly and work second bead over rim using tire levers. Start at a point opposite valve.

8 Work final area of bead over rim while pushing valve inwards to ensure that inner tube is not trapped.

20 After the tire bead is correctly seated on the rim, allow the tire to deflate. Replace the valve core and inflate the tube to the recommended pressure, then tighten the valve stem locknut securely and tighten the cap.

21 It is recommended that a motorcycle tire specialist balances the wheels.

14 Tube tires (wire spoked wheels) – puncture repair

1 Tire tube repair requires a patching kit that's usually available from motorcycle dealers, accessory stores or auto parts stores. Be sure to follow the directions supplied with the kit to ensure a safe repair. Patching should be done only when a new tube is unavailable. Replace the tube as soon as possible. Sudden deflation can cause loss of control and an accident.

2 To repair a tube, remove it from the tire, inflate and immerse it in a sink or tub full of water to pinpoint the leak. Mark the position of the leak, then deflate the tube. Dry it off and thoroughly clean the area around the puncture.

3 Most tire patching kits have a buffer to rough up the area around the hole for proper adhesion of the patch. Roughen an area

slightly larger than the patch, then apply a thin coat of the patching cement to the roughened area. Allow the cement to dry until tacky, then apply the patch.

4 It may be necessary to remove a protective covering from the top surface of the patch after it has been attached to the tube. Keep in mind that tubes made from synthetic rubber may require a special patch and adhesive if a satisfactory bond is to be achieved.

5 Before replacing the tube, check the inside of the tire to make sure the object that caused the puncture is not still inside. Also check the outside of the tire, particularly the tread area, to make sure nothing is projecting through the tire that may cause another puncture. Check the rim for sharp edges or damage. Make sure the rubber trim band is in good condition and properly installed before inserting the tube.

15 Tubeless tires (cast alloy wheels) – general information

1 Tubeless tires are used as standard equipment on VN1500A models, VN1600 Classic models, all Nomad/Classic Tourer models and all Mean Streak models. They are generally safer than tube-type tires but if

problems do occur they require special repair techniques. Refer to the *Pre-ride checks* listed at the beginning of this manual for tire maintenance, and to Chapter 1 for wheel and tire inspection

2 The force required to break the seal between the rim and the bead of the tire is substantial, and is usually beyond the capabilities of an individual working with normal tire irons.

3 Also, repair of a punctured tire and replacement on the wheel rim requires special tools, skills and experience that the average do-it-yourselfer lacks.

4 For these reasons, if a puncture or flat occurs with a tubeless tire, or a new tire is needed, the wheel should be removed from the motorcycle and taken to a dealer service department or a motorcycle repair shop for repair or replacement of the tire. The accompanying illustration sequence can be used as a guide to replace a tubeless tire in an emergency. If you do fit them yourself it is recommended that a motorcycle tire specialist balances the wheels afterwards.

5 When selecting new tires, refer to the tire information in the Owner's Handbook. Ensure that front and rear tire types are compatible, the correct size and correct speed rating; if necessary seek advice from a Kawasaki dealer or tire fitting specialist **(see illustration)**.

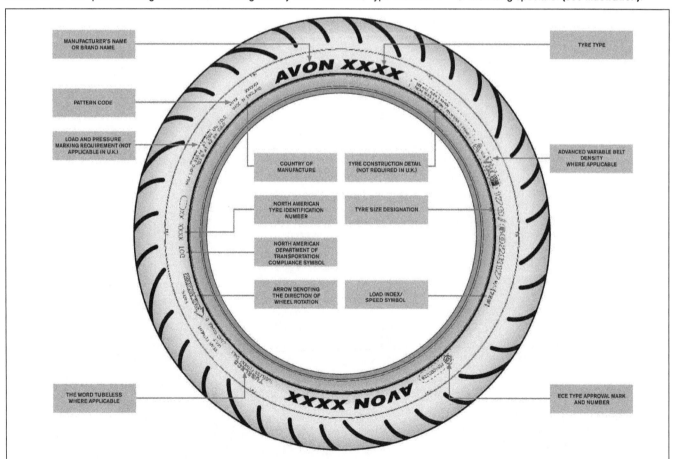

15.5 Common tyre sidewall markings

TIRE CHANGING SEQUENCE - TUBELESS TIRES

Deflate tire. After releasing beads, push tire bead into well of rim at point opposite valve. Insert lever next to valve and work bead over edge of rim.

Use two levers to work bead over edge of rim. Note use of rim protectors.

When first bead is clear, remove tire as shown.

Before installing, ensure that tire is suitable for wheel. Take note of any sidewall markings such as direction of rotation arrows.

Work first bead over the rim flange.

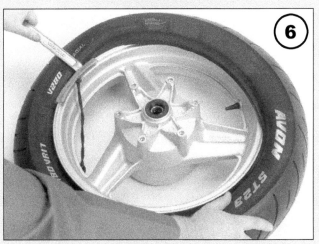

Use a tire lever to work the second bead over rim flange.

Notes

Chapter 8
Frame and bodywork

Contents

Degrees of difficulty

Easy, suitable for novice with little experience	Fairly easy, suitable for beginner with some experience	Fairly difficult, suitable for competent DIY mechanic	Difficult, suitable for experienced DIY mechanic	Very difficult, suitable for expert DIY or professional

1 General information

The machines covered by this manual use a double cradle frame constructed of steel tubing. This Chapter covers the procedures necessary to remove and install the side covers and other body parts.

2 Frame – inspection and repair

1 The frame should not require attention unless accident damage or severe corrosion has occurred. In most cases, frame replacement is the only satisfactory remedy for such damage. A few frame specialists have the jigs and other equipment necessary for straightening the frame to the required standard of accuracy, but even then there is no simple way of assessing to what extent the frame may have been over stressed.

2 After the machine has accumulated a lot of miles, the frame should be examined closely for signs of cracking or splitting at the welded joints. Rust can also cause weakness at these joints. Loose engine mount bolts can

3.1a Remove the C-clip (arrowed) from the bottom of the pivot pin then withdraw the pin from the top

3.1b Note how the return spring ends (arrowed) locate before removing the peg or board

3.2 Footpeg/board bracket bolts (arrowed)

cause ovaling or fracturing of the mounting tabs. Minor damage can often be repaired by welding, depending on the extent and nature of the damage.

3 Remember that a frame which is out of alignment will cause handling problems. If misalignment is suspected as the result of an accident, it will be necessary to strip the machine completely so the frame can be thoroughly checked.

3 Footpegs, floorboards and brackets – removal and installation

1 If it's only necessary to detach the footpeg or floorboard from the bracket, pry the C-clip(s) off the pivot pin(s), slide out the pin(s) and detach the footpeg or floorboard from the bracket **(see illustration)**. Be careful not to lose the spring, and note how its ends locate **(see illustration)**. Installation is the reverse of removal, but be sure to install the spring correctly.

2 If it's necessary to remove the entire bracket from the frame, remove the bolts that secure the bracket to the frame, then detach the footpeg and bracket **(see illustration)**.

3 Installation is the reverse of removal. Make sure all bracket bolts are securely tightened.

4 Sidestand – removal and installation

1 The sidestand is bolted to the frame. An extension spring anchored between them ensures that the stand is held in the retracted position.

2 If you need to remove the stand support the bike securely using an auxiliary stand. Displace the sidestand switch (see Chapter 9) – there is no need to disconnect the wiring unless you want to completely remove the switch.

3 Retract the stand. Note which way round and which way up the spring fits, then unhook it **(see illustration)**.

4 On VN1500A and B models unscrew the nut and lift the stand off its pivot.

5 On all other models unscrew the nut, then unscrew the pivot bolt and remove the stand **(see illustration)**.

6 Installation is the reverse of removal. Clean off all old grease. Apply fresh grease to the pivot shaft and to the contacting surfaces of the stand and bracket. Make sure the spring is in good condition and not over stretched. Make sure the pivot nut is tight. Make sure the spring ends are correctly and securely hooked in place – an accident is almost certain to occur if the stand extends while the machine is in motion.

5 Mirrors – removal and installation

1 To remove a mirror, loosen its locknut. Unscrew the mirror from its mount on the handlebar.

2 Installation is the reverse of removal. Position the mirror as required before tightening the locknut.

6 Seat(s) – removal and installation

VN1500A

1 To remove the front seat unlock it then lift it

4.3 Unhook the springs (arrowed)

up at the back and draw it back, noting how it locates at the front.

2 To remove the rear seat first remove the front seat. Unscrew the two bolts securing the rear seat and draw it forwards to release the tabs at the back.

3 Installation is the reverse of removal.

VN1500B

4 Open the panel behind the seat.

5 Remove two mounting bolts then lift the seat up at the back and draw it back, noting how it locates at the front and lift the seat off.

6 Installation is the reverse of removal.

VN1500 Classic, Classic FI, Nomad/Classic Tourer, Nomad/Classic Tourer FI

7 To remove the front seat unscrew the bolt on each side, then draw the seat forwards and remove it, noting how it locates.

8 To remove the rear seat first remove the front seat. Unscrew the bolt at the front then draw the seat forwards to release the hooks from the bracket on the fender.

9 Installation is the reverse of removal. Make sure the rear seat hooks locate in the bracket and the front seat hook locates under the washer.

VN1600 Classic and Nomad/Classic Tourer

10 To remove the rear seat unscrew the bolt at the back, then draw the seat back and remove it, noting how it locates at the front.

11 To remove the front seat first remove the

4.5 Unscrew the nut (A), then unscrew the pivot bolt (B)

rear seat. Unscrew the bolt at the back then draw the seat back and up to release the tab at the front from under the tank bracket.

12 Installation is the reverse of removal. Make sure the tab at the front of each seat locates under its bracket.

Drifter

13 Unscrew the bolt on each side, and on J models with a dual seat the nut at the rear. Draw the seat forwards to release the hook at the front and remove the seat.

14 Installation is the reverse of removal. Make sure the hook at the front locates under the washer.

Mean Streak

15 Unscrew the bolt on each side and the bolt at the rear. Draw the seat back to release the tab at the front and remove the seat.

16 Installation is the reverse of removal. Make sure the tab at the front locates under the bracket.

---

7 Side covers –
removal and installation

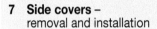

VN1500A and B

1 Unscrew the bolt securing the bottom of the panel.

2 Carefully pull the top of the panel away to release the pegs from the grommets.

3 Installation is the reverse of removal. Make sure all grommets are in good condition. A spray of light oil helps the pegs into the grommets, and will make them easier to release next time.

All other models

4 On the left side, use the ignition key to unlock the latch at the rear of the cover, turning it clockwise a quarter turn **(see illustration)**. Carefully pull the rear of the cover away from the frame to free the peg from the grommet, then move the cover forwards to free the grommets form the pegs **(see illustration)**.

5 On the right side, undo the screw or bolt securing the bottom of the panel **(see illustration)**. Carefully pull the top of the panel

8.2 Release the brake hose clip(s) from the fender

7.4a Unlock the cover using the ignition key

7.5a Undo the screw (arrowed) . . .

away to release the pegs from the grommets, taking care not to catch the panel against the exhaust pipe **(see illustration)**.

6 Installation is the reverse of removal. Make sure all grommets are in good condition. A spray of light oil helps the pegs into the grommets, and will make them easier to release next time.

---

8 Front fender –
removal and installation

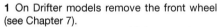

1 On Drifter models remove the front wheel (see Chapter 7).

2 Release the brake hose(s) from the fender **(see illustration)**.

3 Unbolt the fender from the fork legs and draw it off **(see illustrations)**.

4 Installation is the reverse of removal.

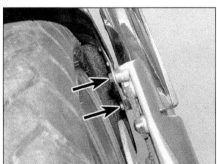

8.3a Front fender bolts (arrowed) – VN1600 Mean Streak

7.4b Pull the rear away then move the cover forwards to free the grommets from the pegs

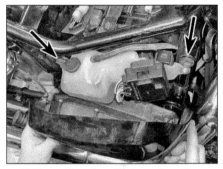

7.5b . . . then free the pegs from the grommets (arrowed)

---

9 Rear fender –
removal and installation

VN1500A and B

1 Remove the seat(s) (see Section 6).

2 Disconnect the electrical connectors for the turn signal lights and tail light.

3 Unbolt the seat back frame and take it off. Remove the rear fender rear section mounting bolts and remove the rear section of the fender, then if required unbolt and remove the front section.

4 Installation is the reverse of removal.

VN1500 Classic and Classic FI

5 Remove the seats (see Section 6).

6 Unscrew the bolts along each side and

8.3b Draw the fender out from between the forks

remove the sub-frame covers and bungee hook brackets.

7 Disconnect the electrical connectors for the tail lights and rear turn signals.

8 Unscrew the bolts securing the front and sides of the fender then draw the fender off the bike.

9 Installation is the reverse of removal.

VN1500 Nomad/Classic Tourer and Nomad/Classic Tourer FI

10 Remove the seats (see Section 6).

11 Remove the saddlebags. Unscrew the saddlebag bracket nuts and bolts and remove the brackets.

12 Unscrew the bolts along each side and remove the sub-frame covers.

13 Disconnect the electrical connectors for the tail lights and rear turn signals.

14 Unscrew the bolts securing the front and sides of the fender then draw the fender off the bike.

15 Installation is the reverse of removal.

VN1600 Classic

16 Remove the seats (see Section 6).

17 Unscrew the bolts along each side and remove the sub-frame covers.

18 Disconnect the electrical connector for the tail lights and rear turn signals, and release the wiring from the tie.

19 Unscrew the bolts securing the front and sides of the fender and the seat band then draw the fender off the bike.

20 Installation is the reverse of removal.

VN1600 Nomad/Classic Tourer

21 Remove the seats (see Section 6).

22 Remove the saddlebags and saddlebag brackets.

23 Unscrew the backrest bracket bolts and remove the backrest.

24 Unscrew the grab-rail/backrest assembly bolts and remove the assembly, then remove the sub-frame covers.

25 Unscrew the saddlebag bracket bolts and remove the brackets.

26 Disconnect the electrical connector for the tail lights and rear turn signals, and release the wiring from the tie.

27 Unscrew the bolts securing the front and sides of the fender then draw the fender off the bike.

28 Installation is the reverse of removal.

Drifter

29 Remove the seat (see Section 6).

30 Unscrew the bolt on each side at the front.

31 On the left side undo the connector cover screw and remove the cover, then disconnect the tail light and rear turn signal wiring connector.

32 Unscrew the fender stay bolts on each side and draw the fender back off the bike.

33 Installation is the reverse of the removal steps.

Mean Streak

34 Remove the seat (see Section 6).

35 Unscrew the bolts on each side and remove the sub-frame covers.

36 Unscrew the bungee hook bracket bolts on each side and remove the brackets.

37 Release the tail light and rear turn signal wiring connector and disconnect it.

38 Unscrew the bolts securing the front and sides of the fender then draw the fender off the bike.

39 Installation is the reverse of the removal steps.

10 Windshield (Nomad/Classic Tourer) – removal, installation and adjustment

Removal and installation

1 Unscrew the windshield bracket bolts on each side and remove the windshield assembly.

2 Installation is the reverse of removal.

Adjustment

3 Slacken the windshield bracket bolts on each side and the lower shield bolts on the front and move the shields up and down as required – there is around 45 mm of up and down adjustment for the main shield, and the lower shield should be set so the gap between the bottom of it and the headlight is 10 mm whatever the position of the main shield. Make sure the shield brackets are at the same height on each side.

Chapter 9
Electrical system

Contents

Degrees of difficulty

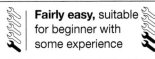

| **Easy,** suitable for novice with little experience | **Fairly easy,** suitable for beginner with some experience | **Fairly difficult,** suitable for competent DIY mechanic | **Difficult,** suitable for experienced DIY mechanic | **Very difficult,** suitable for expert DIY or professional |

Specifications

Battery

VN1500A and B models
  Capacity . . . . 12V, 20Ah (amp-hours), fillable
  Specific gravity. . . . . See Chapter 1
VN1500 Classic and Nomad/Classic Tourer
  Capacity . . . . 12V, 14Ah (amp-hours), maintenance free
All other models
  Type FTZ16-BS
  Capacity . . . . 12V, 18Ah (amp-hours), maintenance free

Charging system

Charging system regulated output
  VN1500A and B models. . . . . 14 volts DC at 6000 rpm
  All other models . . . . 14 to 15 volts DC at 3000 rpm
Alternator un-regulated output
  VN1500A and B models . . . . about 55 volts AC at 3000 rpm
  VN1500 Classic D models . . . . 45 to 65 volts AC at 3000 rpm
  All other models . . . . 60 to 96 volts AC at 3000 rpm
Stator coil resistance . . . . 0.3 to 0.5 ohms

Starter motor

Brush length
  Standard. . . . . 12 mm (15/32 inch)
  Minimum. . . . . 8.5 mm (11/32 inch)
Commutator diameter
  Standard. . . . . 28 mm (1-7/64 inch)
  Minimum. . . . . 27 mm (1-1/16 inch)

Circuit fuse ratings

Main fuse 30A
Circuit fuses (see also illustrations 6.2a and b)
  F1 Ignition. 10A
  F2 Horn. 10A
  F3 Tail 10A
  F4 Head 10A
  F5 Accessory 10A
  F6 Fan
    1500 models. 10A
    1600 models. 15A
  F7 Turn 10A
Fuel injection fuse 15A

Bulb wattage

VN1500A and B models

Headlight . . . . 60/55 watts
City light (where fitted) . . . . 4 watts
Front turn signals
  US, Canada . . . . 23/8 watts
  All others. . . . . 21 watts
Rear turn signals
  US, Canada . . . . 23 watts
  All others. . . . . 21 watts
Speedometer, tachometer lights . . . . 3.4 watts
Indicator lights . . . . 3.0 watts
Tail/brake lights
  US, Canada, ... 27/8 watts
  All others. . . . . 21/5 watts
License plate light (where fitted). . . . . 5 watts

VN1500 Classic

Headlight . . . . 60/55 watts
City light (where fitted) . . . . 4 watts
Front turn signals
  US, Canada . . . . 23/8 watts
  All others. . . . . 21 watts
Rear turn signals
  US, Canada . . . . 23 watts
  All others. . . . . 21 watts
Speedometer lights . . . . 1.7 watts
Indicator lights
  Temperature, oil pressure. . . . . 1.7 watts
  Turn signal . . . . 3.4 watts
  High beam . . . . 3.0 watts
  Neutral . . . . 3.0 watts
Tail/brake lights
  US, Canada
    E1 and E2 models. . . . . 27/8 watts
    E3-on . . . . 21/5 watts
  All others. . . . . 21/5 watts
License plate light (where fitted). . . . . 5 watts

VN1500 Nomad/Classic Tourer

Headlight . . . . 60/55 watts
City light (where fitted) . . . . 4 watts
Front turn signals
  US, Canada . . . . 23/8 watts
  All others. . . . . 21 watts

Bulb wattage (continued)

VN1500 Nomad/Classic Tourer (continued)

Rear turn signals
    US, Canada . . . . 23 watts
    All others. . . . . 21 watts
Speedometer lights . . . . 1.7 watts
Indicator lights
    Temperature, oil pressure . . . . 1.7 watts
    Turn signal . . . . 3.4 watts
    High beam . . . . 3.0 watts
    Neutral . . . . 3.0 watts
Tail/brake lights
    US, Canada
        G1/2 and H1/2 models . . . . 27/8 watts
        G3 models . . . . 21/5 watts
    All others. . . . . 21/5 watts
License plate light (where fitted) . . . . 5 watts

VN1500 Classic FI

Headlight . . . . 60/55 watts
City light (where fitted) . . . . 5 watts
Front turn signals
    US, Canada
        N1 and N2 models . . . . 23/8 watts
        N3-on . . . . 21/5 watts
    All others. . . . . 21 watts
Rear turn signals
    US and Canada N1 and N2 models . . . . 23 watts
    All others. . . . . 21 watts
Instrument lights. . . . . LED
Indicator lights
    Temperature, oil pressure, FI . . . . LED
    Turn signal . . . . 2.0 watts
    High beam . . . . 1.4 watts
    Neutral . . . . 2.0 watts
    Low fuel . . . . 3.0 watts
Tail/brake lights . . . . 21/5 watts
License plate light (where fitted) . . . . 5 watts

VN1500 Nomad/Classic Tourer FI

Headlight . . . . 60/55 watts
City light (where fitted) . . . . 5 watts
Front turn signals
    US, Canada
        L1 and L2 models. . . . . 23/8 watts
        L3-on . . . . 21/5 watts
    All others. . . . . 21 watts
Rear turn signals
    US and Canada L1 and L2 models . . . . 23 watts
    All others. . . . . 21 watts
Instrument lights
    L1 models. . . . . 1.7 watts
    L2-on . . . . LED
Indicator lights
    L1 models
        Temperature, oil pressure, FI . . . . LED
        Turn signal. . . . . 3.4 watts
        High beam . . . . 3.4 watts
        Neutral . . . . 3.4 watts
        Low fuel . . . . 3.0 watts
    L2-on
        Temperature, oil pressure, FI . . . . LED
        Turn signal. . . . . 2.0 watts
        High beam . . . . 1.4 watts
        Neutral . . . . 2.0 watts
        Low fuel . . . . 3.0 watts
Tail/brake lights . . . . 21/5 watts
License plate light (where fitted) . . . . 5 watts

Bulb wattage (continued)

VN1600 Classic and Nomad/Classic Tourer

Headlight	60/55 watts
City light (where fitted)	5 watts
Front turn signals	
US, Canada	21/5 watts
All others	21 watts
Rear turn signals	21 watts
Instrument lights	LED
Indicator lights	
Temperature, oil pressure, low fuel, FI	LED
Turn signal	1.1 watts
High beam	1.1 watts
Neutral	1.1 watts
Tail/brake lights	21/5 watts
License plate light	5 watts

Drifter

Headlight	60/55 watts
City light (where fitted)	5 watts
Front turn signals	
US, Canada	
J1, J2 and R1 models	23/8 watts
R2-on	21/5 watts
All others	21 watts
Rear turn signals	
US and Canada J1, J2 and R1 models	23 watts
All others	21 watts
Instrument lights	
J models	1.7 watts
R models	LED
Indicator lights	
J models	
Temperature, oil pressure, FI	LED
Turn signal	3.4 watts
High beam	3.4 watts
Neutral	3.4 watts
Low fuel	3.0 watts
R models	
Temperature, oil pressure, FI	LED
Turn signal	2.0 watts
High beam	1.4 watts
Neutral	2.0 watts
Low fuel	3.0 watts
Tail/brake lights	21/5 watts
License plate light	5 watts

Mean Streak

Headlight	60/55 watts
City light (where fitted)	5 watts
Front turn signals	
US, Canada	21/5 watts
All others	21 watts
Rear turn signals	21 watts
Instrument lights	1.7 watts
Indicator lights	
Temperature, oil pressure, FI	LED
Turn signal	3.4 watts
High beam	3.4 watts
Neutral	3.4 watts
Low fuel	3.0 watts
Tail/brake lights	21/5 watts
License plate light	5 watts

Torque specifications

Alternator rotor bolt
   VN1500A, B, D, and Classic E1, E2, F1 and F2 models . . . .   59 Nm (43 ft-lbs)
   All other models . . . .   78 Nm (57 ft-lbs)
Alternator cover bolts. . . . .   11 Nm (95 inch-lbs)
Alternator stator screws
   Single stator models. . . . .   13 Nm (113 inch-lbs)
   Twin stator models
      Outer stator. . . . .   13 Nm (113 inch-lbs)
      Inner stator
         VN1500 engines . . . .   13 Nm (113 inch-lbs)
         VN1600 engines . . . .   11 Nm (95 inch-lbs)
Neutral switch. . . . .   15 Nm (11 ft-lbs)
Oil pressure switch. . . . .   15 Nm (11 ft-lbs)
Speed sensor bolt . . . .   10 Nm (87 inch-lbs)

1 General information

The machines covered by this manual are equipped with a 12-volt electrical system with a DC battery that is charged by a three-phase alternator with the permanent magnet rotor mounted on the left-hand end of the crankshaft. On VN1500A, B and Classic D, E1 and F1 models and all Drifter and Mean Streak models the rotor spins around a multi-coil stator in the alternator cover and the output passes to a regulator/rectifier. All other Classic and all Nomad/Classic Tourer models have a double-sided rotor and two stators, with the second mounted on the crankcase, and there are two regulator/rectifiers.

The regulator maintains the charging system output within the specified range to prevent overcharging. The rectifier converts the AC (alternating current) output of the alternator to DC (direct current) to power the lights and other components and to charge the battery.

An electric starter motor is mounted on the front of the engine. The starting system includes the motor, the battery, the starter motor relay, the starter circuit relay (part of the junction box) and the various wires and switches. If the engine stop switch and the ignition switch are both in the ON position, the circuit relay allows the starter motor to operate only if the transmission is in neutral (neutral switch ON) or the clutch lever is pulled to the handlebar (clutch switch ON) and the sidestand is up (sidestand switch ON).
Note: *Keep in mind that electrical parts, once purchased, can't be returned. To avoid unnecessary expense, make very sure the faulty component has been positively identified before buying a replacement part.*

2 Electrical troubleshooting

1 A typical electrical circuit consists of an electrical component, the switches, relays, etc. related to that component and the wiring and connectors that hook the component to both the battery and the frame. To aid in locating a problem in any electrical circuit, wiring diagrams covering all models are included at the end of this Chapter.
2 Before tackling any troublesome electrical circuit, first study the appropriate diagrams thoroughly to get a complete picture of what makes up that individual circuit. Trouble spots, for instance, can often be narrowed down by noting if other components related to that circuit are operating properly or not. If several components or circuits fail at one time, chances are the fault lies in the fuse or ground (earth) connection, as several circuits often are routed through the same fuse and ground connections.
3 Electrical problems often stem from simple causes, such as loose or corroded connections or a blown fuse. Prior to any electrical troubleshooting, always visually check the condition of the fuse, wires and connections in the problem circuit.
4 If testing instruments are going to be utilized, use the diagrams to plan where you will make the necessary connections in order to accurately pinpoint the trouble spot.
5 The best tool for electrical troubleshooting is a digital multimeter **(see illustration)**. Alternative tools include a test light, a continuity tester (which includes a bulb, battery and set of test leads) and a jumper wire, preferably with a circuit breaker incorporated, which can be used to bypass electrical components **(see illustrations)**. Specific checks described later in this Chapter may also require an ohmmeter.
6 Voltage checks should be performed if

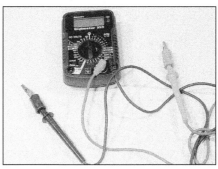

2.5a A digital multimeter can be used for all electrical tests

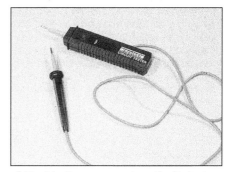

2.5b A battery-powered continuity tester

2.5c A simple test light is useful for voltage tests

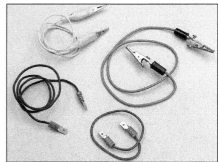

2.5d A selection of insulated jumper wires

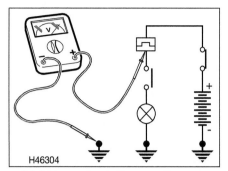

2.6 Voltage check. Connect the meter positive probe to the component and the negative probe to earth

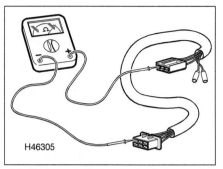

2.9 Wiring continuity check. Connect the meter probes across each end of the same wire

Removal and installation

1 Make sure the ignition is switched OFF. On VN1500A and B models remove the left side cover (see Chapter 8). On all other models remove the seat (the front seat on dual seat models) (see Chapter 8).

2 Unscrew the negative (–) terminal bolt first – where fitted lift up the black insulating cover to access it, then unscrew the bolt and disconnect the lead from the battery **(see illustration)**. Lift up the red insulating cover to access the positive (+) terminal, then unscrew the bolt and disconnect the lead.

3 Disconnect and/or move aside any wiring and connectors that sit on top of the battery.

4 Remove the battery retaining strap or bracket according to model – the bracket is secured by one or two bolts, again according to model **(see illustration)**.

5 Lift the battery from the bike **(see illustration)**.

6 On installation, clean the battery terminals and lead ends with a wire brush, fine sandpaper or steel wool. Reconnect the leads, connecting the positive (+) terminal first. Fit the insulating cover(s).

a circuit is not functioning properly **(see illustration)**. Connect one lead of a test light or voltmeter to either the negative battery terminal or a known good ground (earth). Connect the other lead to a connector in the circuit being tested, preferably nearest to the battery or fuse. If the bulb lights, voltage is reaching that point, which means the part of the circuit between that connector and the battery is problem-free. Continue checking the remainder of the circuit in the same manner. When you reach a point where no voltage is present, the problem lies between there and the last good test point. Most of the time the problem is due to a loose connection. Keep in mind that some circuits only receive voltage when the ignition key is in the ON position.

7 One method of finding short circuits is to remove the fuse and connect a test light or voltmeter in its place to the fuse terminals. There should be no load in the circuit. Move the wiring harness from side-to-side while watching the test light. If the bulb lights, there is a short to ground (earth) somewhere in that area, probably where insulation has rubbed off a wire. The same test can be performed on other components in the circuit, including the switch.

8 A ground (earth) check should be done to see if a component is grounded properly. Disconnect the battery and connect one lead of a self-powered test light (continuity tester) to a known good ground (earth). Connect the other lead to the wire or ground connection being tested. If the bulb lights, the ground is

good. If the bulb does not light, the ground is not good.

9 A continuity check is performed to see if a circuit, section of circuit or individual component is capable of passing electricity through it **(see illustration)**. Disconnect the battery and connect one lead of a self-powered test light (continuity tester) to one end of the circuit being tested and the other lead to the other end of the circuit. If the bulb lights, there is continuity, which means the circuit is passing electricity through it properly. Switches can be checked in the same way.

10 Remember that all electrical circuits are designed to conduct electricity from the battery, through the wires, switches, relays, etc. to the electrical component (light bulb, motor, etc.). From there it is directed to the frame (ground/earth) where it is passed back to the battery. Electrical problems are basically an interruption in the flow of electricity from the battery or back to it.

---

3 Battery – removal and installation, inspection and maintenance

> ⚠ **Warning: Remember, the gas escaping from a charging battery is explosive, so keep open flames and sparks well away from the area. If the gas ignites, the entire battery can explode and spray acid. Also, the electrolyte is extremely corrosive and will damage anything it comes in contact with.**

> **HAYNES HiNT** *Battery corrosion can be kept to a minimum by applying a layer of battery terminal grease or petroleum jelly (Vaseline) to the terminals after the leads have been connected. DO NOT use a mineral based grease.*

7 Install the side cover or seat(s) (see Chapter 8).

Inspection and maintenance

8 VN1500A and B models are fitted with a standard type battery on which regular checks of the electrolyte level and specific gravity should be made – refer to Chapter 1 for details. Also look for sediment, which is the result of sulfation caused by low electrolyte levels, inside the bottom of the battery. These deposits will cause internal short circuits, which can quickly discharge the battery.

9 All other models are fitted with a maintenance free (MF) battery that does not require electrolyte level checks and topping up. However, the following checks should still

3.2 Disconnect the negative (-) lead first, then the positive (+) lead (arrowed)

3.4 Battery retaining bracket bolts (arrowed)

3.5 Carefully lift the battery out – it is quite heavy

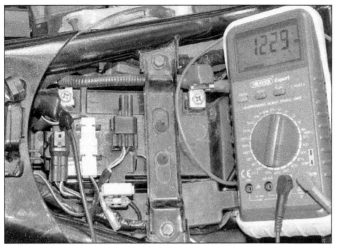

3.14 Checking battery voltage – connect the meter as shown

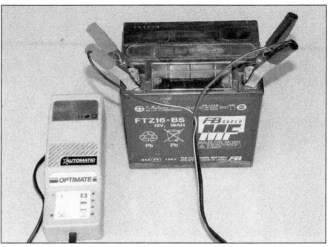

4.13 Battery connected to a charger

be performed. **Note:** *Do not attempt to remove the battery caps to check the electrolyte level or battery specific gravity. Removal will damage the caps, resulting in electrolyte leakage and battery damage.*

10 Check the battery terminals and leads are tight and free of corrosion. If corrosion is evident, clean the terminals as described in Step 6, then protect them from further corrosion (see **Haynes Hint**).

11 Keep the battery case clean to prevent current leakage, which can discharge the battery over a period of time (especially when it sits unused). Wash the outside of the case with a solution of baking soda and water. Rinse the battery thoroughly, then dry it.

12 Look for cracks in the case and replace the battery with a new one if any are found. If acid has been spilled on the frame or battery box, neutralise it with a baking soda and water solution, dry it thoroughly, then touch up any damaged paint.

13 If the motorcycle sits unused for long periods of time, disconnect the leads from the battery terminals, negative (–) terminal first. Refer to Section 4 and charge the battery once every month to six weeks.

14 Check the state of charge of the battery by measuring the voltage present at the battery terminals. Connect the voltmeter positive (+) probe to the battery positive (+) terminal, and the negative (–) probe to the battery negative (–) terminal **(see illustration)**. When fully-charged there should be 12.8 to 13.2 volts present. If the voltage falls much below this remove the battery (see above), and recharge it as described below in Section 4.

4 Battery – charging

1 If the machine sits idle for extended periods or if the charging system malfunctions, the battery can be charged from an external source. Charging procedures for the fillable battery

used on VN1500A and B models are different from the procedures for maintenance-free batteries, which are used on all other models.

Fillable batteries – VN1500A and B models

2 To properly charge the battery, you will need a charger of the correct rating, an hydrometer, a clean rag and a syringe for adding distilled water to the battery cells.

3 The maximum charging rate for any battery is 1/10 of the rated amp/hour capacity. So the maximum charging rate for a 20 amp/hour battery would be 2.0 amps. Few owners will have access to an expensive current controlled charger, so if a normal domestic charger is used check that after a possible initial peak, the charge rate falls to a safe level. If the battery becomes hot during charging **stop**. Further charging will cause damage. Note that there are many bike-specific chargers available from good suppliers that are designed for the maintenance and recovery of motorcycle batteries. They are a worthwhile investment, especially if the bike is not used over winter. Follow the manufacturer's instructions.

4 Do not allow the battery to be subjected to a so-called quick charge (high rate of charge over a short period of time) unless you are prepared to buy a new battery. The heat will warp the plates inside the battery until they touch each other, causing a short circuit.

5 When charging the battery, always remove it from the machine and be sure to check the electrolyte level before hooking up the charger. Add distilled water to any cells that are low.

6 Loosen the cell caps, hook up the battery charger leads (red to positive, black to negative), cover the top of the battery with a clean rag, then, and only then, plug in the battery charger.

7 Allow the battery to charge until the specific gravity is as specified (refer to Chapter 1 for specific gravity checking procedures). The charger must be unplugged and disconnected from the battery when making specific gravity

checks. If the battery overheats or gases excessively, the charging rate is too high. Either disconnect the charger or lower the charging rate to prevent damage to the battery.

8 If one or more of the cells do not show an increase in specific gravity after a long slow charge, or if the battery as a whole does not seem to want to take a charge, it is time for a new battery.

9 When the battery is fully charged, unplug the charger first, then disconnect the leads from the battery. Fit the cell caps and wipe any electrolyte off the outside of the battery case.

> ⚠ *Warning: Remember, the gas escaping from a charging battery is explosive, so keep open flames and sparks well away from the area. If the gas ignites, the entire battery can explode and spray acid. Also, the electrolyte is extremely corrosive and will damage anything it comes in contact with.*

Maintenance-free batteries – all other models

10 Charging a maintenance-free battery requires a digital voltmeter and a variable-voltage charger with a built-in ammeter OR a motorcycle-specific charger designed for the maintenance and recovery of motorcycle batteries, in particular catering for the requirements of heavily discharged MF batteries. The latter is a worthwhile investment, especially if the bike is not used over winter.

11 When charging the battery, always remove it from the machine.

12 Connect a digital voltmeter between the battery terminals and measure the voltage. If terminal voltage is 12.6 volts or higher, the battery does not need charging. If it's lower, recharge the battery.

13 Hook up the battery charger leads (positive lead to battery positive terminal and negative lead to battery negative terminal, then, and only then, plug in the battery charger **(see illustration)**.

14 If using a motorcycle-specific charger, the battery's state of charge will be indicated on

5.1a Junction box fuses – remove the cover for access

5.1b Main fuse (arrowed) – displace the relay and disconnect the wiring connector for access

the charger and the display will indicate when the battery is fully charged.

15 If you have a current-controlled battery charger, set the charge rate to 1/10 of the battery's rated amp/hour capacity, thus for an 18 amp/hour battery the charge rate would be 1.8 amps for 10 hours. If the battery is charged at a higher rate, it could be damaged. If a normal domestic charger is used, check that after a possible initial peak, the charge rate falls to a safe level. If the battery becomes hot during charging **stop**. Further charging will cause damage.

16 Wait 30 minutes after switching off the charger and disconnecting it, then measure voltage between the battery terminals. If it's 12.6 volts or higher, the battery is fully charged. If it's between 12.0 and 12.6 volts, continue charging the battery. If the battery will not accept a charge, or discharges when in use on the motorcycle it should be replaced.

5 Fuses – check and replacement

1 All fuses except the main fuse, and the fuel injection system fuse (where fitted), are fitted in the junction box, located under the seat (front seat on dual seat models) on VN1500A and B and Classic and Nomad/Classic Tourer

5.1c Fuel injection system fuse (arrowed) and its spare

models (i.e. all carburetor models), and behind the right side cover on all others **(see illustration)**. The fuses are protected by a plastic cover, which snaps into place. This box contains the fuses (and spares) which protect the fan, headlight, tail light, turn signals, horn, ignition and accessory circuit wiring. The main fuse is fitted in the starter motor relay, located under the seat (front seat on dual seat models) on VN1500A and B models, and behind the coolant reservoir (behind the right side cover) on all others **(see illustration)** (see Section 26). On fuel injection models the system is protected by its own fuse fitted in a separate holder under the front seat, on top of the battery on Classic FI and Nomad/Classic Tourer FI models, to the rear of the battery on Drifter models, and to the left side of the battery on all others **(see illustration)**.

2 The fuses can be removed and checked visually – if you can't pull the fuse out with your fingertips, use a pair of suitable pliers. A blown fuse is easily identified by a break in the element **(see illustration)**. Each fuse is clearly marked with its rating and must only be replaced by a fuse of the correct rating. A spare fuse of each rating is housed with the fuses in the junction box, or in the case of the fuel injection system fuse in the fuse holder **(see illustrations 5.1a and c)**. If a spare fuse is used, always replace it with a new one so

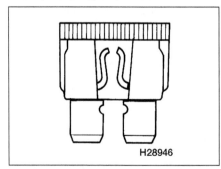

5.2 A blown fuse can be identified by a break in its element

that a spare of each rating is carried on the bike at all times.

3 If a fuse blows, be sure to check the wiring harnesses very carefully for evidence of a short circuit. Look for bare wires and chafed, melted or burned insulation. If a fuse is replaced before the cause is located, the new fuse will blow immediately.

4 Never, under any circumstances, use a higher rated fuse or bridge the fuse block terminals, as damage to the electrical system – including melted wires, ruined components, and fire – could result.

5 Occasionally a fuse will blow or cause an open circuit for no obvious reason. Corrosion of the fuse ends and fuse block terminals may occur and cause poor fuse contact. If this happens, remove the corrosion with a wire brush or emery paper, then spray the fuse end and terminals with electrical contact cleaner.

6 Junction box – check

1 In addition to serving as the fuse block, the junction box is used to house the starter circuit relay (not the starter motor relay), the headlight relay (where fitted), on VN1500A and B models except A9-on the cooling fan relay, and all related diodes. Neither the relays or the diodes are replaceable individually. If one of them fails, the junction box must be replaced with a new one. The headlight relay is fitted to US and Canada models only on VN1500A and B models, to US, Canada and Australia models across the rest of the VN1500 model range, and to all VN1600 models.

2 In addition to the relay checks, the fuse circuits and diode circuits should be checked also, to rule out the possibility of an open circuit condition or blown diode within the junction block as the cause of an electrical problem. Schematics of the junction box and connector terminal identification can be found in the accompanying illustrations **(see illustrations)**.

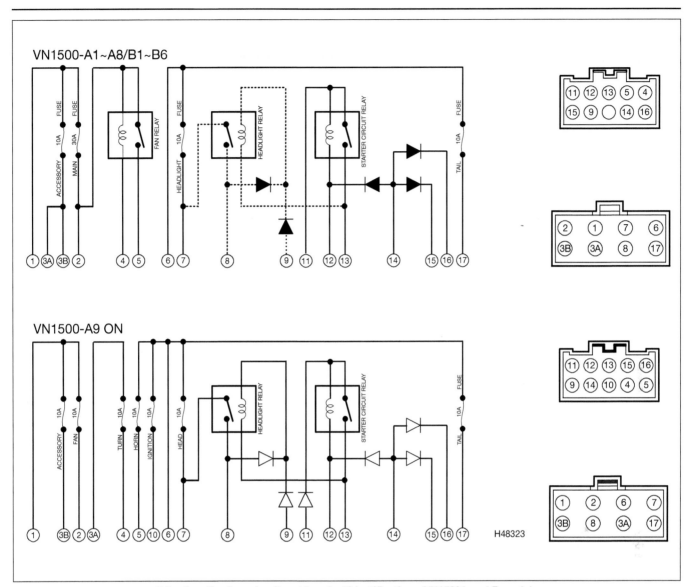

6.2a Junction box circuit and terminal identification – VN1500A and B models

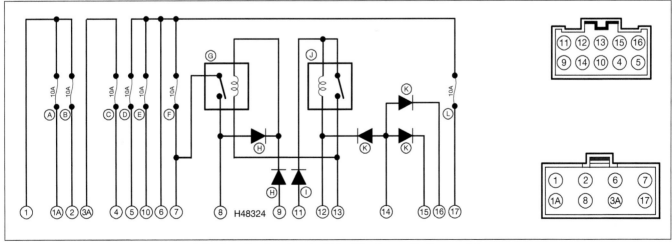

6.2b Junction box terminal identification – all other models

Removal and installation

3 The junction box is located under the seat (front seat on dual seat models) on VN1500A and B and Classic and Nomad/Classic Tourer models (i.e. all carburetor models), and behind the right side cover on all others **(see illustration)**. Remove the seat(s) or side cover (see Chapter 8).

4 Release the junction box and disconnect the wiring connectors from it **(see illustration)**.

Fuse circuit check

5 Remove the junction box (Steps 3 and 4).

6 If the terminals are dirty or bent, clean and straighten them. Using the relevant accompanying table and referring to the relevant junction box circuit diagram for terminal identification, check the continuity across the terminals indicated with an ohmmeter – some should have no resistance and others should have infinite resistance.

VN1500A and B models

METER CONNECTION	METER READING (ohms)
1 – 2	zero
1 – 3B	zero
3A – 4	zero
6 – 5	zero
6 – 7	zero
6 – 10	zero
6 – 17	zero
1 – 7	infinity
1 – 3A	infinity
3A – 8	infinity
8 – 17	infinity

All other models

METER CONNECTION	METER READING (ohms)
1 – 1A	zero
1 – 2	zero
3A – 4	zero
6 – 5	zero
6 – 7	zero
6 – 10	zero
6 – 17	zero
1A – 8	infinity
2 – 8	infinity
3A – 8	infinity
6 – 2	infinity
6 – 3A	infinity
17 – 3A	infinity

7 If the resistance values are not as specified, replace the junction box with a new one.

Diode circuit check

8 Remove the junction box (Steps 3 and 4).

9 Using an ohmmeter, check the resistance across the specified pairs of terminals for your model, then write down the readings:

a) Terminals 13 and 8 (US, Canada and Australia 1500 models (except A and B in Australia); all1600 models)

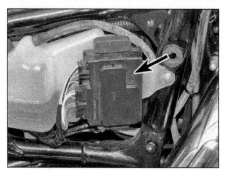

6.3 Junction box (arrowed)

6.4 Release the box from its rubber holder

b) Terminals 13 and 9 (US, Canada and Australia 1500 models (except A and B in Australia); all 1600 models)

c) Terminals 12 and 11 (except VN1500A1 to A8 and B models)

d) Terminals 12 and 14 (all models)

e) Terminals 15 and 14 (all models)

f) Terminals 16 and 14 (all models)

10 Now, reverse the ohmmeter leads and check the resistances again, writing down the readings. The resistances should be low in one direction and at least ten times as high in the other direction. If the readings for any pair of terminals are low or high in both directions, a diode is defective and the junction box must be replaced with a new one.

Relay checks

11 Remove the junction box (Steps 3 and 4).

12 Using an ohmmeter, check the continuity across the terminals indicated in the relevant accompanying tables for your model, first with no battery connected and then with one connected.

13 If the junction box fails any of these tests, it must be replaced with a new one.

VN1500A and B

with battery disconnected

	METER CONNECTION	METER READING (OHMS)
Fan relay	2 – 5	infinity
	4 – 5	infinity
Headlight relay	7 – 8	infinity
	7 – 13	infinity
Starter circuit relay	11 – 13	infinity
	12 – 13	infinity

with battery connected

	METER CONNECTION	BATTERY CONNECTION	METER READING (OHMS)
Fan relay	2 – 5	2 – 4	zero
Headlight relay	7 – 8	9 – 13	zero
Starter circuit relay	11 – 13	11 – 12	zero

All other models

with battery disconnected

	METER CONNECTION	METER READING (OHMS)
Headlight relay	7 – 8	infinity
	7 – 13	infinity
	13 (+) – 9 (-)	not infinity (reading varies)
Starter circuit relay	9 – 11	infinity
	12 – 13	infinity
	13 (+) – 11 (-)	infinity
	12 (+) – 11 (-)	not infinity (reading varies)

with battery connected

	METER CONNECTION	BATTERY CONNECTION	METER READING (OHMS)
Headlight relay	7 – 8	9 – 13	zero
Starter circuit relay	13 (+) – 11 (-)	11 – 12	not infinity (reading varies)

8.1a Undo the screw on each side . . .

8.1b . . . and displace the beam unit

8.2 Disconnect the wiring connector(s)

7 Lighting system – check

Note: *Refer to electrical system fault finding in Section 2, to the wiring diagram for your model at the end of this Chapter, and to the relevant Section for component and connector access information and illustrations.*

1 The battery provides power for operation of the headlight, city light (where fitted), tail light, brake light, license plate light (where fitted), and instrument cluster lights. If none of the lights operate, always check battery voltage before proceeding. Low battery voltage indicates either a faulty battery, low battery electrolyte level (fillable batteries) or a defective charging system. Refer to Chapter 1 for battery checks and Sections 29 through 33 for charging system tests. Also, check the fuses (Section 5) – if there is more than one problem at the same time, it is likely to be a fault relating to a multi-function component, such as one of the fuses governing more than one circuit, or the ignition switch. When checking for a blown filament in a bulb, it is advisable to back up a visual check with a continuity test of the filament as it is not always apparent that a bulb has blown.

Headlight

2 If the headlight does not work, check the fuse first (see Section 5), then unplug the electrical connector for the headlight and use jumper wires to connect the bulb directly to the battery terminals. If the light comes on, the problem lies in the wiring or one of the switches in the circuit. Refer to Sections 19 and 20 for the switch testing procedures, and also the wiring diagrams at the end of this Chapter. Where fitted, also check the headlight relay in the junction box (Section 6).

3 US and Canadian VN1500A and B models use an additional relay in the system, called the reserve lighting unit. On these models, the headlight doesn't come on when the ignition switch is first turned on, but comes on when the starter button is pressed and stays on until the ignition is turned off. The light will go out whenever the starter is operated after the engine has stalled (this prevents excessive strain on the battery). This component is checked by process of elimination – if all other parts and circuits in the lighting system are good, the reserve lighting device is defective. For this reason, it's a good idea to have a Kawasaki dealer check the lighting system before replacing the reserve lighting device. Refer to the wiring diagram at the end of this manual for details of the system.

Tail light/license plate/city lights

4 If one of the lights fails to work, check the bulb and the bulb terminals first, then check for battery voltage at the red wire to the light. If voltage is present, check the black/yellow wire for an open or poor connection to ground (earth).

5 If no voltage is indicated, check the wiring between the tail light, license plate light or city light as appropriate and the ignition switch, then check the switch itself.

Brake light

6 See Section 14 for the brake light circuit checking procedure.

Instrument lights and warning lights

7 See under the relevant Section in this Chapter according to the light and circuit in question, or to Chapter 3 and 4A or 4B for the temperature and fuel warning lights respectively.

Turn signals

8 See Section 13.

8 Headlight and city light bulbs – replacement

1 Undo the screw on each side of the headlight **(see illustration)**. Pull the beam unit out from the bottom, noting how it locates at the top **(see illustration)**.

2 Disconnect the headlight wiring connector, and where fitted the city light wiring connector **(see illustration)**. The beam unit is now free and can be removed to a bench.

3 To replace the headlight bulb remove the dust cover **(see illustration)**. Release the retaining clip and swing it out of the way **(see illustration)**. Remove the bulb, noting how it seats **(see illustration)**.

8.3a Remove the cover . . .

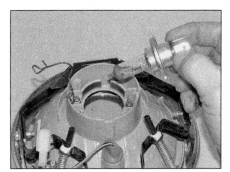

8.3b . . . then release the bulb holder . . .

8.3c . . . and remove the bulb

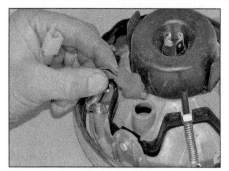

8.4a Pull the bulb holder out . . .

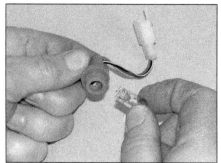

8.4b . . . then pull the bulb out

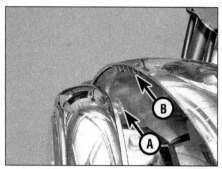

8.5 Make sure the tab (A) on the top of the beam unit locates behind the rib (B) inside the shell

4 To replace the city light bulb pull the holder out of the beam unit, then pull the bulb out of its holder **(see illustrations)**.

5 When fitting the new bulb, reverse the removal procedure. Be sure not to touch the headlight bulb with your fingers – oil from your skin will cause the bulb to overheat and fail prematurely. If you do touch the bulb, wipe it off with a clean rag dampened with rubbing alcohol. Make sure the clip is securely seated and the wiring securely connected. Fit the dust cover with the TOP mark at the top. Make sure the headlight rim screw holes are correctly aligned and its tab locates correctly in the shell **(see illustration)**.

9 Headlight assembly – removal and installation

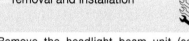

1 Remove the headlight beam unit (see Section 8, Steps 1 and 2).

9.2 Free the wiring from any clamps

9.3a Unscrew the nuts or bolts according to model (Mean Streak shown)

2 Release the wiring from any clamps inside the headlight shell **(see illustration)**.
3 Unscrew the headlight shell mounting bolts and/or nuts, according to model, then displace the headlight shell and feed the wiring out the hole(s) in the back, noting its routing **(see illustrations)**.
4 Installation is the reverse of removal. Adjust the headlight aim (see Section 10).

10 Headlight aim – check and adjustment

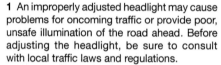

1 An improperly adjusted headlight may cause problems for oncoming traffic or provide poor, unsafe illumination of the road ahead. Before adjusting the headlight, be sure to consult with local traffic laws and regulations.
2 The headlight beam can be adjusted both vertically and horizontally. Before performing the adjustment, make sure the fuel tank has at least a half tank of fuel, and have an assistant sit on the seat.

VN1500A and B models

3 To adjust the horizontal position of the beam, turn the adjuster screw on the upper right side of the headlight rim as required until the beam points straight-ahead. Turning clockwise moves the beam to the left; turning counterclockwise moves the beam to the right.
4 To adjust the vertical position of the beam, turn the adjuster screw on the lower left side of the headlight rim as required until the beam

9.3b Feed the wiring out the back of the shell and remove it

is at the correct height. Turning clockwise moves the beam up; turning counterclockwise moves the beam down.

All other VN1500 models, all Mean Streak models

5 To adjust the horizontal position of the beam, turn the adjuster screw on the lower left side of the headlight rim as required until the beam points straight-ahead. Turning clockwise moves the beam to the left; turning counterclockwise moves the beam to the right.
6 To adjust the vertical position of the beam, turn the adjuster screw on the lower right side of the headlight rim as required until the beam is at the correct height **(see illustration)**. Turning clockwise moves the beam up; turning counterclockwise moves the beam down.

VN1600 models except Mean Streak

7 To adjust the horizontal position of the beam, turn the adjuster screw on the lower right side of the headlight rim as required until the beam points straight-ahead. Turning clockwise moves the beam to the left; turning counterclockwise moves the beam to the right.
8 To adjust the vertical position of the beam, turn the adjuster screw on the lower left side of the headlight rim as required until the beam is at the correct height. Turning clockwise moves the beam up; turning counterclockwise moves the beam down.

10.6 Headlight beam adjuster screw (arrowed)

11.1 Undo the screw(s) and remove the lens

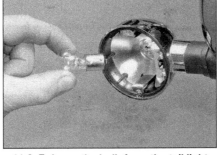

11.2 Release the bulb from the tail light

11.3 Check the rubber seal

11 Turn signal, tail/brake light and license plate light bulbs – replacement

1 Undo screw(s) securing the lens, noting any washer(s), and take off the lens **(see illustration)**.
2 Push the bulb in and turn it counterclockwise (anti-clockwise) to remove it **(see illustration)**. Check the socket terminals for corrosion and clean them if necessary. Line up the pins on the new bulb with the slots in the socket, push in and turn the bulb clockwise until it locks in place. It is a good idea to use a paper towel or dry cloth when handling the new bulb to prevent injury if the bulb should break and to increase bulb life.
3 Make sure the rubber seal is in good condition and correctly seated **(see illustration)** – fit a new one if necessary.
4 Position the lens on the reflector, making sure any tab locates correctly, and fit the screw(s) with any washer(s) previously removed – do not to overtighten the screw(s) as it is easy to crack the lens or strip the threads.

12 Turn signal assemblies – removal and installation

1 The turn signal assemblies can be removed individually in the event of damage or failure.

2 To remove a turn signal assembly, first follow the wiring harness from the turn signal to its electrical connectors, inside the headlight on the front and under the seat on the back – refer to Section 8 or Chapter 8 accordingly. Mark the wires with pieces of numbered tape then unplug the electrical connectors.
3 The front turn signals are secured either around the fork or to a bracket **(see illustrations)**. Ascertain whether you need to remove just the turn signal stem, or whether you need to remove its mounting assembly as well, then undo the relevant fasteners as required and remove the stem or assembly.
4 The rear turn signals are secured either directly to the rear fender or to a bracket mounted on the fender **(see illustration)**. Ascertain whether you need to remove just the turn signal stem, or whether where applicable you need to remove its mounting assembly as well, then undo the relevant fasteners as required and remove the stem or assembly.
5 Note the fitting of any washers, collars and damping rubbers as fitted according to model. Make sure any rubbers are in good condition, or if not replace them with new ones.
6 Installation is the reverse of the removal procedure.

13 Turn signal circuit – check

1 Most turn signal problems are the result of a burned out bulb or corroded socket. This is

especially true when the turn signals function on one side (although possibly too quickly), but fail to work on the other side. If this is the case, first check the bulbs, the sockets and the wiring connectors. If all the turn signals fail to work, check the fuse (see Section 5, except VN1500A1 to A8 and all B models), then the relay on VN1500A and B models and Classic D, E1 and F1 models (Step 2) or self cancelling system components on all other models (Step 3-on). If it is good, the problem lies in the wiring or connectors, or the switch.
2 On VN1500A and B models remove the left side cover (see Chapter 8). On Classic D, E1 and F1 models remove the right side cover (see Chapter 8), then displace and support the coolant reservoir (see Chapter 3). Disconnect the relay wiring connector. Check for battery voltage at the orange/green wire terminal on the loom side of the connector with the ignition ON. If no voltage is present, check the wiring from the relay to the ignition switch for continuity. If voltage is present, short between the orange/green and green wire terminals on the connector using a jumper wire. Turn the ignition ON and operate the turn signal switch, first in one direction, then the other. If the turn signal lights come on in each direction (they won't flash), the switch and light side of the circuit is confirmed good and the relay is confirmed faulty. If the lights do not come on the problem lies in the wiring or connectors, or the switch. Refer to Section 20 for the switch testing procedures, and also to the wiring diagrams at the end of this Chapter.

12.3a To remove the fork-mounted turn signal unscrew the nut and withdraw the bolt . . .

12.3b . . . then expand the holder and remove the signal

12.4 Fender-mounted turn signal nut (arrowed)

13.3 Turn signal control unit (arrowed)

3 All models except VN1500A and B models and Classic D, E1 and F1 models have self canceling turn signals. The circuit comprises the distance sensor in the speedometer and the turn signal control unit. On VN1500 Classic E2-on and F2 models and on VN1500 Nomad/Classic Tourer models remove the fuel tank (see Chapter 4A). On all other models (i.e. all models with fuel injection) remove the right side cover (see Chapter 8), then displace and support the coolant reservoir (see Chapter 3). Disconnect the turn signal control unit wiring connector **(see illustration)**. Check for battery voltage at the orange/green wire terminal on the loom side of the connector with the ignition ON. If no voltage is present, check the wiring from the relay to the ignition switch via the junction box for continuity. If voltage is present, short between the orange/green and orange wire terminals on the connector using a jumper wire. Turn the ignition ON and operate the turn signal switch, first in one direction, then the other. If the turn signal lights come on in each direction (they won't flash), the switch and light side of the circuit is confirmed good, and the fault could be in the control unit. If the lights do not come on the problem lies in the wiring or connectors, or the switch. Refer to Section 20 for the switch testing procedures, and also to the wiring diagrams at the end of this Chapter.

4 Next check the distance sensor. On models with a speedometer cable disconnect the cable from the front wheel. Connect an ohmmeter across the light blue and black/yellow wire terminals on the harness side of the control unit connector. Have an assistant

turn the speedometer inner cable slowly while you observe the meter reading. If the sensor is functioning correctly, the ohmmeter should show continuity four times per wheel revolution. If it doesn't check the wiring between the control unit and the speedometer, and check the cable and the speedometer.

5 On models without a speedometer cable raise the rear wheel off the ground using an auxiliary stand – tie the front brake to the handlebar. Connect a voltmeter to the light blue and black/yellow wire terminals in control unit connector with it connected. Turn the ignition on and have an assistant turn the rear wheel slowly while you observe the meter reading. If the sensor is functioning correctly, the voltmeter reading should fluctuate between 0.5 and 12 volts as the wheel is turned. If it does the distance sensor is proved good. If it doesn't check the wiring between the sensor and control unit, then check the sensor itself.

6 There is no test procedure for the turn signal control unit; if the fault cannot be traced to the distance sensor, switch or wiring and connectors, the control unit should be replaced with a new one.

14 Brake light switches –
check and replacement

Circuit check

1 Before checking the brake light circuit, check the fuse (see Section 5).

2 Using a test light (or voltmeter) connected to a good ground (earth), check for voltage at the brown (VN1500A and B) or red/blue (all other models) wire terminal in the electrical connector to the brake light switch. If there's no voltage present, check the wire between the switch and the junction box (see the wiring diagrams at the end of this manual).

3 If voltage is available, touch the probe of the test light to the other terminal of the switch, then pull the brake lever or depress the brake pedal – if the test light doesn't light up, replace the switch with a new one.

4 If the test light does light, check the wiring between the switch and the brake lights (see the wiring diagrams at the end of this manual).

Switch replacement

Brake lever switch

5 Disconnect the electrical connectors from the switch **(see illustration)**.

6 Remove the mounting screw **(see illustration)** and detach the switch from the brake lever bracket/front master cylinder.

7 Installation is the reverse of the removal procedure. The brake lever switch isn't adjustable.

Brake pedal switch

8 Locate the switch at the brake pedal, follow its wiring harness to the electrical connector and disconnect it **(see illustration)**.

9 Where necessary for access, remove the footpeg or board bracket from the motorcycle (see Chapter 8).

10 Unhook the switch spring. Loosen the adjuster nut, compress the retainer prongs and remove the switch from the bracket.

11 Install the switch by reversing the removal procedure.

12 Adjust the switch by following the procedure described in Chapter 1.

15 Instrument and warning
light housings – removal and
installation

VN1500A and B models

Speedometer housing

1 Remove the headlight (see Section 9).

2 Unscrew the speedometer cable knurled nut from the speedometer and pull the speedometer cable free.

3 Unscrew the speedometer mounting bolts and remove the speedometer.

4 Installation is the reverse of removal.

Fuel gauge housing – VN1500A

5 Unscrew the bolt securing the front of the instrument housing to the tank. Lift the housing up and pull it forward to free it from the tab at the back

6 Disconnect the fuel gauge wiring connector.

7 Installation is the reverse of removal. Make sure the rubber seal for the housing rim is in good condition and correctly fitted.

14.5 Disconnect the wiring connectors ...

14.6 ... then undo the screw (arrowed) and remove the switch

14.8 Rear brake light switch (arrowed)

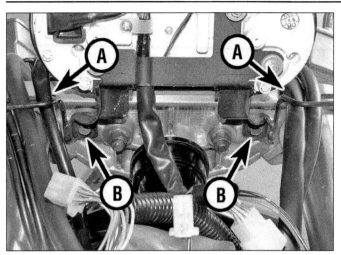

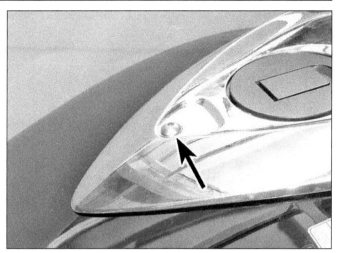

15.24 Free the cables, hose and wiring from the guides (A), then unscrew the bolts (B) and remove the instrument housing

15.26 Unscrew the bolt (arrowed) . . .

Warning light housings

8 Remove the speedometer housing, and on A models the turn signals

9 Unscrew the housing bolts and take the housing off.

10 Installation is the reverse of removal.

VN1500 Classic, Nomad/Classic Tourer, Nomad/Classic Tourer FI L1 models, Drifter J models

11 Unscrew the housing mounting bolt.

12 Push the housing forward to disengage the tab on the housing from the tank.

13 Lift the housing up. Disconnect the wiring connectors and unscrew the speedometer cable knurled nut. Pull the speedometer cable free of the speedometer and lift the housing off.

14 Installation is the reverse of removal. Make sure the rubber damper for the locating tab is in good condition and correctly fitted.

VN1500 Classic FI, Nomad/ Classic Tourer FI L2-on models, Drifter R models

15 Unscrew the housing cover bolt.

16 Lift the back of the cover then push it forward and remove it.

17 Lift the back of the instrument housing up

off its rear locating peg then push it forward off the front pegs. Pull the rubber boot off the wiring connector and disconnect it.

18 Installation is the reverse of removal. Make sure the rubber grommets are in good condition and correctly fitted.

VN1600 Classic and Nomad/ Classic Tourer

19 Undo the housing cover screws and remove the cover.

20 Disconnect the instrument and ignition switch wiring connectors.

21 Unscrew the bolts at the front and remove the instrument assembly from the tank.

22 Installation is the reverse of removal.

Mean Streak

Instrument housing

23 Remove the headlight beam unit (see Section 8). Free the instrument wiring from the clamp and disconnect the connectors (see illustration 9.2). Feed the wiring out the back of the headlight shell.

24 Free the cables, hose and wiring from the guides that are part of the instrument bracket (see illustration). Unscrew the instrument bracket bolts and remove the housing.

25 Installation is the reverse of removal.

Warning light housing

26 Make sure the key is not in the ignition switch. Unscrew the housing cover bolt (see illustration).

27 Lift the back of the cover then pull it back to free the grommet from the peg, lift it up and disconnect the wiring connector (see illustration).

28 Installation is the reverse of removal. Make sure the rubber grommets is in good condition and correctly fitted (see illustration).

16 Meters and gauges, speedometer cable and speed sensor – check and replacement

Check

Fuel gauge (if equipped)

1 Refer to Chapter 4A or 4B.

Speedometer – cable actuated

2 On VN1500A and B models, Classic, Nomad/Classic Tourer, Nomad/Classic Tourer FI L1 models, and Drifter J models the speedometer is driven by a cable running off a drive unit on the front wheel.

3 First check the cable is not broken or disconnected, and its drive unit on the front wheel is working correctly. If all is good, take the instrument to a Kawasaki dealer service department or other qualified repair shop for diagnosis.

Speedometer – electronic

4 On VN1500 Classic FI, Nomad/Classic Tourer FI L2-on models, VN1600 Classic and Nomad/Classic Tourer, Drifter R models and Mean Streak the speedometer is electronic and gets its signals from the speed sensor mounted on the left side of the engine. Special equipment is required to test both the speedometer and the sensor. Before taking them to a dealer make sure the wiring and connectors are all good.

15.27 . . . then displace the housing and disconnect the wiring connector

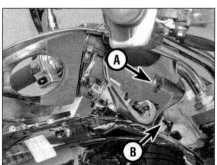

15.28 Check the grommet (A) and make sure it locates over the peg (B)

16.10a Back cover screws (arrowed)

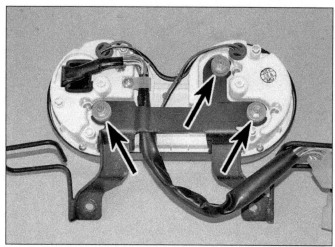

16.10b Unscrew the nuts (arrowed) and detach the bracket

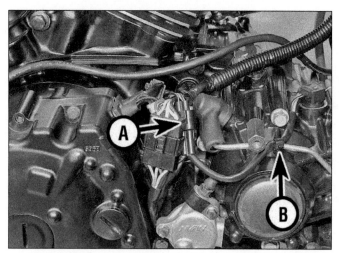

16.16 Disconnect the connector (A) and release the tie (B)

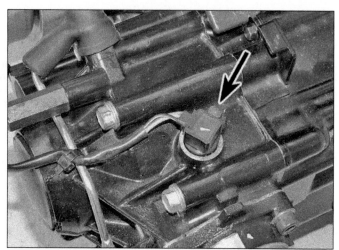

16.17 Unscrew the bolt (arrowed) and remove the sensor

Meter/gauge replacement

5 Remove the housing (see Section 15).
6 On VN1500A and B models undo the trip reset knob screw and pull the knob off. Undo the screws and remove the meter shroud. Pull the bulbholders out. Remove the rubber seal. To remove the fuel gauge on A models mark the location of each wire, then undo the screws and detach them. Pull the bulb holder out. Unscrew the nuts and remove the gauge. Remove the rubber seal.
7 On VN1500 Classic, Nomad/Classic Tourer, Nomad/Classic Tourer FI L1 models, and Drifter J models, undo the trip reset knob screw and pull the knob off. Unscrew the nuts and remove the meter. Mark the location of each wire, then undo the screws and detach them. Pull the bulb holders out, noting which fits where.
8 On VN1500 Classic FI, Nomad/Classic Tourer FI L2-on models, and Drifter R models undo the screws on the back and remove the front cover. Undo the two screws and lift the meter/gauge/warning light units out of

the housing, freeing the FI and oil pressure warning LEDs from the housing. If required disconnect the warning light panel connector and separate it from the meter/gauge unit.
9 On VN1600 Classic and Nomad/Classic Tourer models, unscrew the nuts and detach the meter/gauge unit from the bracket, noting how the grommets locate onto the pegs. Undo the four perimeter screws on the back and remove the front cover. Undo the four remaining screws and lift the meter/gauge unit out of the housing.
10 On Mean Streak models undo the screws and remove the back cover, then unscrew the nuts and detach the meter unit from the bracket, noting how the grommets locate onto the pegs (see illustrations). Undo the five perimeter screws on the back and remove the front cover. Release the wiring, and pull the bulb holders and rubber seal out. Undo the four remaining screws and lift the meter/gauge unit out of the housing and disconnect the wiring connectors.
11 Installation is the reverse of removal.

Speedometer cable replacement

12 Disconnect the speedometer cable from the speedometer (see Section 15).
13 Disconnect the lower end of the speedometer cable from the drive at the front wheel. Note carefully how the cable is routed, then remove it.
14 Installation is the reverse of removal.

Speed sensor replacement

15 Remove the left side engine cover.
16 Disconnect the sensor wiring connector (see illustration). Release the wiring tie.
17 Unscrew the bolt and remove the sensor (see illustration).
18 Check the condition of the O-ring and replace it with a new one if necessary.
19 Installation is the reverse of removal. Fit a new O-ring if necessary. Smear the O-ring with grease. Clean the threads of the bolt and apply a non-permanent thread locking compound. Tighten the sensor bolt to the torque listed in the specifications.

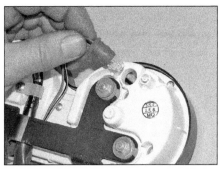

17.3a Pull the bulb holder out . . .

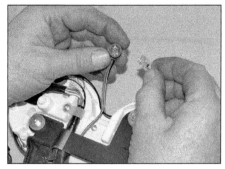

17.3b . . . then pull the bulb out of the holder

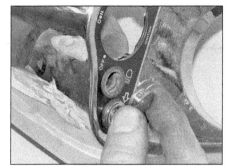

17.5a Remove the cap . . .

17 Instrument and warning light bulbs – replacement

1 Refer to the Specifications at the beginning of the Chapter and see whether the malfunctioning light is a standard bulb or an LED – the LEDs cannot be replaced with new ones. If an LED malfunctions refer to Section 16.

2 If the light being accessed is within an instrument or warning light housing and does not have its own lens cap, access the relevant bulb holder by referring to Sections 15 and 16, and displacing or removing the housing as required according to model.

3 To replace a bulb in a rubber bulb holder without its own lens cap, pull the rubber holder out of its housing, then pull the bulb out of the holder (see illustrations).

4 To replace a bulb in a plastic holder turn the holder anti-clockwise to release it, then pull the bulb out of the holder.

5 To replace a bulb in a rubber bulb holder with its own lens cap, carefully lever the cap off, then pull the bulb holder out, then pull the bulb out of the holder (see illustrations) – where the bulb is recessed use a piece of rubber tubing or similar that fits over the bulb as shown.

6 If the contacts are dirty or corroded, they should be scraped clean and sprayed with electrical contact cleaner before new bulbs are installed.

7 Carefully push the new bulb into position, then fit the holder back into the housing.

18.2 Pull the boot off the switch, then undo the screw (arrowed) and detach the wire

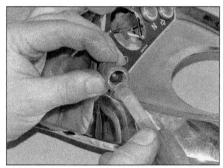

17.5b . . . then pull the bulb holder out. Push a piece of tube over the bulb . . .

18 Oil pressure switch – check and replacement

Check

1 If the oil pressure warning light fails to operate properly, check the oil level and make sure it is correct.

2 If the oil level is correct, disconnect the wire from the oil pressure switch, which is located in the back of the crankcase to the left of the oil filter (see illustration). Turn the ignition switch ON and ground (earth) the end of the wire. If the light comes on, the oil pressure switch is defective and must be replaced with a new one – note that on all except VN1500A and B and Classic D, E1 and F1 models the system is fitted with a three second delay unit

18.6 Unscrew and remove the switch

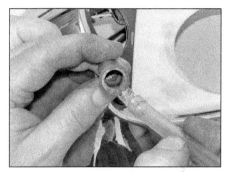

17.5c . . . and pull the bulb out of the holder

to prevent the light coming on during heavy braking and acceleration when oil surge occurs.

3 If the light does not come on, check the oil pressure warning light bulb where fitted (other models have an LED), and check the wiring and connectors between the oil pressure switch, delay unit where fitted, and the light, and between the light and the junction box (see the wiring diagrams at the end of this manual).

4 On all except VN1500A and B and Classic D, E1 and F1 models if all is good so far replace the delay unit with a new one.

Replacement

Oil pressure switch

5 To replace the switch, drain the engine oil (see Chapter 1).

6 Disconnect the wire from the oil pressure switch, which is located in the back of the crankcase to the left of the oil filter (see illustration 18.2). Unscrew the switch from the crankcase (see illustration).

7 Coat the threads of the new switch with silicone sealant, then screw the unit into its hole, tightening it to the torque listed in this Chapter's Specifications. Connect the wire and fit the rubber boot.

8 Fill the crankcase with the recommended type and amount of oil (see Chapter 1). Run the engine and check the operation of the switch, and for any leaks around it.

Delay unit

9 Remove the right side cover (see Chapter 8).

18.11 Oil pressure light delay unit (arrowed)

19.2 Disconnect the ignition switch wiring connector – Mean Streak shown

19.7 Ignition switch bolts (arrowed) – Mean Streak shown

10 Displace and support the coolant reservoir (see Chapter 3).

11 Displace the delay unit and disconnect its wiring connector **(see illustration)**.

12 Installation is the reverse of removal.

19 Ignition switch – check and replacement

⚠️ **Warning: Always disconnect the battery negative (-) lead before checking or removing the ignition switch to prevent the risk of short circuits.**

Check

1 On models with a frame-mounted switch trace the wiring from it and disconnect it at the connector.

2 On models with a tank-mounted switch remove the instrument or warning light housing (see Section 15), then if not already done disconnect the switch wiring connector **(see illustration)**.

3 Using an ohmmeter, check the continuity of the terminal pairs indicated in the wiring diagrams at the end of this manual. Continuity should exist between the terminals connected by a solid line when the switch is in the indicated position.

4 If the switch fails any of the tests, replace it with a new one.

Replacement

5 On models with a frame-mounted switch trace the wiring from it and disconnect it at the connector. Free the wiring from any ties and feed it back to the switch, noting its routing. Remove bodywork components as necessary for access to the switch mounting screws.

6 On models with a tank-mounted switch remove the instrument or warning light housing (see Section 15), then if not already done disconnect the switch wiring connector **(see illustration 19.2)**.

7 Unscrew the bolts and remove the switch **(see illustration)**.

8 Installation is the reverse of removal.

20 Handlebar switches – check

1 Generally speaking, the switches are reliable and trouble-free. Most troubles, when they do occur, are caused by dirty or corroded contacts, but wear and breakage of internal parts is a possibility that should not be overlooked. If breakage does occur, the entire switch and related wiring harness will have to be replaced with a new one, since individual parts are not usually available.

2 The switches can be checked for continuity with an ohmmeter or a continuity test light. Always disconnect the battery ground (earth) lead, which will prevent the possibility of a short circuit, before making the checks.

3 Trace the wiring harness of the switch in question and unplug the electrical connectors – remove the headlight beam unit or fuel tank as required according to model for access **(see illustrations)**.

4 Refer to the wiring diagrams at the end of this manual for switch continuity diagrams. Using the ohmmeter or test light, check for continuity between the terminals of the switch harness with the switch in the various positions. Continuity should exist between the terminals connected by a solid line when the switch is in the indicated position.

5 If the continuity check indicates a problem exists, refer to Section 21, disassemble the switch and spray the switch contacts with electrical contact cleaner **(see illustration)**. If they are accessible, the contacts can be scraped clean with a knife or polished with crocus cloth. If switch components are damaged or broken, it will be obvious when the switch is disassembled.

21 Handlebar switches – removal and installation

1 The handlebar switches are composed of two halves that clamp around the bars. They are easily removed for cleaning or inspection by taking out the clamp screws and pulling

20.3a On some models the switch connectors (arrowed) . . .

20.3b . . . are under the tank on each side of the frame

20.5 Check the switch contacts and connections – clean and spray as required

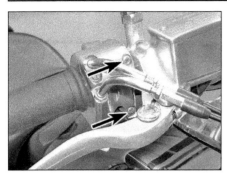

21.1a Switch housing screws (arrowed) – right side

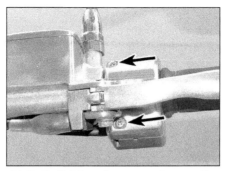

21.1b Switch housing screws (arrowed) – left side

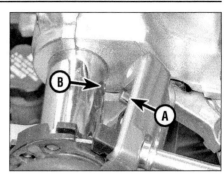

21.3 Locate the peg (A) in the hole (B)

the switch halves away from the handlebars **(see illustrations)**.

2 To completely remove the switches, trace the wiring harness of the switch in question and unplug the electrical connectors – remove the headlight beam unit or fuel tank as required according to model for access **(see illustrations 20.3a and b)**. Release the wiring from any ties and feed it back to the switch, noting its routing. Undo the switch housing screws and detach the housing from the handlebar, noting how it locates. If removing the right side switch housing refer to chapter 4A or 4B according to model and detach the throttle cables.

3 When installing the switches, make sure the wiring harnesses are properly routed and secured to avoid pinching or stretching the wires. Locate the peg on the switch housing in the hole in the handlebar **(see illustration)**. Check and adjust throttle cable operation and freeplay (see Chapter 1).

22 Neutral switch – check and replacement

Check

1 The switch is located in the front bevel gear housing on the left side of the crankcase. The switch is part of the starter interlock safety circuit which prevents or stops the engine running if the transmission is in gear whilst the sidestand is down, and prevents the engine from starting if the transmission is in gear

22.2 Pull the wiring connector off the switch

unless the sidestand is up, and unless the clutch is pulled in.

2 Make sure the transmission is in neutral. On all except Drifter J models remove the shift pedal(s) (see Chapter 2), then remove the left side engine cover **(see illustration 30.10)**. Disconnect the wire from the neutral switch **(see illustration)**. Check the switch is tight in the crankcase. Turn the main switch ON and ground (earth) the end of the wire. If the light comes on, the neutral switch is defective and must be replaced with a new one.

3 If the neutral light fails to operate, first check the bulb (see Section 17). If the bulb is good, check the wiring and connectors in the neutral switch circuit.

4 To confirm the switch is faulty connect one lead of an ohmmeter to a good ground (earth) and the other lead to the post on the switch. When the transmission is in neutral, the ohmmeter should read 0 ohms – in any other gear, the meter should read infinite resistance.

5 If the switch doesn't check out as described, remove it and check the action of the plunger – if it does not move in and out smoothly and freely or is damaged, worn or deformed, replace the switch with a new one. If the neutral light has been working intermittently, try reinstalling it temporarily without its sealing washer. If the light now works consistently, the switch plunger is worn and the switch should be replaced with a new one (don't just leave the old switch in position without the washer).

6 If no problems can be found it is possible

23.8 The bolt (A) is on the top of the bracket on this type of switch – note how the arm locates around the post on the stand (B)

the fault lies with the switch contact plate on the end of the shift drum, inside the crankcase – refer to Chapter 2.

Replacement

7 The switch is located in the front bevel gear housing on the left side of the crankcase. On all except Drifter J models remove the shift pedal(s) (see Chapter 2), then remove the left side engine cover **(see illustration 30.10)**.

8 Disconnect the wire from the neutral switch **(see illustration 22.2)**.

9 Unscrew the neutral switch from the case and remove the sealing washer.

10 Fit the switch using a new sealing washer and tighten it to the torque listed in the Specifications.

23 Sidestand switch – check and replacement

Check

1 Support the bike securely upright using an auxiliary stand. On Drifter J models remove the connector cover on the left side of the engine. On all other models remove the shift pedal(s) (see Chapter 2), then remove the left side engine cover **(see illustration 30.10)**.

2 Follow the wiring harness from the switch to the connector, then disconnect it.

3 Connect the leads of an ohmmeter to the wire terminals on the switch side of the connector.

4 With the sidestand in the up position, there should be continuity through the switch (0 ohms). With the sidestand down, there should be no continuity (infinite resistance).

5 If the switch fails either of these tests, replace it with a new one.

Replacement

6 Support the bike securely upright using an auxiliary stand. Raise the sidestand.

7 Follow the wiring harness from the switch to the connector, then disconnect it. Free the wiring from any ties and feed it down to the switch, noting its routing.

8 Undo the switch mounting screws (VN1500A and B) or bolt (all other models) and remove the switch, noting how its arm engages with the stand **(see illustration)**.

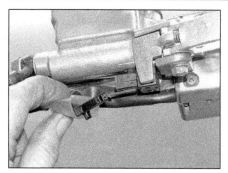

24.2 Disconnect the wiring connector

9 Installation is the reverse of removal. Clean the threads of the screws or bolt and apply some non-permanent thread locking compound.

24 Clutch switch –
check and replacement

Check

1 The clutch switch is mounted under the clutch master cylinder. The switch is part of the starter interlock safety circuit which prevents or stops the engine running if the transmission is in gear whilst the sidestand is down, and prevents the engine from starting if the transmission is in gear unless the sidestand is up and the clutch lever is pulled in. The switch isn't adjustable.
2 To check the switch, disconnect the wiring connector from it **(see illustration)**. Connect the probes of an ohmmeter or a continuity tester to the two switch terminals. With the clutch lever pulled in, continuity should be indicated. With the clutch lever out, no continuity (infinite resistance) should be indicated.
3 If the switch is good, check the other components (sidestand switch, neutral switch, diode block) in the starter safety circuit, and check the wiring between them for continuity, and the connectors for loose or broken connections.

25.1 Horn wiring connectors (A) and mounting bolt (B) – Mean Streak

24.6 Undo the screw (arrowed) and remove the switch

Removal and installation

4 The clutch switch is mounted on the front of the master cylinder.
5 Disconnect the wiring connector from the switch **(see illustration 24.2)**.
6 Undo the single screw securing the switch and remove it, noting how it fits **(see illustration)**.
7 Installation is the reverse of removal. Make sure the switch is correctly located before tightening its screw.

25 Horn(s) –
check and replacement

Check

1 Disconnect the electrical connectors from the horn **(see illustration)**. Using two jumper wires, apply battery voltage directly to the terminals on the horn. If the horn sounds, check the switch (see Section 20) and the wiring between the switch and the horn (see the wiring diagrams at the end of this manual).
2 If the horn doesn't sound, replace it with a new one.

Replacement

3 Detach the electrical connectors and unbolt the horn or its bracket (according to model) from the frame **(see illustration 25.1)**.
4 Installation is the reverse of removal.

26.2 Starter relay (arrowed)

26 Starter motor relay and starter circuit relay – check and replacement

Starter motor relay

Check

1 If the starter circuit is faulty, first check the main fuse (see Section 5).
2 The starter relay is located under the seat (front seat on dual seat models) on VN1500A and B models, and behind the coolant reservoir (behind the right side cover) on all others **(see illustration)**. Remove the seat(s) (see Chapter 8) or displace and support the reservoir (see Chapter 3) according to model.
3 On all except VN1500A and B models displace the relay from its mount. Lift the rubber terminal cover and undo the nut or screw (according to model) securing the starter motor lead **(see illustration)**; position the lead away from the relay terminal. With the ignition switch ON, the engine kill switch in the RUN position, and the transmission in neutral, press the starter switch. The relay should be heard to click.
4 If the relay doesn't click, switch off the ignition and remove the relay as described below; test it as follows.
5 Set a multimeter to the ohms x 1 scale and connect it across the relay's starter motor and battery lead terminals. There should be no continuity. Using a fully-charged 12 volt battery and two insulated jumper wires, connect the positive (+) terminal of the battery to the yellow/red wire terminal of the relay, and the negative (–) terminal to the black/yellow wire terminal of the relay. At this point the relay should be heard to click and the multimeter read 0 ohms (continuity). If this is the case the relay is proved good. If the relay does not click when battery voltage is applied and indicates no continuity (infinite resistance) across its terminals, it is faulty and must be replaced with a new one.
6 If the relay is good, check the heavy gauge cables from the battery to the relay, and from the relay to the starter motor, particularly that their terminals are tight and corrosion-free.
7 Next check for battery voltage at the yellow/

26.3 Lift the cover to access the battery and starter motor leads

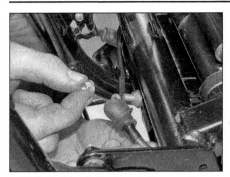

27.3 Pull back the terminal cover then undo the nut and detach the lead

27.4a Unscrew the two bolts . . .

27.4b . . . and remove the starter motor

red wire terminal on the relay wiring connector with the ignition ON, the kill switch in the RUN position and the starter button pressed. If there is no voltage, check the wiring to the junction box, then check the starter circuit relay (Section 6).

8 If voltage is present, check that there is continuity to earth in the black/yellow wire. If not check the wiring and connectors.

Replacement

9 Disconnect the lead from the negative terminal of the battery (see Section 3).

10 The starter relay is located under the seat (front seat on dual seat models) on VN1500A and B models, and behind the coolant reservoir (behind the right side cover) on all others (see illustration 26.2). Remove the seat(s) (see Chapter 8) or displace and support the reservoir (see Chapter 3) according to model.

11 Displace the relay and detach the battery positive lead, the starter lead and the wiring connector from the relay. Remove the main fuse if required (see illustration 5.1b).

12 Installation is the reverse of removal. Reconnect the negative battery lead after all the other electrical connections are made.

Starter circuit relay

13 The starter circuit relay is incorporated in the junction box; refer to the tests described in Section 6.

27 Starter motor – removal and installation

Removal

1 Disconnect the lead from the negative terminal of the battery (see Section 3).

2 For best access to the starter motor remove the radiator (see Chapter 3) – depending on your tools and dexterity you could get away with just displacing it from its mounts to avoid having to drain the cooling system, and where mounted below the radiator you

can displace the regulator/rectifier(s), but to avoid the possibility of damaging the delicate cooling fins it is best to remove the radiator completely.

3 Peel back the rubber terminal cover on the starter motor. Undo the nut securing the starter lead and detach the lead (see illustration).

4 Unscrew the two bolts securing the starter motor to the crankcase (see illustration). Slide the starter motor out and remove it (see illustration) – if it is tight apply gentle leverage with a screwdriver.

5 Remove the O-ring on the end of the starter motor and discard it as a new one must be used.

Installation

6 Fit a new O-ring onto the end of the starter motor, making sure it is seated in its groove (see illustration). Apply a smear of engine oil to the O-ring. Make sure the bottom of the mounting lugs on the motor and tops of the mounts on the engine are clean.

7 Manoeuvre the motor into position and slide it into the crankcase (see illustration 27.4b). Ensure that the starter motor teeth mesh correctly with those of the starter idle/reduction gear. Fit the mounting bolts and tighten them (see illustration 27.4a).

8 Connect the starter lead to the motor and secure it with the nut (see illustration 27.3). Fit the rubber cover over the terminal.

9 Install the remaining components as required according to your removal method.

10 Connect the battery negative (–) lead.

28 Starter motor – disassembly, inspection and reassembly

Check

1 Remove the starter motor (see Section 27). Cover its body in some rag and clamp the motor in a soft-jawed vice – do not overtighten it.

2 Using a fully-charged 12 volt battery and two insulated jumper wires, connect the positive (+) terminal of the battery to the protruding terminal on the starter motor, and the negative (–) terminal to one of the motor's mounting lugs. At this point the starter motor should spin. If this is the case the motor is proved good, though it is worth disassembling it and checking it if you suspect it of not working properly under load.

Disassembly

3 Remove the starter motor (see Section 27).

4 Note any alignment marks between the main housing and the front and rear covers, or make your own if they aren't clear (see illustration).

5 Unscrew the two long bolts and remove

27.6 Fit a new O-ring and lubricate it

28.4 Note the alignment marks (arrowed) or make your own between the housing and the covers

28.5a Unscrew and remove the two bolts (arrowed) . . .

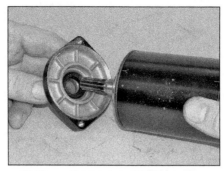

28.5b . . . then remove the front cover

28.6 Remove the rear cover

the front cover **(see illustrations)**. Note the sealing ring and remove it if required **(see illustration 28.25)**.

6 Remove the rear cover **(see illustration)**. Note the sealing ring and remove it if required **(see illustration 28.23a)**. Remove the shim(s) from the cover or the rear end of the armature noting how many are fitted **(see illustration 28.23b)**.

7 Withdraw the armature from the main housing noting that there will some resistance from the pull of the magnets set in the housing **(see illustration)**.

8 At this stage check for continuity between the terminal bolt and each insulated brush – there should be continuity (zero resistance). Check for continuity between the terminal bolt and the housing – there should be no continuity (infinite resistance). If the results are not as described investigate the cause and rectify as necessary – it could be that a brush

wire has become detached or the terminal bolt O-ring or insulator piece or brush piece seat is not as it should be.

9 Noting the correct fitted location of each component, unscrew the nut from the terminal bolt and remove the plain washer, the one large and two small insulating washers **(see illustration 28.21b)**. Remove the brushplate assembly, noting how it locates **(see illustration 28.20b)**. Remove the O-ring and insulator piece from the terminal bolt, then remove the bolt.

10 Remove the brushplate seat from the housing **(see illustration 28.18a)**.

Inspection

11 The parts of the starter motor that are most likely to require attention are the brushes. Measure the length of each brush and compare the results to the length listed in this Chapter's Specifications **(see illustration)**. If any of the

brushes are worn beyond the service limit, fit a new brush set and brushplate. If the brushes are not worn excessively, nor cracked, chipped, or otherwise damaged, they may be reused.

12 Inspect the commutator bars on the armature for scoring, scratches and discoloration. The commutator can be cleaned and polished with crocus cloth, but do not use sandpaper or emery paper. After cleaning, wipe away any residue with a cloth soaked in electrical system cleaner or denatured alcohol. Measure the diameter of the commutator and replace the armature with a new one if worn to the limit specified **(see illustration)**.

13 Using an ohmmeter or a continuity test light, check for continuity between the commutator bars **(see illustration)**. Continuity should exist between each bar and all of the others. Also, check for continuity between the commutator bars and the armature shaft **(see illustration)**. There should be no continuity (infinite resistance) between the commutator and the shaft. If the checks indicate otherwise, the armature is defective and a new starter motor must be obtained – the armature is not available separately.

14 Check the front end of the armature shaft for worn, cracked, chipped and broken teeth. If any are found check the teeth of the idle/reduction gear via the starter orifice in the back of the engine. If the shaft is damaged or worn, a new starter motor must be obtained – the armature is not available separately. Check the bearing on each end of the shaft. If they do not run smoothly replace them with

28.7 Draw the armature out of the housing

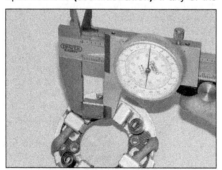

28.11 Measure the length of each brush

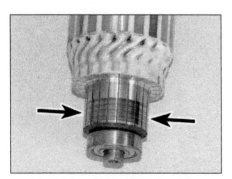

28.12 Measure the diameter of the commutator

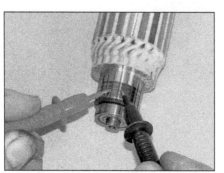

28.13a There should be continuity between the bars . . .

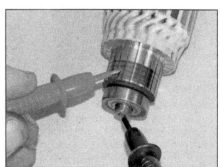

28.13b . . . and no continuity between the bars and the shaft

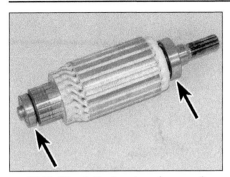

28.14 Check the bearings (arrowed)

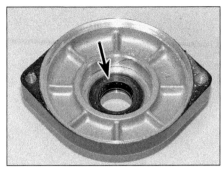

28.15 Check the seal (arrowed) in the front cover

28.18a Fit the brushplate seat . . .

new ones if available **(see illustration)** – ask your dealer or a bearing supplier, otherwise you have to fit a new armature.

15 Inspect the front and rear covers for signs of cracks or wear. Check the oil seal in the front cover for wear and damage **(see illustration)**. If necessary fit a new on if available – ask your dealer or a seal supplier, otherwise you have to fit a new cover.

16 Inspect the magnets in the main housing and the housing itself for cracks.

17 Check the housing sealing rings for signs of deformation and deterioration and replace them with new ones if necessary.

Reassembly

18 Fit the brushplate seat into the housing, then locate the insulator piece **(see illustrations)**.

19 Push the brushes all the way back into their housings and locate the brush spring ends onto the tops of the brushes so they are held retracted **(see illustration)**.

20 Fit the terminal bolt through the brush piece, locating its base in the recess **(see illustration)**. Fit the brushplate, locating the brush piece in its seat, the brush wires in their cut-outs and the locating tab in its cut-out **(see illustrations)**.

21 Fit the O-ring down over the bolt and press it into place between the bolt and the cover **(see illustration)**. Slide the small insulating washers onto the terminal bolt, followed by the large insulating washer and the plain washer **(see illustration)**. Fit the nut onto the terminal bolt and tighten it securely.

28.18b . . . then the insulator piece

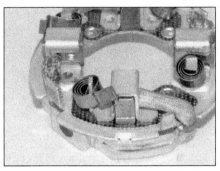

28.19 Push each brush into its housing and place the spring end as shown to keep them retracted

28.20a Fit the terminal bolt . . .

28.20b . . . then fit the brushplate assembly onto the housing . . .

28.20c . . . making sure it locates correctly

28.21a Fit the O-ring over the bolt and against the housing . . .

28.21b . . . then fit the washers and nut as shown

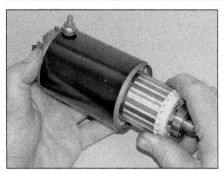

28.22a Guide the armature into the housing . . .

28.22b . . . then relocate the spring ends onto the brushes

28.23a Fit the sealing ring . . .

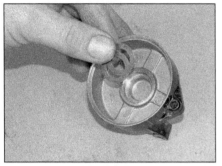

28.23b . . . and the shims, then fit the rear cover

28.25 Fit the front sealing ring

28.26 Fit the long bolts

22 Carefully insert the armature into the housing, keeping a strong hold on both against the draw of the magnets, and keeping the brushplate in position as the commutator fits through it (see illustration). Lift the brush springs off the brushes, push the brushes against the commutator, and set the spring ends against the brushes (see illustration). Check the armature turns.

23 Fit the sealing ring onto the rear of the housing if removed, using a new one if necessary (see illustration). Fit the shim(s) into the rear cover (see illustration). Fit the rear cover, aligning the marks between the cover and housing (see illustration 28.6).

24 Apply a smear of grease to the front cover oil seal lip (see illustration 28.15).

25 Fit the sealing ring onto the front of the housing if removed, using a new one if necessary (see illustration). Slide the front cover into position, aligning the marks made on removal (see illustration 28.5b).

26 Check the marks made on removal are correctly aligned (see illustration 28.4) then fit the long bolts and tighten them (see illustration).

27 Install the starter motor (see Section 27).

29 Charging system testing – general information and precautions

1 If the performance of the charging system is suspect, the system as a whole should be checked first, followed by testing of the individual components (the alternator and the voltage regulator/rectifier). **Note:** *Before beginning the checks, make sure the battery is fully charged and that all system connections are clean and tight.*

2 Checking the output of the charging system and the performance of the various components within the charging system requires the use of special electrical test equipment. A voltmeter or a multimeter is the absolute minimum equipment required. In addition, an ohmmeter is generally required for checking the remainder of the system.

3 When making the checks, follow the procedures carefully to prevent incorrect connections or short circuits, as irreparable damage to electrical system components may result if short circuits occur. Because of the special tools and expertise required, it is recommended that the job of checking the charging system be left to a dealer service department or a reputable motorcycle repair shop.

30 Charging system – output and leakage tests

Caution: Never disconnect the battery cables from the battery while the engine is running. If the battery is disconnected, the alternator and regulator/rectifier will be damaged.

1 To check the charging system output, you will need a voltmeter or a multimeter with a voltmeter function.

2 The battery must be fully charged (charge it from an external source if necessary) and the engine must be at normal operating temperature to obtain an accurate reading.

Regulated output test

3 On VN1500A and B models remove the left side cover (see Chapter 8). On all other models remove the seat (the front seat on dual seat models) (see Chapter 8).

4 Attach the positive voltmeter lead to the battery positive terminal and the negative lead to the battery negative terminal (see illustration). The voltmeter selector switch (if so equipped) must be in a DC volt range greater than 15 volts.

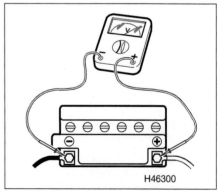

H46300

30.4 Checking regulated voltage output – connect the meter as shown

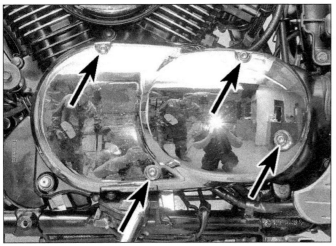

30.10 Unscrew the bolts (arrowed) and remove the cover

30.11 Disconnect the relevant wiring connector(s)

5 Start the engine. Run it at varying speeds up to 6,000 rpm on VN1500A and B models and 3000 rpm on all other models.

6 The charging system output should be within the range listed in this Chapter's Specifications. It should be at the low end of the range at low engine speeds and at the high end of the range at higher engine speeds.

7 If the output is as specified, the charging system is functioning properly.

8 Low voltage output may be the result of damaged windings in the alternator stator coils, loss of magnetism in the alternator rotor or wiring problems. Make sure all electrical connections are clean and tight, then refer below to check the un-regulated output and to Section 31 to check the stator coils.

9 High voltage output, above the specified range, indicates a defective regulator/rectifier (see Section 32).

> **HAYNES HiNT** Clues to a faulty regulator are constantly blowing bulbs, with brightness varying considerably with engine speed, and battery overheating.

Un-regulated output test

Note: Before proceeding refer to the general information on the charging system in Section 1 of this Chapter. On models with a twin stator and regulator/rectifier set-up perform the check given below on each stator in turn.

10 On Drifter J models remove the connector cover on the left side of the engine. On all other models remove the shift pedal(s) (see Chapter 2), then remove the left side engine cover **(see illustration)**.

11 Trace the wiring from the alternator cover on the left-hand side of the engine and disconnect it at the 3-pin connector with the black wires on VN1600 Classic and Nomad/Classic Tourer models and yellow wires on all others **(see illustration)**. Check the connector terminals for corrosion and security.

12 Connect a voltmeter with a 250-volt AC

scale to two of the yellow wire terminals in the alternator connector (as you are measuring the alternator output before it has been rectified from alternating current to direct current, the voltmeter must be able to measure AC).

13 Run the engine at 3000 rpm and note the voltage reading.

14 Take three different measurements between different pairs of wires. In all cases, the voltage should be as listed in this Chapter's Specifications.

a) If one of the readings is low, one coil in the stator is probably defective. This will produce an occasional failure to start due to insufficient battery charge.

b) If each voltage reading is correct, the rectifier/regulator is probably defective. Refer to Section 32.

c) If each voltage reading is low, the alternator may be defective. Test the stator coils as described in Section 31. If the stator coils test OK, the rotor magnets have probably lost magnetism. This can be caused by dropping or hitting the alternator, by leaving the alternator near another source of magnetism, or by age.

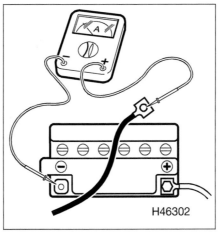

30.16 Checking the charging system leakage rate - connect the meter as shown

Leakage test

Caution: Always connect an ammeter in series, never in parallel with the battery, otherwise it will be damaged. Do not turn the ignition ON or operate the starter motor when the ammeter is connected – a sudden surge in current will blow the meter's fuse.

15 Ensure the ignition is OFF, then disconnect the battery negative (-) lead (see Section 3).

16 Set the multimeter to the Amps function and connect its negative (-) probe to the battery negative (-) terminal, and positive (+) probe to the disconnected negative (-) lead **(see illustration)**. Always set the meter to a high amps range initially and then bring it down to the mA (milli Amps) range; if there is a high current flow in the circuit it may blow the meter's fuse.

17 Battery current leakage should not exceed about 0.1 mA. If a higher leakage rate is shown there is a short circuit in the wiring, although if an after-market immobiliser or alarm is fitted, its current draw should be taken into account. Disconnect the meter and reconnect the battery negative (-) lead.

18 If leakage is indicated, refer to the Wiring Diagrams at the end of this Chapter and systematically disconnect individual electrical components and check the meter after disconnecting each component until the source is identified.

31 Alternator stator coils – resistance test

Note: Before proceeding refer to the general information on the charging system in Section 1 of this Chapter. On models with a twin stator and regulator/rectifier set-up perform the check given below on each stator in turn.

1 If charging system output is low or non-existent, the alternator stator coil windings and leads should be checked for proper continuity. The test can be made with the stator(s) in place on the machine.

2 On Drifter J models remove the connector cover on the left side of the engine. On all other models remove the shift pedal(s) (see Chapter 2), then remove the left side engine cover **(see illustration 30.10)**.

3 Trace the wiring from the alternator cover on the left-hand side of the engine and disconnect it at the 3-pin connector with the black wires on VN1600 Classic and Nomad/Classic Tourer models and yellow wires on all others **(see illustration 30.11)**. Check the connector terminals for corrosion and security.

4 Using a multimeter set to the ohms x 1 (ohmmeter) scale measure the resistance of the stator coils between each pair of yellow wire terminals on the alternator side of the connector, taking a total of three readings.

5 Next check for continuity between each of the wires and the engine.

6 If the coil windings are in good condition the reading(s) should be within the range shown in the Specifications at the start of this Chapter, and there should be no continuity (infinite resistance) between the terminals and ground (earth). If not, the alternator stator coil assembly is at fault and should be replaced with a new one. **Note:** *Before condemning the stator coils, check the fault is not due to damaged wiring between the connector and the coils.*

32.5a Regulator/rectifier (arrowed)

32 Voltage regulator/rectifier(s) – check and replacement

Check

Note: *Before proceeding refer to the general information on the charging system in Section 1 of this Chapter. On models with a twin stator and regulator/rectifier set-up perform the check given below on each regulator/rectifier in turn.*

1 Testing of the voltage regulator/rectifier requires a special Kawasaki tester. Ordinary ohmmeters will produce a variety of readings which may indicate that the regulator/rectifier is defective when it is actually good.

2 If the charging system output voltage in Section 30 was too high, the regulator/rectifier may be defective. It may also be defective if the output was too low and no other cause (alternator or wiring problems) can be found.

3 If you suspect the regulator/rectifier, take it to a dealer service department or other repair shop for further checks, or substitute a known good unit and recheck the charging system output.

Replacement

4 On VN1500A and B models remove the left side cover (see Chapter 8). The regulator/ rectifier is to the rear of the battery. Disconnect the wiring connector, then unscrew the bolts and remove it, displacing or moving aside any other component as required.

5 On Classic D, E1 and F1 models and all Drifter and Mean Streak models the regulator/ rectifier is mounted low on the left side of the bike **(see illustration)**. On Drifter J models remove the connector cover on the left side of the engine. On all other models remove the shift pedal(s) (see Chapter 2), then remove the left side engine cover **(see illustration 30.10)**. Trace the wiring from the regulator/rectifier and disconnect the wiring connector **(see**

illustration 30.11). Release the wiring from any ties and feed it back, noting its routing. Unscrew the four bolts and remove the cover and then the regulator/rectifier **(see illustration)**.

6 On all other Classic models there is one regulator/rectifier mounted low on the left side of the bike and one at the front below the radiator. Remove the shift pedal(s) (see Chapter 2), then remove the left side engine cover **(see illustration 30.10)**. Trace the wiring from the relevant regulator/rectifier and disconnect the wiring connector **(see illustration 30.11)**. Release the wiring from any ties and feed it back, noting its routing. Unscrew the bolts and remove the cover (left side) and the regulator/rectifier.

7 On all Nomad/Classic Tourer models both regulator/rectifiers are mounted at the front below the radiator. Remove the shift pedal(s) (see Chapter 2), then remove the left side engine cover **(see illustration 30.10)**. Trace the wiring from the relevant regulator/rectifier and disconnect the wiring connector **(see illustration 30.11)**. Release the wiring from any ties and feed it back, noting its routing. Unscrew the relevant bolts and remove the regulator/rectifier(s) individually or as an assembly on their bracket, as required.

8 Installation is the reverse of the removal steps.

33 Alternator rotor – removal and installation

VN1500A, B and Classic D, E1 and F1 models and all Drifter and Mean Streak models

Removal

1 Remove the engine from the frame (see Chapter 2).

2 Working in a criss-cross pattern, evenly slacken the alternator outer cover bolts **(see illustration)**. **Note:** *As each bolt is*

32.5b Unscrew the cover bolts and the regulator/rectifier bolts and remove both

33.2 Unscrew the bolts (arrowed) and remove the cover

33.3a Note the alignment of the arm then unscrew the bolt . . .

33.3b . . . and remove the shift linkage

33.4a Unscrew the bolts (arrowed) and remove the cover

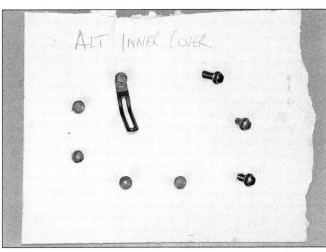

33.4b Store the bolts in a cardboard template

removed, store it in its relative position in a cardboard template of the crankcase halves **(see illustration 33.4b)**. *This will ensure all bolts are installed in the correct location on reassembly.* Draw the cover off the engine, noting that it will be restrained by the force of the rotor magnets – on all except VN1500A and B models hold the shift shaft in place and draw the cover off it, and be prepared to catch any residual oil. Remove and discard the gasket **(see illustration 33.13d)**. Remove the dowels from either the cover or the crankcase if loose.

3 To remove the shift linkage assembly mark the alignment of the linkage arm clamp slit with the shift mechanism shaft, then unscrew the pinch bolt and slide the arm off the shaft and remove the shaft stub from the inner cover **(see illustrations)**.

4 Working in a criss-cross pattern, evenly slacken the alternator inner cover bolts, noting the wiring clamp(s) where fitted **(see illustration)**. **Note:** *As each bolt is removed, store it in its relative position in a cardboard*

template of the crankcase halves **(see illustration)**. *This will ensure all bolts are installed in the correct location on reassembly.* Draw the cover off the engine – be prepared to catch any residual oil. Remove and discard the gasket **(see illustration 33.11a)**. Remove the dowels from either the cover or the crankcase if loose.

5 Remove a spark plug from each cylinder

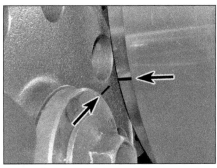

33.5 Turn the engine to align the marks (arrowed) on the rotor and the gear

(see Chapter 1). Turn the engine using a socket on the rotor bolt and align the marks on the left balancer gear and the rotor **(see illustration)** – these marks must be aligned when installing the rotor later.

6 Prevent the alternator rotor from turning, using either a rotor strap (keeping it clear of the raised triggers for the pick-up coils) or a holding tool **(see illustration)** – a holding tool

33.6 Holding the rotor with a strap while unscrewing the bolt

33.8 Remove the spacer then slide the rotor off

33.9a With the wide spline aligned with the rib (arrowed) slide the rotor on . . .

33.9b . . . and turn the balancer gear to align the marks

can locate either in the holes in the rim of the rotor or in the balancer gear, depending on the type available **(see illustration 33.10b)**.

7 With the rotor held unscrew the bolt and remove its washer.

8 Remove the splined spacer, noting how it fits **(see illustration)**. Draw the rotor off the shaft.

Installation

9 Make sure the wide spline on the crankshaft is in line with rib on the crankcase, and if not turn it so it is **(see illustration)**. Make sure that no metal objects have attached themselves to the magnet on the inside of the rotor. Slide the rotor onto the crankshaft, aligning and engaging the wide splines, and turning the balancer gear as required before the teeth engage so the balancer and rotor marks are lined up correctly **(see illustration)**.

10 Slide the spacer onto the shaft with its ramped side innermost, again aligning the wide splines **(see illustration 33.8)**. Lubricate the bolt threads and seating surface and both sides of the washer with molybdenum disulphide oil (engine oil and molybdenum grease mixed in the ratio 10:1). Fit the bolt with its washer and tighten it to the torque listed in this Chapter's Specifications, holding the rotor as before to prevent it turning **(see illustrations)**.

11 Fit the inner cover dowels into the crankcase if removed, then locate a new gasket onto them **(see illustration)**. Fit the inner cover making sure it locates onto the dowels **(see illustration)**. Tighten the cover bolts evenly in a criss-cross sequence to the specified torque.

12 Clean and re-grease the stub end of the linkage shaft then fit it into its bore in the alternator inner cover **(see illustration)**. Fit the linkage arm onto the shift shaft, aligning the marks, and tighten the pinch bolt **(see illustration 33.3a)**.

13 On all except VN1500A and B models check the condition of the shaft seals in the outer cover and replace them with new ones if necessary **(see illustrations)**. Smear them

33.10a Fit the bolt with its washer . . .

33.10b . . . and tighten to the specified torque

33.11a Fit the new gasket onto the dowels (arrowed) . . .

33.11b . . . then fit the inner cover

33.12 Grease the stub before fitting it into its bore

33.13a Lever the old seals out . . .

33.13b . . . and fit new ones, levelling them with a piece of wood

33.13c Smear sealant onto the grommet seating surface (arrowed)

33.13d Fit the new gasket onto the dowels (arrowed) . . .

33.13e . . . then fit the outer cover

with grease. Smear a suitable sealant onto the wiring grommet **(see illustration)**. Fit the outer cover dowels into the crankcase if removed, then locate a new gasket onto them **(see illustration)**. Fit the cover, noting that the rotor magnets will forcibly draw the cover/stator on, making sure it locates onto the dowels. Tighten the cover bolts evenly in a criss-cross sequence to the specified torque.

14 Install the engine (see Chapter 2).

VN1500 Classic E2-on and F2, Classic FI, VN1600 Classic and all Nomad/Classic Tourer models

Removal

15 Remove the engine from the frame (see Chapter 2).

16 Remove the shift pedals (see Chapter 2), then remove the left side engine cover **(see illustration 30.10)**. Disconnect the alternator and pick-up coil wiring connectors **(see illustration 30.11)**.

17 Working in a criss-cross pattern, evenly slacken the alternator outer cover bolts, noting the bracket on VN1600 models **(see illustration 33.2)**. **Note:** *As each bolt is removed, store it in its relative position in a cardboard template of the crankcase halves* **(see illustration 33.4b)**. *This will ensure all bolts are installed in the correct location on reassembly.* Draw the cover off the engine, noting that it will be restrained by the force of the rotor magnets – hold the shift shaft in place and draw the cover off it, and be prepared to catch any residual oil. Remove and discard the gasket **(see illustration 33.13d)**. Remove the dowels from either the cover or the crankcase if loose.

18 Prevent the alternator rotor from turning, using either a rotor strap (keeping it clear of the raised triggers for the pick-up coils) or a holding tool that locates in the holes in the rim of the rotor **(see illustration 33.6)**.

19 With the rotor held unscrew the bolt and remove its washer.

20 Remove the splined spacer, noting how it fits **(see illustration 33.8)**. Draw the rotor off the shaft, noting that it will be restrained by the force of the rotor magnets over the inner stator coils.

Installation

21 Make sure that no metal objects have

attached themselves to the magnet on the inside of the rotor. Slide the rotor onto the crankshaft, aligning and engaging the wide splines, and noting that the force of the magnets will forcibly draw it onto the inner stator.

22 Slide the spacer onto the shaft with its ramped side innermost, again aligning the wide splines **(see illustration 33.8)**. Lubricate the bolt threads and seating surface and both sides of the washer with molybdenum disulphide oil (engine oil and molybdenum grease mixed in the ratio 10:1). Fit the bolt with its washer and tighten it to the torque listed in this Chapter's Specifications, holding the rotor as before to prevent it turning **(see illustration 33.10a and 33.6)**.

23 Check the condition of the shaft seals in the outer cover and replace them with new ones if necessary **(see illustration 33.13a and b)**. Smear them with grease. Smear a suitable sealant onto the wiring grommet **(see illustration 33.13c)**. Fit the outer cover dowels into the crankcase if removed, then locate a new gasket onto them **(see illustration 33.13d)**. Fit the cover, noting that the rotor magnets will forcibly draw the cover/stator on, making sure it locates onto the dowels **(see illustration 33.13e)**. Tighten the cover bolts evenly in a criss-cross sequence to the specified torque, not forgetting to secure the bracket on VN1600 models.

24 Connect the alternator and pick-up coil wiring connectors. Install the left side cover, then the shift pedals (see Chapter 2).

34 Alternator stator(s) – removal and installation

VN1500A, B and Classic D, E1 and F1 models and all Drifter and Mean Streak models

Removal

1 Remove the shift pedals (see Chapter 2), then remove the left side engine cover **(see illustration 30.10)**. Disconnect the alternator and pick-up coil wiring connectors **(see illustration 30.11)**.

2 Working in a criss-cross pattern, evenly

slacken the alternator outer cover bolts **(see illustration 33.2)**. **Note:** *As each bolt is removed, store it in its relative position in a cardboard template of the crankcase halves* **(see illustration 33.4b)**. *This will ensure all bolts are installed in the correct location on reassembly.* Draw the cover off the engine, noting that it will be restrained by the force of the rotor magnets – on all except VN1500A and B models hold the shift shaft in place and draw the cover off it, and be prepared to catch any residual oil. Remove and discard the gasket **(see illustration 33.13d)**. Remove the dowels from either the cover or the crankcase if loose.

3 On all except VN1500A and B models remove the pick-up coils (see Chapter 5).

4 Remove the wiring harness retainer, then release the wiring grommet. Unscrew the stator screws and lift the stator out of the cover **(see illustration)**.

Installation

5 Clean the threads of the stator screws and apply a non-permanent thread locking compound. Tighten the stator screws to the torque listed in this Chapter's Specifications. Make sure the stator and pick-up coil wiring is correctly route and secured and the grommets are smeared with a silicone sealant and seated in the cut-out.

6 On all except VN1500A and B models install the pick-up coils (see Chapter 5).

7 On all except VN1500A and B models check the condition of the shaft seals in the outer cover and replace them with new ones if necessary **(see illustrations 33.13a and b)**. Smear them with grease. Smear a

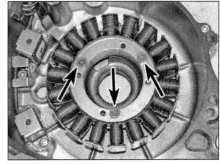

34.4 Alternator stator screws (arrowed)

suitable sealant onto the wiring grommet **(see illustration 33.13c)**. Fit the outer cover dowels into the crankcase if removed, then locate a new gasket onto them **(see illustration 33.13d)**. Fit the cover, noting that the rotor magnets will forcibly draw the cover/ stator on, making sure it locates onto the dowels **(see illustration 33.13e)**. Tighten the cover bolts evenly in a criss-cross sequence to the specified torque.

8 Connect the alternator and pick-up coil wiring connectors. Install the left side cover, then the shift pedals (see Chapter 2).

VN1500 Classic E2-on and F2, Classic FI, VN1600 Classic and all Nomad/Classic Tourer models

Outer stator removal

9 Remove the shift pedals (see Chapter 2), then remove the left side engine cover. Disconnect the alternator and pick-up coil wiring connectors.

10 Working in a criss-cross pattern, evenly slacken the alternator outer cover bolts, noting the bracket on VN1600 models **(see illustration 33.2)**. Note: *As each bolt is removed, store it in its relative position in a cardboard template of the crankcase halves* **(see illustration 33.4b)**. *This will ensure all bolts are installed in the correct location on reassembly.* Draw the cover off the engine, noting that it will be restrained by the force of the rotor magnets – hold the shift shaft in place and draw the cover off it, and be prepared to catch any residual oil. Remove and discard the gasket **(see illustration 33.13d)**. Remove the dowels from either the cover or the crankcase if loose.

11 Remove the pick-up coils (see Chapter 5).

12 Remove the wiring harness retainer, then release the wiring grommet. Unscrew the stator bolts and lift the stator out of the cover,

Outer stator installation

13 Clean the threads of the stator bolts and apply a non-permanent thread locking compound. Tighten the stator bolts to the torque listed in this Chapter's Specifications. Make sure the stator and pick-up coil wiring is correctly routed and secured and the grommets are smeared with a silicone sealant and seated in the cut-out.

14 Install the pick-up coils (see Chapter 5).

15 Check the condition of the shaft seals in the outer cover and replace them with new ones if necessary **(see illustrations 34.13a and b)**. Smear them with grease. Smear a suitable sealant onto the wiring grommet **(see illustration 33.13c)**. Fit the outer cover dowels into the crankcase if removed, then locate a new gasket onto them **(see illustration 33.13d)**. Fit the cover, noting that the rotor magnets will forcibly draw the cover/ stator on, making sure it locates onto the dowels **(see illustration 33.13e)**. Tighten the cover bolts evenly in a criss-cross sequence to the specified torque, not forgetting to secure the bracket on VN1600 models.

16 Connect the alternator and pick-up coil wiring connectors. Install the left side cover, then the shift pedals (see Chapter 2).

Inner stator removal

17 Remove the engine from the frame (see Chapter 2).

18 Remove the alternator rotor (see Section 33).

19 To remove the shift linkage assembly mark the alignment of the linkage arm clamp slit with the shift mechanism shaft, then unscrew the pinch bolt and slide the arm off the shaft **(see illustrations 33.3a and b)**. Draw the linkage shaft out of the inner cover.

20 Working in a criss-cross pattern, evenly slacken the alternator inner cover bolts, noting the wiring clamp(s) where fitted **(see illustration 33.4a)**. Note: *As each bolt is removed, store it in its relative position in a cardboard template of the crankcase halves* **(see illustration 33.4b)**. *This will ensure all bolts are installed in the correct location on reassembly.* Draw the cover off the engine

– be prepared to catch any residual oil. Remove and discard the gasket **(see illustration 33.11a)**. Remove the dowels from either the cover or the crankcase if loose.

21 Release the wiring grommet. Unscrew the stator holder bolts and draw the stator and its holder off the crankcase.

Inner stator installation

22 Clean the threads of the stator bolts and apply a non-permanent thread locking compound Tighten the stator bolts to the torque listed in this Chapter's Specifications. Make sure the stator wiring is correctly routed and secured and the grommet is smeared with a silicone sealant and seated in the cut-out.

23 Fit the inner cover dowels into the crankcase if removed, then locate a new gasket onto them **(see illustration 33.11a)**. Fit the inner cover making sure it locates onto the dowels **(see illustration 33.11b)**. Tighten the cover bolts evenly in a criss-cross sequence to the specified torque.

24 Clean and re-grease the stub end of the linkage shaft then fit it into its bore in the alternator inner cover **(see illustration 33.12)**. Fit the linkage arm onto the shift shaft, aligning the marks, and tighten the pinch bolt **(see illustration 33.3a)**.

25 Install the alternator rotor (see Section 34).

26 Install the engine (see Chapter 2).

35 Wiring diagrams

Prior to troubleshooting a circuit, check the fuses to make sure they're in good condition. Make sure the battery is fully charged and check the lead connections.

When checking a circuit, make sure all connectors are clean, with no broken or loose terminals or wires. When disconnecting a connector, don't pull on the wires – pull only on the connector housings themselves.

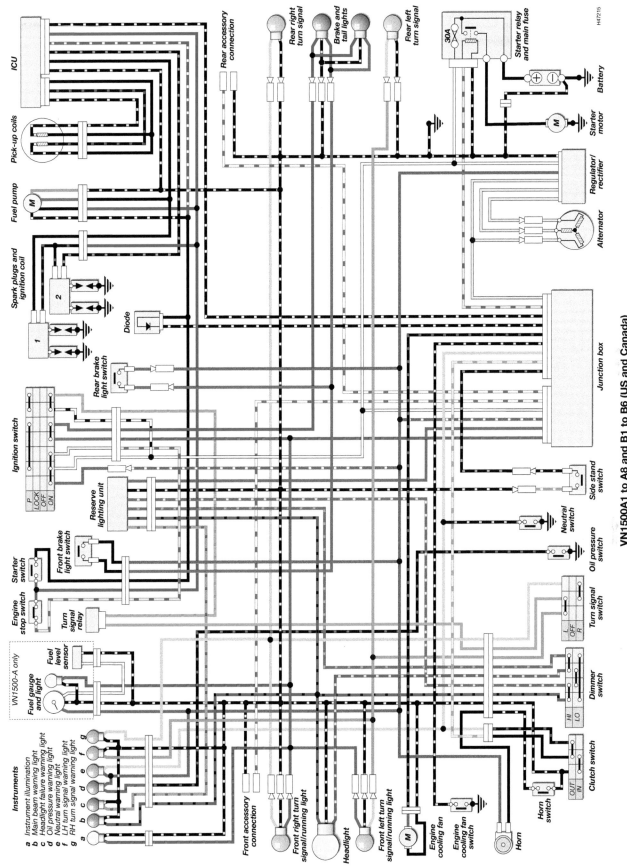

H47215

VN1500A1 to A8 and B1 to B6 (US and Canada)
(for fuse details see illustrations 6.2a and 6.2b in Chapter 9)

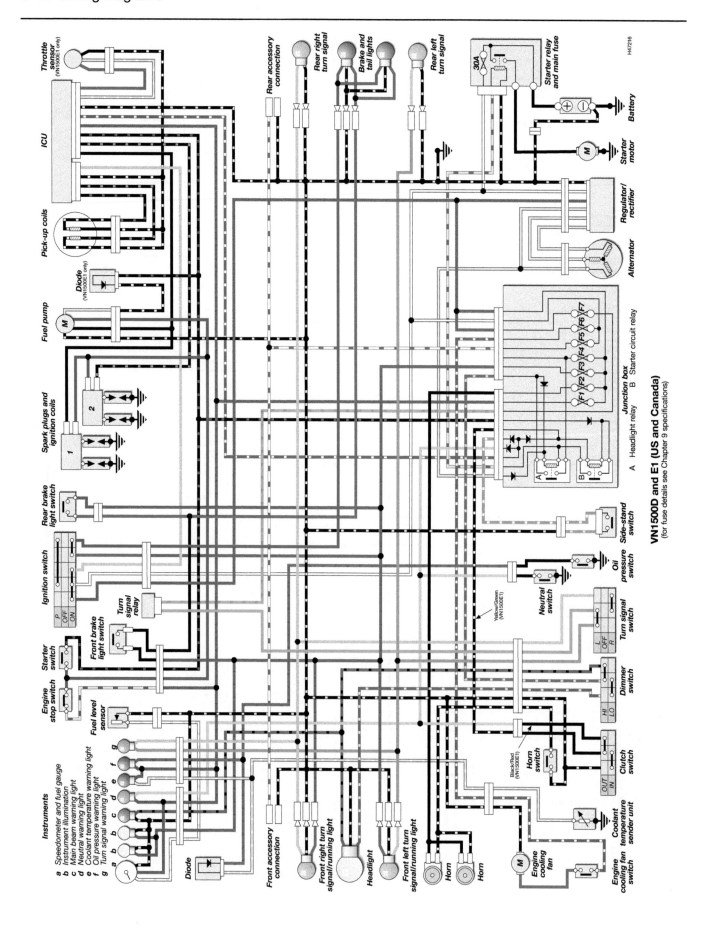

VN1500D and E1 (US and Canada)
(for fuse details see Chapter 9 specifications)

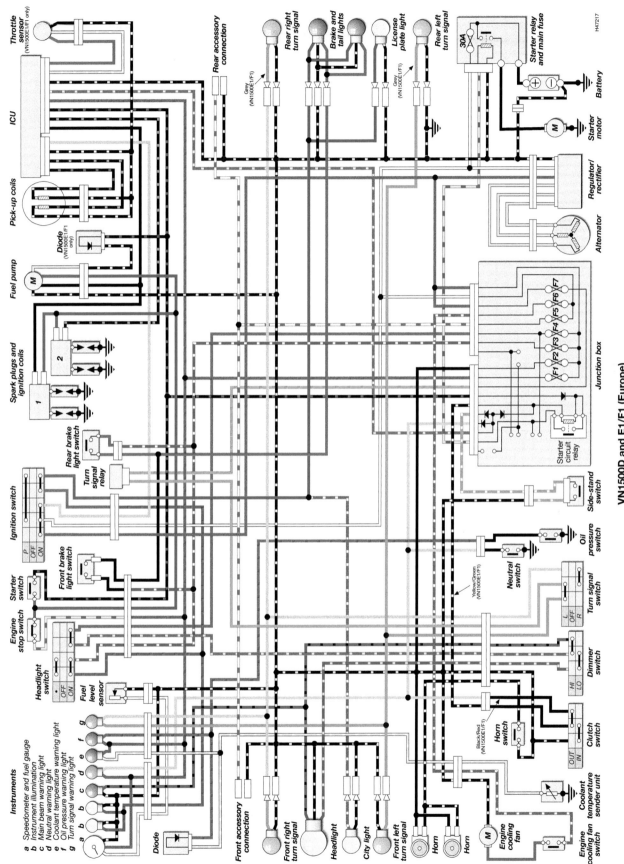

VN1500D and E1/F1 (Europe)
(for fuse details see Chapter 9 specifications)

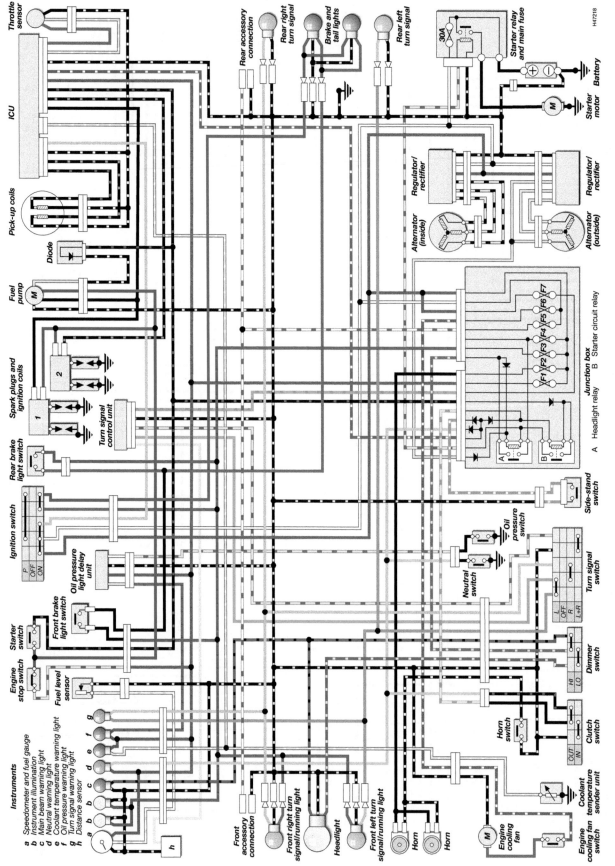

VN1500E2 to E7 (US and Canada) and VN1500G1 to G3 (US and Canada)
(for fuse details see Chapter 9 specifications)

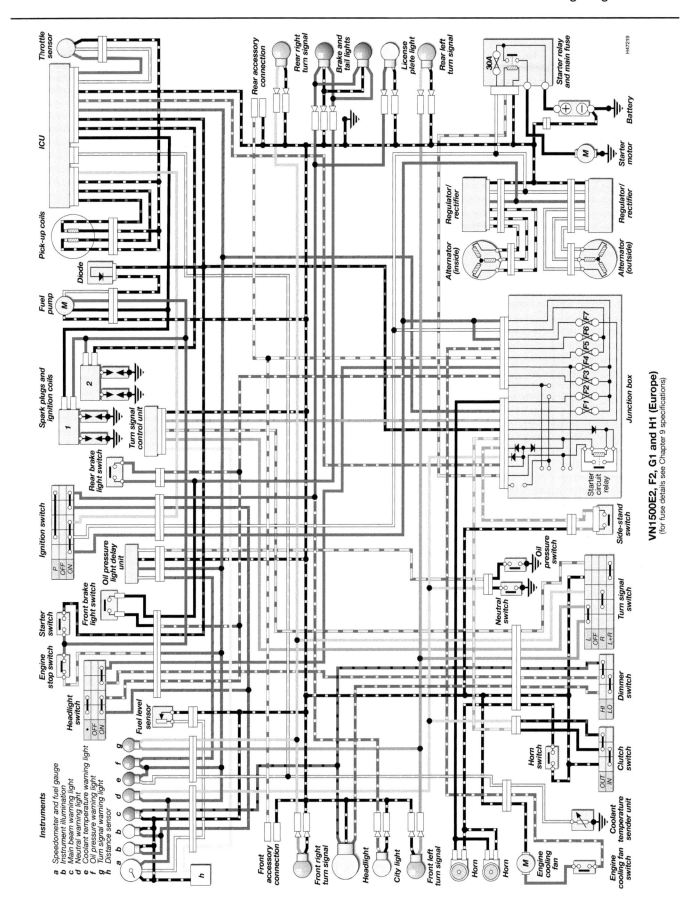

VN1500E2, F2, G1 and H1 (Europe)
(for fuse details see Chapter 9 specifications)

Instruments

a Speedometer and fuel gauge
b Instrument illumination
c Main beam warning light
d Neutral warning light
e Coolant temperature warning light
f Oil pressure warning light
g Turn signal warning light
h Distance sensor

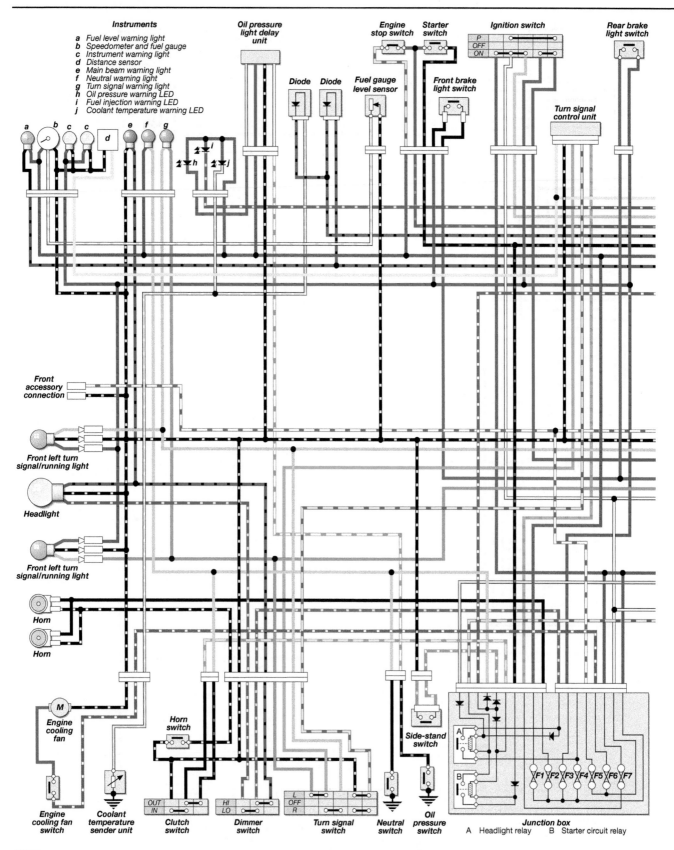

Instruments

a Fuel level warning light
b Speedometer and fuel gauge
c Instrument warning light
d Distance sensor
e Main beam warning light
f Neutral warning light
g Turn signal warning light
h Oil pressure warning LED
i Fuel injection warning LED
j Coolant temperature warning LED

Oil pressure light delay unit

Diode Diode

Fuel gauge level sensor

Engine stop switch Starter switch

Front brake light switch

Ignition switch

Rear brake light switch

Turn signal control unit

Front accessory connection

Front left turn signal/running light

Headlight

Front left turn signal/running light

Horn

Horn

Engine cooling fan

Engine cooling fan switch

Coolant temperature sender unit

Horn switch

Clutch switch

Dimmer switch

Turn signal switch

Neutral switch

Side-stand switch

Oil pressure switch

Junction box
A Headlight relay   B Starter circuit relay

VN1500J1 and L1 (US and Canada)
(for fuse details see Chapter 9 specifications)

H47220

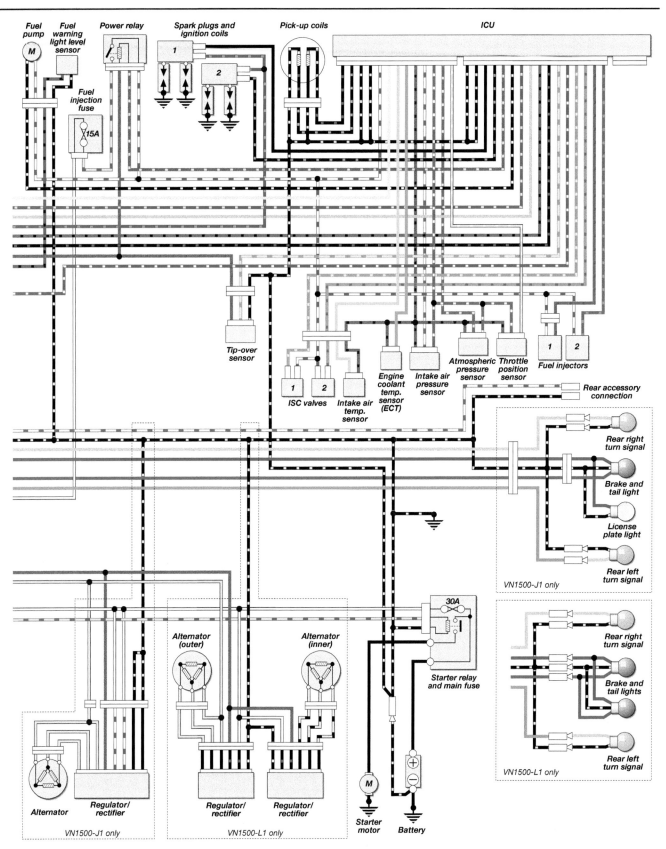

VN1500J1 and L1 (US and Canada)
(for fuse details see Chapter 9 specifications)

H47221

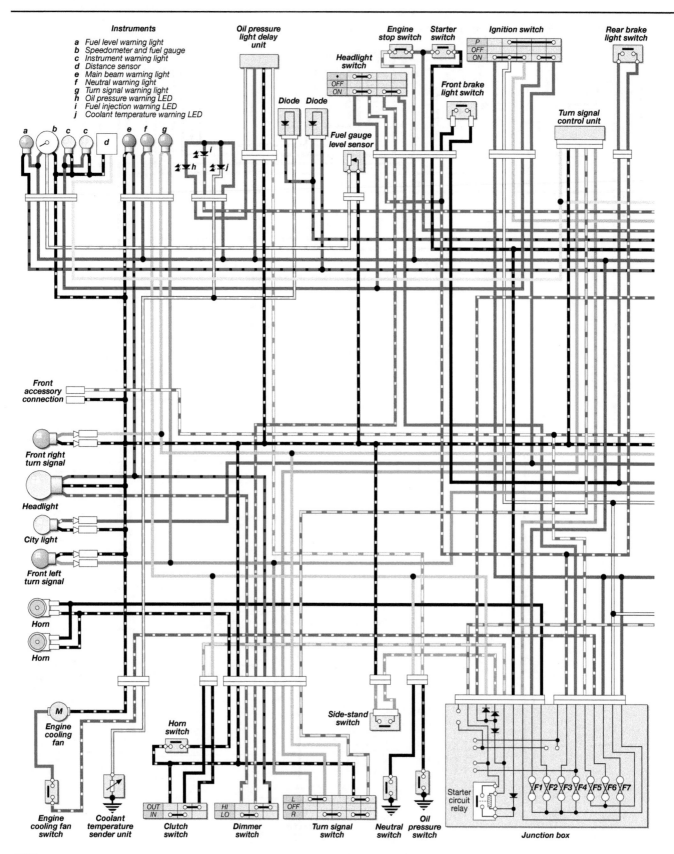

Instruments

a Fuel level warning light
b Speedometer and fuel gauge
c Instrument warning light
d Distance sensor
e Main beam warning light
f Neutral warning light
g Turn signal warning light
h Oil pressure warning LED
i Fuel injection warning LED
j Coolant temperature warning LED

VN1500J1 and L1 (Europe)
(for fuse details see Chapter 9 specifications)

H47222

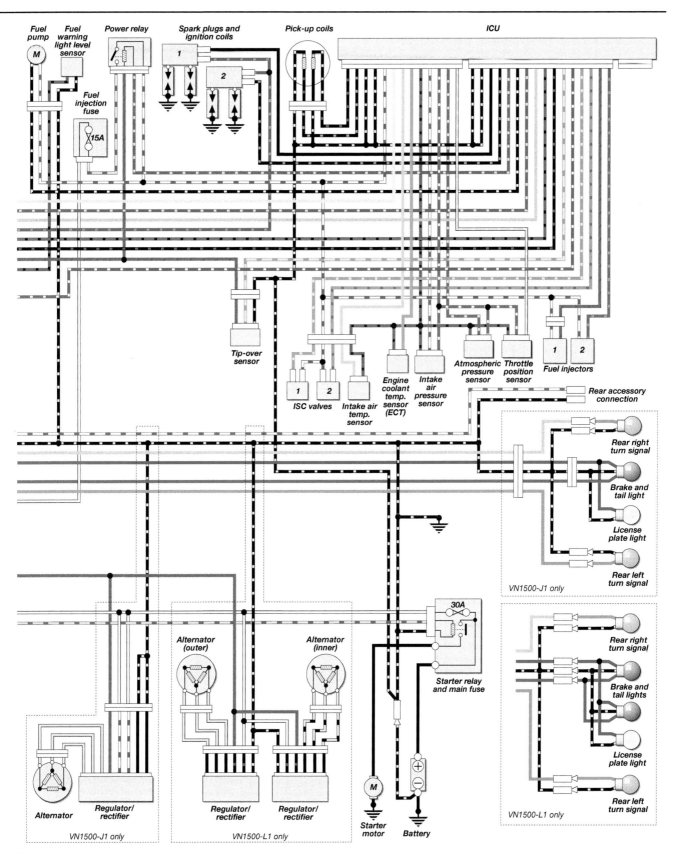

Fuel pump

Fuel warning light level sensor

Power relay

Spark plugs and ignition coils

Pick-up coils

ICU

Fuel injection fuse

15A

Tip-over sensor

ISC valves

Intake air temp. sensor

Engine coolant temp. sensor (ECT)

Intake air pressure sensor

Atmospheric pressure sensor

Throttle position sensor

Fuel injectors

Rear accessory connection

Rear right turn signal

Brake and tail light

License plate light

Rear left turn signal

VN1500-J1 only

Rear right turn signal

Brake and tail lights

License plate light

Rear left turn signal

VN1500-L1 only

Alternator (outer)

Alternator (inner)

30A

Starter relay and main fuse

Alternator

Regulator/ rectifier

Regulator/ rectifier

Regulator/ rectifier

M

Starter motor

Battery

VN1500-J1 only

VN1500-L1 only

H47223

VN1500J1 and L1 (Europe)
(for fuse details see Chapter 9 specifications)

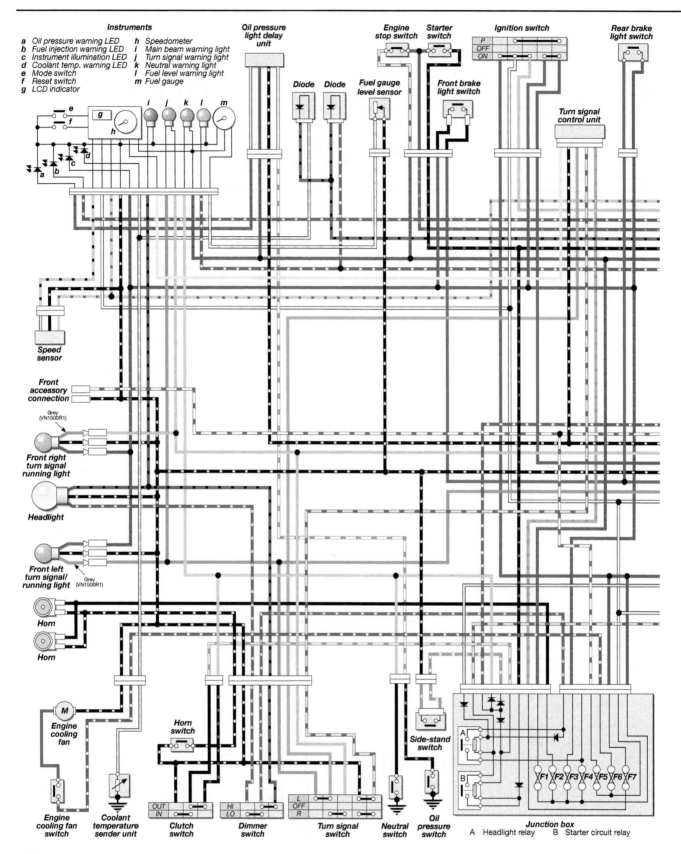

Instruments

a Oil pressure warning LED
b Fuel injection warning LED
c Instrument illumination LED
d Coolant temp. warning LED
e Mode switch
f Reset switch
g LCD indicator
h Speedometer
i Main beam warning light
j Turn signal warning light
k Neutral warning light
l Fuel level warning light
m Fuel gauge

VN1500R1 and R2 (US and Canada)
(for fuse details see Chapter 9 specifications)

H47224

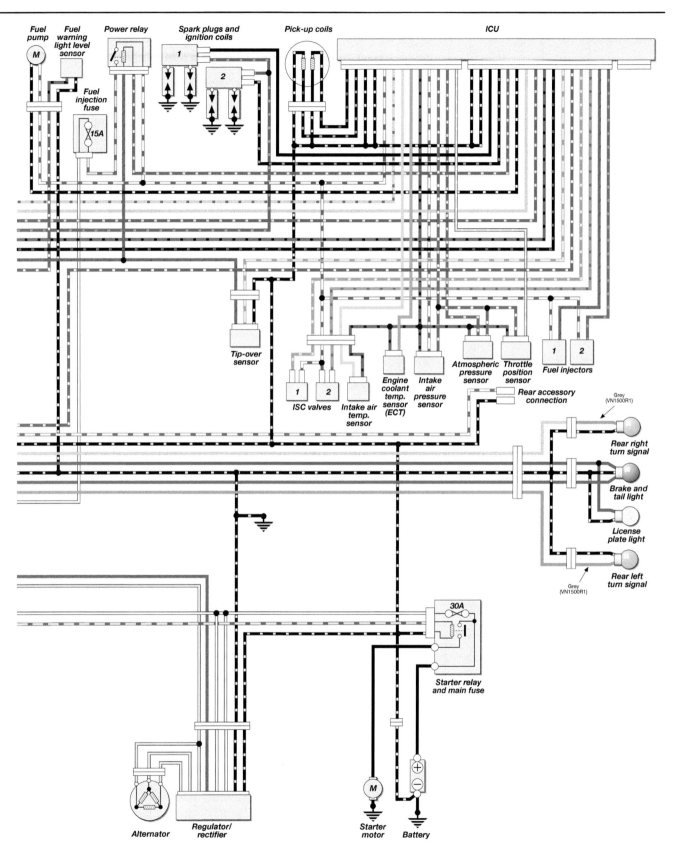

VN1500R1 and R2 (US and Canada)
(for fuse details see Chapter 9 specifications)

H47225

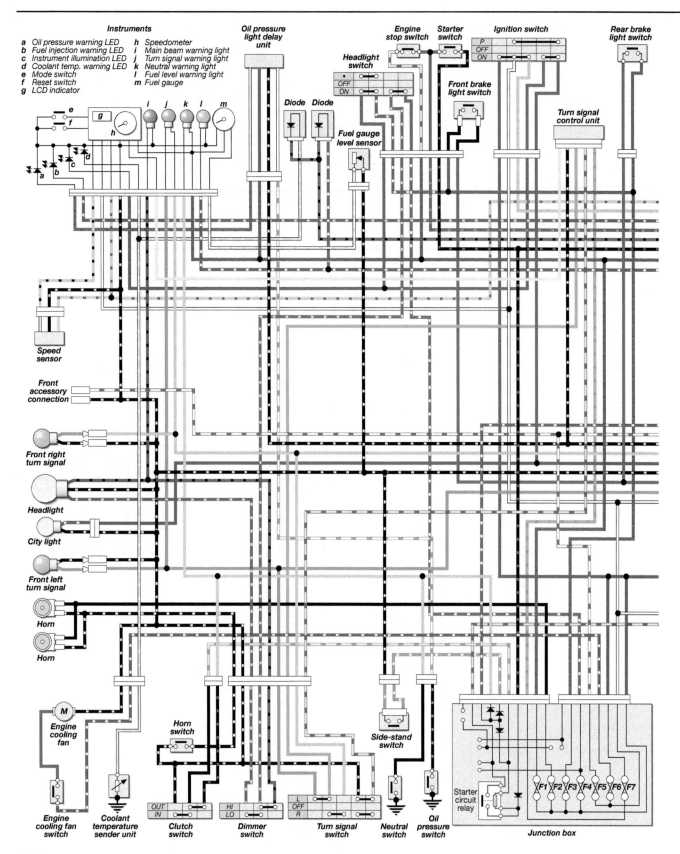

Instruments

a Oil pressure warning LED
b Fuel injection warning LED
c Instrument illumination LED
d Coolant temp. warning LED
e Mode switch
f Reset switch
g LCD indicator

h Speedometer
i Main beam warning light
j Turn signal warning light
k Neutral warning light
l Fuel level warning light
m Fuel gauge

H47226

VN1500R1 (Europe)
(for fuse details see Chapter 9 specifications)

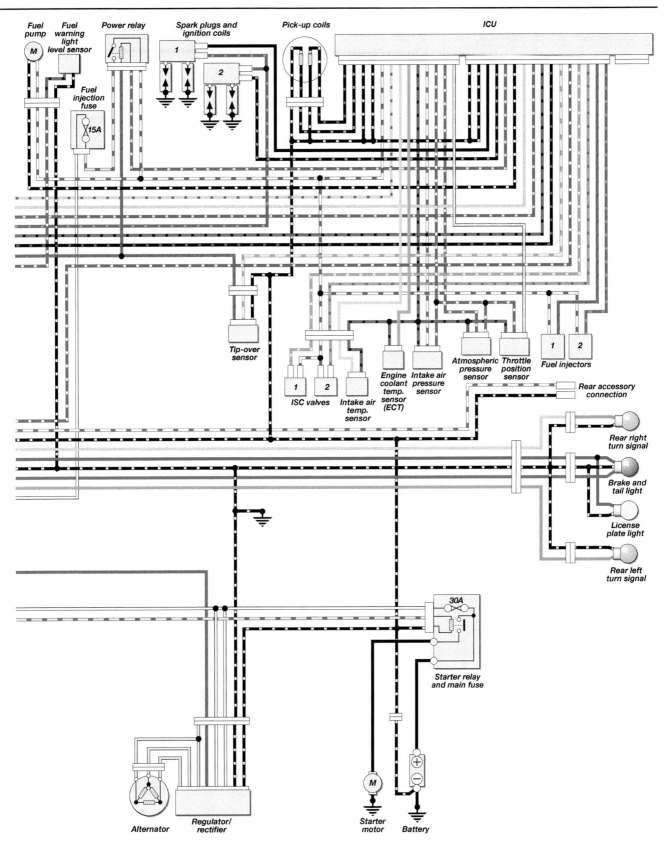

VN1500R1 (Europe)
(for fuse details see Chapter 9 specifications)

H47227

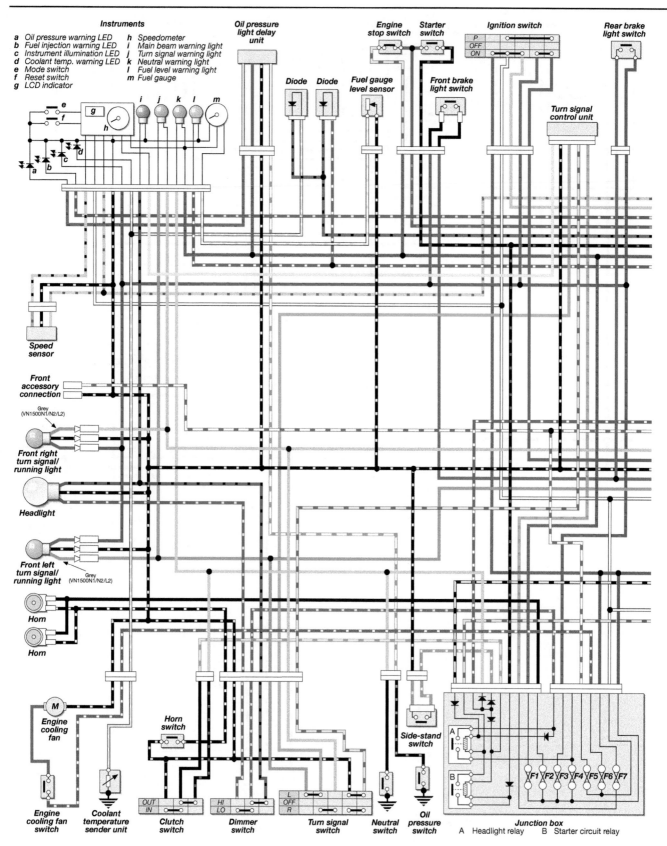

Instruments

a Oil pressure warning LED
b Fuel injection warning LED
c Instrument illumination LED
d Coolant temp. warning LED
e Mode switch
f Reset switch
g LCD indicator

h Speedometer
i Main beam warning light
j Turn signal warning light
k Neutral warning light
l Fuel level warning light
m Fuel gauge

Oil pressure light delay unit

Diode

Diode

Fuel gauge level sensor

Engine stop switch

Starter switch

Front brake light switch

Ignition switch

Rear brake light switch

Turn signal control unit

Speed sensor

Front accessory connection

Grey (VN1500N1/N2/L2)

Front right turn signal/ running light

Headlight

Front left turn signal/ running light

Grey (VN1500N1/N2/L2)

Horn

Horn

Engine cooling fan

Engine cooling fan switch

Coolant temperature sender unit

Horn switch

Clutch switch

Dimmer switch

Turn signal switch

Side-stand switch

Neutral switch

Oil pressure switch

Junction box
A Headlight relay   B Starter circuit relay

F1 F2 F3 F4 F5 F6 F7

H47228

VN1500N and VN1500L2-on (US and Canada)
(for fuse details see Chapter 9 specifications)

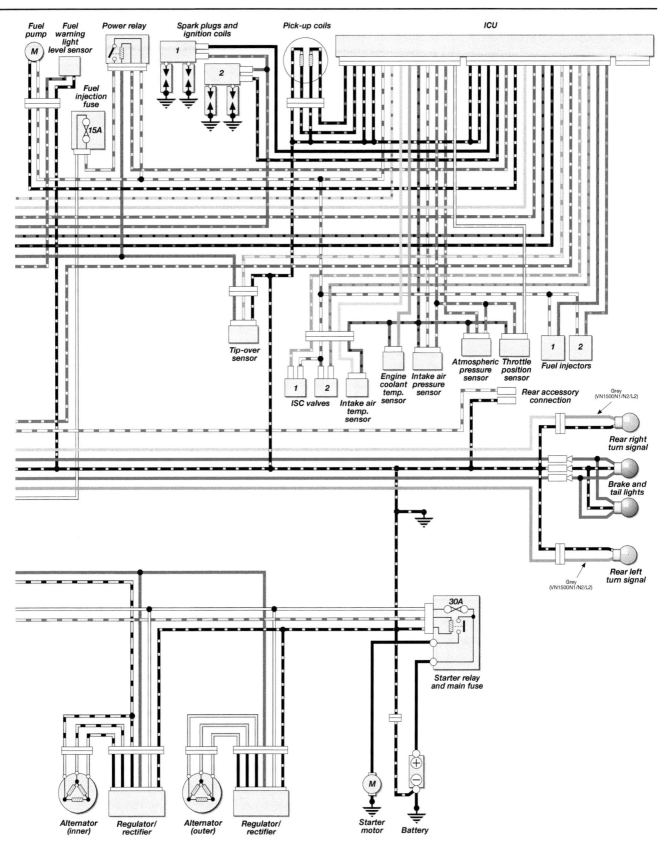

Fuel pump

Fuel warning light level sensor

Power relay

Spark plugs and ignition coils

Pick-up coils

ICU

Fuel injection fuse

15A

Tip-over sensor

ISC valves

Intake air temp. sensor

Engine coolant temp. sensor

Intake air pressure sensor

Atmospheric pressure sensor

Throttle position sensor

Fuel injectors

Rear accessory connection

Grey (VN1500N1/N2/L2)

Rear right turn signal

Brake and tail lights

Grey (VN1500N1/N2/L2)

Rear left turn signal

30A

Starter relay and main fuse

Alternator (inner)

Regulator/ rectifier

Alternator (outer)

Regulator/ rectifier

Starter motor

Battery

H47229

VN1500N and VN1500L2-on (US and Canada)
(for fuse details see Chapter 9 specifications)

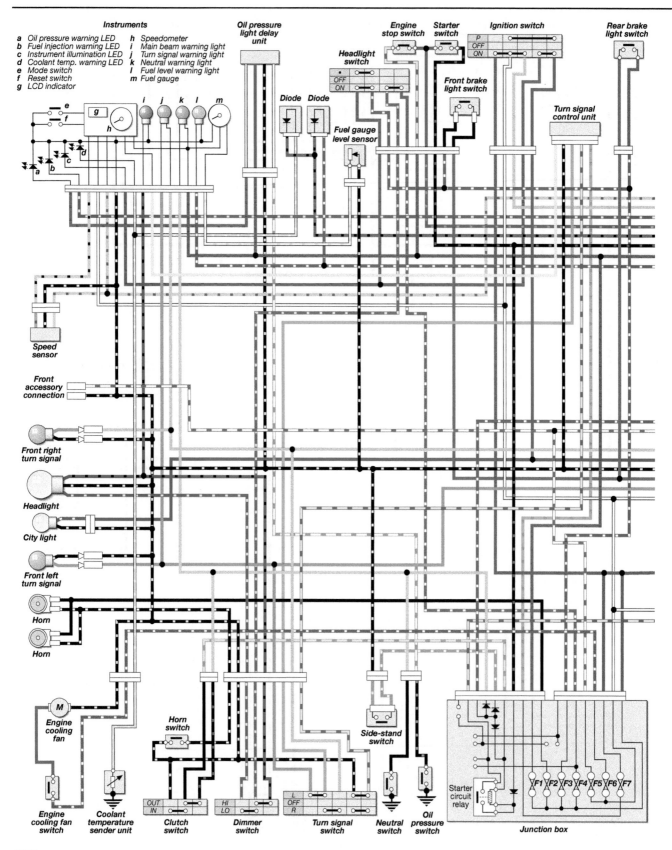

Instruments

a Oil pressure warning LED
b Fuel injection warning LED
c Instrument illumination LED
d Coolant temp. warning LED
e Mode switch
f Reset switch
g LCD indicator
h Speedometer
i Main beam warning light
j Turn signal warning light
k Neutral warning light
l Fuel level warning light
m Fuel gauge

VN1500N and VN1500L2 - on (Europe)
(for fuse details see Chapter 9 specifications)

H47230

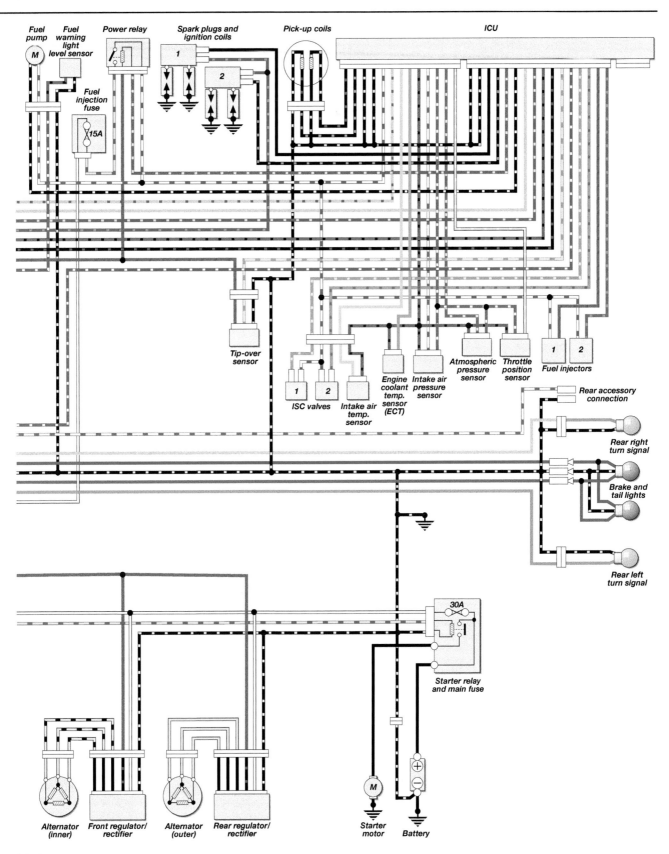

H47231

VN1500N and VN1500L2-on (Europe)
(for fuse details see Chapter 9 specifications)

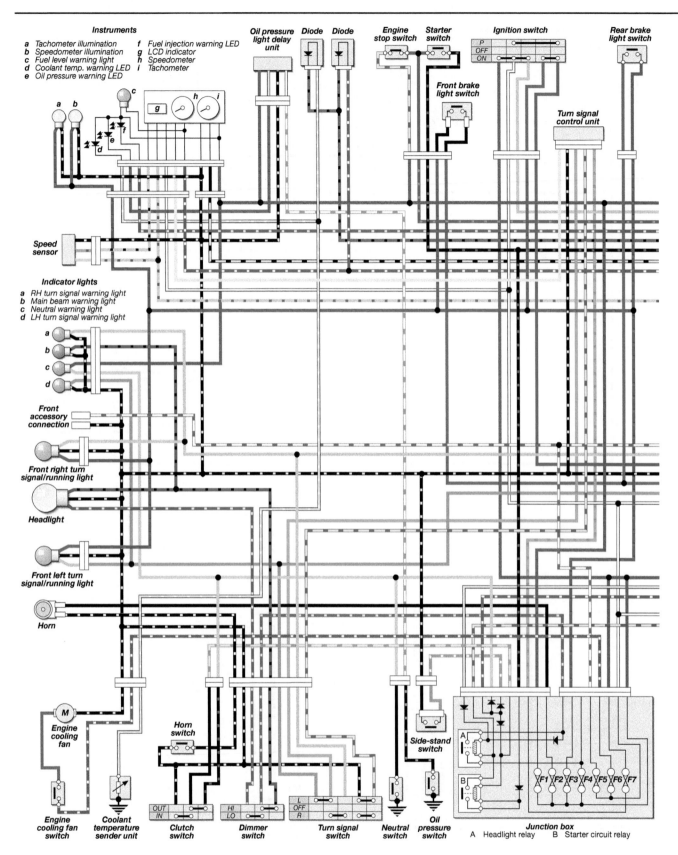

Instruments
a Tachometer illumination
b Speedometer illumination
c Fuel level warning light
d Coolant temp. warning LED
e Oil pressure warning LED
f Fuel injection warning LED
g LCD indicator
h Speedometer
i Tachometer

Indicator lights
a RH turn signal warning light
b Main beam warning light
c Neutral warning light
d LH turn signal warning light

Speed sensor

Front accessory connection

Front right turn signal/running light

Headlight

Front left turn signal/running light

Horn

Engine cooling fan

Engine cooling fan switch

Coolant temperature sender unit

Horn switch

Clutch switch

Dimmer switch

Turn signal switch

Neutral switch

Oil pressure switch

Oil pressure light delay unit

Diode

Diode

Engine stop switch

Starter switch

Front brake light switch

Ignition switch

Rear brake light switch

Turn signal control unit

Side-stand switch

Junction box
A Headlight relay   B Starter circuit relay

H47232

VN1500P (US and Canada)
(for fuse details see Chapter 9 specifications)

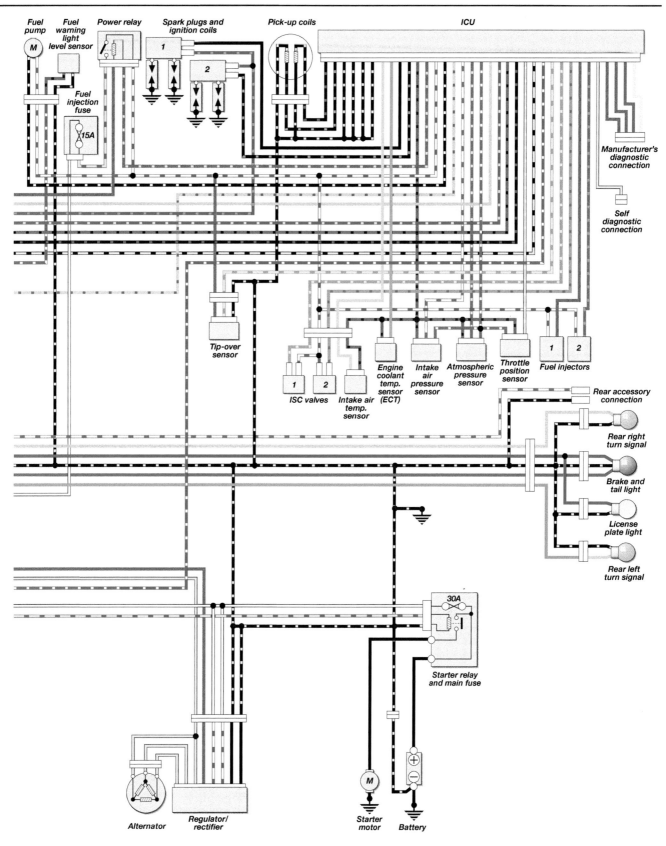

VN1500P (US and Canada)
(for fuse details see Chapter 9 specifications)

H47233

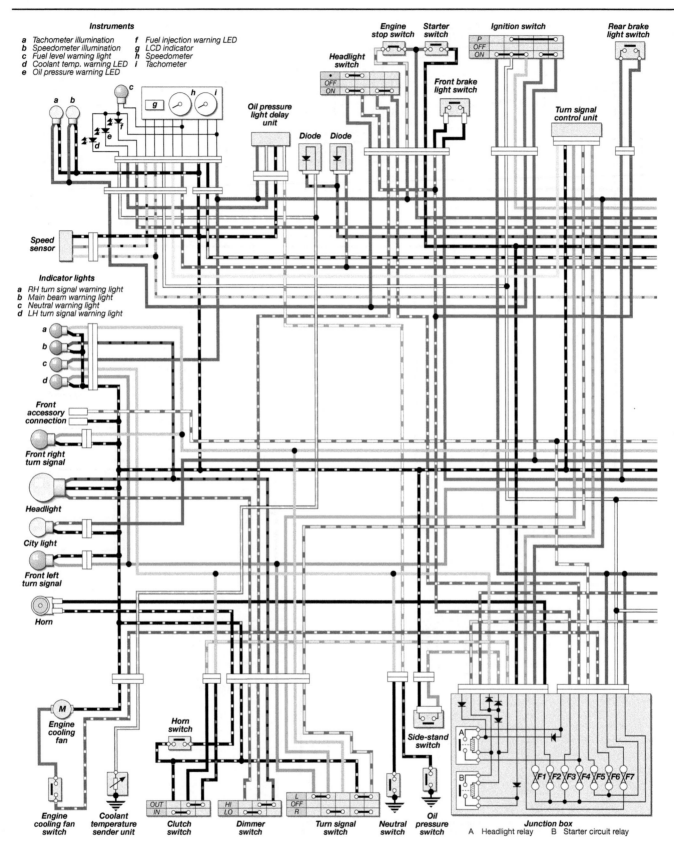

Instruments

a Tachometer illumination
b Speedometer illumination
c Fuel level warning light
d Coolant temp. warning LED
e Oil pressure warning LED
f Fuel injection warning LED
g LCD indicator
h Speedometer
i Tachometer

Indicator lights

a RH turn signal warning light
b Main beam warning light
c Neutral warning light
d LH turn signal warning light

Engine stop switch
Starter switch
Ignition switch
Rear brake light switch
Headlight switch
Front brake light switch
Oil pressure light delay unit
Diode
Diode
Turn signal control unit
Speed sensor
Front accessory connection
Front right turn signal
Headlight
City light
Front left turn signal
Horn
Engine cooling fan
Engine cooling fan switch
Coolant temperature sender unit
Horn switch
Clutch switch
Dimmer switch
Turn signal switch
Side-stand switch
Neutral switch
Oil pressure switch
Junction box
A Headlight relay   B Starter circuit relay

Clutch switch: OUT IN
Dimmer switch: HI LO
Turn signal switch: L OFF R

H47234

VN1500P (Europe)
(for fuse details see Chapter 9 specifications)

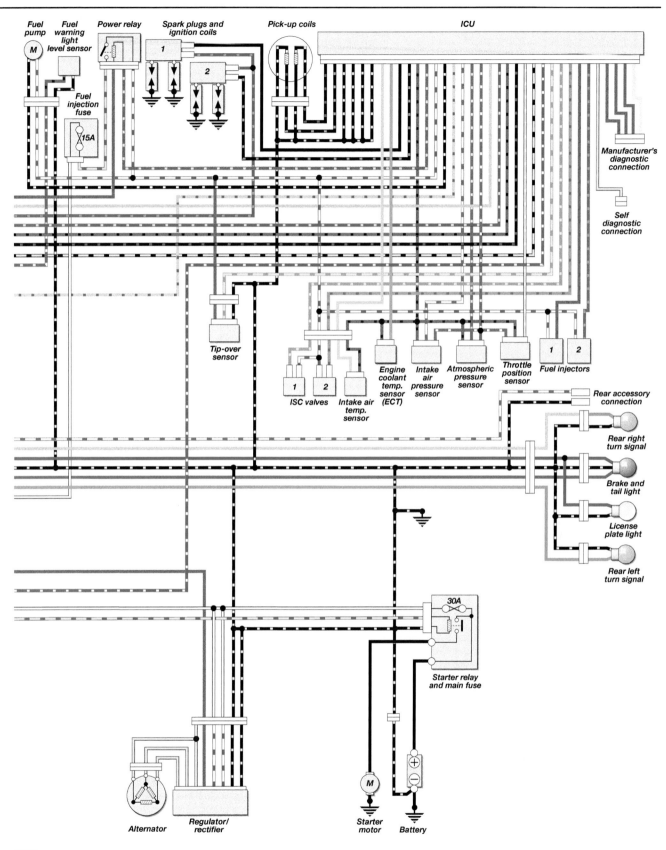

Fuel pump

Fuel warning light level sensor

Power relay

Spark plugs and ignition coils

1

2

Pick-up coils

ICU

Fuel injection fuse

15A

Manufacturer's diagnostic connection

Self diagnostic connection

Tip-over sensor

ISC valves

1   2

Intake air temp. sensor

Engine coolant temp. sensor (ECT)

Intake air pressure sensor

Atmospheric pressure sensor

Throttle position sensor

Fuel injectors

1   2

Rear accessory connection

Rear right turn signal

Brake and tail light

License plate light

Rear left turn signal

30A

Starter relay and main fuse

M

Starter motor

Battery

Alternator

Regulator/rectifier

H47235

VN1500P (Europe)
(for fuse details see Chapter 9 specifications)

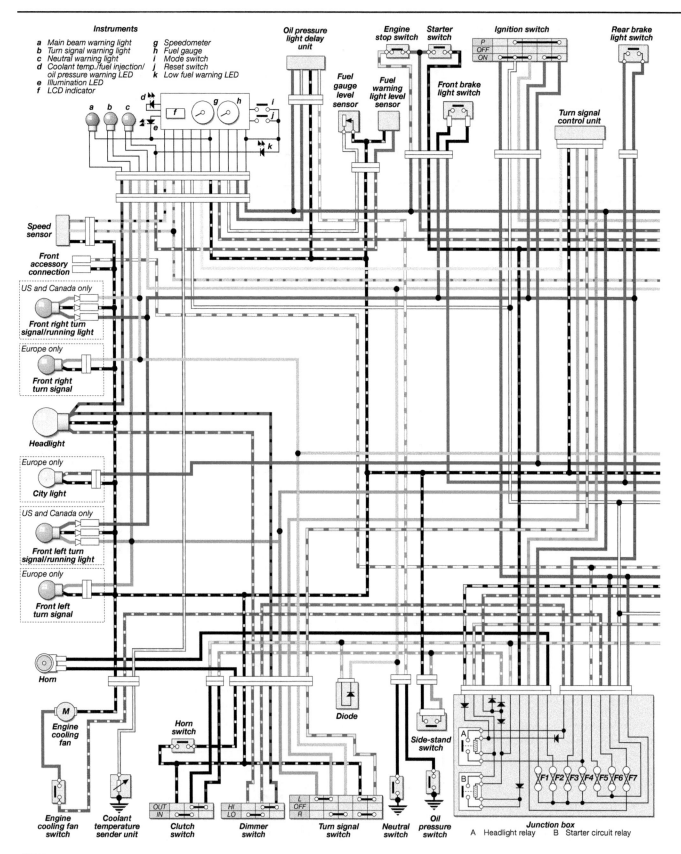

VN1600A and VN1600D
(for fuse details see Chapter 9 specifications)

H47236

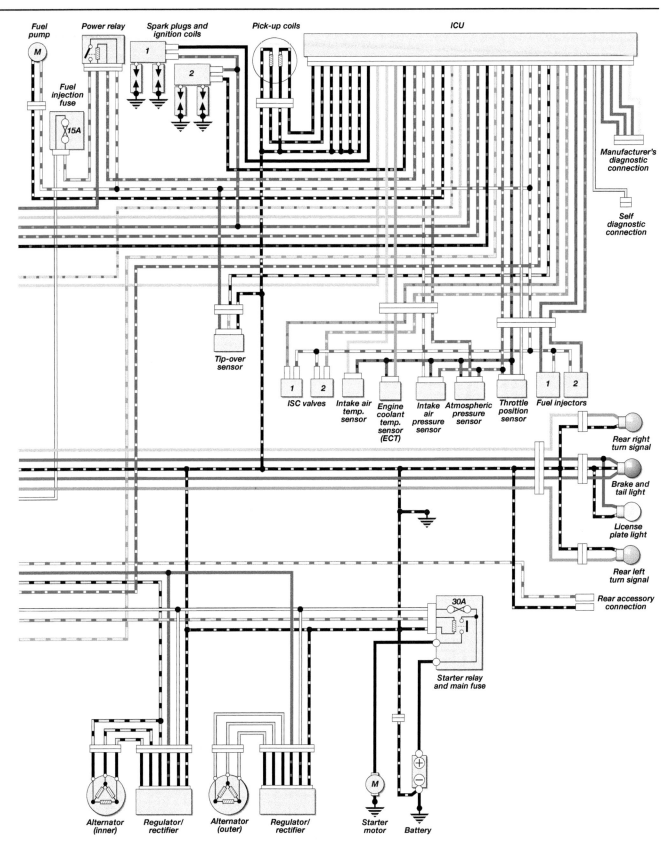

Fuel pump

Power relay

Spark plugs and ignition coils

Pick-up coils

ICU

Fuel injection fuse

15A

Manufacturer's diagnostic connection

Self diagnostic connection

Tip-over sensor

ISC valves

Intake air temp. sensor

Engine coolant temp. sensor (ECT)

Intake air pressure sensor

Atmospheric pressure sensor

Throttle position sensor

Fuel injectors

Rear right turn signal

Brake and tail light

License plate light

Rear left turn signal

Rear accessory connection

30A

Starter relay and main fuse

Alternator (inner)

Regulator/ rectifier

Alternator (outer)

Regulator/ rectifier

Starter motor

Battery

H47237

VN1600A and VN1600D
(for fuse details see Chapter 9 specifications)

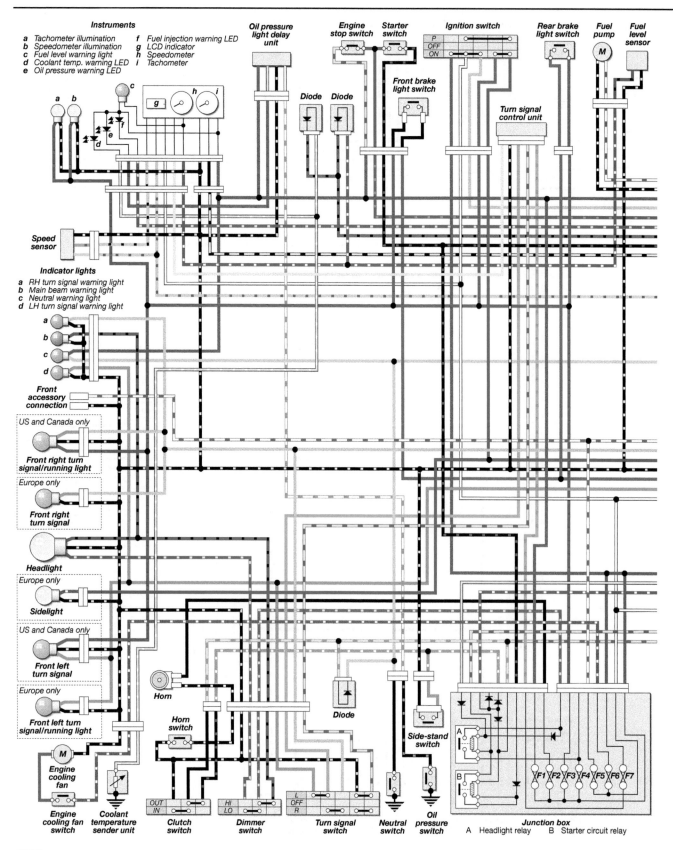

Instruments

a Tachometer illumination
b Speedometer illumination
c Fuel level warning light
d Coolant temp. warning LED
e Oil pressure warning LED
f Fuel injection warning LED
g LCD indicator
h Speedometer
i Tachometer

Indicator lights

a RH turn signal warning light
b Main beam warning light
c Neutral warning light
d LH turn signal warning light

H47238

VN1600B
(for fuse details see Chapter 9 specifications)

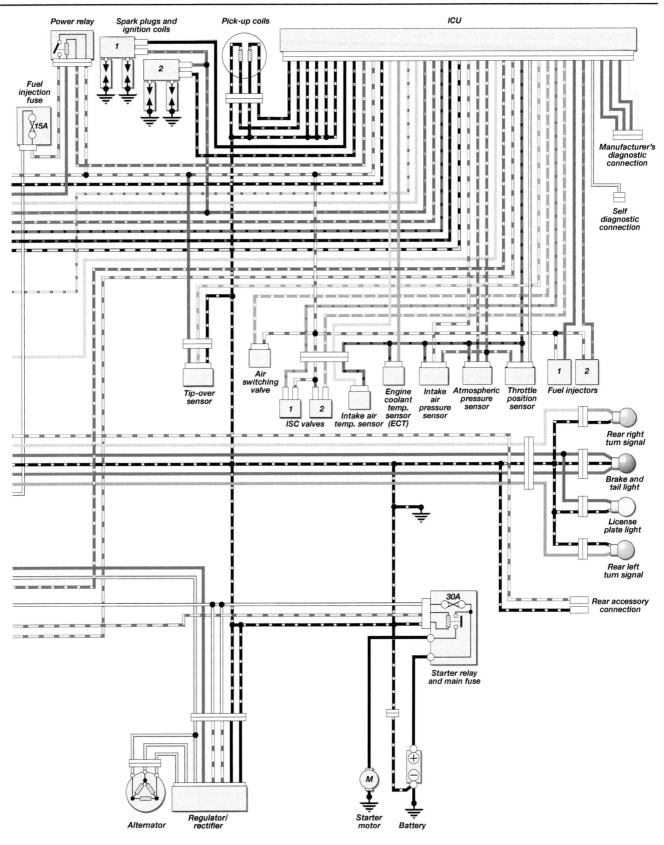

Power relay

Spark plugs and
ignition coils

Pick-up coils

ICU

Fuel
injection
fuse

15A

Manufacturer's
diagnostic
connection

Self
diagnostic
connection

Tip-over
sensor

Air
switching
valve

ISC valves

Intake air
temp. sensor

Engine
coolant
temp.
sensor
(ECT)

Intake
air
pressure
sensor

Atmospheric
pressure
sensor

Throttle
position
sensor

Fuel injectors

Rear right
turn signal

Brake and
tail light

License
plate light

Rear left
turn signal

Rear accessory
connection

30A

Starter relay
and main fuse

Alternator

Regulator/
rectifier

Starter
motor

Battery

H47239

VN1600B
(for fuse details see Chapter 9 specifications)

Reference

Tools and Workshop Tips

● Building up a tool kit and equipping your workshop ● Using tools ● Understanding bearing, seal, fastener and chain sizes and markings ● Repair techniques

Security

● Locks and chains ● U-locks ● Disc locks ● Alarms and immobilisers ● Security marking systems ● Tips on how to prevent bike theft

Lubricants and fluids

● Engine oils ● Transmission (gear) oils ● Coolant/anti-freeze ● Fork oils and suspension fluids ● Brake/clutch fluids ● Spray lubes, degreasers and solvents

Conversion Factors

$$34 \text{ Nm} \times 0.738 = 25 \text{ lbf ft}$$

● Formulae for conversion of the metric (SI) units used throughout the manual into Imperial measures

Storage

● How to prepare your motorcycle for going into storage and protect essential systems ● How to get the motorcycle back on the road

Troubleshooting

● Common faults and their likely causes ● Links to main chapters for testing or repair procedures

Technical Terms Explained

● Component names, technical terms and common abbreviations explained

Index

Buying tools

A toolkit is a fundamental requirement for servicing and repairing a motorcycle. Although there will be an initial expense in building up enough tools for servicing, this will soon be offset by the savings made by doing the job yourself. As experience and confidence grow, additional tools can be added to enable the repair and overhaul of the motorcycle. Many of the specialist tools are expensive and not often used so it may be preferable to hire them, or for a group of friends or motorcycle club to join in the purchase.

As a rule, it is better to buy more expensive, good quality tools. Cheaper tools are likely to wear out faster and need to be renewed more often, nullifying the original saving.

> ⚠ **Warning: To avoid the risk of a poor quality tool breaking in use, causing injury or damage to the component being worked on, always aim to purchase tools which meet the relevant national safety standards.**

The following lists of tools do not represent the manufacturer's service tools, but serve as a guide to help the owner decide which tools are needed for this level of work. In addition, items such as an electric drill, hacksaw, files, soldering iron and a workbench equipped with a vice, may be needed. Although not classed as tools, a selection of bolts, screws, nuts, washers and pieces of tubing always come in useful.

For more information about tools, refer to the Haynes *Motorcycle Workshop Practice Techbook* (Bk. No. 3470).

Manufacturer's service tools

Inevitably certain tasks require the use of a service tool. Where possible an alternative tool or method of approach is recommended, but sometimes there is no option if personal injury or damage to the component is to be avoided. Where required, service tools are referred to in the relevant procedure.

Service tools can usually only be purchased from a motorcycle dealer and are identified by a part number. Some of the commonly-used tools, such as rotor pullers, are available in aftermarket form from mail-order motorcycle tool and accessory suppliers.

Maintenance and minor repair tools

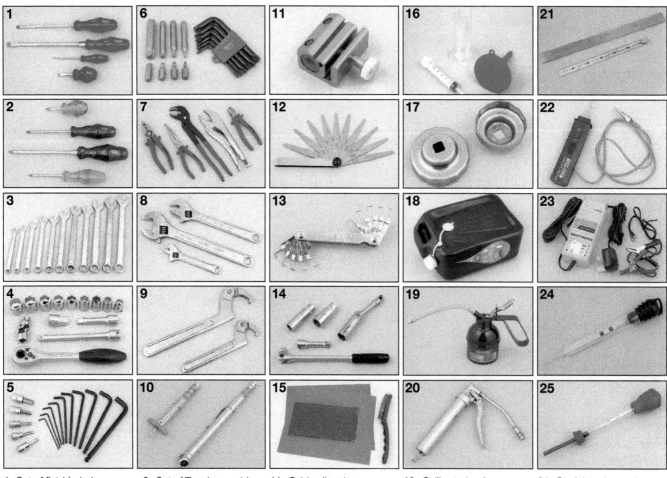

1 Set of flat-bladed screwdrivers
2 Set of Phillips head screwdrivers
3 Combination open-end and ring spanners
4 Socket set (3/8 inch or 1/2 inch drive)
5 Set of Allen keys or bits

6 Set of Torx keys or bits
7 Pliers, cutters and self-locking grips (Mole grips)
8 Adjustable spanners
9 C-spanners
10 Tread depth gauge and tyre pressure gauge

11 Cable oiler clamp
12 Feeler gauges
13 Spark plug gap measuring tool
14 Spark plug spanner or deep plug sockets
15 Wire brush and emery paper

16 Calibrated syringe, measuring vessel and funnel
17 Oil filter adapters
18 Oil drainer can or tray
19 Pump type oil can
20 Grease gun

21 Straight-edge and steel rule
22 Continuity tester
23 Battery charger
24 Hydrometer (for battery specific gravity check)
25 Anti-freeze tester (for liquid-cooled engines)

Repair and overhaul tools

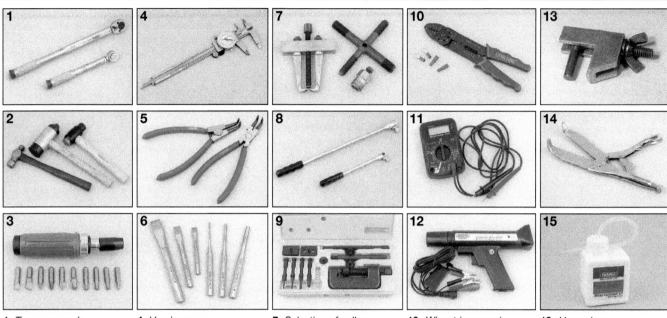

1 Torque wrench
(small and mid-ranges)
2 Conventional, plastic or
soft-faced hammers
3 Impact driver set

4 Vernier gauge
5 Circlip pliers (internal and
external, or combination)
6 Set of cold chisels
and punches

7 Selection of pullers
8 Breaker bars
9 Chain breaking/
riveting tool set

10 Wire stripper and
crimper tool
11 Multimeter (measures
amps, volts and ohms)
12 Stroboscope (for
dynamic timing checks)

13 Hose clamp
(wingnut type shown)
14 Clutch holding tool
15 One-man brake/clutch
bleeder kit

Specialist tools

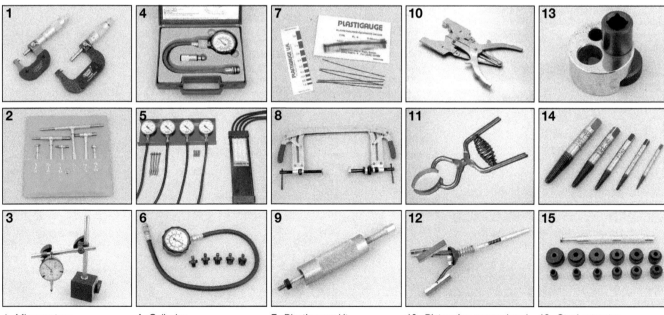

1 Micrometers
(external type)
2 Telescoping gauges
3 Dial gauge

4 Cylinder
compression gauge
5 Vacuum gauges (left) or
manometer (right)
6 Oil pressure gauge

7 Plastigauge kit
8 Valve spring compressor
(4-stroke engines)
9 Piston pin drawbolt tool

10 Piston ring removal and
installation tool
11 Piston ring clamp
12 Cylinder bore hone
(stone type shown)

13 Stud extractor
14 Screw extractor set
15 Bearing driver set

1 Workshop equipment and facilities

The workbench

● Work is made much easier by raising the bike up on a ramp - components are much more accessible if raised to waist level. The hydraulic or pneumatic types seen in the dealer's workshop are a sound investment if you undertake a lot of repairs or overhauls **(see illustration 1.1)**.

1.1 Hydraulic motorcycle ramp

● If raised off ground level, the bike must be supported on the ramp to avoid it falling. Most ramps incorporate a front wheel locating clamp which can be adjusted to suit different diameter wheels. When tightening the clamp, take care not to mark the wheel rim or damage the tyre - use wood blocks on each side to prevent this.
● Secure the bike to the ramp using tie-downs **(see illustration 1.2)**. If the bike has only a sidestand, and hence leans at a dangerous angle when raised, support the bike on an auxiliary stand.

1.2 Tie-downs are used around the passenger footrests to secure the bike

● Auxiliary (paddock) stands are widely available from mail order companies or motorcycle dealers and attach either to the wheel axle or swingarm pivot **(see illustration 1.3)**. If the motorcycle has a centrestand, you can support it under the crankcase to prevent it toppling whilst either wheel is removed **(see illustration 1.4)**.

1.3 This auxiliary stand attaches to the swingarm pivot

1.4 Always use a block of wood between the engine and jack head when supporting the engine in this way

Fumes and fire

● Refer to the Safety first! page at the beginning of the manual for full details. Make sure your workshop is equipped with a fire extinguisher suitable for fuel-related fires (Class B fire - flammable liquids) - it is not sufficient to have a water-filled extinguisher.
● Always ensure adequate ventilation is available. Unless an exhaust gas extraction system is available for use, ensure that the engine is run outside of the workshop.
● If working on the fuel system, make sure the workshop is ventilated to avoid a build-up of fumes. This applies equally to fume build-up when charging a battery. Do not smoke or allow anyone else to smoke in the workshop.

Fluids

● If you need to drain fuel from the tank, store it in an approved container marked as suitable for the storage of petrol (gasoline) **(see illustration 1.5)**. Do not store fuel in glass jars or bottles.

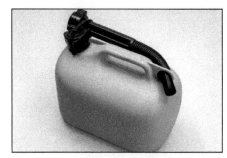

1.5 Use an approved can only for storing petrol (gasoline)

● Use proprietary engine degreasers or solvents which have a high flash-point, such as paraffin (kerosene), for cleaning off oil, grease and dirt - never use petrol (gasoline) for cleaning. Wear rubber gloves when handling solvent and engine degreaser. The fumes from certain solvents can be dangerous - always work in a well-ventilated area.

Dust, eye and hand protection

● Protect your lungs from inhalation of dust particles by wearing a filtering mask over the nose and mouth. Many frictional materials still contain asbestos which is dangerous to your health. Protect your eyes from spouts of liquid and sprung components by wearing a pair of protective goggles **(see illustration 1.6)**.

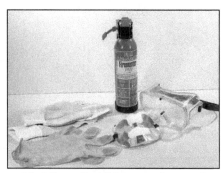

1.6 A fire extinguisher, goggles, mask and protective gloves should be at hand in the workshop

● Protect your hands from contact with solvents, fuel and oils by wearing rubber gloves. Alternatively apply a barrier cream to your hands before starting work. If handling hot components or fluids, wear suitable gloves to protect your hands from scalding and burns.

What to do with old fluids

● Old cleaning solvent, fuel, coolant and oils should not be poured down domestic drains or onto the ground. Package the fluid up in old oil containers, label it accordingly, and take it to a garage or disposal facility. Contact your local authority for location of such sites or ring the oil care hotline.

OIL CARE
FOLLOW THE CODE

Note: It is antisocial and illegal to dump oil down the drain. To find the location of your local oil recycling bank in the UK, call 08708 506 506 or visit www. oilbankline.org.uk

In the USA, note that any oil supplier must accept used oil for recycling.

2 Fasteners -
screws, bolts and nuts

Fastener types and applications

Bolts and screws

● Fastener head types are either of hexagonal, Torx or splined design, with internal and external versions of each type **(see illustrations 2.1 and 2.2)**; splined head fasteners are not in common use on motorcycles. The conventional slotted or Phillips head design is used for certain screws. Bolt or screw length is always measured from the underside of the head to the end of the item **(see illustration 2.11)**.

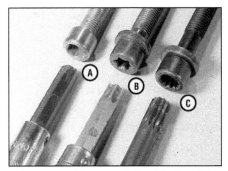

2.1 Internal hexagon/Allen (A), Torx (B) and splined (C) fasteners, with corresponding bits

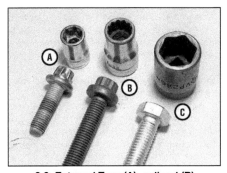

2.2 External Torx (A), splined (B) and hexagon (C) fasteners, with corresponding sockets

● Certain fasteners on the motorcycle have a tensile marking on their heads, the higher the marking the stronger the fastener. High tensile fasteners generally carry a 10 or higher marking. Never replace a high tensile fastener with one of a lower tensile strength.

Washers **(see illustration 2.3)**

● Plain washers are used between a fastener head and a component to prevent damage to the component or to spread the load when torque is applied. Plain washers can also be used as spacers or shims in certain assemblies. Copper or aluminium plain washers are often used as sealing washers on drain plugs.

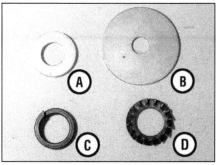

2.3 Plain washer (A), penny washer (B), spring washer (C) and serrated washer (D)

● The split-ring spring washer works by applying axial tension between the fastener head and component. If flattened, it is fatigued and must be renewed. If a plain (flat) washer is used on the fastener, position the spring washer between the fastener and the plain washer.

● Serrated star type washers dig into the fastener and component faces, preventing loosening. They are often used on electrical earth (ground) connections to the frame.

● Cone type washers (sometimes called Belleville) are conical and when tightened apply axial tension between the fastener head and component. They must be installed with the dished side against the component and often carry an OUTSIDE marking on their outer face. If flattened, they are fatigued and must be renewed.

● Tab washers are used to lock plain nuts or bolts on a shaft. A portion of the tab washer is bent up hard against one flat of the nut or bolt to prevent it loosening. Due to the tab washer being deformed in use, a new tab washer should be used every time it is disturbed.

● Wave washers are used to take up endfloat on a shaft. They provide light springing and prevent excessive side-to-side play of a component. Can be found on rocker arm shafts.

Nuts and split pins

● Conventional plain nuts are usually six-sided **(see illustration 2.4)**. They are sized by thread diameter and pitch. High tensile nuts carry a number on one end to denote their tensile strength.

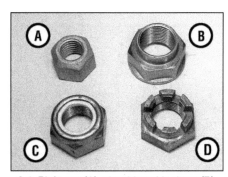

2.4 Plain nut (A), shouldered locknut (B), nylon insert nut (C) and castellated nut (D)

● Self-locking nuts either have a nylon insert, or two spring metal tabs, or a shoulder which is staked into a groove in the shaft - their advantage over conventional plain nuts is a resistance to loosening due to vibration. The nylon insert type can be used a number of times, but must be renewed when the friction of the nylon insert is reduced, ie when the nut spins freely on the shaft. The spring tab type can be reused unless the tabs are damaged. The shouldered type must be renewed every time it is disturbed.

● Split pins (cotter pins) are used to lock a castellated nut to a shaft or to prevent slackening of a plain nut. Common applications are wheel axles and brake torque arms. Because the split pin arms are deformed to lock around the nut a new split pin must always be used on installation - always fit the correct size split pin which will fit snugly in the shaft hole. Make sure the split pin arms are correctly located around the nut **(see illustrations 2.5 and 2.6)**.

2.5 Bend split pin (cotter pin) arms as shown (arrows) to secure a castellated nut

2.6 Bend split pin (cotter pin) arms as shown to secure a plain nut

Caution: If the castellated nut slots do not align with the shaft hole after tightening to the torque setting, tighten the nut until the next slot aligns with the hole - never slacken the nut to align its slot.

● R-pins (shaped like the letter R), or slip pins as they are sometimes called, are sprung and can be reused if they are otherwise in good condition. Always install R-pins with their closed end facing forwards **(see illustration 2.7)**.

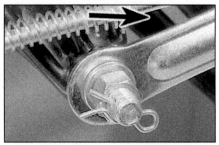

2.7 Correct fitting of R-pin. Arrow indicates forward direction

Circlips (see illustration 2.8)

● Circlips (sometimes called snap-rings) are used to retain components on a shaft or in a housing and have corresponding external or internal ears to permit removal. Parallel-sided (machined) circlips can be installed either way round in their groove, whereas stamped circlips (which have a chamfered edge on one face) must be installed with the chamfer facing away from the direction of thrust load **(see illustration 2.9)**.

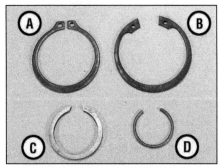

2.8 External stamped circlip (A), internal stamped circlip (B), machined circlip (C) and wire circlip (D)

● Always use circlip pliers to remove and install circlips; expand or compress them just enough to remove them. After installation, rotate the circlip in its groove to ensure it is securely seated. If installing a circlip on a splined shaft, always align its opening with a shaft channel to ensure the circlip ends are well supported and unlikely to catch **(see illustration 2.10)**.

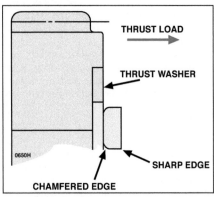

2.9 Correct fitting of a stamped circlip

THRUST LOAD
THRUST WASHER
SHARP EDGE
CHAMFERED EDGE
0650H

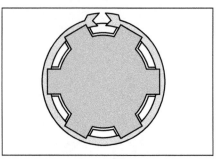

2.10 Align circlip opening with shaft channel

● Circlips can wear due to the thrust of components and become loose in their grooves, with the subsequent danger of becoming dislodged in operation. For this reason, renewal is advised every time a circlip is disturbed.

● Wire circlips are commonly used as piston pin retaining clips. If a removal tang is provided, long-nosed pliers can be used to dislodge them, otherwise careful use of a small flat-bladed screwdriver is necessary. Wire circlips should be renewed every time they are disturbed.

Thread diameter and pitch

● Diameter of a male thread (screw, bolt or stud) is the outside diameter of the threaded portion **(see illustration 2.11)**. Most motorcycle manufacturers use the ISO (International Standards Organisation) metric system expressed in millimetres, eg M6 refers to a 6 mm diameter thread. Sizing is the same for nuts, except that the thread diameter is measured across the valleys of the nut.

● Pitch is the distance between the peaks of the thread **(see illustration 2.11)**. It is expressed in millimetres, thus a common bolt size may be expressed as 6.0 x 1.0 mm (6 mm thread diameter and 1 mm pitch). Generally pitch increases in proportion to thread diameter, although there are always exceptions.

● Thread diameter and pitch are related for conventional fastener applications and the accompanying table can be used as a guide. Additionally, the AF (Across Flats), spanner or socket size dimension of the bolt or nut **(see illustration 2.11)** is linked to thread and pitch specification. Thread pitch can be measured with a thread gauge **(see illustration 2.12)**.

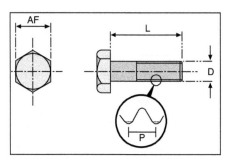

2.11 Fastener length (L), thread diameter (D), thread pitch (P) and head size (AF)

AF
L
D
P

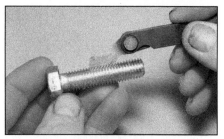

2.12 Using a thread gauge to measure pitch

AF size	Thread diameter x pitch (mm)
8 mm	M5 x 0.8
8 mm	M6 x 1.0
10 mm	M6 x 1.0
12 mm	M8 x 1.25
14 mm	M10 x 1.25
17 mm	M12 x 1.25

● The threads of most fasteners are of the right-hand type, ie they are turned clockwise to tighten and anti-clockwise to loosen. The reverse situation applies to left-hand thread fasteners, which are turned anti-clockwise to tighten and clockwise to loosen. Left-hand threads are used where rotation of a component might loosen a conventional right-hand thread fastener.

Seized fasteners

● Corrosion of external fasteners due to water or reaction between two dissimilar metals can occur over a period of time. It will build up sooner in wet conditions or in countries where salt is used on the roads during the winter. If a fastener is severely corroded it is likely that normal methods of removal will fail and result in its head being ruined. When you attempt removal, the fastener thread should be heard to crack free and unscrew easily - if it doesn't, stop there before damaging something.

● A smart tap on the head of the fastener will often succeed in breaking free corrosion which has occurred in the threads **(see illustration 2.13)**.

● An aerosol penetrating fluid (such as WD-40) applied the night beforehand may work its way down into the thread and ease removal. Depending on the location, you may be able to make up a Plasticine well around the fastener head and fill it with penetrating fluid.

2.13 A sharp tap on the head of a fastener will often break free a corroded thread

● If you are working on an engine internal component, corrosion will most likely not be a problem due to the well lubricated environment. However, components can be very tight and an impact driver is a useful tool in freeing them **(see illustration 2.14)**.

2.14 Using an impact driver to free a fastener

● Where corrosion has occurred between dissimilar metals (eg steel and aluminium alloy), the application of heat to the fastener head will create a disproportionate expansion rate between the two metals and break the seizure caused by the corrosion. Whether heat can be applied depends on the location of the fastener - any surrounding components likely to be damaged must first be removed **(see illustration 2.15)**. Heat can be applied using a paint stripper heat gun or clothes iron, or by immersing the component in boiling water - wear protective gloves to prevent scalding or burns to the hands.

2.15 Using heat to free a seized fastener

● As a last resort, it is possible to use a hammer and cold chisel to work the fastener head unscrewed **(see illustration 2.16)**. This will damage the fastener, but more importantly extreme care must be taken not to damage the surrounding component.

Caution: Remember that the component being secured is generally of more value than the bolt, nut or screw - when the fastener is freed, do not unscrew it with force, instead work the fastener back and forth when resistance is felt to prevent thread damage.

2.16 Using a hammer and chisel to free a seized fastener

Broken fasteners and damaged heads

● If the shank of a broken bolt or screw is accessible you can grip it with self-locking grips. The knurled wheel type stud extractor tool or self-gripping stud puller tool is particularly useful for removing the long studs which screw into the cylinder mouth surface of the crankcase or bolts and screws from which the head has broken off **(see illustration 2.17)**. Studs can also be removed by locking two nuts together on the threaded end of the stud and using a spanner on the lower nut **(see illustration 2.18)**.

2.17 Using a stud extractor tool to remove a broken crankcase stud

2.18 Two nuts can be locked together to unscrew a stud from a component

● A bolt or screw which has broken off below or level with the casing must be extracted using a screw extractor set. Centre punch the fastener to centralise the drill bit, then drill a hole in the fastener **(see illustration 2.19)**. Select a drill bit which is approximately half to three-quarters the

2.19 When using a screw extractor, first drill a hole in the fastener . . .

diameter of the fastener and drill to a depth which will accommodate the extractor. Use the largest size extractor possible, but avoid leaving too small a wall thickness otherwise the extractor will merely force the fastener walls outwards wedging it in the casing thread.

● If a spiral type extractor is used, thread it anti-clockwise into the fastener. As it is screwed in, it will grip the fastener and unscrew it from the casing **(see illustration 2.20)**.

2.20 . . . then thread the extractor anti-clockwise into the fastener

● If a taper type extractor is used, tap it into the fastener so that it is firmly wedged in place. Unscrew the extractor (anti-clockwise) to draw the fastener out.

 *Warning: Stud extractors are very hard and may break off in the fastener if care is not taken - ask an engineer about spark erosion if this happens.*

● Alternatively, the broken bolt/screw can be drilled out and the hole retapped for an oversize bolt/screw or a diamond-section thread insert. It is essential that the drilling is carried out squarely and to the correct depth, otherwise the casing may be ruined - if in doubt, entrust the work to an engineer.

● Bolts and nuts with rounded corners cause the correct size spanner or socket to slip when force is applied. Of the types of spanner/socket available always use a six-point type rather than an eight or twelve-point type - better grip

2.21 Comparison of surface drive ring spanner (left) with 12-point type (right)

is obtained. Surface drive spanners grip the middle of the hex flats, rather than the corners, and are thus good in cases of damaged heads **(see illustration 2.21).**

● Slotted-head or Phillips-head screws are often damaged by the use of the wrong size screwdriver. Allen-head and Torx-head screws are much less likely to sustain damage. If enough of the screw head is exposed you can use a hacksaw to cut a slot in its head and then use a conventional flat-bladed screwdriver to remove it. Alternatively use a hammer and cold chisel to tap the head of the fastener around to slacken it. Always replace damaged fasteners with new ones, preferably Torx or Allen-head type.

HAYNES HiNT

A dab of valve grinding compound between the screw head and screwdriver tip will often give a good grip.

Thread repair

● Threads (particularly those in aluminium alloy components) can be damaged by overtightening, being assembled with dirt in the threads, or from a component working loose and vibrating. Eventually the thread will fail completely, and it will be impossible to tighten the fastener.

● If a thread is damaged or clogged with old locking compound it can be renovated with a thread repair tool (thread chaser) **(see illustrations 2.22 and 2.23)**; special thread

2.22 A thread repair tool being used to correct an internal thread

2.23 A thread repair tool being used to correct an external thread

chasers are available for spark plug hole threads. The tool will not cut a new thread, but clean and true the original thread. Make sure that you use the correct diameter and pitch tool. Similarly, external threads can be cleaned up with a die or a thread restorer file **(see illustration 2.24).**

2.24 Using a thread restorer file

● It is possible to drill out the old thread and retap the component to the next thread size. This will work where there is enough surrounding material and a new bolt or screw can be obtained. Sometimes, however, this is not possible - such as where the bolt/screw passes through another component which must also be suitably modified, also in cases where a spark plug or oil drain plug cannot be obtained in a larger diameter thread size.

● The diamond-section thread insert (often known by its popular trade name of Heli-Coil) is a simple and effective method of renewing the thread and retaining the original size. A kit can be purchased which contains the tap, insert and installing tool **(see illustration 2.25)**. Drill out the damaged thread with the size drill specified **(see illustration 2.26)**. Carefully retap the thread **(see illustration 2.27)**. Install the

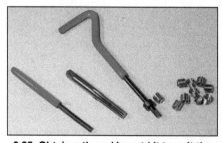

2.25 Obtain a thread insert kit to suit the thread diameter and pitch required

2.26 To install a thread insert, first drill out the original thread . . .

2.27 . . . tap a new thread . . .

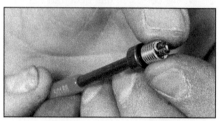

2.28 . . . fit insert on the installing tool . . .

2.29 . . . and thread into the component . . .

2.30 . . . break off the tang when complete

insert on the installing tool and thread it slowly into place using a light downward pressure **(see illustrations 2.28 and 2.29)**. When positioned between a 1/4 and 1/2 turn below the surface withdraw the installing tool and use the break-off tool to press down on the tang, breaking it off **(see illustration 2.30)**.

● There are epoxy thread repair kits on the market which can rebuild stripped internal threads, although this repair should not be used on high load-bearing components.

Thread locking and sealing compounds

● Locking compounds are used in locations where the fastener is prone to loosening due to vibration or on important safety-related items which might cause loss of control of the motorcycle if they fail. It is also used where important fasteners cannot be secured by other means such as lockwashers or split pins.

● Before applying locking compound, make sure that the threads (internal and external) are clean and dry with all old compound removed. Select a compound to suit the component being secured - a non-permanent general locking and sealing type is suitable for most applications, but a high strength type is needed for permanent fixing of studs in castings. Apply a drop or two of the compound to the first few threads of the fastener, then thread it into place and tighten to the specified torque. Do not apply excessive thread locking compound otherwise the thread may be damaged on subsequent removal.

● Certain fasteners are impregnated with a dry film type coating of locking compound on their threads. Always renew this type of fastener if disturbed.

● Anti-seize compounds, such as copper-based greases, can be applied to protect threads from seizure due to extreme heat and corrosion. A common instance is spark plug threads and exhaust system fasteners.

3 Measuring tools and gauges

Feeler gauges

● Feeler gauges (or blades) are used for measuring small gaps and clearances (see illustration 3.1). They can also be used to measure endfloat (sideplay) of a component on a shaft where access is not possible with a dial gauge.

● Feeler gauge sets should be treated with care and not bent or damaged. They are etched with their size on one face. Keep them clean and very lightly oiled to prevent corrosion build-up.

3.1 Feeler gauges are used for measuring small gaps and clearances - thickness is marked on one face of gauge

● When measuring a clearance, select a gauge which is a light sliding fit between the two components. You may need to use two gauges together to measure the clearance accurately.

Micrometers

● A micrometer is a precision tool capable of measuring to 0.01 or 0.001 of a millimetre. It should always be stored in its case and not in the general toolbox. It must be kept clean and never dropped, otherwise its frame or measuring anvils could be distorted resulting in inaccurate readings.

● External micrometers are used for measuring outside diameters of components and have many more applications than internal micrometers. Micrometers are available in different size ranges, eg 0 to 25 mm, 25 to 50 mm, and upwards in 25 mm steps; some large micrometers have interchangeable anvils to allow a range of measurements to be taken. Generally the largest precision measurement you are likely to take on a motorcycle is the piston diameter.

● Internal micrometers (or bore micrometers) are used for measuring inside diameters, such as valve guides and cylinder bores. Telescoping gauges and small hole gauges are used in conjunction with an external micrometer, whereas the more expensive internal micrometers have their own measuring device.

External micrometer

Note: *The conventional analogue type instrument is described. Although much easier to read, digital micrometers are considerably more expensive.*

● Always check the calibration of the micrometer before use. With the anvils closed (0 to 25 mm type) or set over a test gauge (for

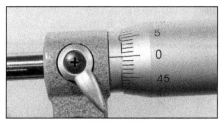

3.2 Check micrometer calibration before use

the larger types) the scale should read zero (see illustration 3.2); make sure that the anvils (and test piece) are clean first. Any discrepancy can be adjusted by referring to the instructions supplied with the tool. Remember that the micrometer is a precision measuring tool - don't force the anvils closed, use the ratchet (4) on the end of the micrometer to close it. In this way, a measured force is always applied.

● To use, first make sure that the item being measured is clean. Place the anvil of the micrometer (1) against the item and use the thimble (2) to bring the spindle (3) lightly into contact with the other side of the item (see illustration 3.3). Don't tighten the thimble down because this will damage the micrometer - instead use the ratchet (4) on the end of the micrometer. The ratchet mechanism applies a measured force preventing damage to the instrument.

● The micrometer is read by referring to the linear scale on the sleeve and the annular scale on the thimble. Read off the sleeve first to obtain the base measurement, then add the fine measurement from the thimble to obtain the overall reading. The linear scale on the sleeve represents the measuring range of the micrometer (eg 0 to 25 mm). The annular scale

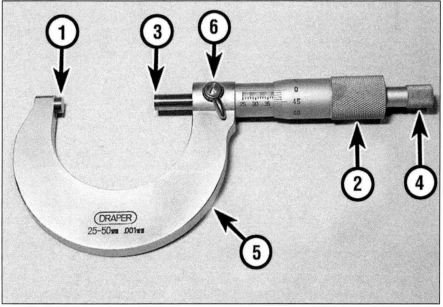

3.3 Micrometer component parts

1 *Anvil*	3 *Spindle*	5 *Frame*
2 *Thimble*	4 *Ratchet*	6 *Locking lever*

on the thimble will be in graduations of 0.01 mm (or as marked on the frame) - one full revolution of the thimble will move 0.5 mm on the linear scale. Take the reading where the datum line on the sleeve intersects the thimble's scale. Always position the eye directly above the scale otherwise an inaccurate reading will result.

In the example shown the item measures 2.95 mm **(see illustration 3.4)**:

Linear scale	2.00 mm
Linear scale	0.50 mm
Annular scale	0.45 mm
Total figure	**2.95 mm**

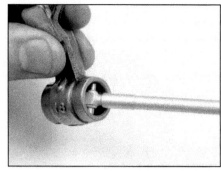

3.5 Micrometer reading of 46.99 mm on linear and annular scales . . .

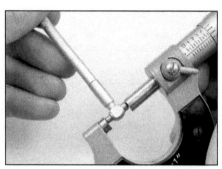

3.7 Expand the telescoping gauge in the bore, lock its position . . .

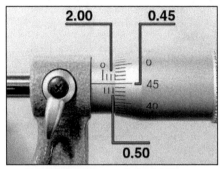

3.4 Micrometer reading of 2.95 mm

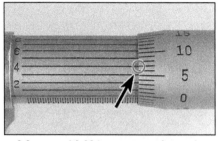

3.6 . . . and 0.004 mm on vernier scale

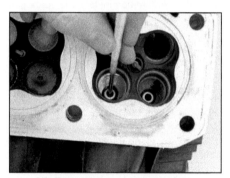

3.8 . . . then measure the gauge with a micrometer

Most micrometers have a locking lever (6) on the frame to hold the setting in place, allowing the item to be removed from the micrometer.

● Some micrometers have a vernier scale on their sleeve, providing an even finer measurement to be taken, in 0.001 increments of a millimetre. Take the sleeve and thimble measurement as described above, then check which graduation on the vernier scale aligns with that of the annular scale on the thimble **Note:** *The eye must be perpendicular to the scale when taking the vernier reading - if necessary rotate the body of the micrometer to ensure this.* Multiply the vernier scale figure by 0.001 and add it to the base and fine measurement figures.

In the example shown the item measures 46.994 mm **(see illustrations 3.5 and 3.6)**:

Linear scale (base)	46.000 mm
Linear scale (base)	00.500 mm
Annular scale (fine)	00.490 mm
Vernier scale	00.004 mm
Total figure	**46.994 mm**

Internal micrometer

● Internal micrometers are available for measuring bore diameters, but are expensive and unlikely to be available for home use. It is suggested that a set of telescoping gauges and small hole gauges, both of which must be used with an external micrometer, will suffice for taking internal measurements on a motorcycle.

● Telescoping gauges can be used to measure internal diameters of components. Select a gauge with the correct size range, make sure its ends are clean and insert it into the bore. Expand the gauge, then lock its position and withdraw it from the bore **(see illustration 3.7)**. Measure across the gauge ends with a micrometer **(see illustration 3.8)**.

● Very small diameter bores (such as valve guides) are measured with a small hole gauge. Once adjusted to a slip-fit inside the component, its position is locked and the gauge withdrawn for measurement with a micrometer **(see illustrations 3.9 and 3.10)**.

Vernier caliper

Note: *The conventional linear and dial gauge type instruments are described. Digital types are easier to read, but are far more expensive.*

● The vernier caliper does not provide the precision of a micrometer, but is versatile in being able to measure internal and external diameters. Some types also incorporate a depth gauge. It is ideal for measuring clutch plate friction material and spring free lengths.

● To use the conventional linear scale vernier, slacken off the vernier clamp screws (1) and set its jaws over (2), or inside (3), the item to be measured **(see illustration 3.11)**. Slide the jaw into contact, using the thumbwheel (4) for fine movement of the sliding scale (5) then tighten the clamp screws (1). Read off the main scale (6) where the zero on the sliding scale (5) intersects it, taking the whole number to the left of the zero; this provides the base measurement. View along the sliding scale and select the division which

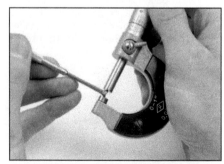

3.9 Expand the small hole gauge in the bore, lock its position . . .

3.10 . . . then measure the gauge with a micrometer

lines up exactly with any of the divisions on the main scale, noting that the divisions usually represents 0.02 of a millimetre. Add this fine measurement to the base measurement to obtain the total reading.

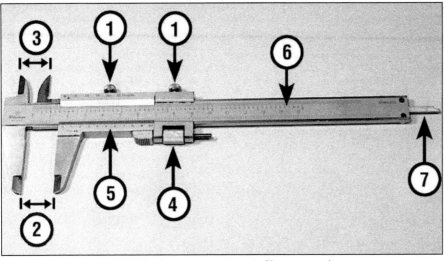

3.11 Vernier component parts (linear gauge)

1 Clamp screws	3 Internal jaws	5 Sliding scale	7 Depth gauge
2 External jaws	4 Thumbwheel	6 Main scale	

In the example shown the item measures 55.92 mm (see illustration 3.12):

Base measurement	55.00 mm
Fine measurement	00.92 mm
Total figure	**55.92 mm**

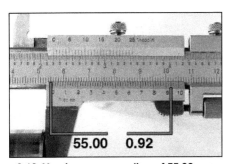

3.12 Vernier gauge reading of 55.92 mm

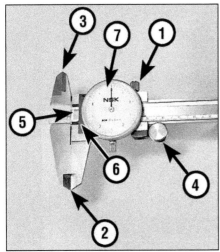

3.13 Vernier component parts (dial gauge)

1 Clamp screw	5 Main scale
2 External jaws	6 Sliding scale
3 Internal jaws	7 Dial gauge
4 Thumbwheel	

● Some vernier calipers are equipped with a dial gauge for fine measurement. Before use, check that the jaws are clean, then close them fully and check that the dial gauge reads zero. If necessary adjust the gauge ring accordingly. Slacken the vernier clamp screw (1) and set its jaws over (2), or inside (3), the item to be measured (see illustration 3.13). Slide the jaws into contact, using the thumbwheel (4) for fine movement. Read off the main scale (5) where the edge of the sliding scale (6) intersects it, taking the whole number to the left of the zero; this provides the base measurement. Read off the needle position on the dial gauge (7) scale to provide the fine measurement; each division represents 0.05 of a millimetre. Add this fine measurement to the base measurement to obtain the total reading.

In the example shown the item measures 55.95 mm (see illustration 3.14):

Base measurement	55.00 mm
Fine measurement	00.95 mm
Total figure	**55.95 mm**

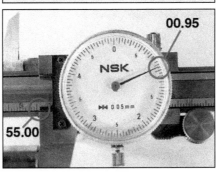

3.14 Vernier gauge reading of 55.95 mm

Plastigauge

● Plastigauge is a plastic material which can be compressed between two surfaces to measure the oil clearance between them. The width of the compressed Plastigauge is measured against a calibrated scale to determine the clearance.

● Common uses of Plastigauge are for measuring the clearance between crankshaft journal and main bearing inserts, between crankshaft journal and big-end bearing inserts, and between camshaft and bearing surfaces. The following example describes big-end oil clearance measurement.

● Handle the Plastigauge material carefully to prevent distortion. Using a sharp knife, cut a length which corresponds with the width of the bearing being measured and place it carefully across the journal so that it is parallel with the shaft (see illustration 3.15). Carefully install both bearing shells and the connecting rod. Without rotating the rod on the journal tighten its bolts or nuts (as applicable) to the specified torque. The connecting rod and bearings are then disassembled and the crushed Plastigauge examined.

3.15 Plastigauge placed across shaft journal

● Using the scale provided in the Plastigauge kit, measure the width of the material to determine the oil clearance (see illustration 3.16). Always remove all traces of Plastigauge after use using your fingernails.

Caution: Arriving at the correct clearance demands that the assembly is torqued correctly, according to the settings and sequence (where applicable) provided by the motorcycle manufacturer.

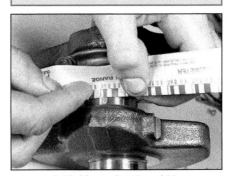

3.16 Measuring the width of the crushed Plastigauge

Dial gauge or DTI (Dial Test Indicator)

● A dial gauge can be used to accurately measure small amounts of movement. Typical uses are measuring shaft runout or shaft endfloat (sideplay) and setting piston position for ignition timing on two-strokes. A dial gauge set usually comes with a range of different probes and adapters and mounting equipment.

● The gauge needle must point to zero when at rest. Rotate the ring around its periphery to zero the gauge.

● Check that the gauge is capable of reading the extent of movement in the work. Most gauges have a small dial set in the face which records whole millimetres of movement as well as the fine scale around the face periphery which is calibrated in 0.01 mm divisions. Read off the small dial first to obtain the base measurement, then add the measurement from the fine scale to obtain the total reading.

In the example shown the gauge reads 1.48 mm (see illustration 3.17):

Base measurement	1.00 mm
Fine measurement	0.48 mm
Total figure	**1.48 mm**

3.17 Dial gauge reading of 1.48 mm

● If measuring shaft runout, the shaft must be supported in vee-blocks and the gauge mounted on a stand perpendicular to the shaft. Rest the tip of the gauge against the centre of the shaft and rotate the shaft slowly whilst watching the gauge reading (see illustration 3.18). Take several measurements along the length of the shaft and record the

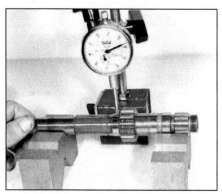

3.18 Using a dial gauge to measure shaft runout

maximum gauge reading as the amount of runout in the shaft. **Note:** *The reading obtained will be total runout at that point - some manufacturers specify that the runout figure is halved to compare with their specified runout limit.*

● Endfloat (sideplay) measurement requires that the gauge is mounted securely to the surrounding component with its probe touching the end of the shaft. Using hand pressure, push and pull on the shaft noting the maximum endfloat recorded on the gauge (see illustration 3.19).

3.19 Using a dial gauge to measure shaft endfloat

● A dial gauge with suitable adapters can be used to determine piston position BTDC on two-stroke engines for the purposes of ignition timing. The gauge, adapter and suitable length probe are installed in the place of the spark plug and the gauge zeroed at TDC. If the piston position is specified as 1.14 mm BTDC, rotate the engine back to 2.00 mm BTDC, then slowly forwards to 1.14 mm BTDC.

Cylinder compression gauges

● A compression gauge is used for measuring cylinder compression. Either the rubber-cone type or the threaded adapter type can be used. The latter is preferred to ensure a perfect seal against the cylinder head. A 0 to 300 psi (0 to 20 Bar) type gauge (for petrol/gasoline engines) will be suitable for motorcycles.

● The spark plug is removed and the gauge either held hard against the cylinder head (cone type) or the gauge adapter screwed into the cylinder head (threaded type) (see illustration 3.20). Cylinder compression is measured with the engine turning over, but not running - carry out the compression test as described in

3.20 Using a rubber-cone type cylinder compression gauge

Fault Finding Equipment. The gauge will hold the reading until manually released.

Oil pressure gauge

● An oil pressure gauge is used for measuring engine oil pressure. Most gauges come with a set of adapters to fit the thread of the take-off point (see illustration 3.21). If the take-off point specified by the motorcycle manufacturer is an external oil pipe union, make sure that the specified replacement union is used to prevent oil starvation.

3.21 Oil pressure gauge and take-off point adapter (arrow)

● Oil pressure is measured with the engine running (at a specific rpm) and often the manufacturer will specify pressure limits for a cold and hot engine.

Straight-edge and surface plate

● If checking the gasket face of a component for warpage, place a steel rule or precision straight-edge across the gasket face and measure any gap between the straight-edge and component with feeler gauges (see illustration 3.22). Check diagonally across the component and between mounting holes (see illustration 3.23).

3.22 Use a straight-edge and feeler gauges to check for warpage

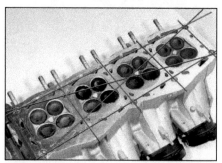

3.23 Check for warpage in these directions

● Checking individual components for warpage, such as clutch plain (metal) plates, requires a perfectly flat plate or piece or plate glass and feeler gauges.

4 Torque and leverage

What is torque?

● Torque describes the twisting force about a shaft. The amount of torque applied is determined by the distance from the centre of the shaft to the end of the lever and the amount of force being applied to the end of the lever; distance multiplied by force equals torque.

● The manufacturer applies a measured torque to a bolt or nut to ensure that it will not slacken in use and to hold two components securely together without movement in the joint. The actual torque setting depends on the thread size, bolt or nut material and the composition of the components being held.

● Too little torque may cause the fastener to loosen due to vibration, whereas too much torque will distort the joint faces of the component or cause the fastener to shear off. Always stick to the specified torque setting.

Using a torque wrench

● Check the calibration of the torque wrench and make sure it has a suitable range for the job. Torque wrenches are available in Nm (Newton-metres), kgf m (kilograms-force metre), lbf ft (pounds-feet), lbf in (inch-pounds). Do not confuse lbf ft with lbf in.

● Adjust the tool to the desired torque on the scale (see illustration 4.1). If your torque wrench is not calibrated in the units specified, carefully convert the figure (see *Conversion Factors*). A manufacturer sometimes gives a torque setting as a range (8 to 10 Nm) rather than a single figure - in this case set the tool midway between the two settings. The same torque may be expressed as 9 Nm ± 1 Nm. Some torque wrenches have a method of locking the setting so that it isn't inadvertently altered during use.

4.1 Set the torque wrench index mark to the setting required, in this case 12 Nm

● Install the bolts/nuts in their correct location and secure them lightly. Their threads must be clean and free of any old locking compound. Unless specified the threads and flange should be dry - oiled threads are necessary in certain circumstances and the manufacturer will take this into account in the specified torque figure. Similarly, the manufacturer may also specify the application of thread-locking compound.

● Tighten the fasteners in the specified sequence until the torque wrench clicks, indicating that the torque setting has been reached. Apply the torque again to double-check the setting. Where different thread diameter fasteners secure the component, as a rule tighten the larger diameter ones first.

● When the torque wrench has been finished with, release the lock (where applicable) and fully back off its setting to zero - do not leave the torque wrench tensioned. Also, do not use a torque wrench for slackening a fastener.

Angle-tightening

● Manufacturers often specify a figure in degrees for final tightening of a fastener. This usually follows tightening to a specific torque setting.

● A degree disc can be set and attached to the socket (see illustration 4.2) or a protractor can be used to mark the angle of movement on the bolt/nut head and the surrounding casting (see illustration 4.3).

4.2 Angle tightening can be accomplished with a torque-angle gauge . . .

4.3 . . . or by marking the angle on the surrounding component

Loosening sequences

● Where more than one bolt/nut secures a component, loosen each fastener evenly a little at a time. In this way, not all the stress of the joint is held by one fastener and the components are not likely to distort.

● If a tightening sequence is provided, work in the REVERSE of this, but if not, work from the outside in, in a criss-cross sequence (see illustration 4.4).

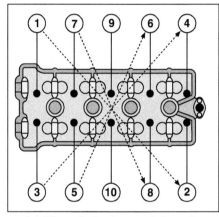

4.4 When slackening, work from the outside inwards

Tightening sequences

● If a component is held by more than one fastener it is important that the retaining bolts/nuts are tightened evenly to prevent uneven stress build-up and distortion of sealing faces. This is especially important on high-compression joints such as the cylinder head.

● A sequence is usually provided by the manufacturer, either in a diagram or actually marked in the casting. If not, always start in the centre and work outwards in a criss-cross pattern (see illustration 4.5). Start off by securing all bolts/nuts finger-tight, then set the torque wrench and tighten each fastener by a small amount in sequence until the final torque is reached. By following this practice,

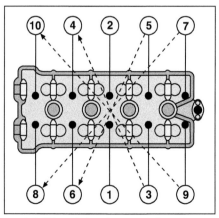

4.5 When tightening, work from the inside outwards

the joint will be held evenly and will not be distorted. Important joints, such as the cylinder head and big-end fasteners often have two- or three-stage torque settings.

Applying leverage

● Use tools at the correct angle. Position a socket wrench or spanner on the bolt/nut so that you pull it towards you when loosening. If this can't be done, push the spanner without curling your fingers around it **(see illustration 4.6)** - the spanner may slip or the fastener loosen suddenly, resulting in your fingers being crushed against a component.

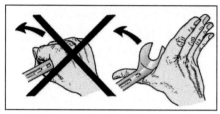

4.6 If you can't pull on the spanner to loosen a fastener, push with your hand open

● Additional leverage is gained by extending the length of the lever. The best way to do this is to use a breaker bar instead of the regular length tool, or to slip a length of tubing over the end of the spanner or socket wrench.
● If additional leverage will not work, the fastener head is either damaged or firmly corroded in place (see *Fasteners*).

5 Bearings

Bearing removal and installation

Drivers and sockets

● Before removing a bearing, always inspect the casing to see which way it must be driven out - some casings will have retaining plates or a cast step. Also check for any identifying markings on the bearing and if installed to a certain depth, measure this at this stage. Some roller bearings are sealed on one side - take note of the original fitted position.
● Bearings can be driven out of a casing using a bearing driver tool (with the correct size head) or a socket of the correct diameter. Select the driver head or socket so that it contacts the outer race of the bearing, not the balls/rollers or inner race. Always support the casing around the bearing housing with wood blocks, otherwise there is a risk of fracture. The bearing is driven out with a few blows on the driver or socket from a heavy mallet. Unless access is severely restricted (as with wheel bearings), a pin-punch is not recommended unless it is moved around the bearing to keep it square in its housing.

● The same equipment can be used to install bearings. Make sure the bearing housing is supported on wood blocks and line up the bearing in its housing. Fit the bearing as noted on removal - generally they are installed with their marked side facing outwards. Tap the bearing squarely into its housing using a driver or socket which bears only on the bearing's outer race - contact with the bearing balls/rollers or inner race will destroy it **(see illustrations 5.1 and 5.2)**.
● Check that the bearing inner race and balls/rollers rotate freely.

5.1 Using a bearing driver against the bearing's outer race

5.2 Using a large socket against the bearing's outer race

Pullers and slide-hammers

● Where a bearing is pressed on a shaft a puller will be required to extract it **(see illustration 5.3)**. Make sure that the puller clamp or legs fit securely behind the bearing and are unlikely to slip out. If pulling a bearing

5.3 This bearing puller clamps behind the bearing and pressure is applied to the shaft end to draw the bearing off

off a gear shaft for example, you may have to locate the puller behind a gear pinion if there is no access to the race and draw the gear pinion off the shaft as well **(see illustration 5.4)**.

> *Caution: Ensure that the puller's centre bolt locates securely against the end of the shaft and will not slip when pressure is applied. Also ensure that puller does not damage the shaft end.*

5.4 Where no access is available to the rear of the bearing, it is sometimes possible to draw off the adjacent component

● Operate the puller so that its centre bolt exerts pressure on the shaft end and draws the bearing off the shaft.
● When installing the bearing on the shaft, tap only on the bearing's inner race - contact with the balls/rollers or outer race with destroy the bearing. Use a socket or length of tubing as a drift which fits over the shaft end **(see illustration 5.5)**.

5.5 When installing a bearing on a shaft use a piece of tubing which bears only on the bearing's inner race

● Where a bearing locates in a blind hole in a casing, it cannot be driven or pulled out as described above. A slide-hammer with knife-edged bearing puller attachment will be required. The puller attachment passes through the bearing and when tightened expands to fit firmly behind the bearing **(see illustration 5.6)**. By operating the slide-hammer part of the tool the bearing is jarred out of its housing **(see illustration 5.7)**.
● It is possible, if the bearing is of reasonable weight, for it to drop out of its housing if the casing is heated as described opposite. If this

5.6 Expand the bearing puller so that it locks behind the bearing . . .

5.7 . . . attach the slide hammer to the bearing puller

method is attempted, first prepare a work surface which will enable the casing to be tapped face down to help dislodge the bearing - a wood surface is ideal since it will not damage the casing's gasket surface. Wearing protective gloves, tap the heated casing several times against the work surface to dislodge the bearing under its own weight **(see illustration 5.8)**.

5.8 Tapping a casing face down on wood blocks can often dislodge a bearing

● Bearings can be installed in blind holes using the driver or socket method described above.

Drawbolts

● Where a bearing or bush is set in the eye of a component, such as a suspension linkage arm or connecting rod small-end, removal by drift may damage the component. Furthermore, a rubber bushing in a shock absorber eye cannot successfully be driven out of position. If access is available to a engineering press, the task is straightforward. If not, a drawbolt can be fabricated to extract the bearing or bush.

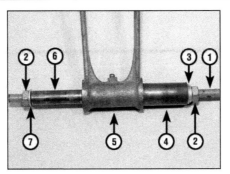

5.9 Drawbolt component parts assembled on a suspension arm

1 Bolt or length of threaded bar
2 Nuts
3 Washer (external diameter greater than tubing internal diameter)
4 Tubing (internal diameter sufficient to accommodate bearing)
5 Suspension arm with bearing
6 Tubing (external diameter slightly smaller than bearing)
7 Washer (external diameter slightly smaller than bearing)

5.10 Drawing the bearing out of the suspension arm

● To extract the bearing/bush you will need a long bolt with nut (or piece of threaded bar with two nuts), a piece of tubing which has an internal diameter larger than the bearing/bush, another piece of tubing which has an external diameter slightly smaller than the bearing/bush, and a selection of washers **(see illustrations 5.9 and 5.10)**. Note that the pieces of tubing must be of the same length, or longer, than the bearing/bush.
● The same kit (without the pieces of tubing) can be used to draw the new bearing/bush back into place **(see illustration 5.11)**.

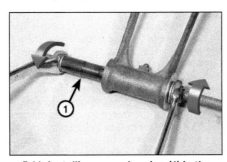

5.11 Installing a new bearing (1) in the suspension arm

Temperature change

● If the bearing's outer race is a tight fit in the casing, the aluminium casing can be heated to release its grip on the bearing. Aluminium will expand at a greater rate than the steel bearing outer race. There are several ways to do this, but avoid any localised extreme heat (such as a blow torch) - aluminium alloy has a low melting point.
● Approved methods of heating a casing are using a domestic oven (heated to 100°C) or immersing the casing in boiling water **(see illustration 5.12)**. Low temperature range localised heat sources such as a paint stripper heat gun or clothes iron can also be used **(see illustration 5.13)**. Alternatively, soak a rag in boiling water, wring it out and wrap it around the bearing housing.

> ⚠️ **Warning: All of these methods require care in use to prevent scalding and burns to the hands. Wear protective gloves when handling hot components.**

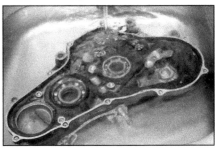

5.12 A casing can be immersed in a sink of boiling water to aid bearing removal

5.13 Using a localised heat source to aid bearing removal

● If heating the whole casing note that plastic components, such as the neutral switch, may suffer - remove them beforehand.
● After heating, remove the bearing as described above. You may find that the expansion is sufficient for the bearing to fall out of the casing under its own weight or with a light tap on the driver or socket.
● If necessary, the casing can be heated to aid bearing installation, and this is sometimes the recommended procedure if the motorcycle manufacturer has designed the housing and bearing fit with this intention.

● Installation of bearings can be eased by placing them in a freezer the night before installation. The steel bearing will contract slightly, allowing easy insertion in its housing. This is often useful when installing steering head outer races in the frame.

Bearing types and markings

● Plain shell bearings, ball bearings, needle roller bearings and tapered roller bearings will all be found on motorcycles (see illustrations 5.14 and 5.15). The ball and roller types are usually caged between an inner and outer race, but uncaged variations may be found.

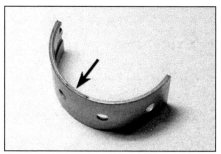

5.14 Shell bearings are either plain or grooved. They are usually identified by colour code (arrow)

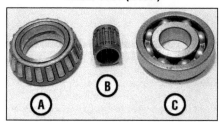

5.15 Tapered roller bearing (A), needle roller bearing (B) and ball journal bearing (C)

● Shell bearings (often called inserts) are usually found at the crankshaft main and connecting rod big-end where they are good at coping with high loads. They are made of a phosphor-bronze material and are impregnated with self-lubricating properties.
● Ball bearings and needle roller bearings consist of a steel inner and outer race with the balls or rollers between the races. They require constant lubrication by oil or grease and are good at coping with axial loads. Taper roller bearings consist of rollers set in a tapered cage set on the inner race; the outer race is separate. They are good at coping with axial loads and prevent movement along the shaft - a typical application is in the steering head.
● Bearing manufacturers produce bearings to ISO size standards and stamp one face of the bearing to indicate its internal and external diameter, load capacity and type (see illustration 5.16).
● Metal bushes are usually of phosphor-bronze material. Rubber bushes are used in suspension mounting eyes. Fibre bushes have also been used in suspension pivots.

5.16 Typical bearing marking

Bearing fault finding

● If a bearing outer race has spun in its housing, the housing material will be damaged. You can use a bearing locking compound to bond the outer race in place if damage is not too severe.
● Shell bearings will fail due to damage of their working surface, as a result of lack of lubrication, corrosion or abrasive particles in the oil (see illustration 5.17). Small particles of dirt in the oil may embed in the bearing material whereas larger particles will score the bearing and shaft journal. If a number of short journeys are made, insufficient heat will be generated to drive off condensation which has built up on the bearings.

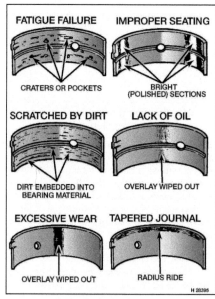

5.17 Typical bearing failures

● Ball and roller bearings will fail due to lack of lubrication or damage to the balls or rollers. Tapered-roller bearings can be damaged by overloading them. Unless the bearing is sealed on both sides, wash it in paraffin (kerosene) to remove all old grease then allow it to dry. Make a visual inspection looking to dented balls or rollers, damaged cages and worn or pitted races (see illustration 5.18).
● A ball bearing can be checked for wear by listening to it when spun. Apply a film of light oil to the bearing and hold it close to the ear - hold the outer race with one hand and spin the inner

5.18 Example of ball journal bearing with damaged balls and cages

5.19 Hold outer race and listen to inner race when spun

race with the other hand (see illustration 5.19). The bearing should be almost silent when spun; if it grates or rattles it is worn.

6 Oil seals

Oil seal removal and installation

● Oil seals should be renewed every time a component is dismantled. This is because the seal lips will become set to the sealing surface and will not necessarily reseal.
● Oil seals can be prised out of position using a large flat-bladed screwdriver (see illustration 6.1). In the case of crankcase seals, check first that the seal is not lipped on the inside, preventing its removal with the crankcases joined.

6.1 Prise out oil seals with a large flat-bladed screwdriver

● New seals are usually installed with their marked face (containing the seal reference code) outwards and the spring side towards the fluid being retained. In certain cases, such as a two-stroke engine crankshaft seal, a double lipped seal may be used due to there being fluid or gas on each side of the joint.

● Use a bearing driver or socket which bears only on the outer hard edge of the seal to install it in the casing - tapping on the inner edge will damage the sealing lip.

Oil seal types and markings

● Oil seals are usually of the single-lipped type. Double-lipped seals are found where a liquid or gas is on both sides of the joint.
● Oil seals can harden and lose their sealing ability if the motorcycle has been in storage for a long period - renewal is the only solution.
● Oil seal manufacturers also conform to the ISO markings for seal size - these are moulded into the outer face of the seal (see illustration 6.2).

6.2 These oil seal markings indicate inside diameter, outside diameter and seal thickness

7 Gaskets and sealants

Types of gasket and sealant

● Gaskets are used to seal the mating surfaces between components and keep lubricants, fluids, vacuum or pressure contained within the assembly. Aluminium gaskets are sometimes found at the cylinder joints, but most gaskets are paper-based. If the mating surfaces of the components being joined are undamaged the gasket can be installed dry, although a dab of sealant or grease will be useful to hold it in place during assembly.
● RTV (Room Temperature Vulcanising) silicone rubber sealants cure when exposed to moisture in the atmosphere. These sealants are good at filling pits or irregular gasket faces, but will tend to be forced out of the joint under very high torque. They can be used to replace a paper gasket, but first make sure that the width of the paper gasket is not essential to the shimming of internal components. RTV sealants should not be used on components containing petrol (gasoline).
● Non-hardening, semi-hardening and hard setting liquid gasket compounds can be used with a gasket or between a metal-to-metal joint. Select the sealant to suit the application: universal non-hardening sealant can be used on virtually all joints; semi-hardening on joint faces which are rough or damaged; hard setting sealant on joints which require a permanent bond and are subjected to high temperature and pressure. **Note:** *Check first if the paper gasket has a bead of sealant*

impregnated in its surface before applying additional sealant.
● When choosing a sealant, make sure it is suitable for the application, particularly if being applied in a high-temperature area or in the vicinity of fuel. Certain manufacturers produce sealants in either clear, silver or black colours to match the finish of the engine. This has a particular application on motorcycles where much of the engine is exposed.
● Do not over-apply sealant. That which is squeezed out on the outside of the joint can be wiped off, whereas an excess of sealant on the inside can break off and clog oilways.

Breaking a sealed joint

● Age, heat, pressure and the use of hard setting sealant can cause two components to stick together so tightly that they are difficult to separate using finger pressure alone. Do not resort to using levers unless there is a pry point provided for this purpose (see illustration 7.1) or else the gasket surfaces will be damaged.
● Use a soft-faced hammer (see illustration 7.2) or a wood block and conventional hammer to strike the component near the mating surface. Avoid hammering against cast extremities since they may break off. If this method fails, try using a wood wedge between the two components.

Caution: If the joint will not separate, double-check that you have removed all the fasteners.

7.1 If a pry point is provided, apply gently pressure with a flat-bladed screwdriver

7.2 Tap around the joint with a soft-faced mallet if necessary - don't strike cooling fins

Removal of old gasket and sealant

● Paper gaskets will most likely come away complete, leaving only a few traces stuck on

Most components have one or two hollow locating dowels between the two gasket faces. If a dowel cannot be removed, do not resort to gripping it with pliers - it will almost certainly be distorted. Install a close-fitting socket or Phillips screwdriver into the dowel and then grip the outer edge of the dowel to free it.

the sealing faces of the components. It is imperative that all traces are removed to ensure correct sealing of the new gasket.
● Very carefully scrape all traces of gasket away making sure that the sealing surfaces are not gouged or scored by the scraper (see illustrations 7.3, 7.4 and 7.5). Stubborn deposits can be removed by spraying with an aerosol gasket remover. Final preparation of

7.3 Paper gaskets can be scraped off with a gasket scraper tool . . .

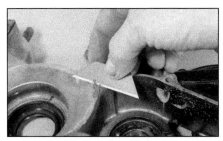

7.4 . . . a knife blade . . .

7.5 . . . or a household scraper

7.6 Fine abrasive paper is wrapped around a flat file to clean up the gasket face

7.7 A kitchen scourer can be used on stubborn deposits

the gasket surface can be made with very fine abrasive paper or a plastic kitchen scourer **(see illustrations 7.6 and 7.7)**.

● Old sealant can be scraped or peeled off components, depending on the type originally used. Note that gasket removal compounds are available to avoid scraping the components clean; make sure the gasket remover suits the type of sealant used.

8 Chains

Breaking and joining final drive chains

● Drive chains for all but small bikes are continuous and do not have a clip-type connecting link. The chain must be broken using a chain breaker tool and the new chain securely riveted together using a new soft rivet-type link. Never use a clip-type connecting link instead of a rivet-type link, except in an emergency. Various chain breaking and riveting tools are available, either as separate tools or combined as illustrated in the accompanying photographs - read the instructions supplied with the tool carefully.

 Warning: The need to rivet the new link pins correctly cannot be overstressed - loss of control of the motorcycle is very likely to result if the chain breaks in use.

● Rotate the chain and look for the soft link. The soft link pins look like they have been

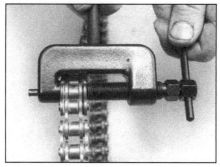

8.1 Tighten the chain breaker to push the pin out of the link . . .

8.2 . . . withdraw the pin, remove the tool . . .

8.3 . . . and separate the chain link

deeply centre-punched instead of peened over like all the other pins **(see illustration 8.9)** and its sideplate may be a different colour. Position the soft link midway between the sprockets and assemble the chain breaker tool over one of the soft link pins **(see illustration 8.1)**. Operate the tool to push the pin out through the chain **(see illustration 8.2)**. On an O-ring chain, remove the O-rings **(see illustration 8.3)**. Carry out the same procedure on the other soft link pin.

> **Caution: Certain soft link pins (particularly on the larger chains) may require their ends to be filed or ground off before they can be pressed out using the tool.**

● Check that you have the correct size and strength (standard or heavy duty) new soft link - do not reuse the old link. Look for the size marking on the chain sideplates **(see illustration 8.10)**.

● Position the chain ends so that they are engaged over the rear sprocket. On an O-ring

8.4 Insert the new soft link, with O-rings, through the chain ends . . .

8.5 . . . install the O-rings over the pin ends . . .

8.6 . . . followed by the sideplate

chain, install a new O-ring over each pin of the link and insert the link through the two chain ends **(see illustration 8.4)**. Install a new O-ring over the end of each pin, followed by the sideplate (with the chain manufacturer's marking facing outwards) **(see illustrations 8.5 and 8.6)**. On an unsealed chain, insert the link through the two chain ends, then install the sideplate with the chain manufacturer's marking facing outwards.

● Note that it may not be possible to install the sideplate using finger pressure alone. If using a joining tool, assemble it so that the plates of the tool clamp the link and press the sideplate over the pins **(see illustration 8.7)**. Otherwise, use two small sockets placed over

8.7 Push the sideplate into position using a clamp

8.8 Assemble the chain riveting tool over one pin at a time and tighten it fully

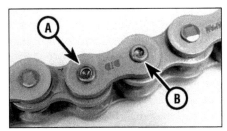

8.9 Pin end correctly riveted (A), pin end unriveted (B)

the rivet ends and two pieces of the wood between a G-clamp. Operate the clamp to press the sideplate over the pins.

● Assemble the joining tool over one pin (following the maker's instructions) and tighten the tool down to spread the pin end securely **(see illustrations 8.8 and 8.9)**. Do the same on the other pin.

 Warning: Check that the pin ends are secure and that there is no danger of the sideplate coming loose. If the pin ends are cracked the soft link must be renewed.

Final drive chain sizing

● Chains are sized using a three digit number, followed by a suffix to denote the chain type **(see illustration 8.10)**. Chain type is either standard or heavy duty (thicker sideplates), and also unsealed or O-ring/X-ring type.

● The first digit of the number relates to the pitch of the chain, ie the distance from the centre of one pin to the centre of the next pin **(see illustration 8.11)**. Pitch is expressed in eighths of an inch, as follows:

8.10 Typical chain size and type marking

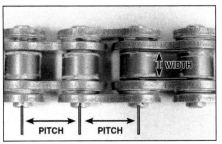

8.11 Chain dimensions

Sizes commencing with a 4 (eg 428) have a pitch of 1/2 inch (12.7 mm)
Sizes commencing with a 5 (eg 520) have a pitch of 5/8 inch (15.9 mm)
Sizes commencing with a 6 (eg 630) have a pitch of 3/4 inch (19.1 mm)

● The second and third digits of the chain size relate to the width of the rollers, again in imperial units, eg the 525 shown has 5/16 inch (7.94 mm) rollers **(see illustration 8.11)**.

9 Hoses

Clamping to prevent flow

● Small-bore flexible hoses can be clamped to prevent fluid flow whilst a component is worked on. Whichever method is used, ensure that the hose material is not permanently distorted or damaged by the clamp.

a) A brake hose clamp available from auto accessory shops **(see illustration 9.1)**.

b) A wingnut type hose clamp **(see illustration 9.2)**.

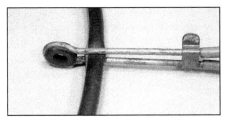

9.1 Hoses can be clamped with an automotive brake hose clamp . . .

9.2 . . . a wingnut type hose clamp . . .

c) Two sockets placed each side of the hose and held with straight-jawed self-locking grips **(see illustration 9.3)**.

d) Thick card each side of the hose held between straight-jawed self-locking grips **(see illustration 9.4)**.

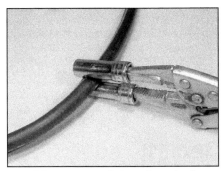

9.3 . . . two sockets and a pair of self-locking grips . . .

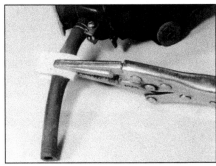

9.4 . . . or thick card and self-locking grips

Freeing and fitting hoses

● Always make sure the hose clamp is moved well clear of the hose end. Grip the hose with your hand and rotate it whilst pulling it off the union. If the hose has hardened due to age and will not move, slit it with a sharp knife and peel its ends off the union **(see illustration 9.5)**.

● Resist the temptation to use grease or soap on the unions to aid installation; although it helps the hose slip over the union it will equally aid the escape of fluid from the joint. It is preferable to soften the hose ends in hot water and wet the inside surface of the hose with water or a fluid which will evaporate.

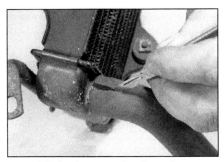

9.5 Cutting a coolant hose free with a sharp knife

Introduction

In less time than it takes to read this introduction, a thief could steal your motorcycle. Returning only to find your bike has gone is one of the worst feelings in the world. Even if the motorcycle is insured against theft, once you've got over the initial shock, you will have the inconvenience of dealing with the police and your insurance company.

The motorcycle is an easy target for the professional thief and the joyrider alike and the official figures on motorcycle theft make for depressing reading; on average a motorcycle is stolen every 16 minutes in the UK!

Motorcycle thefts fall into two categories, those stolen 'to order' and those taken by opportunists. The thief stealing to order will be on the look out for a specific make and model and will go to extraordinary lengths to obtain that motorcycle. The opportunist thief on the other hand will look for easy targets which can be stolen with the minimum of effort and risk.

Whilst it is never going to be possible to make your machine 100% secure, it is estimated that around half of all stolen motorcycles are taken by opportunist thieves. Remember that the opportunist thief is always on the look out for the easy option: if there are two similar motorcycles parked side-by-side, they will target the one with the lowest level of security. By taking a few precautions, you can reduce the chances of your motorcycle being stolen.

Security equipment

There are many specialised motorcycle security devices available and the following text summarises their applications and their good and bad points.

Once you have decided on the type of security equipment which best suits your needs, we recommended that you read one of the many equipment tests regularly carried out by the motorcycle press. These tests compare the products from all the major manufacturers and give impartial ratings on their effectiveness, value-for-money and ease of use.

No one item of security equipment can provide complete protection. It is highly recommended that two or more of the items described below are combined to increase the security of your motorcycle (a lock and chain plus an alarm system is just about ideal). The more security measures fitted to the bike, the less likely it is to be stolen.

Lock and chain

Pros: *Very flexible to use; can be used to secure the motorcycle to almost any immovable object. On some locks and chains, the lock can be used on its own as a disc lock (see below).*

Cons: *Can be very heavy and awkward to carry on the motorcycle, although some types will be supplied with a carry bag which can be strapped to the pillion seat.*

● Heavy-duty chains and locks are an excellent security measure **(see illustration 1)**. Whenever the motorcycle is parked, use the lock and chain to secure the machine to a solid, immovable object such as a post or railings. This will prevent the machine from being ridden away or being lifted into the back of a van.

● When fitting the chain, always ensure the chain is routed around the motorcycle frame or swingarm **(see illustrations 2 and 3)**. Never merely pass the chain around one of the wheel rims; a thief may unbolt the wheel and lift the rest of the machine into a van, leaving you with just the wheel! Try to avoid having excess chain free, thus making it difficult to use cutting tools, and keep the chain and lock off the ground to prevent thieves attacking it with a cold chisel. Position the lock so that its lock barrel is facing downwards; this will make it harder for the thief to attack the lock mechanism.

Ensure the lock and chain you buy is of good quality and long enough to shackle your bike to a solid object

Pass the chain through the bike's frame, rather than just through a wheel . . .

. . . and loop it around a solid object

U-locks

Pros: *Highly effective deterrent which can be used to secure the bike to a post or railings. Most U-locks come with a carrier which allows the lock to be easily carried on the bike.*

Cons: *Not as flexible to use as a lock and chain.*

● These are solid locks which are similar in use to a lock and chain. U-locks are lighter than a lock and chain but not so flexible to use. The length and shape of the lock shackle limit the objects to which the bike can be secured **(see illustration 4)**.

Disc locks

Pros: *Small, light and very easy to carry; most can be stored underneath the seat.*

Cons: *Does not prevent the motorcycle being lifted into a van. Can be very embarrassing if you*

U-locks can be used to secure the bike to a solid object – ensure you purchase one which is long enough

forget to remove the lock before attempting to ride off!

● Disc locks are designed to be attached to the front brake disc. The lock passes through one of the holes in the disc and prevents the wheel rotating by jamming against the fork/brake caliper **(see illustration 5)**. Some are equipped with an alarm siren which sounds if the disc lock is moved; this not only acts as a theft deterrent but also as a handy reminder if you try to move the bike with the lock still fitted.

● Combining the disc lock with a length of cable which can be looped around a post or railings provides an additional measure of security **(see illustration 6)**.

Alarms and immobilisers

Pros: *Once installed it is completely hassle-free to use. If the system is 'Thatcham' or 'Sold Secure-approved', insurance companies may give you a discount.*

Cons: *Can be expensive to buy and complex to install. No system will prevent the motorcycle from being lifted into a van and taken away.*

● Electronic alarms and immobilisers are available to suit a variety of budgets. There are three different types of system available: pure alarms, pure immobilisers, and the more expensive systems which are combined alarm/immobilisers **(see illustration 7)**.
● An alarm system is designed to emit an audible warning if the motorcycle is being tampered with.
● An immobiliser prevents the motorcycle being started and ridden away by disabling its electrical systems.
● When purchasing an alarm/immobiliser system, check the cost of installing the system unless you are able to do it yourself. If the motorcycle is not used regularly, another consideration is the current drain of the system. All alarm/immobiliser systems are powered by the motorcycle's battery; purchasing a system with a very low current drain could prevent the battery losing its charge whilst the motorcycle is not being used.

A typical disc lock attached through one of the holes in the disc

A disc lock combined with a security cable provides additional protection

A typical alarm/immobiliser system

Indelible markings can be applied to most areas of the bike – always apply the manufacturer's sticker to warn off thieves

Chemically-etched code numbers can be applied to main body panels . . .

. . . again, always ensure that the kit manufacturer's sticker is applied in a prominent position

Security marking kits

Pros: *Very cheap and effective deterrent. Many insurance companies will give you a discount on your insurance premium if a recognised security marking kit is used on your motorcycle.*

Cons: *Does not prevent the motorcycle being stolen by joyriders.*

● There are many different types of security marking kits available. The idea is to mark as many parts of the motorcycle as possible with a unique security number (see illustrations 8, 9 and 10). A form will be included with the kit to register your personal details and those of the motorcycle with the kit manufacturer. This register is made available to the police to help them trace the rightful owner of any motorcycle or components which they recover should all other forms of identification have been removed. Always apply the warning stickers provided with the kit to deter thieves.

Ground anchors, wheel clamps and security posts

Pros: *An excellent form of security which will deter all but the most determined of thieves.*

Cons: *Awkward to install and can be expensive.*

● Whilst the motorcycle is at home, it is a good idea to attach it securely to the floor or a solid wall, even if it is kept in a securely locked garage. Various types of ground anchors, security posts and wheel clamps are available for this purpose (see illustration 11). These security devices are either bolted to a solid concrete or brick structure or can be cemented into the ground.

Permanent ground anchors provide an excellent level of security when the bike is at home

Security at home

A high percentage of motorcycle thefts are from the owner's home. Here are some things to consider whenever your motorcycle is at home:
✔ Where possible, always keep the motorcycle in a securely locked garage. Never rely solely on the standard lock on the garage door, these are usual hopelessly inadequate. Fit an additional locking mechanism to the door and consider having the garage alarmed. A security light, activated by a movement sensor, is also a good investment.

✔ Always secure the motorcycle to the ground or a wall, even if it is inside a securely locked garage.
✔ Do not regularly leave the motorcycle outside your home, try to keep it out of sight wherever possible. If a garage is not available, fit a motorcycle cover over the bike to disguise its true identity.
✔ It is not uncommon for thieves to follow a motorcyclist home to find out where the bike is kept. They will then return at a later date. Be aware of this whenever you are returning

home on your motorcycle. If you suspect you are being followed, do not return home, instead ride to a garage or shop and stop as a precaution.
✔ When selling a motorcycle, do not provide your home address or the location where the bike is normally kept. Arrange to meet the buyer at a location away from your home. Thieves have been known to pose as potential buyers to find out where motorcycles are kept and then return later to steal them.

Security away from the home

As well as fitting security equipment to your motorcycle here are a few general rules to follow whenever you park your motorcycle.
✔ Park in a busy, public place.
✔ Use car parks which incorporate security features, such as CCTV.

✔ At night, park in a well-lit area, preferably directly underneath a street light.
✔ Engage the steering lock.
✔ Secure the motorcycle to a solid, immovable object such as a post or railings with an additional lock. If this is not possible,

secure the bike to a friend's motorcycle. Some public parking places provide security loops for motorcycles.
✔ Never leave your helmet or luggage attached to the motorcycle. Take them with you at all times.

Lubricants and fluids

A wide range of lubricants, fluids and cleaning agents is available for motor-cycles. This is a guide as to what is available, its applications and properties.

Four-stroke engine oil

● Engine oil is without doubt the most important component of any four-stroke engine. Modern motorcycle engines place a lot of demands on their oil and choosing the right type is essential. Using an unsuitable oil will lead to an increased rate of engine wear and could result in serious engine damage. Before purchasing oil, always check the recommended oil specification given by the manufacturer. The manufacturer will state a recommended 'type or classification' and also a specific 'viscosity' range for engine oil.

● The oil 'type or classification' is identified by its API (American Petroleum Institute) rating. The API rating will be in the form of two letters, e.g. SG. The S identifies the oil as being suitable for use in a petrol (gasoline) engine (S stands for spark ignition) and the second letter, ranging from A to J, identifies the oil's performance rating. The later this letter, the higher the specification of the oil; for example API SG oil exceeds the requirements of API SF oil. **Note:** *On some oils there may also be a second rating consisting of another two letters, the first letter being C, e.g. API SF/CD. This rating indicates the oil is also suitable for use in a diesel engines (the C stands for compression ignition) and is thus of no relevance for motorcycle use.*

● The 'viscosity' of the oil is identified by its SAE (Society of Automotive Engineers) rating. All modern engines require multigrade oils and the SAE rating will consist of two numbers, the first followed by a W, e.g. 10W/40. The first number indicates the viscosity rating of the oil at low temperatures (W stands for winter – tested at –20ºC) and the second number represents the viscosity of the oil at high temperatures (tested at 100ºC). The lower the number, the thinner the oil. For example an oil with an SAE 10W/40 rating will give better cold starting and running than an SAE 15W/40 oil.

● As well as ensuring the 'type' and 'viscosity' of the oil match the recommendations, another consideration to make when buying engine oil is whether to purchase a standard mineral-based oil, a semi-synthetic oil (also known as a synthetic blend or synthetic-based oil) or a fully-synthetic oil. Although all oils will have a similar rating and viscosity, their cost will vary considerably; mineral-based oils are the cheapest, the fully-synthetic oils the most expensive with the semi-synthetic oils falling somewhere in-between. This decision is very much up to the owner, but it should be noted that modern synthetic oils have far better lubricating and cleaning qualities than traditional mineral-based oils and tend to retain these properties for far longer. Bearing in mind the operating conditions inside a modern, high-revving motorcycle engine it is highly recommended that a fully synthetic oil is used. The extra expense at each service could save you money in the long term by preventing premature engine wear.

● As a final note always ensure that the oil is specifically designed for use in motorcycle engines. Engine oils designed primarily for use in car engines sometimes contain additives or friction modifiers which could cause clutch slip on a motorcycle fitted with a wet-clutch.

Two-stroke engine oil

● Modern two-stroke engines, with their high power outputs, place high demands on their oil. If engine seizure is to be avoided it is essential that a high-quality oil is used. Two-stroke oils differ hugely from four-stroke oils. The oil lubricates only the crankshaft and piston(s) (the transmission has its own lubricating oil) and is used on a total-loss basis where it is burnt completely during the combustion process.

● The Japanese have recently introduced a classification system for two-stroke oils, the JASO rating. This rating is in the form of two letters, either FA, FB or FC – FA is the lowest classification and FC the highest. Ensure the oil being used meets or exceeds the recommended rating specified by the manufacturer.

● As well as ensuring the oil rating matches the recommendation, another consideration to make when buying engine oil is whether to purchase a standard mineral-based oil, a semi-synthetic oil (also known as a synthetic blend or synthetic-based oil) or a fully-synthetic oil. The cost of each type of oil varies considerably; mineral-based oils are the cheapest, the fully-synthetic oils the most expensive with the semi-synthetic oils falling somewhere in-between. This decision is very much up to the owner, but it should be noted that modern synthetic oils have far better lubricating properties and burn cleaner than traditional mineral-based oils. It is therefore recommended that a fully synthetic oil is used. The extra expense could save you money in the long term by preventing premature engine wear, engine performance will be improved, carbon deposits and exhaust smoke will be reduced.

● Always ensure that the oil is specifically designed for use in an injector system. Many high quality two-stroke oils are designed for competition use and need to be pre-mixed with fuel. These oils are of a much higher viscosity and are not designed to flow through the injector pumps used on road-going two-stroke motorcycles.

Transmission (gear) oil

● On a two-stroke engine, the transmission and clutch are lubricated by their own separate oil bath which must be changed in accordance with the Maintenance Schedule.
● Although the engine and transmission units of most four-strokes use a common lubrication supply, there are some exceptions where the engine and gearbox have separate oil reservoirs and a dry clutch is used.
● Motorcycle manufacturers will either recommend a monograde transmission oil or a four-stroke multigrade engine oil to lubricate the transmission.
● Transmission oils, or gear oils as they are often called, are designed specifically for use in transmission systems. The viscosity of these oils is represented by an SAE number, but the scale of measurement applied is different to that used to grade engine oils. As a rough guide a SAE90 gear oil will be of the same viscosity as an SAE50 engine oil.

Shaft drive oil

● On models equipped with shaft final drive, the shaft drive gears are will have their own oil supply. The manufacturer will state a recommended 'type or classification' and also a specific 'viscosity' range in the same manner as for four-stroke engine oil.
● Gear oil classification is given by the number which follows the API GL (GL standing for gear lubricant) rating, the higher the number, the higher the specification of the oil, e.g. API GL5 oil is a higher specification than API GL4 oil. Ensure the oil meets or

exceeds the classification specified and is of the correct viscosity. The viscosity of gear oils is also represented by an SAE number but the scale of measurement used is different to that used to grade engine oils. As a rough guide an SAE90 gear oil will be of the same viscosity as an SAE50 engine oil.
● If the use of an EP (Extreme Pressure) gear oil is specified, ensure the oil purchased is suitable.

Fork oil and suspension fluid

● Conventional telescopic front forks are hydraulic and require fork oil to work. To ensure the forks function correctly, the fork oil must be changed in accordance with the Maintenance Schedule.
● Fork oil is available in a variety of viscosities, identified by their SAE rating; fork oil ratings vary from light (SAE 5) to heavy (SAE 30). When purchasing fork oil, ensure the viscosity rating matches that specified by the manufacturer.
● Some lubricant manufacturers also produce a range of high-quality suspension fluids which are very similar to fork oil but are designed mainly for competition use. These fluids may have a different viscosity rating system which is not to be confused with the SAE rating of normal fork oil. Refer to the manufacturer's instructions if in any doubt.

Brake and clutch fluid

● All disc brake systems and some clutch systems are hydraulically operated. To ensure correct operation, the hydraulic fluid must be changed in accordance with the Maintenance Schedule.
● Brake and clutch fluid is classified by its DOT rating with most motorcycle manufacturers specifying DOT 3 or 4 fluid. Both fluid types are glycol-based and can be mixed together without adverse effect; DOT 4 fluid exceeds the requirements of DOT 3

fluid. Although it is safe to use DOT 4 fluid in a system designed for use with DOT 3 fluid, never use DOT 3 fluid in a system which specifies the use of DOT 4 as this will adversely affect the system's performance. The type required for the system will be marked on the fluid reservoir cap.
● Some manufacturers also produce a DOT 5 hydraulic fluid. DOT 5 hydraulic fluid is silicone-based and is not compatible with the glycol-based DOT 3 and 4 fluids. Never mix DOT 5 fluid with DOT 3 or 4 fluid as this will seriously affect the performance of the hydraulic system.

Coolant/antifreeze

● When purchasing coolant/antifreeze, always ensure it is suitable for use in an aluminium engine and contains corrosion inhibitors to prevent possible blockages of the internal coolant passages of the system. As a general rule, most coolants are designed to be used neat and should not be diluted whereas antifreeze can be mixed with distilled water to provide a coolant solution of the required strength. Refer to the manufacturer's instructions on the bottle.
● Ensure the coolant is changed in accordance with the Maintenance Schedule.

Chain lube

● Chain lube is an aerosol-type spray lubricant specifically designed for use on motorcycle final drive chains. Chain lube has two functions, to minimise friction between the final drive chain and sprockets and to prevent corrosion of the chain. Regular use of a good-quality chain lube will extend the life of the drive chain and sprockets and thus maximise the power being transmitted from the transmission to the rear wheel.
● When using chain lube, always allow some time for the solvents in the lube to evaporate before riding the motorcycle. This will minimise the amount of lube which will

'fling' off from the chain when the motorcycle is used. If the motorcycle is equipped with an 'O-ring' chain, ensure the chain lube is labelled as being suitable for use on 'O-ring' chains.

Degreasers and solvents

● There are many different types of solvents and degreasers available to remove the grime and grease which accumulate around the motorcycle during normal use. Degreasers and solvents are usually available as an aerosol-type spray or as a liquid which you apply with a brush. Always closely follow the manufacturer's instructions and wear eye protection during use. Be aware that many solvents are flammable and may give off noxious fumes; take adequate precautions when using them (see Safety First!).

● For general cleaning, use one of the many solvents or degreasers available from most motorcycle accessory shops. These solvents are usually applied then left for a certain time before being washed off with water.

Brake cleaner is a solvent specifically designed to remove all traces of oil, grease and dust from braking system components. Brake cleaner is designed to evaporate quickly and leaves behind no residue.

Carburettor cleaner is an aerosol-type solvent specifically designed to clear carburettor blockages and break down the hard deposits and gum often found inside carburettors during overhaul.

Contact cleaner is an aerosol-type solvent designed for cleaning electrical components. The cleaner will remove all traces of oil and dirt from components such as switch contacts or fouled spark plugs and then dry, leaving behind no residue.

Gasket remover is an aerosol-type solvent designed for removing stubborn gaskets from engine components during overhaul. Gasket remover will minimise the amount of scraping required to remove the gasket and therefore reduce the risk of damage to the mating surface.

Spray lubricants

● Aerosol-based spray lubricants are widely available and are excellent for lubricating lever pivots and exposed cables and switches. Try to use a lubricant which is of the dry-film type as the fluid evaporates, leaving behind a dry-film of lubricant. Lubricants which leave behind an oily residue will attract dust and dirt which will increase the rate of wear of the cable/lever.

● Most lubricants also act as a moisture dispersant and a penetrating fluid. This means they can also be used to 'dry out' electrical components such as wiring connectors or switches as well as helping to free seized fasteners.

Greases

● Grease is used to lubricate many of the pivot-points. A good-quality multi-purpose grease is suitable for most applications but some manufacturers will specify the use of specialist greases for use on components such as swingarm and suspension linkage bushes. These specialist greases can be purchased from most motorcycle (or car) accessory shops; commonly specified types include molybdenum disulphide grease, lithium-based grease, graphite-based grease, silicone-based grease and high-temperature copper-based grease.

Gasket sealing compounds

● Gasket sealing compounds can be used in conjunction with gaskets, to improve their sealing capabilities, or on their own to seal metal-to-metal joints. Depending on their type, sealing compounds either set hard or stay relatively soft and pliable.

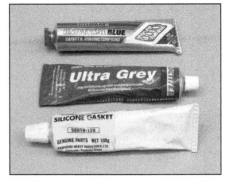

● When purchasing a gasket sealing compound, ensure that it is designed specifically for use on an internal combustion engine. General multi-purpose sealants available from DIY stores may appear visibly similar but they are not designed to withstand the extreme heat or contact with fuel and oil encountered when used on an engine (see 'Tools and Workshop Tips' for further information).

Thread locking compound

● Thread locking compounds are used to secure certain threaded fasteners in position to prevent them from loosening due to vibration. Thread locking compounds can be purchased from most motorcycle (and car) accessory shops. Ensure the threads of the both components are completely clean and dry before sparingly applying the locking compound (see 'Tools and Workshop Tips' for further information).

Fuel additives

● Fuel additives which protect and clean the fuel system components are widely available. These additives are designed to remove all traces of deposits that build up on the carburettors/injectors and prevent wear, helping the fuel system to operate more efficiently. If a fuel additive is being used, check that it is suitable for use with your motorcycle, especially if your motorcycle is equipped with a catalytic converter.

● Octane boosters are also available. These additives are designed to improve the performance of highly-tuned engines being run on normal pump-fuel and are of no real use on standard motorcycles.

Conversion factors

Length (distance)

Inches (in)	x 25.4	= Millimetres (mm)	x 0.0394	=	Inches (in)
Feet (ft)	x 0.305	= Metres (m)	x 3.281	=	Feet (ft)
Miles	x 1.609	= Kilometres (km)	x 0.621	=	Miles

Volume (capacity)

Cubic inches (cu in; in³)	x 16.387	= Cubic centimetres (cc; cm³)	x 0.061	=	Cubic inches (cu in; in³)
Imperial pints (Imp pt)	x 0.568	= Litres (l)	x 1.76	=	Imperial pints (Imp pt)
Imperial quarts (Imp qt)	x 1.137	= Litres (l)	x 0.88	=	Imperial quarts (Imp qt)
Imperial quarts (Imp qt)	x 1.201	= US quarts (US qt)	x 0.833	=	Imperial quarts (Imp qt)
US quarts (US qt)	x 0.946	= Litres (l)	x 1.057	=	US quarts (US qt)
Imperial gallons (Imp gal)	x 4.546	= Litres (l)	x 0.22	=	Imperial gallons (Imp gal)
Imperial gallons (Imp gal)	x 1.201	= US gallons (US gal)	x 0.833	=	Imperial gallons (Imp gal)
US gallons (US gal)	x 3.785	= Litres (l)	x 0.264	=	US gallons (US gal)

Mass (weight)

Ounces (oz)	x 28.35	= Grams (g)	x 0.035	=	Ounces (oz)
Pounds (lb)	x 0.454	= Kilograms (kg)	x 2.205	=	Pounds (lb)

Force

Ounces-force (ozf; oz)	x 0.278	= Newtons (N)	x 3.6	=	Ounces-force (ozf; oz)
Pounds-force (lbf; lb)	x 4.448	= Newtons (N)	x 0.225	=	Pounds-force (lbf; lb)
Newtons (N)	x 0.1	= Kilograms-force (kgf; kg)	x 9.81	=	Newtons (N)

Pressure

Pounds-force per square inch (psi; lbf/in²; lb/in²)	x 0.070	= Kilograms-force per square centimetre (kgf/cm²; kg/cm²)	x 14.223	=	Pounds-force per square inch (psi; lbf/in²; lb/in²)
Pounds-force per square inch (psi; lbf/in²; lb/in²)	x 0.068	= Atmospheres (atm)	x 14.696	=	Pounds-force per square inch (psi; lbf/in²; lb/in²)
Pounds-force per square inch (psi; lbf/in²; lb/in²)	x 0.069	= Bars	x 14.5	=	Pounds-force per square inch (psi; lbf/in²; lb/in²)
Pounds-force per square inch (psi; lbf/in²; lb/in²)	x 6.895	= Kilopascals (kPa)	x 0.145	=	Pounds-force per square inch (psi; lbf/in²; lb/in²)
Kilopascals (kPa)	x 0.01	= Kilograms-force per square centimetre (kgf/cm²; kg/cm²)	x 98.1	=	Kilopascals (kPa)
Millibar (mbar)	x 100	= Pascals (Pa)	x 0.01	=	Millibar (mbar)
Millibar (mbar)	x 0.0145	= Pounds-force per square inch (psi; lbf/in²; lb/in²)	x 68.947	=	Millibar (mbar)
Millibar (mbar)	x 0.75	= Millimetres of mercury (mmHg)	x 1.333	=	Millibar (mbar)
Millibar (mbar)	x 0.401	= Inches of water (inH₂O)	x 2.491	=	Millibar (mbar)
Millimetres of mercury (mmHg)	x 0.535	= Inches of water (inH₂O)	x 1.868	=	Millimetres of mercury (mmHg)
Inches of water (inH₂O)	x 0.036	= Pounds-force per square inch (psi; lbf/in²; lb/in²)	x 27.68	=	Inches of water (inH₂O)

Torque (moment of force)

Pounds-force inches (lbf in; lb in)	x 1.152	= Kilograms-force centimetre (kgf cm; kg cm)	x 0.868	=	Pounds-force inches (lbf in; lb in)
Pounds-force inches (lbf in; lb in)	x 0.113	= Newton metres (Nm)	x 8.85	=	Pounds-force inches (lbf in; lb in)
Pounds-force inches (lbf in; lb in)	x 0.083	= Pounds-force feet (lbf ft; lb ft)	x 12	=	Pounds-force inches (lbf in; lb in)
Pounds-force feet (lbf ft; lb ft)	x 0.138	= Kilograms-force metres (kgf m; kg m)	x 7.233	=	Pounds-force feet (lbf ft; lb ft)
Pounds-force feet (lbf ft; lb ft)	x 1.356	= Newton metres (Nm)	x 0.738	=	Pounds-force feet (lbf ft; lb ft)
Newton metres (Nm)	x 0.102	= Kilograms-force metres (kgf m; kg m)	x 9.804	=	Newton metres (Nm)

Power

Horsepower (hp)	x 745.7	= Watts (W)	x 0.0013	=	Horsepower (hp)

Velocity (speed)

Miles per hour (miles/hr; mph)	x 1.609	= Kilometres per hour (km/hr; kph)	x 0.621	=	Miles per hour (miles/hr; mph)

Fuel consumption*

Miles per gallon (mpg)	x 0.354	= Kilometres per litre (km/l)	x 2.825	=	Miles per gallon (mpg)

Temperature

Degrees Fahrenheit = (°C x 1.8) + 32   Degrees Celsius (Degrees Centigrade; °C) = (°F - 32) x 0.56

It is common practice to convert from miles per gallon (mpg) to litres/100 kilometres (l/100km), where mpg x l/100 km = 282

Preparing for storage

Before you start

If repairs or an overhaul is needed, see that this is carried out now rather than left until you want to ride the bike again.

Give the bike a good wash and scrub all dirt from its underside. Make sure the bike dries completely before preparing for storage.

Engine

● Remove the spark plug(s) and lubricate the cylinder bores with approximately a teaspoon of motor oil using a spout-type oil can (see illustration 1). Reinstall the spark plug(s). Crank the engine over a couple of times to coat the piston rings and bores with oil. If the bike has a kickstart, use this to turn the engine over. If not, flick the kill switch to the OFF position and crank the engine over on the starter (see illustration 2). If the nature on the ignition system prevents the starter operating with the kill switch in the OFF position,

remove the spark plugs and fit them back in their caps; ensure that the plugs are earthed (grounded) against the cylinder head when the starter is operated (see illustration 3).

⚠ *Warning: It is important that the plugs are earthed (grounded) away from the spark plug holes otherwise there is a risk of atomised fuel from the cylinders igniting.*

HAYNES HiNT *On a single cylinder four-stroke engine, you can seal the combustion chamber completely by positioning the piston at TDC on the compression stroke.*

● Drain the carburettor(s) otherwise there is a risk of jets becoming blocked by gum deposits from the fuel (see illustration 4).

● If the bike is going into long-term storage, consider adding a fuel stabiliser to the fuel in the tank. If the tank is drained completely, corrosion of its internal surfaces may occur if left unprotected for a long period. The tank can be treated with a rust preventative especially for this purpose. Alternatively, remove the tank and pour half a litre of motor oil into it, install the filler cap and shake the tank to coat its internals with oil before draining off the excess. The same effect can also be achieved by spraying WD40 or a similar water-dispersant around the inside of the tank via its flexible nozzle.

● Make sure the cooling system contains the correct mix of antifreeze. Antifreeze also contains important corrosion inhibitors.

● The air intakes and exhaust can be sealed off by covering or plugging the openings. Ensure that you do not seal in any condensation; run the engine until it is hot,

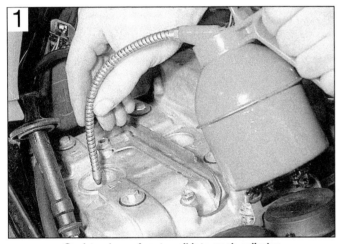

Squirt a drop of motor oil into each cylinder

Flick the kill switch to OFF . . .

. . . and ensure that the metal bodies of the plugs (arrows) are earthed against the cylinder head

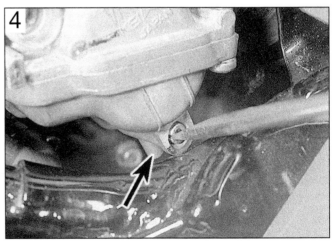

Connect a hose to the carburettor float chamber drain stub (arrow) and unscrew the drain screw

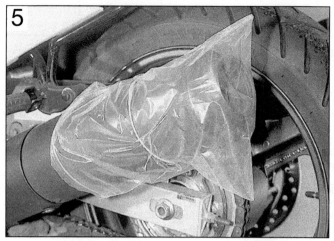

Exhausts can be sealed off with a plastic bag

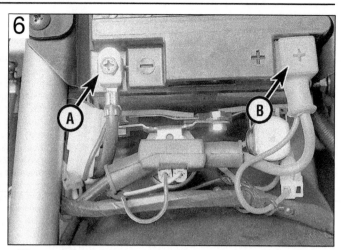

Disconnect the negative lead (A) first, followed by the positive lead (B)

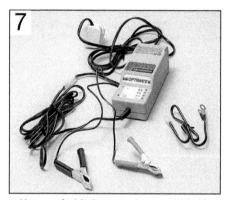

Use a suitable battery charger - this kit also assess battery condition

● Check the electrolyte level and top up if necessary (conventional refillable batteries). Clean the terminals.
● Store the battery off the motorcycle and away from any sources of fire. Position a wooden block under the battery if it is to sit on the ground.
● Give the battery a trickle charge for a few hours every month **(see illustration 7)**.

Tyres

● Place the bike on its centrestand or an auxiliary stand which will support the motorcycle in an upright position. Position wood blocks under the tyres to keep them off the ground and to provide insulation from damp. If the bike is being put into long-term storage, ideally both tyres should be off the ground; not only will this protect the tyres, but will also ensure that no load is placed on the steering head or wheel bearings.
● Deflate each tyre by 5 to 10 psi, no more or the beads may unseat from the rim, making subsequent inflation difficult on tubeless tyres.

Pivots and controls

● Lubricate all lever, pedal, stand and

footrest pivot points. If grease nipples are fitted to the rear suspension components, apply lubricant to the pivots.
● Lubricate all control cables.

Cycle components

● Apply a wax protectant to all painted and plastic components. Wipe off any excess, but don't polish to a shine. Where fitted, clean the screen with soap and water.
● Coat metal parts with Vaseline (petroleum jelly). When applying this to the fork tubes, do not compress the forks otherwise the seals will rot from contact with the Vaseline.
● Apply a vinyl cleaner to the seat.

Storage conditions

● Aim to store the bike in a shed or garage which does not leak and is free from damp.
● Drape an old blanket or bedspread over the bike to protect it from dust and direct contact with sunlight (which will fade paint). This also hides the bike from prying eyes. Beware of tight-fitting plastic covers which may allow condensation to form and settle on the bike.

then switch off and allow to cool. Tape a piece of thick plastic over the silencer end(s) **(see illustration 5)**. Note that some advocate pouring a tablespoon of motor oil into the silencer(s) before sealing them off.

Battery

● Remove it from the bike - in extreme cases of cold the battery may freeze and crack its case **(see illustration 6)**.

Getting back on the road

Engine and transmission

● Change the oil and replace the oil filter. If this was done prior to storage, check that the oil hasn't emulsified - a thick whitish substance which occurs through condensation.
● Remove the spark plugs. Using a spout-type oil can, squirt a few drops of oil into the cylinder(s). This will provide initial lubrication as the piston rings and bores comes back into contact. Service the spark plugs, or fit new ones, and install them in the engine.

● Check that the clutch isn't stuck on. The plates can stick together if left standing for some time, preventing clutch operation. Engage a gear and try rocking the bike back and forth with the clutch lever held against the handlebar. If this doesn't work on cable-operated clutches, hold the clutch lever back against the handlebar with a strong elastic band or cable tie for a couple of hours **(see illustration 8)**.
● If the air intakes or silencer end(s) were blocked off, remove the bung or cover used.
● If the fuel tank was coated with a rust

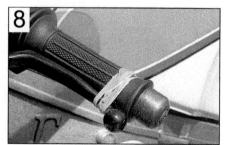

Hold clutch lever back against the handlebar with elastic bands or a cable tie

preventative, oil or a stabiliser added to the fuel, drain and flush the tank and dispose of the fuel sensibly. If no action was taken with the fuel tank prior to storage, it is advised that the old fuel is disposed of since it will go off over a period of time. Refill the fuel tank with fresh fuel.

Frame and running gear

● Oil all pivot points and cables.
● Check the tyre pressures. They will definitely need inflating if pressures were reduced for storage.
● Lubricate the final drive chain (where applicable).
● Remove any protective coating applied to the fork tubes (stanchions) since this may well destroy the fork seals. If the fork tubes weren't protected and have picked up rust spots, remove them with very fine abrasive paper and refinish with metal polish.
● Check that both brakes operate correctly. Apply each brake hard and check that it's not possible to move the motorcycle forwards, then check that the brake frees off again once released. Brake caliper pistons can stick due to corrosion around the piston head, or on the sliding caliper types, due to corrosion of the slider pins. If the brake doesn't free after repeated operation, take the caliper off for examination. Similarly drum brakes can stick due to a seized operating cam, cable or rod linkage.
● If the motorcycle has been in long-term storage, renew the brake fluid and clutch fluid (where applicable).
● Depending on where the bike has been stored, the wiring, cables and hoses may have been nibbled by rodents. Make a visual check and investigate disturbed wiring loom tape.

Battery

● If the battery has been previously removal and given top up charges it can simply be reconnected. Remember to connect the positive cable first and the negative cable last.
● On conventional refillable batteries, if the battery has not received any attention, remove it from the motorcycle and check its electrolyte level. Top up if necessary then charge the battery. If the battery fails to hold a charge and a visual checks show heavy white sulphation of the plates, the battery is probably defective and must be renewed. This is particularly likely if the battery is old. Confirm battery condition with a specific gravity check.
● On sealed (MF) batteries, if the battery has not received any attention, remove it from the motorcycle and charge it according to the information on the battery case - if the battery fails to hold a charge it must be renewed.

Starting procedure

● If a kickstart is fitted, turn the engine over a couple of times with the ignition OFF to distribute oil around the engine. If no kickstart is fitted, flick the engine kill switch OFF and the ignition ON and crank the engine over a couple of times to work oil around the upper cylinder components. If the nature of the ignition system is such that the starter won't work with the kill switch OFF, remove the spark plugs, fit them back into their caps and earth (ground) their bodies on the cylinder head. Reinstall the spark plugs afterwards.
● Switch the kill switch to RUN, operate the choke and start the engine. If the engine won't start don't continue cranking the engine - not only will this flatten the battery, but the starter motor will overheat. Switch the ignition off and try again later. If the engine refuses to start, go through the fault finding procedures in this manual. **Note:** *If the bike has been in storage for a long time, old fuel or a carburettor blockage may be the problem. Gum deposits in carburettors can block jets - if a carburettor cleaner doesn't prove successful the carburettors must be dismantled for cleaning.*

● Once the engine has started, check that the lights, turn signals and horn work properly.

● Treat the bike gently for the first ride and check all fluid levels on completion. Settle the bike back into the maintenance schedule.

This Section provides an easy reference-guide to the more common faults that are likely to afflict your machine. Obviously, the opportunities are almost limitless for faults to occur as a result of obscure failures, and to try and cover all eventualities would require a book. Indeed, a number have been written on the subject.

Successful troubleshooting is not a mysterious 'black art' but the application of a bit of knowledge combined with a systematic and logical approach to the problem. Approach any troubleshooting by first accurately identifying the symptom and then checking through the list of possible causes, starting with the simplest or most obvious and progressing in stages to the most complex. Take nothing for granted, but above all apply liberal quantities of common sense.

The main symptom of a fault is given in the text as a major heading below which are listed the various systems or areas which may contain the fault. Details of each possible cause for a fault and the remedial action to be taken are given. Further information should be sought in the relevant Chapter.

1 Engine doesn't start or is difficult to start

- ☐ Starter motor doesn't rotate
- ☐ Starter motor rotates but engine does not turn over
- ☐ Starter works but engine won't turn over (seized)
- ☐ No fuel flow
- ☐ Engine flooded
- ☐ No spark or weak spark
- ☐ Compression low
- ☐ Stalls after starting
- ☐ Rough idle

2 Poor running at low speed

- ☐ Spark weak
- ☐ Fuel/air mixture incorrect
- ☐ Compression low
- ☐ Poor acceleration

3 Poor running or no power at high speed

- ☐ Firing incorrect
- ☐ Fuel/air mixture incorrect
- ☐ Compression low
- ☐ Knocking or pinging
- ☐ Miscellaneous causes

4 Overheating

- ☐ Engine overheats
- ☐ Firing incorrect
- ☐ Fuel/air mixture incorrect
- ☐ Compression too high
- ☐ Engine load excessive
- ☐ Lubrication inadequate
- ☐ Miscellaneous causes

5 Clutch problems

- ☐ Clutch slipping
- ☐ Clutch not disengaging completely

6 Gearchanging problems

- ☐ Doesn't go into gear, or lever doesn't return
- ☐ Jumps out of gear
- ☐ Overselects

7 Abnormal engine noise

- ☐ Knocking or pinging
- ☐ Piston slap or rattling
- ☐ Valve noise
- ☐ Other noise

8 Abnormal driveline noise

- ☐ Clutch noise
- ☐ Transmission noise
- ☐ Final drive noise

9 Abnormal frame and suspension noise

- ☐ Front end noise
- ☐ Shock absorber noise
- ☐ Brake noise

10 Oil pressure warning light comes on

- ☐ Engine lubrication system
- ☐ Electrical system

11 Excessive exhaust smoke

- ☐ White smoke
- ☐ Black smoke

12 Poor handling or stability

- ☐ Handlebar hard to turn
- ☐ Handlebar shakes or vibrates excessively
- ☐ Handlebar pulls to one side
- ☐ Poor shock absorbing qualities

13 Braking problems

- ☐ Brakes are spongy, don't hold
- ☐ Brake lever or pedal pulsates
- ☐ Brakes drag

14 Electrical problems

- ☐ Battery dead or weak
- ☐ Battery overcharged

1 Engine doesn't start or is difficult to start

Starter motor doesn't rotate

☐ Engine kill switch OFF.

☐ Fuse blown. Check main fuse and starter circuit fuse (Chapter 9).

☐ Battery voltage low. Check and recharge battery (Chapter 9).

☐ Starter motor defective. Make sure the wiring to the starter is secure. Make sure the starter relay clicks when the start button is pushed. If the relay clicks, then the fault is in the wiring or motor.

☐ Starter relay faulty. Check it according to the procedure in Chapter 9.

☐ Starter switch not contacting. The contacts could be wet, corroded or dirty. Disassemble and clean the switch (Chapter 9).

☐ Wiring open or shorted. Check all wiring connections and harnesses to make sure that they are dry, tight and not corroded. Also check for broken or frayed wires that can cause a short to ground (see wiring diagram, Chapter 9).

☐ Ignition switch defective. Check the switch according to the procedure in Chapter 9. Replace the switch with a new one if it is defective.

☐ Engine kill switch defective. Check for wet, dirty or corroded contacts. Clean or replace the switch as necessary (Chapter 9).

☐ Faulty neutral, side stand or clutch switch or diodes. Check the wiring to each switch and the switch itself according to the procedures in Chapter 9, then if necessary check the diodes and starter circuit relay in the junction box.

Starter motor rotates but engine does not turn over

☐ Starter motor clutch defective. Inspect and repair or replace (Chapter 2).

☐ Damaged idler or starter gears. Inspect and replace the damaged parts (Chapter 2).

Starter works but engine won't turn over (seized)

☐ Seized engine caused by one or more internally damaged components. Failure due to wear, abuse or lack of lubrication. Damage can include seized valves, rockers, camshafts, pistons, crankshaft, connecting rod bearings, or transmission gears or bearings. Refer to Chapter 2 for engine disassembly.

No fuel flow

☐ No fuel in tank.

☐ Fuel tank breather hose obstructed.

☐ Fuel filter is blocked (see Chapter 1).

☐ Faulty fuel pump (see Chapter 4A or 4B). On models with fuel injection also check the FI fuse and power relay (see Chapter 4B).

Engine flooded

☐ Starting technique incorrect. On carburettor models, under normal circumstances the machine should start with little or no throttle. When the engine is cold, the choke should be operated and the engine started without opening the throttle. When the engine is at operating temperature, only a very slight amount of throttle should be necessary. On fuel injection models the engine should start with no throttle.

No spark or weak spark

☐ Ignition switch OFF.

☐ Engine kill switch turned to the OFF position.

☐ Battery voltage low. Check and recharge the battery as necessary (Chapter 9).

☐ Spark plugs dirty, defective or worn out. Locate reason for fouled plugs using spark plug condition chart at the end of this manual and follow the plug maintenance procedures (Chapter 1).

☐ Spark plug caps or secondary (HT) wiring faulty. Check condition. Replace either or both components if cracks or deterioration are evident (Chapter 5).

☐ Spark plug caps not making good contact. Make sure that the plug caps fit snugly over the plug ends.

☐ Ignition HT coils defective. Check the coils, referring to Chapter 5.

☐ ICU defective. Refer to Chapter 5 for details.

☐ Pick-up coil defective. Refer to Chapter 5 for details.

☐ Ignition or kill switch shorted. This is usually caused by water, corrosion, damage or excessive wear. The switches can be disassembled and cleaned with electrical contact cleaner. If cleaning does not help, replace the switches (Chapter 9).

☐ Wiring shorted or broken between:
 a) Ignition switch and engine kill switch (or blown fuse)
 b) ICU and engine kill switch
 c) ICU and ignition HT coils
 d) Ignition HT coils and spark plugs
 e) ICU and ignition pick-up coil.

☐ Make sure that all wiring connections are clean, dry and tight. Look for chafed and broken wires (Chapters 5 and 9).

Compression low

☐ Spark plugs loose. Remove the plugs and inspect their threads. Reinstall and tighten to the specified torque (Chapter 1).

☐ Cylinder head not sufficiently tightened down. If the cylinder head is suspected of being loose, then there's a chance that the gasket or head is damaged if the problem has persisted for any length of time. The head nuts should be tightened to the proper torque in the correct sequence (Chapter 2).

☐ Hydraulic valve lifter leaking or damaged. This means that the valve is not closing completely and compression pressure is leaking past the valve. Inspect the lifters (Chapter 2).

☐ Cylinder and/or piston worn. Excessive wear will cause compression pressure to leak past the rings. This is usually accompanied by worn rings as well. A top-end overhaul is necessary (Chapter 2).

☐ Piston rings worn, weak, broken, or sticking. Broken or sticking piston rings usually indicate a lubrication or fuelling problem that causes excess carbon deposits or seizures to form on the pistons and rings. Top-end overhaul is necessary (Chapter 2).

☐ Piston ring-to-groove clearance excessive. This is caused by excessive wear of the piston ring lands. Piston replacement is necessary (Chapter 2).

☐ Cylinder head gasket damaged. If a head is allowed to become loose, or if excessive carbon build-up on the piston crown and combustion chamber causes extremely high compression, the head gasket may leak. Retorquing the head is not always sufficient to restore the seal, so gasket replacement is necessary (Chapter 2).

☐ Cylinder head warped. This is caused by overheating or improperly tightened head nuts. Machine shop resurfacing or head replacement is necessary (Chapter 2).

☐ Valve spring broken or weak. Caused by component failure or wear; the springs must be replaced (Chapter 2).

☐ Valve not seating properly. This is caused by a bent valve (from over-revving or improper valve adjustment), burned valve or seat (improper fuelling) or an accumulation of carbon deposits on the seat (from fuelling or lubrication problems). The valves must be cleaned and/or replaced and the seats serviced if possible (Chapter 2).

1 Engine doesn't start or is difficult to start (continued)

Stalls after starting

☐ Improper choke action.
☐ Ignition malfunction. See Chapter 5.
☐ Carburetor malfunction (see Chapter 4A) or fuel injection system malfunction (see Chapter 4B).
☐ Fuel contaminated. The fuel can be contaminated with either dirt or water, or can change chemically if the machine is allowed to sit for several months or more. Drain the tank (Chapter 4).
☐ Intake air leak. Check for loose carburetor/throttle body intake rubber retaining clips and damaged/disconnected vacuum hoses (Chapter 4A or 4B).
☐ Engine idle speed incorrect. Turn idle adjusting screw until the engine idles at the specified rpm (Chapter 1).
☐ Faulty fuel pump (Chapter 4A or 4B).

Rough idle

☐ Ignition malfunction. See Chapter 5.
☐ Idle speed incorrect. See Chapter 1.
☐ Carburetors not synchronized (VN1500A and B). Adjust them with vacuum gauge or manometer set as described in Chapter 1.
☐ Carburetor malfunction (see Chapter 4A) or fuel injection system malfunction (see Chapter 4B).
☐ Fuel contaminated. The fuel can be contaminated with either dirt or water, or can change chemically if the machine is allowed to sit for several months or more. Drain the tank (Chapter 4).
☐ Intake air leak. Check for loose carburetor/throttle body intake rubber retaining clips and damaged/disconnected vacuum hoses. Replace the intake ducts if they are split or deteriorated (Chapter 4A or 4B).
☐ Air filter clogged. Replace the air filter element (Chapter 1).
☐ Faulty fuel pump (Chapter 4A or 4B).

2 Poor running at low speeds

Spark weak

☐ Battery voltage low. Check and recharge battery (Chapter 9).
☐ Spark plugs fouled, defective or worn out. Refer to Chapter 1 for spark plug maintenance.
☐ Spark plug cap or HT wiring defective. Refer to Chapters 1 and 5 for details on the ignition system.
☐ Spark plug caps not making contact.
☐ Incorrect spark plugs. Wrong type, heat range or cap configuration. Check and install correct plugs listed in Chapter 1.
☐ ICU faulty. See Chapter 5.
☐ Pick-up coil defective. See Chapter 5.
☐ Ignition HT coil defective. See Chapter 5.

Fuel/air mixture incorrect

☐ On carburettor models pilot screws incorrectly set (Chapter 4A)
☐ On carburettor models pilot jet or air passage blocked. Remove and overhaul the carburetors (Chapter 4A).
☐ On fuel injection models fuel injection system malfunction (see Chapter 4B).
☐ Air filter housing poorly sealed. Look for cracks, holes or loose clamps and replace or repair defective parts.
☐ Fuel tank breather hose obstructed.
☐ Intake air leak. Check for loose carburetor/throttle body intake duct retaining clips and damaged/disconnected vacuum hoses. Replace the intake ducts if they are split or deteriorated (Chapter 4A or 4B).

Compression low

☐ Spark plugs loose. Remove the plugs and inspect their threads. Reinstall and tighten to the specified torque (Chapter 1).
☐ Cylinder head not sufficiently tightened down. If the cylinder head is suspected of being loose, then there's a chance that the gasket and head are damaged if the problem has persisted for any length of time. The head nuts should be tightened to the proper torque in the correct sequence (Chapter 2).
☐ Hydraulic valve lifter leaking or damaged. This means that the valve is not closing completely and compression pressure is leaking past the valve. Inspect the lifters (Chapter 2).
☐ Cylinder and/or piston worn. Excessive wear will cause compression pressure to leak past the rings. This is usually accompanied by worn rings as well. A top-end overhaul is necessary (Chapter 2).
☐ Piston rings worn, weak, broken, or sticking. Broken or sticking piston rings usually indicate a lubrication or fuelling problem that causes excess carbon deposits or seizures to form on the pistons and rings. Top-end overhaul is necessary (Chapter 2).
☐ Piston ring-to-groove clearance excessive. This is caused by excessive wear of the piston ring lands. Piston replacement is necessary (Chapter 2).
☐ Cylinder head gasket damaged. If a head is allowed to become loose, or if excessive carbon build-up on the piston crown and combustion chamber causes extremely high compression, the head gasket may leak. Retorquing the head is not always sufficient to restore the seal, so gasket replacement is necessary (Chapter 2).
☐ Cylinder head warped. This is caused by overheating or improperly tightened head nuts. Machine shop resurfacing or head replacement is necessary (Chapter 2).
☐ Valve spring broken or weak. Caused by component failure or wear; the springs must be replaced (Chapter 2).
☐ Valve not seating properly. This is caused by a bent valve (from over-revving or improper valve adjustment), burned valve or seat (improper fuelling) or an accumulation of carbon deposits on the seat (from fuelling, lubrication problems). The valves must be cleaned and/or replaced and the seats serviced if possible (Chapter 2).

Poor acceleration

☐ Carburetor malfunction (see Chapter 4A) or fuel injection system malfunction (see Chapter 4B).
☐ Engine oil viscosity too high. Using a heavier oil than that recommended in Chapter 1 can damage the oil pump or lubrication system and cause drag on the engine.
☐ Brakes dragging. Usually caused by debris which has entered the brake piston seals, or from a warped disc or drum or bent axle. Repair as necessary (Chapter 7).

3 Poor running or no power at high speed

Firing incorrect

☐ Air filter restricted. Clean or replace filter (Chapter 1).
☐ Spark plugs fouled, defective or worn out. See Chapter 1 for spark plug maintenance.
☐ Spark plug caps or HT wiring defective. See Chapters 1 and 5 for details of the ignition system.
☐ Spark plug caps not in good contact. See Chapter 5.
☐ Incorrect spark plugs. Wrong type, heat range or cap configuration. Check and install correct plugs listed in Chapter 1.
☐ ICU unit defective. See Chapter 5.
☐ Pick-up coil defective. See Chapter 5.
☐ Ignition coil defective. See Chapter 5.

Fuel/air mixture incorrect

☐ Carburetor malfunction (see Chapter 4A) or fuel injection system malfunction (see Chapter 4B).
☐ Air filter clogged, poorly sealed, or missing (Chapter 1).
☐ Air filter housing poorly sealed. Look for cracks, holes or loose clamps, and replace or repair defective parts.
☐ Fuel tank breather hose obstructed.
☐ Intake air leak. Check for loose carburetor/throttle body intake duct retaining clips and damaged/disconnected vacuum hoses. Replace the intake ducts if they are split or deteriorated (Chapter 4A or 4B).

Compression low

☐ Spark plugs loose. Remove the plugs and inspect their threads. Reinstall and tighten to the specified torque (Chapter 1).
☐ Cylinder head not sufficiently tightened down. If the cylinder head is suspected of being loose, then there's a chance that the gasket and head are damaged if the problem has persisted for any length of time. The head nuts should be tightened to the proper torque in the correct sequence (Chapter 2).
☐ Hydraulic valve lifter leaking or damaged. This means that the valve is not closing completely and compression pressure is leaking past the valve. Inspect the lifters (Chapter 2).
☐ Cylinder and/or piston worn. Excessive wear will cause compression pressure to leak past the rings. This is usually accompanied by worn rings as well. A top-end overhaul is necessary (Chapter 2).
☐ Piston rings worn, weak, broken, or sticking. Broken or sticking piston rings usually indicate a lubrication or fuelling problem that causes excess carbon deposits or seizures to form on the pistons and rings. Top-end overhaul is necessary (Chapter 2).
☐ Piston ring-to-groove clearance excessive. This is caused by excessive wear of the piston ring lands. Piston replacement is necessary (Chapter 2).

☐ Cylinder head gasket damaged. If a head is allowed to become loose, or if excessive carbon build-up on the piston crown and combustion chamber causes extremely high compression, the head gasket may leak. Retorquing the head is not always sufficient to restore the seal, so gasket replacement is necessary (Chapter 2).
☐ Cylinder head warped. This is caused by overheating or improperly tightened head nuts. Machine shop resurfacing or head replacement is necessary (Chapter 2).
☐ Valve spring broken or weak. Caused by component failure or wear; the springs must be replaced (Chapter 2).
☐ Valve not seating properly. This is caused by a bent valve (from over-revving or improper valve adjustment), burned valve or seat (improper fuelling) or an accumulation of carbon deposits on the seat (from fuelling or lubrication problems). The valves must be cleaned and/or replaced and the seats serviced if possible (Chapter 2).

Knocking or pinging

☐ Carbon build-up in combustion chamber. Use of a fuel additive that will dissolve the adhesive bonding the carbon particles to the crown and chamber is the easiest way to remove the build-up. Otherwise, the cylinder heads will have to be removed and decarbonized (Chapter 2).
☐ Incorrect or poor quality fuel. Old or improper grades of fuel can cause detonation. This causes the piston to rattle, thus the knocking or pinging sound. Drain old fuel and always use the recommended fuel grade.
☐ Spark plug heat range incorrect. Uncontrolled detonation indicates the plug heat range is too hot. The plug in effect becomes a glow plug, raising cylinder temperatures. Install the proper heat range plug (Chapter 1).
☐ Improper air/fuel mixture. This will cause the cylinders to run hot, which leads to detonation. An intake air leak can cause this imbalance. See Chapter 4A or 4B.

Miscellaneous causes

☐ Throttle valve doesn't open fully. Adjust the throttle grip freeplay (Chapter 1).
☐ Clutch slipping. May be caused by loose or worn clutch components. Refer to Chapter 2 for clutch overhaul procedures.
☐ Engine oil viscosity too high. Using a heavier oil than the one recommended in Chapter 1 can damage the oil pump or lubrication system and cause drag on the engine.
☐ Brakes dragging. Usually caused by debris which has entered the brake piston seals, or from a warped disc or bent axle. Repair as necessary.

4 Overheating

Engine overheats

- ☐ Coolant level low. Check and add coolant (Chapter 1).
- ☐ Leak in cooling system. Check cooling system hoses and radiator for leaks and other damage. Repair or replace parts as necessary (Chapter 3).
- ☐ Thermostat sticking open or closed. Check and replace as described in Chapter 3.
- ☐ Faulty pressure cap. Remove the cap and have it pressure tested (Chapter 3).
- ☐ Coolant passages clogged. Have the entire system drained and flushed, then refill with fresh coolant.
- ☐ Water pump defective. Remove the pump and check the components (Chapter 3).
- ☐ Clogged radiator fins. Clean them by blowing compressed air through the fins from the rear of the radiator.
- ☐ Cooling fan or fan switch fault (Chapter 3).

Firing incorrect

- ☐ Spark plugs fouled, defective or worn out. See Chapter 1 for spark plug maintenance.
- ☐ Incorrect spark plugs.
- ☐ ICU defective. See Chapter 5.
- ☐ Faulty pick-up coil. See Chapter 5.
- ☐ Faulty ignition coil. See Chapter 5.

Fuel/air mixture incorrect

- ☐ Carburetor malfunction (see Chapter 4A) or fuel injection system malfunction (see Chapter 4B).
- ☐ Air filter clogged, poorly sealed, or missing (Chapter 1).
- ☐ Air filter housing poorly sealed. Look for cracks, holes or loose clamps, and replace or repair defective parts.
- ☐ Fuel tank breather hose obstructed.
- ☐ Intake air leak. Check for loose carburetor/throttle body intake duct retaining clips and damaged/disconnected vacuum hoses. Replace the intake ducts if they are split or deteriorated (Chapter 4A or 4B).

Compression too high

- ☐ Carbon build-up in combustion chamber. Use of a fuel additive that will dissolve the adhesive bonding the carbon particles to the piston crown and chamber is the easiest way to remove the build-up. Otherwise, the cylinder heads will have to be removed and decarbonized (Chapter 2).
- ☐ Improperly machined head surface or installation of incorrect gasket during engine assembly.

Engine load excessive

- ☐ Clutch slipping. Can be caused by damaged, loose or worn clutch components. Refer to Chapter 2 for overhaul procedures.
- ☐ Engine oil level too high. The addition of too much oil will cause pressurization of the crankcase and inefficient engine operation. Check Specifications and drain to proper level (Chapter 1).
- ☐ Engine oil viscosity too high. Using a heavier oil than the one recommended in Chapter 1 can damage the oil pump or lubrication system as well as cause drag on the engine.
- ☐ Brakes dragging. Usually caused by debris which has entered the brake piston seals, or from a warped disc or drum or bent axle. Repair as necessary.

Lubrication inadequate

- ☐ Engine oil level too low. Friction caused by intermittent lack of lubrication or from oil that is overworked can cause overheating. The oil provides a definite cooling function in the engine. Check the oil level (Chapter 1).
- ☐ Poor quality engine oil or incorrect viscosity or type. Oil is rated not only according to viscosity but also according to type. Some oils are not rated high enough for use in this engine. Check the Specifications section and change to the correct oil (Chapter 1).

Miscellaneous causes

- ☐ Modification to exhaust system. Most aftermarket exhaust systems cause the engine to run leaner, which makes it run hotter.

5 Clutch problems

Clutch slipping

☐ Friction plates worn or warped. Overhaul the clutch assembly (Chapter 2).

☐ Plain plates warped (Chapter 2).

☐ Clutch diaphragm spring broken or weakened. An old or heat-damaged (from slipping clutch) spring should be replaced (Chapter 2). Check spring height.

☐ Clutch pushrod bent. Check and, if necessary, replace (Chapter 2).

☐ Clutch center or housing unevenly worn. This causes improper engagement of the plates. Replace the damaged or worn parts (Chapter 2).

Clutch not disengaging completely

☐ Clutch release hydraulic system needs bleeding (Chapter 2) or fluid level low (Pre-ride checks).

☐ Clutch plates warped or damaged. This will cause clutch drag, which in turn will cause the machine to creep. Overhaul the clutch assembly (Chapter 2).

☐ Clutch spring tension inadequate. Check the spring height (Chapter 2).

☐ Engine oil deteriorated. Old, thin, worn out oil will not provide proper lubrication for the plates, causing the clutch to drag. Replace the oil and filter (Chapter 1).

☐ Engine oil viscosity too high. Using a heavier oil than recommended in Chapter 1 can cause the plates to stick together, putting a drag on the engine. Change to the correct weight oil (Chapter 1).

☐ Clutch housing bearing seized. Lack of lubrication, severe wear or damage can cause the bearing to seize on the input shaft. Overhaul of the clutch, and perhaps transmission, may be necessary to repair the damage (Chapter 2).

☐ Loose clutch center nut. Causes housing and center misalignment putting a drag on the engine. Engagement adjustment continually varies. Overhaul the clutch assembly (Chapter 2).

6 Gearchanging problems

Doesn't go into gear or lever doesn't return

☐ Clutch not disengaging. See above.

☐ Shift fork(s) bent or seized. Often caused by dropping the machine or from lack of lubrication. Overhaul the transmission (Chapter 2).

☐ Gear(s) stuck on shaft. Most often caused by a lack of lubrication or excessive wear in transmission bearings and bushings. Overhaul the transmission (Chapter 2).

☐ Gear shift drum binding. Caused by lubrication failure or excessive wear. Replace the drum and bearing (Chapter 2).

☐ Gear shift lever pawl spring weak or broken (Chapter 2).

☐ Gear shift lever broken. Splines stripped out of lever or shaft, caused by allowing the lever to get loose or from dropping the machine. Replace necessary parts (Chapter 2).

☐ Gear shift mechanism stopper arm broken or worn. Full engagement and rotary movement of shift drum results. Replace the arm (Chapter 2).

☐ Stopper arm spring broken. Allows arm to float, causing sporadic shift operation. Replace spring (Chapter 2).

Jumps out of gear

☐ Shift fork(s) worn. Overhaul the transmission (Chapter 2).

☐ Gear groove(s) worn. Overhaul the transmission (Chapter 2).

☐ Gear dogs or dog slots worn or damaged. The gears should be inspected and replaced. No attempt should be made to service the worn parts.

Overselects

☐ Stopper arm spring weak or broken (Chapter 2).

☐ Return spring post broken or distorted (Chapter 2).

7 Abnormal engine noise

Knocking or pinging

☐ Carbon build-up in combustion chamber. Use of a fuel additive that will dissolve the adhesive bonding the carbon particles to the piston crown and chamber is the easiest way to remove the build-up. Otherwise, the cylinder heads will have to be removed and decarbonized (Chapter 2).

☐ Incorrect or poor quality fuel. Old or improper fuel can cause detonation. This causes the pistons to rattle, thus the knocking or pinging sound. Drain the old fuel and always use the recommended grade fuel.

☐ Spark plug heat range incorrect. Uncontrolled detonation indicates that the plug heat range is too hot. The plug in effect becomes a glow plug, raising cylinder temperatures. Install the proper heat range plug (Chapter 1).

☐ Improper air/fuel mixture (carburettor models). This will cause the cylinders to run hot and lead to detonation. Blocked carburetor jets or an air leak can cause this imbalance. See Chapter 4A.

Piston slap or rattling

☐ Cylinder-to-piston clearance excessive. Caused by improper assembly. Inspect and overhaul top-end parts (Chapter 2).

☐ Connecting rod bent. Caused by over-revving, trying to start a badly flooded engine or from ingesting a foreign object into the combustion chamber. Replace the damaged parts (Chapter 2).

☐ Piston pin or piston pin bore worn or seized from wear or lack of lubrication. Replace damaged parts (Chapter 2).

☐ Piston ring(s) worn, broken or sticking. Overhaul the top-end (Chapter 2).

☐ Piston seizure damage. Usually from lack of lubrication or overheating. Replace the pistons and cylinders, as necessary (Chapter 2).

☐ Connecting rod bearing clearance excessive. Caused by excessive wear or lack of lubrication. Replace worn parts.

Valve noise

☐ Hydraulic lifters faulty or need bleeding (see Chapter 2).

☐ Valve spring broken or weak. Check and replace weak valve springs (Chapter 2).

☐ Camshaft or cylinder head worn or damaged. Lack of lubrication at high rpm is usually the cause of damage. Insufficient oil or failure to change the oil at the recommended intervals are the chief causes. Since there are no replaceable bearings in the head, the head itself will have to be replaced if there is excessive wear or damage (Chapter 2).

Other noise

☐ Cylinder head gasket leaking.

☐ Exhaust pipe leaking at cylinder head connection. Caused by improper fit of pipe(s) or loose exhaust nuts. All exhaust fasteners should be tightened evenly and carefully. Failure to do this will lead to a leak.

☐ Crankshaft runout excessive. Caused by a bent crankshaft (from over-revving) or damage from an upper cylinder component failure. Can also be attributed to dropping the machine on either of the crankshaft ends.

☐ Engine mounting bolts loose. Tighten all engine mount bolts (Chapter 2).

☐ Crankshaft bearings worn (Chapter 2).

☐ Camchain, tensioner or guides worn. Replace according to the procedure in Chapter 2.

8 Abnormal driveline noise

Clutch noise

☐ Clutch outer drum/friction plate clearance excessive (Chapter 2).
☐ Loose or damaged clutch spring holder (Chapter 2).

Transmission noise

☐ Bearings worn. Also includes the possibility that the shafts are worn. Overhaul the transmission (Chapter 2).
☐ Gears worn or chipped (Chapter 2).
☐ Metal chips jammed in gear teeth. Probably pieces from a broken clutch, gear or shift mechanism that were picked up by the gears. This will cause early bearing failure (Chapter 2).

☐ Engine oil level too low. Causes a howl from transmission. Also affects engine power and clutch operation (Chapter 1).

Final drive noise

☐ Final drive oil level low. Top up with the correct oil (Chapter 1).
☐ Front bevel gear or final drive gears or their bearings worn or damaged. Remove the relevant housing and check for play and damage (Chapter 6).
☐ Universal joint on driveshaft worn (Chapter 6).

9 Abnormal frame and suspension noise

Front end noise

☐ Low fluid level or improper viscosity oil in forks. This can sound like spurting and is usually accompanied by irregular fork action (Chapter 6).
☐ Spring weak or broken. Makes a clicking or scraping sound. Fork oil, when drained, will have a lot of metal particles in it (Chapter 6).
☐ Steering head bearings loose or damaged. Clicks when braking. Check and adjust or replace as necessary (Chapters 1 and 6).
☐ Triple clamps loose. Make sure all clamp bolts are tightened to the specified torque (Chapter 6).
☐ Fork tube bent. Good possibility if machine has been dropped. Replace tube with a new one (Chapter 6).
☐ Front axle bolt or axle pinch bolts loose. Tighten them to the specified torque (Chapter 7).
☐ Loose or worn wheel bearings. Check and replace as needed (Chapter 7).

Shock absorber noise

☐ Fluid level incorrect. Indicates a leak caused by defective seal. Shock will be covered with oil. Replace shocks or seek advice on repair from a Kawasaki dealer (Chapter 6).
☐ Defective shock absorber with internal damage. This is in the body of the shock and can't be remedied. The shocks must be replaced (Chapter 6).
☐ Bent or damaged shock body. Replace the shocks (Chapter 6).

Brake noise

☐ Squeal caused by dust on brake pads. Usually found in combination with glazed pads. Clean using brake cleaning solvent (Chapter 7).
☐ Contamination of brake pads. Oil, brake fluid or dirt causing brake to chatter or squeal. Clean or replace pads (Chapter 7).
☐ Pads glazed. Caused by excessive heat from prolonged use or from contamination. Do not use sandpaper/emery cloth or any other abrasive to roughen the pad surfaces as abrasives will stay in the pad material and damage the disc. A very fine flat file can be used, but pad replacement is suggested as a cure (Chapter 7).
☐ Disc warped. Can cause a chattering, clicking or intermittent squeal. Usually accompanied by a pulsating lever and uneven braking. Replace the disc (Chapter 7).
☐ Loose or worn wheel bearings. Check and replace as needed (Chapter 7).

10 Oil pressure warning light comes on

Engine lubrication system

☐ Engine oil pump defective, blocked oil strainer screen or failed relief valve. Carry out oil pressure check (Chapter 2).

☐ Engine oil level low. Inspect for leak or other problem causing low oil level and add recommended oil (Pre-ride checks).

☐ Engine oil viscosity too low. Very old, thin oil or an improper weight of oil used in the engine. Change to correct oil (Chapter 1).

☐ Camshaft or journals worn. Excessive wear causing drop in oil pressure. Replace cam and/or cylinder head. Abnormal wear could be caused by oil starvation at high rpm from low oil level or improper weight or type of oil (Chapter 1).

☐ Crankshaft and/or bearings worn. Same problems as above. Check and replace crankshaft and/or bearings (Chapter 2).

Electrical system

☐ Oil pressure switch defective. Check the switch according to the procedure in Chapter 9. Replace it if it is defective.

☐ Oil pressure warning light circuit defective. Check for pinched, shorted, disconnected or damaged wiring (Chapter 9).

11 Excessive exhaust smoke

White smoke

☐ Piston oil ring worn. The ring may be broken or damaged, causing oil from the crankcase to be pulled past the piston into the combustion chamber. Replace the rings with new ones (Chapter 2).

☐ Cylinders worn, cracked, or scored. Caused by overheating or oil starvation. Install new cylinders or rebore (Chapter 2).

☐ Valve oil seal damaged or worn. Replace oil seals with new ones (Chapter 2).

☐ Valve guide worn. Perform a complete valve job (Chapter 2).

☐ Engine oil level too high, which causes the oil to be forced past the rings. Drain oil to the proper level (Chapter 1 and Pre-ride checks).

☐ Head gasket broken between oil return and cylinder. Causes oil to be pulled into the combustion chamber. Replace the head gasket and check the head for warpage (Chapter 2).

☐ Abnormal crankcase pressurization, which forces oil past the rings. Clogged breather is usually the cause.

Black smoke (carburetor models)

☐ Air filter clogged. Clean or replace the element (Chapter 1).

☐ Carburetor flooding. Remove and overhaul the carburetor(s) (Chapter 4A).

☐ Main jet too large. Remove and overhaul the carburetor(s) (Chapter 4A).

☐ Choke cable stuck (Chapter 4A).

☐ Fuel level too high. Check the fuel level (Chapter 4A).

12 Poor handling or stability

Handlebar hard to turn

☐ Steering head bearing adjuster nut too tight. Check adjustment as described in Chapter 1.

☐ Bearings damaged. Roughness can be felt as the bars are turned from side-to-side. Replace bearings and races (Chapter 6).

☐ Races dented or worn. Denting results from wear in only one position (e.g., straight ahead), from a collision or hitting a pothole or from dropping the machine. Replace races and bearings (Chapter 6).

☐ Steering stem lubrication inadequate. Causes are grease getting hard from age or being washed out by use of pressure washers. Disassemble steering head and repack bearings (Chapter 6).

☐ Steering stem bent. Caused by a collision, hitting a pothole or by dropping the machine. Replace damaged part. Don't try to straighten the steering stem (Chapter 6).

☐ Front tire air pressure too low (Pre-ride checks).

Handlebar shakes or vibrates excessively

☐ Tires worn or out of balance (Chapter 7).

☐ Swingarm bearings worn. Replace worn bearings (Chapter 6).

☐ Wheel rim(s) warped or damaged. Inspect wheels for runout (Chapter 7).

☐ Wheel bearings worn. Worn front or rear wheel bearings can cause poor tracking. Worn front bearings will cause wobble (Chapter 7).

☐ Handlebar clamp bolts loose (Chapter 6).

☐ Fork yoke bolts loose. Tighten them to the specified torque (Chapter 6).

☐ Engine mounting bolts loose. Will cause excessive vibration with increased engine rpm (Chapter 2).

Handlebar pulls to one side

☐ Frame bent. Definitely suspect this if the machine has been dropped. May or may not be accompanied by cracking near the bend. Replace the frame (Chapter 8).

☐ Wheels out of alignment. Caused by improper location of axle spacers or from bent steering stem or frame (Chapters 6 and 8).

☐ Swingarm bent or twisted. Caused by age (metal fatigue) or impact damage. Replace the arm (Chapter 6).

☐ Steering stem bent. Caused by impact damage or by dropping the motorcycle. Replace the steering stem (Chapter 6).

☐ Fork tube bent. Disassemble the forks and replace the damaged parts (Chapter 6).

☐ Fork oil level uneven. Check and add or drain as necessary (Chapter 6).

Poor shock absorbing qualities

☐ Too hard:
   a) Fork oil level excessive (Chapter 6).
   b) Fork oil viscosity too high. Use a lighter oil (see the Specifications in Chapter 6).
   c) Fork tube bent. Causes a harsh, sticking feeling (Chapter 6).
   d) Shock shaft or body bent or damaged (Chapter 6).
   e) Fork internal damage (Chapter 6).
   f) Shock internal damage.
   g) Tire pressure too high (Pre-ride checks).

☐ Too soft:
   a) Fork or shock oil insufficient and/or leaking (Chapter 6).
   b) Fork oil level too low (Chapter 6).
   c) Fork oil viscosity too light (Chapter 6).
   d) Fork springs weak or broken (Chapter 6).
   e) Shock internal damage or leakage (Chapter 6).

13 Braking problems

Brakes are spongy, don't hold

☐ Air in brake line. Caused by inattention to master cylinder fluid level (see Pre-ride checks) or by leakage. Locate problem and bleed brakes (Chapter 7).

☐ Pad or disc worn (Chapters 1 and 7).

☐ Brake fluid leak. See paragraph 1.

☐ Contaminated pads. Caused by contamination with oil, grease, brake fluid, etc. Clean or replace pads. Clean disc thoroughly with brake cleaner (Chapter 7).

☐ Brake fluid deteriorated. Fluid is old or contaminated. Drain system, replenish with new fluid and bleed the system (Chapter 7).

☐ Master cylinder internal parts worn or damaged causing fluid to bypass (Chapter 7).

☐ Master cylinder bore scratched by foreign material or broken spring. Repair or replace master cylinder (Chapter 7).

☐ Disc warped. Replace disc (Chapter 7).

Brake lever or pedal pulsates

☐ Disc warped. Replace disc (Chapter 7).

☐ Axle bent. Replace axle (Chapter 7).

☐ Brake caliper bolts loose (Chapter 7).

☐ Wheel warped or otherwise damaged (Chapter 7).

☐ Wheel bearings damaged or worn (Chapter 7).

Brakes drag

☐ Master cylinder piston seized. Caused by wear or damage to piston or cylinder bore (Chapter 7).

☐ Lever binding. Check pivot and lubricate (Chapter 7).

☐ Brake caliper piston seized in bore. Caused by wear or ingestion of dirt past deteriorated seal (Chapter 7).

☐ Brake caliper mounting bracket pins corroded – sliding type caliper. Clean off corrosion and lubricate (Chapter 7).

☐ Brake pad damaged. Material separated from backing plate. Usually caused by faulty manufacturing process or from contact with chemicals. Replace pads (Chapter 7).

☐ Pads improperly installed (Chapter 7).

14 Electrical problems

Battery dead or weak

☐ Battery faulty. Caused by sulfated plates which are shorted through sedimentation. Also, broken battery terminal making only occasional contact (Chapter 9).

☐ Battery leads making poor contact (Chapter 9).

☐ Load excessive. Caused by addition of high wattage lights or other electrical accessories.

☐ Ignition switch defective. Switch either grounds internally or fails to shut off system. Replace the switch (Chapter 9).

☐ Regulator/rectifier defective (Chapter 9).

☐ Alternator stator coil open or shorted (Chapter 9).

☐ Wiring faulty. Wiring grounded or connections loose in ignition, charging or lighting circuits (Chapter 9).

Battery overcharged

☐ Regulator/rectifier defective. Overcharging is noticed when battery gets excessively warm (Chapter 9).

☐ Battery defective. Replace battery with a new one (Chapter 9).

☐ Battery amperage too low, wrong type or size. Install manufacturer's specified amp-hour battery to handle charging load (Chapter 9).

A

ABS (Anti-lock braking system) A system, usually electronically controlled, that senses incipient wheel lockup during braking and relieves hydraulic pressure at wheel which is about to skid.

Aftermarket Components suitable for the motorcycle, but not produced by the motorcycle manufacturer.

Allen key A hexagonal wrench which fits into a recessed hexagonal hole.

Alternating current (ac) Current produced by an alternator. Requires converting to direct current by a rectifier for charging purposes.

Alternator Converts mechanical energy from the engine into electrical energy to charge the battery and power the electrical system.

Ampere (amp) A unit of measurement for the flow of electrical current. Current = Volts ÷ Ohms.

Ampere-hour (Ah) Measure of battery capacity.

Angle-tightening A torque expressed in degrees. Often follows a conventional tightening torque for cylinder head or main bearing fasteners **(see illustration)**.

Angle-tightening cylinder head bolts

Antifreeze A substance (usually ethylene glycol) mixed with water, and added to the cooling system, to prevent freezing of the coolant in winter. Antifreeze also contains chemicals to inhibit corrosion and the formation of rust and other deposits that would tend to clog the radiator and coolant passages and reduce cooling efficiency.

Anti-dive System attached to the fork lower leg (slider) to prevent fork dive when braking hard.

Anti-seize compound A coating that reduces the risk of seizing on fasteners that are subjected to high temperatures, such as exhaust clamp bolts and nuts.

API American Petroleum Institute. A quality standard for 4-stroke motor oils.

Asbestos A natural fibrous mineral with great heat resistance, commonly used in the composition of brake friction materials. Asbestos is a health hazard and the dust created by brake systems should never be inhaled or ingested.

ATF Automatic Transmission Fluid. Often used in front forks.

ATU Automatic Timing Unit. Mechanical device for advancing the ignition timing on early engines.

ATV All Terrain Vehicle. Often called a Quad.

Axial play Side-to-side movement.

Axle A shaft on which a wheel revolves. Also known as a spindle.

B

Backlash The amount of movement between meshed components when one component is held still. Usually applies to gear teeth.

Ball bearing A bearing consisting of a hardened inner and outer race with hardened steel balls between the two races.

Bearings Used between two working surfaces to prevent wear of the components and a build-up of heat. Four types of bearing are commonly used on motorcycles: plain shell bearings, ball bearings, tapered roller bearings and needle roller bearings.

Bevel gears Used to turn the drive through 90°. Typical applications are shaft final drive and camshaft drive **(see illustration)**.

Bevel gears are used to turn the drive through 90°

BHP Brake Horsepower. The British measurement for engine power output. Power output is now usually expressed in kilowatts (kW).

Bias-belted tyre Similar construction to radial tyre, but with outer belt running at an angle to the wheel rim.

Big-end bearing The bearing in the end of the connecting rod that's attached to the crankshaft.

Bleeding The process of removing air from an hydraulic system via a bleed nipple or bleed screw.

Bottom-end A description of an engine's crankcase components and all components contained there-in.

BTDC Before Top Dead Centre in terms of piston position. Ignition timing is often expressed in terms of degrees or millimetres BTDC.

Bush A cylindrical metal or rubber component used between two moving parts.

Burr Rough edge left on a component after machining or as a result of excessive wear.

C

Cam chain The chain which takes drive from the crankshaft to the camshaft(s).

Canister The main component in an evaporative emission control system (California market only); contains activated charcoal granules to trap vapours from the fuel system rather than allowing them to vent to the atmosphere.

Castellated Resembling the parapets along the top of a castle wall. For example, a castellated wheel axle or spindle nut.

Catalytic converter A device in the exhaust system of some machines which converts certain pollutants in the exhaust gases into less harmful substances.

Charging system Description of the components which charge the battery, ie the alternator, rectifer and regulator.

Circlip A ring-shaped clip used to prevent endwise movement of cylindrical parts and shafts. An internal circlip is installed in a groove in a housing; an external circlip fits into a groove on the outside of a cylindrical piece such as a shaft. Also known as a snap-ring.

Clearance The amount of space between two parts. For example, between a piston and a cylinder, between a bearing and a journal, etc.

Coil spring A spiral of elastic steel found in various sizes throughout a vehicle, for example as a springing medium in the suspension and in the valve train.

Compression Reduction in volume, and increase in pressure and temperature, of a gas, caused by squeezing it into a smaller space.

Compression damping Controls the speed the suspension compresses when hitting a bump.

Compression ratio The relationship between cylinder volume when the piston is at top dead centre and cylinder volume when the piston is at bottom dead centre.

Continuity The uninterrupted path in the flow of electricity. Little or no measurable resistance.

Continuity tester Self-powered bleeper or test light which indicates continuity.

Cp Candlepower. Bulb rating commonly found on US motorcycles.

Crossply tyre Tyre plies arranged in a criss-cross pattern. Usually four or six plies used, hence 4PR or 6PR in tyre size codes.

Cush drive Rubber damper segments fitted between the rear wheel and final drive sprocket to absorb transmission shocks **(see illustration)**.

Cush drive rubbers dampen out transmission shocks

D

Degree disc Calibrated disc for measuring piston position. Expressed in degrees.

Dial gauge Clock-type gauge with adapters for measuring runout and piston position. Expressed in mm or inches.

Diaphragm The rubber membrane in a master cylinder or carburettor which seals the upper chamber.

Diaphragm spring A single sprung plate often used in clutches.

Direct current (dc) Current produced by a dc generator.

Decarbonisation The process of removing carbon deposits - typically from the combustion chamber, valves and exhaust port/system.

Detonation Destructive and damaging explosion of fuel/air mixture in combustion chamber instead of controlled burning.

Diode An electrical valve which only allows current to flow in one direction. Commonly used in rectifiers and starter interlock systems.

Disc valve (or rotary valve) A induction system used on some two-stroke engines.

Double-overhead camshaft (DOHC) An engine that uses two overhead camshafts, one for the intake valves and one for the exhaust valves.

Drivebelt A toothed belt used to transmit drive to the rear wheel on some motorcycles. A drivebelt has also been used to drive the camshafts. Drivebelts are usually made of Kevlar.

Driveshaft Any shaft used to transmit motion. Commonly used when referring to the final driveshaft on shaft drive motorcycles.

E

Earth return The return path of an electrical circuit, utilising the motorcycle's frame.

ECU (Electronic Control Unit) A computer which controls (for instance) an ignition system, or an anti-lock braking system.

EGO Exhaust Gas Oxygen sensor. Sometimes called a Lambda sensor.

Electrolyte The fluid in a lead-acid battery.

EMS (Engine Management System) A computer controlled system which manages the fuel injection and the ignition systems in an integrated fashion.

Endfloat The amount of lengthways movement between two parts. As applied to a crankshaft, the distance that the crankshaft can move side-to-side in the crankcase.

Endless chain A chain having no joining link. Common use for cam chains and final drive chains.

EP (Extreme Pressure) Oil type used in locations where high loads are applied, such as between gear teeth.

Evaporative emission control system Describes a charcoal filled canister which stores fuel vapours from the tank rather than allowing them to vent to the atmosphere. Usually only fitted to California models and referred to as an EVAP system.

Expansion chamber Section of two-stroke engine exhaust system so designed to improve engine efficiency and boost power.

F

Feeler blade or gauge A thin strip or blade of hardened steel, ground to an exact thickness, used to check or measure clearances between parts.

Final drive Description of the drive from the transmission to the rear wheel. Usually by chain or shaft, but sometimes by belt.

Firing order The order in which the engine cylinders fire, or deliver their power strokes, beginning with the number one cylinder.

Flooding Term used to describe a high fuel level in the carburettor float chambers, leading to fuel overflow. Also refers to excess fuel in the combustion chamber due to incorrect starting technique.

Free length The no-load state of a component when measured. Clutch, valve and fork spring lengths are measured at rest, without any preload.

Freeplay The amount of travel before any action takes place. The looseness in a linkage, or an assembly of parts, between the initial application of force and actual movement. For example, the distance the rear brake pedal moves before the rear brake is actuated.

Fuel injection The fuel/air mixture is metered electronically and directed into the engine intake ports (indirect injection) or into the cylinders (direct injection). Sensors supply information on engine speed and conditions.

Fuel/air mixture The charge of fuel and air going into the engine. See **Stoichiometric ratio**.

Fuse An electrical device which protects a circuit against accidental overload. The typical fuse contains a soft piece of metal which is calibrated to melt at a predetermined current flow (expressed as amps) and break the circuit.

G

Gap The distance the spark must travel in jumping from the centre electrode to the side electrode in a spark plug. Also refers to the distance between the ignition rotor and the pickup coil in an electronic ignition system.

Gasket Any thin, soft material - usually cork, cardboard, asbestos or soft metal - installed between two metal surfaces to ensure a good seal. For instance, the cylinder head gasket seals the joint between the block and the cylinder head.

Gauge An instrument panel display used to monitor engine conditions. A gauge with a movable pointer on a dial or a fixed scale is an analogue gauge. A gauge with a numerical readout is called a digital gauge.

Gear ratios The drive ratio of a pair of gears in a gearbox, calculated on their number of teeth.

Glaze-busting see **Honing**

Grinding Process for renovating the valve face and valve seat contact area in the cylinder head.

Gudgeon pin The shaft which connects the connecting rod small-end with the piston. Often called a piston pin or wrist pin.

H

Helical gears Gear teeth are slightly curved and produce less gear noise that straight-cut gears. Often used for primary drives.

Installing a Helicoil thread insert in a cylinder head

Helicoil A thread insert repair system. Commonly used as a repair for stripped spark plug threads **(see illustration)**.

Honing A process used to break down the glaze on a cylinder bore (also called glaze-busting). Can also be carried out to roughen a rebored cylinder to aid ring bedding-in.

HT (High Tension) Description of the electrical circuit from the secondary winding of the ignition coil to the spark plug.

Hydraulic A liquid filled system used to transmit pressure from one component to another. Common uses on motorcycles are brakes and clutches.

Hydrometer An instrument for measuring the specific gravity of a lead-acid battery.

Hygroscopic Water absorbing. In motorcycle applications, braking efficiency will be reduced if DOT 3 or 4 hydraulic fluid absorbs water from the air - care must be taken to keep new brake fluid in tightly sealed containers.

I

lbf ft Pounds-force feet. An imperial unit of torque. Sometimes written as ft-lbs.

lbf in Pound-force inch. An imperial unit of torque, applied to components where a very low torque is required. Sometimes written as in-lbs.

IC Abbreviation for Integrated Circuit.

Ignition advance Means of increasing the timing of the spark at higher engine speeds. Done by mechanical means (ATU) on early engines or electronically by the ignition control unit on later engines.

Ignition timing The moment at which the spark plug fires, expressed in the number of crankshaft degrees before the piston reaches the top of its stroke, or in the number of millimetres before the piston reaches the top of its stroke.

Infinity (∞) Description of an open-circuit electrical state, where no continuity exists.

Inverted forks (upside down forks) The sliders or lower legs are held in the yokes and the fork tubes or stanchions are connected to the wheel axle (spindle). Less unsprung weight and stiffer construction than conventional forks.

J

JASO Quality standard for 2-stroke oils.

Joule The unit of electrical energy.

Journal The bearing surface of a shaft.

K

Kickstart Mechanical means of turning the engine over for starting purposes. Only usually fitted to mopeds, small capacity motorcycles and off-road motorcycles.

Kill switch Handebar-mounted switch for emergency ignition cut-out. Cuts the ignition circuit on all models, and additionally prevent starter motor operation on others.

km Symbol for kilometre.

kmh Abbreviation for kilometres per hour.

L

Lambda (λ) sensor A sensor fitted in the exhaust system to measure the exhaust gas oxygen content (excess air factor).

Lapping see **Grinding**.
LCD Abbreviation for Liquid Crystal Display.
LED Abbreviation for Light Emitting Diode.
Liner A steel cylinder liner inserted in a aluminium alloy cylinder block.
Locknut A nut used to lock an adjustment nut, or other threaded component, in place.
Lockstops The lugs on the lower triple clamp (yoke) which abut those on the frame, preventing handlebar-to-fuel tank contact.
Lockwasher A form of washer designed to prevent an attaching nut from working loose.
LT Low Tension Description of the electrical circuit from the power supply to the primary winding of the ignition coil.

M

Main bearings The bearings between the crankshaft and crankcase.
Maintenance-free (MF) battery A sealed battery which cannot be topped up.
Manometer Mercury-filled calibrated tubes used to measure intake tract vacuum. Used to synchronise carburettors on multi-cylinder engines.
Micrometer A precision measuring instrument that measures component outside diameters **(see illustration)**.

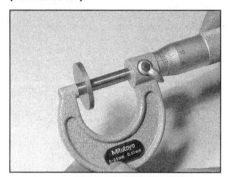

Tappet shims are measured with a micrometer

MON (Motor Octane Number) A measure of a fuel's resistance to knock.
Monograde oil An oil with a single viscosity, eg SAE80W.
Monoshock A single suspension unit linking the swingarm or suspension linkage to the frame.
mph Abbreviation for miles per hour.
Multigrade oil Having a wide viscosity range (eg 10W40). The W stands for Winter, thus the viscosity ranges from SAE10 when cold to SAE40 when hot.
Multimeter An electrical test instrument with the capability to measure voltage, current and resistance. Some meters also incorporate a continuity tester and buzzer.

N

Needle roller bearing Inner race of caged needle rollers and hardened outer race. Examples of uncaged needle rollers can be found on some engines. Commonly used in rear suspension applications and in two-stroke engines.
Nm Newton metres.
NOx Oxides of Nitrogen. A common toxic pollutant emitted by petrol engines at higher temperatures.

O

Octane The measure of a fuel's resistance to knock.
OE (Original Equipment) Relates to components fitted to a motorcycle as standard or replacement parts supplied by the motorcycle manufacturer.
Ohm The unit of electrical resistance. Ohms = Volts ÷ Current.
Ohmmeter An instrument for measuring electrical resistance.
Oil cooler System for diverting engine oil outside of the engine to a radiator for cooling purposes.
Oil injection A system of two-stroke engine lubrication where oil is pump-fed to the engine in accordance with throttle position.
Open-circuit An electrical condition where there is a break in the flow of electricity - no continuity (high resistance).
O-ring A type of sealing ring made of a special rubber-like material; in use, the O-ring is compressed into a groove to provide the sealing action.
Oversize (OS) Term used for piston and ring size options fitted to a rebored cylinder.
Overhead cam (sohc) engine An engine with single camshaft located on top of the cylinder head.
Overhead valve (ohv) engine An engine with the valves located in the cylinder head, but with the camshaft located in the engine block or crankcase.
Oxygen sensor A device installed in the exhaust system which senses the oxygen content in the exhaust and converts this information into an electric current. Also called a Lambda sensor.

P

Plastigauge A thin strip of plastic thread, available in different sizes, used for measuring clearances. For example, a strip of Plastigauge is laid across a bearing journal. The parts are assembled and dismantled; the width of the crushed strip indicates the clearance between journal and bearing.
Polarity Either negative or positive earth (ground), determined by which battery lead is connected to the frame (earth return). Modern motorcycles are usually negative earth.
Pre-ignition A situation where the fuel/air mixture ignites before the spark plug fires. Often due to a hot spot in the combustion chamber caused by carbon build-up. Engine has a tendency to 'run-on'.
Pre-load (suspension) The amount a spring is compressed when in the unloaded state. Preload can be applied by gas, spacer or mechanical adjuster.
Premix The method of engine lubrication on older two-stroke engines. Engine oil is mixed with the petrol in the fuel tank in a specific ratio. The fuel/oil mix is sometimes referred to as "petroil".
Primary drive Description of the drive from the crankshaft to the clutch. Usually by gear or chain.
PS Pfedestärke - a German interpretation of BHP.
PSI Pounds-force per square inch. Imperial measurement of tyre pressure and cylinder pressure measurement.
PTFE Polytetrafluroethylene. A low friction substance.

Pulse secondary air injection system A process of promoting the burning of excess fuel present in the exhaust gases by routing fresh air into the exhaust ports.

Q

Quartz halogen bulb Tungsten filament surrounded by a halogen gas. Typically used for the headlight **(see illustration)**.

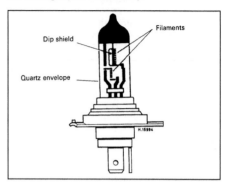

Quartz halogen headlight bulb construction

R

Rack-and-pinion A pinion gear on the end of a shaft that mates with a rack (think of a geared wheel opened up and laid flat). Sometimes used in clutch operating systems.
Radial play Up and down movement about a shaft.
Radial ply tyres Tyre plies run across the tyre (from bead to bead) and around the circumference of the tyre. Less resistant to tread distortion than other tyre types.
Radiator A liquid-to-air heat transfer device designed to reduce the temperature of the coolant in a liquid cooled engine.
Rake A feature of steering geometry - the angle of the steering head in relation to the vertical **(see illustration)**.

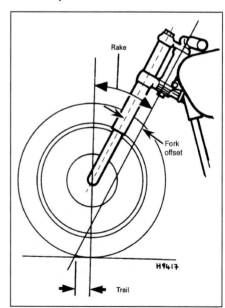

Steering geometry

Rebore Providing a new working surface to the cylinder bore by boring out the old surface. Necessitates the use of oversize piston and rings.

Rebound damping A means of controlling the oscillation of a suspension unit spring after it has been compressed. Resists the spring's natural tendency to bounce back after being compressed.

Rectifier Device for converting the ac output of an alternator into dc for battery charging.

Reed valve An induction system commonly used on two-stroke engines.

Regulator Device for maintaining the charging voltage from the generator or alternator within a specified range.

Relay A electrical device used to switch heavy current on and off by using a low current auxiliary circuit.

Resistance Measured in ohms. An electrical component's ability to pass electrical current.

RON (Research Octane Number) A measure of a fuel's resistance to knock.

rpm revolutions per minute.

Runout The amount of wobble (in-and-out movement) of a wheel or shaft as it's rotated. The amount a shaft rotates 'out-of-true'. The out-of-round condition of a rotating part.

S

SAE (Society of Automotive Engineers) A standard for the viscosity of a fluid.

Sealant A liquid or paste used to prevent leakage at a joint. Sometimes used in conjunction with a gasket.

Service limit Term for the point where a component is no longer useable and must be renewed.

Shaft drive A method of transmitting drive from the transmission to the rear wheel.

Shell bearings Plain bearings consisting of two shell halves. Most often used as big-end and main bearings in a four-stroke engine. Often called bearing inserts.

Shim Thin spacer, commonly used to adjust the clearance or relative positions between two parts. For example, shims inserted into or under tappets or followers to control valve clearances. Clearance is adjusted by changing the thickness of the shim.

Short-circuit An electrical condition where current shorts to earth (ground) bypassing the circuit components.

Skimming Process to correct warpage or repair a damaged surface, eg on brake discs or drums.

Slide-hammer A special puller that screws into or hooks onto a component such as a shaft or bearing; a heavy sliding handle on the shaft bottoms against the end of the shaft to knock the component free.

Small-end bearing The bearing in the upper end of the connecting rod at its joint with the gudgeon pin.

Spalling Damage to camshaft lobes or bearing journals shown as pitting of the working surface.

Specific gravity (SG) The state of charge of the electrolyte in a lead-acid battery. A measure of the electrolyte's density compared with water.

Straight-cut gears Common type gear used on gearbox shafts and for oil pump and water pump drives.

Stanchion The inner sliding part of the front forks, held by the yokes. Often called a fork tube.

Stoichiometric ratio The optimum chemical air/fuel ratio for a petrol engine, said to be 14.7 parts of air to 1 part of fuel.

Sulphuric acid The liquid (electrolyte) used in a lead-acid battery. Poisonous and extremely corrosive.

Surface grinding (lapping) Process to correct a warped gasket face, commonly used on cylinder heads.

T

Tapered-roller bearing Tapered inner race of caged needle rollers and separate tapered outer race. Examples of taper roller bearings can be found on steering heads.

Tappet A cylindrical component which transmits motion from the cam to the valve stem, either directly or via a pushrod and rocker arm. Also called a cam follower.

TCS Traction Control System. An electronically-controlled system which senses wheel spin and reduces engine speed accordingly.

TDC Top Dead Centre denotes that the piston is at its highest point in the cylinder.

Thread-locking compound Solution applied to fastener threads to prevent slackening. Select type to suit application.

Thrust washer A washer positioned between two moving components on a shaft. For example, between gear pinions on gearshaft.

Timing chain See **Cam Chain.**

Timing light Stroboscopic lamp for carrying out ignition timing checks with the engine running.

Top-end A description of an engine's cylinder block, head and valve gear components.

Torque Turning or twisting force about a shaft.

Torque setting A prescribed tightness specified by the motorcycle manufacturer to ensure that the bolt or nut is secured correctly. Undertightening can result in the bolt or nut coming loose or a surface not being sealed. Overtightening can result in stripped threads, distortion or damage to the component being retained.

Torx key A six-point wrench.

Tracer A stripe of a second colour applied to a wire insulator to distinguish that wire from another one with the same colour insulator. For example, Br/W is often used to denote a brown insulator with a white tracer.

Trail A feature of steering geometry. Distance from the steering head axis to the tyre's central contact point.

Triple clamps The cast components which extend from the steering head and support the fork stanchions or tubes. Often called fork yokes.

Turbocharger A centrifugal device, driven by exhaust gases, that pressurises the intake air. Normally used to increase the power output from a given engine displacement.

TWI Abbreviation for Tyre Wear Indicator. Indicates the location of the tread depth indicator bars on tyres.

U

Universal joint or U-joint (UJ) A double-pivoted connection for transmitting power from a driving to a driven shaft through an angle. Typically found in shaft drive assemblies.

Unsprung weight Anything not supported by the bike's suspension (ie the wheel, tyres, brakes, final drive and bottom (moving) part of the suspension).

V

Vacuum gauges Clock-type gauges for measuring intake tract vacuum. Used for carburettor synchronisation on multi-cylinder engines.

Valve A device through which the flow of liquid, gas or vacuum may be stopped, started or regulated by a moveable part that opens, shuts or partially obstructs one or more ports or passageways. The intake and exhaust valves in the cylinder head are of the poppet type.

Valve clearance The clearance between the valve tip (the end of the valve stem) and the rocker arm or tappet/follower. The valve clearance is measured when the valve is closed. The correct clearance is important - if too small the valve won't close fully and will burn out, whereas if too large noisy operation will result.

Valve lift The amount a valve is lifted off its seat by the camshaft lobe.

Valve timing The exact setting for the opening and closing of the valves in relation to piston position.

Vernier caliper A precision measuring instrument that measures inside and outside dimensions. Not quite as accurate as a micrometer, but more convenient.

VIN Vehicle Identification Number. Term for the bike's engine and frame numbers.

Viscosity The thickness of a liquid or its resistance to flow.

Volt A unit for expressing electrical "pressure" in a circuit. Volts = current x ohms.

W

Water pump A mechanically-driven device for moving coolant around the engine.

Watt A unit for expressing electrical power. Watts = volts x current.

Wear limit see **Service limit**

Wet liner A liquid-cooled engine design where the pistons run in liners which are directly surrounded by coolant **(see illustration)**.

Wet liner arrangement

Wheelbase Distance from the centre of the front wheel to the centre of the rear wheel.

Wiring harness or loom Describes the electrical wires running the length of the motorcycle and enclosed in tape or plastic sheathing. Wiring coming off the main harness is usually referred to as a sub harness.

Woodruff key A key of semi-circular or square section used to locate a gear to a shaft. Often used to locate the alternator rotor on the crankshaft.

Wrist pin Another name for gudgeon or piston pin.

Note: *References throughout this index are in the form - "Chapter number" • "Page number"*

Preserving Our Motoring Heritage

< The Model J Duesenberg Derham Tourster. Only eight of these magnificent cars were ever built – this is the only example to be found outside the United States of America

Almost every car you've ever loved, loathed or desired is gathered under one roof at the Haynes Motor Museum. Over 300 immaculately presented cars and motorbikes represent every aspect of our motoring heritage, from elegant reminders of bygone days, such as the superb Model J Duesenberg to curiosities like the bug-eyed BMW Isetta. There are also many old friends and flames. Perhaps you remember the 1959 Ford Popular that you did your courting in? The magnificent 'Red Collection' is a spectacle of classic sports cars including AC, Alfa Romeo, Austin Healey, Ferrari, Lamborghini, Maserati, MG, Riley, Porsche and Triumph.

A Perfect Day Out

Each and every vehicle at the Haynes Motor Museum has played its part in the history and culture of Motoring. Today, they make a wonderful spectacle and a great day out for all the family. Bring the kids, bring Mum and Dad, but above all bring your camera to capture those golden memories for ever. You will also find an impressive array of motoring memorabilia, a comfortable 70 seat video cinema and one of the most extensive transport book shops in Britain. The Pit Stop Cafe serves everything from a cup of tea to wholesome, home-made meals or, if you prefer, you can enjoy the large picnic area nestled in the beautiful rural surroundings of Somerset.

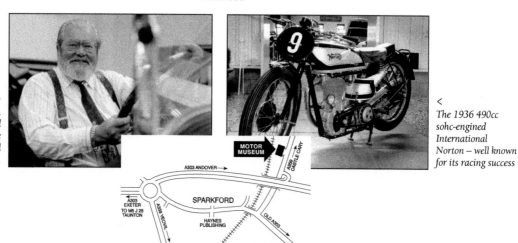

> John Haynes O.B.E., Founder and Chairman of the museum at the wheel of a Haynes Light 12.

< The 1936 490cc sohc-engined International Norton – well known for its racing success

The Museum is situated on the A359 Yeovil to Frome road at Sparkford, just off the A303 in Somerset. It is about 40 miles south of Bristol, and 25 minutes drive from the M5 intersection at Taunton.
Open 9.30am - 5.30pm (10.00am - 4.00pm Winter) 7 days a week, *except Christmas Day, Boxing Day and New Years Day*
Special rates available for schools, coach parties and outings Charitable Trust No. 292048